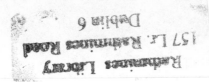
Items should be returned on or before the last date shown below. Items not already requested by other borrowers may be renewed in person, in writing or by telephone. To renew, please quote the number on the barcode label. To renew online a PIN is required. This can be requested at your local library.
Renew online @ **www.dublincitypubliclibraries.ie**
Fines charged for overdue items will include postage incurred in recovery. Damage to or loss of items will be charged to the borrower.

**Leabharlanna Poiblí Chathair Bhaile Átha Cliath
Dublin City Public Libraries**

Baile Átha Cliath
Dublin City

Rathmines Branch Tel: 4973539
Brainse Ráth Maonas Fón: 4973539

Date Due	Date Due	Date Due
29/1/14		

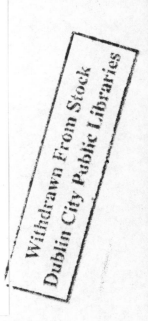
IRISH ACADEMIC PRESS
DUBLIN

First published in 2013 by Irish Academic Press

8 Chapel Lane
Sallins
Co. Kildare,
Ireland

British Library Cataloguing in Publication Data
An entry can be found on request

ISBN: 978 0 7165 3183 8 (cloth)
ISBN: 978 0 7165 3186 9 (paper)
ISBN: 978 0 7165 3187 6 (ebook)

Library of Congress Cataloging-in-Publication Data
An entry can be found on request

Printed in Ireland by SPRINT-print Ltd.

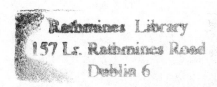
For my wonderful parents
Áine and Gerry Kelly

&

In memory of Lieutenant Stephen Kirby
Royal Welsh Fusiliers
(1957–1979)

Contents

Acknowledgements

I would like to thank the various archival institutions in Ireland and abroad. I am particularly grateful to the staff of the School of History and Archives, University College Dublin, for all their kind assistance over the past several years. I must also extend my thanks to the numerous individuals who freely gave their time to discuss their own personal recollections of events central to my research; they include, Kenneth Bloomfield, Harry Boland, Richard Booth, Mary Colley, Ciarán Ó Cuinn, Liam Cullen, Pádraig Faulkner, Garret FitzGerald, Martin Mansergh and Micheál Martin.

I must also record my thanks to the following individuals: Matthew Kelleher (my American friend and scholar), Michael Laffan, Kate Breslin, Ronan Fanning (my original PhD supervisor prior to his retirement in 2007), Seamus Helferty, Denis Dolan, Jenny Campbell, Helena Cotter, Lisa Hyde and Ruairi Byrne. Special thanks must be extended to my PhD internal examiner, Diarmaid Ferriter and my external examiner, Fearghal McGarry.

The support of my friend and colleague Bryce Evans has proved an invaluable resource during the final part of this project. Our discussions of Irish history and politics, over a sociable drink on a Friday evening, was always entertaining and fulfilling. I am especially indebted to Michael Kennedy. Michael supervised the final three years of my PhD studies, the basis of which forms a large part of this monograph. His expertise and depth of knowledge in the field of modern Irish history is paralleled by very few. His guidance and constructive criticism was always measured and most appreciated.

To my family my most earnest thanks are offered. My mother and father, Áine and Gerry and my younger brother Conor, are an inspiration. I must acknowledge the precious hours given by my mother to read over numerous drafts of my work. To my father I can only offer, which would never be enough, my admiration for the sacrifices that he has made for me – mam and dad, I am eternally grateful for your support and love down through the years.

List of Abbreviations

BO	Bodleian Library, Oxford
CJ	Northern Ireland Files
DE	Dáil Éireann, official debates
DFA	Department of Foreign Affairs
DO	Dominions Office
DT	Department of the Taoiseach
FCO	Foreign and Commonwealth Office
HO	Home Office
IRA	Irish Republican Army
NAI	National Archives of Ireland, Dublin
NAUK	National Archives of United Kingdom, London
NLI	National Library of Ireland, Dublin
PREM	Prime Minister's Office
PRONI	Public Records Office of Northern Ireland
SE	Seanad Éireann, official debates
UBSC	University of Birmingham Special Collections, Birmingham
UCDA	University College Dublin Archives, Dublin
UO	University of Oxford, Oxford
WR	War Office

NB. Note on Punctuation: Readers should note that, in general, this study has followed the *Irish Historical Studies* rules for capital letters and punctuations. The use of a capital U for Unionists or Unionism denotes organised unionism, i.e. the Ulster Unionist Party; the use of lower case, unionist opinion, etc., refers to those citizens of Northern Ireland who wished to maintain the Union between Great Britain and Northern Ireland. Likewise, a capital N for Nationalists refers to organised nationalism, i.e. the Nationalists Party in Northern Ireland; the use of lower case, nationalist opinion, etc., refers to the nationalist population of Northern Ireland who opposed the partition of Ireland. The use of lower case is, likewise, used to refer to political/government positions associated with politicians and civil servants, i.e. the use of lower case is used when referring to 'taoiseach' and 'prime minister'. The use of capitals is employed to refer to government departments, i.e. 'the Department of the Taoiseach' and 'the Commonwealth and Relations Office'.

Note on Primary Sources

The availability of archival material never before correlated into a single study of Fianna Fáil's views towards Northern Ireland has greatly helped to fill in the gaps in our understanding of the topic under examination. This monograph provides the first original in-depth analysis of Fianna Fáil's private and public attitude to partition and Northern Ireland from 1926 to 1971.

Given the tradition of Fianna Fáil not to commit the most sensitive material to paper, a practice espoused by de Valera personally, historians are inevitably left with gaps in research possibilities regarding Northern Ireland policy.[1] For instance, there was reluctance to record discussions on Northern Ireland at Fianna Fáil meetings of the parliamentary party and the National Executive. This is naturally frustrating. The records may show that on occasions 'special' parliamentary party meetings convened to discuss Northern Ireland policy. Such meeting could go on for hours and sometimes into the early hours of the morning. Yet, all the record shows, at best, are several lines denoting decisions reached.[2] This approach continued at cabinet level as all that was recorded were decisions made and not the details of what was discussed.

Until relatively recently there has been a dearth of primary source material relating to Fianna Fáil and its leaders.[3] Over the past two decades, however, additional archival documentation has become available to researchers. In particular, this work takes advantage of the availability of Fianna Fáil Party Papers and the personal papers of Eamon de Valera, Frank Aiken, Seán MacEntee and Patrick Hillery, all deposited in the University College Dublin Archives (UCDA).[4]

As Seán Lemass left very little personal archival papers[5] the Fianna Fáil Party collection is of particular importance.[6] The collection contains the files from Lemass's period as director of organisation from 1954 to 1957 and the files during his presidency of the party from 1959 to 1966.[7] As very few of the first generation of Fianna Fáil politicians left any papers open to researchers, the availability of the above archival documentation has proved an invaluable resource to this researcher. Access to an unpublished memoir of Gerald Boland has also provided this researcher with a unique insight into the private attitude of a senior Fianna Fáil politician.[8]

Government files from the National Archives of Ireland (NAI), specifically the Department of the Taoiseach (DT) and Department of Foreign Affairs (DFA), also represent a significant part of the work. Additional archival material from the National Archives of United Kingdom (NAUK), primarily files from the Foreign and Commonwealth Office (FCO), Prime Minister's Office (PREM), Dominions Office (DO) and Northern Ireland Office (CJ), have also proved a valuable resource. The Public Records Office of Northern Ireland (PRONI) has likewise been utilised.[9] The personal papers of Clement Attlee[10] and Neville Chamberlain[11] have also provided a unique insight into the private views of the British government towards Fianna Fáil, partition, and the Irish Republican Army (IRA).

A major component of this work examines Fianna Fáil grass-roots' attitude to Northern Ireland and considerable time was devoted to an analysis of regional newspapers. This venture, although time consuming, was highly productive. By analysing local newspapers, in conjunction with access to local Fianna Fáil Party files,[12] this research offers a micro examination of the varying attitude among Fianna Fáil grass-roots in relation to partition and Northern Ireland. In particular, the *Kerryman*, *Tipperary Star*, *Connacht Tribune* and *Anglo-Celt* operated as a gauge towards understanding grass-roots support (and opposition) for Fianna Fáil governments' stance on partition and the IRA.[13]

Interviews with influential figures directly related to this book have also proved of vital benefit, helping to underpin some central arguments offered by this research. I was fortunate to interview retired and serving Fianna Fáil government ministers, including the late Pádraig Faulkner and Dermot Ahern. I also interviewed and corresponded with past taoisigh, notably the late Garret FitzGerald and Bertie Ahern. The inside information provided by retired and serving civil servants and political advisers also proved a worthwhile resource, particularly the views of Kenneth Bloomfield. The interviews and phone conversations that I had with Harry Boland will stay with me for a long time; Harry's insight into the minefield of internal Fianna Fáil party politics was always both objective and fascinating.

NOTES

1. See John Bowman's observations, John Bowman, *De Valera and the Ulster Question, 1917–1973* (Oxford: Oxford University Press, 1982), 2–3.

2. See, for example, University College Dublin Archives (UCDA) Fianna Fáil Party Papers, P176/446, meeting of Fianna Fáil parliamentary party 'especially arranged to discuss partition', 27 Oct. 1954. See also UCDA P176/446, meeting of Fianna Fáil parliamentary party, 15 Jan. 1957.

3. See Eunan O'Halpin, 'Parliamentary party discipline and tactics: the Fianna Fáil archives, 1926–32', *Irish Historical Studies*, Vol. XXX (1996–7), 583.

4. The Fianna Fáil Party collection (P176) was deposited in UCDA in 2000; the Eamon de Valera Papers (P150) and Frank Aiken Papers (P104) were made available to the public by UCDA in 2003 and 1999, respectively. The Seán MacEntee Papers (P67) was made available to researchers during the 1990s, while the Patrick Hillery Papers (P205) became available in 2011/12.

5. The only known available archival material concerning Lemass (not including files from the National Archives of Ireland (NAI)) are held by the Mr John O'Connor and Mr Jack O'Brien. Entitled 'Lemass family papers' the files contain miscellaneous correspondence, photographs and documents. The 'Colm Barnes papers', in the possession of Mr Colm Barnes also contain some notes of conversations with Lemass and his contemporaries. See John Horgan, *Seán Lemass, The Enigmatic Patriot* (Dublin: Gill and Macmillan, 1999), notes on 'Manuscript sources', 399.

6. During the course of my research the ability to consult the minutes of the Fianna Fáil National Executive meetings (P176/344–350) and parliamentary party meetings (P176/444–448) proved an invaluable resource. See O'Halpin's comments concerning the 'outstanding' availability of the Fianna Fáil Party Papers to researchers. O'Halpin, 'Parliamentary party discipline and tactics', 585–590.

7. See, for example, UCDA P176/51–76; UCDA P176/348, P176/447–448; and P176/945.

8. Mr. Harry Boland, son of the late Gerald Boland, kindly granted this author permission to access his father's unpublished handwritten memoirs. Boland wrote his memoirs (on Seanad Éireann headed paper) during the early/mid-1960s (a copy of Boland's memoir is in the possession of this author).

9. See Bibliography for a comprehensive inventory of referenced primary sources.

10. The Clement Attlee Papers are located at Bodleian Library, University of Oxford.

11. The Neville Chamberlain Papers are located at University of Birmingham, Special Collections (main library).

12. The Fianna Fáil Party collection contains an extensive sub-section on the Fianna Fáil organisation at grass-roots level. The files are arranged on a county-by-county basis, in alphabetical order by county. See UCDA P176/51–71 Constituency Files 1937–1954 and P176/311–344. The collection also holds the files of the General Secretary and National Organiser. These files reveal how closely the party administration remained in contact with its grass-roots and how effectively they oversaw the party's machinery. See UCDA P176/266–310, files of Fianna Fáil General Secretary and National Organiser.

13. See Bibliography for a comprehensive list of newspapers.

Index of Key Terms and Political Bodies

- The **Ard Chomhairle** (National Executive) is the supreme governing body of Fianna Fáil, when the Ard Fheis is not in session. It contains the most senior members of Fianna Fáil and is chaired by the party president. The body has the power to deal with and determine all matters and questions while the Ard Fheis is not in session. Most recently, among others, the body consists of a president, five vice-presidents, two honorary secretaries, two honorary treasurers, three members of government (or the front bench if in opposition) to be nominated by the leader of the party, five members of the parliamentary party (non-members of the government or of the front bench), a committee of twenty (non-members of the parliamentary party) to be elected by the Ard Fheis and three (non-members of the parliamentary party) shall be co-opted by the Ard Comhairle.
- The **Ard Fheis** (national conference); plural **Ard Fheiseanna** (conferences) is the supreme governing and legislative body of Fianna Fáil, which is convened annually, in as far as is practicable, by the National Executive. Most recently, among others, the body consists of three delegates from each registered cumann; three delegates from each registered Comhairle Ceantair and registered Comhairle Dáilcheantair; party members of the National Executive, the Dáil and Seanad, the European Parliament, local County Councils, City Councils, Borough Councils and Town Councils.
- The **Clár** (Agenda) is a central feature of the annual Fianna Fáil Ard Fheis. The Clár outlines (in a heading format) the various aspects/events/procedures of the party conference.
- The **Comhairle Ceantair** (District Council) the Comhairle Ceantair consists of a secretary and two delegates from each registered

cumann in the area. No public representative is permitted to be an officer of the Comhairle Ceantair. Its duties are to supervise, direct and advise the registered cumainn in its area. To arrange conventions for the selection of candidates for election to local authorities and to carry out loyally any instructions issued to it from bodies over it.

- The **Comhairle Dáilcheantair** (Constituency Council) is important as it represents a fixed number of delegates from each cumann in a particular constituency (in recent years the Council consists of a Cathoirleach (Chairman), secretary and three delegates from each Comhairle Ceantair in the Constituency; consisting of a least one woman and one man). Local TDs, members of the European Parliament, Senators and Councillors who are members of a cumann in the constituency, have the right to attend and speak at all meetings of the Comhairle Dáilcheantair, but do not have the right to vote unless they are delegates to the Comhairle Dáilcheantair. This body directs the organisation of the Constituency with a view to contesting elections and selects candidates for the Dáil, European and Local elections. In Fianna Fáil's case, cumann secretaries are *ex officio* members of the council. In recent years the Constituency Council also has a youth committee known as the Coiste Ógra Comhairle Dáilcheantair which is governed in accordance with the current Fianna Fáil National Youth Scheme.

- The **Cumann** (branch); plural **Cumainn** (branches). The Fianna Fáil Party is organised at grass-roots level on the basis of local branches, usually contiguous with parishes in rural areas and with groups of streets in urban areas. Each cumann consists of not less than ten members at least 50% of whom must reside or work in the cumann area. The geographic extent of the cumann shall be a parish area or a polling place (voting place). Where an existing cumann has more than 4,000 voters, the need for additional cumainn shall be considered by the Comhairle Ceantair/ Comhairle Dáilcheantair/ Ard Chomhairle. It is the duty of a cumann to promote the interests of the organisation in its area, and secure public support for its programme.

- The **Ógra Fianna Fáil** (young-wing of Fianna Fáil) is the young-wing of the party. Its members are constituted to hold positions on the Comhairle Ceantair (in the form of a youth committee 'Coiste Ógra Comhairle Ceantair') and the Comhairle Dáilcheantair (again in the form of a youth committee 'Coiste Ógra Comhairle

Dáilcheantair'). Each year (when possible) a National Ógra Fianna Fáil Ard Fheis (National Youth Conference) is held; as well as an annaul Coiste Ógra Comhairle Dáilcheantair (to be held in each constituency).

Introduction

'Maybe we were far too rigid in our approach [to partition], too tenacious of our point of view, too proud to temporise or placate ... whatever may have been the reason, we made no headway: so our successors must start from "square one"'.

[Seán MacEntee, 1970][1]

When the Troubles broke out in Northern Ireland in the late 1960s Fianna Fáil was hopelessly ill-prepared for the ensuing crisis. For almost half a century, since Fianna Fáil's establishment in 1926, the movement had pursued an impractical, naive and at times deluded strategy towards partition and Northern Ireland. This strategy was impractical because Fianna Fáil relied upon a mixture of outdated and ad-hoc policies to form the crux of the party's approach to partition; it was naive because the party – particularly in the post-war era – maintained that the British government had a moral obligation to help deliver Irish unity; and, lastly, deluded because Fianna Fáil continually ignored the strength of opposition from Ulster Unionism for a united Ireland.

The above quotation from Seán MacEntee, a founding father of Fianna Fáil, vividly exposed that for more than a generation Fianna Fáil remained 'far too rigid' in its attitude towards Northern Ireland. Constrained by its own perceived ideological obligations to the ghosts of Irish nationalism and its anti-partitionist past, the party made 'no headway' on partition. There was a sustained reluctance within Fianna Fáil to deal with the political realities of a divided Ireland. By the late 1960s partition was in existence for almost half a century and a generation had grown up who had never lived in a united Ireland. Fianna Fáil, nevertheless, was incapable of acknowledging this reality. The party, as MacEntee bemoaned, was 'too proud' and stubborn to commit itself to a realistic and workable Northern Ireland policy.

Formal partition of Ireland dates from June 1921, when the Northern Ireland parliament, as provided for in the Government of

Ireland 'Partition' Act of 1920, was officially opened. Under the terms of the Act, two parliaments, one in Belfast the other in Dublin, were established with powers of local self-government. Irish nationalists, on both side of the newly formed border, reacted furiously to news of the Act's passing. It was described as 'odious', 'insidious' and that the Act violated 'the laws of God and nature'.[2] The leader of Sinn Féin and president of Dáil Éireann, Eamon de Valera described the Act as fostering '... political and religious rancour, which would divide Ireland into antagonistic parts ...'[3] Northern nationalists were equally forthright, Rev. Dean McGlinchey said that the object of the 'Partition Act' was to 'kill the Irish movement' and to '... carve up Ireland'.[4] Joseph Devlin, leader of Northern Nationalism, condemned the legislation as an 'outrage' and 'wantonly insane'.[5]

The Act granted local autonomy, under a 'home rule' parliament to the six North-Eastern counties of Ulster (Antrim, Armagh, Down, Fermanagh, Londonderry and Tyrone). The new Northern Ireland state held its first general election in May 1921. Unionists secured forty seats to a mere six Sinn Féin and six Nationalists seats; thus, Ulster Unionists acquired an overwhelming majority, which characterised Northern Ireland politics for the subsequent fifty years. The following month, in June 1921, Sir James Craig was elected the first prime minister of Northern Ireland. Thereafter, the traditional North–South partitionist divide, which was present long before the passing of the Government of Ireland Act, was given a legal and political permanence that hitherto never existed.

Simultaneously, in the newly created twenty-six county state of Southern Ireland, the revitalised Sinn Féin Party refused to contest the general election in May 1921, as stipulated under the terms of the Government of Ireland Act. The degree of self-governance conferred by the Act fell far short of Sinn Féin demands. Control of defence, foreign policy and finance remained with Westminster. Instead the party used the general election of 1921 as a means of electing the second Dáil Éireann. This 'independent' parliament, which the British refused to recognise, was established under the banner of the Irish republic in January 1919. In total, 124 Sinn Féin candidates were elected unopposed in the general election in May 1921.

The signing of the Anglo-Irish Treaty of December 1921, negotiated between Lloyd George's coalition government in London and a delegation of Sinn Féin, led by Arthur Griffith and the charismatic Michael Collins, copper fastened the partition of Ireland. Although the treaty conferred much more independence upon what was to become the Irish Free State than had ever been contemplated under the terms of the Government of Ireland Act, the Dáil and Irish Nationalist leaders were hopelessly unable to prevent the Act's implementation in Northern Ireland. In truth, partition rarely assumed much importance during the protracted negotiations between London and Dublin throughout the latter part of 1921. Indeed, the central issues in these negotiations, as in the subsequent treaty debates and the civil war, were symbolic: the question of status, the crown and the republic.[6]

De Valera's refusal to support the Dáil's ratification of the Anglo-Irish Treaty, passed by the narrow margin of sixty-four votes to fifty-seven, spelled the beginning of a dark period in Ireland's recent history, a traumatising and bloody civil war. Although some attempts through an electoral pact were made by de Valera and Collins to stop the drift into armed conflict, the die was cast. De Valera demanded that only a sovereign republic constituted Ireland's legitimate aspiration. Collins, on the other hand, maintained that the Anglo-Irish Treaty and the establishment of a dominion parliament in Dublin, represented a 'stepping stone' to the attainment of the Irish republic. As ever, the partition question did not factor heavily in the political discourse during this period.

The civil war, lasting from June 1922 to the summer of 1923, witnessed the tearing apart of families, brothers fought against one another, homes and businesses were destroyed and political executions were carried out by both pro and anti-treaty forces. Besides the loss of men such as Cathal Brugha, Harry Boland and Erskine Childers, perhaps the greatest tragedy of the civil war was the death of Michael Collins, who was shot and killed in an ambush at Béal na mBláth, Co. Cork in August 1922. The war was finally brought to an end following an order from the chief of staff of the IRA and future co-founder of Fianna Fáil, Frank Aiken, to 'dump arms'. The civil war cost the Irish Free State approximately £17m and material destruction was estimated at about £30m. When the anti-treatyite casualties were added to those of the Irish army, the total number killed during the fighting was estimated to be between 4,000 and 5,000.[7]

In the aftermath of the civil war the division between those who formed the pro-treaty party (Cumann na nGaedheal from 1923 to 1933 and Fine Gael thereafter) and the anti-treaty party, retaining the name Sinn Féin until 1926, when de Valera founded Fianna Fáil, resulted in a long lasting divide in the politics of Southern Ireland. Henceforth, politically, or more appropriately electorally, the question of partition and the quest for Irish unity was utilised by the political class in the South to galvanise popular grass-roots support and to woo recalcitrant 'republicans' back into parliamentary politics. Fianna Fáil, 'the Republican Party' and Fine Gael, 'the United Ireland' Party, as their respective subtitles suggested, attempted to create the image that a united Ireland lay at the centre of their ideology. Fianna Fáil, in particular, was the master of this political illusion. De Valera wrapped the Irish tricolour around Fianna Fáil and depicted the movement as the 'nationalist' party and the custodians of the aspiration for Irish unity.

During Fianna Fáil's early years from 1926 to 1932, on suitable occasions, the party played the anti-partitionist card. But behind the hollow rhetoric of anti-partitionism, de Valera and his fellow 'soldiers of destiny' intentionally ignored partition. Attention was instead focused on securing and maintaining a Fianna Fáil government in the twenty-six counties. Although Fianna Fáil's self-proclaimed 'first political objective' was to secure a united Ireland, no realistic policies were actually implemented to fulfil this primary objective.[8] Indeed, de Valera routinely confessed that Fianna Fáil were unable to offer any 'clear way' to end partition.[9]

From 1932 successive Fianna Fáil governments implemented social and economic policy reforms, dismantled Ireland's constitutional links with Great Britain, introduced a new Irish constitution in 1937 and successfully maintained Irish neutrality during the Second World War. However, on the question of Irish reunification Fianna Fáil was incapable of formulating a realistic and official long-term Northern Ireland policy. Instead, under the authoritarian leadership of de Valera, the party reverted to the comforts of anti-partitionism, habitually describing the continued maintenance of partition as a 'crime',[10] that the North–South border was an 'unnatural boundary'.[11]

Juxtaposed to the Fianna Fáil governments' use of anti-partition throughout the 1930s and 1940s, de Valera also wished to secure support from the party rank-and-file for a more 'realistic' attitude to partition. All government resources, he routinely argued, must be first focused on the twenty-six counties before attention could be turned to Northern Ireland.[12] The advancement of this policy had obvious attractions for de Valera as it permitted consecutive Fianna Fáil cabinets to ignore partition down through the years.

The Fianna Fáil leadership believed that to think too much about Northern Ireland was a dangerous exercise because it could expose the party's inability to fulfil its promise of a thirty-two county republic.

Therefore, despite its place at the core of Fianna Fáil's ideology, the partition question was deliberately submerged. By keeping the issue off the political agenda, de Valera and his successor as Fianna Fáil leader, Seán Lemass, were eager to maintain a level of harmony within Fianna Fáil. This is a significant point: afraid that the emotive subject of partition might cause an irreconcilable split within the party, the leadership were reluctant to ever formulate a coherent and long-term Northern Ireland policy. Consequently, the Fianna Fáil apparatus, from cabinet ministers, backbench TDs, county councillors and grass-roots party members, were left confused and uneducated towards what actually constituted official Northern Ireland policy that could transform with the times.

The outbreak of violence in Northern Ireland in the late 1960s, however, meant that partition could no longer be ignored. Consequently, between 1969 and 1971, under the leadership of Jack Lynch, Fianna Fáil was brought face to face with one of its most blatant contradictions – the gap between the party's habitual pronouncements of its desire for a united Ireland and the reality that the organisation could offer no practical solutions to deliver this objective. When the violence intensified throughout Northern Ireland in the summer of 1969 Fianna Fáil's bluff was called. For a generation, senior Fianna Fáil politicians had sold the myth that the party offered the best chance of securing an end to partition. Yet, as violence engulfed Northern Ireland this myth quickly unwound. Party members throughout the country began to question – many for the first occasion – what actually constituted Fianna Fáil's official Northern Ireland policy. Significantly, a division appeared between those who maintained that only constitutional means could undo partition and those within the party who advocated that the use of physical force was a legitimate policy.

The crisis surrounding the Irish government's response to the Battle of the Bogside in August 1969 revealed that Fianna Fáil had no realistic Northern Ireland policy. This split was first exposed during the infamous cabinet meeting of the afternoon of 13 August 1969. At the meeting Fianna Fáil ministers passionately debated whether the use of physical force constituted official Fianna Fáil Northern Ireland policy. Taoiseach, Jack Lynch, with the support of the majority of his ministers, argued that the use of violence was not a legitimate policy of Fianna Fáil. Lynch's assertion was correct, officially, since the late 1920s — the Fianna Fáil leadership resolutely opposed the use of violence on the grounds that its use was impractical.[13] Nevertheless, a consortium of anti-partitionist ministers, led by Neil Blaney, Charles J. Haughey and Kevin Boland argued that physical force had always represented official Fianna Fáil policy and that the outbreak of violence on the streets of Derry was an opportune time to force London to agree to Irish unity.[14]

The division at cabinet level spread like a cancer throughout the Fianna Fáil organisation from 1969 to 1971. There was, as described by Conor Cruise O'Brien, an infectious and dangerous sickness that was quickly infecting every part of the Fianna Fáil apparatus from cabinet ministers to grass-roots. O'Brien pointed the finger of blame at Blaney and the anti-partitionist-wing of Fianna Fáil. These people, he exclaimed, had publicly advocated force to end partition.[15] Therefore, due to an absence of a coherent and official Northern Ireland policy, Fianna Fáil members were able to interpret how *they* defined policy; the anti-partitionists within the organisation argued that physical force was an acceptable policy. It was a harrowing time for Fianna Fáil. Privately, minister for external affairs, Patrick Hillery admitted that the party was beginning to 'crumble'.[16]

The divide between the constitutionalists and militants created a vacuum which left many within Fianna Fáil confused towards what denoted official party policy *vis á vis* the use of force. From Fianna Fáil backbench TDs and county councillors, down to the local grass-roots cumainn, members tried to piece together what was the party's official Northern Ireland policy. In May 1970, Labour TD for Dublin North Central, Michael O'Leary, aptly described the inherent ambiguity within Fianna Fáil. He accused Fianna Fáil of never having 'a policy on unity'.[17] The problem of 'Fianna Fáil policy on unity', he said 'is that one did not exist'.[18] He elaborated, that in public Fianna Fáil spoke of a 'commitment to a peaceful solution and in private that there was this secret conviction that force could be used in certain circumstances'. Many Fianna Fáil members throughout the country, he said, adhere to this 'interpretation' of policy.[19] O'Leary's observations were, indeed, an accurate appraisal.

As the violence continued in Northern Ireland a vocal minority within Fianna Fáil allowed emotion to cloud their judgement. Lynch, himself, admitted that 'no other political topic' generated 'more emotion than the subject of partition'; the maintenance of partition, he said, 'eats into the Irish consciousness like a cancer'.[20] Throughout Ireland a cohort of party members from grass-roots to elected representative resigned from Fianna Fáil in protest at the government's failure to pursue a 'stronger' Northern Ireland policy, including Kevin Boland.[21] The Fianna Fáil government was accused by party supporters of abandoning the 'last vestige of Republicanism'.[22]

In the aftermath of the Fianna Fáil Ard Fheis in February 1971, under a rejuvenated Lynch, the government confidently commanded that only peaceful means could deliver Irish reunification. Physical force was unequivocally ruled out.[23] Thereafter, Lynch's conciliatory relationship with Ulster Unionism, his demands on London to implement reforms in Northern Ireland and his support for the creation of a power-sharing executive between Unionists and Nationalists, formed the basis of Fianna Fáil's 'peaceful' Northern Ireland policy for the remainder of his leadership until his resignation in 1979.[24] Henceforth, Fianna Fáil, Fine Gael and the Labour Party, shared a bi-partisan non-violent Northern Ireland policy; it is for this reason that the book concludes in 1971 (the concluding chapter offers an overview of Fianna Fáil's Northern Ireland policy from 1971 to 1979). Of course, there were differences of emphasis among the three rival Southern political parties on the emotive subject of Northern Ireland.[25] Nevertheless, there was an agreement among all mainstream parties in the Republic of Ireland that Irish unity could only be brought about by peaceful methods and that this was a long-term strategy.

A GAP IN THE HISTORIOGRAPHY: FIANNA FÁIL, PARTITION AND NORTHERN IRELAND, 1926–1971

Although Fianna Fáil has been criticised for ignoring Northern Ireland, no study has examined the reasons for the party's inability to formulate a workable Northern Ireland policy from 1926 to 1971.[26] This book answers this question. It is the first study to analyse the historical reasons why Fianna Fáil was unable to devise and implement a lucid and indeed realistic Northern Ireland policy from 1926 to 1971. Uniquely, it explores Fianna Fáil's attitude towards Northern Ireland from the perspective of the entire apparatus of the organisation, from grass-roots up to county councillors, backbench TDs and cabinet ministers.

To date, the historiography concentrated on examining Fianna Fáil's policies towards Northern Ireland in the context of the outbreak of the Troubles in the late 1960s and the ensuing Peace Process of the late 1980s and 1990s.[27] Perhaps the best-known study of Fianna Fáil's attitude towards Northern Ireland, prior to the early 1970s, is John Bowman's, *De Valera and the Ulster Question, 1917–1973*.[28]

Although an important contribution, Bowman dealt with Eamon de Valera's partition strategy and did not offer an all-encompassing history of Fianna Fáil's Northern Ireland policy from 1926 to 1971. Besides Bowman, those who have explored Fianna Fáil's Northern Ireland policy prior to the late 1960s have dealt with the subject on an ad-hoc, selective basis.[29]

For example, Michael Kennedy's 2000 seminal publication, *Division and Consensus, the Politics of Cross-Border Relations in Ireland, 1925–1969*, examined the Fianna Fáil governments' attitude to Northern Ireland in the overall context of North–South cross-border co-operation from 1925 to 1969. His publication, however, did not explore Fianna Fáil's Northern Ireland policy at party level, instead concentrating on the formation of policy at government and departmental level.[30] Donnacha Ó Beacháin's publication, *Destiny of Soldiers, Fianna Fáil, Irish Republicanism and the IRA, 1926–1973*, offered an excellent survey of Fianna Fáil's ideological evolution from its revolutionary origins to the party's periods in government from the 1930s to the early 1970s.[31] This study, nonetheless, did not examine Fianna Fáil's overall strategy to partition, particularly in relation to the party's views towards Ulster Unionism, Northern Nationalism and anti-partitionist movements in Great Britain.

Likewise, Noel Whelan's dry survey history of Fianna Fáil, scarcely examined the party's attitude to Northern Ireland prior to the 1970s.[32] Other, more partisan studies, have attempted to trace Fianna Fáil's attitude to partition and Northern Ireland. Notably, Kevin Boland's 'propagandists' publications, as labelled by Patrick Hillery,[33] were heavily critical of Fianna Fáil's 'abandonment' of its traditional Northern Ireland policy.[34] There are also gaps in our understanding of Fianna Fáil's longstanding association with Northern Nationalism. The party's relationship with Northern Nationalists was considered in separate studies by Brendan Lynn, Enda Staunton and Eamon Phoenix.[35] These authors did not trace, in adequate detail, Fianna Fáil's determination to prevent Northern Nationalists' involvement in Dublin's Northern Ireland policy from the late 1920s onwards.

Henry Patterson and John Horgan produced important studies on Seán Lemass and Northern Ireland, respectively.[36] Their works focused on Lemass's attitude towards Northern Ireland as taoiseach from 1959 to 1966. Neither study explored his evolving views towards Northern Ireland from the mid-1920s to the 1950s. A number of recent biographies of leading Fianna Fáil politicians, particularly John Walsh's fine work on Patrick Hillery and Dermot Keogh's study of Jack Lynch provided an important insight into Fianna Fáil's attitude to Northern Ireland.[37] Nevertheless they offered limited analysis of Fianna Fáil's stance on Northern Ireland during the period under investigation; gaps, therefore, remain in relation to the party's views on partition.

More general literature on Irish nationalism and partition has, likewise, only touched on Fianna Fáil's attitude towards Northern Ireland. Perhaps the finest work to date on Irish nationalism by Richard English, *Irish Freedom, the History of Nationalism in Ireland*, did not consider Fianna Fáil's attitude to partition and Northern Ireland.[38] Likewise, D. George Boyce's scholarly study, *Nationalism in Ireland*, refrained from analysing Fianna Fáil's stance on Northern Ireland.[39] General studies of pan-European nationalism, chiefly those by Ernest Gellner, Elie Kedourie and Eric J. Hobsbawm, have also neglected to explore the nature of Irish nationalism, particularly at Irish party politics level.[40]

Clare O'Halloran's excellent study of partition and Irish nationalism explored the realities of partition for Irish nationalist from 1920 to 1949. In a similar pattern to this book O'Halloran stripped away the rhetoric of Irish nationalism and revealed the emptiness of much nationalist posturing; needless to say, little was said of Fianna Fáil's attitude to Northern Ireland during the 1960s and early 1970s.[41] M.W. Heslinga, Michael Laffan, Denis Gwynn and Frank Gallagher examined particular features of the partition of Ireland, including historical, geographical and conceptual characteristics. Nonetheless, these studies predominantly fell outside the time-frame of this work and thus did not consider Fianna Fáil's attitude to partition and Northern Ireland.[42] This book, therefore, fills in many of the missing gaps and is a welcome and long overdue study of modern Irish nationalism and partition from the perspective of Fianna Fáil, the most powerful and electorally successful Irish political party of the twentieth century.

THE FIANNA FÁIL ELITE, PARTITION AND NORTHERN IRELAND

The attitudes and policies of two men, Eamon de Valera and Seán Lemass, are central to this book. These two colossal figures of twentieth-century Irish history dominated Fianna Fáil's thinking on partition for a generation. De Valera, so often described as an 'enigma', almost singlehandedly directed the party's Northern Ireland policy from 1926 to 1959.[43] Lemass, likewise, during his period of Fianna Fáil leader from 1959 to 1966, dictated the party's Northern

Ireland strategy. Importantly, the book also examines, among others, the public and private views of Frank Aiken, Seán MacEntee and Jack Lynch in relation to Northern Ireland. As the research reveals, although impeded by the forceful personalities of de Valera and Lemass, these men felt strongly about partition and were not afraid to criticise or attempt to revise Fianna Fáil's traditional attitude to partition.

How does one assess de Valera's attitude to partition and Northern Ireland? The answer to this question represents a minefield for historians; some have criticised de Valera as simply not having a Northern Ireland policy,[44] that he ignored partition, not understanding what was involved.[45] Yet, it is unfair to arraign him before the bar of history for failing to achieve that what he, personally, never actually claimed to be able to achieve. Instead de Valera should be examined, not in the comfort of retrospect, but in the context in which he lived. What he can certainly be criticised for – and as this book reveals – throughout his political career is following a confused and muddled approach to partition. His single mindedness and dictatorial control meant that under his leadership Fianna Fáil was incapable of modifying its Northern Ireland policy. As he expressed himself: 'whenever I wanted to know what the Irish people wanted I had only to examine my own heart and it told me straight off what the Irish people wanted. I, therefore, am holding to this policy ...'[46]

De Valera admitted towards the end of his life that it was the threat of partition that first prompted his involvement in politics.[47] His entire political thinking was 'dominated by partition'.[48] As United Kingdom Representative to Ireland, Lord Rugby (formerly, Sir John Maffey) alleged in 1947, partition 'eats into Mr. de Valera's soul'.[49] Writing in 1975, Seán MacEntee recalled that in almost every exchange, 'formal or informal, between him and his British counterparts, there recurred, like the clanging of a bell, one theme: Partition, Partition, Partition! Every argument came back to it, every decision was affected by it'.[50] Indeed, in the Department of the Taoiseach de Valera kept on his wall of his office a map of Ireland in black with a white blemish representing the North-East corner to 'point out the wrong wrought by partition to our nation and our people'.[51]

De Valera was an autocrat within the cabinet and the party when it came to Northern Ireland policy. Under his watchful eye, Fianna Fáil constructed a republican orthodoxy that became sacrosanct. Built on ambiguity, his entire approach to Northern Ireland was based on the principle that Irish reunification was simply inevitable and that an historic nation could not remain divided eternally.[52] It was, however, this form of nationalist thinking that bedevilled his approach to Northern Ireland. By the 1950s partition had been in existence for nearly forty years. A generation had grown up knowing only a divided Ireland. De Valera, however, still maintained that partition could not last indefinitely.

De Valera was admired and even worshipped by many Fianna Fáil supporters.[53] Nevertheless, his 'very charismatic hold over both his colleagues and followers'[54] did not entail unconditional support for his Northern Ireland policy. This book reveals that he was routinely criticised by disgruntled supporters. Party members often expressed frustration and on occasions anger that Fianna Fáil was ignoring the Holy Grail of Irish nationalism: the fulfilment of the party's promise of a thirty-two county Irish Republic. At the party's annual Ard Fheiseanna, for example, de Valera was habitually heckled by delegates for failing to end partition.[55]

Throughout de Valera's long career he freely admitted that he could offer no immediate solution to partition.[56] Instead he maintained that Fianna Fáil offered the best chance to secure Irish unity. Although during the early years of Fianna Fáil's existence he did not rule out the use of physical force to end partition, by the late 1920s he resolutely opposed the use of violence.[57] For the remainder of his political career he maintained that the coercion of Ulster Unionists was a foolish exercise that had no hope of success.[58]

Not until the 1950s, impelled by Lemass, did Fianna Fáil attempt to revise its anti-partitionist approach to Northern Ireland. Even then, de Valera remained openly sceptical. His sudden change of heart by the mid-1950s had more to do with Britain's hardening stance in support of the Northern Ireland government, than his genuine wish to forge friendlier relations with Ulster Unionists. In fact, when de Valera retired as Fianna Fáil leader in 1959 Irish unity was little more than a political mirage.

Lemass's succession to de Valera as leader heralded a new chapter in Fianna Fáil's relationship with partition and Ulster Unionism. Lemass's stance on Northern Ireland was a welcome breath of fresh air after a generation of stale anti-partitionism. By the 1950s he increasingly recognised that Fianna Fáil's Northern Ireland policy under de Valera, particularly his policies towards Ulster Unionism, had entrenched rather than helped to remove partition. A founding member of Fianna Fáil, Lemass had witnessed the damage that the party's approach to Northern Ireland had caused over the preceding years. So often described as a 'pragmatist' he believed that the rhetoric of Irish nationalism had proved counter-productive.[59] Rather than helping to end partition, he was convinced that Fianna Fáil's anti-partitionist approach to Northern Ireland had entrenched the physical and psychological divide between Dublin and Belfast.

This book contends that on becoming taoiseach Lemass's quest for the economic salvation of Ireland became intrinsically linked with his Northern Ireland policy. Although his intervention was important, the fact remained that when he retired in 1966, he too left behind him no coherent or official long-term Northern Ireland policy for Fianna Fáil. His stance on Northern Ireland was instead based on short-term motivations. His desire to encourage cross-border relations and particularly the removal of trade barriers between Dublin and Belfast was the central motivation for his approach towards Northern Ireland. He did not consider the long-term implications of his strategy. His revision of the party's Northern Ireland policy was, as is argued, to prove innovative, but ultimately unofficial. Confronted by the traditionalist-wing of Fianna Fáil, Lemass was continually impeded as he attempted to revise core principles of the party's stance on Northern Ireland. For example, his progressive use of political terminology and his constitutional *de facto* recognition of Northern Ireland were never officially endorsed by Fianna Fáil under his leadership. Instead the central elements of Lemass's Northern Ireland policy remained informal and ambiguous.

The contribution of Frank Aiken to Fianna Fáil's approach to Northern Ireland is also an underlying theme of this book. Although his involvement with the North was more subtle than that of either de Valera or Lemass, he was an important figure. More than any other of de Valera's colleagues, the South Armagh native held similar views to 'his chief' on the subject of Northern Ireland.[60] He was viewed, by some, as a man of 'very limited intelligence', whose 'hatred of Britain blinkered his vision'.[61] Throughout the 1930s and into the early 1950s he followed an anti-partitionist policy: like de Valera he routinely demanded a British declaration in support of Irish unity; that Ulster Unionists did not have the right to vote themselves out of a united Ireland; and that a federal agreement between Belfast and Dublin constituted a workable solution for an end to partition.

Nevertheless, while he may have been perceived as the 'the most anglophobic' senior member of Fianna Fáil,[62] by the mid-1950s, he realised that the party's anti-partitionist approach towards Northern

Ireland had proved a fruitless exercise. Indeed, it would be incorrect to portray Aiken simply as an anti-partitionist bigot, a politician that could not deal with the practicalities of a partitioned Ireland.[63] Aiken, albeit reluctantly, appreciated that a change in direction was needed. The problem he faced, however, was that like de Valera, he was unable to offer any innovative proposals on how to deal with Northern Ireland.

Under Lemass's leadership from 1959 onwards it is a noteworthy point that Aiken was increasingly silent on the issue of Northern Ireland. Instead, his preoccupation turned towards Ireland's role at the United Nations. He believed that Northern Ireland was a 'constitutional issue' and thus not his business.[64] While there was an unspoken 'antipathy' between Aiken and Lemass, the former was content to follow the latter's approach towards Northern Ireland.[65] It is true that Aiken did not support Lemass's initiative to use the term 'Northern Ireland' to replace that of the 'Six-Counties', nor did he wish to concede constitutional recognition to Northern Ireland. He did, however, by 1965, offer no objection to Lemass's visit to Belfast to meet Northern Ireland prime minister, Terence O'Neill and, like Lemass, encouraged Northern Nationalists to assume the position of the official opposition party at Stormont.

This work also unearths Seán MacEntee's attitude towards Fianna Fáil's stance on Northern Ireland. Although his nuances on the North were subtle, like Lemass he represented the realist-wing within Fianna Fáil on the emotive issue of partition. A Belfast-born founding member of the party, he lamented in later life that the issue of Northern Ireland had become 'a dead controversy' Within the organisation by the late 1920s.[66] Speaking in 1979 he noted that as 'a Northerner, partition was one of the supreme issues'.[67] He was opposed to de Valera's anti-partitionist approach towards Ulster Unionists and in particular argued that the Fianna Fáil sponsored 1948/49 worldwide anti-partition campaign was a disaster.

By the early 1950s, in the mould of Lemass, but in contrast to de Valera and Aiken, he encouraged Fianna Fáil to follow a more realistic approach to Northern Ireland. Anti-partitionism, he believed, should be replaced with North–South co-operation. Although it is widely recorded that MacEntee and Lemass could be bitter opponents on social and economic issues,[68] on the subject of Northern Ireland they held similar views. As is demonstrated, he supported Lemass's revision of political terminology in reference to Northern Ireland, advanced the argument that constitutional concessions should be made by Dublin so as to entice Ulster Unionists into a united Ireland and supported granting official *de facto* recognition to Northern Ireland.

Jack Lynch's involvement with Northern Ireland has puzzled historians over the past fifty years. Although his record on Northern Ireland may seem confused at times, he did remain consistent on three points. Firstly, he always remained convinced that Irish unity was a long-term aspiration rather than a short to medium-term policy. Secondly, he resolutely and consistently rejected the use of physical force as a legitimate policy to secure Irish unity. Thirdly, by the turn of the 1970s, he was pragmatic enough to realise that in the intermediate period a powersharing executive between Ulster Unionists and Northern Nationalists was necessary.

Lynch, however, differed from Lemass on two fronts. In the mould of de Valera, he placed far greater emphasis on British responsibility to end partition. For example, speaking in Tipperary in October 1968, he argued that fundamentally 'partition arose out of British policy'.[69] Addressing the General Assembly of the United Nations, in October 1970, he again insisted that 'Britain had a responsibility'.[70] Secondly, unlike Lemass, who placed greater emphasis on encouraging cross-border relations between Dublin and Belfast, rather than exposing the widespread discrimination of Northern Catholics, by the turn of the 1970s Lynch repeatedly demanded wholesale legislative reforms in Northern Ireland.[71]

* * *

In conclusion, Fianna Fáil's failure to achieve its central goal of ending partition never embarrassed the party or prompted much self criticism. Under de Valera and subsequently Lemass, Fianna Fáil was content to ignore Northern Ireland. As this book illustrates, only when the issue was reawakened, usually on foot of a renewed IRA campaign in Northern Ireland or as a consequence of Lemass's wish to foster stronger cross-border co-operation, did Fianna Fáil give any consideration to Irish reunification: but these overtures towards Northern Ireland were always based on short-term motivations. The party created a myth that it genuinely wished to implement policies that could deliver the goal of Irish unity. In reality, Fianna Fáil was always motivated by self-interest and by short-term political manoeuvring.

By the early 1970s, on the issue of Northern Ireland, Jack Lynch wished to portray the image that Fianna Fáil had always followed, as he said, a 'realistic policy' in relation to partition.[72] He exclaimed that Fianna Fáil realised that it could not 'ignore the existence and strength of Unionist sentiment'.[73] Lynch's hypothesis was fatally flawed. The sobering truth was that since 1926 Fianna Fáil had ignored the strength among Ulster Unionism against a united Ireland and refused to deal realistically with partition. Lynch opportunistically argued that his Northern Ireland policy could be 'traced' back to Lemass.[74] He boastfully spoke of how his Fianna Fáil government have 'adopted and developed the policy expressed by Mr. Lemass and, before him, Mr. de Valera'.[75] Lynch was, indeed, telling the truth. Like his predecessors, during the early years of his leadership, Fianna Fáil remained deluded in its attitude towards partition and Northern Ireland. This delusion was not acknowledged until the early 1970s. It had taken the almost irreconcilable split of 1969 to 1971 within Fianna Fáil to occur before the party finally realised that it needed to construct and adhere to a long-term, realistic and non-violent Northern Ireland policy.

Addressing a gathering of Fianna Fáil grass-roots in November 1971, in a rare public display of self-deprecation, prominent Fianna Fáiler and minister for finance and the gaeltacht, George Colley acknowledged that his party's reluctance to formulate a coherent Northern Ireland policy had merely helped to entrench partition. 'We must face the fact', he said, 'in the years since partition we, in the South, have done relatively little to bridge the gap that divides our communities ... that for all practical purposes most of us in the South maintained an attitude of rigid righteousness, making no real effort to understand the deep fear, the terrified insecurity that sustains the beleaguered attitude among the Unionists'.[76] Over thirty years previously, in February 1938, Seán MacEntee made a similar frank admission. Reflecting on Fianna Fáil's attitude to partition and Northern Ireland in the aftermath of the Anglo-Irish Agreement of 1938, MacEntee, similarly lamented that Fianna Fáil 'never had a considered [Northern Ireland] policy'. 'It has always been', he said 'an affair of hasty improvisations, a matter of fits and starts'.[77]

Colley's and MacEntee's pronouncements were rare, but accurate, acknowledgements that their party had ignored Northern Ireland for a generation. Prior to 1971, Fianna Fáil, as is argued, never had a 'considered' Northern Ireland policy. There was a sustained reluctance within the party to deal with partition on a pragmatic and rational basis. On the subject of Northern Ireland a sense of 'rigid righteousness' and of arrogance prevailed within the organisation. The chapters below examine the many reasons why Fianna Fáil was unable to formulate a workable and realistic Northern Ireland policy from 1926 to 1971.

NOTES

1. See *Irish Press*, 22 Jan. 1970.
2. See comments by 'our London reporter', *Irish Independent*, 11 May 1921 & C. Lehane, *Irish Independent*, 2 & 5 May 1921.
3. See statement by de Valera. *Anglo-Celt*, 28 May 1921.
4. See comments by Rev. Dean McGlinchey. *Freeman's Journal*, 21 May 1921.
5. See open letter signed by Joseph Devlin and other leading Northern nationalists. *Freeman's Journal*, 7 May 1921.
6. Michael Laffan, *The Partition of Ireland, 1911–1925* (Dundalk: Dundalgan Press, 1983), 80–83.
7. Dermot Keogh, *Twentieth Century Ireland, Nation and State* (Dublin: Gill and Macmillan, 1994), 17.
8. See University College Dublin Archives (UCDA) Fianna Fáil Party Papers, P176/28, de Valera's 'National policy' speech at the inaugural meeting of Fianna Fáil, La Scala Theatre, Dublin, 16 May 1926.
9. See UCDA P176/740, record of de Valera's Presidential address, Fianna Fáil Ard Fheis, 24 Nov. 1926. See also UCDA P176/745, copy of de Valera's Presidential address, Fianna Fáil Ard Fheis, 27 Oct 1931 and lastly, Dáil Éireann speech by de Valera, 19 July 1951. See Maurice Moynihan, *Speeches and Statements by Eamon de Valera* (Dublin: Gill and Macmillan 1980), 541–544. See also record of radio broadcast by de Valera, 14 May 1954, in Moynihan, *Speeches and Statements by Eamon de Valera*, 566–570.
10. See comments by Fianna Fáil TD, Frank Fahey. *The Irish Times*, 14 Feb. 1929.
11. See comments by Fianna Fáil TD, Patrick J. Rutledge. *The Irish Times*, 7 Feb. 1929.
12. See, for example, de Valera's comments at the 1933 Fianna Fáil Ard Fheis. UCDA P176/747, record of Fianna Fáil Ard Fheis, 8–9 Oct. 1933.
13. See, for example, de Valera's comments. *Irish Independent*, 14 Sept. 1927. See also de Valera's remarks during two separate Dáil debates. Dáil Éireann debate (DE) 3 May 1933. Vol. 27, cols. 439–440 & DE, 19 Nov. 1936. Vol. 64, cols. 731–732. See also Lemass's Oxford Address, 15 Oct. 1959. Reprinted, *The Irish Times*, 16 Oct. 1959 and his remarks during a Dáil debate in 1961. DE, 6 Dec. 1961. Vol. 192, col. 1213.
14. See John Walsh, *Patrick Hillery, The Official Biography* (Dublin: New Ireland, 2008), 174.
15. See comments by O'Brien. DE, 8 May 1970. Vol. 248, col. 888.
16. National Archives of the United Kingdom (NAUK) Foreign and Commonwealth Office (FCO) 33/1596, British Ambassador to Ireland, John Peck to Sir Stewart Crawford, Foreign and Commonwealth Office, 1 June 1971.
17. See comments by O'Leary. DE, 8 May 1970. Vol. 246, col. 1133.
18. DE, 8 May 1970. Vol. 246, col. 1117.
19. DE, 8 May 1970. Vol. 246, col. 1117.
20. See Lynch's Presidential address at the Fianna Fáil Ard Fheis, 17 Jan. 1970. See Jack Lynch, *Speeches and Statements, Irish Unity Northern Ireland Anglo-Irish Relations, August 1969 – October 1971* (Dublin, Government information bureau, 1972), 16.
21. See NAUK FCO 33/1596, letter entitled 'defection in Fianna Fáil', issued by D.E.S. Blatherwick, British Embassy, Dublin, 19 Aug. 1971.
22. See NAUK FCO 33/1596, letter entitled 'new Republican Party', issued by D.E.S. Blatherwick, British Embassy, Dublin, 19 Aug. 1971.
23. See Lynch's Presidential address, Fianna Fáil Ard Fheis, 20 Feb. 1971. Lynch, *Speeches and Statements, Irish Unity Northern Ireland Anglo-Irish Relations*, 41–48.

24. See NAUK FCO 33/1596, copy of speech by Lynch at a dinner of the South Louth Comhairle Ceantair, Fianna Fáil, at Fairways Hotel, Dundalk, 28 May 1971. See also Lynch's comments, UCDA P176/448, meeting of Fianna Fáil parliamentary party, 22 Sept. 1971.

25. For an overview of Fine Gael's position on Northern Ireland from Aug. 1969 to Feb. 1973, see Garret FitzGerald, *All in a Life, Garret FitzGerald, An Autobiography* (Dublin: Gill and Macmillan, 1991), 88–111. For an overview of the Labour Party's attitude to Northern Ireland from 1969 to 1973, see Niamh Puirséil, *The Irish Labour Party, 1922–73* (Dublin: UCD Press, 2007), 288–299.

26. See Kieran Allen, *Fianna Fáil and Irish Labour, 1926 To The Present* (London: Pluto Press, 1997), 15–16; James Downey, *Irish Times* supplement 'Fifty Years of Fianna Fáil', 19 May 1976. See also Richard Dunphy, *The Making of Fianna Fáil Power in Ireland* (Oxford: Oxford University Press, 1995), 8.

27. See, for example, Catherine O'Donnell, *Fianna Fáil, Irish Republicanism and the Northern Ireland Troubles, 1968–2005* (Dublin: Irish Academic Press, 2007); Paul Arthur, 'Anglo-Irish relations and the Northern Ireland problem', *Irish Studies in International Affairs*, Vol. 2 (1985), 37–59; and John Coakley (ed.), *Changing Shades of Orange and Green: Redefining the Union and the Nation in Contemporary Ireland, Perspectives in British-Irish Studies* (Dublin: UCD Press, 2002).

28. John Bowman, *De Valera and the Ulster Question, 1917–1973* (Oxford: Oxford University Press, 1982).

29. See Tom Gallagher, 'Fianna Fáil and partition 1926–84', *Éire – Ireland*, Vol. 20, No.1 (1985): 39–57; T. Ryle Dwyer, 'Eamon de Valera and the partition question', in (eds.) J. P. O'Carroll and John A. Murphy, *De Valera and His Times* (Cork: Cork University Press, 1986), 74–91; and lastly, David Harkness, 'The north and de Valera', in Sidney Poger (ed.), *The "De Val-Era" in Ireland, 1916–1975* (Boston: Northeastern University Press, 1984), 78–81.

30. Michael Kennedy, *Division and Consensus, The Politics of Cross-Border Relations in Ireland, 1925–1969* (Dublin: Institute for Public Administration, 2000). See also Etain Tannam, *Cross-Border Co-operation in the Republic of Ireland and Northern Ireland* (New York: St Martin's Press, 1999).

31. Donnacha Ó Beacháin, *Destiny of the Soldiers: Fianna Fáil, Irish Republicanism and the IRA, 1926–1973* (Dublin: Gill and Macmillan, 2011).

32. Noel Whelan, *Fianna Fáil, A Biography of the Party* (Dublin: Gill and Macmillan, 2011).

33. See UCDA Patrick Hillery Papers P205/101, see Hillery's handwritten diary entry, 13 Jan. 1978.

34. See Kevin Boland, *The Rise and Decline of Fianna Fáil* (Dublin: Mercer Press, 1982), 70–72. See also Boland, *Under Contract with the Enemy* (Dublin: Mercer Press, 1988).

35. Brendan Lynn, *Holding the Ground: the Nationalist Party in Northern Ireland, 1945–72* (Aldershot: Ashgate, 1997); Lynn, 'The Irish Anti-Partition League and the political realities of partition', *Irish Historical Studies*, Vol. XXXIV, No. 135 (May 2005), 321–332; Lynn, 'Revising northern nationalism, 1960–1965: the Nationalist Party's response', *New Hibernia Review*, Vol. 4, No. 3 (autumn, 2000), 78–92; Enda Staunton, *The Nationalists of Northern Ireland, 1918–1973* (Dublin: Columba Press, 2001); and lastly, Eamon Phoenix, *Northern Nationalism, Nationalists Politics, Partition and the Catholic Minority in NI, 1890–1940* (Ulster Historical Foundation, 1994).

36. Henry Patterson, 'Seán Lemass and the Ulster Question, 1959–65', *Journal of Contemporary History*, Jan. 1999; 34 (1) 145–159 and John Horgan, *Seán Lemass, The Enigmatic Patriot* (Dublin: Gill and Macmillan, 1999), 270–286. For other recommended works on Lemass's views on Northern Ireland see Bryce Evans, *Seán Lemass, Democratic Dictator* (Cork: Collins Press, 2011) and Tom Garvin, *Judging Lemass, The Measure of the Man* (Dublin: Royal Irish Academy, 2009).

37. Walsh, *Patrick Hillery, The Official Biography* and Dermot Keogh, *Jack Lynch, A Biography* (Dublin: Gill and Macmillan, 2008). See also Tom Feeney, *Seán MacEntee, A Political Life* (Dublin: Irish Academic Press, 2009); Dwyer, *Nice Fellow, Jack Lynch* (Cork: Mercier Press, 2001); and James Downey, *Lenihan, His Life his Loyalties* (Dublin: New Island Books, 1998).

38. See Richard English, *Irish Freedom, The History of Nationalism in Ireland* (London: Pan Macmillan, 2007), 327–330 & 354–355.
39. George D. Boyce, *Nationalism in Ireland* (London: Gill and Macmillan, 1991). See also Tom Garvin, *The Evolution of Irish Nationalist Politics* (Dublin: Gill and Macmillan, 2005).
40. See Ernest Gellner, *Nations and Nationalism* (London: Verso, 2006); Elie Kedourie, *Nationalism* (London: Hutchinson, 1993); Eric J. Hobsbawm, *Nations and Nationalism since 1780* (London: Cambridge University Press, 1990). See also John Hutchinson and Anthony D. Smith (eds.), *Nationalism* (Oxford: Oxford University Press, 1994) and Gellner, *Nationalism* (London: Weidenfeld and Nicolson, 1997).
41. Clare O'Halloran, *Partition and the Limits of Irish Nationalism* (New Jersey: Humanities Press International, Inc., 1987).
42. M.W. Heslinga, *The Irish Border As a Cultural Divide* (Netherlands: Van Gorcum Assen, 1979); Laffan, *The Partition of Ireland, 1911–1925*; Denis Gwynn, *The History of Partition, 1912–1925* (Dublin: Browne and Nolan, 1950); and lastly, the partisan study by Frank Gallagher, *The Indivisible Island, The History of Partition of Ireland* (London: Gollancz, 1957).
43. See the *Catholic Digest*, 'De Valera at 70', 1952 and Bowman, *De Valera*, 1.
44. J.J. Lee, *Ireland 1912–1985, Politics and Society* (Cambridge: Cambridge University Press, 1989), 368.
45. John A. Murphy, 'The Achievements of Eamon de Valera', in O'Carroll and Murphy (ed.), *De Valera and His Times*, 12.
46. See *The Irish Times*, 30 Aug. 1975.
47. The Earl of Longford and Thomas P. O'Neill, *Eamon de Valera* (London: Hutchinson, 1970), 470.
48. NAUK Dominions Office (DO) 35/7853, note of the British Ambassador to Ireland, Alexander Clutterbuck's observations of de Valera, 3 July 1959.
49. NAUK DO 35/3926, conversation between de Valera and Rugby reported back to the CRO, 16 Oct. 1947. Maffey was British Representative to Ireland from 1939 to 1949.
50. UCDA Seán MacEntee Papers P67/ 475–478, Seán MacEntee, 'The man I knew', *Iris, Fianna Fáil*, winter 1975 (draft copy).
51. UCDA Eamon de Valera Papers P150/2964, confidential memorandum by de Valera, 1 Sept. 1948.
52. See John Bowman's observation: 'inevitability of Irish unity', Bowman, *De Valera*, 305–06.
53. See UCDA P176/294, Lemass from unidentified Co. Kerry Fianna Fáil supporter, 20 Dec. 1955. See also Gallagher, 'Fianna Fáil and Partition 1926–84', 48–49 and David Thornley's comments of Fianna Fáil supporters' loyalty to the party leadership. *The Irish Times*, 1 April 1965.
54. Gallagher, 'Fianna Fáil and Partition 1926–84', 48.
55. See coverage of the 1954 Fianna Fáil Ard Fheis, *Irish Press*, 13 Oct. 1954. See also coverage of the 1955 Fianna Fáil Ard Fheis. *Irish Press*, 23 Nov. 1955.
56. See de Valera's comments: DE, 22 Aug. 1921. Vol. 4, col. 33; and DE, 29 May 1935. Vol. 56, col. 2114. See also *Irish Independent*, 13 Oct. 1954.
57. At the First Fianna Fáil Ard Fheis, in 1926, in an attempt to win over a sceptical anti-partitionist audience, de Valera did not rule out the use of violence as a method to restore a united Ireland. 'I never said, and am not going to say, that force is not a legitimate weapon for a nation to use in striving to win its freedom'. See UCDA P176/737, 1926 Fianna Fáil Ard Fheis, 24 Nov. 1926. By the 1930s, wishing to distance himself away from the IRA, de Valera's views had altered; at the 1931 Fianna Fáil Ard Fheis his tone emphasised the need for realism. He said that 'force was out of the question. Were it feasible, it would not be desirable'. UCDA P176/42, 1931 Fianna Fáil Ard Fheis, Oct. 1931.
58. See UCDA P150/2075, copy of de Valera's Presidential speech, 1957 Fianna Fáil Ard Fheis, 19 Nov. 1957.
59. See *Irish Times*, 12 May 1971. See also UCDA Todd Andrews Papers P91/158, Edward Mac Aonraoi to Todd Andrews, dated '1980' (reference to Lemass's personality and traits).

60. That said, in the late 1920s and against the wishes of de Valera, Aiken argued that the use of physical force was a legitimate policy to secure Irish unity. By the early 1930s, however, he rejected this policy. See UCDA Frank Aiken Papers P104/1499, copy of 'A call to unity' by Frank Aiken, 19 June 1926.

61. Raymond James Reynold, 'David Gray, the Aiken mission, and Irish neutrality, 1940–41', *Diplomatic History*, Vol. 9, No. 1 (winter, 1985): 55–71; 67.

62. Ronan Fanning, *Dictionary of Irish Biography*, Frank Aiken (Dublin: Cambridge University Press, 2010), 55.

63. For example Henry Patterson wrote that Aiken was reported by some of his own Fianna Fáil colleagues to be a 'bigot'. He also contends that Aiken was 'a bastion of traditional anti-partitionism'. See Patterson, *Ireland Since 1939*, 61 & 157.

64. Fanning, *Dictionary of Irish Biography*, Frank Aiken, 55.

65. Fanning, *Dictionary of Irish Biography*, Frank Aiken, 55.

66. See Terence de Vere White's interview with Seán MacEntee, *The Irish Times* supplement 'Fifty Years of Fianna Fáil', 19 May 1976.

67. *The Irish Times*, 13 Dec. 1979.

68. See for example John Horgan's observations in Horgan, *Seán Lemass*, 183 and Tom Garvin, *Preventing the Future, Why was Ireland so Poor for so Long?* (Dublin: Gill and Macmillan, 2004), 144–145.

69. National Archives of Ireland (NAI) Department of Taoiseach (DT) 2000/6/657, speech by Lynch, Tipperary town, 8 Oct. 1968.

70. See Lynch, *Speeches and Statements, Irish Unity Northern Ireland Anglo-Irish Relations*, 33–35.

71. See Lynch's speech, Dáil Éireann, 28 July 1970, and Lynch's Presidential address, Fianna Fáil Ard Fheis, 20 Feb. 1971. Lynch, *Speeches and Statements, Irish Unity Northern Ireland Anglo-Irish Relations*, 26–29 & 41–48, respectively.

72. Speech by Jack Lynch, Dáil Éireann, 30 July 1970. See Lynch, *Speeches and Statements, Irish Unity Northern Ireland Anglo-Irish Relations*, 30.

73. Speech by Jack Lynch, Dáil Éireann, 30 July 1970. See Lynch, *Speeches and Statements, Irish Unity Northern Ireland Anglo-Irish Relations*, 30.

74. See Lynch's comments at a meeting of the Fianna Fáil parliamentary party, 22 Sept. 1971. UCDA P176/448, meeting of Fianna Fáil parliamentary party, 22 Sept. 1971.

75. Speech by Jack Lynch, Dundalk, 28 May 1971. See Lynch, *Speeches and Statements, Irish Unity Northern Ireland Anglo-Irish Relations*, 55.

76. See NAUK FCO 33/1596, record of address by Colley, Cáirde Fáil Luncheon meeting, Jury's Hotel, Dublin, 18 Nov. 1971.

77. UCDA P67/155, (draft) MacEntee to de Valera, 17 Feb. 1938.

1

1926–1937

'I am getting old ... but I am young enough yet to see a Republic functioning in Ireland'.

[Eamon de Valera, 9 Nov. 1933] [1]

FIANNA FÁIL, IRISH UNITY AND ANTI-PARTITIONISM, 1926–1932

Fianna Fáil, the 'Republican Party', formally established in May 1926, was born out of the ashes of the fiasco surrounding the boundary commission agreement in 1925. Founded by a group of disenfranchised anti-treatyites and led by the charismatic and sole surviving commandant of the Easter 1916 Rising, Eamon de Valera, Fianna Fáil portrayed itself as the embodiment of Irish republicanism. From its inception Fianna Fáil was determined to create a political hegemony – to accommodate republican sympathisers, draw in the petty bourgeoisie and win support from the urban working classes, the small farmers and the rural peasantry. The party incorporated a powerful blend of social justice, economic protectionism and Catholicism under the banner of Irish nationalism. Paraphrasing his republican idol Pádraig Pearse, in April 1926, de Valera asserted that Fianna Fáil's *raison d'être* was to see 'his country politically free, and not only free but truly Irish as well'.[2]

An unauthorised draft report of the boundary commission agreement, published in the British Tory *Morning Post* in November 1925, accurately predicted that the boundary commission, originally devised under the terms of the Anglo-Irish Treaty of 1921, would make only minor transfers of territory to both the Free State and Northern Ireland.[3] To the bewilderment of the Dublin government the commission recommended a relatively insignificant adjustment of the border, with the transfer of some 130,000 acres and 24,000 people from Northern Ireland to the Free State. The report also envisaged a smaller transfer of land and people from the South to the North.[4] There was outrage and confusion in Dublin and the Irish government's representative, Ulster Catholic, Eóin MacNeill promptly resigned from the boundary commission.

In the end, following retracted negotiations in London, on 3 December 1925, an agreement was reached revoking the powers of article twelve of the Anglo-Irish Treaty of 1921. The border between Dublin and Belfast, therefore, remained unchanged and the powers of the Council of Ireland – the legislative vehicle that nationalist Ireland hoped would facilitate Irish unity – were transferred to the government of Northern Ireland.[5] The Bill to enact the boundary commission agreement was presented to the Dáil on 7 December and although it lead to some heated debates, after several days of discussions, it was passed by a margin of fifty-two votes to fifteen, on 15 December.[6]

Thereafter, the Cumann na nGaedheal cabinet dropped Northern Ireland with indecent haste. De Valera, leader of the anti-treaty Sinn Féin movement, quickly filled the vacuum left by the Free State's indifference on the partition question, depicting himself as the guardian of nationalist Ireland. When news of the Bill's passing reached de Valera he was furious and condemned the decision in language that bordered on incitement. This categorical affirmation of partition, he declared, demonstrated 'how futile merely verbal protest is'. The subject of partition, he maintained, was the supreme question in Irish politics.[7] His patriotic outbursts against the continued partition of Ireland were not unwarranted, considering that by signing the agreement the Cumann na nGaedheal government had arguably granted *de facto* recognition to Northern Ireland. Therefore, although the Free State government disagreed with partition, they had reluctantly accepted its permanence, at least in the immediate period.

De Valera anticipated that the debacle surrounding the boundary commission agreement would entice anti-treaty Sinn Féin supporters to reconsider their abstentionist policy. Since the foundation of the Free State in 1921 anti-treaty Sinn Féin's refusal to take the 'oath of allegiance to a foreign power' was sacrilegiously adhered to by party members.[8] In the aftermath of the boundary commission agreement debacle, at a meeting of the Comhairle na dTeachtaí (the republican government of the 'Council of Deputies' set up to rival Dáil Éireann), prominent Sinn Féin deputies, including TD for Kerry, Austin Stack and TD for Roscommon, Gerald Boland, argued that the party should enter Dáil Éireann and vote against the boundary commission agreement Bill. Boland subsequently wrote that he felt that the time had arrived to 'take our proper place in the life of the country'.[9] Although the Stack/Boland proposal was rejected by Republican TD for Cork-Borough, Mary MacSwiney, Boland told those present at the meeting of the Comhairle na dTeachtaí that '… in my view we would be blamed by future generations, not for being responsible for partition, but for allowing it to be agreed to when there was a very good chance of defeating the Bill'.[10]

De Valera, as ever treading a cautious line, refused to back the Stack/Boland proposal; although it is widely recorded that for some time prior to the boundary commission agreement de Valera had already favoured taking the oath of allegiance and that he used the fiasco as an excuse to persuade the Sinn Féin Party to abandon abstentionism.[11] Asked by MacSwiney if he would support the proposal, de Valera remained tight-lipped. Instead he suggested that a special gathering of the Sinn Féin Ard Fheis should convene to consider the movement's abstentionist policy.[12] Between late 1925 and the early months of 1926, de Valera took soundings on support for a more flexible and less doctrinaire opposition to the Free State. By this stage a split within the Sinn Féin movement was firmly on the cards, with intelligence reports claiming that 'a number of Irregulars are in favour of entry to the Dáil'.[13]

In March 1926, the specially arranged Sinn Féin Ard Fheis duly met. De Valera proposed a motion that if the oath of allegiance was abolished Sinn Féin elected representatives would take their seats in Dáil Éireann. This Ard Fheis, Gerald Boland later recorded, signalled the moment that 'the time had arrived to adopt a realistic attitude on political matters'.[14] Like de Valera, he was left disappointed. After protracted discussions the resolution to end abstentionism was narrowly defeated. The radical Roscommon priest Fr Michael O'Flanagan challenged de Valera's motion, proposing an amendment rejecting entry to the hated Free State parliament at all cost.[15]

De Valera turned the defeat to his benefit and in a decisive act broke away from the doctrinaires within Sinn Féin, resigning as president of the party. In May 1926, with the aid of the young Seán Lemass and a cohort of loyal followers, de Valera launched a new political movement, Fianna Fáil. In almost every parish Fianna Fáil rapidly built up a loyal rank-and-file support base through the establishment of an impressive network of cumainn, which by November 1927 stood at 1,307.[16] It was a 'national movement' rather than a political party. In the words of Kevin Boland, it was 'not a normal political party because it had this noble and historic ideal', an ideal to secure an independent, free and united Ireland.[17]

The choice of name, Fianna Fáil, the 'Republican Party', was significant: the ancient name of Fianna Fáil indicated continuity with the 'spirit and devotion' of the Irish Volunteers founded in 1913.[18] It was the name of a short-lived bulletin edited and largely written by Terence McSwiney for the supporters of the Cork volunteers opposed to Irish participation in the First World War.[19] Fianna Fáil's sub-title, 'the Republican Party' was equally important. It denoted the movement's commitment to the establishment of a thirty-two county Republic. In reality, the choice of name represented a compromise. De Valera wanted Fianna Fáil; Lemass favoured the Republican Party. De Valera's younger lieutenant argued that the people would not know what Fianna Fáil meant and he also suspected that their opponents would distort the Irish letters Fáil into the English word 'fail'.[20] In the end de Valera's choice prevailed over Lemass's less romantic proposal, albeit in a compromise formula, in which both titles were used.

At the inaugural meeting of Fianna Fáil, held at La Scala Theatre, Dublin, on 16 May 1926, de Valera outlined the fundamental aims of the new organisation; foremost among them were the reunification of Ireland and the restoration of the Irish language. 'The first political objective ... of our organisation', he announced, 'is to secure the unity and the independence of Ireland'. 'To me', he explained, 'the unity of Ireland was the first essential to any hope of independence. As long as part of Ireland is cut off, there is no use in talking about independence'. Greeted with a furore of applause from those assembled, he proclaimed that 'We do not accept partition as being a thing that has been accepted by the will of the Irish people. That is our position'.[21]

Although on paper the ending of partition represented Fianna Fáil's number one objective, from 1926 onwards, de Valera admitted that he was unable to offer any immediate solution to the problem. 'Personally', he explained at the inaugural meeting of Fianna Fáil in May 1926, 'I knew there is no clear out way of solving this problem'. If any man, he said, was able to find a 'clear out solution of that problem, it would be no problem at all. That is a fact'.[22] He continued this theme at the inaugural Fianna Fáil Ard Fheis, later that year, in November 1926. Irish unity, he said, could not be solved overnight.[23] He also claimed that Irish nationalists were not at fault for failing to end partition. Rather, he laid the blame squarely at the feet of the London government; an accusation which remained a staple diet of his Northern Ireland policy throughout his political career. The British, he explained, with all the strength of its Empire, were Ireland's main opponents in securing a united Ireland.[24]

Therefore, unable to offer an immediate solution for ending partition and faced with stalwart British opposition – not to mention Ulster Unionists' rejection – of a united Ireland, de Valera spelt out the crux of Fianna Fáil's Northern Ireland policy. In the immediate term, the party must focus all resources on securing a Republican government in the twenty-six counties, which by its deeds, would build up Ireland's economic and social strength. Once Ireland's industrial and social potency was 'far superior' than that of Northern Ireland, de Valera argued, only then would the British government be compelled to agree to Irish unity.[25] In the run up to the Irish general election of June 1927, at which Fianna Fáil secured forty-four seats, de Valera reiterated the basis of his Northern Ireland policy to a correspondent of the *Daily Mail*: 'if we in the Twenty-Six Counties built up a sound national economy, raised standards of living and generally made the country a place to be proud of, I believe that the people of the Six-Counties would be anxious to join us'.[26]

Although he never dared to admit it publicly, this approach was a version of Michael Collins's stepping stone policy to the attainment of a united Ireland, which the anti-treaty republicans, led by de Valera, had previously rejected. Henceforth, Fianna Fáil would work within the parameters of the state, if only with the objective of changing it. Under de Valera's leadership Fianna Fáil was to be republican, but not doctrinaire, claiming continuity, but avoiding commitment to the past.[27] Some years later de Valera informed Michael McInerney of *The Irish Times* that in the aftermath of the boundary commission agreement the former realised that the Irish people 'were not going to turn away from the Dáil, the Southern Parliament of the Free State Assembly'.[28] Therefore, he came to the conclusion that he must either continue to oppose the apparatus of the Free State or reluctantly acknowledge its legitimacy. Fianna Fáil's decision in 1927 to end its abstentionist policy and take the hated oath of allegiance to the British King is a point in question. Following the assassination of deputy prime minister and minister for home affairs, Kevin O'Higgins, in August 1927, the Free State government introduced legislation obliging elected TDs to take their seats in the Dáil or forfeit them.

Initially, de Valera was reluctant to enter Dáil Éireann unless the oath of allegiance was first removed. Gerald Boland recalled that de Valera was particularly anxious not to further antagonise the IRA, because of the movement's continued support for abstentionism and bitter opposition to the Free State apparatus. Boland noted that the Fianna Fáil hierarchy held several meetings to consider the issue, at which he spoke in favour of entering Dáil Éireann. De Valera, however, remained evasive on the issue. Boland subsequently described his leader's non-committal attitude as 'foolish'.[29] In an attempt to placate de Valera's reservations, Boland held secret discussions with prominent members of the IRA, comprised of Moss Twomey, Andy Cooney and Seán Russell (the discussions took place at Russell's home in the North Strand, Dublin). Boland explained that de Valera was eager to secure assurances that the IRA would remain 'inactive', if Fianna Fáil entered Dáil Éireann. After prolonged discussions they agreed to de Valera's request.[30] Twomey subsequently recorded that by their actions Fianna Fáil had 'abandoned orthodoxy republicanism'. Nonetheless, he was 'not very angered' by the decision, as he too believed that abstentionism was by then a 'futile and wrong' policy.[31]

After much soul searching and assured of the IRA's passive resistance de Valera made one of the most important decisions of his political career. On Friday 12 August 1927, reported by the *Irish Independent* as 'a tense day of excitement', de Valera escorted forty-two of his fellow Fianna Fáil deputies through the gates of Leinster House.[32] Describing Fianna Fáil's decision to end its policy of abstentionism as 'painful and humiliating' de Valera argued that to do otherwise would have lead to 'civil war'.[33] Accordingly, he entered Dáil Éireann removed the Bible to a far corner of the room, covered the oath in the register with some papers and signed.[34] It was an astonishing chain of events, in a matter of a few months, the hated oath of allegiance was transformed from an 'oath to partition', into a mere 'empty formula'.[35] In the words of the British *Daily News*, 'Fianna Fáil can never be itself again'.[36]

Under de Valera's skilful management the abandonment of abstentionism closed the gap between Fianna Fáil's self-declared ideological principles and the realities of contemporary politics. For a cohort of senior Fianna Fáil figures de Valera's *volte face* was a base betrayal of the republican orthodoxy. In protest at the decision to take the oath, Hanna Sheehy Skeffington and Dorothy Macardle resigned from the Fianna Fáil National Executive.[37] Macardle was left furious at the decision; de Valera reportedly gave her his 'solemn promise' that he would not take the oath of allegiance.[38] A selection of Fianna Fáil grass-roots were, likewise, displeased by de Valera's actions and at the party's second Ard Fheis, in November 1927, the rank-and-file tolerated rather than supported their leader's pragmatic decision.[39]

By 1927, as Fianna Fáil deputies accustomed themselves to the day-to-day routine of the opposition benches, partition was rarely discussed. True to his word, de Valera's attention and that of his party, was instead concerned with the immediate issues of the day in the twenty-six counties. A general election pamphlet from 1927 typified the party's preoccupation. It outlined Fianna Fáil's central policies if elected to government. Partition was not mentioned. Rather the pamphlet focused on the removal of the oath of allegiance, retaining the land annuities and emigration.[40] From the outset the Fianna Fáil parliamentary party rarely discussed partition. At its inaugural gathering in June 1927, de Valera proposed that all elected Fianna Fáil TDs sign a form undertaking to support the party 'in every action it takes to secure the independence of a united Ireland'.[41] Behind this hollow ritualistic pledge, however, partition was ignored throughout Fianna Fáil's years in opposition from 1926 to 1932.

During these years on the opposition benches de Valera's preoccupation, as with most ambitious politicians, was the attainment of power: to secure and consolidate a Fianna Fáil government in the twenty-six counties. The party forged ahead, founding numerous sub-committees to examine economic, agricultural and industrial policy; nonetheless, no such committee was formed to examine partition.[42] The Fianna Fáil leadership's preoccupation with economic and social considerations meant that there was little time to consider the question of Irish unity. Through the use of radical rhetoric de Valera was determined to win a wide electoral base. Therefore, the party hierarchy focused much of its time and resources propagating the party's economic nationalism, which emphasised economic self-sufficiency with the growth of native industries. The party publicly condemned the encroachment of foreign investment in Ireland, attacked the parasitical banking network and opposed the payment of land annuities.[43] The party also asserted that Ireland must create a unique society that was built on the social and conservative principles of Catholicism. Under de Valera, Catholicism and nationalism were to be fused together to create a society constructed around social justice.[44]

Despairingly, by the turn of the 1930s, Fianna Fáil TDs were more inclined to protest at the standard of food in the Oireachtas restaurant than to discuss partition.[45] The party's self-declared 'number one objective' was not debated at parliamentary party meetings,[46] nor was there any partition resolution placed on the Clár at consecutive Fianna Fáil Ard Fheiseanna between 1929 and 1932.[47] De Valera was instead preoccupied with dampening down any expectation that the attainment of Irish unity was a short-term objective. For instance, at the 1931 Ard Fheis, he stated that 'as regards to partition, I see no immediate solution'.[48] Instead, he merely repeated the crux of Fianna Fáil's Northern Ireland policy first articulated in 1926: the 'only hope', he said, for an end to partition, 'was good government in the Twenty-Six Counties and such social and economic conditions here as will attract the majority in the Six-Counties to throw their lot with us'.[49]

Although reluctant to maintain a debate on partition within Fianna Fáil, in the public domain, de Valera created the impression that the party was the custodians of the aspiration for Irish unity. In the words of Fianna Fáil deputy for Dublin-North, Seán T. O'Kelly speaking in the Dáil in October 1927, only a Fianna Fáil government could get Ireland 'back on its feet' and bring the 'curse' of partition to an end.[50] This witnessed the emergence of a second defining feature of Fianna Fáil's Northern Ireland policy during the early years of the party's existence: the use of anti-partitionism. Aspirational in character, under de Valera, the party propagated the 'evils' and 'crime' of partition.[51] Anti-partitionism was a tool employed by Fianna Fáil to reassure nationalist Ireland that the party was determined to end partition. This policy remained at the core of Fianna Fáil's approach to Northern Ireland for a generation and was not finally abandoned until the early-1950s. Behind the bravado, however, such expressions of anti-partitionism exposed the limitations of Fianna Fáil's Northern Ireland policy.

The debacle surrounding de Valera's arrest by the Royal Ulster Constabulary (RUC), while on a visit to Northern Ireland in 1929, revealed the shortcomings of such anti-partitionism. Under the 1924 Northern Ireland Prohibition Act, de Valera was prohibited from entering or residing in the counties of Armagh, Down, Fermanagh, Tyrone, Londonderry and the city of Belfast; the only region of Northern Ireland he was permitted entry was county Antrim. In February 1929, he defied this Act and returned to Northern Ireland, accepting an invitation to open a Gaelic bazaar in Belfast.[52] Soon afterwards he was arrested by RUC officers at Goraghwood train station, near Newry. He was then transported to Belfast and placed in prison. At his court hearing, adhering to the Irish Republican tradition of a martyr in a 'foreign' courtroom, de Valera refused to recognise 'that this court has any authority'.[53] Speaking only in Irish, he was sentenced to one month's imprisonment. He was then offered to be released as long as he promised not to enter Northern Ireland again without permission – he refused.[54] He was duly charged for contravention of the exclusion order which had been issued against him five years before and was sentenced to one month's imprisonment.[55]

Fianna Fáil's reaction to this incident bore all the hallmarks of a publicity stunt designed to embarrass the Free State government and keep afresh in nationalist Ireland's mind Fianna Fáil's commitment to ending partition. The vast majority of speeches delivered in the wake of de Valera's arrest attacked Cumann na nGaedheal ministers for allegedly turning their back on partition. Seán T. O'Kelly led the protests against the government and selected the president of the executive council, William T. Cosgrave for particular criticism. Fianna Fáil deputies were left infuriated by Cosgrave's remarks in the Dáil, on 20 February 1929, that his government had 'no jurisdiction' in relation to de Valera's arrest and therefore could not 'interfere with the administration of law in Northern Ireland'.[56]

O'Kelly was incensed and taunted the government with jibes, 'What have you done? What protests have you made?'. 'All you have managed to do', O'Kelly exclaimed, was to send 'begging letters' to Ulster Unionists and crawl on 'your knees' pleading for clemency.[57] The government, he shouted across the Dáil chamber, should be 'ashamed' of itself for failing to tackle partition.[58] He was left to bemoan that the Cumann na nGaedheal government had accepted partition 'agreed to it, mentally, morally and physically'.[59] Fianna Fáil TD for Cork-East, Martin Corry was equally forthright, accusing Cumann na nGaedheal ministers of having no 'backbone'.[60] According to Fianna Fáil propaganda the Cumann na nGaedheal government had 'sold the population of six of our Northern counties into slavery to the English enemy'.[61]

Outside the Dáil, de Valera's incarceration evoked a tidal wave of anti-partitionist protests from a consortium of senior Fianna Fáil figures. Deputy for Mayo-North, Patrick J. Rutledge (who assumed the role of Fianna Fáil leader during de Valera's imprisonment) noted that de Valera's arrest emphasised the existence of the 'unnatural boundary between the Six-Counties and the Free State'. He asserted that Irish unity was only achievable if a Fianna Fáil government held power.[62] Seán MacEntee, TD for Dublin-County, was equally incensed by de Valera's arrest. A Belfast native, MacEntee was unlike the vast majority of his party colleagues in that he was aware of Northern realities and the scale of discrimination levelled against Northern Ireland Catholics. He later claimed that it was the singular act of the partition of Ireland, not the oath of allegiance, which made him so vehemently opposed to the Anglo-Irish Treaty of 1921.[63] 'We will not rest content', he noted in the aftermath of de Valera's arrest, 'until we have the Republican flag floating not alone over Cave Hill, but on Stormont'.[64]

At a meeting of the Fianna Fáil National Executive, on 7 February 1929, MacEntee won unanimous support for his resolution, which denounced de Valera's arrest as 'a violation of the right of an Irish citizen to visit and speak in any part of Ireland'. On behalf of Fianna Fáil, the resolution continued, 'we call upon Irishmen in every country to unite in manifesting their resentment towards this act of tyranny, inspired by the enemies of a United Ireland'.[65] Deputy for Carlow-Kilkenny, Thomas Derrig, also proposed a resolution calling on Fianna Fáil to organise a public meeting in Dublin to protest at de Valera's arrest, while P. T. McGinley proposed a resolution that those sympathetic to Irish unity should abstain from purchasing goods from Belfast.[66] Although after some discussions the latter two proposals were rejected, the following week an estimated 5,000 people attended a rally at College Green, Dublin, to protest at de Valera's arrest.[67]

Perhaps the largest protest came from Seán Lemass. Eager to play the anti-partitionist card he expressed his outrage upon learning of de Valera's imprisonment. He labelled Ulster Unionists as 'bigots' and argued that the episode provided all the evidence needed that there could be no stability or peace in Ireland until Fianna Fáil had 'definitely established not merely independence, but political and territorial unity as well'.[68] In words, echoing those of his party leader, he said that partition was the 'greatest wrong ever perpetrated by Britain against the Irish people'.[69]

Lemass was not simply interested on beating the anti-partitionist drum and at the National Executive meeting on 7 February he insisted that given 'the new situation now existing' Fianna Fáil must establish a 'special committee' to reconsider the party's Northern Ireland policy.[70] Lemass's appeals for the party to reconsider its Northern Ireland policy were, however, politely ignored. Instead a watered-down version of his resolution was passed by the National Executive, which agreed to appoint a committee 'to consider how best to increase the effectiveness of public protest against the arrest of Mr de Valera'.[71]

At local county council level several resolutions were passed protesting against de Valera's arrest and the continued maintenance of partition. At a 'special meeting' of Limerick Corporation, attended by eighteen members, councillor M.C. Ford moved a resolution demanding that 'all Irishmen who stand for the unity of Ireland to cooperate in any action that may be taken to prevent the sale of Six County products'.[72] At a meeting of Cork County Council, Fianna Fáil TD for Cork-West and founding member of the movement, Tommy Mullins, spoke of the deplorable actions of the Northern Ireland government, while at Carrickmacross Urban Council, Co. Monaghan, a special meeting denounced the actions of the Ulster Unionist 'bigots'.[73] Similar protests and the passing of resolutions occurred at county council meetings in counties Leitrim, Donegal, Longford, Kerry, Westmeath, Kildare, Clare and Cavan.[74]

Upon his release from prison de Valera depicted the affair as a propaganda triumph for Fianna Fáil, as it brought a 'substantial accretion of strength and prestige' to the party.[75] It lay bare, he proclaimed, 'the foundations of force and repression on which the present order in Ireland rests'.[76] Behind such anti-partitionist rhetoric, however, the episode merely reinforced Fianna Fáil's inability to make any inroads towards ending partition. Neither the British nor Northern Ireland governments gave Fianna Fáil's protests much consideration. In truth, besides the occasional outbursts of anti-partitionism, Fianna Fáil was not interested in implementing any actual workable policies to help end partition. This was evidentially apparent given de Valera's refusal to extend the Fianna Fáil organisation into Northern Ireland. Given that Sinn Féin was organised in Northern Ireland and remembering the very *raison d'être* for Fianna Fáil's existence was to achieve a united Ireland, the party hierarchy's hesitation to extend across the border came as a surprise and disappointment to many party members.

IDEOLOGY VS. PRAGMATISM: FIANNA FÁIL AS A NORTHERN IRELAND POLITICAL PARTY

At the inaugural Fianna Fáil Ard Fheis in November 1926 de Valera categorically ruled out the extension of the party into Northern Ireland.[77] Speaking to party's rank-and-file he pleaded with supporters to adhere to his policy. While acknowledging that 'Fianna Fáil was intended to be an all-Ireland organisation', he argued that Southern nationalists 'should take cognisance of the fact that the conditions in the Twenty-Six Counties and the Six-Counties were different and they require different treatment'.[78] The honorary secretary's report, issued at the Ard Fheis, disclosed that the general organising committee 'had not attempted actively' to organise the party in Northern Ireland.[79]

In typical de Valera speak he maintained that in principle he wanted Fianna Fáil to enter Northern Ireland, however, this could only be achieved when the right circumstances arose. 'The time to start organising in the Six-Counties', he explained, 'would depend on the conditions there'. Pointing out that 'Republicans were in the majority in the Twenty-Six Counties', the situation was different in Northern Ireland, as 'unfortunately the majority vote in the Six-Counties was neither Republican or Nationalist and therefore the problem was different'.[80] This policy, of non-intervention in Northern Ireland politics, was to remain a staple part of de Valera's attitude to partition throughout his reign as party leader.

It was a policy decision, however, which frustrated many within Fianna Fáil, including some senior party members and grass-roots. At the 1926 Ard Fheis the party's two honorary secretaries, Seán Lemass and Gerald Boland requested that the Fianna Fáil National Executive 'be directed to endeavour to effect an arrangement for the preservation of the unity of the Republican movement in the counties of Antrim, Armagh, Derry, Fermanagh and Tyrone'.[81] It was envisaged that once this was achieved the road would be then clear for Fianna Fáil to remodel itself on an all-Ireland thirty-two-county basis.

De Valera, however, rejected the Lemass/Boland motion. Instead, after some arm twisting, he managed to withdraw the resolution and in its place secured agreement that 'as a preliminary to the establishment of the Fianna Fáil organisation in the Six-Counties area a representatives conference of Republicans in that area be convened ...'[82] In the event that an agreement could not be reached among Northern nationalist representatives and Fianna Fáil, it was agreed that the party's National Executive 'be directed to take immediate steps to establish Fianna Fáil in that area'.[83]

Lemass was eager, initially at least, to examine the possibility of extending Fianna Fáil across the border, but given de Valera's opposition he realised he would have to bide his time. At a meeting of the party's National Executive in January 1928, Lemass and MacEntee expressed their willingness to meet representatives of the Nationalist Party in Northern Ireland, in the hope that they could 'discuss the possibility of co-operation'.[84] On foot of the National Executive's deliberations and following a request from Cahir Healy, MP for South Fermanagh, in early February 1928, it was agreed that Lemass would lead a Fianna Fáil delegation to Northern Ireland to hold discussions with the newly formed Nationalist political organisation.[85]

Later that month a committee of prominent Fianna Fáil members, including Lemass, Gerald Boland and Seán T. O'Kelly, travelled to Northern Ireland to investigate the possibility of the party contesting the forthcoming Northern Ireland elections. On two separate visits the Fianna Fáil delegation met a collection of prominent Northern nationalists,[86] in order to gain 'first hand information' of the current state of affairs in Northern Ireland.[87] Northern Catholics welcomed the proposal with open arms. Bishop of Clogher, Co. Tyrone, Dr Patrick McKenna reported that the 'time was opportune for setting up' Fianna Fáil in Northern Ireland.[88] Moreover, in February 1928 Lemass travelled to London to consider the 'possibility' of extending the organisation in England.[89] Indeed, by this period Fianna Fáil had a branch in Sydney, Australia.[90]

However, following their explanatory talks, Lemass and O'Kelly advised that any attempts at 'getting a united political action' between Northern Nationalists and Fianna Fáil should be postponed.[91] The Fianna Fáil committee reported that

> whilst many individuals are anxious that Fianna Fáil should take the initiative and actively organise the area from Headquarters, the general view among Republicans is that an essential step to the realisation of national unity will be a political victory by Republicans in the South, and that it will be wise policy not to divert our energies from that objective ... although Fianna Fáil would give all possible assistance to Northern Nationalist candidates, such an effort would be more likely to give results if it originated within that area, than if it originated in Dublin.[92]

Although Lemass noted that local efforts had been made to establish cumainn in Northern Ireland, with some success particularly in Co. Derry,[93] the party hierarchy (no doubt under de Valera's orders) maintained that the organisation should leave aside any ambitions of contesting Northern Ireland elections until Fianna Fáil secured a 'political victory' and entered government in the South. Consequently, while Lemass noted that Fianna Fáil would 'work with any Nationalist party who would seek fearlessly and honestly to end partition', behind the bravado, he wished to distance the party away from Northern nationalists.[94] Speaking at the Fianna Fáil Ard Fheis in November 1929 (at which there was no partition resolution on the Clár) Lemass and Boland reported that '... any effort to organise Republicans' in Northern Ireland 'would be more likely to give results if it originated in the North-East than in Dublin ...'[95]

The Fianna Fáil hierarchy's reluctance to extend across the border at this time may have also been influenced by the party's poor organisational activities during 1929. Disappointment was expressed with the level of finance achieved through national collections and the number of registered cumainn had declined dramatically.[96] In such circumstances it is perhaps understandable that de Valera sought to consolidate the party's organisation base in the Free State, rather than diverting scarce resources to Fianna Fáil's political ambitions in Northern Ireland.

When Fianna Fáil entered government in 1932 the party no longer maintained a debate on the issue.[97] Although de Valera won a seat as an abstentionist MP for South Down in 1933, his was an isolated case. No other Fianna Fáil TD was willing to follow suit on the grounds that the party's aim was to 'consolidate ... not divide' Northern Nationalism.[98] De Valera's election was a symbolic gesture, the only concrete effect of which was to deprive the nationalists of South Down of their MP, since de Valera was too occupied as minister for external affairs and president of the Irish Free State, to worry himself with their concerns.[99]

Speaking on the eve of the Northern Ireland general election in 1933, de Valera personally recorded that 'Fianna Fáil has no intention of putting forward candidates in the Six-Counties in the coming elections'.[100] Although he announced his habitual pledge to bring partition to an 'end as speedily as possible', he rejected the proposition of extending Fianna Fáil across the border. The political conditions in Northern Ireland, he explained, 'are today very different to those in the Twenty-Six [Counties]. These differences cannot be ignored in framing the general national policy'. Fianna Fáil, he noted, was not in a position to enter Northern Ireland politics until there was 'substantial agreement upon a common policy' from Northern Nationalists.[101]

In January 1934, the secretary of the Department of the President, Seán O'Muineacháin, rejected a request from Cahir Healy that Fianna

Fáil intervene in the forthcoming by-elections in Belfast Central, and counties Tyrone and Fermanagh. O'Muineacháin explained that while Fianna Fáil 'is ready to co-operate in any movement which is likely to bring partition to an end', de Valera was adamant that Fianna Fáil 'will take no initiative in the way of intervention in differences of opinion among Six County anti-partitionists'. 'These are matters for decision', O'Muineacháin wrote, 'in the areas immediately concerned' and thus were not Dublin's responsibility.[102]

The following year in October 1935, Archdeacon P.P. Tierney, of St Michael's Enniskillen, Co. Fermanagh, wrote to the Fianna Fáil National Executive reporting rumours that Fianna Fáil had given 'silent approval' to Republican candidates in the Fermanagh-Tyrone Northern Ireland elections.[103] National Executive members promptly replied to Archdeacon Tierney's letter, stating that it was the unanimous view of the executive that Fianna Fáil had no intention of interfering in the forthcoming election in Tyrone-Fermanagh. The letter explained that the matter was 'for the decision by the Nationalists of that area'. 'We have not taken or supported', it continued, 'and we do not propose to take or support, any action which might prevent the attainment of that result'.[104]

Throughout the 1930s Eamonn Donnelly persistently called on Fianna Fáil to be remodelled on an all-Ireland basis and was reportedly 'incensed' at de Valera's refusal to extend the party across the border.[105] Donnelly had served as Sinn Féin chief organiser during the early 1920s and was a founder member of Fianna Fáil.[106] First elected to the Northern Ireland Parliament as Sinn Féin MP for Co. Armagh from 1925 to 1929, he was elected Fianna Fáil TD for Laois-Offaly in 1933. At the Fianna Fáil Ard Fheis in November 1933, he heckled de Valera and shouted, 'What about the North?'[107]

Despite such occasional outbursts by the late 1930s de Valera maintained his opposition to the extension of Fianna Fáil across the border. In January 1938 he turned down an offer to run as a candidate for South Down in the forthcoming election;[108] seemingly not wanting to agitate further Ulster Unionists or the British government while the Anglo-Irish negotiations were taking place, and also because he had come to believe that anti-partitionist candidates should boycott the election.[109] In July 1939, at a meeting of the Fianna Fáil parliamentary party, he 'advised' members not to agree to select two Fianna Fáil candidates to run in the approaching Northern Ireland elections.[110]

During the Second World War the idea that Fianna Fáil should be remodelled on an all-Ireland basis was continually rejected by the party hierarchy. At the 1939, 1944 and 1945 Ard Fheiseanna, Fianna Fáil supporters expressed their anger that the organisation had failed to establish political branches of the party in Northern Ireland.[111] At the 1944 conference, for example, a delegate of the Seán Ó Ceallaigh cumann, Dublin North-West, remarked how it had always struck him as 'extraordinary that Fianna Fáil had never tackled organising in the Six-Counties' or had not contested recent Northern Ireland elections. He said that 'they had a cumann in Scotland but none in the lost province'.[112]

In the post-war period the Fianna Fáil leadership refused to budge on the issue. At the Fianna Fáil Ard Fheis in November 1945, Fr McCormack demanded that Fianna Fáil be extended into Northern Ireland; his request, however, was rejected by de Valera. Gerald Boland dubiously remarked that the extension of Fianna Fáil across the border would 'not be feasible for obvious reasons'.[113] In 1948, at a meeting of the party's internal National Executive publicity sub-committee, Eoin Ryan and Basil Clancy 'recommended that the organisation be extended into the Six Co. Area'. Their requests were once again politely ignored by de Valera.[114] This theme continued during the Fianna Fáil Ard Fheiseanna in 1949 and 1953, as grass-roots appeals 'for the extension of the Fianna Fáil organisation into the North', were opposed by the party hierarchy.[115]

Speaking in 1953, de Valera admitted that Fianna Fáil had considered the establishment of the organisation in Northern Ireland, but decided that it would be 'far better to stand aside, and to allow the people of the Six-Counties to form a political organisation which would suit their own needs'. If Fianna Fáil crossed the border, he explained, it was likely to 'create more difficulties than the solution of difficulties, and would be very unwise'. 'The people in the Six-Counties', he said, 'have different problems from a political point of view'.[116] He was adamant that such a venture was politically futile considering that from a practical point of view little success could be made given Ulster Unionist dominance of Northern Ireland politics. Citing the widespread instances of gerrymandering of the electoral system by Ulster Unionists throughout Northern Ireland, de Valera maintained it would be 'impossible' for Fianna Fáil to carry out its programme.[117]

Tommy Mullins, Fianna Fáil's general secretary from 1945 to 1973, admitted shortly before his death in 1976 that Fianna Fáil's decision not to extend into Northern Ireland was a major 'mistake'. 'Representatives from the North', he explained, 'advised us that it would only worsen matters if we organised Fianna Fáil in the North. We accepted this advice ... but looking back I feel we did the wrong thing. We should have organised there long ago'.[118] According to Donegal Fianna Fáil stalwart Neil Blaney it was no accident that Fianna Fáil did not emerge as an all-Ireland party. Blaney noted that, in his view, Dublin-based Ulstermen active in the party prevented the organisation from extending into Northern Ireland. He accused Fianna Fáil heavyweights Seán MacEntee and Frank Aiken, together with Senators Joseph Connolly and Denis McCullough of leading the case against forming the party on an all-Ireland basis.[119]

From a purely practical standpoint there would have been many advantages to establishing Fianna Fáil across the border. Of course it would have taken considerable time, effort and finances to establish a professional cumainn system in Northern Ireland, nonetheless, the rewards would have been considerable. Once the branches were set up and managed accordingly, they would be self-financing and could contribute to the upkeep of party headquarters in Dublin. The propaganda value of transforming into an all-Ireland organisation would have also increased Fianna Fáil's national appeal and reinforced the notion that the party remained the custodians for the aspiration for Irish unity.

For many supporters the Fianna Fáil leadership's reluctance to establish the party in Northern Ireland represented a paradox; Fianna Fáil was preaching anti-partitionism and unity, the orthodox policy for such a party would be to organise throughout the thirty-two counties and adopt an abstentionist policy in the Northern Ireland elections. Under de Valera's guidance, pragmatic considerations took priority over ideological aspirations. Believing that Fianna Fáil would have little chance of electoral success if the party organised in Northern Ireland, but instead further split an already fragmented nationalist electorate, grass-roots demands for the party's extension were thus ignored. Most significantly, as is discussed below, de Valera's fixation with securing and maintaining power in the South meant that the question of partition and the attainment of a united Ireland remained in the political doldrums.

PARTITION AND 'REALISM': FIANNA FÁIL
IN GOVERNMENT, 1932–1937

Sensing that Irish unity was not a primary concern for the vast majority of the Irish electorate, partition did not feature as a major issue during the 1932 election campaign in the twenty-six counties. Instead Fianna Fáil fought the campaign on a promise to bring improvements in economic conditions and to implement its 'Republican' programme for government. When partition was mentioned it was always as a footnote to more topical matters, including the oath of allegiance, the land annuities, emigration and unemployment.[120] When the votes were counted Fianna Fáil emerged as the largest party in the Dáil, with seventy-two seats and with the support of the Labour Party formed a new government; Fianna Fáil was to hold power for almost forty of the next fifty-four years. De Valera assumed both the position as president of the executive council and minister for external affairs. By securing the latter appointment de Valera made sure that he assumed responsibility for Anglo-Irish relations and partition policy.

In accordance with Fianna Fáil's approach to Northern Ireland since 1926, on entering government de Valera reiterated that nationalist Ireland needed to remain realistic. Before attention could be turned to securing an end to partition, he maintained, all resources must be allocated towards implementing Fianna Fáil's economic, social and political programme in the twenty-six counties. At the 1933 Fianna Fáil Ard Fheis, for example, de Valera pleaded with the party faithful to follow his 'policy regarding the re-establishment of the Republic'. A strategy, he said, which relied on realism and patience.[121] Speaking at a gathering of the Fianna Fáil parliamentary party in mid-January 1934, he again emphasised the need for a sense of 'realism' towards securing a united Ireland. He explained to deputies the difficulties of ending partition and appealed to party members to realise that it was 'the Fianna Fáil Party that was making the real National advance and that we should not encourage a false attitude ...' What was instead needed, he asserted, was a sense of perspective.[122]

This muddled belief that attention should be first focused on securing independence in the South before turning one's attention to the North, was commonly adhered to by Fianna Fáil members. During the 1933 general election campaign, for instance, outgoing minister for commerce and industry, Seán Lemass spoke of how the 'triumphant nationalism of the people of the South' would eventually secure the 'unity of our historic country'.[123] Likewise, Aodh de Blacam, a member of the Fianna Fáil National Executive, propagated the 'evil effects of partition' and pointed out the economic, moral and social benefits that those living in the South retained over their Northern neighbours. Born in London, but with family roots in Newry, Co. Down, de Blacam moved to Ireland in 1912 to work as a freelance journalist. He was believed to be a 'rural idealist', who had resented de Valera for his failure to fulfil his dreams of re-unified Gaelic-medieval agrarian society.[124] Writing in the Irish Jesuit journal *Studies* in 1934, de Blacam factiously wrote that 'while Newry's mills are all but stopped, bus loads of workers go daily over the Border from Newry to employment in the rapidly-growing industries in Dundalk'. An example, he noted 'which brings home the universal contrast between decline in the Six-Counties and development in the Twenty Six'.[125]

Both men's comments exposed the futility of Fianna Fáil's strategy towards Northern Ireland. Bordering on delusional, the idea that an economically prosperous twenty-six county Ireland would eventually compel Ulster Unionists to agree to a united Ireland was endemic amongst the Irish nationalist political elite. Since the enactment of partition, economic factors were regarded by Irish nationalists as the most influential in bringing partition to an end. Throughout the 1920s Cumann na nGaedheal had drawn on the observation that 'economic factors will overthrow artificial barriers'.[126]

On coming to power in 1932 de Valera continued to endorse the rhetoric of the economic merits for ending partition. Speaking in the Dáil in 1933, having admitted he had no immediate solution to partition, he instead maintained that Irish reunification would eventually be achieved by means of economic enticement of Ulster Unionists.[127] Two years later, in May 1935, again addressing his Dáil colleagues, de Valera confessed that 'we have no plan ... which we can inevitably bring about the union of this country'. Describing partition as a 'disaster and a shame', he returned to his worn-out pronouncement that an economically prosperous twenty-six counties would prove irresistible to Northern Ireland Protestants.[128]

In truth, Fianna Fáil's espousal of native economic ownership and self-sufficiency made little economic sense. There was not enough native capital or expertise to allow for Irish ownership and successful self-sufficiency at the same time. This did not matter to de Valera. Political not economic factors dictated his thinking. It was still politically attractive to stress Sinn Féinish self-reliance through such policies and they were rigidly adhered to by consecutive Fianna Fáil governments throughout the 1930s and 1940s.[129]

The idea that a prosperous Ireland in the twenty-six counties would be enough to end partition at some stage in the future had obvious attractions for de Valera, since it entailed that no specific Northern Ireland policies would have to be adopted. Fianna Fáil could ignore partition and concentrate on politics in the South of

Ireland, while claiming to be striving towards Irish unity (as revealed by Fianna Fáil's reluctance to enter Northern Ireland politics). Journalist, pacifist and the author of a 1936 biography of de Valera, Desmond Ryan sceptically wrote that during the mid-1930s a cohort of 'small industrialists behind Fianna Fáil' acquired a vested interest in maintaining partition, since 'tariffs blunt the competition of the powerful and long-established Ulster industrialists'.[130]

There remained one stumbling block to de Valera's fanciful notion that a prosperous industrialised South could eventually entice Northern Ireland into a united Ireland: Northern Ireland Protestants. Throughout the inter-war period de Valera refused to acknowledge Ulster Unionists' legitimate opposition to Irish unity. Thus, the Belfast authorities were to be ignored, their political aspirations sneered at and their legitimacy ridiculed. On a practical level, on assuming power, cross-border co-operation with the Northern Ireland government, a subject which had featured occasionally on the Cumann na nGaedheal cabinet agenda, vanished from the cabinet discussions of the Fianna Fáil administrations of the 1930s.[131] Rather, de Valera viewed the partition question as a matter solely for the Dublin and London governments. 'If Britain', he said in the Dáil in June 1934, 'did not actively assist in maintaining and keeping up that spirit that maintains partition today ... the union of this country would come inevitably'.[132] Indeed, speaking in the Dáil in May 1937, de Valera reaffirmed his conviction that without the interference of British politicians partition would inevitably fizzle out.[133]

The perception that the ending of partition rested in the hands of the British government rather than Ulster Unionists was widespread within Fianna Fáil. In 1934 Eamonn Donnelly, Fianna Fáil TD for Laois-Offaly, stated that London, not Belfast, must be the focus of the Irish government in the national drive to end partition; a point which de Valera wholeheartedly supported.[134] It was not until after the Second World War that de Valera reluctantly conceded that the support of Ulster Unionists was required if partition was to be ended.[135] In the meantime, however, the Belfast authorities were to be bypassed. Although de Valera might have seen himself as the realist within Fianna Fáil, attempting to educate ill-informed supporters on the complexities of the partition question, he was unable to recognise that his own pronouncements on the subject, further alienated Ulster Unionists. In fact, Fianna Fáil's twin national aims, the reunification of Ireland and the revival of the Gaelic language merely compounded Ulster Unionists' opposition to Irish unity. De Valera was blissfully unaware that the two policies were irreconcilable, even mutually contradictory, since the more Gaelic Southern Ireland became the more it differed from and repelled Ulster Unionists.

De Valera's calls for realism and to focus on fulfilling Southern interests before turning their attention towards Northern Ireland was not solely confined to Fianna Fáil. George O'Brien's 1936 publication, *The Four Green Fields*, argued that the question of partition and of the constitutional status of the Free State should not become the main preoccupation of political parties in the South:

> It would be most regrettable if the continuance of partition were to waste the energy of the people of the Free State, which is badly needed for the material and cultural restoration ... Ireland has covered three of her four fields, and it is more important that she should till them profitably than she should continue to dissipate her energy in discussing their tenure, or in deploring the temporary exclusion of the fourth field.[136]

For some within Fianna Fáil, de Valera's appeals for realism and patience provided all the evidence needed that the organisation was neglecting the Holy Grail of securing a thirty-two county all-Ireland Republic. In May 1934, at a meeting of the Fianna Fáil parliamentary party, in which de Valera was absent, Eamonn Donnelly attacked his leader's neglect of Northern Ireland policy. Donnelly proposed the establishment of a special sub-committee to review partition and in particular Fianna Fáil strategy towards the forthcoming Northern Ireland elections.[137] The previous year, in August 1933, Donnelly had similarly requested that a special meeting of the National Executive be held to 'consider the attitude to the Fianna Fáil organisation towards a general election which is to be held in the near future in North-East Ulster'.[138] On both occasions, however, Donnelly's insistence that new life be inserted into the party's stale Northern Ireland policy was ignored by senior figures within the organisation. Under de Valera's watchful eye, Donnelly's requests were politely ignored and the proposed sub-committee never convened.[139]

Instead with Fianna Fáil's attention firmly fixated on the twenty-six counties, de Valera implemented his blueprint to secure Ireland's sovereignty: the dismantling of the 1921 Anglo-Irish Treaty. Privately, Frank Aiken noted that the Fianna Fáil government were determined to systematically dismantle the treaty 'at any cost'.[140] Aided by the Department of External Affairs, under the guidance of its secretary

Joseph Walshe, the Fianna Fáil government's first measure focused on the removal of article seventeen of the 1921 constitution, which made the oath of allegiance obligatory on the members entering Dáil Éireann. In private correspondence with London de Valera ridiculed the 1921 Anglo-Irish Treaty and pinpointed the oath for particular criticism, describing it as 'an intolerable burden'.[141]

Coinciding with this new Bill was de Valera's determination to retain the land annuities, hitherto handed over to the British government under consecutive land acts of the late nineteenth and early twentieth centuries. The Fianna Fáil government also adopted a policy of non-co-operation with the King's representative in Ireland, the governor-general, James MacNeill. Aiken boastfully exclaimed that his government wished to 'put him [O'Neill] in his place'.[142] In protest to the government's ostracising policy, MacNeill resigned in October 1932 and was replaced by de Valera's personally selected appointment, a Protestant disciple of Irish nationalism, Domhnall Ó Buachalla.

Such unilateral actions by the new government infuriated London and precipitated a sharp deterioration in Anglo-Irish relations. In the context of partition, as is examined below, it merely confirmed Fianna Fáil's inability to secure Irish unity. Thus, although de Valera put in motion a campaign which would ultimately pave the way for Ireland's constitutional sovereignty in the twenty-six counties, the fate of the six North-Eastern counties remained a side issue.

FIANNA FÁIL, THE BRITISH GOVERNMENT AND PARTITION, 1932–1937

London's immediate response to the Fianna Fáil government's retention of the land annuities was to impose a 20% tax on imports from the Irish Free State, a measure that provoked a similar levy on English exports. This incident marked the commencement of the 'economic war' between the two countries, which was to last until the signing of the Anglo-Irish Agreement in 1938. Essentially, a political rather than an economic dispute, the debacle between London and Dublin reinforced Whitehall's opposition to Irish unity.

Throughout 1932, in a series of negotiations, de Valera acted unilaterally to restructure Ireland's constitutional and financial relationship with Britain. A stalemate, however, was reached by the end of the year following a series of abortive British–Irish meetings in London in October.[143] During these early negotiations partition remained to the forefront of de Valera's mind.[144] Despite his protests, however, the British refused to be drawn on the question of Irish unity. He was thus left frustrated and disappointed and following the conclusion of negotiations with his British colleagues he reaffirmed that for as long as partition remained, no overall settlement could be agreed between Dublin and London.[145] The British were left unperturbed by de Valera's protests, remaining equally resolute: in their minds the reunification of Ireland was a distant prospect rather than an immediate concern. Indeed, the partition question was not raised during a meeting between de Valera and British prime minister, Ramsay MacDonald in July 1932.[146]

De Valera failed, or simply chose not to recognise, that his bold affirmations of independence, such as his withholding of land annuities, proved counter-productive in the drive to end partition. As Centre Party TD for Roscommon, Frank MacDermott pointed out in the Dáil in 1935, de Valera's attempts to dismantle the treaty, he said, only helped to 'consolidate partition'.[147] De Valera ignored such warnings and throughout the 1930s undertook a campaign to convince London that their strategic interests would be best served by a stable, peaceful, independent and united Ireland. In the words of Joseph Walshe, Ireland's 'immediate policy' towards London 'must be the restoration of the unity of Ireland'.[148] In negotiations with London, de Valera continually used the 'outrage' of partition as a justification for a new constitutional relationship between Britain and Ireland.[149]

The negotiations of the 'coal-cattle pact' in 1934 marked one small area of improvement in Anglo-Irish relations. However, the broader political issue of Ireland's constitutional relationship with the Commonwealth and the issue of the settlement of the annuities remained in the way of harmonious relations between Dublin and London. By March 1935, spurred on by the imminent arrival of the new secretary of state for dominion affairs, Malcolm MacDonald, de Valera attempted to find an impasse on the partition question. The Earl of Granard, a member of the Irish Free State Senate, forwarded a proposal to the Dominions Office, which he alleged had the 'approval of the Irish government ... and would settle the Irish deadlock provided that the British and Northern Ireland governments would assent to it'.[150]

The Granard proposal advanced the establishment of a sovereign, federal Irish Commonwealth, composed of two dominions, North and South, both externally associated with the British Commonwealth.

Based on a federal agreement, both the Irish and Northern Ireland governments would continue to exercise their 'present powers in their own territories'. Thus, although the 'State Parliaments' in Dublin and Belfast would retain their present powers, their members would also elect an Irish Commonwealth parliament which would control 'the transferred powers of North and South and also such other common services as the North and South may decide to surrender to it, e.g. agriculture'. Granard noted that the proposals were drawn up by a close friend of de Valera and that the solution advocated would meet the fundamental requirements of all three parties, the British, Ulster unionists and the Irish nationalists.[151] Granard recorded that Ulster would secure 'political peace', and trade with the South and would also 'give England a present of an Irish settlement'. For Irish nationalists, such a solution would meet 'the unquenchable Irish desire for nationhood'. The Commonwealth parliament would elect a President, who would be an Irish citizen, and be responsible for the assent of Bills of the Commonwealth and the state parliaments.[152]

Although London initially gave the Granard proposal some consideration, after a period they came to the conclusion that the offer was an elaborated version of de Valera's 'external association', as enshrined in his famous Document No. 2 of 1921.[153] In this document (which was considerably altered between December 1921 and 1923) de Valera advanced the principle that in return for a united Ireland the Northern Ireland government would retain its own parliament in Belfast and powers currently held by Westminster would be transferred to the Irish government.[154] In the fifteen years between 1921 and 1935 de Valera's views on Northern Ireland and partition had changed little and he genuinely (and naively) believed that this compromise of his republican beliefs would lead to a united Ireland. Ulster Unionists had no interest in de Valera's latest federal offer to help end partition, having turned down a similar proposal offered by Aodh de Blacam, a senior Fianna Fáil member obsessed with the idea of a united Ireland. Writing in *The Irish Times* in January 1935, under the pseudonym, 'Pacificus', de Blacam praised de Valera's recent 'conception' of the Commonwealth as a 'smaller League of Nations' and had mooted the possibility of the United States becoming a member of a wider Anglo-Celtic Commonwealth.[155] Ulster Unionists, however, categorically rejected de Blacam's offer.[156]

Faced with yet another statement in Anglo-Irish relations, de Valera returned to his habitual protests; that relations between Dublin and London would remain unfriendly until inroads were made on partition. During discussions with British permanent secretary to the treasury, Sir Warren Fisher, in early October 1936, de Valera was forthright: no agreement between Dublin and London would be 'acceptable to the Irish people' unless substantial concessions were made on the partition question.[157] At a subsequent meeting between Irish high commissioner to London, John W. Dulanty and a selection of British officials, the former recorded that 'de Valera wished to make it absolutely clear that no agreement could be finally reached until Irish unity was delivered'.[158]

The crisis surrounding the abdication of King Edward VIII following the death of his father King George V, in December 1936, proved pivotal in de Valera's quest at finally dismantling Ireland's last remaining constitutional link with the British Crown. On 11 December, while the Commonwealth was in crisis, de Valera introduced and the Dáil passed both the constitution (amendment no. twenty-seven) Act 1936 and the executive authority (external relations Act). The passage of these Acts was a milestone which marked five years of continuous and comprehensive redefinition of British–Irish relations. The former Act ended the functions of the monarch in relation to internal affairs in the Irish Free State; all internal references to the King and the Governor General were deleted from the constitution. The latter gave authority for the continued exercise by the monarch, on the advice of the Executive Council, of functions relating to the external relations of the Irish Free State. It bought into being the external association of the Irish Free State with the Commonwealth; a relationship that lasted until 1949. The Act provided for the continuance of existing diplomatic relations, whereby all foreign diplomats in Dublin would continue to be accredited to the British sovereign.[159]

De Valera's decision that all foreign representatives in Ireland would remain accredited to the King was based on two salient points. Firstly, he believed to remove the King completely would have raised international complications 'of a high order' and in particular he was concerned with maintaining diplomatic relations with the Vatican and the United States of America. Secondly, it was his view that keeping this 'shadowy' link with Britain might help towards the ultimate reunification of Ireland.[160] Although the British government expressed their opposition to de Valera's new legislation, in the aftermath of the abdication crisis and with the growing foreign policy problems in Europe, they chose not to react. It was a classical case of appeasement on behalf of London and most certainly gave de Valera a proud sense of satisfaction. Yet, the question of partition remained unanswered, the British government unwilling to budge on the issue in the face of fierce Ulster Unionist opposition and as the threat of war lingered over Europe.

FIANNA FÁIL, PHYSICAL FORCE AND THE IRA, 1926–1936

It is important to examine de Valera's attitude to the use of physical force to end partition and his relationship with the IRA if one is to understand Fianna Fáil's strategy to Irish reunification during the 1930s. During the early months of Fianna Fáil's existence, in an attempt to placate the republican hardliners within the organisation and to win support from disenfranchised Sinn Féin and IRA members, de Valera did not rule out the use of force to secure a united Ireland. At the inaugural Fianna Fáil Ard Fheis in 1926 he argued that physical force was morally justifiable as a 'legitimate weapon' to end partition.[161] This statement was consistent with de Valera's traditional policy towards the use of physical force. As a surviving commandant of the 1916 Easter Rising he always maintained that armed insurrection was morally justified. On suitable occasions he was not afraid to threaten Ulster Unionists with coercion. For example, speaking to a gathering on Dublin's Westmoreland Street, in July 1917, he recorded that 'if Ulster stood in the way of the attainment of Irish freedom Ulster should be coerced'.[162]

Nonetheless, by the turn of the 1920s, he rejected the physical force policy on the grounds that it would not succeed.[163] In particular, the horrors of the civil war, together with Britain's military superiority, convinced him of the futile practicalities of the use of armed insurrection. On a trip to America in March 1927, where there was a strong lobby in favour of the use of force, de Valera made a distinction between the moral justification for force and the rejection of force on the grounds that it was unfeasible and counter-productive. During a speech in Boston he asked his audience: 'Do you think that the Irish people are so mean that after all this fighting for seven and a half centuries they are now going to be content to have Six-Counties of their ancient territory cut off?.'[164] This speech was characteristic of de Valera's pronouncements on the issue of physical force during his American tour. On several occasions, while addressing his American audiences, he stated or implied that peace could not be established as long as partition lasted. However, he never actually advocated the use of force as a legitimate weapon to end partition.[165]

De Valera continued this theme on his return to Ireland. Throughout the Irish general election of September 1927 he resolutely rejected the physical force-line. Questioned about his interview with the *Manchester Guardian* in June 1927, in which he had threatened to 'punish Ulster', he made it clear in an election advertisement that 'what Fianna Fáil does not stand for: attacking the North east: Fianna Fáil does not stand for attacking "Ulster". It will except the existing realities, but will work resolutely to bring partition to an end'.[166] Indeed, in the run up to the 1927 Irish general election, with the support of the Fianna Fáil National Executive, he refused an invitation from the IRA army council that Fianna Fáil, Sinn Féin and the IRA come together for the purpose 'to effect co-ordination for the coming elections'.[167] Writing in Fianna Fáil's press organ the *Nation* in January 1928, in unambiguously constitutional terms, de Valera declared that his party was 'committed to a policy of political action rather than revolution to achieve its aim of an independent Ireland'.[168] It was a policy, Seán MacEntee later recalled, which de Valera rigorously pursued 'of weaning Republicanism from the gun'.[169]

De Valera's denunciation of the use of physical force was greeted with resentment from some with Fianna Fáil, including a cohort of senior figures. At the 1926 and 1927 Fianna Fáil Ard Fheiseanna some grass-roots delegates from Dublin demanded that the organisation take a more 'forceful' interest on the partition issue.[170] Indeed, at the 1928 Ard Fheis, the Erskine Childers cumann, Dublin City North issued a resolution (which was passed) requesting that Fianna Fáil reaffirm 'its determination to continue the struggle for the attainment of a Republic for the whole of Ireland and calls upon our Dáil members to adopt a more fighting and militant policy' towards partition.[171]

Within Fianna Fáil it was apparent that many members, if not outward supporters, were at the very least sympathetic to the IRA's endorsement of physical force to end partition. At the 1931 Ard Fheis several speakers, including two TDs and three members of the National Executive, expressed broad sympathy with the IRA and their willingness to use violence to secure Irish unity. Con Murphy of the National Executive, although favouring a peaceful solution, noted that the IRA had a 'moral right' to resist foreign domination and in that way they were 'one with Fianna Fáil'.[172] Throughout the early years of Fianna Fáil's existence party members routinely protested at the imprisonment of IRA members on 'trumped up charges'. Robert Briscoe, Fianna Fáil deputy for Dublin-South, for instance, accused the Special Branch of encouraging young men in the West of Ireland to rob banks so as to smear republicans.[173] In Dáil Éireann, Fianna Fáil deputies regularly asked Dáil questions about ill-treatment of IRA men and the harassment of republican supporters.[174]

Most tellingly, Frank Aiken expressed unease at de Valera's categorical rejection of the use of violence. A founding member of Fianna Fáil, he had fought on the anti-treaty side during the civil war, commanding the fourth Northern division of the IRA, eventually succeeding Liam Lynch as chief of staff, a post he held until 1925. He was a prominent Fianna Fáil figure from the outset and well-respected by party grass-roots. In June 1926 Aiken produced a memorandum, 'A call for unity', which he requested be issued to party delegates at the 1927 Fianna Fáil Ard Fheis. Under de Valera's direct orders, however, the document was not circulated; de Valera having noted that given Aiken's current mission in America to secure financial support for Fianna Fáil, the time was not opportune to make the document public.[175]

Nonetheless, following Aiken's intervention the memorandum was eventually published in mid-1927. Its contents revealed Aiken's opposition to some of de Valera's central policies in relation to partition. The former argued that the use of physical force, if peaceful means failed, was a legitimate policy in the quest for Irish unity. Not only this, but he also expressed his opposition to de Valera's federal offer to Ulster Unionists. 'Ireland', Aiken wrote:

> is being controlled by two unlawful governments, whose ministers deny their sovereignty and unity ... we have to get the people to make it clear again that their wishes are to get rid of foreign authority and partition and to have a free and independent government in control of the whole 32 counties Republic of Ireland ... it is our duty to do this by peaceful means if we can, and to prepare for war if we are denied the right to do it peacefully.[176]

Aiken's attitude was not unique. The following year, in April 1927, an editorial in the *Nation* directly questioned de Valera's constitutional crusade against the use of armed force. If Fianna Fáil's 'programme of peaceful penetration' for a united Ireland was not achieved, the passage warned, 'revolution' would ultimately follow.[177]

Seán Lemass's often quoted (and misrepresented) Dáil Éireann speech of March 1928 encapsulated Fianna Fáil's inherent ambiguity on the issue of constitutional politics. 'Fianna Fáil', he declared, 'is a slightly constitutional party. We are perhaps open to the definition of a constitutional party, but before anything else we are a Republican party'.[178] In this speech Lemass recorded that Fianna Fáil's adoption of constitutional methods was not an end in itself, but a means to achieving a united Ireland; if constitutional policies failed, then military action was not illegitimate. Prior to his death in August 1922, Michael Collins had likewise asserted that if peaceful means failed, in the last resort, the use of violence was a legitimate policy in the national drive to end partition.[179]

By 1929, the new editor of the *Nation* and de Valera's trusted friend, Frank Gallagher, sought to clarify Fianna Fáil's attitude towards the use of physical force. He stated that the party did not 'renounce the doctrine of physical force for achieving the freedom of Ireland', however, he explained that such a policy was inappropriate at the present time.[180] De Valera was left unstirred by the rumblings of discontent within Fianna Fáil and by the beginning of the 1930s he doggedly opposed the use of physical force. Speaking at the 1931 Fianna Fáil Ard Fheis, he was unequivocal: 'Force is out of the question, were it feasible, it would not be desirable'.[181]

Despite de Valera's missionary zeal against the use of physical force, on the eve of Fianna Fáil's entry to government in 1932, many supporters remained reluctant to endorse their leader's constitutional crusade. In particular, Fianna Fáil's ambivalent relationship with the IRA left a sizeable proportion of party members sympathetic to the ideals of physical force nationalism. At the 1931 Easter 1916 Rising commemorations, for example, two thousand members of the Dublin brigade of the IRA marched through Dublin city, led by Fianna Fáil deputy for Dublin-North, Oscar Traynor. This was followed by the highlight of the republican calendar, in June of that year, the oration at the grave of Irish republicanism's founding father, Theobald Wolfe Tone, in Bodenstown, Co. Kildare.[182] Together, Fianna Fáil and IRA members were present *en masse* to pay homage to the ideals and aspirations of the Irish nationalist tradition; a tradition which glorified militant republicanism.

Throughout the 1932 election campaign Fianna Fáil maintained its ambivalent relationship with the IRA; although de Valera resolutely declined to forge a formal alliance between his party, Sinn Féin and the IRA.[183] Many IRA supporters lent a hand, as canvassers and as self-appointed guardians of Fianna Fáil meetings, in some areas extending this role to break up meetings of its opponents.[184] For instance, in Dublin, the third battalion of the IRA undertook election work in their various areas, canvassing in Donnybrook, Rathgar, and Ranelagh. It is estimated that, in total, Fianna Fáil secured an additional 5,000 extra election workers across the state due to the IRA's intervention.[185] Significantly, at this time Fianna Fáil never attempted to distance itself from the IRA; aware that the party could attract a large number of disaffected republicans into the Free State constitutional arena, many of whom had become bewildered with the IRA's campaign.

Disillusioned anti-treatyites saw Fianna Fáil as a legitimate vehicle towards acceptance of the independent Irish state. Not only this, but many already within Fianna Fáil were slow to sever their connections with the IRA. For instance, a number of high-ranking Fianna Fáil members were regular contributors to the IRA publication, *An Phoblacht*. A small, but vocal, minority of Fianna Fáil supporters 'hedged their bets' by retaining dual membership of the party and the IRA. As Donnacha Ó Beacháin explained, as Fianna Fáil and the IRA drew their support from the same 'republican reservoir, each fed off the other'.[186]

Fianna Fáil's election victory in March 1932 was welcomed by the IRA; the latter happy to see the demise of the hated pro-treaty Cumann na nGaedheal government. For the first several months of the Fianna Fáil government's existence relations between both movements remained amicable. In de Valera's first government he appointed former chief of staff of the IRA, Aiken as minister for defence; a shrewd move, calculated to test the loyalty of the army, while at the same time mollifying radical republicans. Between mid-February and early March of 1932, high-level discussions took place between Fianna Fáil and the IRA.[187] The purpose of the meetings was to see if both movements could agree upon a common national programme in the attainment of an Irish Republic. Aiken proposed that the two movements should be 'fused at once'. Such a fusion, he argued, would 'double' their strengths and provide a huge boost to republican morale.[188] Aiken's main concern was to bring the IRA under government control and thus neutralise the movement's threat to the state. De Valera remained sceptical of these discussions and while he kept his election promise to release all republican prisoners, he was left frustrated at the IRA's refusal to be absorbed into the Free State army.

For the meantime any tensions remained in the background and when de Valera called a snap general election in 1933 the IRA, with the support of *An Phoblacht*, called on the electorate, albeit reluctantly, to return Fianna Fáil to government.[189] The honeymoon period, however, soon ended. Upon Fianna Fáil's return to government de Valera was eager to cut all remaining ties with the IRA and to distance Fianna Fáil away from the argument that physical force was a legitimate weapon to end partition. Speaking in the Dáil in May 1933 de Valera reaffirmed that Irish unity could only be secured 'by peaceful means, not by armed force'.[190] Although the British government had been alarmed at Fianna Fáil's rise to power, de Valera notified London of his party's commitment to finding a peaceful solution to partition.[191] Indeed, speaking on de Valera's behalf in May 1936, secretary for the Department of External Affairs, Joseph Walshe, reassured London that the idea that a Fianna Fáil government wished to use physical force to secure Irish unity did not exist expect in 'the imagination of some Tory propagandists'.[192]

The advent of the Blueshirts shortly after Fianna Fáil's rise to power afforded de Valera with a perfect opportunity to consolidate his control over the hardliners within his own party and against the IRA.[193] In implementing repressive legislation against the Blueshirts, which culminated with the banning of the movement in 1933, de Valera extended the legislation to curtail the actions of the IRA. Coupled with the absorption of many republicans into the paid service of the state machinery, through employment in the Free State army, the police and civil service, together with the introductions of pensions for those who fought on the anti-treaty side during the civil war, de Valera masterfully absorbed many of the IRA into the state apparatus.[194]

By the turn of 1934 relations between Fianna Fáil and the IRA were increasingly strained. With a safe parliamentary majority, de Valera stepped up his campaign against the IRA. At a meeting of the Fianna Fáil parliamentary party in January 1934 he requested that deputies dispel the perception that the IRA was advancing the 'National principles' greater than Fianna Fáil.[195] At a subsequent parliamentary party meeting in March of that year, he informed deputies that in the future 'National advancement' could only be made through a government with 'National principles'. He explained that a 'great deal' of Fianna Fáil's success in the future depended on the 'proper organisation of the New Military force'.[196] *An Phoblacht* was increasingly seized or censored by the Fianna Fáil government and every week brought new cases of IRA prisoners tried before the non-jury military tribunal.[197] At the 1936 Fianna

Fáil party conference, facing pressure from some delegates to take a more active involvement with ending partition, de Valera stressed that partition 'cannot be done by force'.[198] Speaking several days later in the Dáil he once again stipulated that 'force is out of the question. That is nothing new for us to say. We have admitted it at all times ...'.[199]

Following unproductive discussions with the IRA leader, Seán Russell, in April 1935, de Valera decided that his government must take action against the movement. Eventually, in June 1936 the IRA was outlawed, its chief of staff, Moss Twomey, having been already arrested. The movement's publicity organ, *An Phoblacht*, was also banned. Some within Fianna Fáil were outraged by the decision. Seán Hayes TD resigned from the party in protest.[200] Other senior Fianna Fáil figures still publicly endorsed, as legitimate, the use of physical force to secure Irish unity. For example, in the run up to the 1937 Irish general election, Fianna Fáil backbencher and veteran of the 1916 Easter Rising, Richard Walsh, claimed that 'Fianna Fáil had no objection to the use of force to achieve Irish independence provided peaceful methods failed'.[201] Despite the occasional backlash from Fianna Fáil supporters, for the meantime, de Valera's constitutional nationalism won out over the IRA's brand of physical force nationalism. It was a battle, however, which de Valera and Fianna Fáil could never decisively win. As this book illustrates, the history of Fianna Fáil's relationship with the IRA ranged, in varying degrees, from sympathetic to antagonistic. The pledge to end partition, which was so central to the ideological composition of Fianna Fáil and the IRA, meant that both routinely vied with one another for the custodianship of Irish republicanism.

THE 1937 IRISH CONSTITUTION AND PARTITION

With the IRA declared illegal de Valera turned his attention again to the question of Ireland's constitutional sovereignty. The new 1937 Irish constitution (*Bunreacht na hÉireann*) marked the fulfilment of a fifteen-year campaign to remodel Ireland's constitutional position. Building on both the constitution amendment Act and external relations Act of 1936 the new constitution was a culmination of de Valera's campaign, started in December 1921, with Document No. 2, to revise the Anglo-Irish Treaty. *Bunreacht na hÉireann* represented the embodiment of the Catholic nationalist tradition, which de Valera personified in public life and reflected recent papal encyclicals. Belfast and London opposed the new constitution, while opposition parties in Dáil Éireann, likewise, initially refused to support de Valera's realignment of Ireland's constitutional stance. Nevertheless, after much protest, the Dáil approved the new constitution in June 1937 and it was narrowly carried by a referendum in July of that year (although the new constitution did not officially come into effect until 29 December 1937).

Articles two and three of the constitution marked the high point of Fianna Fáil's official anti-partitionism. For the first time the irredentist claim to Northern Ireland was given a legal form and permanence which it had hitherto lacked. In articles two and three the characteristic ambiguities and contradictions of nationalist ideology were restated in their most authoritative form. Article two claimed for the nation, jurisdiction over the entire island, thus, this nebulous entity declared that those who lived in counties Armagh and Derry were just as much as part of the nation as those living in counties Cork or Kerry. Paradoxically, however, article 3 accepted that *de facto* the laws of the state could only be exercised in the twenty-six counties 'pending the reintegration of the national territory'.

It was de Valera's assertion in article three of a territorial claim to Northern Ireland which exposed the very essence of his anti-partitionism and his disregard for Ulster Unionism. The political explanation of this clause (in de Valera's mind at least) was that the constitution was a statement *inter alia* of the position of Ireland in the world from an Irish nationalist perspective, which believed that there should be one state for the entire Irish nation.[202] Therefore, de Valera supposed that the nation, as distinct from the state, had rights. He maintained that Irish people living in the Free State and in Northern Ireland together formed the Irish nation; that a nation had a right to unity of territory in some form, be it as a unitary or federal state and that the Government of Ireland Act of 1920, though legally binding, was a violation of that natural right to unity which was superior to positive law.[203]

Consequently, this national claim to unity existed not in the legal, but in the political order and was one of the rights which were envisaged in article two; it was expressly saved by article 3, which stated the areas to which the laws enacted by the parliament established by the constitution applied.[204] Illogically, by claiming jurisdiction over the whole island, in line with ideological orthodoxy, the document also contained an acknowledgement of the existence of partition; though at the same time reiterating the worn-out cliché that unity was inevitable and that partition would eventually disappear.[205]

In October 1936, writing to Joseph Walshe, John Dulanty explained the motives behind de Valera's decision to insert articles two and three into the new constitution. 'In the absence of any proposal for an all-Ireland settlement', Dulanty wrote, de Valera had decided to proceed with the constitution with the aim 'to establish now such a relationship with the members of the British Commonwealth of nations that, in the event of the Six-counties voluntarily accepting union with the rest of Ireland, the constitution would not necessarily require amendment'. De Valera, according to Dulanty, envisaged that the constitution would embrace the principle of Irish unity and 'would represent the nearest approach that we could now make to the creation of a constitutional system which would satisfy public opinion in the Irish Free State'.[206]

De Valera's assumption that Northern Ireland would eventually 'voluntarily' enter a united Ireland revealed his blatant disregard towards the traditions and political principles of Ulster Unionism. Northern Protestants' reaction to the new constitution was one of anger, confusion and thereafter indifference. On first hearing news of the new constitution, Ulster Unionists were convinced that de Valera had torn up the tripartite treaty of 1925 with its apparent guarantees of Northern Ireland's political and territorial integrity.[207] In fact, Northern Ireland prime minister, Lord Craigavon, did not place much emphasis on articles two and three. He considered them objectionable but not worthy of much notice. They made, he said, 'not a pin of difference' to Northern Ireland's position.[208]

The Catholic ethos of the constitution, as enshrined in article forty-four and which recognised the 'special position' of the Catholic Church, further exposed the contradictory nature of Fianna Fáil's attitude towards the Northern Protestants. It was, as John Bowman outlined, the 'most formal expression of the contradiction at the core of Fianna Fáil's strategy on unification: their attempt at nation-building on a specifically republican, Catholic, Gaelic model ...'.[209] Ulster Unionists' opposition to Irish unity was, therefore, completely ignored. De Valera simply refused to acknowledge that in Northern Ireland the Protestant majority did not wish to be a part of a united Irish state.

Speaking in the Dáil in May 1937 Senator Frank MacDermott (nominated by the taoiseach) warned de Valera of the alienating effect that the Catholic ethos of the constitution would have upon

Northern Protestants. 'Article 44', he said, offered 'no basis for unity with the North and contains various provisions tending to prolong partition'.[210] MacDermott was left to bemoan that the constitution was designed solely for Southern nationalist consumption and ignored the way of life of the one million Protestants in Northern Ireland over whom it claimed sovereignty.[211]

Additionally, article 15.2, which dealt with the legislature of the state, recorded that provisions may be made by law for the 'creation or recognition of subordinate legislature and for the powers and functions of these legislatures'. This was drafted with the possible reunification with Northern Ireland in mind; just as Northern Ireland was a subordinate legislature within the United Kingdom until 1972. Under this clause it would be recognised as a subordinate legislature in an all-Ireland state. During a meeting with British officials in September 1936, Dulanty explained that de Valera's aim in devising article 15. 2. would be to establish a relationship with the members of the British Commonwealth of nations, so that in the event of the 'Six-Counties voluntarily accepting union with the rest of Ireland, the constitution would not necessarily require amendment'.[212] Given that the Belfast authorities had only a few years previously, rejected the Granard proposal of 1935 de Valera's latest federal offer merely reinforced his myopia towards Ulster Unionist political sensibilities.

The new constitution represented a further retreat from reality into the refuge of hollow anti-partitionism, helping to entrench rather than end partition. For de Valera, however, it gave him greater authority to claim the South's legitimate right for a united Ireland and helped lessen the pressure on Fianna Fáil to defend its record on partition. In a speech in June 1937, before the plebiscite on the constitution was held, de Valera gave evidence of the only practical function of articles two and three, when responding to a heckler: 'Somebody has asked me about the Six-Counties', he said, 'my reply is to get a copy of the new constitution. There is in it an assertion that the national territory is the whole of Ireland and not part of it'.[213] Frank Aiken, likewise, declared that the new constitution gave the Irish people their first occasion of 'declaring that this whole nation of Ireland is a sovereign, independent and democratic State'. In a blatant rejection of Northern Protestants' opposition to the constitution, he opportunistically noted that its enactment expressed 'not alone the ideas of the vast majority of the people in the South but of the vast majority of the people in the North, if the truth were known'.[214]

Besides Senator Frank MacDermott's protests there were others who greeted the new constitution with a distinct sense of caution. During the draft stages of the constitution articles two and three drew particular criticism from the secretary of the Department of Finance, J. J. McElligott. A veteran of the 1916 Easter Rising, he found articles two and three to be irredentist in tone. The claim to territory 'which does not belong to us', he wrote, gave a 'permanent place in the Constitution to a claim to *Hibernia Irredenta*'.[215] Peadar O'Donnell, Irish nationalist and committed socialist, rejected de Valera's constitution on the grounds that it merely created a Catholic state in the South and rejected the political aspirations of Northern Protestants; thus giving its tacit consent to the copper-fastening of partition.[216]

Tellingly, inside Fianna Fáil, some expressed their opposition to the new constitution. Gerald Boland believed that it would inevitably lead to a greater divide between Dublin and Belfast. He was so upset by the constitution that he reportedly tendered his resignation to de Valera, asserting that 'this is a constitution under which Wolfe Tone could not live as a free citizen'. Boland even warned de Valera that unless the constitution was modified to meet his concerns he would emigrate from Ireland with his family.[217] Boland subsequently wrote in the early 1960s that it never seems to have 'occurred to those who claimed and still claim that the constitution applied to all Ireland: that if the Six-Counties had to vote on it the constitution would have been defeated'. 'I personally', he noted, 'was and am against a written constitution. Britain and the Six-Counties get on very well without one ...'[218] On first receiving a draft of the constitution, Seán MacEntee reportedly argued that articles two and three, particularly the South's territorial claim over Northern Ireland, would cause offence to Northern Protestants; a point which he felt de Valera was slow to pick up on.[219]

For others within Fianna Fáil the new constitution did not go far enough in its anti-partitionism; Eamonn Donnelly was again de Valera's main antagonist. In Donnelly's mind article three of the new constitution signalled a base betray of Irish republicanism. He demanded a unilateral step: for the formal declaration of a united Ireland in the new constitution. He argued that the constitution should omit article three's *de facto* acceptance on interim partition, while inserting a clause within article two, permitting Northern Nationalist MPs seats in the Dáil.[220] Although Donnelly's requests were initially rejected by de Valera at the Fianna Fáil Ard Fheis in November 1936, he was determined to force the issue on the agenda.[221] At a meeting of the National Executive in December 1936 he gave notice of a motion requesting that a special Ard Fheis be called in early February 1937 to discuss the forthcoming constitution, with 'special reference to partition and that Representatives from the North-East Ulster be asked to attend'. After discussion Donnelly's request was granted.[222]

The National Executive duly reconvened on 1 February 1937 to discuss Donnelly's motion. Following prolonged (and no doubt protracted) discussions, Donnelly withdrew his original motion and in its place proposed that an 'all Ireland convention be called before the constitution is introduced and that steps be taken to approach again the question of the reunification of Ireland'. De Valera then assumed chairmanship of the meeting and following further 'long discussions', which lasted until 8.30pm, Donnelly's motion was overwhelmingly rejected by twenty-one votes to four.[223]

Although frustrated, Donnelly was not yet defeated and later that year in November, at a meeting of the party's National Executive, gave notice of a motion requesting that the Fianna Fáil organisation, 'as is at present constituted, be remodelled and made applicable to all Ireland under its present title, or, if necessary, under another name ...'[224] In addition, Donnelly recommended three further policy initiatives. Firstly, that Fianna Fáil should contest 'all Parliamentary seats in Northern Ireland at coming general elections'; secondly, that the party hold a 'general election in South Ireland on the same date'; and lastly, to establish 'an all-Ireland National Party under the leadership of Mr Eamon de Valera with headquarters in Dublin'.[225]

Over the following weeks Donnelly's motion was debated at two meetings of the National Executive.[226] However, on Donnelly's own accord (and presumably after some arm twisting) he withdrew the motion.[227] Thereafter, the motion was never again debated at a meeting of the National Executive.[228] Donnelly was infuriated, in his mind, de Valera and his fellow cabinet colleagues cared little for the plight of Northern Ireland Catholics and were content to ignore the partition question. Speaking in the Dáil in May 1937 he frustratingly insisted that partition was the 'predominant national issue. Nothing else counts; nothing else matters ...'[229] He eventually fell out with the Fianna Fáil hierarchy because of article 3 of the 1937 constitution. He later publicly lamented that the constitution was 'torpedoed' by article 3.[230]

* * *

In conclusion, the initial ten years of Fianna Fáil's existence marked a meteoric rise in the fortunes of the once destitute anti-treaty republicans. Under de Valera's watchful eye Fianna Fáil assumed the mantle of the defenders of Irish republicanism in the twenty-six counties. De Valera constructed an image of Fianna Fáil as the 'national' or patriotic party. Although the Fianna Fáil governments of the 1930s were relatively successful in their policy of 'dismantling the treaty' in the South, the partition question was deliberately ignored. Behind the hollow ritualistic pledges to secure a united Ireland, de Valera and his party hierarchy intentionally sidestepped the issue of Irish reunification. To excuse themselves for this blatant contradiction the Fianna Fáil leadership habitually argued that attention could only be turned to Northern Ireland once Ireland's industrial and social strength was built up in the twenty-six counties. Indeed, during a private lunch with Erskine and Rita Childers before he left the Irish presidency in 1973, de Valera reportedly confessed that because he had been 'so absorbed in building up the South after independence' he had completely failed to find a solution to partition.[231]

As is demonstrated in the following chapter, in the aftermath of the Anglo-Irish Agreement of 1938, in which Ireland's sovereignty was secured, partition – in the public dominion at least – became Fianna Fáil's central priority. The Fianna Fáil government's failure to secure an end to partition during the Anglo-Irish Agreement negotiations resulted in a tirade of opposition to the party's Northern Ireland policy, from within Fianna Fáil, Northern Nationalists and IRA supporters. In response, the Fianna Fáil government sponsored an anti-partition campaign in Ireland and Great Britain to create the impression that the party was making a conciliatory effort to end partition. In fact, the opposite was the truth. In reality, the party was always motivated by self-interest and by short-term political manoeuvring. As is explained, during the Second World War, Fianna Fáil's commitment to safeguarding Irish neutrality outweighed any perceived ideological loyalties to achieve Irish unity.

NOTES

1. *Irish Press*, 9 Nov. 1933.
2. See University College Dublin Papers UCDA Eamon de Valera Papers, P150/2009, speech by de Valera, 14 April 1926.
3. Under article twelve of the Anglo-Irish Treaty of 1921 the Northern Ireland government retained her existing status, as defined by the provisions of the Government of Ireland Act

of 1920. However, article twelve also made provisions for the establishment of a boundary commission, which would revise the border at a later date. It was not until November 1924, nearly three years after the treaty was signed, that the boundary commission began its investigation. Northern Ireland refused to appoint a commissioner, therefore, the British and Dublin governments agreed that London should select a commissioner on behalf of Northern Ireland. The Irish government appointed minister for education, Eóin MacNeill as their representative on the commission, J. R. Fisher assumed the role as Northern Ireland commissioner and Richard Feetham, a South African judge, chaired the proceedings. For an overview of the boundary commission's investigations see Michael Laffan, *The Partition of Ireland, 1911–1925* (Dundalk: Dundalgan Press, 1983), 99–105.

4. Alvin Jackson, *Home Rule, an Irish History, 1800–2000* (London: Phoenix, 2003), 247.

5. Under the terms of the Government of Ireland Act of 1920 the Council of Ireland was established. It was envisaged that the Council of Ireland would consist of equal representatives from the Dublin and Belfast governments and would deal with matters of common interest between both jurisdictions.

6. Michael Kennedy, *Division and Consensus: The Politics of Cross-Border Relations in Ireland, 1925–1969* (Dublin: Institute for Public Administration, 2000), 18.

7. See de Valera's comments, *An Phoblacht*, Dec. 1925.

8. See UCDA Fianna Fáil Party Papers P176/22, copy of de Valera's public statement in relation to his decision to convene a special gathering of the Sinn Fein Ard Fheis, 15 Jan. 1926.

9. Gerald Boland's unpublished memoirs, marked, 1 (a). Boland wrote his handwritten memoirs (on Seanad Éireann headed paper) during the early/mid-1960s.

10. Gerald Boland's unpublished memoirs, marked, 1 (a).

11. See, for example, J. J. Lee, *Ireland, 1912–1985, Politics and Society* (Cambridge: Cambridge University Press, 1989), 151 & Ryle. T Dwyer, *De Valera: The Man and the Myths* (Dublin, 1992), 136.

12. Gerald Boland's unpublished memoirs, marked, 1 (a)

13. Bryce Evans, *Seán Lemass, Democratic Dictator* (Cork: Collins Press, 2011), 49.

14. Gerald Boland's unpublished memoirs, marked, 2 (a).

15. Evans, *Seán Lemass*, 49.

16. See UCDA P176/741, record of 'reports of proceedings', 1927 Fianna Fáil Ard Fheis, 24–25 Nov. 1927.

17. Kevin Boland, *The Rise and Decline of Fianna Fáil* (Dublin: Mercier Press, 1982), 33.

18. UCDA P150/2011, record of interview by de Valera, 17 April 1926. Although the official Irish title of the Irish Volunteers was Óglaigh na hEireann, they were often called by Irish speakers 'Fianna Fáil' and the initials 'F.F.' were incorporated in the Volunteer badge.

19. Martin Mansergh, 'Fianna Fáil and Republicanism in the Twentieth Century', Iseult Honohan (ed.) *Republicanism in Ireland: Confronting Theories and Traditions* (Manchester: Manchester University Press, 2008), 107.

20. See 'The name and the game', *The Irish Times*, 19 May 1976.

21. UCDA P176/28, de Valera's 'National policy' speech at the inaugural meeting of Fianna Fáil, La Scala Theatre, Dublin, 16 May 1926. De Valera made a similar argument at the 1926 Fianna Fáil Ard Fheis. 'Do you think', he noted, 'the leopard was going to change its spots over night ... it was obvious to me ... that the Treaty would mean a division and a partition of this country, and therefore I was against it'. UCDA P176/740, record of 1926 Fianna Fáil Ard Fheis.

22. UCDA P176/28, de Valera's 'National policy' speech at the inaugural meeting of Fianna Fáil, La Scala Theatre, Dublin, 16 May 1926.

23. UCDA P176/740, record of de Valera's Presidential address, Fianna Fáil Ard Fheis, 24 Nov. 1926.

24. UCDA P176/28, de Valera's 'National policy' speech at the inaugural meeting of Fianna Fáil, La Scala Theatre, Dublin, 16 May 1926.

25. See, for example, UCDA P176/28, de Valera's 'National policy' speech at the inaugural meeting of Fianna Fáil, La Scala Theatre, Dublin, 16 May 1926 & UCDA P150/2047, record of de Valera's 'closing speech', Fianna Fáil Ard Fheis, 25 Nov. 1926.

26. *Daily Mail*, 22 June 1927.
27. See, for example, de Valera's comments at the 1927 Fianna Fáil Ard Fheis. UCDA, P150/2048 record of de Valera's Presidential address, Fianna Fáil Ard Fheis, 24 Nov. 1927.
28. *The Irish Times*, 19 May 1976.
29. Gerald Boland's unpublished memoirs, marked, 4 (a) and 5 (a).
30. Gerald Boland's unpublished memoirs, marked, 7 (a).
31. See Brian Hanley, *The IRA, 1926–1936* (Dublin: Four Courts Press, 2002), 117–118.
32. *Irish Independent*, 13 Aug. 1927.
33. Dick Walsh, *The Party, Inside Fianna Fáil* (Dublin: Gill and Macmillan, 1986), 16–17.
34. Walsh, *The Party, Inside Fianna Fáil*, 16–17.
35. See the *Nation*, 4 June 1927, 2 July 1927 and 20 Aug. 1927, respectively.
36. Quoted in the *Irish Independent*, 13 Aug. 1927.
37. Donnacha Ó Beacháin, *Destiny of the Soldiers: Fianna Fáil, Irish Republicanism and the IRA, 1926–1973* (Dublin: Gill and Macmillan, 2011), 68.
38. Gerald Boland's unpublished memoirs, marked, 9 (a).
39. See UCDA P176/741, record of 1927 Fianna Fáil Ard Fheis, 24–25 Nov. 1927.
40. UCDA P176/830, copy of Fianna Fáil 1927 general election pamphlet.
41. UCDA P176/442, meeting of Fianna Fáil parliamentary party, 22 June 1927.
42. See UCDA P176/442–444, record of meetings of Fianna Fáil parliamentary party, 1927–1932.
43. See Kieran Allen, *Fianna Fáil and Irish Labour, 1926 to the Present* (London: Pluto Press, 1997), 16–23.
44. Allen, *Fianna Fáil and Irish Labour, 1926 to the present*, 23–24.
45. The minutes of the parliamentary party are littered with references to the Oireachtas restaurant, Northern Ireland, however, was rarely discussed. See P176/442–444, record of Fianna Fáil parliamentary party meetings, 1927–1931.
46. UCDA P176/443–444, record of Fianna Fáil parliamentary party meetings, 1929–1932.
47. See UCDA P176/743–746, record of Fianna Fáil Ard Fheiseanna, 1929–1932.
48. UCDA P176/745, copy of de Valera's Presidential address, 27 Oct. 1931.
49. UCDA P176/745, copy of de Valera's Presidential address, 27 Oct. 1931.
50. Dáil Éireann debate (DE) 11 Oct. 1927. Vol. 21, cols. 27–28.
51. See, for example, comments by Fianna Fáil TDs, Robert Briscoe and Frank Fahey. *The Irish Times*, 14 Feb. 1929.
52. See UCDA P176/37, file relating to de Valera's arrest in Northern Ireland, Feb. 1929.
53. *The Irish Times*, 7 Feb. 1929.
54. *The Irish Times*, 7 Feb. 1929.
55. In Oct. 1924, under the 1924 Prohibition Act, de Valera was arrested while in Newry, but was later released. The following week he returned to Northern Ireland where he spoke at St Columb's Hall, Co. Derry. He was again arrested. *Belfast Newsletter*, 6 Feb. 1926.
56. DE, 20 Feb. 1929. Vol. 28, col. 1.
57. DE, 20 Feb. 1929. Vol. 28, cols. 133–134.
58. DE, 20 Feb. 1929. Vol. 28, col. 134.
59. DE, 20 Feb. 1929. Vol. 28, cols. 134.
60. DE, 20 Feb. 1929. Vol. 28, col. 32.
61. *Nation*, 27 April 1929.
62. *The Irish Times*, 7 Feb. 1929.
63. See 'MacEntee's fruitful career', *Irish Press*, 26 May 1976.
64. *Nation*, 23 Feb. 1929.
65. UCDA P150/218, meeting of Fianna Fáil National Executive, 7 Feb. 1929.
66. UCDA P150/218, meeting of Fianna Fáil National Executive, 7 Feb. 1929 (please note that the minutes of the Fianna Fáil National Executive from 1926 to 1938 are contained within the Eamon de Valera Papers and *not* the Fianna Fáil Party Papers).
67. *The Irish Times*, 14 Feb. 1929.
68. See UCD P176/37 and *The Irish Times*, 14 Feb. 1929.

69. *The Irish Times*, 14 Feb. 1929.
70. UCDA P150/218, meeting of Fianna Fáil National Executive, 7 Feb. 1929.
71. See UCDA P150/218, meeting of Fianna Fáil National Executive, 14 Feb. 1929. The following members were appointed to the new 'special committee': Seán O'Donovan, P. O'Fathagh [*sic*], Tom Gallivan, Robert Brennan and Seán Brady. It is unclear if the committee ever convened.
72. *Irish Independent*, 15 Feb. 1929.
73. See *Irish Independent*, 15 Feb. 1929.
74. See *Irish Independent*, 15 & 16 Feb. 1929.
75. See de Valera's comments. UCDA P176/743, record of 1929 Fianna Fáil Ard Fheis.
76. See de Valera's comments. UCDA P176/743, record of 1929 Fianna Fáil Ard Fheis.
77. At the 1926 Ard Fheis de Valera rejected a proposal that Fianna Fáil establish itself in Northern Ireland on the grounds that 'he did not see how that organisation could give a direction to anybody ...' *The Irish Times*, 26 Nov. 1926.
78. *The Irish Times*, 26 Nov. 1926.
79. UCDA P176/740, record of Honorary Secretary's Report, 1st Fianna Fáil Ard Fheis, 24 Nov. 1926.
80. *The Irish Times*, 26 Nov. 1926.
81. UCDA P176/740, record of 1926 Fianna Fáil Ard Fheis.
82. UCDA P176/740, record of 1926 Fianna Fáil Ard Fheis.
83. UCDA P176/740, record of 1926 Fianna Fáil Ard Fheis.
84. UCDA P150/2117, meeting of Fianna Fáil National Executive, 19 Jan. 1928.
85. UCDA P150/2117, meeting of Fianna Fáil National Executive, 2 Feb. 1928.
86. As reported by Cahir Healy to Joseph Devlin the Fianna Fáil delegation met, among others, 'Father Coyle [parish priest, Devenish, Co. Fermanagh], Devlin, McAllister – Ballymena [MP Co. Armagh] and Donnelly [Alex Donnelly, MP]'. See Public Records Office of Northern Ireland (PRONI) Cahir Healy Papers D2991/A/1/75, Healy to Devlin, 8 Feb. 1928.
87. UCDA P176/742, record of Honorary Secretary's Report, 3rd Fianna Fáil Ard Fheis, 1 Oct. 1928.
88. Public Records office of Northern Ireland (PRONI) Chair Healy Papers D2991/A/1/75, Healy to Devlin, 8 Feb. 1928.
89. UCDA P176/742, record of Honorary Secretary's Report, 3rd Fianna Fáil Ard Fheis, 1 Oct. 1928.
90. See UCDA P150/2047, meeting of Fianna Fáil National Executive, 2 Dec. 1926.
91. UCDA P150/2117, meeting of Fianna Fáil National Executive, 17 Feb. 1928.
92. UCDA P176/742, record of Honorary Secretary's Report, 3rd Fianna Fáil Ard Fheis, 1 Oct. 1928.
93. UCDA P176/742, record of Honorary Secretary's Report, 3rd Fianna Fáil Ard Fheis, 1 Oct. 1928.
94. *The Irish Times*, 14 Feb. 1929.
95. UCDA P176/743, record of 1929 Fianna Fáil Ard Fheis.
96. Ó Beacháin, *Destiny of the Soldiers*, 97.
97. At the 1932 Fianna Fáil Ard Fheis the possibility of extending Fianna Fáil into Northern Ireland was not debated. See UCDA 176/746, record of 1932 Fianna Fáil Ard Fheis.
98. John Bowman, *De Valera and the Ulster Question, 1917–1973* (Oxford: Oxford University Press, 1982), 133.
99. Clare O'Halloran, *Partition and the Limits of Irish Nationalism* (New Jersey: Humanities Press International, Inc., 1987), 154.
100. UCDA P150/1997, de Valera's attitude re: Northern Ireland elections, 17 Nov. 1933.
101. UCDA P150/1997, interview given by de Valera on 'Fianna Fáil's attitudes towards the Six-Counties Elections', 17 Nov. 1933.
102. PRONI D2991/B/52/8, O'Muineachain to Healy, Jan. 1934 (date omitted).
103. UCDA P150/2123, meeting of Fianna Fáil National Executive, 30 Oct. 1935.

104. UCDA P150/2123, meeting of Fianna Fáil National Executive, 30 Oct. 1935. However, the following month at the meeting of the National Executive, following an interview with 'Messers O'Connor and Devlin', members agreed to subscribe £100 to the election fund to fight the Tyrone–Fermanagh seat. UCDA P150/2123, meeting of Fianna Fáil National Executive, 11 Nov. 1935.
105. See Bowman, *De Valera*, 133. See also UCDA P176/345, meeting of the Fianna Fáil National Executive, 8 Nov. 1937.
106. *Newry Journal*, 2 Jan. 1945.
107. *Irish Press*, 9 Nov. 1933. See also Tom Gallagher, 'Fianna Fáil and partition 1926–84', *Éire – Ireland*, Vol. 20, No.1 (1985): 39–57; 35–36.
108. *Irish Press*, 28 Jan. 1938.
109. Bowman, *De Valera*, 171.
110. UCDA P176/444, meeting of Fianna Fáil parliamentary party, 13 July 1939.
111. For a record of a series of partition resolutions at the 1939, 1944 and 1945 Fianna Fáil Ard Fheiseanna see *Irish Press*, 13 Dec. 1939, 11 Oct. 1944, & 7 Nov. 1945.
112. This was the opinion of F. McDonald, Dublin. *The Irish Times*, 11 Oct. 1944.
113. *Irish Press*, 7 Nov. 1945.
114. UCDA P176/384, meeting of Fianna Fáil National Executive publicity sub-committee, 15 March 1948.
115. See, for example, *The Irish Times*, 16 June 1949 & 15 Oct. 1953.
116. *The Irish Times*, 15 Oct. 1953.
117. *The Irish Times*, 16 June 1949.
118. Gallagher, 'Fianna Fáil and partition 1926–84', 34–35.
119. Gallagher, 'Fianna Fáil and partition 1926–84', 33.
120. See, for example, de Valera's speeches in Co. Clare, 8 Feb. 1932 and Co. Kerry, 10 Feb. 1932. *Irish Independent*, 8 & 10 Feb. 1932. See also, Eamon de Valera, *Recent Speeches and Broadcasts* (Dublin: Talbot Press, 1933), 9–14.
121. UCDA P176/747, record of Fianna Fáil Ard Fheis, 8–9 Oct. 1933. De Valera reiterated this policy approach during a Dáil debate in April 1934. See DE 20 April. 1934. Vol. 51, cols. 2145–2146.
122. UCDA P176/444, meeting of Fianna Fáil parliamentary party, 10 Jan. 1934.
123. *Irish Press*, 24 Jan. 1933.
124. Patrick Maume, 'Anti-Machiavel: Three Ulster Nationalists of the Age of De Valera', *Irish Political Studies*, 14 (1999), 43–63.
125. Aodh de Blacam, 'Some thoughts on partition', *Studies, An Irish Quarterly Review* (Vol. XXIII, 1934), 559–576; 573.
126. This was the opinion of Seán Milroy, Cumann na nGaedheal TD. See O'Halloran, *Partition and the Limits of Irish Nationalism*, 159.
127. Speech by de Valera. DE, 1 March 1933. Vol. 46, cols. 188–192.
128. Speech by de Valera. DE, 29 May 1935. Vol. 56, cols. 2114–2115.
129. Richard English, *Irish Freedom, the History of Nationalism in Ireland* (London: Pan Macmillan, 2007), 319–320.
130. See UCDA Desmond Ryan Papers LA10/D/201, biographical material on de Valera. The title of the biography was *Unique Dictator, a Study of Eamon de Valera* (Dublin, 1936).
131. Kennedy, *Division and Consensus*, 44.
132. Speech by de Valera. DE, 13 June 1934. Vol. 52, col. 282.
133. Speech by de Valera. DE, 19 May 1937. Vol. 67, cols. 706–707.
134. See speech by Eamonn Donnelly and reply from de Valera. DE, 13 June 1934. Vol. 52 No. 2, cols 282–283.
135. See Chapter Four, pp.147-155.
136. George O'Brien, *The Four Green Fields* (Dublin: Talbot Press, 1936), 145 & 151.
137. The committee was to comprise of Donnelly, Rice, Smith, J. Doherty and Neil Blaney. UCDA P176/444, Fianna Fáil parliamentary meeting, 30 May 1934.
138. UCDA P150/2122, meeting of National Executive, 14 Aug. 1933.

139. There are no records, either from the minutes of the Fianna Fáil parliamentary party or National Executive, which refer to this sub-committee. See UCDA P176/444 and UCDA P150/2123, respectively.
140. UCDA Moss Twomey Papers P69/52 (56), record of conversation between Aiken, Tom Barry, Seán MacBride and Gilmore, 16 July 1932.
141. See de Valera's comments to J. H. Thomas, 5 April 1932. In Catriona Crowe, Ronan Fanning, Michael Kennedy, Dermot Keogh and Eunan O'Halpin, *Documents on Irish Foreign Policy 1937–1939* (Vol. IV) (Dublin: Royal Irish Academy, 2006), 281–282.
142. UCDA P69/52 (56), record of conversation between Aiken, Tom Barry, Seán MacBride and Gilmore, 16 July 1932.
143. See, for example, National Archives of Ireland (NAI) Department of Foreign Affairs (DFA) Secretary's File S1/4, minutes of first meeting of the conference between the representatives of the Irish Free State and the British government, 14 Oct. 1932; NAI DFA Secretary's File S1, minutes of second meeting of the conference between the representatives of the Irish Free State and the British government, 14 Oct. 1932; NAI DFA Secretary's File S1/4, minutes of third meeting of the conference between the representatives of the Irish Free State and the British government, 15 Oct. 1932; and NAI DFA Secretary's File S1, minutes of fourth meeting of the conference between the representatives of the Irish Free State and the British government, 15 Oct. 1932.
144. See, for example, NAI DFA Secretary's files S1, minute of conversation between de Valera and Dulanty, 18 March 1932; NAI Department of Taoiseach (DT) S2264, de Valera to J. H. Thomas (London), 5 April, 1932; NAI DFA Secretary's Files S1, de Valera to J. H. Thomas (London) 2 July 1932; UCDA P150/226, minutes of meeting between de Valera and Ramsay MacDonald, 15 July 1932.
145. See NAI DFA Secretary's File S1, minutes of fourth meeting of the conference between the representatives of the Irish Free State and the British government, 15 Oct. 1932.
146. UCDA P150/226, minutes of meeting between de Valera and Ramsay MacDonald, 15 July 1932.
147. DE, 10 April 1935 Vol. 55 No. 16, cols. 2262–2263.
148. NAI DFA (unregistered papers), Walshe to Seán T. O'Ceallaigh, date unknown, late Sept. or early Oct. 1932.
149. See, for example, NAI DT S2264, de Valera to J. H. Thomas, 5 April 1932.
150. Bowman, *De Valera and the Ulster Question*, 119.
151. Bowman, *De Valera and the Ulster Question*, 119–120.
152. Bowman, *De Valera and the Ulster Question*, 119–120.
153. Bowman, *De Valera and the Ulster Question*, 121.
154. Under de Valera's federal offer, contained with Document No. 2, clause XVI did not recognise or accept the principle of partition, but offered a federal solution in the attainment of a united Ireland. See Eamon de Valera, *The Alternative to 'the Treaty': Document No. 2* (Dublin, 1923). A copy is available from UCDA P176/944.
155. *The Irish Times*, 1 Jan. 1935.
156. See *The Times*, 2 Jan. 1935 and *Belfast Newsletter*, 1 Jan. 1935.
157. UCDA P150/2335, note recording conversation between de Valera and Fisher, 6 Oct. 1936. See also UCDA P150/2179, Dulanty to Walshe, 15 Sept. 1936.
158. UCDA P150/2179, meeting between Dulanty, Fisher, Grattan Bushe, Harding and Wilson, 15 Sept. 1936. See also UCDA P150/2179, Dulanty to Walshe recording a meeting between the former and Sir N. E. Warren Fisher, Sir Horace J. Wilson and Sir Edward J. Harding, 8 Sept. 1936 and NAI 2003/17/181, Seán Murphy to Dulanty, 11 Sept. 1936.
159. See Crowe, Fanning, Kennedy, Keogh and O'Halpin, *Documents on Irish Foreign Policy 1937–1939* (Vol. IV), xi–xii.
160. Earl of Longford and Thomas P. O'Neill, *Eamon de Valera* (London: Hutchinson, 1970), 293.
161. At the 1st Fianna Fáil Ard Fheis, in 1926, de Valera stated: 'I never said, and am not going to say, that force is not a legitimate weapon for a nation to use in striving to win its freedom'. See UCDA P176/737, 1926 Fianna Fáil Ard Fheis, 24 Nov. 1926.

162. See comments by de Valera. *Freeman's Journal*, 16 July 1917.
163. See comments by de Valera. DE, 22 Aug. 1921. Vol. 4 cols. 28–29.
164. See Bowman, *De Valera and the Ulster Question*, 103.
165. See Bowman, *De Valera and the Ulster Question*, 103.
166. See *Irish Independent*, 14 Sept. 1927.
167. See UCDA P69/48 (31)-(37), record of correspondence between secretary of the IRA army council and Fianna Fáil leadership, May 1927.
168. *Nation*, 28 Jan. 1928.
169. *The Irish Times*, 23 July 1974.
170. See partition resolutions issued by M. O Mhellain Craobh Dublin City and Thomas Ashe Craobh, Dublin City (1926 Fianna Fáil Ard Fheis) and North Dublin City Comhairle Ceanntair (1927 Fianna Fáil Ard Fheis), respectively, UCDA P176/740–741.
171. UCDA P176/742, record of 1928 Fianna Fáil Ard Fheis.
172. *Irish Press*, 28 Oct. 1931.
173. Hanley, *The IRA, 1926–1936*, 118.
174. Hanley, *The IRA, 1926–1936*, 118.
175. UCDA Frank Aiken Papers P104/1499, copy of 'A call to unity' by Frank Aiken, 19 June 1926. See also UCDA P69/144 for an additional copy.
176. UCDA P104/1499, copy of 'A call to unity' by Frank Aiken, 19 June 1926.
177. *Nation*, 14 April 1928.
178. DE, 12 March 1928. Vol. 22, cols. 1615–1616.
179. Laffan, *The Partition of Ireland, 1911–1925*, 98.
180. *Nation*, 10 Aug. 1929.
181. UCDA P176/745, record of 1931 Fianna Fáil Ard Fheis. See also speech by de Valera, *Irish Press*, 17 March. 1932.
182. Ó Beacháin, *Destiny of the Soldiers*, 105.
183. See P69/52 (53), secretary of the IRA army council to Tom Barry, 19 July 1932.
184. Ó Beacháin, *Destiny of the Soldiers*, 105.
185. Hanley, *The IRA, 1926–1936*, 125.
186. Ó Beacháin, *Destiny of the Soldiers*, 85.
187. See P69/52 (53)-(61), record of meetings and correspondence between Aiken, Tom Barry and the IRA army council, March-July 1932.
188. UCD P104/1322, Aiken to IRA army council, 19 Feb. 1932. See also Hanley, *The IRA, 1926–1936*, 126.
189. See *An Phoblacht* for the month of Jan. 1933.
190. DE, 3 May 1933. Vol. 27, cols. 439–440.
191. See, for example, National Archives of United Kingdom (NAUK), Dominions Office (DO) 35/398/6, Sir Edward J. Harding's record of conversation with Dulanty, 19 Feb. 1934; the latter noted that de Valera would not 'exercise' coercion to win Irish unity.
192. UCDA P150/2183, Walshe to de Valera, 2 May 1936.
193. Officially called the Army Comrade's Association, later the National Guard, the Blueshirts were paramilitary and fascist in form, with drilling and uniforms (mimicking the Italian Blackshirts and German Brownshirts) and fascist salutes and slogans. Led by Eoin O'Duffy, previously commissioner of the Garda Síochána, the Blueshirts were outlawed in 1933. Its members, however, along with the National League, were absorbed into Cumann na nGaedheal, leading to the establishment of a new party, Fine Gael.
194. Ó Beacháin, *Destiny of the Soldiers*, 134–135.
195. UCDA P176/444, meeting of Fianna Fáil parliamentary party, 10 Jan. 1934.
196. UCDA P176/444, meeting of Fianna Fáil parliamentary party, 22 March 1934.
197. Hanley, *The IRA, 1926–1936*, 136.
198. See UCDA P150/2057, de Valera's handwritten preparatory comments marked 'Britain 2', Nov. 1936.
199. DE, 19 Nov. 1936. Vol. 64, cols. 731–732.
200. See *An Phoblacht*, 4 July 1936.
201. *Irish Press*, 15 June 1937.

202. The 1937 Irish constitution was actually very similar to the later Federal German constitution, the preamble to which spoke of the 'entire German people' and stated that the people of the Federal Republic adopted that constitution 'also act[ing] on behalf of those Germans to whom participation was denied'.
203. James Casey, *Constitutional Law in Ireland* (London: Sweet and Maxwell, 1992), 31.
204. Casey, *Constitutional Law in Ireland*, 31.
205. O'Halloran, *Partition and the Limits of Irish Nationalism*, 175.
206. NAI DFA 2003/17/181, Dulanty to Walshe, 14 Oct. 1936.
207. Graham Walker, *A History of the Ulster Unionist Party, Protest, Pragmatism and Pessimism* (Manchester: Manchester University Press, 2004), 79.
208. Kennedy, *Division and Consensus*, 58.
209. Bowman, *De Valera and the Ulster Question*, 128.
210. DE, 11 May 1937. Vol. 52. No. 2, col. 76.
211. DE, 11 May 1937. Vol. 52. No. 2, cols. 76–84.
212. See UCDA P150/2179, Dulanty to Walshe, 15 Sept. 1936 and NAI DFA 2003/17/181, Dulanty to Walshe, 14 Oct. 1936. See also UCDA P150/2335, note of conversation between de Valera and Fisher, 6 Oct. 1936.
213. O'Halloran, *Partition and the Limits of Irish Nationalism*, 177.
214. Speech by Aiken. DE, 14 June 1937. Vol. 68, No. 2, cols. 386–387.
215. See Dermot Keogh, *Twentieth Century Ireland, Nation and State* (Dublin: Gill and Macmillan, 1994), 98 and Ronan Fanning, *The Irish Department of Finance* (Dublin: Institute for Public Administration, 1978), 267. See also NAI DT S9715B, response of the Department of Finance to the first draft of the Constitution, 23 March 1937.
216. See Niall Carson, *Beginnings and Blind Alleys: The Bell, 1940–1954*, 139. (Unpublished 2011 PhD thesis, available from the University of Liverpool).
217. Gallagher, 'Fianna Fáil and Partition 1926–84', 38–39.
218. Gerald Boland's unpublished memoirs, marked, 14 (b).
219. Tom Feeney, *Seán MacEntee, a Political Life* (Dublin: Irish Academic Press, 2009), 237.
220. See comments by Donnelly. *Irish Press*, 4 Nov. 1936.
221. See *Irish Press*, 4 Nov. 1936.
222. UCDA P176/345, meeting of the National Executive, 21 Dec. 1936.
223. UCDA P176/345, meeting of National Executive, 1 Feb. 1937. See also UCDA P176/345, meeting of National Executive, 4 Jan. 1937.
224. UCDA P176/345, meeting of National Executive, 8 Nov. 1937.
225. UCDA P176/345, meeting of National Executive, 8 Nov. 1937.
226. See UCDA P176/345, meetings of National Executive, 8 & 22 Nov. 1937.
227. UCDA P176/345, meeting of National Executive, 22 Nov. 1937.
228. UCDA P176/345, record of meetings of National Executive, 6 Dec. 1937 – 3 Jan. 1938.
229. Speech by Donnelly, DE, 11 May 1937. Vol. 67, No. 1, cols. 105–118.
230. *Irish Press*, 13 April 1939.
231. See 'Dev's Confession', *The Irish Times* 29 Jan. 1981.

2

1938–1945

'... What is the party's official policy on this matter [Northern Ireland policy]? We don't know what to say'.

[Fianna Fáil National Executive memorandum,
19 Sept. 1938] [1]

THE ANGLO-IRISH AGREEMENT AND THE FIANNA FÁIL NATIONAL EXECUTIVE, 1938–1939

The signing of the Anglo-Irish Agreement of April 1938 represented a watershed for Fianna Fáil's approach to Northern Ireland. The Agreement ended the economic war with Britain and allowed a reduction in tariffs; settled the financial dispute over the land annuities, the Irish government agreeing to pay a lump-sum of £10 million; and most importantly, by the Irish regaining control of three naval ports, Lough Swilly, Berehaven and Cobh, Ireland was in a position to remain neutral in the likely event of a future war. The issue of partition, however, remained unresolved. With Ireland's sovereignty secured under the terms of the Agreement, the ending of partition, as de Valera stated, assumed priority.[2] 'No other question', he declared, 'now interested the Irish people more than partition'.[3] Effectively, as Clare O'Halloran argued, with substantial progress made in the area of sovereignty, 'the spotlight turned on partition, more than in the past, as the last unattained nationalist goal'.[4]

Throughout de Valera's participation in the Anglo-Irish negotiations, which first commenced during secret discussions with British dominions secretary, Malcolm MacDonald, in January 1937, the former habitually insisted that his remaining great objective was the ending of partition.[5] He was reportedly 'obsessed' by partition.[6]

In a meeting with MacDonald in mid-September 1937, de Valera 'emphasised' that partition was the 'fundamental and vital' question in regard to relations between Dublin and London'.[7] The 'supreme importance of a United Ireland', de Valera recorded, was the Fianna Fáil government's central priority.[8]

In talks with the British prime minister, Neville Chamberlain, in January 1938, de Valera argued that he could not agree to a common British–Irish defence agreement that would 'smell of defence co-operation' unless there was 'substantial progress' towards terminating partition.[9] A stalemate thus ensued. The British were unwilling to offer any concessions on partition, while Dublin refused to enter into a military defence co-operation agreement, citing Ulster Unionists' opposition in support of Irish unity.[10] Indeed, upon first receiving news of de Valera's secret meeting with MacDonald, Northern Ireland prime minister, Lord Craigavon was unequivocal: he publicly pronounced that Irish unity was impossible.[11]

Therefore, as the Anglo-Irish negotiations drew to a close de Valera was confronted with a dilemma. While he had won economic concessions and secured Ireland's sovereignty, he found that the British had no intention of agreeing to end partition. He faced the choice of rejecting proposals which were to Ireland's benefit simply because his ultimate aspiration of Irish unity had failed to be delivered. The Anglo-Irish Agreement has often been described as a triumph for de Valera. John Bowman argued that de Valera, retrospectively, saw it as his 'greatest achievement'.[12] Desmond Ryan, a surviving participant of the 1916 Easter Rising, wrote that the success of the Agreement would permit de Valera to be regarded as the 'strongest and greatest of Irish national leaders since [Charles Stewart] Parnell'.[13] The return of full control of the Irish ports was indeed a significant accomplishment. However, de Valera's semi-official biographers, The Earl of Longford and Thomas P. O'Neill, remarked that de Valera did not view the Agreement as a political success.[14] As he came away from London they record that he was 'far from jubilant'. Partition weighed heavily on his mind. He felt, they wrote, 'heartily disappointed at making no real progress on the partition question'.[15]

Why is there a difference between Bowman and that of the account by Longford and O'Neill? As a consummate reader of the Irish mind de Valera was conscious that many Irish nationalists viewed the negotiations as the opportune occasion to end partition. Therefore, to admit publicly that the Agreement represented a great success for him personally, given that he was unable to deliver any concessions on partition, would have invariably left him open to the accusation that he had neglected partition. It is true that on his return from London, following the close of the negotiations, de Valera did exploit the economic and military success of the Agreement, particularly during the general election of June 1938. He was, however, reluctant to maintain a debate on the lack of progress made on partition during the negotiations.[16]

On his return to Dublin on board the Holyhead to Dún Laoghaire mail-boat following the close of the negotiations with the British, he could not hide his genuine disappointment having failed to secure any concessions on partition. 'I confess', he wrote, 'that it is something of a heartbreak that it has not been possible to include this question [partition] ...'. While rejoicing that the Agreement would allow 'for a better understanding' between the people of Britain and Ireland, he could not be entirely happy until 'the full solution is reached ... a completely free united Ireland'.[17] Speaking in the Dáil on 29 April, he admitted that because he was unable to undo partition during the negotiations, the Agreement was a 'bad and poor document'.[18] Indeed, in correspondence with American president, Franklin D. Roosevelt, de Valera wrote that because the Agreement had failed to resolve the partition issue, a 'complete reconciliation' between Ireland and Britain 'remains still for the future'.[19]

To defend his approach to partition during the 1938 negotiations was difficult, particularly as in the wake of his discussions with the British he realised he had no policy which was likely to succeed. During preliminary discussions with the secretary to the Irish government, Maurice Moynihan, de Valera acknowledged that he could offer no immediate solution to partition.[20] Therefore, faced with the fact that he could not win support for Irish unity from the British government, de Valera instead sought to reaffirm and officially recorded for posterity, Ireland's legitimate claim for an end to partition. This approach, however, was not enough to satisfy the extremists within Fianna Fáil or the IRA. Chamberlain privately noted that de Valera had admitted that he was 'so nervous as to the criticism' he would receive following the signing of the Agreement.[21]

This explains the motives behind the timing of de Valera's announcement of a new Fianna Fáil anti-partition campaign in Great Britain and Northern Ireland – in the very week that the discussions with the British government concluded. If he was unable to bring about Irish unity in the short-term, he would at the very least give the impression that Fianna Fáil offered the best chance of ending partition. Propaganda, therefore, became his preferred policy. His strategy was to accentuate his fundamental objection to partition and to seek its termination.

In the weeks leading up to the signing of the Agreement, working closely with his minister for defence, Frank Aiken, de Valera began to form the nucleus of the party's new approach to Northern Ireland. On 28 March 1938, at a meeting of the party's National Executive publicity sub-committee, it was first recommended that Fianna Fáil commence an anti-partition campaign to educate public opinion in Great Britain and Northern Ireland of the partition of Ireland.[22] Aiken was appointed chairman, while Pádraic Ó Máille (Leas Chathaoirleach of the Seanad, 11 May 1938 to 22 July 1938), Erskine Childers (elected Fianna Fáil TD for Athlone-Longford at the 1938 Irish general election in April 1938), John McCann (elected Fianna Fáil TD for Dublin South following a by-election victory in June 1939), and Aodh de Blacam (discussed below) made up the remainder of the sub-committee.[23]

Aiken's presence gave the committee's recommendations substantial credibility. Since coming to power in 1932 he was a leading figure within consecutive Fianna Fáil cabinets and was known to be one of de Valera's 'closest friends',[24] 'politically devoted' to 'his chief'.[25] His contemporary and opposition colleague, Fine Gael's James Dillon believed Aiken to be 'a Northern bigot ... intolerant and dictatorial'.[26] Most revealing was the private opinion of Aiken's own cabinet colleague, minister for lands, Gerald Boland. Writing in 1962 he recalled that Aiken was a 'condescending ... menace'.[27] Boland remarked that during Fianna Fáil's early years Aiken wanted to be 'as usual the big noise', but really he was only 'a selfish show man'.[28] The British recorded that due to his 'Northern background' Aiken was reported to 'feel strongly about partition'.[29] Some have observed that Aiken was perceived as 'the most anglophobic of de Valera's ministers', and as a consequence was omitted from the Irish delegation during the Anglo-Irish negotiations.[30]

Irrespective of how others viewed Aiken, his relationship with de Valera was 'almost symbiotic'.[31] It is apparent that the new anti-partition drive was engineered by de Valera and Aiken; the latter acting as a mediator for the former. Speaking at a meeting of the party's National Executive, on 28 March 1938, on the evening that the sub-committee first proposed the creation of the anti-partition campaign, Aiken 'verbally' encouraged the National Executive committee members to endorse the new anti-partition policy.[32]

On 24 April 1938, the day before the Anglo-Irish Agreement was signed, the Fianna Fáil National Executive publicity sub-committee convened on the advice of de Valera to discuss partition. On the conclusion of the meeting the sub-committee issued a four-point recommendation, which formed the basis of the newly conceived anti-partition campaign:

> (1) That an organisation, to be known as the Anti-Partition of Ireland League, be founded in Britain.
> (2) That an organiser, or two, be sent to organise a Convention of the principal Irish supporters in England and Scotland, for the purpose of electing Officers and preparing for the Anti-Partition Campaign.
> (3) That the Taoiseach be asked to write a book, or foreword to a book, on the partition question which would sell as 1/-.
> (4) That one of the principal activities of the Anti-Partition League was the dissemination of the book throughout Ireland. [33]

Henceforth, anti-partition propaganda constituted the basis of Fianna Fáil's Northern Ireland policy. Members of the publicity sub-committee argued that a new approach was essential given that the party's approach to Northern Ireland was absent of 'definite guidelines'. 'Every day', a memorandum produced on behalf of the committee read, 'influential Irish residents in England come to our secretary and ask ... what is the party's official policy on this matter [Northern Ireland policy]? We don't know what to say'. [34]

De Valera now sought to answer this question. Since he was unable to offer any immediate solution to partition, he would instead inform public opinion in Great Britain and Northern Ireland of the 'facts' of partition. [35] As he later pronounced 'were we to get the facts known to the citizens of Britain ... it would be inconceivable that the majority of people in Britain would allow partition to remain'. [36]

De Valera's decision to initiate a fresh anti-partition drive reflected pressure that he had encountered from within Fianna Fáil. By instructing the National Executive publicity sub-committee to formulate a series of new policy initiatives on Northern Ireland he made a pre-emptive strike to curtail any anticipated backlash, both within Fianna Fáil and from the wider nationalist community, concerning his inability to secure concessions on partition during the Anglo-Irish negotiations. This was de Valera's cue for an anti-partition propaganda offensive.

Two years previously, in March 1936, de Valera had ruled out the prospect of undertaking an anti-partition campaign, stating that such a policy '... would be a mere demonstration and would not produce any practical results'.[37] The situation, however, had now changed. Faced with the prospect of widespread discontent because of his perceived failure to end partition, he realised that a new path was necessary. Indeed, during preliminary Anglo-Irish negotiations with MacDonald, in September 1937, de Valera warned his colleague that if concessions were not won on partition, he would be forced to 'consider definitely a campaign to inform British and world opinion' of the injustice of partition.[38]

In January 1938 a cohort of Fianna Fáil TDs expressed their disappointment at the nature of the talks on partition during the Anglo-Irish negotiations.[39] De Valera personally informed MacDonald that some Fianna Fáil deputies recorded that they might lose their seats or that there may have even been a split in the party if no progress was made on partition.[40] Upon de Valera's return to Ireland he was forced to speak at length on the partition issue at a meeting of the Fianna Fáil parliamentary party.[41] Senior cabinet ministers, in particular minister for lands, Gerald Boland and minister for posts and telegraphs, Oscar Traynor, were reportedly unwilling to support the Agreement with London unless a settlement on partition was made.[42]

Writing to his sister, Ida, in March 1938, Chamberlain explained the dilemma de Valera faced. Referring to a previous meeting between himself and de Valera, he noted that his Irish colleague 'was clearly much impressed and anxious to accept [the Agreement] but very doubtful about his colleagues'. Indeed, Chamberlain reported that according to de Valera the reaction from many of the Fianna Fáil cabinet to the terms of the Agreement was 'appalling'.[43] Fianna Fáil veteran TD for Cork-East, Martin Corry, speaking in the Dáil following the signing of the Agreement, offered his own solution to partition. 'I personally am in favour of storing up sufficient poison gas', he informed stunned opposition deputies, 'so that when you get the wind in the right direction you can start at the Border and let it travel, and follow it'.[44]

Most tellingly Belfast-born Catholic and minister for finance, Seán MacEntee, prepared a draft letter of resignation from the government, in February 1938. He wrote the letter in protest at de

Valera's demands during the negotiations that any attempt to settle the trade dispute with London would first have to involve the British government taking 'effective steps' to end partition.[45] Known to be 'prone to contradiction and argument',[46] MacEntee refrained from sending his letter of resignation at the last minute. Its contents, nevertheless, revealed his opposition to Fianna Fáil's attitude towards Northern Ireland. The party, he wrote in regard to partition 'never had a considered policy'. 'It has always been', he bemoaned 'an affair of hasty improvisations, a matter of fits and starts'.[47] For the past six years, he said, the Fianna Fáil government 'have done nothing' to secure Irish unity, but rather helped to entrench the divide between Dublin and Belfast.

The 'partition problem', MacEntee continued, 'cannot be solved except with the consent of the majority of the Northern non-Catholic population. It certainly cannot be solved by their coercion'. Thus, he believed that the partition question (for the immediate term at least) must be placed to one side. Attention, he said, should instead be given towards obtaining an agreement with London, which would secure Ireland's neutrality in the face of the impending European war.[48] Although usually inclined to concede full deference on lines of policy to de Valera, MacEntee could not remain tight-lipped on the subject of Northern Ireland. De Valera's efforts, he believed, during the negotiations to compel the British to 'force' Northern Protestants to enter a united Ireland were nonsensical. It had resulted, he said, 'in the essential unity and confidence of the cabinet ... being destroyed'.[49] Rather than harping on about partition and maintaining that it was solely Britain's responsibility to bring about Irish unity, MacEntee wrote, 'we should ... re-establish some contacts with the representatives of the Six County majority and create that atmosphere in which we can begin to talk politics'.[50]

A selection of grass-roots Fianna Fáil supporters held reservations at de Valera's perceived failure to gain any concessions on partition during the Anglo-Irish negotiations. Resolutions 'poured into' de Valera's office denouncing any settlement which failed to tackle partition.[51] Opposition Fine Gael deputy for Cork-North, Timothy Linehan mockingly reported that Fianna Fáil cumainn throughout the length of the country were 'shrieking in holy horror even at the very idea of a settlement' that failed to end partition.[52] At a meeting of the Fianna Fáil Tipperary Comhairle Ceantair (District Council) party Senator Seán Hayes lamented that because partition was not settled the Agreement was not 'completely satisfactory'.[53] Following the signing of the Agreement, at meetings of Kilkenny and Limerick Corporations, respectively, some local county councillors exclaimed as 'disgraceful' de Valera's neglect of partition.[54] Councillor O'Hanrahan, speaking at a meeting of the Kilkenny Corporation, noted that 'we have nothing to congratulate ourselves on ... the Six-Counties are still outside our land'.[55]

Outside Fianna Fáil circles there were many others who were also disappointed by the lack of progress on partition. Madam Maud Gonne Edith MacBride was reportedly furious upon hearing news of de Valera's apparent failure to gain concessions on partition during the negotiations. In particular she lamented that Irish newspapers had drawn insufficient attention to the conduct under which her 'fellow-Irishmen were suffering in the Six-Counties'.[56] Some regional newspapers expressed disappointment that the Agreement had 'ignore[ed] the North ... the thorny question of partition has not been touched'.[57] The *Anglo-Celt*, in a single line, grieved that 'nothing has been done with reference to partition'.[58] At a meeting of Cavan County Council, the vice-chairman, Mr. E. MacDonnell and his fellow County Councillor, J. P. Mc Kiernan demanded that the Irish government approach Adolf Hitler and the German Nazi Party to help solve partition.[59]

Rev. T. Maguire, a Roman Catholic priest from Newtownbutler, Co. Fermanagh, and a member of the United Ireland Party, said that like the Anglo-Irish Treaty of 1921 the Irish people had been 'sold again by the settlement of the so-called economic war'.[60] Maguire, referred to in British circles as a 'rabid anti-partitionist' epitomised the sense of frustration that many nationalists throughout Ireland felt towards the unresolved issue of partition.[61] Nonetheless, apart from such occasional outbursts of anti-partitionism the general public in the South welcomed the Agreement.[62] Indeed, in his letter to de Valera, MacEntee noted that the country at large was 'looking for a settlement, expects to get one, and does not regard partition as more than a theoretical obstacle to a practical agreement'.[63]

For Northern Nationalists the negotiations with the British naively raised their expectations that de Valera would find a permanent solution to partition. During a meeting in London, in February 1938, a delegation of Northern Nationalist, led by MP for South Fermanagh, Cahir Healy, pressed de Valera to ensure that partition was placed at the centre of the negotiations.[64] The delegation expressed their 'outrage' that the 'historic Irish nation' was divided by the British government, noting that it would be a betrayal if de Valera settled the trade and defence disputes, but ignored partition.[65] De Valera was reluctant to commit himself to a pledge to end partition and instead reassured Healy and his colleagues that he would 'bring the facts to the attention of the British government'.[66]

Although traditionally sympathetic to the plight of Northern Nationalists and a publicist of their grievances, de Valera always saw the dangers of aligning with any political alliance which possibly could erode his strict personal control of Fianna Fáil's Northern Ireland policy. In reality, since Fianna Fáil's establishment de Valera was more than happy to ignore the plight of Northern Nationalists. His excuse was that they must wait until Fianna Fáil was in power. As Fianna Fáil TD Thomas Derrig noted in March 1929, 'We can do no more at present ... than show our sympathy to them'.[67] This position proved considerably beneficial for de Valera as it absolved him from tackling the Northern minority problem and allowed him to 'concentrate totally on Free State issues without appearing to be ignoring the Northern nationalists as Cumann na nGaedheal were doing'.[68]

Upon securing power, Fianna Fáil remained reluctant to involve themselves with Northern Nationalists. The party's traditional anti-partitionist rhetoric was not translated into active policy from 1932 onwards. Besides the occasional expression of sympathy or anti-partitionist outburst, the Fianna Fáil governments' attitude towards the Northern minority differed little from those of the previous Cumann na nGaedheal administration. Throughout the 1920s the Cumann na nGaedheal cabinet distanced itself from the plight of Northern Catholics. Thus, overwhelmed by the Northern Ireland government's repressive measures and ignored by Dublin, the Northern minority realised that they must fend for themselves. Writing in 1922 Cahir Healy bemoaned of the South's neglect of Northern Catholics: 'we must', he wrote, 'look after ourselves'.[69]

This policy of keeping Northern Nationalists at arm's length continued unabated under the Fianna Fáil governments of the 1930s. De Valera made this clear in correspondence with Healy in 1934. Pressed by Healy for a statement on Fianna Fáil's policy towards Northern Catholics, de Valera noted that while the party would co-operate with their northern comrades towards ending partition, the party would not be drawn 'in the way of intervention in differences of opinion among the six-county anti-partitionists ...'.[70] Indeed, de Valera had resisted pressure from Northern nationalists to raise the political and social grievances of the Catholic minority at the League of Nations in Geneva, apart from a fleeting reference by Seán T. O'Kelly to the 'shameful partition of Ireland'.[71] As Clare O'Halloran observed, 'professions of support and sympathy were Fianna Fáil's only reaction to the problem'.[72]

Privately, on hearing news of the Anglo-Irish Agreement, Northern Nationalists were incensed. Healy again led the protests. In a letter to Eamonn Donnelly he noted that 'De Valera made a civil war about the difference between Documents 1 and 2, but he is not prepared to say "boo" to Chamberlain over the loss of the six counties!'.[73] In public, Northern Nationalists' reaction was more reserved. They issued a public statement expressing their 'disappointment' that de Valera had failed to secure an end to partition.[74] Arguably for the first time, due to his inability to secure concessions on partition, Northern Nationalists seriously questioned de Valera's position as the leader of Irish nationalism and the man best suited to deliver Irish unity.[75] On de Valera's return to Dublin from London, Northern Ireland Senator, for Fermanagh/Tyrone, John McHugh bemoaned that de Valera 'had no real' Northern Ireland policy and was merely using the Catholic minority of Northern Ireland 'for his own purposes'.[76]

De Valera's decision, therefore, to endorse a new anti-partition campaign was a pragmatic decision. It aimed to counteract criticism from Irish nationalists, both within the Fianna Fáil organisation and North and South of the border, towards the Irish government's lack of progress on partition during the Anglo-Irish negotiations. Some historians have argued that de Valera's central motive for the creation of the anti-partition campaign was to 'establish internationally a clear sense of Irish grievance that would allow him to justify Irish neutrality' in the anticipated war.[77] This analysis fails to grasp the complexities internally within Fianna Fáil, which effectively compelled de Valera to initiate his anti-partition crusade. In a desperate attempt to reassure Irish nationalists that Fianna Fáil offered the best chance of securing Irish reunification he turned to the sterile use of anti-partitionism.

THE FIANNA FÁIL ANTI-PARTITION SUB-COMMITTEE, 1938

Following Fianna Fáil's general election victory in June 1938 and a break for the traditional summer Dáil recess, the party's National Executive convened on 10 October 1938, at party headquarters, Mount Street, Dublin, to hold a 'special meeting' to discuss partition. Chaired by de Valera, National Executive members considered the recommendations on partition issued on behalf of the National Executive publicity sub-committee the previous March and April 1938. Members first decided that Fianna Fáil, in future, would co-operate with the anti-partition movements in Northern Ireland in organising anti-partition demonstrations.[78] Significantly, members additionally agreed that the party would establish an anti-partition sub-committee to 'consider the most effective means to organise public opinion in England on the question of partition'.[79]

This new anti-partition sub-committee first convened immediately after the meeting of the National Executive; the committee then continued to meet on a fortnightly basis, thirty-one times in total, until its final meeting in September 1939.[80] Oscar Traynor was appointed chairman, while known vocal anti-partitionist deputies, including Fianna Fáil Senator Margaret Pearse, Aodh de Blacam and Eamonn Donnelly were also appointed to the committee.[81] Traynor was a political heavyweight within the Fianna Fáil cabinet. He had taken part in the 1916 Easter Rising and subsequent War of Independence and was well respected by grass-roots supporters. Most importantly, from de Valera's standpoint, while upset at not having secured an end to partition during the Anglo-Irish talks, he was unconditionally loyal to 'his chief'. His presence, therefore, as chairman ensured that he was able to keep a watchful eye over proceedings.

Margaret Pearse was the sister of Pádraig Pearse and was believed to have been critical of de Valera's approach to partition and particularly of his hardening attitude to the IRA from 1939 to 1940.[82] De Blacam, an original member of the party's publicity sub-committee, represented the 'vociferous anti-partitionists' arm of Fianna Fáil.[83] Described by Northern dramatist, Louis J. Walsh as a republican 'doctrinaire',[84] de Blacam's opposition to de Valera's Northern Ireland policy eventually lead to his defection to Clann na Poblachta in December 1947.

It was Donnelly's presence on the committee, in particular, which was most interesting considering that he was a traditional critic of Fianna Fáil's approach to Northern Ireland. Throughout the 1930s he had been a consistent thorn in the side of de Valera over the party's approach to Northern Ireland.[85] According to Cahir Healy, Donnelly's presence on the National Executive gave Nationalist representatives a voice.[86] Although a long time member of the Fianna Fáil elite, by 1937 he fell out with the party hierarchy because of article three of the 1937 constitution.[87]

During a speech in the Dáil, in May 1937, Donnelly demanded that the government establish a 'special partition department'. 'Partition and partition alone', he insisted, was the only subject that should concern Irish nationalists, 'nothing else matters'.[88] In Dublin in September 1938, under the auspices of the North-Dock Fianna Fáil cumann, Donnelly spoke of the Fianna Fáil government's neglect of Northern Ireland policy. He argued that if 'resolutions, speeches, lectures, debates and manifestos could end partition, it would have disappeared long since'. 'Irish nationalists', he proclaimed, 'had been wasting their time'.[89]

The appointment of Donnelly, Pearse and de Blacam ensured that the committee was not merely to comprise of a series of 'yes men', but instead was to represent a vocal, and at times, hostile grouping of Fianna Fáil supporters, at variance with the party's approach to Northern Ireland. Given Donnelly's repeated denunciation of Fianna Fáil's approach to Northern Ireland it is not altogether surprising that de Valera assumed an effective veto over any policy decisions recommended by the new anti-partition sub-committee. Although not a member of the sub-committee, any decisions taken at meetings of the committee first required de Valera's personal consent before becoming official policy.[90] In reality, real control of Fianna Fáil's Northern Ireland policy lay exclusively with de Valera. The formation of the committee was a charade, established in the wake of the Anglo-Irish Agreement to demonstrate to Fianna Fáil members that the party was undertaking a new Northern Ireland strategy.

That this new Northern Ireland policy initiative was organised and financed under the auspices of Fianna Fáil and not the government or Oireachtas in Leinster House, further indicated de Valera's wish to maintain a firm hold over policy. He was reluctant to share the anti-partition stage with Opposition parties. During the initial months of the campaign the anti-partition sub-committee agreed to allocate £100 respectively, from the Fianna Fáil coffers, to the London, Liverpool, Manchester and Glasgow branches of the League to pay the salary of an Organiser in each district.[91]

Some within Fianna Fáil expressed their objection to the party maintaining sole control of the anti-partition drive. In August 1939 a collection of unidentified Fianna Fáil Senators wrote to the party's National Executive forwarding a resolution calling for the anti-partition campaign to be 'directed by the Department of External Affairs on behalf of the Government'. They noted that any expenses incurred should be 'a charge on the State funds'.[92] At a previous meeting of the National Executive in February 1939 Donnelly forwarded a motion, seconded by de Blacam, that the National Executive should transfer control of the party's anti-partition campaign to the custody of the government.[93]

Irrespective of financial concerns, Donnelly believed that Fianna Fáil's monopoly on the anti-partition campaign merely represented opportunism within the party. This new anti-partition drive, Donnelly believed, was being used by de Valera and his cabinet colleagues merely for political gain. 'The undoing of partition', Donnelly recorded, was 'not the monopoly of any Irish political party. It was a national issue'.[94] At a meeting of the anti-partition sub-committee in July 1939 he moved a resolution calling for an 'All Party meeting in Dublin'.[95] His endeavours, however, came to nothing as de Valera rejected his colleague's request.[96] Donnelly was left to exclaim, 'there is no co-ordinated effort to direct the anti-partition activities along lines to meet with eventual success'.[97]

THE FORMATION OF THE ANTI-PARTITION OF
IRELAND LEAGUE OF GREAT BRITAIN

As originally specified by the National Executive publicity sub-committee in March 1938, the chief task of the anti-partition sub-committee was to supervise and safeguard the formation of a new anti-partition movement in the major cities of Great Britain to be known as the Anti-Partition of Ireland League of Great Britain.

On 11 October 1938 de Valera wrote to the members of the anti-partition sub-committee instructing that branches of the new League should be formed in London, Liverpool, Manchester and Glasgow. He noted that the method to be adopted would be to get in contact with a number of 'suitable people who would form an organisation committee for their own immediate areas'. He explained, 'You know the sort of people required ... the people who would have the greatest influence in their neighbourhood and would be most effective in converting British opinions against partition'.[98]

During the initial months of the anti-partition drive de Valera took it upon himself to assume responsibility for co-ordinating the campaign. He devised the constitution, rules and regulations for the Anti-Partition of Ireland League of Great Britain.[99] Under his instructions, Fianna Fáil TD for Waterford and parliamentary secretary to the taoiseach and to the minister for external affairs,

Patrick J. Little, travelled to London to interview 'special organisers' who would assume management for each branch of the League.[100] De Valera also secured the services of Liam MacMahon, a Manchester native, who had helped to establish the Irish Self-Determination League in 1919.[101] By November 1938 three branches of the League were formed in London, while in Liverpool a new branch of the League was established under the auspices of the Council of Irish Societies.[102] In March 1939 the League held its first annual conference, with representatives from London, Manchester, Liverpool and Glasgow attending.[103]

With the apparatus of the new League formed, members of the anti-partition sub-committee focused their attentions towards sending suitable speakers to Britain and Northern Ireland to speak at anti-partition meetings and rallies. During its relatively short existence the sub-committee sent several prominent Fianna Fáil personalities to address such meetings. De Valera's son, Vivion de Valera, travelled to Northern Ireland and Manchester;[104] party deputy for Dublin County, Seán Brady visited Liverpool,[105] while Fianna Fáil general secretary, Erskine Childers spoke in Northern Ireland and Liverpool.[106]

Spurred on by the anti-partition campaign in the major British cities, Northern Nationalists enthusiastically embraced de Valera's anti-partition drive. Under de Valera's direct orders he informed Northern Nationalists that it was imperative to hold anti-partition meetings as quickly as possible.[107] Throughout 1938 and early 1939 numerous meetings were held across Northern Ireland from counties Derry to Armagh; on one occasion Childers was detained and later released by police while speaking at an anti-partition meeting in the village of Newtownbutler, Co. Fermanagh.[108]

Parallel with the anti-partition drive in the United Kingdom and Northern Ireland an anti-partition campaign was initiated throughout the South of Ireland. In Co. Kilkenny in June 1939, a new Anti-Partition branch was established, at which Fianna Fáil TDs minister for education, Thomas Derrig and Erskine Childers spoke against the use of force.[109] Over the subsequent months additional Anti-Partition branches were founded in counties Limerick[110] and Tipperary.[111] In July 1939 large rallies were held in counties Dublin and Cork to protest against partition; in Dublin alone, it was reported that over '1,000 old IRA men' were on parade in College Green.[112]

The anti-partition sub-committee also devoted a substantial amount of its energies towards the commissioning and production of anti-partition propaganda material. Pamphlets, articles and newspapers were all produced by the sub-committee during its short existence. Over 2,000 of Henry Harrison's pamphlet, *The Partition of Ireland, How Britain is Responsible*, and 5,000 copies of the pamphlet, *The Unity of Ireland, Speeches by de Valera to the Seanad Éireann*, were distributed by the committee to the various anti-partition bodies in Great Britain and Northern Ireland.[113] It was also decided that a weekly bulletin would be compiled by the Publicity Department of Fianna Fáil, containing information on partition to be forwarded to each branch of the Anti-Partition of Ireland League of Great Britain.[114]

In the early weeks of October 1938, with the anti-partition campaign underway, de Valera decided to open up a second front to his Northern Ireland strategy. His attention now turned directly to Ulster Unionists, believing, naively, that he had one more ace card to play towards persuading Belfast to agree to a united Ireland.

DE VALERA'S FEDERAL PROPOSAL, OCTOBER 1938

On 17 October 1938, in an interview in the *Evening Standard*, de Valera outlined proposals for a federal solution between Dublin and Belfast. A federal offer had formed a staple ingredient of Fianna Fáil's approach to Northern Ireland since 1926 and remained conventional party policy for the subsequent three decades.[115] The proposal rested on the premise that the Northern Ireland government would retain its own parliament in Belfast and powers currently held by Westminster would be transferred to the Irish government.[116] In fact, the proposal offered little new, as de Valera had previously proposed giving local autonomy to the Northern Ireland parliament provided that Ulster Unionists were willing to enter an all-Ireland parliament in Dublin, in his infamous Document No. 2 of 1921.[117]

The proposal was immediately rejected by Ulster Unionists. They had no interest in any of de Valera's initiatives. Speaking in 1938, the Northern Ireland prime minister, Lord Craigavon, typified Ulster Unionist reaction to de Valera's overtures: 'civil war would follow any attempts to meet Mr. de Valera's manifesto on a united Ireland'.[118] In particular, de Valera's unwillingness to grant Belfast economic concessions during the 1938 Anglo-Irish Agreement had left a bitter taste in the mouths of Ulster Unionists.

More than any other of Dublin's policies, protectionism was greeted with the sharpest hostility by Belfast. The economic nationalism as espoused by de Valera had little appeal to Ulster Unionists whose more industrialised economy was dependent on export markets which could not be filled by the Irish market in the South. Indeed, Fianna Fáil's economic policies provided Ulster Unionists with powerful circumstantial evidence that the Irish government would 'cheerfully and rapidly destroy their economy in their interests of securing Irish unity'.[119] De Valera was certainly aware that the high tariffs of the 1930s gave an economic 'edge' to partition. He, nevertheless, was not prepared to offer Belfast preferential treatment to Northern Ireland imports.[120]

Significantly, de Valera also failed to realise the negative effect that the newly established Fianna Fáil sponsored anti-partition campaign in Britain had for Dublin's relationship with Belfast. The anti-partition campaign, which propagated the illegality of the Northern Ireland state and exposed the Stormont government's discrimination practices against the Catholic minority of Northern Ireland, merely lent weight to Ulster Unionists' objection to entering a united Ireland. In discussions with de Valera, Chamberlain 'frankly' explained to the former of how the Dublin sponsored anti-partition campaign had merely 'multiplied his [de Valera's] own difficulties'. The campaign, Chamberlain noted, confirmed that de Valera 'had not a single friend in Northern Ireland'.[121] Indeed, within Ulster Unionist circles de Valera was commonly regarded with contempt; writing in 1938, Walter Duff, a Unionist sympathiser living in America, described de Valera as 'that half-breed Spaniard'.[122]

THE DONNELLY-CAMP OF FIANNA FÁIL CHALLENGE
DE VALERA'S NORTHERN IRELAND POLICY

The unattractiveness of de Valera's federal offer to Ulster Unionists was compounded by his inability to maintain a united front within the Fianna Fáil organisation on the partition issue. From the outset Eamonn Donnelly routinely made demands on the anti-partition sub-committee that were at variance with official, or more appropriately de Valera's, Northern Ireland policy.[123] In January 1939, at a meeting of the sub-committee, Donnelly moved a motion in favour of the establishment of an 'Anti-Partition Monster meeting' in Dublin, for Easter of that year.[124] Between February and May 1939 Donnelly placed the motion on the Clár on a further several occasions. On each occasion, however, the motion was referred to de Valera, who was openly reluctant to give an answer.[125]

Donnelly's request for a monster meeting was scheduled to take place in the immediate days prior to de Valera's anticipated trip to

America, on the invitation of American president, F. D. Roosevelt to attend the New York World's Fair. For Donnelly, therefore, the anti-partition meeting was logical given de Valera's anticipated anti-partition drive in America, where he had planned a six-week coast-to-coast tour during May 1939. De Valera, however, was forced to cancel his American anti-partition tour because of the British threat of conscription to Northern Ireland in April 1939.

Members of the National Executive[126] and grass-roots supporters had also requested that a monster meeting be convened at the earliest possible moment 'to draw [the] attention of the public to the partition question'.[127] De Valera was reluctant to endorse holding an anti-partition rally in Dublin. Traynor informed sub-committee members that de Valera was unable to agree to the proposal on the grounds that 'in the circumstances it would be advisable to postpone any steps for the organising of such a meeting for the present'.[128]

For a cohort of disgruntled Fianna Fáil supporters de Valera's stance on partition was perceived to have become sterile and inactive. His unwillingness to consider the holding of a monster meeting, which was supported by the majority of members on the National Executive, served to prove to Donnelly and his fellow anti-partitionists that the formation of the anti-partition sub-committee had been an exercise in the optics of illusion. Irrespective of what de Valera might say in public, ultimately Northern Ireland policy lay exclusively under his control. Real power rested with de Valera. Cahir Healy was left to complain that on partition de Valera was an 'individualist', who would not allow others play a part in policy formation.[129] This dictatorial control over Northern Ireland policy was, however, the breaking point for a consortium of anti-partitionist members, no longer willing to blindly adhere to de Valera's diktat.

It was de Valera's speech on partition, delivered to the Seanad in February 1939, which precipitated a showdown between the Fianna Fáil leadership and a cohort of anti-partitionists within the organisation. Originally laid down by Senators Frank MacDermott (Independent) and Ernest Henry Alton (Independent, University of Dublin), on 26 January 1939, a Seanad motion on partition had appealed for more friendly relations between Dublin and Belfast.[130] This motion, however, was subsequently amended by Fianna Fáil Senator Seán O'Donovan. In its place he demanded that the British government, her armed forces and administrative officials should immediately evacuate Northern Ireland and that the Irish government would assume control of 'that section of Irish territory'.[131] O'Donovan, a veterinary surgeon by profession, was well respected within Fianna Fáil circles and as chairman of the Tomas Ó Cléirigh cumann, Dublin North-East, had written to the party's National Executive in May 1939 offering a five-point memorandum on the recent anti-partition campaign.[132]

During a passionate and at times antagonistic debate in the Seanad, which occurred over two days (26 January and 7 February), de Valera spoke passionately against the use of force to secure Irish unity. He would not permit himself to be drawn into a debate on the Fianna Fáil government's Northern Ireland policy, maintaining that policy was already 'largely embodied in the Constitution'.[133] Senators shouted down one another during heated exchanges. Senator John MacLoughlin (Industrial and Commercial Panel) accused de Valera of offering 'no policy except a policy of "wobble" on the partition question'. He lamented that there was a 'ring of insincerity about the whole business,' Fianna Fáil, he felt, were a bunch of 'prevaricators and quibblers'.[134]

De Valera's frank admission during the Seanad debate that he did not favour a united Ireland if that meant 'sacrificing the Irish language' was evidence for the anti-partitionists that he was out of touch with the partition debate.[135] Donnelly and de Blacam were infuriated with de Valera's comments. His admission was viewed as a bridge too far, exposing, as Donnelly in particular viewed it, a prime example of Fianna Fáil's neglect of Northern Ireland policy. Consequently, on 13 February, a week after de Valera's Seanad speech, at the request of Donnelly, the National Executive convened to hold a 'special meeting' on partition. Over thirty people were present, including several frontbench TDs, Aiken, Boland, Childers, Traynor and Patrick J. Rutledge. The meeting was chaired by de Valera, while also in attendance was a selection of anti-partitionists, Donnelly, de Blacam, party TD for Donegal West, Cormac Breslin and Senators Margaret Pearse, Seán O'Donovan and Christopher Michael Byrne.

At the behest of Donnelly and seconded by de Blacam, a motion was moved, mirroring that of Senator O'Donovan the previous week, which asserted that the Irish government reiterate 'our claim to the whole of Ireland' and demand that the British evacuate Northern Ireland.[136] In what had become almost synonymous whenever de Valera chaired a meeting of the National Executive, members had a 'long discussion' on the motion; however 'no decision was reached'.[137]

De Valera was evidently under severe pressure from a faction of anti-partition party members to take a more aggressive approach to Northern Ireland. At the party's annual Ard Fheis the previous November, delegates had forwarded over twenty resolutions to party headquarters demanding that 'all necessary steps be taken to end partition'.[138] During the conference de Valera had categorically ruled out the use of force to secure Irish unity. He informed those in attendance that he was not prepared to 'shift an inch' from this policy. 'If the organisation wants to have a shift from it', he pronounced – hinting at his possible resignation – 'then they will have to get other people' to run Fianna Fáil.[139]

His response to members of the National Executive, the circumstantial evidence suggests, would have been identical to his repeated statements at the party annual Ard Fheiseanna against physical violence to end partition.[140] The formation of the anti-partition sub-committee, rather than offering a coherent policy towards Northern Ireland, had in reality revealed a simmering disagreement among party members, which threatened to boil over at any moment.

THE TERMINATION OF THE ANTI-PARTITION OF IRELAND LEAGUE OF GREAT BRITAIN AND THE RE-EMERGENCE OF THE IRA, 1939

Irrespective of the criticism that de Valera faced from within Fianna Fáil towards partition, it was the IRA's decision to renew its military campaign in Great Britain in January 1939 and the outbreak of the Second World War in September of the same year, which ultimately proved disastrous for his 1938 Northern Ireland policy.

Under the leadership of the militarist Seán Russell, the IRA made 'a declaration of war on the United Kingdom' and commenced a series of bombing campaigns in several major British cities. In July 1939 the British House of Commons introduced legislation to quell the Republican threat. The Fianna Fáil government also counteracted the danger posed by the IRA and in 1939 enacted 'the Offences Against the State Act'. The passing of the legislation allowed for the creation of special criminal courts and increased police powers to search, arrest and detain suspected IRA members.

Privately, de Valera habitually warned London that the British government's failure to tackle partition was a considerable factor in the renewed IRA campaign.[141] He spoke of the 'unbelievable narrow-mindedness' of British ministers and officials in respect of seeking a solution to partition.[142] The announcement by the British government in April 1939 that conscription was to possibly apply to the people of Northern Ireland further lent to de Valera's belief that London's policy towards Ireland was encouraging IRA violence. De Valera was known to be 'very perturbed' by Chamberlain's announcement. He warned that the introduction of conscription in Northern Ireland 'can only be regarded as an act of war against our nation and will provoke the bitterest hostility to England wherever there are Irishmen throughout the world'.[143]

Writing to Chamberlain in April 1939 de Valera reported that 'a large section of our people, particularly the young ... are led to see hope only in Britain's weakness'. 'The intensification of feeling here and amongst our people in the United States', he wrote, 'means it is imperative to act quickly lest it is too late to save the situation'.[144] In correspondence with Malcolm MacDonald, de Valera repeated similar sentiments regarding a failure to end partition. 'It is vital', he informed MacDonald 'that the temptation to our young people to try to cut this Gordian knot be removed quickly. In a short while, it may be too late'.[145]

For London, the Fianna Fáil sponsored anti-partition campaign was perceived to have helped drive support for the IRA. MacDonald reported that there was a great feeling of 'uneasiness' and 'irritation' throughout Britain towards the anti-partition campaign. He noted that many people could not distinguish between the Irish government's policy and that of the IRA.[146] Indeed, de Valera's semi-official biographers' record that the re-emergence of the IRA 'blew high-sky any hopes which de Valera had of convincing British public opinion' that partition should be ended.[147]

In some Irish circles de Valera's sponsored anti-partition campaign was equally dismissed as ill-advised. Senator Frank MacDermott (nominated by the Taoiseach), an ardent critic of Fianna Fáil's Northern Ireland policy, believed that the campaign had merely encouraged 'very strong, very violent and very inflammatory statements'. Citing Eamonn Donnelly as an example of the anti-partitionist mindset inherent within Fianna Fáil, MacDermott pleaded with de Valera to realise that anti-partition speeches only 'do more harm than good'.[148]

It was the outbreak of the Second World War in September 1939 that brought de Valera's anti-partition campaign to a grinding halt. On 1 September Germany invaded Poland. Two days later, on 3 September, the British and French declared war on Nazi Germany. De Valera reacted immediately to the unfolding crisis. Prior to the British and French declaration of war, on 2 September, de Valera declared Ireland's neutrality during a sitting of Dáil Éireann. The taoiseach introduced two Bills – the First Amendment of the Constitution Bill and the draconian Emergency Powers Bill; it was necessary to amend articles 28.3.3 of the constitution to provide for the declaration of a state of emergency during a time when armed conflict was taking place without the participation of the state.[149] This was the origin of the anodyne description of the Second World War as the 'Emergency' in Irish public discourse.

At an emergency Fianna Fáil parliamentary party meeting, convened at 4am on the morning of 3 September, de Valera outlined the Irish government's policy of neutrality. Addressing over forty elected representatives he assured those present that Irish neutrality would be vigorously pursued and that the question of partition would never be far from the government's mind.[150]

On 11 September, at what transpired to be the final meeting of the anti-partition sub-committee until 1946, de Valera ordered the closure of all branches of the Anti-Partition of Ireland League of Great Britain. Traynor remarked that 'no good purpose could now be served by continuing the League's activities as originally planned'.[151] Interestingly the reasons given by de Valera for the termination of the League were because of financial irregularities and specifically the 'unsatisfactory state' of the organisation in London'.[152] De Valera informed the London branch of the League that he was 'not satisfied' with the manner in which the sums guaranteed for the organiser's salary had been disbursed.[153]

Financial concerns, albeit de Valera may have genuinely held, nonetheless allowed him to conceal the *bona fide* reasons for terminating the government's anti-partition campaign. His real motives can be summarised in three points: (a) due to the outbreak of the Second World War de Valera was determined to consolidate his control over the government's official stance on Northern Ireland and focus all available resources on neutrality; (b) as a direct consequence of the renewed IRA campaign in Britain, de Valera believed that the anti-partition campaign in Britain was a useless exercise; and lastly (c) due to the lack of direct and personal control to which de Valera held over the Anti-Partition of Ireland League of Great Britain he no longer wished to support external anti-partition movements.

THE INTERNAL DEBATE: THE EMERGENCY, FIANNA FÁIL AND NORTHERN IRELAND, 1939–1940

The historiography of Fianna Fáil's approach to partition during the Emergency has concentrated on the government's determination to preserve Irish neutrality irrespective of British assertions that partition would be ended if Ireland agreed to enter the war on the side of the Allies.[154] Historians have failed to examine the persistent disagreements among Fianna Fáil supporters towards de Valera's wartime approach to Northern Ireland, which represented a genuine threat to the stability of the party.[155] Some writers have incorrectly argued that the outbreak of war allowed the partition issue to fade into its customary position, into the background.[156]

Evidentially, the maintenance of neutrality was the Fianna Fáil government's main concern during the war. Indeed 'neutrality', as noted by John Bowman, 'now took precedence over anti-partitionism in Irish politics'.[157] Nevertheless, the outbreak of the war increased expectations for a cohort of anti-partitionists within Fianna Fáil that the ending of partition was imminent. Traditionally 'England's difficulty was seen as Ireland's opportunity' and it was within this context that a section of Fianna Fáil members viewed partition.

Eamonn Donnelly argued that if Fianna Fáil did not reunite the country while the war was on, 'they could whistle for it afterwards'.[158] Speaking in October 1940 he opportunistically remarked that the partition of Ireland would end once 'Britain took home the descendants of the Planters who were living in the lands of the old Irish'.[159] Other party members were even terser. Joseph Brennan, a Donegal native and future frontbench party TD, from a 'strongly Republican family'[160] noted that Fianna Fáil's approach to partition was like that of the armies on the Western front: 'They were continually getting ready, but making no effort to obtain their great objective'.[161]

At Fianna Fáil's first war-time Ard Fheis, in December 1939, de Valera faced stern criticism from party delegates – some who had advocated the use of force – towards the party's perceived lacklustre movement on partition.[162] The *Irish Press* recorded that a 'Ding-dong debate' among the rank-and-file occurred on the subject of the party's approach to Northern Ireland policy, in which 'wordy blows were given and taken'.[163] In his defence, de Valera informed delegates of the formation of the anti-partition sub-committee, established the previous year in October 1938, which he promised would tackle partition. His words fell on deaf ears. Some of the party faithful in attendance accused de Valera of establishing the committee in a cynical attempt to appease the anti-partitionist within the organisation; as we have learned above their accusations were entirely warranted.[164]

During the initial months of 1940, as a 'phoney war' lingered on between Britain, France and Germany, with either side unwilling to mount a major military offensive, the partition question, likewise, remained inactive. This drastically changed by April 1940 as the Fianna Fáil National Executive witnessed unprecedented examples of senior party figures directly challenging de Valera's authority on Northern Ireland policy. On 1 April 1940 Donnelly moved a motion and seconded by Joseph O'Connor that a 'special Ard Fheis' be convened for the purpose of reviewing partition. Correspondence was read also from grass-roots cumainn from counties Galway, Monaghan and Dublin inquiring about the Fianna Fáil government's current stance on Northern Ireland and appealing for immediate action to be taken to bring partition to an end.[165]

In an attempt to placate the hardliners within Fianna Fáil, particularly those that advocated the use of force to secure Irish unity, Erskine Childers wrote an open letter to the editor of the *Irish Press* in mid-April 1940. An original member of the Fianna Fáil National Executive anti-partition sub-committee established in March 1938, Childers was a firm supporter of de Valera's stance on partition. In a rare occurrence Childers publicly outlined the Fianna Fáil government's 'plan' to end partition. 'The campaign for unity', he said, 'must be slow, constructively organised and carefully thought out'. In a cryptic message to the anti-partitionists within Fianna Fáil he noted that this policy, if to prove successful, 'must be faced by everyone'. Childers outlined four 'elements for an end to partition', which were a basic reaffirmation of de Valera's personal attitude to Irish unity.[166]

Firstly, in what had come to constitute Fianna Fáil's stance on partition since the party's foundation, Childers maintained that the 'growth of prosperity and national discipline in the 26 Counties' was essential before attention could be turned towards the question of Irish unity. Southern Ireland, he argued, first needed to build up a strong economic foundation if Ulster Unionists were to ever agree to an end to partition. Secondly, he wrote that the British must 'withdraw' support for the maintenance of partition. Thirdly, he argued that the use of propaganda was central to Fianna Fáil's partition strategy. This policy, he said, must have assistance from the Dublin government and must 'have the desired effect; not mere propaganda for propaganda's sake'. And lastly, he explained that Fianna Fáil would need to see definite signs from within the Northern Ireland state that there was 'support for unity' and the sufficient 'growth' of Northern nationalists over the coming decades.[167]

Childers's letter once again exposed the naivety of the Fianna Fáil government's attitude to partition. Although Childers's calls for patience and constraint were merited, like de Valera, he failed to realise the alienating effect that the use of propaganda had upon Ulster Unionism. Additionally, his calls for 'support for unity' within Northern Ireland (and this no doubt included the support of Northern Protestants) was nonsensical at a time when the Northern Ireland state was a committed partner with London in the war against the Axis Powers.

Simultaneously, Childers's pronouncements were greeted with disdain by many of his own senior Fianna Fáil members. Again it was Donnelly who expressed his contempt for the current government's stance on Northern Ireland. 'When? Oh When', he wrote, 'will we get politicians from the Twenty-Six Counties to recognise the problem of Partition for what it truly is'. Donnelly was particularly perturbed by Childers's remarks that the 'solution to partition would take time, barring some extraordinary change of circumstance'.[168] Donnelly was not alone in his protests. At a meeting of the Fianna Fáil National Executive in early May 1940, Frank Sherwin proposed that a 'special meeting of the National Executive be called to consider the partition question and that the Taoiseach be requested to attend the meeting'.[169] De Valera, however, declined the request. Gerald Boland spoke on his leader's behalf. He explained that because de Valera 'was very much occupied' he could not find it 'convenient' for the moment to attend a special meeting of the National Executive to consider the question of partition.[170]

It was a period when there were heightened expectations within Fianna Fáil that Irish unity was an attainable objective. In early May 1940, as Winston Churchill was appointed British prime minister and as German forces invaded France and the Low Countries, Seán Lemass and James Ryan were despatched to London to negotiate a new trade agreement with the British government. Their presence had raised hope from the Donnelly-wing of the party that possible talks on partition may have been on the agenda. They were, however, to be disappointed. Although British secretary of state for dominion affairs and future prime minister, Anthony Eden expressed 'a general desire to see the end of partition ...' only passing consideration was allocated to the subject during the course of the meeting.[171] Apart from secretary for the Department of External Affairs, Joseph Walshe's protests, neither Lemass nor Ryan were reported to have even raised partition during the discussions.[172] Lemass, in particular, seemed far more concerned with economic matters, chiefly securing trade concessions, rather than badgering about a united Ireland.

For the anti-partitionists within Fianna Fáil this meeting between senior British and Irish ministers was yet another example that partition was being ignored by the party hierarchy. De Valera's reluctance to maintain a debate on partition exposed his determination not to allow a section of Fianna Fáil members to hijack Northern Ireland policy at the expense of undermining his war-time policy of neutrality. He would not permit the opportunists within the party to dictate the Irish government's stance on Irish unity at a time when there was a genuine concern at government level that German forces, with the support of the IRA, were making preparations to invade Ireland.[173]

CONSTITUTIONALISTS VS. MILITANTS: FIANNA FÁIL
AND THE IRA, 1939–1945

The disagreements among senior Fianna Fáil members on the issue of partition came to the boil as a result of the government's war-time policy towards the IRA. The known attempts by the IRA to plan a joint invasion of Northern Ireland with the support of Nazi Germany further compounded de Valera's anxiety. Although the IRA plans were perceived as 'amateurish ... childish ... and completely useless', de Valera saw the IRA's willingness to align itself with Berlin as further indication of his need to reaffirm to the Irish people the futility of the use of force to end partition.[174] Following the outbreak of the IRA campaign in early 1939 and throughout the war years de Valera maintained an almost missionary zeal to persuade public opinion against support for the IRA and the use of physical force to end partition. It was a time when he routinely called for 'national discipline'[175] and spoke of his belief that physical force was not a legitimate policy in the national drive to secure a united Ireland.[176]

Speaking at a Fianna Fáil Comhairle Dáilcheantair in the border county of Cavan in February 1940, de Valera made clear his war-time policy against the IRA. 'The use of force by a secret group', he said, 'can only hurt and harm'.[177] Speaking in Tralee, Co. Kerry, in late June 1940, de Valera pleaded with rank-and-file Fianna Fáil members to remember that 'at the moment we have five-sixths of our island free in every sense of the word', patience and restraint would deliver Irish unity, not illegal organisations, which, he argued, only jeopardise the stability of the state.[178] Aiken, similarly, spoke of the IRA as a 'crazy' and 'reckless group' that defied the government and people of Ireland.[179]

By the late 1930s the vast majority of Fianna Fáil members had left behind their ideological baggage of securing Irish unity by force.

Politics instead reigned supreme and militancy was off the agenda. Nevertheless, for de Valera and his government the IRA posed a serious challenge to the political stability of the state. The preservation of Irish sovereignty was paramount, thus, in de Valera's eyes, the merciless suppression of the IRA was entirely justified. The government's actions, however, were not welcomed by a small cohort within Fianna Fáil, many of whom held a sneaking respect for the IRA.

The division between the constitutionalists and militants within Fianna Fáil surfaced following de Valera's decision in January 1940 to enact further legislation against the IRA under 'The Emergency Powers Act'.[180] The Act enabled the government to introduce internment without trial.[181] During the war years over 500 IRA suspects were interned, while a further 600 were committed under 'the Offences Against the State Act'.[182] Eamonn Donnelly again led the protests against the Fianna Fáil government for its action against the IRA. Addressing a gathering at the Mansion House in Dublin, in early 1940, he spoke in defence of two convicted IRA men, Peter Barnes and James McCormack, who were sentenced to death for their suspected part in the Coventry bombing of 1939.[183]

It was the execution during the course of the war of six IRA men and the death of a further three while on hunger-strike that resulted in many Fianna Fáil members questioning their loyalty to the organisation.[184] In particular, the impending death of hunger striker Patrick McGrath in late 1939, a veteran of the 1916 Easter Rising, witnessed an 'outpouring of emotion within republican circles and a *crise de conscience*' within the Fianna Fáil government.[185] Gerald Boland later confessed that by September 1940 the government was faced with a possible division over its handling of the IRA. He recalled that the old revolutionary comrades within the cabinet were faced by 'a terrible moment of truth when actions and words had to bear some firm, ruthless, policy...'.[186]

Many within Fianna Fáil, remembering their own recent past, were profoundly uneasy about action taken against the IRA. Seán Lemass, who was allegedly close to breaking with the government on the issue, was reminded by his mother that the IRA men were doing precisely what he had done and others had done a quarter of a century earlier.[187] During the war, founding member of Fianna Fáil and Lord Mayor of Dublin (1939–1941) Kathleen Clarke, resigned from the party because of the government's war-time policy against the IRA.[188] Indeed, Fianna Fáil Senator Margaret Pearse, a member of the Fianna Fáil national executive anti-partition sub-committee founded in 1938, wrote to de Valera in November 1939, to protest at the '... tragedy ... if Paddy [McGrath] dies now'.[189]

If not openly supportive of the IRA, many Fianna Fáil members were sympathetic of their cause. United Kingdom representative to Ireland from 1939 to 1949, Sir John Maffey [later Lord Rugby], writing shortly after the conclusion of the war, eloquently described the serious problem posed for the Fianna Fáil government because of public sympathy for the IRA:

> politics are swayed by emotions and emotions swayed by hysteria ... you have crowds are marchings [*sic*] and bands and Requiem masses which summons Irish men and women to active sympathy for one more Irish patriot, one who has died because the Union Jack still flies in Ulster. All this inferentially condemns the de Valera government for its apparent acceptance of this final wrong to Ireland.[190]

Under de Valera, Fianna Fáil was never able to fully divorce the organisation away from an aggressively militant stance towards partition. Although in the minority, a cohort of Fianna Fáil backbench TDs, county councillors and grass-roots members allowed themselves to be 'swayed' by emotion and believed that the use of violence, in the right circumstances, was a legitimate policy.

THE JUNE 1940 'OFFER': DE VALERA, FIANNA FÁIL ANTI-PARTITIONISTS AND NORTHERN NATIONALISTS

During late June and early July 1940 de Valera held secret negotiations with the British government concerning Ireland's possible entry into the war in return for substantial movement on partition. Significantly these negotiations represented the most serious move by the British government since the enactment of partition, twenty years before, to offer Irish unity in return for Ireland ending its policy of neutrality. In fact, the negotiations of June 1940 was the last occasion, until the outbreak of the Troubles in Northern Ireland in the late 1960s, that the British government were to seriously contemplate granting Irish unity.[191]

In late June 1940, minister for health, Malcolm MacDonald, visited Dublin to hold top-secret discussions with de Valera. During this tense month, when the threat of a German invasion of the British Isles was a very real possibility, London desperately sought to convince Ireland to enter the war and in particular secure control of Ireland's ports. Secretly, the British considered securing control of the ports by force if necessary and viewed MacDonald's visit to Dublin as a last throw of the dice to acquire Ireland's support for the war effort.[192] It was a period when there was a real sense of fear and panic of invasion in official circles in Dublin. The leaders of Fine Gael urged de Valera to abandon neutrality in return for British action on partition.[193] Media speculation did little to help the sense of paranoia. The *Kerryman* proclaimed that the British might possibly invade Ireland. The paper noted that London could easily 'manufacture a "German plot" as they did in 1918; they could provoke an "incident" or imagine a "grievance" ... to justify seizing our territory'.[194]

The talks between MacDonald and de Valera focused on Ireland's possible entry into the war on the side of the United Kingdom and her Allies in return for two central points. Firstly, MacDonald explained that a declaration would be issued by the British accepting the 'principle of a united Ireland'. Secondly, for the immediate establishment of a joint body, which would include representatives from Dublin and Belfast to 'work out the constitutional and other practical details of the union of Ireland ...'[195] Both Aiken and Lemass, who were present during parts of the negotiations with MacDonald, were recorded to have, like de Valera, given little serious consideration to the British offer; Aiken was reported to have drowned out any attempts by Lemass to contribute to the discussions.[196] Indeed, it was subsequently reported in British circles that Aiken 'believed in a German victory and probably hoped for it'.[197]

On 4 July 1940, after considerable deliberation with his cabinet, de Valera ultimately rejected the British 'purely tentative' offer, as he noted privately to Chamberlain, on the premise that the Ulster Unionists held an effective veto on a united Ireland, which Dublin believed was irrespective of the British government's genuine willingness to see partition ended.[198] Instead de Valera put a counter offer on the table; an offer he must have realised London would reject out-of-hand. He proposed that the British agree to the 'immediate establishment of a single sovereign all-Ireland parliament', which would be 'free to decide all matters of national policy, internal and external'. This new all-Ireland parliament, de Valera explained, would thus have the mandate to declare the whole of Ireland as neutral. 'On the basis of unity and neutrality', he noted, 'we could mobilise the whole of the manpower of this country for the national defence'. Such a policy, he said, 'would provide the surest guarantees against any part of our territory being used as a base for operations against Britain'.[199] Not surprisingly, the British refused to give the counter proposal even a moment's consideration.

Irrespective of the cabinet's ultimate rejection of the British proposal, for the anti-partitionists within Fianna Fáil, London's willingness to offer Irish unity stirred up the expectation that an end to partition was imminent. The Fianna Fáil National Executive was again the vehicle which party members forced de Valera to reconsider the government's war-time Northern Ireland policy. On 8 July 1940, forty party members convened for a 'special meeting' of the National Executive to deliberate partition.[200] In attendance were known anti-partitionists, Donnelly, Pearse, Breslin, Joseph Boyle, Frank Sherwin and party Senators, Christopher Michael Byrne,[201] and the Donegal Fianna Fáil stalwart, Neal Blaney (father of Neil Blaney).

From the outset of the meeting heated arguments occurred between de Valera and his supporters and the Donnelly anti-partitionist brigade. On several occasions de Valera tried to 'explain the line of policy' that the government were following in relation to partition, as the minutes of the meeting politely phrased it. The anti-partitionists, however, were in no mood to compromise. Sherwin put forward a proposal demanding that periodical meetings of the National Executive be convened on a regular basis, so that grass-roots supporters could be kept up-to-date with the government's war-time approach to partition.[202] It was an initiative, however, that de Valera was unwilling to entertain. Since the outbreak of the war he had been reluctant to debate the partition issue with senior Fianna Fáil members, never mind the party's grass-roots.

De Valera's reluctance to maintain a debate on partition within the organisation was made glaringly apparent following his decision to cancel the Fianna Fáil Ard Fheis, scheduled for late 1940. On 16 September 1940, at a meeting of the Fianna Fáil National Executive, de Valera notified those in attendance that he believed the time was not appropriate to hold the party's annual conference.[203] This was a classical de Valera manoeuvre to neutralise the opposition from within Fianna Fáil towards his war-time Northern Ireland policy. He did not want to allow the anti-partitionists within the organisation a platform to voice their views on partition – particularly given that some delegates had advocated the use of force to end partition at the previous conference in 1939. In fact, Fianna Fáil did not again hold an annual conference until 1943, when de Valera felt sufficiently reassured of Ireland's security. But even then, de Valera advised delegates at the

1943 Ard Fheis against a prolonged debate on the issue of partition.[204]

De Valera's cancelling of the party's 1940 Ard Fheis signalled his determination to retain control of the Fianna Fáil government's Northern Ireland policy. Donnelly, in particular, was incensed by de Valera's decision. In protest he resigned from the Fianna Fáil National Executive soon after. Addressing a Mansion House anti-partitionist rally in November 1940 he bemoaned that the Fianna Fáil government were ignoring partition and demanded that the British government immediately 'hand over at once' Tyrone, Fermanagh, East Down, South Down and Derry City.[205] Disillusioned, Donnelly cut all ties with Fianna Fáil and instead decided to run for Sinn Féin in a Northern Ireland by-election in 1942, where he was successfully elected abstentionist MP for Falls Division.[206]

Donnelly's departure, one can assume, was privately welcomed by de Valera. The records reveal that upon Donnelly leaving the Fianna Fáil National Executive, the partition question dramatically ceased to be an issue under debate at meetings of the Executive. Tellingly, unlike the previous several years, from February 1941 to March 1945, the subject of Northern Ireland was not deliberated at meetings of the National Executive, or indeed at meetings of either the parliamentary party or cabinet.[207] The available records show that the subject of Northern Ireland was, likewise, ignored at grass-roots level.[208]

De Valera's attitude towards Northern Nationalists during the war further emphasised his unwillingness to let Northern Ireland policy fall outside his control. Cahir Healy had agreed to organise a series of anti-partition rallies in Northern Ireland during 1938 to coincide with de Valera's anti-partition campaign in mainland Britain and in the South of Ireland.[209] When war broke out in 1939, however, Northern Nationalists and de Valera parted ways; de Valera's attention instead turned towards preserving Irish neutrality in the twenty-six counties. As Enda Staunton remarked by this period 'Northern Nationalists were nobody's children'.[210]

In a meeting between de Valera and a delegation of Northern Nationalists, led by Cahir Healy, during the early months of the war, de Valera made his attitude clearly known. The retention of Irish independence in the twenty-six counties, de Valera said, was of such value that 'the loss of it could not be risked in any effort to reintegrate the country'. The Northern delegation, who had declared that de Valera claimed a moral right 'to speak for all Ireland', were left dumbfounded. On being asked about a possible German invasion of Northern Ireland, de Valera was unambiguous. His government's policy would be simply to protect twenty-six county territory. Northern Nationalists, de Valera concluded, could 'decide for themselves what attitude to take up'.[211]

Although attempts were made by Northern Nationalists to establish closer relations with Dublin during the war years, de Valera was reluctant to permit them a voice in Fianna Fáil's Northern Ireland policy. In truth, as one Fianna Fáil grass-root member noted in October 1939, the Dublin government had 'forgotten' about Northern Catholics and that 'as far as we are concerned they might as well be living in the South Sea Islands'.[212] Privately, Nationalist MP for Foyle-Derry, Patrick Maxwell and Healy,[213] expressed their sense of abandonment by the Fianna Fáil government. Writing in June 1940, Maxwell noted that 'it was now more obvious than ever' that Northern Catholics were 'left to their own devices. And it was now time something was done by ourselves'.[214] Healy, writing in the *Irish Press* in September 1944, was more forceful. He recalled that like 1925, when the 'first party washed its hands' of Northern Nationalists, Fianna Fáil was now doing the same.[215]

While Northern Nationalists' and Eamonn Donnelly's outspoken comments on partition continued uncensored during the war, their criticism became increasingly marginalised.[216] Donnelly's public pronouncements that the Fianna Fáil leadership had told him 'in polite language to go to hell',[217] were suffocated by de Valera's determination not to allow his Northern Ireland policy to be hijacked by a select grouping of renegade party supporters. During the 1943 and subsequent 1944 general elections, which saw Fianna Fáil return to government on both occasions, partition was not a major issue of either campaign.[218] De Valera's priority was neutrality. He was determined, irrespective of complaints from party members that he had neglected partition during the war,[219] to maintain discipline and focus all government resources on the stability of the state. It would be incorrect, however, to say that de Valera completely neglected the partition issue during the final years of the war. Privately, he routinely raised the subject with Sir Maffey whenever the opportunity arose.[220]

* * *

In conclusion, when the war ended in Europe in May 1945 the Fianna Fáil government faced the sobering reality that partition was copper-fastened. Although during the late 1930s and early 1940s the British government had considered granting Irish unity, by the conclusion of the war, circumstances had changed drastically. London's wartime indebtedness to Belfast, together with the strategic importance of Northern Ireland, gave to the Ulster Unionists a security which they had not known since partition had been first enacted. As Sir Maffey expressed to London in 1943, 'in her post-war relationships England would not forget while she was fighting for her life Dublin harboured Axis legations and interned British airmen'.[221]

Therefore, unable to offer any instant end to partition, by 1945 de Valera returned to his pre-war strategy towards Northern Ireland, a Fianna Fáil sponsored anti-partition drive. If he could offer no immediate solution to partition (as had been the case in the aftermath of the Anglo-Irish Agreement of 1938) de Valera was determined to retain the impression that Fianna Fáil was the custodian of the aspiration for Irish unity. As is discussed in the following chapter, this was de Valera's cue to undertake his much anticipated worldwide anti-partition propaganda campaign.

NOTES

1. University College Dublin Archives (UCDA) Fianna Fáil Party Papers P176/384, meeting of National Executive publicity sub-committee, 19 Sept. 1938. Memorandum produced on behalf of the committee by de Blacam.
2. See comments by de Valera. Dáil Éireann debate (DE), 27 April 1938. Vol. 71, cols. 36–37.
3. *Irish Press*, 23 Nov. 1938.
4. Clare O'Halloran, *Partition and the Limits of Irish Nationalism* (New Jersey: Humanities Press International, Inc., 1987), 181.
5. See UCDA Eamon de Valera Papers P150/2349, record of conversation between de Valera and MacDonald, 14 Jan. 1937. See also UCDA P150/2349, record of conversation between de Valera and MacDonald, 15 Sept. 1937.
6. UCDA P150/2349, see comments by MacDonald, 17 Sept. 1937.
7. UCDA P150/2349, record of conversation between de Valera and MacDonald, 17 Sept. 1937.
8. See, for example, UCDA P150/2179, Dulanty to de Valera, 26 Jan. 1938 and UCDA P150/2183, Joseph Walshe to de Valera, 25 Jan. 1938.
9. UCDA P150/2489, de Valera to Walshe, 21 Jan. 1938.
10. See, for example, UCDA P150/2349, record of conversation between de Valera and MacDonald, 17 Sept. 1937 and UCDA P150/2183, Walshe to de Valera, 3 Jan. 1938.
11. See comments by Craigavon. *Irish Independent*, 16 Jan. 1937.
12. John Bowman, *De Valera and the Ulster Question, 1917–1973* (Oxford: Oxford University Press, 1982), 181. See also Terry de Valera, *A Memoir, Terry de Valera* (Dublin: Currach Press, 2005), 203.
13. UCDA Desmond Ryan Papers LA10/D/203, 'De Valera and Chamberlain agree to differ'. April/May 1938.
14. The Earl of Longford and Thomas P. O'Neill, *Eamon de Valera* (London: Hutchinson,

1970), 324.

15. Longford and O'Neill, *Eamon de Valera*, 325.

16. See Dáil Éireann debates on the Anglo-Irish Treaty, 27–29 April 1938. DE, 27–29 April. Vol. 71. See also *Irish Press* during June 1938.

17. UCDA P150/2511, handwritten notes by de Valera, 23 April 1938.

18. See comments by de Valera. DE, 29 April 1938. Vol. 71, cols. 429–430.

19. UCDA P150/2836, de Valera to Roosevelt, 22 April 1938.

20. UCDA P150/2487, memorandum from Maurice Moynihan to de Valera, 'Conference with British Minister, January 1938', Jan. 1938.

21. University of Birmingham Special Collections (UBSC) Neville Chamberlain Papers (NCP) 18/1/1051–70, Neville Chamberlain to Ida Chamberlain, 1 May 1938.

22. UCDA P176/384, meeting of National Executive publicity sub-committee, 28 March 1938.

23. UCDA P176/384, meeting of National Executive publicity sub-committee, 28 March 1938.

24. Longford and O'Neill, *Eamon de Valera*, 463.

25. This was the opinion of a secret Central Intelligence Agency (CIA) report dated 1 April 1949. See Seán Cronin, *Washington's Irish Policy 1916–1986* (Dublin: Anvil Books, 1987), 254–255.

26. Maurice Manning, *James Dillon, a Biography* (Dublin: Wolfhound Press, 1999), 160–161.

27. Gerald Boland's unpublished memoirs, marked, 6 (x) and 7(x).

28. Gerald Boland's unpublished memoirs, marked, 2 (b) and 12 (a).

29. National Archives of the United Kingdom (NAUK) Foreign and Commonwealth Office (FCO) 33/1599, this was the opinion of British Ambassador to Ireland (1970–73), John Peck, May 1971.

30. Ronan Fanning, *Dictionary of Irish Biography*, Frank Aiken (Dublin: Cambridge University Press, 2010), 54.

31. See Máire Cruise O'Brien, *The Same Age as the State* (Dublin: O'Brien Press, 2003), 217.

32. UCDA P176/346, meeting of National Executive, 28 March 1939. As members were undecided Aiken again 'verbally' discussed the proposal at the subsequent National Executive meeting the following month. UCDA P176/346, meeting of National Executive, 11 April. 1939.

33. UCDA P150/1998, meeting of National Executive publicity sub-committee, 24 April 1938.

34. UCDA P176/384, meeting of National Executive publicity sub-committee, 19 Sept. 1938. Memorandum produced on behalf of the committee by de Blacam.

35. Speech by de Valera, Fianna Fáil North-West Comhairle Ceanntair, Gresham Hotel, Dublin. *Irish Press*, 24 April 1939.

36. See comments by de Valera. *Irish Press*, 24 April 1939.

37. UCDA P176/444, meeting of parliamentary party, 12 March 1936.

38. UCDA P150/2349, record of conversation between de Valera and MacDonald, 17 Sept. 1937.

39. At a cabinet meeting on 7 Jan. 1938, a discussion on partition occurred and it was agreed by ministers that 'any agreement which does not include the restoration of the Six-Counties will not be regarded as disposing completely of the matters at issue between Ireland and Britain'. Moynihan referred to a cabinet meeting 'of Friday last, the 7th', at which ministers decided on the above point. See UCDA P150/2487, memorandum from Maurice Moynihan to de Valera, 'Conference with British Minister, January 1938', Jan. 1938.

40. Bowman, *De Valera*, 170.

41. While the minutes of the parliamentary meeting do not record that a disagreement occurred among deputies over partition, given the known division within the party on the issue, it seems certain that a heated debate occurred. UCDA P176/444, meeting of Fianna Fáil parliamentary party, 28 April 1938. See also UCDA P176/444, meeting of Fianna Fáil parliamentary party, 25 April 1938.

42. This was the opinion of Seán MacEntee. See UCDA Seán MacEntee Papers P67/155, (drafted) MacEntee to de Valera, 17 Feb. 1938.

43. UBSC NCP 18/1/1051–70, Neville Chamberlain to Ida Chamberlain, 13 March 1938.

44. See comments by Corry. DE, 29 April 1938. Vol. 71, cols. 315–318.
45. UCDA P67/155, (draft) MacEntee to de Valera, 17 Feb. 1938.
46. Terry De Valera, *A Memoir*, 205.
47. UCDA P67/155, (draft) MacEntee to de Valera, 17 Feb. 1938.
48. UCDA P67/155, (draft) MacEntee to de Valera, 17 Feb. 1938.
49. UCDA P67/155, (draft) MacEntee to de Valera, 17 Feb. 1938.
50. UCDA P67/155, (draft) MacEntee to de Valera, 17 Feb. 1938.
51. Longford and O'Neill, *Eamon de Valera*, 317.
52. See comments by Linehan. DE, 29 April 1938. Vol. 71, cols. 340–341.
53. *Tipperary Star*, 30 April 1938.
54. This was the opinion of Kilkenny councillor Mr O'Hanrahan (forename unknown). See *Kilkenny Journal*, 7 May 1938. See also *Limerick Echo* 30 April 1938, report of Limerick Corporation meeting, held 28 April 1938.
55. *Kilkenny Journal*, 7 May 1938.
56. *Irish Press*, 27 April 1938.
57. *Tipperary Star*, 30 April 1938.
58. *Anglo-Celt*, 30 April 1938.
59. *Irish Press*, 22 Sept. 1938.
60. *Irish Press*, 13 Dec. 1939.
61. See NAUK Home Office (HO) 144/22162, Home Office memorandum: 'Cahir Healy', Oct. 1941.
62. See coverage of the signing of the Agreement, *Irish Press*, 28–30 April 1938; *Kerryman*, 30 April 1938; and *Limerick Echo,* 30 April 1938.
63. UCDA P67/155, (draft) MacEntee to de Valera, 17 Feb. 1938.
64. Longford and O'Neill, *Eamon de Valera*, 321.
65. UCDA P150/2499, record of meeting between de Valera and a 'delegation of six county House of Commons and Senate' Northern Nationalists, 25 Feb. 1938.
66. UCDA P150/2499, record of meeting between de Valera and a 'delegation of Six County House of Commons and Senate' Northern Nationalists, 25 Feb. 1938.
67. See comments by Derrig. *Irish Independent*, 26 March 1929.
68. O'Halloran, *Partition and the Limits of Irish Nationalism*, 88.
69. Michael Laffan, *The Partition of Ireland, 1911–1925* (Dundalk: Dundalgan Press, 1983), 98.
70. Eamon Phoenix, *Northern Nationalism, Nationalist Politics, Partition and the Catholic Minority of Northern Ireland, 1890–1940* (Ulster Historical Foundation, 1994), 380.
71. Phoenix, *Northern Nationalism*, 380.
72. O'Halloran, *Partition and the Limits of Irish Nationalism*, 88.
73. Phoenix, *Northern Nationalism*, 386.
74. *Anglo-Celt*, 30 April 1938.
75. For an analysis of de Valera's relationship with Northern Nationalists during the 1920s and 1930s, see Enda Staunton, *The Nationalists of Northern Ireland, 1918–1973* (Dublin: Columba Press, 2001), 74–142.
76. Staunton, *The Nationalists of Northern Ireland*, 137.
77. Henry Patterson, *Ireland Since 1939, the Persistence of Conflict* (Dublin: Penguin Ireland, 2006), 30.
78. UCDA P176/345, meeting of National Executive, 10 Oct. 1938.
79. UCDA P176/345, meeting of National Executive, 10 Oct. 1938.
80. UCDA P176/40, record of National Executive anti-partition sub-committee meetings, Oct. 1938 – Sept. 1939.
81. UCDA P176/345, meeting of National Executive, 10 Oct. 1938. Liam Pedlar was also appointed to the committee, as was Seán Bonner in May 1939. See UCDA P176/346, meeting of National Executive, 19 May 1939.
82. Ronan Fanning, '"The Rule of Order": Eamon de Valera and the IRA, 1923–1940', in J. P O'Carroll and John A. Murphy (eds.), *De Valera and his Times* (Cork: Cork University Press, 1986), 169.
83. O'Halloran, *Partition*, 52. For an example of de Blacam's anti-partitionist views see Aodh

de Blacam, 'Some thoughts on partition', *Studies, An Irish Quarterly Review* (Vol. XXIII, 1934), 559–576.

84. PRONI D2991/B/66/1, Wash to Cahir Healy, 22 Feb. 1938.
85. See, for example, UCDA P176/345, meetings of National Executive, 21 Dec. 1936 and 8 Nov. 1937.
86. Bowman, *De Valera*, 185.
87. See Chapter One, p.57.
88. See speech by Donnelly. DE, 11 May 1937. Vol. 67, cols. 105–118.
89. *Irish Press*, 22 Sept. 1938. In July 1938 Donnelly was arrested at his home in Ballinacraig, Newry, under the Northern Ireland Exclusion Order, for defying an order excluding him from Northern Ireland. *Newry Journal*, 2 Jan. 1945.
90. See UCDA P150/1998, Seámus O'Daímím to de Valera, 11 May 1938.
91. UCDA P176/40, meeting of 18th anti-partition sub-committee, 13 March 1939 and UCDA P176/346, meetings of National Executive, 3 April and 1 May 1939.
92. UCDA P176/346, meeting of National Executive, 28 Aug. 1939.
93. UCDA P176/346, meeting of National Executive, 13 Feb. 1939. Two years previously, in May 1937, Donnelly had similarly demanded that 'a special Governmental Department be set up for the purpose of uniting and co-ordinating all the anti-partition forces in Ireland, North and South irrespective of political or religious outlook ...'; his request was ignored. Speech by Eamonn Donnelly. DE, 11 May 1937. Vol. 67, cols. 114–115.
94. *Irish Press*, 22 Sept. 1938.
95. UCDA P176/40, meeting of 27th anti-partition sub-committee, 17 July1939.
96. UCDA P176/40, meeting of 28th anti-partition sub-committee, 31 July 1939.
97. See comments by Donnelly. *Irish Press*, 22 Sept. 1938.
98. UCDA P176/38, de Valera to members of the anti-partition sub-committee, 11 Oct. 1938. See also UCDA P150/1998, undated and unsigned letter; yet most probably de Valera's instructions.
99. For a copy of the rules and regulations of the League see UCDA P176/38.
100. UCDA 176/345, meeting of National Executive, 14 Nov. 1938. See also UCDA P176/40, meeting of 3rd and 5th anti-partition sub-committee, 31 Oct. and 14 Nov. 1938.
101. Longford and O'Neill, *Eamon de Valera*, 340.
102. UCDA P176/40, meeting of 1st anti-partition sub-committee, 10 Oct. 1938.
103. See UCDA P176/39.
104. UCDA P176/40, meeting of 3rd, 4th & 9th anti-partition sub-committee, 31 Oct., 4 Nov. and 19 Dec. 1938.
105. *Irish Press*, 20 March 1939. Vivion de Valera was elected to Dáil Éireann as a Fianna Fáil TD for Dublin North-West at a by-election in Dec. 1945. He remained a Fianna Fáil TD for various Dublin constituencies until 1982.
106. UCDA P176/40, meeting of 3rd, 4th & 9th anti-partition sub-committee, 31 Oct., 4 Nov. and 19 Dec. 1938.
107. See PRONI D2991/B/144/4, Healy to secretary of Cavan Executive of Fianna Fáil, Bernard Fay, 28 Oct. 1938.
108. Staunton, *The Nationalists of Northern Ireland*, 140.
109. *Irish Press*, 22 June 1939.
110. *Irish Press*, 24 Aug. 1939.
111. *Irish Press*, 23 Oct. 1939.
112. *Irish Press*, 7 July 1939.
113. UCDA P176/40, meeting of 16th, 17th and 18th anti-partition sub-committee, 27 Feb., 6 March and 13 March 1938.
114. UCDA P176/40, meeting of 23rd anti-partition sub-committee, 15 May 1939.
115. During de Valera's remaining years as leader, until his retirement from active politics in 1959 and subsequently under the leaderships of Seán Lemass (1959–1966) and Jack Lynch (1966–1979), respectively, a federal solution constituted a central feature of Fianna Fáil's Northern Ireland policy until the introduction of Direct Rule to Northern Ireland by Westminster in Feb. 1972. See de Valera's Presidential speech, 1954 Fianna Fáil Ard Fheis, *Irish Press*, 13 Oct. 1954; see Lemass's speech, *One Nation*, to the Oxford Union,

15 Oct. 1959, *The Irish Times*, 16 Oct. 1959; and lastly, See Lynch's 'Tralee speech', 20 Sept. 1969, *The Irish Times*, 21 Sept. 1969.

116. *Evening Standard*, 17 Oct. 1938.

117. See Eamon de Valera, *The alternative to 'the Treaty': Document No. 2* (Dublin, 1923). A copy is available from UCDA P176/944.

118. David Harkness, 'The North and de Valera', in *The "De Val-Era" in Ireland, 1916–1975*, (ed.) Sidney Poger (Boston: Northeastern University Press 1984), 77.

119. John Horgan, *Seán Lemass, the Enigmatic Patriot* (Dublin: Gill and Macmillan, 1999), 79.

120. Tom Gallagher, 'Fianna Fáil and Partition 1926–84', *Éire – Ireland*, Vol. 20, No.1 (1985), 39.

121. UBSC NCP 18/1/1091, Neville Chamberlain to Ida Chamberlain, 26 March 1939.

122. See PRONI Ellison Spence Papers D2481/1/3/41, Walter Duff, Duffmont, Milwaukee, Oregon, USA, to John Graham, 22 Oct. 1938.

123. At the second meeting of the sub-committee in late Oct. 1938, Donnelly requested that the government should seek to encourage Irish voters, permitted to vote in the British general election, to 'vote in favour of those candidates ... that offer their support to the ending of partition'. The motion was 'referred to President-de Valera'. It was never again to be discussed by the committee members. UCDA P176/40, meeting of 2nd anti-partition sub-committee, 24 Oct. 1938.

124. UCDA P176/40, meeting of 13th anti-partition sub-committee, 30 Jan. 1939.

125. See UCDA P176/40, meeting of 14th, 15th and 23rd anti-partition sub-committee, 6 Feb., 20 Feb. and 15 May 1939.

126. At a meeting of the Fianna Fáil National Executive in July 1939 members requested that a 'monster meeting' be held to coincide with de Valera's scheduled trip to America. See UCDA P176/346, meeting of National Executive, 31 July 1939.

127. See comments by honorary secretary of Fianna Fáil Dublin South-city Comhairle Ceanntair, Gearoid O'Murchadha. UCDA P176/346, meeting of National Executive, 3 July 1939.

128. UCDA P176/40, meeting of 28th anti-partition sub-committee, 31 July 1939.

129. PRONI D2991/B/144/33, Healy to Rev. T. Maguire, (date omitted, late 1930s).

130. Seanad Éireann debate (SE), 26 Jan. 1939. Vol. 22, cols. 807–811.

131. SE, 7 Feb. 1939. Vol. 22, cols. 920–921. See also speech by O'Donovan. *Irish Press*, 22 Sept. 1938.

132. UCDA P176/346, meeting of National Executive, 15 May 1939.

133. See comments by de Valera. SE, 7 Feb. 1939. Vol. 22, col. 988.

134. SE, 26 Jan. 1939. Vol. 22, col. 865.

135. SE, 7 Feb. 1939. Vol. 22, cols. 988–989.

136. UCDA, P176/346, meeting of National Executive, 13 Feb. 1939.

137. UCDA, P176/346, meeting of National Executive, 13 Feb. 1939.

138. UCDA P176/749, record of Fianna Fáil Ard Fheis, 23 & 24 Nov. 1938.

139. *Irish Press*, 23 Nov. 1938.

140. At a subsequent meeting of the National Executive Fianna Fáil Senators William Quirke and P. Ó'Máille forwarded a motion calling for Fianna Fáil members to participate at anti-partition meetings in Northern Ireland and that all speakers should be prepared for arrest and imprisonment in Northern Ireland. UCDA P176/346, meeting of National Executive, 11 Sept. 1939.

141. UCDA P150/2548, de Valera to Chamberlin, 12 April 1939.

142. UCDA P150/2571, meeting between Walshe and A. Eden, 10 Sept. 1939. Walshe expressed de Valera's views to Eden.

143. Memorandum from Joseph P. Walshe of the instructions received from Eamon de Valera for transmission to John W. Dulanty, 26 April 1939. In Catriona Crowe, Ronan Fanning, Michael Kennedy, Dermot Keogh and Eunan O'Halpin, *Documents on Irish Foreign Policy 1937–1939* (Vol. IV) (Dublin: Royal Irish Academy, 2006), 445–446.

144. UCDA P150/2548, de Valera to Chamberlain, 12 April 1939.

145. UCDA P150/2553, de Valera to MacDonald, 13 April 1939.

146. Memorandum by John Leydon on co-operation with Northern Ireland, 2 Dec. 1938.

In Crowe, Fanning, Kennedy, Keogh and O'Halpin, *Documents on Irish Foreign Policy 1937–1939* (Vol. IV), 369–370.

147. Longford and O'Neill, *Eamon de Valera*, 342.
148. See speech by MacDermott. SE, 26 Jan. 1939. Vol. 22, col. 809.
149. Dermot Keogh, *Twentieth Century Ireland, Nation and State* (Dublin: Gill and Macmillan, 1994), 109.
150. UCDA P176/444, record of meeting of parliamentary party, 3 Sept. 1939.
151. UCDA P176/40, meeting of 30th anti-partition sub-committee, 11 Sept. 1939.
152. UCDA P176/40, meeting of 29th anti-partition sub-committee, 28 Aug. 1939.
153. UCDA P176/40, meeting of 19th anti-partition sub-committee, 3 April 1939.
154. See Robert Fisk, *In Time of War* (London, 1983), 110–469; Brian Girvin, *The Emergency: Neutral Ireland 1939–45* (London: Gill and Macmillan, 2006), 320–321; Bowman, *De Valera*, 208–266; and lastly, Patterson, *Ireland Since 1939*, 50–75.
155. See T. R. Dwyer, 'Eamon de Valera and the Partition Question', in O'Carroll and Murphy (eds.), *De Valera and his Times*, 85–86; and Richard Dunphy, *The Making of Fianna Fáil Power in Ireland* (Oxford: Oxford University Press,1995), 280–284.
156. See O'Halloran, *Partition*, 182.
157. Bowman, *De Valera*, 215.
158. See comments by Donnelly. *Belfast Newsletter*, 13 Dec. 1940.
159. See comments by Donnelly. *Irish Press*. Oct. 1940.
160. NAUK FCO 33/1599, confidential profile of Joseph Brennan, British Embassy, Dublin, May 1971.
161. See comments by Brennan. *Irish Press*, 13 Dec. 1939.
162. J. Kelly P.C, Wolfe-Tone cumann, North-Dublin city, questioned de Valera as to why force was not a legitimate policy. *Irish Press*, 13 Dec. 1939.
163. *Irish Press*, 14 Dec. 1939.
164. *Irish Press*, 13 Dec. 1939.
165. Honorary secretary of Fianna Fáil East Galway Comhairle Dáilcheantair, P. Purcell and secretary of the party's Monaghan cumann, E. O'h-Annlain, inquired what steps were being taken to carry out a resolution adopted by the previous Ard Fheis regarding the use of Radio Éireann for propaganda in respect to partition. A letter was read from honorary secretary of Fianna Fáil County Dublin Comhairle Dáilcheantair, J. J. Clare relating the opinion of party members in relation to anti-partition activities. UCDA P176/345, meeting of National Executive, 1 April 1940.
166. See Childers's letter to the editor 'Towards unity'. *Irish Press*, 18 April 1940.
167. See Childers's letter to the editor 'Towards unity'. *Irish Press*, 18 April 1940.
168. See Donnelly's letter to the editor. *Irish Press*, 13 April 1940.
169. The proposal was seconded by Joseph Boyle. UCDA P176/345, meeting of National Executive, 6 May 1940. Members of the National Executive for 1940 were Boland, O'Kelly, Seamus O'Rian, Rutledge, Senator William Quirke, Breslin, Pedlar, Little, Traynor, Pearse, de Blacam, and Donnelly.
170. UCDA P176/345, meeting of National Executive, 10 June 1940.
171. See UCDA P150/2571, record of meeting between UK and Éire ministers, dated 1 May 1940.
172. UCDA P150/2571, record of meeting between UK and Éire ministers, dated 1 May 1940. See also Bowman, *De Valera*, 214–215.
173. See UCDA P150/2458, Chamberlain to de Valera, 12 June 1940.
174. For a detailed account of the IRA association with the Nazis and the relationship between the Dublin and the Berlin governments during the Second World War see Eunan O'Halpin, *M15 and Ireland, 1939–1945* (Dublin, *Irish Academic Press*, 2003), 30–102 and O'Halpin, 'British Intelligence, the Republican Movement and the IRA's German Links, 1935–45', in Fearghal McGarry (ed.), *Republicanism in Modern Ireland* (Dublin: UCD Press, 2003), 108–131. See also Patterson, *Ireland Since 1939*, 52–56.
175. UCDA P150/2591, record of speech by de Valera at a Fianna Fáil by-election convention, Galway-West, 13 May 1940.
176. See speech by de Valera. *Irish Press*, 17 April 1939.

177. UCDA P150/2584, record of speech by de Valera at a Fianna Fáil county convention, Co. Cavan, 18 Feb. 1940.
178. See comments by de Valera. *Kerryman*, 29 June 1940.
179. See comments by Aiken. *Irish Press*, 6 May 1940.
180. For an account of the Fianna Fáil government's relationship with the IRA during World War II see Caoimhe Nic Dháibhéid, 'Throttling the IRA: Fianna Fáil and the subversive threat, 1939–1945', in *From Parnell to Paisley, Constitutional and Revolutionary Politics in Modern Ireland*, (eds.) Caoimhe Nic Dháibhéid and Colin Reid (Dublin: Irish Academic Press, 2010), 116–138.
181. Fanning, *The Rule of Order: Eamon de Valera and the IRA, 1923–1940*, 170.
182. Patterson, *Ireland Since 1939*, 54. See also John Maguire, *IRA Internments and the Irish Government: Subversives and the State, 1939–1962* (Dublin: Irish Academic Press, 2008).
183. *Newry Reporter*, 2 Jan. 1945.
184. George Plant was executed in March 1942 for the killing of an alleged IRA informer. He had fought on the anti-treaty side during the civil war. Five other IRA men were executed during the war and another three were allowed to die on hunger strike. Paddy McGrath and Thomas Harte died in Mountjoy Sept. 1940; Richard Goss died in Port Laoise in Aug. 1941; and Charlie Kerins died in Mountjoy in Feb. 1944.
185. Nic Dháibhéid, *Throttling the IRA: Fianna Fáil and the Subversive Threat, 1939–1945*, 118.
186. See 'Gerald Boland's story', *Irish Press*, 9 Oct. 1968.
187. Patterson, *Ireland Since 1939*, 54–55.
188. Horgan, *Lemass*, 108.
189. National Archives of Ireland (NAI) Department of the Taoiseach (DT) S 11515, Margaret Pearse to de Valera, 15 Nov. 1939.
190. See NAUK DO 35/2094, memorandum recording meeting between de Valera and Sir Maffey, 18 May 1946.
191. On one further occasion, on the night of the Pearl Harbour attack, at 2.00am on 8 Dec. 1941, British prime minister, Winston Churchill purportedly offered a far less tangible proposal for a united Ireland. Via telegram he informed de Valera that Ireland had a chance to become a 'Nation Once Again'. But this message was sent when Churchill was intoxicated by alcohol and was thus judiciously ignored by de Valera. See Diarmaid Ferriter, *Judging Dev, a Reassessment of the Life and legacy of Eamon de Valera* (Dublin: Royal Irish Academy, 2007), 154. See also UCDA P150/2632, de Valera's 'recollections' of Churchill's 'offer', 10 Dec. 1941.
192. Privately, Neville Chamberlain conceded that if the Irish government did not agree to allow the British gain control of the Irish ports 'we shall have to seize the Irish ports back by force'. See UBSC NCP 18/1/1164, Neville Chamberlain to Ida Chamberlain, 7 July 1940.
193. Patterson, *Ireland Since 1939*, 57.
194. *Kerryman*, 13 July 1940.
195. UCDA P150/2548, record of MacDonald's meeting with de Valera, 26 June 1940.
196. Bowman, *De Valera*, 230.
197. NAUK Prime Minister's Office (PREM) 8/824, character profile of Frank Aiken, 1947.
198. UCDA P150/2548, see de Valera's comments to Chamberlain, 4 July 1940. See also UCDA P150/2548, Chamberlain to de Valera, 29 June 1940. See also Paul Bew (ed.), *The memoir of David Gray: A Yankee in De Valera's Ireland* (Dublin: Royal Irish Academy, 2012), xviii-xxii & xxviii-xxix.
199. UCDA P150/2548, de Valera to Chamberlain, 4 July 1940.
200. UCDA P176/345, meeting of National Executive, 8 July 1940.
201. At a previous National Executive meeting Byrne had requested that a 'special meeting' of the National Executive be held to discuss partition. The motion was seconded by T. Breslin. UCDA P176/345, meeting of National Executive, 24 June 1940.
202. UCDA P176/345, meeting of National Executive, 8 July 1940.
203. UCDA P176/345, meeting of National Executive, 16 Sept. 1940.

204. De Valera having been reported as stating: 'no I do not want to speak about it anymore'. He reassured delegates that he was doing everything 'humanly possible' to end partition. *Irish Press*, 29 Sept. 1943.

205. See comments by Donnelly. *Irish Press*, 20 Nov. 1940.

206. *Newry Reporter*, 2 Jan. 1945.

207. See also UCDA P176/346–346, record of National Executive meetings, 1941–1945. See also UCDA P176/446, record of the parliamentary meetings, 1941–1945. See also NAI Government Cabinet Minutes, TAOIS/G3/9, record of cabinet meetings, 1941–1945.

208. See UCDA P176/51–71, record of Fianna Fáil constituency files, 1937–1954.

209. Patterson, *Ireland Since 1939*, 30.

210. Staunton, *The Nationalists of Northern Ireland*, 143.

211. The Archives of the Archdiocese of Armagh (ARCH), The Cardinal Joseph MacRory Papers, ARCH/11/3, 1. Report of meeting between de Valera and delegation of Northern Ireland Nationalists, undated, between Sept. 1939 and May 1940. I wish to thank Mr Clive Abbott for providing me with the above information.

212. This view was expressed by an unidentified Fianna Fáil member at a meeting of the Anti-Partition Council of Tipperary. See *Irish Press*, 23 Oct. 1939.

213. Healy spent time in Brixton prison during the war from July 1941 to Dec. 1942 under the terms of the Defence Regulation Act 18B. See Cahir Healy, *Times* obituary, *Times* 10 Feb. 1970.

214. Staunton, *The Nationalists of Northern Ireland, 1918–1973*, 144.

215. *Irish Press*, 29 Sept. 1944.

216. Speaking at the Fianna Fáil Ard Fheis in Oct. 1944, Donnelly again complained that the Irish government had neglected partition and the Northern nationalist community. *Irish Press*, 11 Oct. 1944.

217. *Irish News*, 29 April 1944.

218. The *Irish Press* contained minimal reference to partition during the 1943 and 1944 election campaigns. See *Irish Press* April/May 1943, and May 1944. See also UCDA P150/2101, general election pamphlet 1944, which made no reference to partition.

219. This was the opinion of a Fianna Fáil grass-roots member from Dublin, J. Brennan. *Irish Press*, 29 Sept. 1943.

220. See NAUK DO 35/2069, meeting between de Valera and Sir Maffey, 23 Feb. 1943; NAUK DO 35/2081, meeting between de Valera and Sir Maffey, (date unknown) Nov. 1944; NAUK DO 35/2086, meeting between de Valera and Sir Maffey, 21 March 1945; and lastly, NAUK DO 35/2088, meeting between de Valera and Sir Maffey, 6 July 1945. See also comments by de Valera. *Irish Press*, 28 Jan. 1942.

221. See NAUK DO 35/2069, memorandum from the secretary of state for Dominion Affairs to the War Cabinet, 27 Feb. 1943. See also comments by de Valera. *Irish Press*, 28 Jan. 1942.

3

1945–1951

'A traveller through anxious times.'

[Rugby to de Valera, 18 Feb. 1948] [1]

AN IDEA REBORN: THE GENESIS OF DE VALERA'S WORLDWIDE
ANTI-PARTITION CAMPAIGN, 1945–1946

At the conclusion of the Second World War the issue of partition represented a conundrum for de Valera. Given that the British would not budge on partition and having previously admitted that he had no immediate solution to secure Irish unity,[2] de Valera instead returned to his pre-war policy of asserting that a Fianna Fáil government represented the best chance, when the 'circumstances arose', of ending partition.[3] A reportedly 'thin and worn out' leader,[4] de Valera publicly accorded that partition might not be ended 'for a considerable period'.[5] He instead maintained that the only viable strategy towards Northern Ireland, in the medium-term, was to recommence the anti-partition propaganda campaign which had been prematurely cancelled because of the outbreak of war in 1939. He believed the commencement of a campaign would help 'inform public opinion' and make 'it clear' to the people of America and Britain that partition was unjust.[6]

De Valera's decision to reignite an anti-partition propaganda campaign was also because he wanted to counteract any possible criticism from within Fianna Fáil. During the war, as discussed in the previous chapter, de Valera had successfully controlled the anti-partitionist-wing within the party, led by Eamonn Donnelly. When the war ended in Europe, de Valera was again confronted by a selection of party supporters, who demanded that immediate steps be taken to end partition. In early May 1945, at a meeting of the Fianna Fáil parliamentary party, Fianna Fáil TD for Cork-West, Ted O'Sullivan asked that the 'party be informed of what steps the government are taking and what policy it is intended to adopt to secure the return of the Six-Counties to the Nation'.[7]

At a meeting of the party's National Executive the previous March members had expressed frustration at the lack of progress on partition. Fianna Fáil TD for Dublin North-West and a member of the anti-partitionist wing of the party, John O'Connor, had requested that the National Executive appoint an anti-partition sub-committee to keep 'the question of the partition of our country constantly before the public'.[8] Grass-roots members equally reported their sense of despondency over de Valera's Northern Ireland policy. In November 1945, a disgruntled Fianna Fáil supporter demanded that the British army leave Northern Ireland immediately.[9] Indeed, some rank-and-file members lamented that the Fianna Fáil government 'was not sufficiently mobilised' to tackle partition.[10] In the run up to the 1945 Ard Fheis partition resolutions poured in from Fianna Fáil cumainn throughout the country, which pleaded with the government to take firmer action to deliver a united Ireland.[11]

As was the case following the signing of the Anglo-Irish Agreement in 1938, the reawakening of the partition debate, at party level, was de Valera's cue to initiate his anti-partition propaganda campaign. Significantly, at both the 1945 and 1946 Fianna Fáil Ard Fheiseanna de Valera orchestrated a preconceived scheme to ensure that a worldwide anti-partition campaign was selected as the central plank of the party's official post-war Northern Ireland policy. Confronted by mounting criticism from the party's grass-roots de Valera sought to appease the anti-partitionists within the party. On behalf of the party's National Executive he included a partition resolution on the Clár at the 1945 Ard Fheis. It read:

> This Ard Fheis believes that the time has come to launch a worldwide propaganda campaign to expose the inconsistency, futility and injustice of the partition of Ireland, and to demonstrate that a united and free Ireland would necessarily be an ardent supporter of any scheme for the promotion of a world peace and progress.[12]

Tellingly, the following year at the 1946 Ard Fheis, the first partition resolution was almost identical to that tabled, at the behest of the party's National Executive, at the previous party conference in 1945.

This was not a coincidence.[13] Issued on behalf of the Carrigaline Comhairle Dáilcheantair, South-East Cork cumann, it declared 'this Ard Fheis believes the time is right for a worldwide publicity drive to expose the injustice and futility of partition'.[14] De Valera manipulated the working procedures of the Ard Fheiseanna in 1945 and 1946 and intentionally ensured that the number one partition resolution at both party conferences called for the commencement of a worldwide anti-partition campaign. This was a pre-emptive strike by the party leadership to ensure that an anti-partition propaganda campaign was to form the nucleus of Fianna Fáil's official Northern Ireland policy in the post-war era.

Kevin Boland, a Fianna Fáil cabinet minister from 1957 to 1970, recalled that such 'manipulating' of the Ard Fheis procedures was a common occurrence. It was not unusual for the party hierarchy to insert 'bogus' resolutions. Party delegates, he said, were happy to adhere to this procedure, as they 'did not want details ... did not want discussion', but merely wanted 'to endorse the "leader" and go home'.[15] 'Rigged or not', Boland wrote, 'this was the Fianna Fáil Ard Fheis. It was the appropriate body to change the policy of the party. It was the only body which had the authority to decide fundamental policy'.[16] This blatant disregard for the working procedure of the Ard Fheis, which is officially the supreme governing authority of Fianna Fáil, highlighted de Valera's determination that policy matters would remain under his authoritarian control. In practice, despite some lip-service to the proposition, the partition resolutions put forward at the annual conference were no more than 'guides to party opinion'.[17] In reality, decisions on Northern Ireland policy remained solely with de Valera and him alone.

A minority, but vocal, cohort of Fianna Fáil members ridiculed de Valera's decision to reignite his anti-partition campaign as outdated and unproductive. At the party's 1946 Ard Fheis disgruntled delegates expressed a feeling of 'dissatisfaction ... at the slow progress of the organisation in securing the freedom and independence of Ireland'.[18] A delegate from Gweedore, Co. Donegal noted that his fellow cumann members had a 'hate' for partition.[19] During the first day of the conference several cumann representatives asserted that they had not merely attended as 'yes men' or to approve 'blindly' the party's Northern Ireland policy.[20]

In late October 1946, in an attempt to demonstrate to party members that the Fianna Fáil hierarchy was continually reviewing its strategy towards Northern Ireland, de Valera ordered that the

National Executive establish a new sub-committee on partition. In reality, the formation of the committee bore all the hallmarks of the optics of illusion over substance. Motivated by short-term consideration its establishment was a cunning move by de Valera to create the impression that the Fianna Fáil leadership was responding to grass-roots pressure to formulate a strategy on Northern Ireland. The opposite, however, was the truth. In fact, the committee was a defunct legislator devoid of any real influence.

As de Valera had previously done in 1938, faced with mounting criticism from party members, he established a sub-committee on partition to demonstrate that the party hierarchy was listening to grass-roots qualms on the partition issue. At a meeting of the party's National Executive, on 26 October 1946, de Valera announced to those present that a new partition sub-committee was to be formed.[21] This was only the second occasion since early 1941[22] that Northern Ireland policy was discussed at the National Executive.[23] Not since September 1939, over seven years previously, had a sub-committee on partition gathered.

The new sub-committee convened on 25 November 1946. De Valera chaired the meeting; also in attendance were Fianna Fáil TDs Oscar Traynor and Patrick John Little, Senator Margaret Pearse and Aodh de Blacam, William McMahon and Liam Pedlar.[24] As the meeting got underway it was obvious that de Valera was determined to retain a firm grip over the committee's *modus operandi*. He began by reading a 'report' outlining how he envisaged the committee would operate.[25] Thereafter, the sub-committee convened on only five other occasions between November 1946 and May 1947.[26] Besides a decision to send a speaker on behalf of the National Executive to an anti-partition rally in Liverpool, the committee devised no new policy initiatives towards Northern Ireland.[27]

The formation of the partition sub-committee was a tactical ploy by de Valera to create the impression that the Fianna Fáil hierarchy were listening to party supporters concerns on the lack of progress on partition. In fact, the committee had no authority to decide the party's partition strategy; this always remained the sole responsibility of de Valera. This episode highlighted the degree of control that de Valera held over his party colleagues and emphasised his obsession with maintaining absolute control over Northern Ireland policy. One could not but agree with the observation of C.S. (Todd) Andrews who succinctly noted that for all practical purposes 'Dev *was* the executive because his rulings were never questioned'.[28]

For one member of the newly established partition committee, de Blacam, the refusal of de Valera to share Northern Ireland policy was the deciding factor for his resignation from Fianna Fáil. Like Eamonn Donnelly's resignation from Fianna Fáil in 1944, de Blacam cited the party's inability to tackle partition as an insult to nationalist Ireland. In December 1947, the Newry native defected from Fianna Fáil to Clann na Poblachta because of a disagreement with members of the Fianna Fáil National Executive over rural depopulation and his disillusionment towards the party's Northern Ireland strategy.[29] Speaking to the *Irish Press* in January 1948 he bemoaned that de Valera and his ex-Fianna Fáil colleagues 'had no plan to end partition'.[30]

ONE STEP FORWARD, TWO STEPS BACKWARDS: FIANNA FÁIL AND NORTHERN NATIONALISTS, 1945–1948

The conclusion of the war brought Fianna Fáil's relationship with Northern Nationalists back on the political agenda. By the mid-1940s Northern Nationalist politicians, directed by Nationalist MP for South-Fermanagh, Cahir Healy viewed Dublin's Northern Ireland policy with scepticism. De Valera, customarily revered in Northern Nationalist circles, was now seen as inactive on partition; Northern Nationalists increasingly felt that Southern politicians, irrespective of what they might say in public, cared little for the plight of their Northern neighbours. The deciding factor for Northern Nationalists to finally break free from the Fianna Fáil government's grip and pursue their own strategy towards Northern Ireland came in the aftermath of the 1944 Fianna Fáil Ard Fheis, held in October. During the first day of the conference Eamonn Donnelly, then an abstentionist MP for the Falls Division, Belfast, demanded that the Fianna Fáil government establish a committee on partition, which would be represented by all mainstream nationalist opinion throughout Ireland. Donnelly explained that

> he came with a message that there was now a more united front among Six-County Nationalist representatives and that they were getting together to hammer out proposals for presentation at the 'psychological moment'. They would ask representatives of the principal Southern parties to help on that committee.[31]

In mid-November 1944, a month after the Ard Fheis, Nationalist MP for Foyle Derry, Patrick Maxwell, wrote to congratulate de Valera for passing a resolution to establish 'a National Council' that would consist of an all-Ireland selection of nationalist opinion.[32] De Valera, however, had no intention of forming such a committee and within days of receiving Maxwell's letter, replied that Fianna Fáil would not agree to Northern Nationalists sitting on a partition committee under the auspices of the Irish government.[33]

De Valera's latest unwillingness to offer Northern Nationalists a share of the anti-partition stage, effectively compelled Maxwell and his Northern associates to embark on their own anti-partition strategy, independent of the Fianna Fáil government. In November 1945, upwards of 480 'nationally minded' Northern Nationalist delegates attended a convention in St Patrick's Hall, Dungannon Co. Tyrone, to inaugurate a new organisation, 'The Irish Anti-Partition League'.[34] Those present included elected representatives of each of the Six-Counties of Northern Ireland, local councillors and Nationalist members of the Northern Ireland government and the British House of Commons.

The event was presided over by the prominent barrister and Nationalist MP for Mourne Co. Down, James McSparran. McSparran was elected chairman and Nationalist MP for South-Armagh, with Malachy Conlon, as full-time secretary of the new organisation. Encouraged because of the election success of the Labour Party in Britain the movement was founded in an attempt at the 'construction of a broad, grassroots movement capable of providing a focus of political unity for the Catholic minority'.[35]

This establishment of the League was to mark a new departure for partition and was importantly not as a result of de Valera or his Fianna Fáil colleagues; it was after all, partly due to Eamonn Donnelly's interventionist tactics.[36] Thus, the re-emergence of the anti-partition drive by Northern Nationalists was initiated without the consent or guidance of the Fianna Fáil government. Whereas before Northern Nationalists had blindly pledged their alliance to de Valera as Ireland's 'national leader' – believing that Fianna Fáil were the true custodians of Irish republicanism – this was no longer the situation.

Enda Staunton argued that de Valera's attitude to the new League was 'one of welcome'. He remarked that upon hearing of the League's formation de Valera pronounced that it was 'one of the best things he had ever heard'.[37] Such observations, however, fail to distinguish between de Valera's *support* for a new coherent anti-partition movement in Northern Ireland and his *willingness* to permit

Northern Nationalists an effective platform to influence Fianna Fáil's Northern Ireland policy.

The formation of the League fitted nicely into de Valera's attempts to reignite his anti-partition campaign throughout Great Britain and Northern Ireland. Fianna Fáil members would be permitted to speak at anti-partition rallies organised on behalf of the new League, prior to receiving official clearance from party headquarters. However, the Northern Ireland anti-partition movement was to be treated as an independent organisation and not affiliated to the Fianna Fáil government. The new organisation could be effectively used by de Valera to fulfil his policy of drumming up support in Northern Ireland for his anti-partition campaign. This in no way implied that he was to permit Northern Nationalists an opportunity to devise Northern Ireland policy: that was to remain firmly within his own grasp.

De Valera's reluctance to offer Northern Nationalists an effective voice on Fianna Fáil's Northern Ireland policy rested not merely on his dislike of sharing the anti-partition stage – although this was the central driving force – but also on his belief that Northern Nationalists should not become involved in Southern politics. In particular, de Valera was adamant that Northern Nationalist MPs would not be permitted a right of access to Dáil Éireann. Since Fianna Fáil's entry into government in 1932, de Valera maintained that Northern Nationalist politicians had no functional role to play in Southern politics. In 1933, for example, de Valera informed Cahir Healy and Joe Devlin that their requests that Northern Nationalist MPs have right of access to Dáil Eireann were impractical.[38]

Within Fianna Fáil, during the 1930s, Eamonn Donnelly had led the calls for Northern Nationalist elected representatives to take seats in the Dáil, but de Valera had quelled such requests.[39] Throughout the remainder of the 1940s and during the 1950s the issue was routinely brought up by Northern Nationalists. De Valera, however, categorically ruled out the prospect that Northern Nationalists might gain access to the Dáil on every occasion that it arose.[40] For de Valera such a move would amount to representation without taxation for the Northern electorate and there would be the possibility that Northern Nationalist MPs would take sides between Dáil parties which would not be in the national interest. Indeed, Northern Nationalists, de Valera said 'would have none of the responsibility, although they would have the opportunity of voting on either side of the house'.[41]

In the run up to the 1948 general election Clann na Poblachta returned to the idea of permitting Northern Ireland Nationalists to take a full and active role in Southern politics. Founded two years previously in 1946, Clann na Poblachta viewed itself as the moral voice of Irish republicanism that embodied both a social consciousness and a nationalistic pedigree.[42] Subsequently described by the British Embassy in Dublin as 'a semi lunatic fringe of Irish republicanism'[43] the party's emergence ensured that the 'green card' had slipped from Fianna Fáil's grasp. Led by former chief of staff of the IRA, Seán MacBride, the son of the 1916 executed Irish rebel, John MacBride, the party, as expressed by Seán Lemass, offered a considerable electoral challenge to Fianna Fáil.[44]

The most significant reference to Northern Ireland during the 1948 election campaign was Clann na Poblachta's pledge that if elected the party would demand that Northern Nationalist MPs be allowed entry to the Dublin parliament.[45] Writing to Cahir Healy, MacBride described the proposal as the 'most constructive ever put forward', believing it could help unite the anti-partition movement in Northern Ireland.[46] Noel Hartnett, a barrister who had once held a seat on the Fianna Fáil National Executive, but had been sacked by the Fianna Fáil government some years earlier, was one of the more vocal Clann na Poblachta spokesmen on partition. As editor of the party's paper *Clann* and director of elections for the organisation, he stated that it was irrational that 'the opening of the Dáil to the elected parliamentarian representatives of the people of the Six-Counties' had still not occurred.[47]

Fianna Fáil immediately rejected the proposal. The party's National Executive issued a statement declaring that partition could not be solved by such 'mock remedies'.[48] As mentioned above, de Valera was adamant that the participation of Northern Nationalist elected representatives in Southern politics was impractical. Seán MacEntee insisted that the proposals were 'absurd'. He noted that if Northern Nationalist MPs had full voting rights it could mean that the, 'government should undertake extending its authority over all Ireland, even if by arms'.[49] MacBride reminded his political opponents that he was not calling for such measures, but instead foresaw the 'nomination of Northern MPs to the Seanad and their being granted a mere right of audience in the Dáil'.[50]

Aodh de Blacam, a recent defector from Fianna Fáil to Clann na Poblachta, ridiculed de Valera's reluctance to consider the proposal. Speaking at a Clann na Poblachta meeting in Drogheda, Co. Louth in mid-January 1948, de Blacam accused Fianna Fáil of 'a terrible desertion from the principles of 1932'. 'Fianna Fáil ministers', he said, 'say they have no plan to end Partition'. He continued:

They are now trying to curb our plan. Our plan is to do what the first Dáil did, to invite representatives of all Ireland into the Legislature and when they come, we will say to the world, are you going to permit a foreign power to occupy the territory from which these men come?[51]

The defection of de Blacam demonstrated to de Valera the genuine threat posed by Clann na Poblachta in undermining Fianna Fáil's approach to Northern Ireland. Thus, in early December 1947, de Valera ordered that the National Executive issue a letter to every registered Fianna Fáil cumann, reaffirming the party's Northern Ireland policy. The letter sharply attacked Clann na Poblachta. It reminded Fianna Fáil members that partition would need 'something more than clever words to solve it'. Describing Clann na Poblachta's approach to partition as 'silly', the letter pronounced that the organisation which had been 'patient ... the movement which without bloodshed, got back the Ports, would get back the Six-Counties'.[52]

During the closing stages of the election campaign, in mid-January 1948, a loyal Fianna Fáil grass-roots supporter from Dublin's North Strand, Gilbert Hughes, wrote to the *Irish Press* to defend his party's stance on Northern Ireland. Describing himself as 'one of the rank-and-file doing the spade-work from twenty years in Fianna Fáil', he attacked, as 'childish', Clann na Poblachta's plan to end partition. In particular, he refuted de Blacam's assertions that Fianna Fáil had 'repudiated the Republic'. Fianna Fáil, Hughes said, succeeded in securing 'a Republic in the Twenty-Six Counties in spite of slander' and was the best party placed to secure the unity of Ireland.[53] Captain Henry Harrison also issued a leaflet, *Ireland's danger and national leadership*, in defence of de Valera's record on partition. 'What is the case against de Valera?', he wrote, 'In what can he be alleged to have failed Ireland?' 'Partition was not of his making ... and his leadership still offers the best hope of curing it'. Harrison concluded, 'it should be left to de Valera to complete the struggle of the centuries'.[54]

Despite attempts by the Fianna Fáil leadership and rank-and-file to discredit Clann na Poblachta's policy initiatives on Northern Ireland, the fact remained that under de Valera's leadership his party was content to ignore the plight of Northern Nationalists. The Fianna Fáil government's unwillingness to permit Northern Nationalists a right of access to Dáil Éireann exposed the party's deep rooted prejudice towards their Northern neighbours. Northern Nationalists, the Fianna Fáil leadership believed, should get on with their own business in Northern Ireland and leave it to Southern politicians to find a solution to partition.

Polling day for the general election was 4 February 1948. The results proved a calamity for Fianna Fáil. When the Dáil assembled on 18 February de Valera found himself voted out of office by a combination of Fine Gael, Clann na Poblachta, Clann na Talmhan, Labour, National Labour and eleven of the twelve independents. Although no coalition strategy was agreed before polling day, in the aftermath of the election and desperate to see Fianna Fáil out of power, they all came together to form the First-Inter Party government. For the first occasion in sixteen years Fianna Fáil was in opposition.

DEV'S TOUR, STAGE 1: FROM NEW YORK
TO NEW DELHI, MARCH – JUNE 1948

Fianna Fáil's general election defeat came as a shock to de Valera. Senior Fianna Fáil politician Gerald Boland recalled that Fianna Fáil ministers, including de Valera, had 'all loved power' and were bitterly disappointed to be relegated to opposition.[55] Although disorientated, de Valera felt some relief at not having the constraints of government on his shoulders. Privately, Lord Rugby [formerly Sir John Maffey] noted that because de Valera no longer held power, 'he had not the responsibility'.[56] Free from the day-to-day commitments of government duties, de Valera decided to finally undertake his much anticipated anti-partition worldwide campaign. In March 1948 he commenced the first stage of his anti-partition tour. He left his deputy leader and vice-chairman of the party, Seán Lemass, to lead Fianna Fáil during his absence from Ireland.[57]

Over the subsequent four months, accompanied by his loyal lieutenant and member of the Fianna Fáil front-bench, Frank Aiken, de Valera travelled almost 50,000 miles, visiting America, Australia, New Zealand and India. The first stop was the country of his birth America. He arrived in New York on 4 March 1948. It was almost twenty years since de Valera last visited America. The Irish delegation was greeted with an enthusiastic welcome from Irish-Americans. Frank Gallagher, director of the Government Information Bureau from 1939 to 1948, recalled that a parade through New York's main thoroughfares in honour of de Valera was the biggest seen since the end of the Second World War.[58]

De Valera travelled 10,000 miles over three weeks, visiting Boston, Chicago, Detroit, Los Angeles, Oklahoma, San Francisco and

Philadelphia. Gallagher recalled that half a million people marched in Boston to welcome de Valera[59] (according to the *Boston Sunday Press* the more realistic number of those present to welcome de Valera to Boston was 250,000).[60] In San Francisco Gallagher reminisced that 1,000 horsemen were present at the welcoming precession to greet de Valera and Aiken upon their arrival.[61] Writing to his wife Maud, who remained in Ireland, Aiken enthusiastically captured the welcome that the Irish delegation received. Their visit to America, he exclaimed, was the 'like of which was never before seen'.[62]

De Valera's campaign in America highlighted that anti-partition propaganda had now become more important than ever before for Fianna Fáil. The tour was the ideal opportunity to propagate the anti-partitionist orthodoxy that laid claim to Northern Ireland as the sundered Six-Counties. De Valera's speeches in America had four dominant themes: that the partition of Ireland was illegal; that the British government should make a declaration in support of Irish unity; the need for a federal solution to end partition; and attacking the Ulster Unionist government of Northern Ireland.

That Ireland was illegally divided constituted the majority of de Valera's anti-partition speeches while in America. In every city, town and village he visited he spoke of the 'crime' of a divided Ireland and against the 'illegality' of partition.[63] He routinely declared that Northern Ireland was 'not a historic entity'[64] and instead exclaimed that partition had divided 'the ancient nation of Ireland'.[65] De Valera repeatedly pronounced that no one in Ireland, including the unionist population, had voted for what they termed the 'Partition Act'.[66]

De Valera's demand that the British government make a declaration in support of Irish unity was based on the assumption that because London had imposed partition it had a moral responsibility to find an ultimate solution to the 'Irish question'.[67] In America he demanded that Britain face its 'moral obligations' and help end partition.[68] Speaking in San Francisco he was unequivocal: Ireland had been 'mutilated' by the British government creating a situation where partition was the 'outstanding cause of quarrel' between Britain and Ireland.[69] Addressing the members of the Massachusetts Senate and House of Representatives he explained that it was the British who 'occupied part of our country' and demanded that the British leave Northern Ireland.[70] De Valera's demands that Britain make a declaration in support of Irish unity were unrealistic in the post-war climate. As a consequence of Irish neutrality, together with

Northern Ireland's war-time efforts and the strategic position of the region in any future war, London maintained that Irish unity was an unattainable short-term objective.

A third ingredient of de Valera's speeches during his visit to America was his proposal for a federal solution to help end partition. Speaking in Tulsa, Oklahoma and later in San Francisco, he explained that a federal agreement could be a 'measure towards the unity of Ireland',[71] as it offered the 'best hope' of ending partition.[72] Over the previous two decades de Valera had proposed granting local autonomy to the Northern Ireland parliament provided that Ulster Unionists were willing to enter an all-Ireland parliament in Dublin. Not for the first or last time, Ulster Unionists unequivocally rejected de Valera's latest federal offer. In a leaflet, *Ulster's right to reply*, published in October 1948, Northern Ireland prime minister, Sir Basil Brooke, firmly reiterated that Northern Protestants would 'never consent' to Dublin's proposal of a federal agreement.[73]

A final component of de Valera's anti-partition speeches while in America was his attack of Ulster Unionism. He accused the Ulster Unionist Party of political myopia. He maintained that the concept of democracy had been 'flouted'[74] and demanded that a plebiscite be held in Northern Ireland to highlight that the Catholic minority wished for a united Ireland.[75] His attack on Ulster Unionists was endemic during his campaign and merely helped to propagate the notion that unionism and Irishness were incompatible – that there could only be one or the other.

Such actions revealed the naivety of de Valera's approach to partition: he ridiculed those whom he admitted he required to achieve Irish unity. Seán O'Faoláin, writing several years earlier in 1941, recorded that this form of nationalist anti-partitionist thinking had only consolidated rather than help end partition. 'The problem', he wrote, 'was not primarily the problem of partition', instead he argued that '... it calls not so much for the destruction of the political Border so much as for a mental Barrier'.[76] De Valera was himself a victim of this mindset, in which he was unable to acknowledge Ulster Unionists' psychological detest for the prospect of a united Ireland. Indeed, veteran nationalist John J. Horgan compared de Valera's campaign against Ulster Unionism to the picking of a sore on one's face – 'the more you pick at the wound the more septic it becomes'.[77] Although Horgan's assessment was unsympathetic, there was no doubting that de Valera's campaign merely helped to entrench the political and psychological divide between Dublin and Belfast.

Speaking in 1947, de Valera had acknowledged that the support of Ulster Unionists was required if partition was to be undone.[78] In the post-war climate he hoped that he could 'persuade' the Northern Ireland majority to enter a united Ireland.[79] He failed, however, to realise that the two sides of Fianna Fáil's Northern Ireland policy contradicted one another. On the one hand, de Valera sought to build a relationship of goodwill which he hoped could persuade 300,000 Ulster Unionists to agree to a united Ireland. On the other, the Fianna Fáil sponsored worldwide anti-partition campaign sought to expose the 'evils of partition' and reveal the extent to which Ulster Unionists discriminated against the Catholics of Northern Ireland.

This mindset personified de Valera's entire approach to partition and illustrated why Ulster Unionists perceived de Valera as belonging to what John H. Herz epitomised as 'the exclusivist, xenophobic, expansionist, oppressive' school of nationalists.[80] De Valera was viewed as the 'bogeyman' of Ulster Unionism and was openly despised by many Northern Ireland Protestants. He failed to understand the scale of the problem facing him: the depth of antipathy that Ulster Unionists felt towards his republican ideal. In Ulster Unionist circles he was ridiculed as the main obstacle to better relations between Belfast and Dublin. In his 1948 leaflet, *Partition, why not?*, Rev. J.G. MacManaway embodied Ulster Unionists' revulsion of de Valera. Not only had de Valera's 'anti-British attitude and actions alienated the Ulster people', but, according to MacManaway, de Valera's policy of neutrality and insistence on the use of the Gaelic language in schools and government, made it impossible for cordial relations between Southern nationalists and Northern unionists.[81]

De Valera failed to acknowledge that Northern Ireland's integration into the British welfare state, within three years of the end of the Second World War, had further strengthened Ulster Unionists' case against entering a united Ireland. Compared to citizens in the South of Ireland, people of Northern Ireland were enjoying a comprehensive health service and increased sickness and pension benefits.[82] Moreover, the weak Irish economy was further evidence to Ulster Unionists for rejecting any calls from Dublin for Irish unity. The economic protectionism policy of Fianna Fáil governments since the 1930s appealed little to Ulster Unionism. Northern Ireland's industrialised economy, which witnessed a boom during the war years and which depended heavily on an export markets, could not be sustained in a protectionist all-Ireland market.

Politically, de Valera's American speeches were a failure. The Dominions Office in London, which kept a file on de Valera's trip to America, reported that 'Mr de Valera's United States tour had little effect in influencing general United States opinion on the Irish partition issue'.[83] The Commonwealth Office recorded on de Valera's American tour that 'Irish politics seemed to have ceased to be an issue of the moment to the mass of Americans'.[84] The British Consul General at Los Angeles reported that de Valera's visit to that city 'caused remarkably little excitement and received only slight publicity in the local Press'.[85] Indeed, the British Consul at Detroit noted that de Valera's speech at a lunch was 'more of an historical summary than an attempt to arouse any remaining anti-British sentiment'.[86] Lord Rugby personally expressed his contempt for de Valera's anti-partition tour. 'So far as he [de Valera] personally is concerned', Rugby wrote, 'his unbridled and unstatemanlike [*sic*] lowered his status here. A sign comment frequently heard is "the spell is broken."'[87]

The director of the US State Department's Office of European Affairs, Jack Hickerson, informed the newly appointed American minister to Ireland, George Garrett, that America's attitude towards Ireland in the light of recent world events was 'that any interference on our part in the issue [partition] would, of course, be construed as an affront to the United Kingdom'.[88] De Valera was aware that the American government had no interest for his anti-partition propaganda campaign, or indeed Dublin's calls for Irish unity. During a brief interview with American president, Harry S. Truman, de Valera refrained from mentioning partition.[89] Despite this, he failed to recognise that his anti-partition propaganda campaign bolstered the State Department's opinion that the question of Irish reunification was a concern for the Dublin and London governments and thus was 'not a problem in which the United States might properly concern itself'.[90]

From America, in late April 1948, de Valera commenced the next leg of his anti-partition journey, where over several weeks he visited Australia and New Zealand. On the invitation of Rev. Daniel Mannix, Archbishop of Melbourne and former president of St Patrick's College, Maynooth, de Valera and Aiken arrived in Sydney on 28 April. Mannix was a lifelong friend of de Valera and was only one of a few members of the Catholic Church hierarchy that had any sympathy for de Valera and his anti-treaty Republican forces during the last turbulent months of the civil war.[91] From Australia, on 24 May, de Valera travelled to New Zealand, where he had a two-hour meeting in Wellington with New Zealand prime-minister, Peter Fraser.[92]

During his stay in the Southern hemisphere de Valera's speeches were once more characteristically based on stressing the 'cruel injustice of partition'.[93] Speaking in Melbourne, Australia, to a gathering of approximately 20,000 people, he said partition was 'deeply resented by his people' and its continued existence was a 'grievous wound'.[94] In Auckland, New Zealand, Ireland's troubled relationship with Britain was a central theme of de Valera's speeches. The 'only outstanding question between Britain and Éire', he said, 'was that of partition'.[95] He confessed that until Irish unity was achieved it would be impossible to establish good relations between the Irish and British governments.[96]

De Valera's campaign in the Southern hemisphere was a flop. Although he reported to Dublin that he received 'an enthusiastic' reception, he did concede that there were not many Irish of first generation in either Australia or New Zealand.[97] While Aiken was eager to inform Dublin that 'the people here are delighted to see Dev for the first time', the reality was an altogether different story.[98] Indeed, despite Aiken's description of the Southern hemisphere tour as a 'magnificent' success, in truth, the anti-partition propaganda campaign was not well received by the vast majority of either Australians or New Zealanders.[99] Writing from Australia to the Commonwealth Office in London, E. J. Williams noted that 'despite Catholic Church interference Dev's tour of Australia does not appear to have been very successful'.[100] Williams explained that given the lack of enthusiasm for de Valera's visit he would 'doubt whether he [de Valera] regarded his visit as much of a success'.[101] Irish minister plenipotentiary to Australia, Thomas J. Kiernan, reported that the Australian people seemed little interested in de Valera's tour.[102]

The high commissioner for the United Kingdom in New Zealand, Patrick Duffy, recorded that de Valera's visit had caused Fraser 'some embarrassment'.[103] He said that during a meeting between de Valera, Aiken and the New Zealand cabinet, the latter felt that they were 'being lectured' by the Irish delegation.[104] The mayor of Wellington, was recorded to have 'flatly declined' to offer de Valera a civic reception on the latter's request.[105] Kathleen Barrett, an Irish descendent from Wellington wrote to Dublin that the subject of partition was 'anathema in this country'.[106] Indeed, one concerned New Zealander, writing from Samoa in 1950, informed the Irish government of the 'complete ignorance' of Irish history and cultural heritage by the people of New Zealand.[107]

The main issue of contention for many of the Australian and New Zealand population was Ireland's decision to remain neutral during the Second World War. According to reports from British officials in Australia, de Valera's visit 'provided evidence of little sympathy for Éire's attitude during the war ...'[108] On several occasions de Valera was forced to defend Ireland's policy of neutrality. He reminded his audiences that 'until Ireland had complete independence, it would be strange to ask her to join a crusade to gain independence for other countries'.[109] He asked 'why should Ireland enter a war in which she would not be able to defend herself?'[110] His arguments, however, were not sympathetically received by his hosts. This was not unexpected considering that over one million Australians and approximately 200,000 New Zealanders had fought under the flag of the Commonwealth during the Second World War.

From Australia, de Valera and Aiken arrived at the next destination of their anti-partition propaganda campaign, Calcutta, India, on 14 June 1948. Unlike the guarded reception which de Valera had received from the American, Australian and New Zealand governments, his arrival was warmly welcomed by the Indian government. Aiken reported that upon first arriving in Calcutta, 'we were met by a huge crowd who nearly tore Mr. de Valera to pieces'.[111] On their first night in Calcutta, de Valera and Aiken dined with the governor of Bengal, Chakravarthi Rajagopalachari. The following day the Irish delegation travelled to Delhi were they lunched with the governor general of India, Lord Louis Mountbatten; Aiken recalled that on their arrival Lord Mountbatten and his wife were in the process of 'packing up to leave and we had the interesting experience of being the last guests of the British regime'.[112]

This reception was followed later in the day with a meeting with Indian prime minister, Jawaharlal Nehru.[113] De Valera had a 'long chat' with Nehru and the Irish delegation enjoyed a meal at the prime minister's home.[114] Aiken recalled that Nehru and de Valera exchanged prison experiences.[115] Privately, Nehru expressed to de Valera his 'deep sympathy' for the partition of Ireland and remarked that he saw Ireland an ally to India in her quest for independence from Britain.[116] There were marked similarities between the partitioning of Ireland and India as both countries had been within the British Imperial system and in each case partition took place coincidentally in time with a transfer of power, although limited in the Irish case, to indigenous authorities.[117]

De Valera's visit to India was a welcome respite from the apathetic reception he had received from the American and Southern hemisphere authorities. In reality, however, de Valera's anti-partition campaign abroad exposed the short-term limitations of the use of propaganda. By the time he reached India he was confronted with the startling realisation that the international community cared little for Irish unity. A British official noted that de Valera's stay in India, given the lack of an Irish audience, 'would deprive Mr de Valera of any field for anti-partition propaganda'.[118] Although his anti-partition campaign received widespread coverage in the Irish newspapers thanks to the Fianna Fáil organ the *Irish Press*,[119] the fact was that propaganda offered only superficial success: de Valera's anti-partition propaganda campaign abroad did nothing to help accelerate Irish unity.

De Valera was, first and foremost, a politician and thus his anti-partition campaign abroad was predominately for home consumption in Ireland, and not necessarily intended to offer any immediate solution to partition. Rugby reported back to London that an unidentified minister of the Irish government speaking on de Valera's anti-partition tour said that in the pursuit to secure his reputation as the custodian of Irish unity 'the man will do all the damage he can'.[120]

Nevertheless, even if an anti-partition propaganda campaign was the best way to practise his trade while in opposition, de Valera's methods merely confirmed that he was unable to deal with the political reality: in the short to medium term Irish unity was unattainable. Ironically, it was possibly de Valera's greatest achievement – securing and maintaining Irish neutrality during the Second World War – which had altered the circumstances so drastically. He failed to grasp that due to Ireland's neutrality and the strategic importance of the island in the event of a future war, Britain and indeed America, would not permit a united Ireland. Simply put, Ireland's 'splendid isolation' meant her continued division. His time abroad showed his inability to foster a new approach to Northern Ireland. His placing of the blame for partition on the shoulders of the British government and his continued portrayal of Ireland as a wounded victim, showed him to be politically sterile on the issue of Irish unity. This approach was, after all, a reincarnation of his Northern Ireland policy of the early 1920s.

DEV'S TOUR STAGE 2: IRELAND & BRITAIN, OCTOBER 1948 – MARCH 1949

After a four-month absence, in late June 1948, de Valera and Aiken returned to Ireland to attend the 19th Fianna Fáil Ard Fheis at the Mansion House in Dublin. No Ard Fheis was held the previous year, as it had been postponed due to the general election. Over 1,000 delegates attended and resolutions on partition poured in from grass-roots condemning the continuing division of Ireland; a resolution issued on behalf of East Donegal Comhairle Dáilcheantair, announced that 'this Ard Fheis condemns the hypocrisy of the British government in continuing to maintain partition in Ireland by military force and subventions while condemning partition in other lands'.[121]

In Ireland, as he had done abroad, de Valera continued his habitual ceremony against partition. His Presidential address on the night of 23 June to the party faithful, which lasted over ninety minutes, denounced partition as 'rotten'.[122] On his return to Ireland, whether it was in the Dáil or attending a local rally, de Valera repeatedly reassured his supporters that 'the outstanding political problem at the present moment was the reunification of our country'[123] and that the 'the boundary must go'.[124]

In October 1948, accepting an invitation from the Anti-Partition of Ireland League of Great Britain, de Valera commenced the second stage of his anti-partition propaganda campaign. The monthly bulletin the *United Irishmen* announced that 'the general topic of conversation amongst the Irish population of Britain at the moment is Dev's Tour'.[125] From October 1948 to February 1949 de Valera travelled to Britain, where he visited a series of centres of the Irish Diaspora. He opened his campaign at a monster meeting in Liverpool, and over the subsequent weeks attended similar anti-partition rallies in Glasgow, Cardiff, Cambridge and Manchester. After a break for Christmas, in February 1949, he travelled to Birmingham, Newcastle, London and Sheffield.[126]

De Valera's speeches on partition throughout his time in Britain were as much about confirming as about converting opinions. The perception of Northern Ireland as a British garrison helped to reinforce de Valera's argument that Ireland was illegally divided. He spoke of the presence of a military force stationed in Northern Ireland holding down the Catholic minority. Routinely he explained that Britain held the border with 'a chain of customs posts and customs officials'.[127] He demanded: 'stop coercing Ulster'.[128] Addressing a gathering in Newcastle-upon-Tyne he called on his audience to remember that it was a 'fundamental crime to divide a nation'.[129] In Birmingham he claimed that Northern Ireland was controlled by '13,000 armed agents of the Orange Gestapo, under the guise of Special Constables ...'[130] At Glasgow University he forcefully declared that the 'Six-Counties is ours, not yours ... Britain which occupies the Six of our Counties is an aggressor ... get out, leave our territory'.[131] Arthur H. Johnson, a concerned Ulster Unionist sympathiser from Northampton, a large market town in the East Midlands of England, informed the Stormont government that 'this fellow de Valera is on the war path in Northampton'.[132]

De Valera was determined that his audiences would be aware that the propaganda drive against partition was being 'vigorously protected by Fianna Fáil'.[133] In vindication of the anti-partition propaganda campaign abroad, de Valera believed that he had increased the volume of informed opinion of the evils of partition 'where throughout the world people of our race are to be found'.[134] Always a believer in the power of international opinion – and willing to ignore any limitations in a policy of total propaganda[135] – de Valera stressed that the phrase 'partition must go' must henceforth be on every 'Irishman's lips, to be used on every appropriate occasion'.[136]

The main motivation for de Valera to maintain the anti-partition propaganda campaign in Britain was based on a wish to inform public opinion throughout the world of the injustice of partition. He also saw his speeches helping to head off the growth in popularity of Clann na Poblachta and to curb IRA republican extremism in Ireland. As a consummate reader of the nationalist mind, de Valera's speeches were intended to remind people in Ireland that Fianna Fáil were the true custodians of Irish republicanism. In this volatile climate for national drive to end partition, de Valera realised that a threat of the use of violence was a legitimate worry. For example, Peadar Cowan, Independent TD for Dublin North-East, who had resigned from Clann na Poblachta in July 1948, had argued in the Dáil that the Irish government should use force to end partition.[137]

De Valera failed to acknowledge – or simply choose not to recognise – that his anti-partition propaganda campaign and aggressive speeches had helped encourage violence. Catholic Archbishop of Dublin from 1940 to 1971, John Charles McQuaid remembered that de Valera's anti-partition propaganda campaign had provoked the younger generation in Ireland to sympathise with IRA violence. Privately he believed that de Valera's speeches were 'all humbug'.[138]

Speaking in Manchester, in late November 1948, de Valera was reported to have spoken in favour of the use of force to end partition. Although his remarks were censored by the *Irish Press*, the British Embassy in Dublin recorded that *The Irish Times* had printed de Valera's speech in its entirety.[139] According to *The Irish Times*, de Valera said that the use of force to end partition, using the American civil war as an example, was sometimes the 'only available means'.[140]

Seán MacEntee later recalled that harsh anti-partition speeches, such as those made by de Valera, merely drove some young people into taking their own 'unauthorised and unguided action'. MacEntee said he always urged de Valera to 'stay away from the North. It is the only way'.[141]

The Belfast government, which kept a file on de Valera's 'anti-partition activities in Great Britain', sought to counteract any possible publicity that de Valera would secure during his anti-partition campaign.[142] The Stormont authorities had received reports from the Ulster Office in London that de Valera was making 'embarrassing speeches' during his tour of Britain.[143] Under the authority of Northern Ireland minister for finance, John Maynard Sinclair, it was decided that the Ulster Unionist Party and not the Northern Ireland government would initiate a 'counter-publicity' policy against de Valera's anti-partition campaign. Sinclair noted that a 'government department cannot appropriately engage in controversy with individual party leaders, or other private persons – thus we must work through the Ulster Unionist Party'.[144] Sinclair specified that 'Ulster's war effort' and the 'fact that the vast majority of our own people desire to remain in the UK', should constitute the central message of Ulster Unionists' counter-publicity campaign.

Arrangements were also made for the holding of counter-publicity meetings and demonstrations by Ulster Unionists in 'the various places visited by Mr. de Valera'.[145] It was also proposed that the Ulster Unionists should link up with the numerous Ulster Associations in the major cities of London, Liverpool, Glasgow, Manchester and Birmingham. The use of the British Broadcasting Corporation (BBC), the production of 'special pamphlets', an advertising campaign and a series of lectures were also mooted as strategies to counteract de Valera's campaign in Britain.[146]

If de Valera's trip to America had not been a success in propaganda terms, his campaign in Britain was doubly difficult. Hugh Delargy, British Labour politician and chairman of the Anti-Partition of Ireland League of Great Britain, who had been present at the majority of the major meetings in Britain when de Valera spoke, recalled that 'enormous and enthusiastic meetings they are, in the biggest cities'. However, in retrospect, he believed that

they were all flops. They were not political meetings at all. They were tribal rallies: tribesmen met to greet the Old

Chieftain. The melodies of 1916 were played. A few IRA veterans, with their Black and Tan medals, formed guards of honour. Sympathetic Englishmen who attended went away bewildered.[147]

The Irish high commissioner to London, John W. Dulanty informed officials in Dublin that de Valera's visit to Britain had not been altogether successful. Dulanty explained that although 7,000 people attended a rally in Liverpool, with many of them paying as much as twelve shillings to attend, their early enthusiasm quickly waned because of de Valera's 'indulging in a lengthy statistical survey'.[148] *The Irish Times* recorded that throughout de Valera's 'long tours, his speeches have been almost unexceptional'.[149] Secret intelligence reports from the Chief Constable, Lancashire, unenthusiastically reported that 'mostly Irish people attended' de Valera's meetings, which were 'boring'.[150] The most common criticism aimed at de Valera was that he was preaching his anti-partition message to the converted. Indeed, Desmond Ryan, who had fought alongside de Valera during the 1916 Rising, recorded that the anti-partition campaign only seemed to 'shout with the converted'.[151]

DE VALERA'S REACTION TO THE REPEAL OF THE EXTERNAL RELATIONS ACT

As de Valera continued his propaganda offensive in Britain, in Ireland the Inter-Party government sought to steal some of Fianna Fáil's thunder on the partition issue. In September 1948, during a state visit to Canada, taoiseach, John A. Costello confirmed reports that the government intended to repeal the external relations Act and that Ireland would be leaving the Commonwealth.[152] Costello, Seán MacBride and William Norton, leading figures in the main coalition parties, Fine Gael, Clann na Poblachta and Labour, had all been bitter opponents of the external relations Act which had been passed by the Fianna Fáil government in 1936.

The principal area of contention was that the Act recognised the King as the symbol of the co-operation within the Commonwealth and confirmed certain of his functions in external affairs. As Ronan Fanning stated, whatever else divided them, the Inter-Party government 'shared a common impulse to make an affirmation of independence as resounding as the Fianna Fáil affirmations of the thirties'.[153] For

Fine Gael the announcement was a means to which the party finally removed the stain of its previous period in government in the 1920s when, as Cumann na nGaedheal, it had acquired a reputation as the pro-British party and of supporting partition.

De Valera was unsure of the merits for repealing the Act. He was pessimistic about the benefits of such a move, having always justified Ireland's tenuous link with the Commonwealth, through the external relations Act, on the grounds that the Act embodied necessary 'bait' for Ulster unionists.[154] However, before leaving office, in late 1947 he had contemplated repealing the Act and instructed the attorney general, Cearbhall Ó Dálaigh, to draft a Bill entitled, 'The Presidential (International Powers and Functions) Bill'.[155] In October 1947 de Valera privately informed Rugby that he might repeal the Act as 'it had done no good'.[156]

Unlike his opposition colleagues, de Valera realised that secession from the Commonwealth did not necessarily follow from repeal of the external relations Act. At this very time British officials were suggesting to India that they use the external relations Act as a basis for staying in the Commonwealth. India accepted this proposal in April 1948 and agreed to recognise the King as the head of the Commonwealth and as a symbol of free association of Commonwealth people.[157] The available evidence suggests that, if in government, de Valera would have chosen to follow the Indian model and keep Ireland 'associated' with the Commonwealth.[158] However, Costello was determined to repeal the Act and informed de Valera that the Inter-Party government intended to withdraw from the Commonwealth, and in its place to introduce the 'Republic of Ireland Act'. The Act declared that the *description* of the state would be the 'Republic of Ireland'. However, the Act did not change the official name of the state (this remained Ireland or Éire in Irish).

While de Valera's semi-official biographers record that he 'rejoiced as one who saw in the action of the government the ending of a long controversy', privately de Valera believed that the Inter-Party government's decision was not necessary.[159] He argued that Ireland was at this moment a Republic; in all but name, at least. 'There is no King of the state either internally or externally', he wrote, 'our executive authority and power internal and external lies with the government'.[160] Speaking in the Dáil, in November 1948, he confessed that the decision might entrench partition rather than help end it, as it severed a last tangible link with Ulster Unionists.[161] In London, in June 1949, he doggedly maintained that

Ireland 'already had a Republic since 1936. No doubt our state was a Republic'.[162]

Writing personally to Costello, in early April 1948, de Valera refused an offer from the Inter-Party government to deliver an address to mark the coming into operation of the Republic of Ireland Act, scheduled for Easter Monday, 18 April. His reluctance was based on the premise that he could never participate 'in any such ventures' as the Act did not merit a national celebration.[163] He believed that 'complete freedom could not be obtained by the blowing of trumpets and the firing of guns'.[164] De Valera had strong feelings against celebrating any political or constitutional event short of the full reunification of the whole island as a Republic. At a meeting of the Fianna Fáil parliamentary party he instructed deputies to oppose the amendment of the Republic of Ireland Act, which provided for the 'institution of a national holiday on the day of the coming of the Bill into operation'.[165] The very use of the name 'Republic' agitated de Valera as he felt that the term was sacred and could only be used when the entire island of Ireland was united.[166] Leading Northern Nationalists agreed with de Valera's diagnosis. James McSparran, Nationalist MP for Mourne from 1945 to 1958 and chairman of the Anti-Partition League, turned down Costello's invitation to speak at the celebration rally, 'as he did not regard the occasion as one for rejoicing'.[167]

The Inter-Party government's performance, from Costello's Ottawa announcement to the inaugural Easter Sunday parade, perturbed de Valera greatly. He was bemused at Costello's short-sightedness and believed, in the words of Gerald Boland, that the government had acted in an 'infamous fashion to misrepresent the position ... misused by our political opponents in propaganda'.[168] De Valera was to later claim that all the Republic of Ireland Act had done was to 'give the map makers a convenient name to write across the face of this part of Ireland'.[169] John W. Dulanty noted that in this new political climate 'any hope of a constitutional or democratic solution had all but gone'.[170] Northern Nationalist representatives were reported to have felt that the episode had been a blunder of judgement, that the 'repeal of the External Relations Act had put them back years'.[171]

Both London and Belfast equally expressed their bemusement of the Inter-Party government's handling of the entire affair. British prime minister, Clement Attlee privately wrote that the Republic of Ireland Act would only increase the 'difficulty in arriving at any agreement on the partition question'.[172] Rugby later conceded that he was 'staggered' by Costello's actions. He believed that it had the effect of 'crushing a delicate fabric', accusing Costello of proclaiming a 'form of warfare'.[173] The Inter-Party government's actions were reported in British circles as being 'abrupt, amateurish and ill prepared'.[174] Indeed, writing in the 1960s the Earl of Longford (formerly Lord Pakenham), a former leading British Labour MP and co-author of de Valera's semi-official biography, described the affair as merely 'an unhappy accident of history'.[175] Within Ulster Unionist circles the Inter Party government's decision was met with condescending bemusement. John Edward Warnock, Northern Ireland attorney general from 1949 to 1956, later recalled how he did not think that anyone would have been so 'politically immature'.[176] According to Joseph Lee, the Irish government's performance, from the repeal of the external relations Act to the declaration of the Republic of Ireland Act, was a shambles from start to finish and 'perhaps the most inept diplomatic exhibition in the history of the State'.[177]

De Valera must accept part of the responsibility for the Irish government's decision to repeal the Act and remove Ireland from the Commonwealth. His anti-partition propaganda campaign forced the hand of the Inter-Party government to play the 'green card'. As Rugby pointed out to London, 'each party must now outdo its rivals in a passionate crusade for Irish unity'.[178] Rugby previously noted 'the Party which does best on the Irish election platform is ... the Party which can put up the hottest anti-British slogan. Blessed are the users of partition'.[179] Irish politicians, he explained, 'strain every nerve to achieve total divorce ... they get that urge with their mother's milk'.[180] Indeed, a British file recorded that members of Dáil Éireann were 'tumbling over one another in their haste to climb onto the Republican band-wagon'.[181]

The repeal of the Act had major consequences for Fianna Fáil's Northern Ireland policy. As is examined below, the Inter-Party government's decision compelled a reluctant Labour government in Britain to introduce counter legislation, the 'Ireland Act', in May 1949. The Ireland Act came as a bitter blow to de Valera. The doctrine of consent, which was enshrined within the Act, reassured Northern Ireland's constitutional position within the United Kingdom and effectively gave Ulster Unionists a veto over Irish unity. The impact that this counter legislation had for partition was dramatic. De Valera was confronted by the reality that the pursuit for Irish unity had become a long-term aspiration rather than a medium-term policy.

'TOTAL PROPAGANDA': THE ALL-PARTY
ANTI-PARTITION COMMITTEE

The Inter-Party government's decision to repeal the external relations Act and declare Ireland a Republic was the first occasion since Fianna Fáil's establishment that the party had been seriously challenged on the partition issue. Its minister for external affairs, Seán MacBride, now sought to ensure that the Inter-Party government would control Northern Ireland policy. On entering government MacBride had become anxious that the partition issue was being used for party purposes as a result of de Valera's anti-partition propaganda campaign.[182] Thus, in April 1948, he decided that Northern Ireland policy would be taken out of the hands of the government and handed over nominally to the newly formed All-Party Anti-Partition Committee.

The committee consisted of the four major political parties, Fine Gael, Labour, Clann na Poblachta and Fianna Fáil. Conor Cruise O'Brien, a civil servant within the Department of External Affairs at the time and who was present at the first meeting of the committee, observed that MacBride's decision to take the main responsibility for Northern Ireland policy away from the Department of External Affairs and instead share the responsibility with the opposition parties was an attempt by the minister for external affairs to reconcile differences he had with de Valera.[183] However, this assumption only tells half the story and it seems that McBride's central motive was his determination that Fianna Fáil would no longer exploit the freedom of opposition to embarrass the government on its Northern Ireland policy. Simply put, if all parties sat under the auspices of a partition committee, the chance to exploit government mistakes and make political capital from them was limited.

An unsigned and undated directive outlined the purpose of the committee. It read:

> The task of the committee should be primarily to assist in the creation of public opinion favourable to the unification of the country, in Ireland, Britain, in the United States, Australia and in such other parts of the world as may, from time to time, be expedient.[184]

The inaugural gathering of the committee was held on 27 January 1949. In attendance at the Mansion House in Dublin were Costello,

MacBride, tánaiste and minister for social welfare, William Norton, minister for education, General Richard Mulcahy, de Valera, Aiken and Fianna Fáil TD for Cavan, Patrick Smith.[185] Given de Valera's past lack of support in any anti-partition initiative that fell outside his personal control his support for the committee was limited. Unlike his successor at the Department of Taoiseach, de Valera would have never permitted opposition parties a role in the formation of government policy on partition.[186] De Valera, however, subsequently noted that if Fianna Fáil refused to participate in the committee the party could have been left 'open to a great deal of misrepresentation' which would have proven to be 'harmful'.[187] In fact, de Valera faced criticism from within Fianna Fáil for his decision to participate on the committee. Joseph Brennan, a future TD for Donegal-West and minister, accused de Valera of 'acquiescing in the blunders of the government'.[188] Michael Yeats, a member of the party's National Executive, felt that by Fianna Fáil joining the committee it 'had led to results not foreseen'.[189]

A backroom staff led by Frank Gallagher, the so-called 'Irish Goebbels',[190] and the 'master propagandist',[191] was employed by the committee to produce anti-partition propaganda literature. Examples of books produced were, *Finances of Partition*, by Labhrás Ó Nualláin, and Gallagher's, *The Indivisible Island*. Numerous pamphlets on discrimination and gerrymandering in Northern Ireland were also produced such as, *Ireland's Right to Unity*, *The Orange Card* and *Discrimination: A Study of Injustice to a Minority*. The production of well-packaged and readily accessible printed material revealed the committees' understanding of the need to present their case against partition professionally and competently. The elaborate production was matched by sophisticated analysis which, through the use of graphs and maps, highlighted 'systematic manipulation of electoral boundaries' within Northern Ireland.[192]

However, the arguments used were those of long established anti-partitionist agenda. The emphasis was on highlighting the 'artificial' boundary of the border that divided the South from the 'lost Six-Counties' and explaining the 'illegality' of British military forces in Northern Ireland.[193] In fact, the production of anti-partition literature by the All-Party Anti-Partition Committee was similar to those devised by the Irish government sponsored North-Eastern Boundary Bureau from 1923 to 1925, which relied upon lengthy statistical surveys and diagrams to demonstrate the illegality of partition.[194]

The first public initiative of the All-Party Anti-Partition Committee was for the organisation of a campaign fund outside local churches, in support of Northern Nationalists anti-partitionist candidates in the Northern Ireland general election set for 10 February 1949. Northern Ireland prime minister, Sir Basil Brooke, announced that 'partition was to the main issue' of the general election.[195] Cross-border tensions had grown since de Valera's anti-partition propaganda campaign to America and Britain. He had overplayed his hand in his relationship with the Ulster Unionists. His tour of America had annoyed Stormont immensely, resulting in a return of megaphone diplomacy between Dublin and Belfast.

On his return to Ireland, de Valera had defended his trips abroad and rejected comments made by Brooke on the subject of discrimination.[196] In defence of his anti-partition propaganda campaign de Valera reminded Brooke that he 'may be assured that the campaign against partition ... will be continued in full blast in every country where people of our race dwell until partition is ended'.[197] Such pressure, however, did little to help already strained relations. Indeed, Brooke said that the purpose of the election was 'to make it clear to all beyond a doubt' that the desire of Northern Ireland was to remain part of the United Kingdom.[198]

By early February 1949 the fundraising campaign for Northern Nationalist candidates had collected over £42,000.[199] The financial success of the campaign was not matched in the election itself, as Northern Nationalists performed poorly at the polls. The net result of Southern politicians' interference in the Northern Ireland election was disastrous and merely seemed to contribute to the Ulster Unionist Party achieving one of the greatest victories in its history. The Northern Ireland Labour Party was all but wiped out at the polls and after its defeat decided to publicly declare its support for partition, while reactionaries regained the ascendancy within the Ulster Unionist Party.[200] The very concept of collecting funds was brought into question, as the *Manchester Guardian* warned 'what the Zinoviev letter did for the English Tories in 1924, the anti-partition fund can do for the Orangemen in 1949'.[201] This was also the opinion of an Ulster Unionist source, which confirmed to *The Irish Times* that it was 'worth 60,000 votes to us' and it would shake 'apathetic unionists ... out of their complacency'.[202]

The importance of the committee, in the context of Fianna Fáil's Northern Ireland policy, was that it demonstrated to de Valera the futility of Dublin's involvement in Northern Ireland politics. The financial assistance offered to Northern Nationalist candidates during the British general election had proved disastrous. Consequently, when

Fianna Fáil entered government in 1951 de Valera ordered that the All-Party Anti-Partition Committee would no longer offer financial assistance to Northern Nationalists.[203] Tellingly, by September 1951 de Valera effectively wound-up the Committee.[204]

'YOU HAVE CARVED UP OUR COUNTRY': DE VALERA AND THE IRELAND ACT

By the summer of 1949 de Valera's anti-partition propaganda campaign took on a new level of intensity – it was a change in direction for which he was unprepared. The catalyst was the British government's decision to introduce an Act to safeguard the constitutional position of the Northern Ireland government within the United Kingdom. London's wish to introduce the Act was built on two salient points. The first was in direct response to the Irish government's official declaration of the Republic of Ireland Act the previous April, which resulted in intensive lobbying from Ulster Unionists for the British to make a counter-declaration;[205] the second was due to Dublin's decision not to join the North Atlantic Treaty Organisation (NATO) in January 1949.[206]

The Inter-Party government's decision to reject the offer of joining NATO was based on the premise that any military alliance involving the British – who the Irish maintained were responsible for partition – was entirely 'repugnant and unacceptable' to the Irish people.[207] De Valera was in agreement, having publicly announced that Fianna Fáil would only support Ireland's involvement in NATO if 'Ireland was united'.[208] For London, Dublin's refusal to participate in NATO made it impossible for Whitehall to retain a 'detached attitude' on partition, as Ireland's refusal had implications for the wider security question of defending the North Atlantic.[209] The American government held similar reservations, viewing Ireland's refusal to join NATO as merely strengthening their perception of the strategic value of Northern Ireland in the case of a future world war, and therefore for the need to maintain a partitioned Ireland.[210]

On 3 May 1949, the British government formally announced, under the title, 'The Ireland Act':

> That Northern Ireland remains part of His Majesty's dominions and of the United Kingdom ... that in no event will Northern Ireland ... cease to be part of His Majesty's

dominions and of the United Kingdom without the consent of parliament of Northern Ireland.[211]

Despite fierce objections from the Friends of Ireland – a selection of British Labour politicians sympathetic to Irish unity, founded in 1945 – which included Ulster-born MPs Geoffrey Bing and Hugh Delargy, the government drove through the legislation with considerable ease.[212] Whitehall's decision to introduce the 'Ireland Act' initiated a crisis in Anglo-Irish relations that had both immediate implications for de Valera's anti-partition propaganda campaign and ultimately long-lasting consequences for Fianna Fáil's Northern Ireland policy.

De Valera was in London at the time of the declaration and the statement seemed to perturb him immensely. He felt that the Act was further evidence of the poisoning effect of partition on Anglo-Irish relations.[213] On the day of its announcement de Valera delivered a speech at Fleet Street in London. Placing the blame squarely on the British government, he passionately declared:

> You have carved up our country … it is a very bad day for relations between Ireland and Britain when the British government should choose at this stage to introduce a Bill telling us that partition is going to be perpetual.[214]

De Valera's anti-partition propaganda speeches took on a new level of intensity not before seen during his propaganda campaign. He believed that the British had embarked on a 'mad course' and instead of cementing good relations with Ireland they had chosen to 'blow them up'.[215] He lamented that the British had given Irishmen and women 'a slap in the face'.[216] He found it 'hard to believe' and that 'it makes one desperate'.[217] Speaking at a huge protest rally against the introduction of the Ireland Act held on O'Connell Street, Dublin, on 13 May 1949, he bitterly remarked that 'the hatred of foreign rule has been burned into the hearts of the people of our race'.[218] Within days of the announcement secretary of the Department of External Affairs, Freddie Boland contacted London urging the British government to make a statement that it would support an agreement between Dublin and Belfast on partition. Widely respected within British circles as 'forceful, pleasant and highly intelligent',[219] London rejected Boland's request. The Home Office notified Boland that any such statement was 'inexpedient'. He was informed that such a statement would be used by the Dublin government and de Valera 'in support of the anti-partition campaign'.[220]

The previous year de Valera had called on the British to 'express her wish to have partition ended'.[221] A year on, the political landscape had drastically changed. A core element of Fianna Fáil's traditional Northern Ireland policy, a British declaration in support of Irish unity, was effectively left in pieces. Throughout the previous sixteen months of de Valera's anti-partition propaganda campaign, abroad and in Ireland, he had habitually demanded that the British make a declaration in favour of Irish unity. With the passage of the Ireland Act, however, he admitted in the Dáil, that rather than making such a declaration 'we have got the contrary assertion now ... Britain does not want us united'.[222]

The Act effectively witnessed the passing of the veto of Irish unity from London to the custody of the Ulster Unionists. De Valera believed that the Act was an 'ingenious system' providing the British with two vetoes on Irish unity; the first through the London parliament, the second through Belfast.[223] Aiken was likewise furious upon hearing of London's decision. Writing privately to Attlee, he passionately compared Britain's justification for a partitioned Ireland to that of Hitler's rationale for invading 'Sudetenland, Czechoslovakia, Austria and Poland'. The British maintenance of partition, he wrote, 'undermined the morale', of not merely Irishmen and women, but of all 'Europeans'.[224]

In private correspondence with Brooke, Attlee explained that because of Irish 'aggression' in the context of Dublin's anti-partition campaign and the Republic of Ireland Act, he was fully prepared 'to make it clear' that the British government condemned Ireland's interference in Northern Ireland affairs.[225] Attlee was personally extremely unhappy towards the Irish government's Northern Ireland policy and in particular identified de Valera's 'intensified' anti-partition campaign as embittering Dublin's relations with London and Belfast. He found it 'ludicrous' to suggest that 'if the anti-partitionists had their way and Northern Ireland were made part of the Irish Republic, there would be a united Ireland'.[226] In reference to Northern Ireland Protestants, he explained that 'there would be no real unity with a large minority which would feel that it has been coerced and betrayed'.[227]

Significantly, the introduction of the Act forced de Valera to acknowledge that his use of propaganda to help end partition had proved futile. Not since the introduction of the Government of Ireland Act in 1920 had partition been so resolutely confirmed. From this moment onwards, arguably as never before, de Valera was forced to concede that the ending of partition was a long-term aspiration rather than a medium-term objective. Instead of encouraging and nurturing support for ending partition, his campaign exposed Irish nationalists' inability to influence British policy on partition. Speaking at the Fianna Fáil Ard Fheis in June 1949, he pessimistically explained: 'I would like to repeat what Mr [Seán] Lemass has already said, that those who promise you that you will have this done in two or three months are fooling you; are playing upon your credulity'.[228] Indeed, all he could offer party delegates, in the drive to end partition, was a request to write to 'our friends abroad' in the hope that they might use their influence to secure Irish unity![229]

Thus, in 1950, de Valera *abandoned* his anti-partition propaganda campaign. On visits to Birmingham, Cardiff and Newry in the early months of 1950, de Valera did not speak of partition.[230] Similarly, during visits to France, Switzerland, Italy, Greece and Israel, in April 1950, once again he decided not to mention partition in any of his speeches.[231] In Ireland he was likewise reluctant to continue his anti-partition mission. In Bruree Co. Limerick, in June 1950, in front of a crowd of over 10,000 people, de Valera spoke predominately on the need 'to work for the [Irish] language'; partition was ignored.[232] Although the All-Party Anti-Partition Committee continued to meet during de Valera's remaining months in opposition, usually once a month, no new policy initiatives were devised and instead attention was given to maintaining correspondence with the anti-partition movement in Britain.[233]

By 1950 de Valera was confronted with the reality that London was simply not interested in Dublin's demands for Irish unity. The Inter-Party government's handling of the external relations Act had forced a reluctant British government to initiate an interventionist policy towards Ireland. However, with the constitutional position of Northern Ireland guaranteed, with the introduction of the Ireland Act, Whitehall wished to retain a *laissez faire* stance. Speaking on the eve of the British general election in February 1950, in which the Labour Party secured victory, Attlee stated that the question of the partition of Ireland was 'a matter that must be settled by the Irish themselves'.[234] Deputy prime minister and leader of the House of Commons, Herbert Morrison was of the same belief: 'don't get us into a tangle, we'll talk about Ireland when the Irish agree among themselves'.[235] De Valera was left to lament that 'from a political party point of view' British parties 'disliked having to touch it [partition]'.[236]

* * *

In conclusion, de Valera's use of propaganda as a tool to preach the injustice of partition was a policy of futility. As Aldous Huxley poetically noted 'the propagandist is a man who canalises an already existing stream. In a land where there is no water, he digs in vain'.[237] De Valera was digging in vain. Perhaps he realised this. He never again embarked on an international anti-partition tour. He had learned a valuable lesson that propaganda only offered superficial success. The 'sore thumb' approach of stressing the 'injustice' and 'crime' of a partitioned Ireland had ran its course. Ernest Blythe eloquently appraised the futility of de Valera's anti-partition propaganda campaign: 'our speeches and articles about the injustice of partition ... must be likened to the shooting off of good ammunition at the smoke-trail of a ship which has passed by and is long out of range'.[238]

During the Irish general election campaign in the summer of 1951 de Valera was noticeably silent on the partition issue.[239] Gone were the hostile sound bites of previous years. As is discussed in the following chapter, upon Fianna Fáil's return to government in May 1951, de Valera dismantled the anti-partition apparatus abroad and in Ireland. Significantly, for Fianna Fáil's Northern Ireland policy the use of anti-partition propaganda was replaced by a new policy of 'persuasion'. Aimed directly at encouraging cross-border co-operation between Dublin and Belfast, particularly on economic matters, Fianna Fáil attempted to implement a more practical Northern Ireland policy. Privately, de Valera admitted that 'a more realistic attitude' to partition was needed.[240]

NOTES

1. University College Dublin Archives (UCDA) Eamon de Valera Papers P150/2940, Lord Rugby to de Valera, 18 Feb. 1948.
2. UCDA P150/2487, memorandum from Maurice Moynihan to de Valera, 'Conference with British Minister, January 1938', Jan. 1938.
3. *Irish Press*, 19 Oct. 1948.
4. National Archives of United Kingdom (NAUK) Dominion Office (DO) 35/2094, memorandum recording meeting between de Valera and Maffey, 18 May 1946.
5. *Irish Press*, 11 Oct. 1944.

6. See de Valera's comments. Dáil Éireann debate (DE), 24 June 1947. Vol. 107, col. 84.

7. UCDA Fianna Fáil Party Papers P176/446, meeting of parliamentary party, 3 May 1945.

8. UCDA P176/346, meeting of National Executive, 12 March 1945.

9. This was the opinion of John Kelly, Dublin. *The Irish Times*, 7 Nov. 1945.

10. This was the opinion of the Seámus O'Sullivan, Fianna Fáil Cork Borough Comhairle Dáilceanntair. *Irish Press*, 11 Oct. 1944.

11. See UCDA, P176/753, record of partition resolutions issued on behalf of Fianna Fáil cumainn to party headquarters, Nov. 1945.

12. *The Irish Times*, 7 Nov. 1945.

13. Garret FitzGerald (interview 19 Jan. 2009) and Pádraig Faulkner (interview 10 July 2006) confirmed that it was not unknown for political parties to ask a particular party branch to submit a resolution on behalf of party headquarters.

14. See *Irish Press*, 9 Oct. 1946.

15. Kevin Boland, *The Rise and Decline of Fianna Fáil* (Dublin, 1982), 140–142.

16. Boland, *The Rise and Decline of Fianna Fáil*, 140–142.

17. Basil Chubb, *A Source Book of Irish Government* (Dublin: Institute for Public Administration, 1969), 213.

18. This was the opinion of C. O' Leary, South-East Cork. *Irish Press*, 9 Oct. 1946.

19. This was the opinion of Seán Ua Fearraidhe, Gweedore cumann, Donegal. UCDA P176/754, record of 1946 Fianna Fáil Ard Fheis, 8–9 Oct. 1946.

20. *Irish Press*, 9 Oct. 1946.

21. UCDA P176/346, meeting of National Executive, 21 Oct. 1946.

22. In March 1945, John O'Connor had requested that a new anti-partition committee be formed. UCDA P176/346, meeting of National Executive, 12 March 1945.

23. UCDA P176/345–346, record of meetings of National Executive, Jan. 1941–Oct. 1946.

24. Traynor, de Blacam and Pearse were present at the inaugural meeting of the original sub-committee on partition on 10 Oct. 1938.

25. UCDA P176/346, meeting of sub-committee on partition, 25 Nov. 1946.

26. The sub-committee on partition convened on 25 Nov. 1946, 8 Jan., 7 Feb. and 22 May 1947 (the records state that the committee met on a further one occasion between Feb. and May 1948, although no date is given). See UCDA P176/346, record of National Executive meetings, Nov. 1946 – May. 1947.

27. UCDA P176/346, meeting of National Executive, 21 Oct. 1946.

28. Andrews was a member of Fianna Fáil's National Executive during the late 1920s. C.S. Andrews, *Man of No Property* (Dublin, New Ireland, 2001), 235.

29. See UCDA P176/835, meeting of Fianna Fáil National Executive, 13 Nov. 1947.

30. *Irish Press*, 19 Jan. 1948.

31. *Irish Press*, 11 Oct. 1944.

32. National Archives of Ireland (NAI) Department of the Taoiseach (DT) S 9361A, Patrick Maxwell to de Valera, 17 Nov. 1944.

33. NAI DT S 9361A, Moynihan to Maxwell, 30 Nov. 1944.

34. *Irish Press*, 15 Nov. 1945.

35. Brendan Lynn, 'The Irish Anti-Partition League and the Political Realities of Partition', *Irish Historical Studies*, Vol. XXXIV, No. 135 (May, 2005), 321–332; 325.

36. John Bowman, *De Valera and the Ulster Question* (Oxford: Oxford University Press, 1982), 258.

37. Enda Staunton, *The Nationalists of Northern Ireland 1918–73* (Dublin: Columba Press, 2001), 144.

38. Clare O'Halloran, *Partition and the Limits of Irish Nationalism* (New Jersey: Humanities Press International, Inc., 1987), 152.

39. See, for example, Donnelly's comments, *Irish Press*, 4 Nov. 1936.

40. At a meeting of the Fianna Fáil's parliamentary party, in Feb. 1949, deputies discussed the 'request from Eddie McAteer MP for a seat in the Dáil … it was decided no action should be taken'. See UCDA P176/446, meeting of Fianna Fáil parliamentary party, 17 Feb. 1949. At a meeting of the 'Party Committee' of Fianna Fáil in Oct. 1950 a similar

proposal from Irish Anti-Partition Association was rejected. See UCDA P176/451, meeting of Fianna Fáil Party Committee, 17 Oct. 1950. See also UCDA P176/446, meetings of the parliamentary party, 27 Oct. 1950 and 11 April 1951. At both meetings de Valera again rejected a request from Northern Nationalists for access to the Dáil.

41. Speech by de Valera. *The Irish Times*, 16 June 1949.
42. Eithne McDermott, *Clann na Poblachta* (Cork: Cork University Press, 1998), 5.
43. See NAUK DO 35/7943, British Embassy, Dublin secret report, 23 July 1959.
44. Speech by Lemass. *Irish Press*, 4 June 1946.
45. UCDA Sighle Humphreys Papers P106/2165, Clann na Poblachta 1948 general election leaflet.
46. Staunton, *The Nationalists of Northern Ireland*, 162.
47. UCDA John A. Costello Papers P190/415, copy of *Clann*, 21 Dec. 1947.
48. UCDA P176/835, document issued on behalf of the Fianna Fáil National Executive, Dec. 1947.
49. Bowman, *De Valera*, 264.
50. Bowman, *De Valera*, 265.
51. *Irish Press*, 19 Jan. 1948.
52. UCDA P176/835, document issued on behalf of the Fianna Fáil National Executive, Dec. 1947.
53. See Gilbert Hughes comments. *Irish Press*, 14 & 20 Jan. 1948.
54. UCDA Donnchadh Ó'Briain Papers P83/33, typescript copy Captain Henry Harrison, *Ireland's Danger and National Leadership*.
55. See *Gerald Boland's story – 11*, *Irish Press*, 19 Oct. 1968.
56. UCDA P150/2940, de Valera to Rugby, 27 Feb.1948.
57. UCDA P150/2944, meeting of the Fianna Fáil parliamentary party, 26 Feb. 1948. At this meeting de Valera was elected, unanimously, chairman of the party and its leader in Dáil Eireann. Seán Lemass was elected vice-chairman and deputy leader.
58. National Library of Ireland (NLI) Frank Gallagher Papers MS 18375 (2).Unpublished biography of Eamon de Valera.
59. NLI Gallagher Papers, MS 18375 (2).
60. *Boston Sunday Post*, 28 March 1948. The paper's front headline noted '250,000 in hub hail de Valera'.
61. NLI Gallagher Papers, MS 18375 (2).
62. UCDA Frank Aiken P104/4823, Aiken to Maud Aiken, 1 April 1948.
63. *Irish Press*, 26 Oct. 1948.
64. Speech by de Valera, New York, 3 April 1948. See Maurice Moynihan, *Speeches and Statements by Eamon De Valera 1917–1973* (Dublin, 1980), 497–505.
65. UCDA P150/2947, speech by de Valera, 13 April 1948.
66. Speech by de Valera. *Irish Press*, 26 Oct. 1948.
67. Speech by de Valera. DE, 24 June 1947. Vol. 107, cols. 78–81.
68. Speech by de Valera, Los Angeles. *Irish Press*, 18 March 1948.
69. Speech by de Valera, San Francisco. *Irish Press,* 17 March 1948.
70. UCDA P150/2948, speech by de Valera, 30 March 1948.
71. Speech by de Valera, Tulsa, Oklahoma. *Irish Press*, 12 March 1948
72. Speech by de Valera, San Francisco. *Irish Press*, 17 March 1948.
73. See UCDA P150/1996, copy of leaflet, *Ulster's Right to Reply*, Oct. 1948.
74. Speech by de Valera. *Irish Press*, 3 April 1948.
75. Speech by de Valera, *Irish Press*, 26 Oct. 1948.
76. See Seán O'Faoláin, 'Ulster', *The Bell*, Vol. 2, No. 4 (July, 1941), 4.
77. UCDA Ernest Blythe Papers P24/1924, John J. Horgan to Ernest Blythe, 3 Nov. 1950.
78. See de Valera's comments. DE, 24 June 1947. Volume 107, cols. 79–82.
79. DE, 24 June 1947. Volume 107, cols. 79–82.
80. Bowman, *De Valera*, 317.
81. See UCDA P150/1996, a copy of the Rev. J. G. MacManaway's leaflet, *Partition, Why Not?* (Issued on behalf of the Ulster Unionist Council, 1948).

82. Henry Patterson, *Ireland Since 1939, the Persistence of Conflict* (Dublin: Penguin Ireland, 2006), 120.

83. Kate O'Malley, *Ireland, India and Empire, Indo-Irish Radical Connections, 1919–1964* (Manchester: Manchester University Press, 2008), 159.

84. NAUK DO 35/3938, Lord Innverchapel to Bevin, 16 April 1948.

85. NAUK DO 35/3938, Lord Innverchapel to Bevin, 16 April 1948.

86. NAUK DO 35/3938, Lord Innverchapel to Bevin, 16 April 1948.

87. NAUK DO 35/3928, Rugby to Eric Machtig, 15 April 1948.

88. Seán Cronin, *Washington's Irish Policy 1916–1986* (Dublin: Anvil Books, 1987), 193.

89. Cronin, *Washington's Irish Policy 1916–1986*, 193.

90. UCDA P104/4564, American assistant secretary of the State Department, Ernest A. Gross to Senator Henry Cabot Lodge Jr., 11 Aug. 1949.

91. See Moynihan, *Speeches and Statements by Eamon de Valera*, 107–109.

92. Speech by de Valera. *Irish Press,* 1 May 1948.

93. Speech by de Valera. *Irish Press,* 1 May 1948.

94. Speech by de Valera. *The Sun,* 4 May 1948.

95. Speech by de Valera. *Auckland Star,* 25 May 1948.

96. Speech by de Valera. *Evening Post,* 26 May 1948.

97. UCDA P155/75, de Valera to his personal secretary, Kathleen O'Connell, 14 May 1948.

98. UCDA P104/4828, Aiken to Maud Aiken, 14 May 1948.

99. UCDA P104/4767, Aiken to Kiernan, Irish legation, Canberra, Australia, 5 Oct. 1948.

100. NAUK DO 35/3929, Williams to Sir E. Machtig, 25 June 1948.

101. NAUK DO 35/3929, Williams to Sir E. Machtig, 11 June 1948.

102. NAI Department of Foreign Affairs (DFA) 305/14/21, Kiernan to unknown recipient in the Department of Foreign Affairs, autumn/winter, 1948.

103. NAUK DO 35/3931, Duffy to secretary of Commonwealth and Relations Office, Philip Noel-Baker, 1 June 1948.

104. NAUK DO 35/3931, Duffy to Noel-Baker, 1 June 1948.

105. NAUK DO 35/3931, Duffy to Noel-Baker, 1 June 1948.

106. NAI DFA 305/14/21, Barrett to A. T. Dryer, Sydney Australia, 9 April 1951.

107. NAI DFA 305/14/21, C. Smith O'Brien Gardiner to Seán MacBride, 7 April 1950.

108. NAUK DO 35/3929, Williams to Sir E. Machtig, 11 June 1948.

109. Speech by de Valera. *Irish Press,* 15 June, 1948.

110. Speech by de Valera. *Southern Cross,* 26 May 1948.

111. UCDA P104/4767, Aiken to Kiernan, Irish legation, Canberra, Australia, 5 Oct. 1948.

112. UCDA P104/4767, Aiken to Kiernan, Irish legation, Canberra, Australia, 5 Oct. 1948.

113. UCDA P150/2955, itinerary of de Valera's visit to India, 14 June 1948.

114. UCDA P104/4767, Aiken to Kiernan, Irish legation, Canberra, Australia, 5 Oct. 1948.

115. UCDA P104/4837, Aiken to Maud Aiken, 17 June 1948.

116. UCDA P150/2955, Nehru to de Valera, 18 June 1948. Nehru devoted several chapters of his work, *Glimpses into World History,* to de Valera and Ireland's fight for independence. See Jawaharlal Nehru, *Glimpses of World History* (India, 1934).

117. Nicholas Mansergh, *The Prelude to Partition: Concepts and Aims in Ireland and India* (Cambridge: Cambridge University Press, 1976), 5–6.

118. NAUK DO 35/3930, Jmcf [sic] to Rumbold, 28 May 1948.

119. See *Irish Press,* March–June 1948.

120. NAUK DO 35/3928, Rugby to Eric Machtig, 9 April 1948.

121. At the 1948 Fianna Fáil Ard Fheis ten similar partition resolutions were issued by grass-roots. See UCDA P176/755, 1948 Fianna Fáil Ard Fheis.

122. *The Irish Times,* 23 June 1948.

123. DE, 6 Aug. 1948. Vol. 122, col. 2420.

124. *Clare Champion,* 21 Aug. 1948.

125. UCDA P150/1996, copy of *United Ireland,* Vol. 1 No. 12, a monthly bulletin published by the Anti-Partition of Ireland League of Great Britain, Sept.–Oct. 1948.

126. UCDA P150/2968, record of de Valera's visit to Britain, Oct. 1948 – Feb. 1949.

127. See *Ireland's Right to Unity* (Dublin, 1950), 9.
128. *Irish Press*, 26 Oct. 1948.
129. Speech by de Valera, Newcastle-upon-Tyne. *Sunday Independent*, 14 Feb. 1949.
130. *Daily Mirror*, 31 Jan. 1949.
131. Speech by de Valera, Glasgow. *Irish Press*, 19 Oct. 1948.
132. Public Records Office of Northern Ireland (PRONI) Cabinet File (Cab) 9B/201/5, Arthur H. Johnson, the Grange, Flore, Northampton, addressed to the Northern Ireland government, 10 March 1949.
133. *Irish Press*, 19 Oct. 1948.
134. UCDA P150/2956, address by de Valera to the Fianna Fáil W.B. Yeats cumann in the Mansion House, Dublin, 7 Feb. 1949.
135. Bowman, *De Valera*, 274.
136. UCDA P150/2956, address by de Valera to the W.B. Yeats cumann, 7 Feb. 1949.
137. DE, 25 Nov. 1948. Vol. 113, col. 508.
138. UCDA P24/1390, Ernest Blythe to Lionel Booth, 1 March 1955. The former recalled a conversation he had with McQuaid in mid-1955.
139. NAUK DO 35/3933, record of de Valera's visit to the United Kingdom.
140. See *The Irish Times,* 23 Nov. 1948. See also *Irish Press* 23 Nov. 1948.
141. *The Irish Times*, 13 Dec. 1979.
142. From the available records it is apparent that the Northern Ireland government kept at least one file on de Valera's anti-partition campaign in Great Britain. See PRONI Cab 9B/201/5, Northern Ireland file re: 'Anti-Partition Campaign', 1948.
143. See PRONI Cab 9B/201/5, Ulster Office, London to Adams, Stormont Castle, Belfast (undated).
144. PRONI Cab 9B/201/5, memorandum by Sinclair 'Mr. de Valera's proposed tour: possibilities of counter-publicity', (undated).
145. PRONI Cab 9B/201/5, note by Sinclair on 'Anti-Partition activities in Great Britain', 9 July 1948.
146. PRONI Cab 9B/201/5, memorandum by Sinclair 'Mr. de Valera's proposed tour: possibilities of counter-publicity', (undated).
147. Bowman, *De Valera*, 274–275.
148. NAI DFA 305/14/108, Dulanty to Frederick Boland, 19 Feb. 1949.
149. *The Irish Times*, 23 Nov. 1948.
150. NAUK Security Service Files (KV) 2/515, report from Chief Constable, Lancashire to the Inspector General Royal Ulster Constabulary (RUC), undated.
151. See UCDA Desmond Ryan Papers LA10/D/207, 'Frank Gallagher', marked 'suppressed'. Date unknown.
152. Earl of Longford and Thomas P. O'Neill, *Eamon de Valera* (London: Hutchinson, 1970), 432.
153. Ronan Fanning, 'Raison d'état and the evolution of Irish foreign policy', in Michael Kennedy and Joseph Morrison Skelly (eds.), *Irish Foreign Policy 1919–66, from Independence to Internationalism* (Dublin: Four Courts Press, 2000), 308–326: 320.
154. Bowman, *De Valera*, 268.
155. See UCDA P150/2970. Under the advice of de Valera a Bill was drawn up entitled 'The Presidential (International Powers and Functions) Bill, 1947'. It contained within its text six sections. It was actually very similar to the 'Republic of Ireland Bill 1948', except it did not contain Section 2 of the latter – 'The Republic Act'. Typed copy of 'The Presidential (International Powers and Functions) Bill, 1947', signed by Cearbhall Ó Dálaigh, Irish attorney-general, 21 Oct. 1947.
156. NAUK DO 35/3926, record of meeting between de Valera and Rugby, 16 Oct. 1947.
157. Deirdre McMahon, 'Ireland, the empire, and the commonwealth', in Kevin Kenny (ed.), *Ireland and the British Empire* (Oxford, Oxford University Press, 2004), 182–219: 214.
158. McMahon, 'Ireland, the empire, and the commonwealth', 215. See also Dermot Keogh, *Twentieth Century Ireland, Nation and State* (Dublin: Gill and Macmillan, 1994), 190.
159. Longford and O'Neill, *Eamon de Valera*, 432.

160. UCDA P150/3703, a collection of miscellaneous and undated handwritten pages by de Valera.
161. DE, 24 Nov. 1948. Vol. 113, cols. 348–398.
162. UCDA P150/2982, copy of transcript of an interview between de Valera and Giorgio Sansa, 20 June 1949.
163. UCDA P150/2990, de Valera to Costello, 7 April 1949.
164. Speech by de Valera. *Irish Press*, 13 June 1949.
165. See UCDA P176/446, meeting of Fianna Fáil parliamentary party, 2 Dec. 1948.
166. Speech by de Valera, 1945 Fianna Fáil Ard Fheis. *The Irish Times*, 7 Nov. 1945.
167. *The Irish Times*, 15–16 March 1949.
168. Speech by Gerald Boland. *Irish Press*, 23 May 1949.
169. Speech by de Valera, Listowel, Co. Kerry. *Irish Press*, 29 Feb. 1956.
170. See Joe McNabb, '*More Rancour than Reason*', the Irish Government's Policy on Partition, *1948–51* (unpublished 2000 M.Litt. thesis available from UCDA).
171. UCDA P104/2579, record on confidential monthly reports by Captain Seamus McCall to the Committee of the All-Party Anti-Partition Conference.
172. University of Oxford (UO) Bodleian Library (BL) Clement Attlee Papers MS. Dep. 83 Fols. 76–80, handwritten notes by Attlee concerning the 'Ireland Bill', undated.
173. UCDA P150/2940, Rugby to de Valera, 22 April 1957.
174. NAUK Northern Ireland Files (CJ) 1/55, note of British views concerning the Irish government's decision to repeal the External Relations Act, date unknown.
175. See comments by Lord Pakenham, *Sunday Observer*, 8 Jan. 1961.
176. *The Irish Times*, 5 May 1960.
177. J.J. Lee, *Ireland 1912–1985, Politics and Society* (Cambridge: Cambridge University Press, 1989), 301.
178. Bowman, *De Valera*, 269.
179. NAUK DO 35/3926, record of meeting between de Valera and Rugby, 16 Oct. 1947.
180. NAUK DO 35/3926, record of meeting between de Valera and Rugby, 16 Oct. 1947.
181. NAUK CJ 1/55, note of British views concerning the Irish government's decision to repeal the External Relations Act, date unknown.
182. NAI DT S 9361A, memorandum issued on behalf of Seán MacBride, 29 April 1948.
183. Conor Cruise O'Brien, *Memoir my Life my Times* (Dublin: Poolbeg Press, 1999), 143–144.
184. See UCDA P104/4668.
185. UCDA P104/8630, meeting of the All-Party Anti-Partition Committee, Jan. 1949. See also *Irish Independent*, 28 Jan. 1948.
186. See UCDA P176/40, record of 27th meeting of the National Executive anti-partition sub-committee, 31 July 1939.
187. *The Irish Times*, 2 Nov. 1950.
188. *Irish Press*, 2 Nov. 1950.
189. *Irish Press*, 1 Nov. 1950.
190. This was the opinion of David Gray, American representative to Ireland. See Bowman, *De Valera*, 259–260.
191. This was the opinion of Desmond Ryan. See UCDA LA10/D/207, 'Frank Gallagher', marked 'suppressed'. Date unknown.
192. *Ireland's Right to Unity* (Dublin, 1950), 1.
193. *Ireland's Right to Unity* (Dublin, 1950), 1.
194. The bureau produced an elaborate book, *Handbook of the Ulster Question*, complete with detailed maps and chapters on the historical, economic and political background to partition, while a *Weekly Bulletin* was also circulated. O'Halloran, *Partition and the Limits of Irish Nationalism*, 113.
195. *Irish Press*, 28 Jan. 1949.
196. UCDA P150/2947, copy of de Valera's reply to Sir Basil Brooke's statement, date unknown.
197. UCDA P150/2947, copy of de Valera's reply to Sir Basil Brooke's statement, date unknown.

198. Speech by Brooke. *Irish Press*, 28 Jan. 1949.
199. *Irish Independent*, 4 Feb. 1949.
200. Donal Barrington, *Uniting Ireland*, Tuairim Pamphlet (Dublin, 1957), 9 (Available from NAI DT S 9361G).
201. Lynn, 'The Irish Anti-Partition League and the Political Realities of Partition', 331.
202. Lynn, 'The Irish Anti-Partition League and the Political Realities of Partition', 331.
203. See UCDA P104/8608, secretary of the Irish Anti-Partition League, Seán McNally, to Aiken, 17 June 1952.
204. From Sept. 1951 to Nov. 1955 the Committee met on only three occasions, finally winding up in Oct. 1972 after holding a further three meetings UCDA P104/8639–8655, record of 39th – 46th meetings of the All-Party Anti-Partition Committee, 28 Sept. 1951–26 Oct. 1971. In 1977, Fianna Fáil deputies George Colley and Richie Ryan were appointed as committee members, following the deaths of de Valera and Costello. Nevertheless, according to the archival records, post-1972, the committee never again convened. See UCDA P104/8663–8673.
205. See NAUK Cabinet Files (Cab) 2/1842, this file contains several letters from Brookeborough requesting the British government to make a declaration in support of the Northern Ireland government following the introduction by Dublin of the Republic of Ireland Act.
206. Throughout 1948 intensive negotiations had taken place in Washington concerning the desire of the major Western powers to form a strategic and military alliance (to be known as NATO) in the face of the threat from Communism.
207. Ronan Fanning, 'Small states, large neighbours: Ireland and the United Kingdom', *Irish Studies in International Affairs*, Vol. 9 (1998), 21–29: 26.
208. Speech by de Valera. *The Irish Times*, 22 March 1949.
209. Bowman, *De Valera*, 27.
210. Fanning, 'Small states, large neighbours: Ireland and the United Kingdom', 27.
211. *Irish Press*, 4 May 1949.
212. Aaron Edwards, 'Social democracy and partition: the British Labour Party and Northern Ireland, 1951–64', *Journal of Contemporary History*, Oct. 2007; 42 (4), 596.
213. Longford and O'Neill, *Eamon de Valera*, 434.
214. *Irish Press*, 4 May 1949.
215. Speech by de Valera, Ennis Co. Clare. *Irish Press*, 9 May 1949.
216. Speech by de Valera. DE, 10 May 1949. Vol. 115, cols. 809–810.
217. Speech by de Valera. *Irish Press*, 9 May 1949.
218. Speech by de Valera. *Irish Press*, 14 May 1949.
219. NAUK Foreign and Commonwealth Office (FCO) 33/1599, confidential profile of Freddie Boland, British Embassy, Dublin, May 1971.
220. UO BL Attlee Papers MS. Dep. 82 Fols. 150, Helsby (Home Office) to Attlee's private office, 6 May 1949.
221. Speech by de Valera. *Irish Press*, 23 June 1948.
222. Speech by de Valera. DE, 10 May 1949. Vol. 115, col. 813.
223. *Ireland's Right to Unity* (Dublin, 1950), 10.
224. See UCDA, P104/4649, Aiken to Attlee, undated, May 1949 (It is unclear if Aiken sent a version of this letter to Attlee).
225. UO BL Attlee Papers MS. Dep. 82 Fols. 176–77, memorandum entitled 'Ireland Bill Defence of Northern Ireland', undated.
226. UO BL Attlee Papers MS. Dep. 82 Fols. 256–57, memorandum entitled 'Secret Ireland Bill – Partition Question', undated.
227. UO BL Attlee Papers MS. Dep. 82 Fols. 256–57, memorandum entitled 'Secret Ireland Bill – Partition Question', undated.
228. Speech by de Valera, Fianna Fáil Ard Fheis. *Irish Press*, 15 June 1949.
229. *Irish Press*, 15 June 1949.
230. *Irish Press*, 26 Jan. 1950, 27 Jan. 1950 and 3 Feb. 1950.
231. UCDA P150/2996–2997, record of de Valera's anti-partition world tour; section III, July 1948–April 1951.

232. *Irish Press*, 26 June 1950.

233. UCDA P104/8636–8642, record of 24th – 39th All-Party Anti-Partition Committee meetings, 8 Feb. 1950–28 Sept.1951.

234. *Irish Press*, 22 Feb. 1950. Speech by Clement Attlee. Attlee subsequently noted that 'Mr Costello's Government made it impossible to do anything'. See UCDA, P104/4525, M.L. Skentelbury, charge d'Affaires at Canberra, to Seán Nunan, secretary to the Department of External Affairs, concerning a trip made by Clement Attlee to Australia, 22 Oct. 1954.

235. *Irish Press*, 18 Feb. 1950. Speech by Herbert Morrison.

236. UCDA P150/2957, 'confidential memorandum' from de Valera to Costello, Sept. 1950.

237. Aldous Huxley quoted in David Welch, *The Third Reich, Politics and Propaganda* (London: Routledge, 2002), 9.

238. UCDA P24/1769, Blythe, *Towards a Six-County Dominion?*, Aug. 1949.

239. See *Irish Press*, May 1951.

240. UCDA P104/8035, record of conversation between de Valera, Aiken and Lord Pakenham in Dublin, 2 May 1952.

4

1951–1955

'We should encourage a policy of persuasion [in relation to partition] as against a policy of pressure'.

[Ernest Blythe, Feb. 1953][1]

PARTITION BEYOND THE 'SORE THUMB' APPROACH

Most studies of Fianna Fáil's attitude towards Northern Ireland have ignored the 1950s.[2] These authors have instead interpreted events as a period of stagnancy between the disputes that characterised Fianna Fáil's anti-partition policy during the 1940s and Seán Lemass's progressive Northern Ireland policy in the 1960s. In fact, the 1950s saw alterations in Fianna Fáil's Northern Ireland policy, particularly in the field of cross-border co-operation. By the early 1950s the Fianna Fáil government sought to replace Dublin's traditional anti-partitionist stance towards Ulster Unionists with a new Northern Ireland policy of North–South co-operation. Although its impact was not immediate, as Michael Kennedy noted, looking at the longer term 'it could be argued that this was the beginning of a road to the Lemass-O'Neill meeting of 1965; in the short term it was evident that change was in the air'.[3]

This gradual 'change' of seeking to move Fianna Fáil away from sterile anti-partitionism to instead encourage cross-border co-operation was an important policy development on the partition issue. However, in reality, Fianna Fáil was incapable of implementing a new long-term Northern Ireland strategy. During the early to mid-1950s, apart from some moves to promote economic relations with Belfast, no substantial progress was made by de Valera and his cabinet colleagues towards the attainment of a united Ireland. Inhibited by its own ingrained reverence to the traditional nationalist anti-partionist orthodoxy and concerned by the renewed IRA activity, Fianna Fáil, all but ignored partition. Instead, the issue was submerged, away from the threat of public scrutiny.

Fianna Fáil's return to government in May 1951 witnessed the party's return to two central tenets of its traditional approach to Northern Ireland. In August 1951, a confidential memorandum was circulated to all heads of Irish diplomatic missions abroad asserting that in the context of the Korean War and the polarisation between Communist East and Capitalist West the Fianna Fáil government directed that the end of partition was to be secured by two processes. Firstly, that London should make a declaration in support of Irish unity; and secondly, that the best method to secure an end to partition was a federal agreement between Dublin and Belfast.[4]

The memorandum exposed the Fianna Fáil government's inability to formulate a realistic long-term Northern Ireland policy in the post-war period. Under de Valera's leadership the party failed to realise that with the introduction of the 1949 Ireland Act, the passing of the veto on Irish unity had effectively transferred from London to the custody of the Ulster Unionists. Within weeks of entering government de Valera's wish to secure a declaration in favour of Irish unity and his offer of a federal agreement was rejected by the British government. When either he or the new minister for external affairs, Frank Aiken, raised the issue of partition with London they were greeted by a wall of silence.[5] British politicians now disliked, 'having to touch it [partition]'.[6] There was reluctance in London to even meet de Valera, knowing that they would inevitably be greeted with 'the familiar text of partition'.[7]

The plight of Fianna Fáil was further exasperated following the arrival of a Conservative led government in October 1951. Irish Ambassador in London, Freddie Boland noted that the Conservative and Labour governments' attitudes to Irish unity were 'just the same in substance', with neither party wishing to 'touch partition'.[8] In February 1952, during a rare meeting between Aiken and the secretary of state for commonwealth relations, Lord Ismay, the latter informed an infuriated Aiken that partition could not be discussed by 'minnows like himself [Lord Ismay]'.[9] The subsequent year, in 1953, during a courtesy lunch in London between de Valera and British prime minister, Winston Churchill, partition was ignored. Churchill made it abundantly obvious to his 'old adversary' that Irish unity could only be secured by the consent of Ulster Unionists.[10]

London's unwillingness to maintain a debate on partition forced the Fianna Fáil government to initiate a new Northern Ireland policy, which sought to 'let the temperature drop', as noted by Seán Nunan of the Department of External Affairs.[11] De Valera grudgingly admitted that Fianna Fáil's previous policy of 'sterile anti-partitionism',[12] as recorded by Seán O'Faoláin, historian and author, had proved disastrous, further increasing the division between North and South. The 'sore thumb'[13] approach of continually stressing the injustice of partition, as espoused by Aiken's predecessor in the Department of External Affairs, Seán MacBride, was a tactic that Fianna Fáil believed had run its course. Henceforth, as Aiken outlined in October 1952, since becoming minister for external affairs, his 'policy' was directed towards letting 'the temperature drop to a point at which Partition could be ended on the basis of reason and goodwill'.[14]

Within Fianna Fáil, chiefly at cabinet level, there was a realisation that the party's previous anti-partition policy had proved ineffective. In 1952, minister for finance, Seán MacEntee, spoke of the necessity to follow a more realistic approach to Northern Ireland. 'We have to recognise', he said, 'that it is a problem which calls, not for wild and spectacular speeches, but for long and prudent statesmanship'. Unity can only be achieved, he remarked, by 'bonds of goodwill'.[15] Grass-roots members advised that the issue of partition should be left 'in the hands of Mr. de Valera'.[16] Adhering to the official party-line, which objected to the use of force, one Fianna Fáil grass-roots member remarked that 'the gun' would only lead to civil war. Irish nationalists would not be 'fighting against the British but against their fellow Irishmen in the North'.[17]

Privately, Aiken routinely admitted that the Fianna Fáil government could 'not expect any immediate spectacular results' on the partition issue.[18] In discussions with London, de Valera, likewise, confessed that 'no sensational progress could be made in the immediate future on partition'.[19] Indeed, speaking in Dáil Eireann in July 1951, he acknowledged that he could not 'promise' that partition would be solved 'within six months or two years or any specific time'.[20] A similar view was expressed by MacEntee[21] and Lemass.[22]

Given London's refusal to sustain a debate on Irish unity, Fianna Fáil's attention therefore turned towards Belfast and Ulster Unionists: this was to mark a significant shift in policy. As early as 1947, in the context of the changed political landscape of post-war Anglo-Irish relations, de Valera had recorded that a 'concurrence of wills' between London, Dublin and Belfast was required if partition was to be undone.[23] However, under de Valera, Fianna Fáil never offered any practical examples of how Dublin was to win support for Irish unity from Ulster Unionists. In the four years since 1947, Dublin's anti-partition campaign had further widened the divide between North and South. As the party of government, the Fianna Fáil leadership realised that it must try and bridge the gap that had developed between Dublin and Belfast over the previous several years.

Significantly, the Fianna Fáil hierarchy moved away from a policy of supposing that partition existed merely by the virtue of only the political, economic and military power of the British government. De Valera now recognised, reluctantly, that Fianna Fáil could no longer ignore the extent of the opposition to Irish unity by Ulster Unionists. Whether he liked it or not, politics was not an exact science and the hand of friendship was necessary if the Ulster Unionists were to be ever convinced that their future lay in a united Ireland. The advancement of cross-border economic co-operation between North and South was Fianna Fáil's desired new approach to Northern Ireland.

FROM OPPOSITION RHETORIC TO REALPOLITIK: FIANNA FÁIL AND NORTH–SOUTH CO-OPERATION

Dublin's sudden shift in emphasis from London to Belfast marked an important cornerstone of Fianna Fáil's approach to Northern Ireland in the early 1950s. Guided by a policy of 'persuasion', specifically on issues of cross-border economic co-operation, the party tried to reassure Ulster Unionists of the benefits of an economically and politically unified Ireland. Fianna Fáil targeted three areas of cross-border co-operation of particular importance, the Great Northern Railway (GNR), the Erne Hydro Electric Scheme and the Foyle Fisheries. While some historians contend that it was the Second Inter-Party government that first 'placed increasing emphasis on co-operation' as a central feature of its Northern Ireland policy, this is inaccurate.[24] In fact, it was the Fianna Fáil government of 1951 to 1954 that initially attempted to remodel Dublin's anti-partition approach to Northern Ireland to face the new politico-economic realities of the 1950s. This new initiative was led personally by de Valera and Aiken.

Under the previous Inter-Party government little effort in the sphere of cross-border co-operation, except for negotiations to save the GNR,[25] had been made to forge more cordial relations with Ulster Unionists, in the hope that they could eventually be enticed into a united Ireland. Instead, as recorded by Freddie Boland, the

Inter-Party government's approach to Northern Ireland of the 'mere venting of moral indignation was no policy for anyone who was really sincere in his desire to achieve a solution and bring partition to an end'.[26] Under the new Fianna Fáil government, Dublin followed a more pragmatic and persuasive policy towards Ulster Unionists. The 'whole aim of Fianna Fáil's approach', as recorded by Boland in discussions with Lord Pakenham in late 1951, was to 'bring about the political circumstances and the climate of opinion, which would make the ending of partition easier and more feasible'.[27] This was to be achieved, he explained, by 'direct dealings with Dublin and Belfast in connection with the Erne development, Foyle Fisheries and the Great Northern Railway'.[28] In May 1952, during a meeting with Pakenham, de Valera remarked that his Fianna Fáil government was 'taking every opportunity of developing a habit of collaboration between North and South, (e.g. the Great Northern Railway, the Erne H.E Scheme, the Foyle Fisheries)'.[29]

This approach was not entirely new. As early as 1933 the Fianna Fáil government had sanctioned the possibility that the Electricity Supply Board (ESB) might access, in the case of an emergency, a supply of electricity from Northern Ireland.[30] In 1936 the drainage of Lough Erne was discussed in Dublin by officials from the Office of Public Works, the Department of Fisheries and the Stormont Ministry for Finance.[31] Furthermore, with the threat of war, officials in the Department of External Affairs pressed de Valera for the need to 'get closer collaboration with the Six-County Government' in the areas of transport, food control and petrol storage.[32] During the war years North–South discussions also took place concerning the Erne hydroelectric scheme.[33]

The Fianna Fáil government's willingness to work side by side with Ulster Unionists on issues of mutual cross-border concern showed that behind the anti-partition bravado Dublin was eager to openly engage with the Northern Ireland government for the first time since the December 1925 London agreement, which was signed in the aftermath of the boundary commission fiasco. Nonetheless, de Valera's new policy of persuasion was fraught with numerous difficulties; not least due to the extent that it was greeted with scepticism from Ulster Unionists. Ernest Blythe's article, *Towards a Six-County Dominion?*, acidly appraised why Ulster Unionists viewed de Valera's latest policy towards Northern Ireland as a veiled attempt to secure Irish unity. Blythe, himself brought up in a unionist household in a 'strongly Orange area', believed that it would be virtually impossible to hope that the '... Protestant Unionists in the Six-Counties can ever be kicked into a Republic'.[34]

Commenting on the role of religion Blythe wrote that '... we must realise that the true basis of partition is religious bigotry, and the fears and suspicions which go with it, all adding to a fanatical resolve not to be put under a Catholic Parliament and government'.[35] Indeed, the debacle over the Mother and Child controversy,[36] which had only reinforced Ulster Unionists' beliefs that the Stormont Parliament would 'never place its neck under the feet of any ecclesiastical hierarchy', had further created a divide between Dublin and Belfast.[37] There was an almost childish naivety endemic within Fianna Fáil, centred on the belief that because the Dublin government offered Ulster Unionists economic concessions on cross-border co-operation, Belfast would simply agree to a united Ireland. The Fianna Fáil government, therefore, grudgingly conceded that the support of Ulster Unionists was required to secure an end to partition. Yet, this concession on behalf of Fianna Fáil was always half-hearted. Under de Valera the party was unable to acknowledge that Ulster Unionists held the veto on Irish unity and only with their consent could partition be ended.

Although Northern Ireland prime minister, Basil Brooke (raised to the peerage as Lord Brookeborough in 1952) was not entirely immune to the Fianna Fáil overtures for cross-border co-operation, he would not agree to formal North–South relations while Dublin refused to recognise the constitutional position of Northern Ireland. In June 1951 he spoke of a 'hands across the border' policy, citing recent advances in 'matters of common interest, such as transport, fisheries and drainage'.[38] His pronouncements were, however, always measured by a warning that cross-border co-operation, on a significant scale, could never occur before recognition was granted.[39] Northern Ireland minister for finance, Brian Maginess, repeated similar sentiments, reiterating that his government was not prepared to discuss partition and as a matter it had been 'finally determined'.[40] De Valera was equally stubborn. He publicly replied to Ulster Unionists' demands, by remarking that he would always favour co-operation with Belfast, but that Dublin would never acknowledge the constitutional status of Northern Ireland.[41]

Fianna Fáil's *rapprochement* towards Ulster Unionism was detested by a large cohort of Northern Ireland Catholics. Perhaps the greatest difficulty of inducing certain large sections of the Catholic community to accept and work a policy of persuasion arose from the fact that it would mean abandoning the idea of abolishing the Northern

Ireland parliament or a campaign to reduce its area of jurisdiction. Likewise, a policy of persuasion was psychologically difficult for the Catholics of Northern Ireland to adopt when they were suffering from discrimination and injustice at the hands of the Ulster Unionist government.

Within Fianna Fáil there was considerable unease at the organisation's new attempts to forge cordial relations with Belfast. At the 1952 Fianna Fáil Ard Fheis, which de Valera did not attend as he was in Utrecht, Netherlands, for an operation on his eyes, Lemass and other leading Fianna Fáil ministers received criticism due to their 'hobnobbing and fraternising with usurpers' from Northern Ireland.[42] In defence of the party's new North–South policy of co-operation, MacEntee remarked that 'Fianna Fáil must work with the North to advance any interest which is common'. Condemning those delegates present for criticising party policy, he pronounced that Irish nationalists 'must recognise that the economic progress and development of the North is as much in our interests as the economic development of the South'.[43] MacEntee's comments won the endorsement of his fellow cabinet members. Nonetheless, for the anti-partitionists within Fianna Fáil, such incidents of 'hobnobbing' provided further evidence that the party hierarchy had turned its back on finding a permanent solution to partition.

At the party Ard Fheiseanna in 1951, 1952 and 1953 grass-roots supporters issued several resolutions demanding that the government 'take all practical steps to bring partition to an end'.[44] De Valera and his ministers were accused of 'taking the matter for granted'.[45] At the 1951 Ard Fheis, for example, a vocal minority of delegates even issued a resolution requesting the party use force to secure Irish unity.[46] In June 1951, a disgruntled Irish nationalist from Co. Cavan, Eric D. O'Gowan, wrote to Nationalist MP for South-Fermanagh, Cahir Healy expressing his contempt for Fianna Fáil's attitude to partition. 'Fianna Fáil', he said, 'pay lip service to the reunification ideal ... I don't believe Dublin wants to see an end to partition'.[47]

In 1953, de Valera received several letters from grass-root Fianna Fáil supporters calling for the government to take a more 'active' approach to partition.[48] Later that year in December, Patrick McSorley from Strabane, Co. Tyrone wrote to de Valera pleading that he tackle partition: 'You saved us from conscription and from military service', he said, 'now please do something to save us from partition'.[49] Although isolated incidents, the unrest at grass-roots by a minority of the party faithful, was a vivid reminder to de Valera of the need to retain a firm hold of the party's Northern Ireland strategy.

Upon entering government in May 1951 the Fianna Fáil hierarchy did not wish to debate Northern Ireland policy. At party level the issue was politely ignored. At meetings of the Fianna Fáil parliamentary party and National Executive partition was rarely discussed; except on sporadic occasions when the issue of permitting Northern Nationalists access to the Dáil was raised.[50] In October 1951, at an event in the Capitol Theatre, Dublin, to mark Fianna Fáil's Silver Jubilee, partition was given only a minor footnote; instead the party hierarchy focused on the economy.[51] The following year, at the Fianna Fáil Ard Fheis in November 1952, partition was once again merely given minor consideration by the party leadership.[52] This theme continued at the 1953 party Ard Fheis. Addressing delegates during his Presidential speech de Valera failed to mention partition. In its place he reminded rank-and-file members of the importance of agriculture, industry, emigration and foreign trade.[53]

At government level partition was also ignored. From November 1951 to February 1953 Fianna Fáil deputies did not raise partition in Dáil Éireann,[54] while from September 1951 to November 1955, the All Party Anti-Partition Committee met on only three occasions.[55] In correspondence with Cahir Healy in 1953 Seán MacBride wrote that 'partition here [is] in the doldrums. Neither de Valera nor Aiken even mention [it] introducing their estimates – which is the usual occasion for a declaration of policy in regard to it'. McBride lamented: 'we had only one meeting of the Mansion House Committee [All-Party Anti-Partition Committee] in the last twelve months, and were are told by de Valera that it was proposed   AQ3 to wind it up soon'.[56]

The Fianna Fáil leadership's determination to censor a debate on the issue of Northern Ireland was logical at a time when the government was attempting to encourage cross-border co-operation with Belfast. Fianna Fáil sought to follow a more cautious approach towards its Northern Ireland strategy and not to permit the anti-partitionists within the party a platform to voice their objections to Dublin's overtures to Belfast. The division between the Fianna Fáil leadership and the anti-partitionists is a further explanation for why the party was unable to formulate a long-term Northern Ireland policy. The Fianna Fáil hierarchy always had to look over its shoulder, afraid that to make too many concessions to Ulster Unionists would create a divide within the party.

FIANNA FÁIL, THE ANTI-PARTITION OF IRELAND LEAGUE OF GREAT BRITAIN AND NORTHERN NATIONALISTS

Fianna Fáil's reluctance to maintain an internal debate on partition was equally matched by the party's determination not to permit external anti-partition movements a voice on Dublin's Northern Ireland policy. Within weeks of returning to government in May 1951 de Valera ordered that Dublin would no longer financially support the Anti-Partition of Ireland League of Great Britain. This was not a completely new policy. Although it was Fianna Fáil that had first established the League in 1938, in the post-war government from 1945 to 1948, de Valera categorically refused to any longer officially endorse or offer financial assistance to the League.[57] Indeed, in 1948, he informed the League that the Irish government and not external anti-partition organisations, held control over 'national policy'.[58]

Moreover, as a member of the All-Party Anti-Partition Committee, during the height of the Dublin sponsored anti-partition campaign from 1948 to 1949, de Valera's support of the League was always tinted with a sense of indifference. His reluctance stemmed from his belief that Northern Ireland policy was a matter solely for the Irish government. External anti-partition movements would be consulted if needed, but otherwise they should know their place.

In May 1951 Alf Havekin, honorary secretary of the League in Manchester, wrote on separate occasions to de Valera and Aiken, respectively, for an appeal for funds for the Anti-Partition of Ireland League of Great Britain.[59] The following year, in July 1952, Havekin once again wrote to Aiken warning that the League was on brink of financial ruin. 'After the payment of salaries to the organisation secretary and typist', he said, 'the total resources in the hands of the trustees and hon. treasurer are in the region of £40'.[60] The problems were further compounded due to the impending resignation of Tadhg Feehan, organiser and secretary of the League, who according to Freddie Boland was the backbone of the organisation.[61]

The previous year, in mid-June 1951, Boland warned Seán Nunan of the current difficulties faced by the anti-partition movements in Britain and Northern Ireland:

> I am afraid that the drying up of funds of the All Party Committee is going to put the Anti-Partition Organisations in this country and the Six-Counties in a bit of a fix to know how they are going to carry on their work … In the

> course of lunch Seán Nally [secretary of the Anti-Partition of
> Ireland League in Northern Ireland] told me funds of their
> organisation are down to two or three hundred pounds ...
> something has to be done or we will have to sack the secretary,
> typist and generally speaking let the whole organisation go
> overboard ... as I am sure will be obvious to you in any case –
> the collapse of the Anti-Partition Organisation, either here or
> elsewhere, owing to a lack of funds, would confront us with a
> very difficult situation and would, no doubt, be followed by a
> vociferous chorus of that unreasonable criticism which we so
> often hear from the Irish abroad that the Irish Government is
> 'failing to give a lead' in the Anti-Partition campaign.[62]

The letter was a severe warning that the entire anti-partition
campaign in Britain and Northern Ireland was in serious financial
trouble. Freddie Boland believed that the League throughout
Britain, which by 1951 had about 3,500 members, organised into
roughly 130 branches, faced 'a difficult task as the British press pays
very scant attention'.[63] The League had produced over 120,000
anti-partition pamphlets to be circulated throughout Britain, yet
it was unclear whether there was much support for the current
campaign.[64]

Following a further request from the League for financial assistance
in January 1952 Aiken travelled to Britain. With the assistance of
Boland, he scheduled a gathering of prominent Irish professionals
and businessmen in London to raise funds for the League. Although
Boland described the event as 'very satisfactory', the opposite,
in fact, was the truth. Only 37 people, half of the invited guests,
actually attended. In all, £293.1.0 was raised through subscriptions.
However, of the sum of the monies gathered, £73.14.1, was spent on
'expenses'.[65]

The event compounded Aiken's belief that for all good intentions
the League was beginning to run out of steam. Thereafter, he decided
that the Irish government would no longer financially subsidise the
League's activities.[66] Alf Havekin was incensed by Aiken's decision.
In correspondence with Tadhg Feehan, Havekin lamented that such
actions could spell the end of the organisation.[67] Freddie Boland
privately commented that it was 'better to make a concentrated effort
in the London area' as there was little enthusiasm in the remainder of
Britain for the League's anti-partition campaign.[68] Following a visit
to London, Patrick J. Little, Fianna Fáil TD for Waterford, reported

to Dublin that the current position of the anti-partition organisation was 'weak, very weak in numbers and effective personnel'. The main difficulty, he explained, was the 'ignorance of the issue [partition]' and the movement's less than adequate efforts to exclude undesirables including 'Communists', from the organisation.[69]

The Northern Nationalists' anti-partition campaign was likewise in danger of petering out. By 1951 the League was on the verge of falling apart. It had no consistent policy and no way of enforcing it. Its MPs decided their own policies without reference to the organisation. It had one MP attending and one abstaining at Westminster and two MPs abstaining and seven attending intermittently at Stormont.[70] Although as a member of the All-Party Anti-Partition Committee de Valera had allocated finances for Northern Nationalists to contest the 1950 British general election and permitted Fianna Fáil members to speak at various anti-partition rallies in Northern Ireland,[71] upon de Valera's return to government, relations soon deteriorated between Dublin and Northern Nationalists.

In June 1952, the secretary of the Irish Anti-Partition League, Seán McNally, wrote to Aiken requesting financial assistance from Dublin from the coffers of the All Party Anti-Partition Committee funds. McNally warned that 'the matter has become more critical ... it would be rather disastrous we think in the interest of unity if we were unable to maintain the office that we have'.[72] Although there is no available record that de Valera officially rejected McNally's request, it is apparent that by late 1951 the Fianna Fáil government had decided to no longer financially support the League. In September 1951, Seamus McCall,[73] Dublin's 'eyes and ears' in Northern Ireland, presented a confidential memorandum to Aiken that offered a critical assessment of the Anti-Partition League in Northern Ireland. McCall noted that the financial assistance provided by the All Party Anti-Partition Committee, a reported total of £4,000, to Northern Nationalist candidates during the previous British general election campaign held in February 1950, had been 'too generous'. He remarked that the end result was that 'it encouraged far too much "hospitality", degraded election workers into demanding Rolls Royces (more or less) for jobs, which, in the old days, willing lads would have done on bicycles'.[74] He even alluded to the possible misuse of funds by some Northern Nationalists: 'I can't for the life of me see what it was reasonably spent on in South Tyrone and Fermanagh, or that it affected the result to any appreciable degree either there or in Mid-Ulster'.[75]

This was de Valera's excuse to cease support for the Anti-Partition League in Northern Ireland. He had become increasingly sceptical of external anti-partition movements in Great Britain and Northern Ireland. Following the disastrous 1948/1949 anti-partition campaign, Fianna Fáil wished to distance itself from the use of stale anti-partition propaganda. This was a natural consequence following de Valera's new policy of nurturing cross-border co-operation between Dublin and Belfast. In particular, he believed that the All-Party Anti-Partition Committee's financial support of Northern Nationalist anti-partitionist candidates in the 1949 Northern Ireland general election had proved a political failure, as the Ulster Unionist Party secured one of its greatest victories in its history. Indeed, the disastrous showing by Northern Nationalists demonstrated that the monies offered by Dublin had been wasted.

Most revealingly, although by 1951 the All Party Anti-Partition Committee held approximately £75,000 in the bank, de Valera would not permit the funds to be allocated to anti-partition movements.[76] Speaking in Sheffield in February 1952, parliamentary secretary to the minister for lands, Jack Lynch, asserted that anti-partition movements in Britain and Northern Ireland must be 'completely self-sufficient'. 'What was required for success', Lynch noted, was not financial support from Dublin, but 'the spirits of patriotism, self-reliance, [and] self-sacrifice'.[77] From this moment onwards Dublin's Northern Ireland policy was to be dictated exclusively by the Irish government. For Fianna Fáil there was a palpable realisation that to support external anti-partition movements was to sabotage the party's new policy of encouraging economic relations between North and South.

NORTHERN IRELAND AND THE 'DOMINION STATUS' DEBATE

By October 1952, as de Valera turned seventy years old, his bleak feeling on the prospect of Irish unity remained. Given Britain's reluctance to undertake a debate on partition and Ulster Unionists' lukewarm response to Fianna Fáil's offer of cross-border co-operation, he was anxious to again kite fly his offer of a federal proposal to end partition. Speaking to the German News Agency on the day of his seventieth birthday, he maintained that the powers which the British Parliament retained over Northern Ireland 'should be transferred to an All-Ireland Parliament'. If this was done, he said, the Northern Ireland Parliament 'could continue to function with its existing power as a local parliament'.[78]

His return to a proposal that Ulster Unionists' vehemently opposed revealed his inability to find a solution to partition. His anxiety was further increased because of growing apprehensions from the Dublin government that Westminster was considering granting Northern Ireland Dominion status. If accorded, Northern Ireland would abandon the system of a 'home rule' devolved government imposed under the 1920 Government of Ireland Act and instead secure internal self-rule. Dominion status would therefore permit Northern Ireland politicians to make most decisions without reference to Westminster. De Valera believed that the granting of Dominion status to Northern Ireland could 'perpetuate partition'.[79] If granted Ulster Unionists, similar to the Fianna Fáil governments of the 1930s, might use their Dominion status as an instrument to confirm Belfast's independence. Such a move would naturally have long-lasting consequences for partition as Northern Ireland's permanency would be copper-fastened.

Ernest Blythe had previously noted that because of Dublin's 1948/49 anti-partition campaign, which had created substantial embarrassment for the British government, the next British counter-move would be to give Dominion status to Northern Ireland. He envisaged that Northern Ireland would possibly be renamed 'Ulster', as desired by Stormont, and that the new dominion would be encouraged to join NATO.[80] The Ulster Unionist Party had previously considered the possibility. Northern Ireland prime minister, James Craig toyed with the idea in the inter-war years and the debate was enlivened after 1945, when the pressure of conforming to Clement Attlee's socialist Labour government created strains within unionism.[81]

Henry Patterson remarked that because of the pro-Keynesian policies of both the Labour and Conservative governments in the post-war period, which accepted a large amount of government planning and direction, Ulster Unionists had become anxious about their constitutional position. Their anxiety stemmed from the fact that Northern Ireland did not fit the Keynesian model of a largely urban and industrialised society. Northern Ireland instead contained a small-scale agricultural sector and was a medium-sized business region.[82] Moreover, some within the Ulster Unionist Party felt that rather than benefiting from the post-war welfare settlement, Northern Ireland was, in fact, being over-taxed to support a large range of benefits that its citizens would not receive.[83]

Therefore, there was a belief by some in London that the only way to avoid a major constitutional crisis was to possibly negotiate a much larger degree of independence for Northern Ireland in the form of the

Dominion status enjoyed by Australia and Canada.[84] Brookeborough, however, had no intention of seeking Dominion status, particularly as he did not want to lose the major financial benefits that flowed to the Northern Ireland Exchequer through a series of agreements negotiated with the Treasury in London since 1946.[85]

Nevertheless, throughout 1950 and 1951 de Valera was gravely concerned about the consequences for partition if Northern Ireland was granted Dominion status. In September 1951, during a meeting with Northern Ireland Labour Party MP for Belfast Central, Frank Hanna, he enquired whether the granting of Dominion status 'would be desirable or undesirable from the point of view of ending partition'.[86] Hanna noted that the development of social legislation under a Labour government in Britain, involving similar developments in Northern Ireland, was disliked by the leading Ulster Unionists. If Labour forced its 'more leftist tendencies' upon Stormont, Hanna said, then Ulster Unionists might very well push for Dominion status. He believed that such a division would be welcomed by Dublin as it would create a degree of separation between London and Belfast.[87]

Indeed, Geoffrey Bing, a radical Labour MP, who had been born in Northern Ireland and was sympathetic to the plight of the Northern Ireland Catholics, remarked to Freddie Boland, that 'Dominion status would inevitably lend to the ending of partition'.[88] 'The present arrangement', Bing said, 'gave the people in Belfast the best of both worlds – they remained an integral part of the United Kingdom and yet enjoyed effective control of all aspects of their internal affairs which really mattered to them'.[89]

The 'Dominion debate' revealed the inability of the Fianna Fáil government to make any inroads towards ending partition. Dublin found itself increasingly marginalised by a confident Ulster Unionist government that was eager to express its autonomy. Although Belfast's overtures towards securing Dominion status had faded by the mid-1950s, Ulster Unionists had demonstrated that they now held the ace card on partition. The passing of the Ireland Act in 1949, together with the possible threat of securing Dominion status, was a harsh reminder to de Valera that – whether he liked it or not – Ulster Unionists held the veto over Irish unity. Although Dublin might habitually complain to London about the maintenance of partition, this was, however, a waste of time. Belfast would now have to become Dublin's main priority.

Ulster Unionists believed de Valera's latest attempt to encourage North–South co-operation was merely a veiled plot aimed at securing some concessions on partition. Their scepticism was warranted. Behind the façade of seeking to encourage cross-border co-operation with the Stormont government and ending its anti-partition propaganda campaign, the Fianna Fáil government's Northern Ireland policy had changed little in a generation. De Valera still maintained the British government, irrespective of the passing of the Ireland Act, had a moral obligation to make a declaration in support of Irish unity; that a federal agreement constituted a workable solution to partition; that Ulster Unionists had no right to vote themselves out of a united Ireland; and lastly, that Fianna Fáil would not recognise the constitutional position of Northern Ireland.

In reality, no effort was made by the Fianna Fáil leadership to revise and implement a long-term Northern Ireland policy. Senior Fianna Fáil members were instead content to concede that they could not 'promise' when partition would be solved.[90] They were happy to ignore partition, to submerge the issue and keep it away from public scrutiny. The outbreak of IRA activity in Northern Ireland in the summer of 1954, however, reawakened the partition debate within the Fianna Fáil organisation. As is analysed below, the renewed IRA campaign exposed a major fault-line between the Fianna Fáil leadership, its elected representatives and grass-roots supporters on the issue of partition and in particular, the use of physical force to secure Irish unity.

THE IRA, PARTITION AND NORTHERN IRELAND: THE FIANNA FÁIL HIERARCHY VS. GRASS-ROOTS

Fianna Fáil's defeat at the 1954 general election came as a bitter disappointment, with the party returning to the opposition benches for the second time in over three years. In May of that year, a Fine Gael led coalition, with John A. Costello as taoiseach, assumed control of the government. The Fianna Fáil hierarchy's willingness to support the new Inter-Party government's crushing of the IRA epitomised, for a small, but vocal, cohort of party members, that the 'Republican Party' had abandoned its primary objective of attaining a united Ireland. Many Fianna Fáil members, particularly the younger generation, were extremely frustrated and fed up with the party's perceived inability to make any inroads towards the undoing of partition.

Since the Second World War the IRA had been dormant. In 1954 it commenced a series of raids against army barracks in Northern Ireland and Britain, in order to stockpile weapons for a forthcoming campaign.

In June 1954 IRA volunteers raided Gough Barracks in Co. Armagh and made off with a large quantity of weapons.[91] A further raid occurred in October when a detachment carried out a raid on Omagh Military Barracks. The raids and other republican activities caused legitimate worries for the Fianna Fáil leadership that some supporters might desert the party and join ranks with the IRA. As noted by Barry Flynn the renewed IRA activity, which received widespread publicity, made it considerably easier for the IRA to recruit young men who had become 'enamoured by the romanticism of the republican cause'.[92]

On 28 October 1954, in a show of rare cross-party support between Fianna Fáil and Fine Gael, de Valera and Costello delivered passionate speeches in the Dáil that reaffirmed the Irish government's objection to the use of force to secure an end to partition.[93] Their speeches, to the consternation of some within Fianna Fáil, confirmed the *modus vivendi* that both parties had reached on the issue of physical force and the IRA, together with Dublin's bipartisan attitude towards Northern Ireland.[94]

De Valera's perceived alignment with Fine Gael on the issue of Northern Ireland was seized upon by the party's 'Republican' rivals, Sinn Féin and Clann na Poblachta. The president of Sinn Féin, Tomás MacGiolla, opportunistically remarked that de Valera and Costello had 'thrown off their masks and re-echoed the words of [Daniel] O'Connell, that Ireland was not worth the shedding of a drop of blood. But the drop of blood had been shed at Omagh'.[95] MacGiolla criticised the pacifist policies of the Fianna Fáil and Fine Gael parties, asserting that the Irish people were entitled to resist aggression by any means in their power.[96] Extravagant promises were made by Sinn Féin activists that the party would tackle the job of ending the border with 'guns in their hands and within three years would make the Six-Counties so hot that England would not be able to hold them'.[97]

In November 1954 Sinn Féin published a pamphlet attacking Fianna Fáil's Northern Ireland policy. Disturbingly the pamphlet attempted to convince members of Fianna Fáil that the time had now come: 'when you must act – Get rid of your leaders or Get out of Fianna Fáil'.[98] Specifically, the pamphlet singled out Lionel Booth for personal attention, criticising his demands that 'extraditions and penal measures' be taken against IRA members.[99] Booth, a Fianna Fáil councillor for Dún Laoghaire-Rathdown, Protestant and respected businessman, had grown increasingly irritated at Irish citizens' sympathy for the IRA and his party's inability to formulate a coherent

Northern Ireland policy.[100] A 'decent and helpful' politician,[101] he had pleaded with Fianna Fáil rank-and-file members that they should want 'unity and not simply the abolition of the border'.[102]

During October and November 1954, Booth had written several articles for *The Irish Times* in which he expressed the futility of violence to end partition. In particular, he concentrated a large part of his writing on denouncing the actions of the IRA, describing the movement as 'irresponsible'.[103] His articles had also been critical of the Inter-Party government's approach to the sensitive issue of political offenders who escaped across the border from Northern Ireland into the Republic. He wrote that the offenders had been 'treated simply as rather naughty, but forgivable, impulsive children'.[104]

Booth was a 'man ploughing a lonely furrow';[105] a minority voice within Fianna Fáil who was willing to publicly expose Irish nationalists' inability to deal with partition on a rational basis. He felt compelled to condemn those Fianna Fáil supporters who would 'deliver the usual nonsense about partition'.[106] He had courageously entered politics on the premise that he could give a voice to the Protestant minority within the Republic. For too long, he felt, the Protestant community had been reluctant to participate in Southern political life and instead remain on the periphery. This, he argued, had merely widened the gap between the two religious communities. Privately, Booth confessed that his willingness to criticise his fellow Fianna Fáil members would inevitably leave him alienated within the organisation. Nevertheless, he felt that this was a small price to pay if he was able to arouse a debate within party circles on partition.[107]

Leader of Clann na Poblachta, Seán MacBride had also jumped on the anti-Fianna Fáil bandwagon. In early February 1955, speaking at a University College Dublin (UCD) Literary and Debating Society's symposium, he opportunistically remarked that 'a process of rapid disintegration had been taking place in the Fianna Fáil Party'.[108] He noted that de Valera's 'alliance' with Fine Gael in the Dáil had 'alienated all Republican support from Fianna Fáil'.[109] Clann na Poblachta's monthly bulletin, *Clann*, denounced Fianna Fáil's 'retrogression' on the national issue. It pronounced that the party had made a 'spectacular alliance' with Fine Gael on the 'basis of doing nothing about partition'.[110]

Clann na Poblachta accused the 'new' Fine Gael-Fianna Fáil alliance 'as helping to maintain the *status quo*'. 'In effect', *Clann* argued, 'they told the people of the Six-Counties: Go home, take an Oath of Allegiance to the British Crown and accept partition'.[111]

The bulletin enclosed Booth's recently published articles in *The Irish Times* and reminded party activists 'don't forget it ... please give it or send it to some member of Fianna Fáil in your area. They should be given an opportunity of knowing the policy of their leaders'.[112]

Of even greater concern for the Fianna Fáil hierarchy than those offered by Sinn Féin and Clann na Poblachta were the increased rumblings from Fianna Fáil grass-roots. The Dublin region was worst affected. Discussions on partition occurred at Fianna Fáil cumann meetings throughout Dublin.[113] On 2 November, the same day that one of Booth's articles appeared in *The Irish Times*, Seán Brady, veteran Fianna Fáil TD in the same constituency as Booth, Dún Laoghaire-Rathdown, wrote to Lemass. He informed Lemass that many members of Booth's constituency believed his recent public pronouncements in the national press were 'detrimental to the interests of Fianna Fáil'.[114] The letter warned that Booth had shown that he did 'not possess those republican qualities which are characteristic of the Fianna Fáil organisation'.[115]

Brady was a prominent Fianna Fáil figure within Dún Laoghaire-Rathdown. He had been a member of Dáil Éireann since 1927 and as David Andrews recalled had such a degree of influence over his constituents that they 'never questioned' his decisions.[116] Brady's protests forced Lemass to intervene on Booth's behalf. Writing to Brady, he noted that Booth's opinions had been misrepresented. Lemass, attempting to act as a mediator, said he would ask Booth to write another article to the press to remove 'a great deal of misunderstanding'.[117] The available evidence confirms that Lemass did not write to Booth requesting that his colleague clarify his original comments.[118] This was not to be the last occasion that Lemass was compelled to intervene on Booth's behalf. As is discussed in the following chapter, in January 1957, Booth again caused outrage among a minority of his constituency by speaking out against Fianna Fáil members who offered support to the IRA.

The unrest among Fianna Fáil grass-roots members of Dún Laoghaire-Rathdown became so serious that in early April 1955 de Valera summoned a meeting of the Dún Laoghaire-Rathdown Comhairle Dáilcheantair. At the meeting he reminded those present that Booth's public announcements were fully in accordance with the party's approach to current IRA activity. In typical de Valera fashion he managed to make all present give 'their word that they would take immediate steps to end the prevailing contention regarding certain actions of the Councillor Booth [sic]'.[119] In private de Valera warned Booth that, although he agreed with his colleague's public pronouncements concerning the IRA, more caution would need to be taken so as to appease those anti-partitionist elements within Dún Laoghaire-Rathdown.[120]

It was not only the Dublin region where Fianna Fáil grass-roots expressed their distaste of the party's stance against the IRA. In early 1955, Lemass received further letters from despondent grass-roots members in Co. Wexford, some of whom demanded, considering Fianna Fáil's 'republican outlook', that the party use 'every opportunity as forcibly as possible' as a means of solving partition.[121] In March 1955 a worried party supporter from Co. Waterford informed Lemass that at a recent debate on partition at a local meeting of a Law and History symposium at Carrick-on-Suir, Co. Tipperary, a large number of young people, between the ages of 18 to 25, had made insults towards de Valera because of Fianna Fáil's failure to end partition.[122] Moreover, the British Embassy in Dublin reported that de Valera had refused to attend an undergraduate debating society meeting at UCD. De Valera's refusal, the report noted, was because he did not want to debate 'the arguments for and against the use of force to find a solution to the Irish problem'.[123] The British Embassy recorded that de Valera's non-attendance was greeted with 'boos from the gathering', with chants of de Valera 'the Hangman'.[124]

Some within Fianna Fáil were clearly reluctant to condemn the latest IRA activity. There was an almost sneaking respect for this new young generation of 'Volunteers' who were willing to use physical force to secure Irish unity. If not openly supportive of the IRA, many Fianna Fáil members were sympathetic to their cause. The Irish Ambassador in London, Freddie Boland, privately conceded that the Irish government found it difficult to deal with public opinion in the Republic towards the IRA. Boland explained that although the majority condemned the IRA, they were not 'wholly unsympathetic'.[125]

The British Embassy in Dublin offered an insight towards the Southern politicians' inherent sympathy for the renewed IRA campaign. The British Ambassador to Ireland from 1955 to 1959, Alexander Clutterbuck noted that it was generally conceded by politicians in Dáil Éireann that 'the new IRA men though misguided are not mere ruffians and scallywags; they are for the most part young idealists with genuinely patriotic aims'. Clutterbuck explained that Irish politicians contribute 'by complaining and agitating incessantly about partition while seeming to be quite without any firm and sympathetic policy towards its ending'.[126] In reference to the inherent sympathy for the IRA Clutterbuck noted that

> this may be particularly true in a country intensely interested in politics, full of emotional nationalism, isolated from the broader problems of the world, and brought up to revere a tradition of secret, violent revolutionaries: in such conditions there will be much latent support for them, while opposition will be half-hearted, or suppressed for fear of political or even physical danger.[127]

As is discussed in the following chapter, by early 1957, as the IRA border-campaign (1956–1962) intensified, a vocal minority of 'emotional' Fianna Fáil members and indeed its elected representatives, not merely offered sympathy for the IRA, but openly supported the activities of this 'secret and violent' illegal movement.

A LOST OPPORTUNITY: THE NATIONAL EXECUTIVE STANDING-COMMITTEE ON PARTITION MATTERS

The widespread criticism levelled at the Fianna Fáil hierarchy by the anti-partitionists within the organisation was the catalyst for a radical departure in relation to the party's Northern Ireland policy. On the evening of 8 November 1954, for the first occasion in over three years, the Fianna Fáil National Executive convened to discuss the party's approach towards Northern Ireland.[128] De Valera chaired the meeting and deputies discussed the resolution on partition, successfully issued on behalf of the Donegal Comhairle Dailcheantair, at the Fianna Fáil Ard Fheis the previous October 1954. The resolution had requested that the party's 'National Executive take the steps to ensure that the strength of Fianna Fáil was used more effectively in the effort to end partition'.[129] This resolution had not originally contained a reference to the National Executive.

In fact, in early September 1954, Lemass contacted Fianna Fáil TD for Donegal-West, Joe Brennan, to inform his colleague that the resolution submitted by Brennan's Comhairle Dáilcheantair had been placed on the Clár as the number one resolution on partition.[130] The resolution was restrained and had called for the party to secure the unity of Ireland by peaceful means.[131] Lemass, however, intentionally altered the resolution and inserted a reference to the party's National

Executive. Although subtle on the exterior, Lemass's intervention was hugely significant. This was a premeditated manoeuvre by Lemass to secure that the Fianna Fáil hierarchy would retain sole responsibility for the party's development of Northern Ireland policy.

During the National Executive meeting on 8 November, following Lemass's suggestion, it was agreed that de Valera would nominate a committee of five to 'deal with all aspects of the matter [partition]'.[132] The committee was to become known as the 'standing-committee on partition matters'.[133] The establishment of the committee so quickly after the Ard Fheis was no coincidence, but had been hastily arranged by Lemass in an attempt to quell simmering discontent within Fianna Fáil because of the lack of progress on partition. In the context of the party hierarchy's hard-line stance against the IRA, at the October 1954 Ard Fheis, a vocal anti-partitionist wing within the party expressed anger at the lack of progress towards the undoing of partition.[134]

This growing frustration finally came to the boil as a direct consequence of de Valera's Presidential address at the party Ard Fheis on the night of 23 October 1954. During his speech he appealed to delegates to reject any resolution that would 'encourage young people to resort to arms'. He reminded those in attendance at the party conference that physical force could not secure Irish unity.[135] To the amazement of some of those present he admitted that he did not think it 'is possible to point out steps' that would 'inevitably lead to the end of partition'.[136] He went as far as to inform delegates that 'I have to admit that our efforts to make for a solution of that sort have come to nought'.[137] His speech, as reported by *The Irish Times*, did not have the support of a number of 'wild-men' within Fianna Fáil.[138]

De Valera's comments infuriated a cohort of anti-partitionists within the Fianna Fáil parliamentary party. On 27 October, de Valera was forced to arrange a day-long meeting of the parliamentary party to discuss Northern Ireland policy.[139] The meeting began at 11.00am and did not end until late into the night; this was the first occasion in four years that Northern Ireland was deliberated at a meeting of the parliamentary party.[140] At the gathering, heated exchanges occurred among deputies over the recent IRA attacks and Fianna Fáil's general attitude towards partition. De Valera came under strong pressure from his fellow deputies to re-examine Fianna Fáil's stance on partition and it was agreed that a special meeting of the party, scheduled for 18 November, would be arranged to 'consider the whole question of partition'.[141]

It is within this context that Lemass instigated the establishment of the new Fianna Fáil National Executive standing-committee on partition matters. The formation of the committee, only ten days before the scheduled 'special meeting' of the Fianna Fáil parliamentary party on 18 November, was no coincidence. Instead it was an orchestrated manoeuvre by the party hierarchy to demonstrate to disgruntled party deputies that an asserted effort was being made to tackle partition.[142]

Lemass's chairmanship of the committee was a defining moment in the evolution of Fianna Fáil's approach to Northern Ireland. Over the previous two decades he had remained relatively silent on partition and had rarely become involved with internal policy formation; this was not surprising considering de Valera's personal control over the issue. By the beginning of the 1950s Lemass's attitude seemed to alter considerably. It was no coincidence that this sudden shift coincided with Lemass's *de facto* control of Fianna Fáil. From a practical standpoint Lemass was running the show and de Valera increasingly permitted his lieutenant to assume responsibility for the organisation. With de Valera's old age and blindness his capacity to rule had began to wane and Lemass progressively emerged as the real power behind the throne.[143] Indeed, in May 1957, two years before de Valera's retirement as Fianna Fáil president, he stood down as chairman of the parliamentary party and appointed Lemass as his successor.[144]

Following Fianna Fáil's return to opposition in 1954 Lemass was given the job as national organiser.[145] He embraced his new position like a man half his age. He was a combination of 'organiser, strategist, and a one-man research bureau'.[146] He believed that Fianna Fáil were the architects and custodians of national policy and was determined that the party would retain the mantle of a 'national movement' rather than a political machine.[147] Without the constraints of ministerial duties to contend with he was freer to devote his time and labour to the formulating and developing of policy. He helped establish new committees to examine economic matters, emigration patterns and social issues. Significantly, his most radical policy initiative was on Northern Ireland.

In late January 1955, Cork-man Thomas Mullins, the 'third-grandfather'[148] of Fianna Fáil and general secretary of the organisation, sent letters to Lemass, Frank Aiken, Seán Moylan, Seán MacEntee, Kevin Boland, Liam Cunningham, Charles J. Haughey and Lieut. Colonel Matthew Feehan. The letters notified the eight men that on de Valera's instructions each had been appointed to a new standing-committee on partition matters.[149] The members were a mixture between the old brigade of Fianna Fáil and a new breed of the party's members, commonly referred to in political circles as 'mohair-suited Young Turks'.

Lemass was appointed chairman, while the presence of Aiken, MacEntee and Cork North TD, Moylan was predictable. The three men had (except for de Valera and Lemass) held the most influential portfolios in previous Fianna Fáil governments. Liam Cunningham's appointment had more to do with geography than anything else. He was a border-county Fianna Fáil deputy for Inishowen, Donegal North-East; an essential factor if the committee was to have credibility among party deputies. Subsequently described by the British Embassy in Dublin, as holding extremely strong views on partition,[150] in December 1954, Cunningham wrote to Fianna Fáil headquarters to request that the organisation make a greater effort to end partition.[151]

The presence of Boland, Haughey and Feehan on the committee was further example of Lemass's determination to bring some 'new blood' into Fianna Fáil. Earlier in 1954 the three men had been appointed by Lemass to the party's organisation committee and had travelled throughout the Republic with the task of pruning the organisation of any dead wood and listening to what policy areas truly mattered to grass-roots members.[152] Their appointment, however, did not survive the suspicions of some of the party's senior members. Kevin Boland's father Gerald Boland subsequently wrote that Lemass's motives were based on a more 'sinister agenda to undermine the older members of the government'. Boland bemoaned that Lemass had consciously collected a team of young men, 'who could be easily controlled'.[153]

Between September 1954 and January 1955, in his role as Fianna Fáil national organiser, Lemass contacted the honorary secretary of every registered cumann in the country and had asked each cumann to submit any views that its members had on either local or national issues.[154] In this context, at least two memoranda on partition were sent to Fianna Fáil headquarters. On 15 January 1955, honorary secretary of the Tomas Ó Cléirigh cumann Dublin North-East, Charles J. Haughey sent a memorandum to party headquarters.[155] On 20 January 1955, Matthew Feehan sent a second memorandum.[156] Before the inaugural meeting of the standing committee on partition-matters Lemass ordered that each member receive a copy of both the Ó Cléirigh and Feehan memoranda.[157] The memoranda, examined below, demonstrate the divergence of opinion within Fianna Fáil on what constituted official Northern Ireland policy.

PARTITION MEMORANDA ISSUED BY THE TOMAS Ó CLÉIRIGH
CUMANN, DUBLIN NORTH-EAST AND BY MATTHEW FEEHAN

The Tomas Ó Cléirigh cumann memorandum, six pages in length, was
an aggressive and provocative policy document – if it had been made
public, its contents could have proved explosive. Besides Haughey,
the Ó Cléirigh cumann contained a number of influential Fianna Fáil
members. Party Senator, Cork-man Seán O'Donovan, was chairman
of the cumann;[158] George Colley, a future deputy leader of the party;
his father Harry Colley, TD for Dublin North-East; Oscar Traynor,
also a TD for Dublin North-East; and Harry Boland, brother of Kevin
Boland and son to Gerald Boland.[159]

It was Haughey's involvement with the Ó Cléirigh cumann
which was most interesting. Although he had no traditional Fianna
Fáil roots, through his friendship with both George Colley and in
particular Harry Boland (with whom he ran a successful accountancy
practice) that Haughey's political career first began. In 1948, before
the general election, he was convinced by Boland and Colley to join
them in the Ó Cléirigh cumann.[160] Haughey was an active member of
cumann affairs from the start. With other young members he became
involved in the writing of a pamphlet, *Firinne Fáil*, on Fianna Fáil
policy and outlook.[161] In September 1951, he cemented his links with
Fianna Fáil, following his marriage to Maureen Lemass, the eldest
daughter of Seán Lemass.

Although he was well received within Fianna Fáil circles as an
emerging protégée and the son-in-law of the second most powerful
man in the party, Haughey's early attempts to break into national
politics were a failure. At the 1951 general election and again in
1954 he ran unsuccessfully as a Fianna Fáil candidate in Dublin
North-Central. He was, however, in 1953 co-opted onto the Dublin
Corporation; although he had to suffer the ignominy of losing his
seat on the Corporation in the local government elections in 1955.[162]
By 1954, although relatively unknown outside North Dublin, he
had steadily climbed the Fianna Fáil ladder in his own constituency,
securing the position as honorary secretary of the Ó Cléirigh cumann
and honorary secretary of the Dublin Comhairle Dailcheantair.

Insofar as his Northern connections influenced Haughey, they were
unlikely to have encouraged moderation. Both his parents came from
Swatragh, Co. Derry. His father, Seán joined the IRA after 1916 and
was involved in the War of Independence in Ulster. He subsequently
fought on the pro-treaty side during the Civil War, later joining the

Free State army in the early 1920s. Speaking in 2006, shortly before his death, Haughey admitted that his father had been 'a committed supporter of Cumann na nGaedheal', and that he was 'very [Michael] Collins'.[163] Seán Haughey's allegiance to the pro-treaty side was something which Frank Aiken, a founding father of Fianna Fáil, had never forgiven him. This greatly influenced Aiken's detestation of his son, whom he saw as a 'Free-Stater' opportunist in Fianna Fáil clothes.[164] Most revealing, although Aiken's retirement from active politics in February 1973 was publicly put down to medical reasons, his real motivation for stepping down as Fianna Fáil TD for Louth was because of the organisation's decision to ratify Haughey as a Fianna Fáil candidate for the 1973 general election. Aiken, according to his son Frank, believed Haughey was the 'wrong sort' of person 'who my father would not have admired as being representative of the men who set up Fianna Fáil'.[165]

Haughey's mother Sarah McWilliams was also involved in the War of Independence and her family remained close to the IRA thereafter; her brother, Pat McWilliams, was interned during the Second World War in Northern Ireland.[166] As a child, during visits to the strongly republican area of South Derry, Haughey had personally witnessed the sectarian riots of 1935 in Maghera and the heavy-handed approach of the B Specials.[167] During the 1930s, at his family home in Belton Park Road on Dublin's Northside, Northern Ireland politics was the focus of much debate and his parents regularly 'kept open house for friends and visitors from the North'.[168] In later life he recalled that his family were 'deeply embedded in the Northern Ireland situation'.[169]

On Victory in Europe (VE) Day on 8 May 1945 Haughey, then a young commerce student at University College Dublin, is remembered for a celebrated incident outside Trinity College where students hoisted a Union Flag on the roof and burned a tricolour. In retaliation Haughey, along with a friend, Seamus Sorohan, climbed up a lamppost outside Trinity College on College Green and burnt a Union Flag. Their actions led to a minor riot.[170] During the late 1940s Haughey served as a Lieutenant in the Fórsa Cosanta Áitiúil (FCÁ).[171] He had toyed with the idea of an army career[172] and was a commissioned officer of the FCÁ up until he resigned in 1957 on being elected a TD.[173]

Unfortunately, the Ó Cléirigh memorandum is not signed – therefore one will never be able to state definitively that Haughey wrote or co-wrote it. Nonetheless, the fact that the memorandum is written in the plural, suggests that its contents represent the *collective* viewpoint of the members of the Tomas Ó Cléirigh cumann.[174] Indeed, the very fact that Haughey, in his capacity as honorary secretary of the Ó Cléirigh cumann, sent the memorandum directly to the Fianna Fáil National Executive reinforces the argument that he most likely endorsed its contents.[175] Moreover, the military tone and content of the memorandum adds weight to the belief that Haughey, given his position as a commissioned officer in the FCÁ, had a hand in its formation.

Given the poor and at times antagonistic relationship that subsequently developed between Haughey and Colley and their respective families, it has proved difficult to decipher the precise role of the two men in the production of the memorandum.[176] Haughey's son, Seán Haughey, is adamant that 'there is nothing to suggest' that his father contributed to the Ó Cléirigh memorandum. In correspondence with this author he stated that there is no copy of the memorandum in the private papers of Charles J. Haughey, and suggested that George Colley was the possible author.[177]

Despite Seán Haughey's claims that his father had no part to play in the memorandum's formation, there is contrary evidence to suggest otherwise.[178] Two former members of the Ó Cléirigh cumann disagree with Seán Haughey's claim. Harry Boland, a member of Ó Cléirigh cumann during the period in question said he would be 'very surprised' if Haughey did not produce the memorandum. He explained that Haughey and George Colley worked closely with one another and although he could not recall the memorandum in question, both men were in charge of policy development.[179] Mary Colley, wife to George Colley, is 'convinced' that Haughey and her husband devised the memorandum. She recalled in a 2009 interview with this author that the two men would spend hours together discussing Northern Ireland and remembers that Haughey came to her home on several occasions during late 1954 and early 1955, where he and Colley formulated the memorandum in question.[180]

The memorandum was produced in the aftermath of the 1954 Fianna Fáil Ard Fheis, held in October of that year. As mentioned above, in the context of the renewed IRA violence, at this party conference, de Valera had not only rejected the use of violence as a legitimate policy to end partition, but he had also admitted he could offer no immediate solution to partition.[181] Harry Boland, who was in attendance during the 1954 Ard Fheis, recalled in a 2008 interview that 'many young folks within Fianna Fáil had become disillusioned' because so little progress was being made to undo partition. He remembered that at this Ard Fheis a cohort of delegates, particularly those of a younger age, openly expressed their frustration at the lack of action on partition from the Fianna Fáil hierarchy.[182] Boland remarked that along with Haughey and Colley, he felt that 'nothing was happening on the North' and that the time had arrived to initiate a fresh approach to partition.[183] Indeed, the previous September 1954, on behalf of the Ó Cléirigh cumann, Haughey issued a resolution requesting that 'the National Executive submit to the Ard Fheis proposals for a positive line of action on partition'.[184]

It was within this sense of despondency and frustration that Haughey decided to submit the Ó Cléirigh memorandum to the Fianna Fáil National Executive. The memorandum's central thesis advocated physical force as a legitimate method to secure Irish unity. The memorandum's preamble declared that de Valera's recent Ard Fheis speech, 'made it clear' that partition could not be ended by 'diplomatic measures'. Therefore, the only 'policy open to us which gives reasonable hope of success', it explained, was the use of force.[185] 'Outside the Organisation', the memorandum declared:

> There is a noticeable and growing discontent with National Inaction in relation to Partition. This Cumann believed that this feeling is particularly widespread even at present, and that the question of Partition will become a major issue for the younger generation of Irish people, at any rate within the next five years ... At present, young people who feel strongly on this question of Partition have not outlet [sic] for their feelings of national outrage except the I.R.A ... We believe it is the duty of the Fianna Fáil Organisation to provide the leadership and the organisation of such national feeling, and that if it should fail to do so, it will be responsible for the consequences.[186]

Four policies contained within the memorandum stand out for particular attention. Firstly, the memorandum advised that the Irish government, in conjunction with the Irish army, should enact a campaign of guerrilla warfare in Northern Ireland. It argued:

> An important preparation would, of course, be in the military sphere. While there is a reasonable hope that negotiations could be forced before the necessity for military action arose,

nevertheless it would be criminally negligent to embark on the campaign without having made preparations in our power to deal with every contingency likely to arise. In this connection, we advocate the lying-in of the greatest possible stocks of arms and ammunitions suitable for guerrilla warfare, the closest possible study of British military installations likely to be of particular importance in relation to the areas in which the campaign will be carried out ...[187]

The memorandum envisaged that the government-sponsored military guerrilla campaign would concentrate its resources on one or two areas in Northern Ireland with Catholic majorities (most probably situated in counties Derry and Armagh). It noted that by concentrating government and army resources on one or more nationalist areas the following advantages could be won: (a), 'From the point of view of the international propaganda, we can claim that we are merely trying to enforce the will of the people in the area'; and (b) the memorandum argued that 'The area or areas concerned being contiguous to the Border can be more easily dealt with and kept in communication with the other portion of the Six-counties'.[188] It explained that an objection to this policy might be advanced on the grounds that the 'concentration of our efforts on one or two nationalist areas would be tantamount to the abandonment of the remainder of the Six-Counties'. 'Such an argument', it noted, 'would be unrealistic, since there is ample precedent for a step-by-step policy in our past history, e.g. the taking over of the ports was not regarded as an abandonment of our claim on the Six-Counties ...'[189]

Secondly, once the envisaged guerrilla campaign was underway the memorandum proposed that the Irish government, with the support of Northern Ireland Catholics, should commence a campaign of civil disobedience (in those selected areas). Such a campaign, the memorandum noted:

should be controlled and directed by the Irish Government, either openly or secretly. The object of such a campaign would be to create an international incident which could not be ignored by the British Government. The campaign would be based on that adopted by Sinn Féin, i.e. non-recognition of British or Stormont sovereignty in the area or areas selected;

non-recognition of the Courts, and the setting-up of 'Sinn
Fein' Courts; the withholding of rates and taxes ...[190]

Indeed, during a private meeting between George Colley and de
Valera, at the 1954 Fianna Fáil Ard Fheis, Colley had asked de Valera's
opinions on the possibility of creating an 'incident on the border',
which would bring international attention to partition. De Valera
was quick to reject Colley's hypothesis. He rhetorically inquired if
Colley would be prepared to be a 'G [Green] Special, who like the
B-Specials, would have to enforce the rule of law on the Protestant
population of Northern Ireland?'[191]

The campaign was to be based on that adopted by Sinn Féin during
the War for Independence. Paradoxically, the concept of arranging a
programme of civil disobedience had also been considered by the
leaders of the IRA in the run up to the renewed activity of the mid-
1950s, but the army council decided under Seán Cronin's influence
to opt for a guerrilla campaign.[192]

Thirdly, the memorandum explained that Northern nationalists
or 'local forces' should be organised and supplied with arms and
ammunition. It was envisaged that these 'local forces' would:

> Work in conjunction with the Army in making simulated
> and diversionary attacks on British military installations
> if required, plans for the destruction of official British and
> Stormont records in regard to rates and taxes in the selected
> areas etc. It would of course be essential to organise nationalist
> opinion in the Six-counties in general and in the selected
> areas or areas in particular. We believe that given a positive
> policy with full support from the South, both materially and
> spiritually, the necessary co-operation will be obtained from
> the Northern Nationalists.[193]

The similarities between the IRA campaign at the time and the
proposals put forward by the Ó Cléirigh cumann were interesting. Both
advocated a method of guerrilla warfare against their 'oppressors'.
This entailed a policy of the destruction of vital communications and
a concentration of superior numbers of men at a decisive time and
location. To foreshadow events in the near future, the memorandum's
reference to the importance of British military installations was to
become a key aspect of the IRA's 'Operation Harvest' campaign. The

campaign commenced in 1956, focusing on the destruction of British transmitter posts, road and rail and any 'enemy' vehicles that were found.[194]

Finally, the memorandum also envisaged the establishment of a committee to examine social welfare, education, industry, taxation and 'current laws that would be necessary upon the anticipated assimilation of one or two of the border counties of Northern Ireland and in the eventual reunification of Ireland'.[195] It noted that:

> a committee of experts on International Law should also be asked to advise on the legal effect of open support by the Irish Government of persons engaged in the campaign of civil disobedience; the question of the use of our regular armed forces in Six-counties; and aiding and possibly arming of irregular forces on active service in Six-counties, etc., and the pointing out of loopholes whereby difficulties involved can be overcome. In this connection, your attention is drawn to the action of the Egyptian Government which unofficially organised a liberation army, consisting of irregular volunteers, but which is believed by many to have consisted mainly of regular army units.[196]

The memorandum offered an appraisal for the justification and implementation of a physical force policy to help secure Irish unity. It argued that the use of violence had and still did constitute official Fianna Fáil policy. Unfortunately no record exists recording the reaction from within Fianna Fáil to the Ó Cléirigh memorandum. Nevertheless, the fact that Haughey most likely had a part to play in its formation and given that he was appointed as a member of the standing-committee for partition matters, there is evidence to suggest that the Fianna Fáil hierarchy did give the memorandum due consideration; if to merely use it as a central reason for the necessity to formulate a realistic and indeed official Northern Ireland policy.

The second memorandum on partition issued by Matthew Feehan offered a more practical and less provocative analysis of Fianna Fáil's attitude towards Northern Ireland. Feehan, a founding member of the *Sunday Press*, was known to be close to Lemass[197] and in late-December 1954, had received a request from Mullins to enquire if he 'had any practical suggestions on partition'.[198] Five pages in length, the majority of Feehan's points were consistent with Fianna Fáil's strategy towards Northern Ireland at the time.[199]

Under the heading 'General Considerations', the memorandum stated that it 'is now apparent that the Anti-Partition campaign has failed'. [200] Feehan, thus, argued that an 'effort must be made to reach the rank-and-file of the Unionists. They are ordinary men and women and our task is to convince them that their destiny lies with the rest of Ireland'. 'Unity', he explained, 'will not be based on a perfect solution'. Concessions would therefore need to be offered to Ulster unionists. [201] On the emotive issue of the use of force to end partition, Feehan was unequivocal: '... It is necessary to clear the air and place beyond all doubt' that military means was out of the question. [202]

The memorandum concluded by outlining how Fianna Fáil, in its efforts to achieve unity, would be required to make concessions to Northern Ireland Protestants. Specifically, possible changes to the 1937 Irish constitution would be necessary and the federal solution would be revived 'even if it was a mere gesture'. [203] While a re-examination of the 'South's social welfare compared to the North's would be required', Feehan concluded, in the tradition of Lemass, by questioning how reunification would affect the tariff protection policy and what 'effect would the introduction of Northern industry have on the South's existing industry'? [204]

On reflection, Feehan's memorandum was extremely forward thinking and one can understand why his views were issued to the party's National Executive for consideration. In fact, a number of the proposals, as is discussed below, were endorsed by the standing-committee on partition matters.

PARTITION MEMORANDUM ISSUED ON BEHALF OF THE
STANDING-COMMITTEE ON PARTITION MATTERS, APRIL 1955

Between the first meeting of the standing-committee on partition matters in early February 1955 and the second gathering in early April, detailed research was carried out by the committee members concerning Fianna Fáil's Northern Ireland policy. [205] Stemming directly from the two meetings a revolutionary memorandum was produced by Lemass and his colleagues. The memorandum recorded that committee members fully endorsed the proposals contained within and instructed the Fianna Fáil National Executive to 'issue a statement on Partition on the following lines or alternatively to incorporate such a statement in any publication dealing with Fianna Fáil's policy and programme'. [206]

The memorandum outlined eight practical policies that Fianna Fáil ought to follow regarding its Northern Ireland policy. Under Lemass's pioneering guidance the committee examined, in specific detail, the political, religious, economic, social and cultural dimensions of Fianna Fáil's strategy towards Northern Ireland. The points represented a victory of pragmatism over dogma. The memorandum's preamble declared that 'It was the purpose of Fianna Fáil to advocate and apply the following policy towards the realisation of the primary aim of the national effort as set out above':

(1) To maintain and strengthen wherever possible, all links with the Six-County majority, especially economic and cultural links, to encourage contacts between the people of both areas in every field, and to demonstrate that widespread goodwill for the Six-County majority can be fostered by such contacts.

(2) To discourage and prevent any course of action which would have the effect of embittering relations between the people of both areas, or making fruitful economic and cultural contacts more difficult.

(3) To keep constant in mind, in relation to all aspects of twenty-six county internal policy and administration, the prospect of the termination of partition and so to direct them as to avoid or minimise the practical problems that may arise when partition is ended.

(4) To eliminate as far as possible all impediments to the free movement of goods, persons, and traffic across the Border and particularly to alter the Customs Law so as to permit of the entry into the twenty-six counties free of Customs duty and subject to no more onerous conditions than apply to twenty-six county products, all goods of bona fide Six-County origins.

(5) To encourage the establishment of joint authorities to manage affairs of common interest, including transport, electricity generations and distributions, sea lights and marks, drainage programmes and tourist development.

(6) To co-ordinate with the Six-County authorities in arrangements for Civil Defence, including movement of population from threatened areas in time of war.

(7) To arrange, if possible, with the Six-County authorities for joint commercial and tourist publicity abroad, and to invite

periodic consultation of all such matters of common interest. (8) To urge on the people of the twenty-six counties the desirability of giving to the Six-County majority of such assurances as to their political and religious rights in a United Ireland as may reasonably be required, and as to the maintenance of local autonomy in respect of such matters as may be desired by them.[207]

Points (1) to (3) were consistent with current Fianna Fáil thinking on Northern Ireland and maintained the 'concurrence of wills' philosophy was the only viable method available to the party to secure Irish unity; that Dublin must work in tangent with London and Belfast, via economic and cultural contacts, if partition was to be successfully ended. Points (4) to (7) originated from Lemass's personal views on the economic practicalities between North and South and specifically the need for the lifting of tariffs and the opening up of the island of Ireland to free trade.

Point (4) proposed the ending of tariffs against Northern Ireland goods and the establishment of a free trade area between North and South. Such a proposal was a logical progression in the context of the post-war economic climate. Ireland's traditional tariff-based protectionist policy ran in variance with the economic realities of an export-led open-market system that encouraged foreign investment. The early 1950s was a period when tens of thousands of Irish people left Ireland in the hope to find work abroad – almost an eighth of the population emigrated by the end of the decade. It was within the context of this new severe economic climate that Lemass believed Fianna Fáil needed to adapt its approach to Northern Ireland.

Since the late 1930s Lemass had grown increasingly sceptical of Fianna Fáil's protectionist economic policy towards Northern Ireland. As early as 1938 he personally wrote to de Valera advocating the need for closer cross-border economic co-operation between Dublin and Belfast. De Valera, however, declined Lemass's offer of North–South co-operation.[208] In the post-war period Lemass continued his self-appointed mission to end the imposed tariff barrier between the two jurisdictions and in its place create an open market free-trade area between North and South.

On visits to Bonn, West Germany, in 1952, he spoke of how partition had prevented the industrial North and the agricultural South from becoming an 'excellent economy'. Citing the Erne development, the Foyle Fisheries and the GNR scheme as examples, he noted that the 'problems of partition are being approached in a practical spirit'.[209] The Bonn speech highlighted the link in Lemass's thinking between economic development and partition. He believed that closer economic co-operation between North and South would 'help to contribute to the wealth and the development of the whole Island', thus eventually encouraging the 'voluntary unity of Ireland'.[210] The following year, in the autumn of 1953, he travelled to America and Canada to preside over the formal opening of the office of the Irish Export Promotion Board. His visit across the Atlantic to develop Irish exports and investment opportunities in the United States was notable for the emphasis he placed on partition.[211] His time abroad revealed the differences which were beginning to emerge between himself and de Valera in relation to Northern Ireland.

Unlike the vast majority of his Fianna Fáil colleagues Lemass was aware that the end of a tariff system, the encouragement of foreign capital and the opening up of Ireland to free trade was essential for the creation of a prosperous Ireland. Therefore, as Michael Kennedy recorded the development of economic links with Northern Ireland was a 'logical first step towards breaking out of protectionism towards free trade'.[212] More than anything else the economy guided Lemass's attitude towards Northern Ireland. As the British government previously recorded, Lemass's 'cool headed ... sensible and more pragmatic' approach to partition, as compared 'to contemporaries in politics', convinced him that only when Ireland secured economic prosperity could attention be turned towards Irish unity.[213] Indeed, as early as 1947, London had signalled Lemass out as an example of an Irish politician eager to forge ahead with an industrial policy: a man 'of sound practical sense, not swayed by political emotion'.[214]

Lemass's wish to promote North–South economic co-operation confirmed Gerald Boland's subsequent observation that in some way Lemass was 'different' from the rest of his party colleagues, that he was a 'real businessman'.[215] Sentimentality had no place in his attitude to Northern Ireland. He was also unique from his Fianna Fáil colleagues in that he had by 1953 acquired, through his personal relationship with Northern Ireland minister for commerce, William McCleery, 'good first-hand knowledge' of dealings with the Belfast government, something his superior, de Valera, did not have.[216] Although 'de Valera's right hand man' he was determined to make Ireland not merely politically, but economically independent.[217]

Indeed, as is argued later in this book, on becoming leader of Fianna Fáil in 1959 Lemass's first major policy development on partition was his offer to the Northern Ireland government of a thirty two-county free trade area between North and South for goods of Irish or Northern Ireland origin.[218] Under de Valera's leadership, however, the proposal was repeatedly ignored. This was not surprising considering that it was under his Fianna Fáil administration in the early 1930s that the Irish erected tough tariffs against Northern Ireland goods, which effectively denied Northern Irish manufacturers and distributors access to the Southern market. In reality, de Valera's reluctance to consider the proposal signalled his inability to grasp the economic and political realities of the post-war environment.

The policies outlined in points (5), (6) and (7) were further examples of Lemass's willingness to re-examine Fianna Fáil's traditional stance of Northern Ireland. Upon entering government in 1951 Fianna Fáil had been willing to encourage cross-border co-operation with Belfast in relation to the GNR, the Erne Hydro Electric Scheme and the Foyle Fisheries. Such policy initiatives, however, soon petered out because of de Valera's refusal to acknowledge the constitutional position of Northern Ireland. Under Lemass's stewardship the committee advised that the Fianna Fáil government attempt to side step the thorny constitutional issue and instead encourage Dublin and Belfast to work alongside one another on issues of mutual practical concern, including transport, commercial and civil defence issues.

Lastly, point (8) dealt with the sensitive issue of the possibility that constitutional concessions might be required if Irish unity was to be secured.[219] Namely that a review of article 44 of the Irish constitution should be undertaken; this dealt with 'the special position of the Catholic Church'. Additionally, the committee recommended that a review of articles 2 and 3, which claimed territorial jurisdiction over the whole of the island of Ireland, be re-examined, in an effort to encourage the Northern Ireland Protestant majority to enter a united Ireland under a federal agreement. Lemass had previously stated that in order to facilitate the Ulster unionists into a united Ireland, many of whom feared that Irish unity would lead to 'discrimination on religious or other grounds' the Irish government would need to produce, 'any reasonable guarantees … whatever constitutional or other safeguards … if partition was to be ended'.[220]

The committee's willingness to re-examine the constitutional relationship between Dublin and Belfast was a brave gamble and highlighted the difficulty that the progressive-wing of Fianna Fáil faced. It is known that some in the party, including Lemass, Feehan and Lionel Booth, realised that the Protestant community of Northern

Ireland held the 'key to the solution' and without first winning their support, 'nothing could ever be achieved'.[221] Importantly, Lemass was one of a few within Fianna Fáil to appreciate that the combination of Catholic social values and the territorial claim to the whole of the island as enshrined in the 1937 Irish constitution had cemented the alienation of Ulster Unionists over the previous two decades, thus entrenching partition.

For many within Fianna Fáil, however, the 1937 Irish constitution was sacrosanct. Any attempts to amend the 'special position of the Catholic Church' would have been extremely problematic; not least considering the authoritarian control of the Catholic Church.[222] Attempts to revise articles two and three would have been met with fierce resistance from the fundamentalists within the party, who viewed any attempted alterations as a 'sell out' and the abandonment of the republican tradition. Although de Valera was the main advocate of a federal solution to help end partition, he held opposite views to Lemass on the issue of making constitutional concessions. This was not altogether unexpected as de Valera had been the main instigator of the 1937 Irish constitution, which had in effect withdrawn the *de facto* recognition of the 1925 boundary agreement between the Dublin and Belfast governments, by asserting the thirty-two county national claim.[223]

The proposal was, however, not altogether impractical. Seán MacEntee had previously noted that the people of Ireland 'should turn their attention to the constitution which may be a future barrier to the unity of the Irish people'.[224] Ernest Blythe had also announced that he would 'like to see changes made in the Constitution which would remove the suggestion that Dáil Éireann had rights to the jurisdiction in the Six-Counties'.[225]

An important omission from the memorandum was that no reference was made to Britain's role in maintaining partition. De Valera had repeatedly asserted that it was the British government who had imposed partition, and therefore it was the British who could ultimately end it.[226] This continued policy of ramming the partition quandary down the throats of the British, at every given opportunity, had become a fruitless exercise. The British Ambassador to Ireland from 1951 to 1955, Sir Walter Hankinson believed that the Irish government approach was 'emotional and unreasoning'. He lamented 'it is always the North or Britain which is to blame and never themselves'.[227]

Hankinson had succinctly but unknowingly pointed out differences between Lemass and de Valera. Lemass intentionally decided not to include a reference to Britain's role. This was to become a hallmark of his Northern Ireland policy during Lemass's period as taoiseach as he relegated the British state 'to a distinctly secondary role'.[228] Lemass, unlike de Valera, was not a prisoner of his past. He was guided by practical considerations. Indeed, a file from the British Embassy in Dublin records that while a 'boy in the 1916 Rising he is not dominated by a sense of grievance and frustration which characterises so many of the older generation of Irish politicians'.[229]

Henry Patterson has put forward the theory that Lemass became receptive to innovatory thinking within Irish nationalism. Examples of this fresh thinking on partition were works such as Ernest Blythe's, *The Smashing of the Border* (1955) and Michael Sheehy's, *Divided We Stand: A Study of Partition*, (1955).[230] Sheehy, for instance, alluded to the internal roots of the partition settlement and played down the role of the British.[231] Sheehy remarked that the Republic maintained that 'England imposed partition against the wishes of both Northern Protestants and Southern Catholics. Consequently the South maintains that the obligation to remove partition lies on England'. 'This view', he wrote, 'is based on a wholly untenable interpretation of the history of partition'. 'The partition policy of the Southern Government', he concluded, 'is in grave need of revision'.[232] Privately, Lemass would have agreed with Sheehy's pessimistic diagnosis.

On 6 April 1955, Lemass sent de Valera the committee's memorandum and proposed that the National Executive should endorse the recommendations as official Fianna Fáil Northern Ireland policy.[233] Within twenty-four hours de Valera wrote back to Lemass and was swift to reject the proposals. The former noted that 'whilst I agree a great deal of it does not seem to be open to serious objection, some of the steps suggested are not so, and are of more than doubtful value'. De Valera explained that the memorandum '... would certainly give rise to very serious controversy and would possibly make confusion worse confounded amongst the nationalists of the Six-Counties'. He, therefore, informed Lemass that its contents must be 'kept as a private norm. Publicity might in fact defeat the purpose of the scheme'.[234]

The fundamental picture of de Valera was a leader desperately trying to maintain control of Fianna Fáil's Northern Ireland policy and not willing to listen to even his closest colleagues. It must have been a difficult task for Lemass to contain his frustration. The episode revealed the differences that had developed between both men. Lemass bestowed a brutal frankness, unsentimental pragmatism and a desire for decision; this was in marked contrast to de Valera's instinct for caution and consensus.[235] Importantly, the event highlighted de Valera's ability to reign in his younger colleague on policy matters. Lemass later admitted that no one else, but de Valera, had ever been able to make him 'change his outlook on an important matter'.[236] Although the proposals were not to become official Fianna Fáil Northern Ireland policy in the immediate future, the seeds of change had been sown. Lemass was to later acknowledge that the craft of policy development was a slow process that was 'never born complete with arms and eyes and legs overnight. It's something that grows over a long time'.[237] In fact, the proposals contained within points (4) to (8) were ten years ahead of their time and were remarkably similar to the policies that Lemass advocated during his presidency of Fianna Fáil from 1959 to 1966.

There is evidence that de Valera did not believe the proposals of the committee to be obsolete as in 1958 he asked to view the memorandum.[238] In the intermediate period, however, he decided to shelve the committee's recommendations. One must acknowledge that he must have found himself in a difficult position. Given the revived IRA campaign and the seemingly ambiguous support of a significant proportion of Irish people to the recent spate of IRA violence, the current political climate was not the appropriate time to announce such new policy initiatives. Publication of the proposals would have left Fianna Fáil open for further criticism that it had abandoned its traditional republican pledge to secure a united Ireland. Additionally, with the rise of Sinn Féin, de Valera was aware that the party's emergence could eat into Fianna Fáil's core vote.[239]

* * *

In conclusion, Fianna Fáil's approach to Northern Ireland from 1951 to 1955 was encapsulated by the party hierarchy's attempts to abandon its traditional anti-partitionist strategy towards Northern Ireland and replace it with a policy of persuasion. Aimed directly at Ulster Unionists, Fianna Fáil sought to encourage cross-border co-operation between Belfast and Dublin. De Valera's overtures, however, were greeted with scepticism from the Ulster unionist community. Ernest Blythe accurately recorded Northern Protestants' disdain for Fianna Fáil's policy of 'persuasion': 'it could have easily be represented as equivalent to bending the knee to the bully'.[240]

De Valera's approach to Northern Ireland was equally detested by a small, but vocal, element with his own organisation. For a selection of party members the renewed IRA campaign was viewed as merely a continuation of Ireland's quest to secure a united Ireland. Indeed, in some supporters' eyes, Ireland's recent history, the 1916 Easter Rising, the War of Independence and the civil war, meant that 'political' violence was a legitimate course of action. Indeed, as is examined in the following chapter, the nationwide sympathy and support offered for the renewed IRA activity meant that the Fianna Fáil hierarchy were forced to pursue a delicate line on Northern Ireland.

NOTES

1. See University College Dublin Archives (UCDA) Ernest Blythe Papers P24/1327, Blythe to general secretary, Irish Anti-Partition League, Belfast, P. F. Mc Gill, 10 Feb. 1953.
2. See John Bowman, *De Valera and the Ulster Question 1919–1973* (Oxford: Oxford University Press, 1982), 281–295; Clare O'Halloran, *Partition and the Limits of Irish Nationalism* (New Jersey: Humanities Press International, Inc., 1987), 185–186; Ronan Fanning, 'Anglo-Irish relations: partition and the British dimension in historical perspective', *Irish Studies in International Affairs*, Vol. 2 (1985), 1–20; Paul Arthur, 'Anglo-Irish relations and the Northern Ireland problem', *Irish Studies in International Affairs*, Vol. 2 (1985), 37–50. See also, Donnacha Ó Beacháin, *Destiny of the Soldiers: Fianna Fáil, Irish Republicanism and the IRA, 1926–1973* (Dublin: Gill and Macmillan, 2011), and Etain Tannam, *Cross-Border Co-operation in the Republic of Ireland and Northern Ireland* (New York: St Martin's Press, 1999).
3. Michael Kennedy, *Division and Consensus: The Politics of Cross-Border Relations in Ireland, 1925–1969* (Dublin: Institute for Public Administration, 2000), 156.
4. National Archives of Ireland (NAI) Department of Foreign Affairs (DFA) 305/14/192, confidential memorandum on partition signed by Seán Nunan, 21 Aug. 1951.
5. UCDA Frank Aiken Papers P104/8724, conversation between Aiken and Lord Ismay, 14 Feb. 1952. See also NAI DFA P203/1, conversation between Boland and Lord Pakenham, 29 Nov. 1951.
6. UCDA Eamon de Valera Papers P150/2970, document entitled: 'Membership and Representation on Inter-Parliamentary Groups', record of meeting between de Valera and a collection of British MPs, 9 Feb. 1949.
7. See National Archives of the United Kingdom (NAUK) Dominions Office (DO) 35/2095, Sir. John Maffey to Dominions Office, 26 July 1946.
8. UCDA P104/8033, Boland to Nunan, 22 Jan. 1952.
9. UCDA P104/8724, conversation between Aiken and Lord Ismay, 14 Feb. 1952.
10. See The Earl of Longford and Thomas P. O'Neill, *Eamon de Valera* (London: Hutchinson, 1970), 442–443.
11. See Seán Nunan's comments. NAI DFA 305/14/192, confidential memorandum on partition signed by Seán Nunan, 21 Aug. 1951.
12. See Seán O'Faoláin's comments. *The Irish Times*, 30 May 1955.
13. See Conor Cruise O'Brien, *Memoir my Life my Times* (Dublin: Poolbeg Press, 1999), 162.
14. UCDA P104/8037, meeting between Aiken and Lord Salisbury, Leader of the House of Lords, 28 Oct. 1952.
15. Speech by MacEntee. *Irish Press*, 5 Nov. 1952.
16. This was the view of Mr. S. O'Sullivan, Father Dominic cumann, Cork-Borough. See *Irish Press*, 7 Nov. 1951.
17. This was the opinion of E. Little, Co. Carlow. See *Irish Press*, 7 Nov. 1951.

18. See UCDA P104/8037, meeting between Aiken and Lord Salisbury, Leader of the House of Lords, 28 Oct. 1952.
19. UCDA P104/8035, meeting between de Valera, Aiken and Pakenham in Dublin, 2 May 1952.
20. Speech by de Valera, 19 July 1951. See Maurice Moynihan, *Speeches and Statements by Eamon de Valera* (Dublin, 1980), 541–544. See also record of radio broadcast by de Valera, 14 May 1954, in Moynihan, *Speeches and Statements by Eamon de Valera, 566–570.*
21. At the 1951 Fianna Fáil Ard Fheis, MacEntee explained that 'some of us are old now and may not live to see the problem solved, but at least in our life-time as long as we live and breathe we are going to work to end it'. *Irish Press,* 7 Nov. 1951.
22. Speaking to a gathering of Fianna Fáil supporters in Dublin, Lemass remarked that he 'was not going to attempt to say how partition will end'. *Irish Press,* 30 Jan. 1953.
23. Speech by de Valera. Dáil Éireann debate (DE), 24 June 1947. Vol. 107, col. 79.
24. See Kennedy, *Division and Consensus,* 151 and 154–155. See also Tannam, *Cross-Border Co-operation,* 48–50.
25. See Kennedy, *Division and Consensus,* 124–131.
26. NAI DFA P203/1, meeting between Boland and Pakenham, 29 Nov. 1951.
27. NAI DFA P203/1, meeting between Boland and Pakenham, 29 Nov. 1951.
28. NAI DFA P203/1, meeting between Boland and Pakenham, 29 Nov. 1951.
29. UCDA P104/8035, meeting between de Valera, Aiken and Pakenham in Dublin, 2 May 1952.
30. Kennedy, *Division and Consensus, 53.*
31. Kennedy, *Division and Consensus, 55.*
32. Kennedy, *Division and Consensus, 73.*
33. Kennedy, *Division and Consensus, 92–102.*
34. UCDA P24/1769, Blythe, *Towards a Six-County Dominion?.*
35. UCDA P24/1769, Blythe, *Towards a Six-County Dominion?.*
36. For an overview of the Mother and Child controversy see Diarmaid Ferriter, *The Transformation of Ireland 1900–2000* (London, Profile Books, 2004), 501–504.
37. See speech by Basil Brooke, Dungannon, co. Tyrone. *Irish Press,* 20 Oct. 1951.
38. Quoted in Kennedy, *Division and Consensus,* 152.
39. See comments by Brooke. *Northern Whig,* 25 June 1951.
40. See comments by Maginess. *The Irish Times,* 18 Feb. 1954.
41. See comments by de Valera. *Northern Whig,* 25 June 1951.
42. This was the opinion of M. T. Fitzgerald, Dublin South-East. See *Irish Press,* 5 Nov. 1952.
43. *Irish Press,* 5 Nov. 1952.
44. This resolution was issued by Hugh McClean, East-Donegal. *Irish Press,* 7 Nov. 1951. See also *Irish Press,* 5 Nov. 1952 and *The Irish Times,* 15 Oct. 1953.
45. This was the opinion of Mr O'Sullivan, the Father Dominic cumann, Cork-Borough. *Irish Press,* 5 Nov. 1952.
46. At the 1951 Fianna Fáil Ard Fheis, Joe Dowling, future Fianna Fáil frontbench spokesman, Dublin South-West and member of the Bernard Curtin cumann, Inchicore, Dublin, put forward the most provocative resolution which called on the use of force to end partition. *Irish Press,* 7 Nov. 1951.
47. Public Records Office of Northern Ireland (PRONI) Cahir Healy Papers D2991/B/53/8, O'Gowan, Bellamont Forest, Cottehill, Co. Cavan, to Healy, 22 June 1951.
48. See NAI Department of the Taoiseach (DT) 97/9/1271, Government policy: letters of advice and criticism, 1953–1956.
49. See NAI DT 97/9/1271, Patrick McSorley, 58 Newtownkennedy, Strabane, Co. Tyrone, to de Valera, 13 Dec. 1953.
50. See UCDA Fianna Fáil Party Papers P176/446, record of Fianna Fáil parliamentary party meetings, 1951–1954. See also UCDA P176/347, records of meetings of the National Executive, 1951–1954. Moreover, the party's official newspaper *Gléas* likewise did not make a reference to Northern Ireland in any of its publications from 1951 to 1954. UCDA P176/985, 3 to 4 issues of *Gléas* were published each year.

51. See *Irish Press*, 21 Oct. 1951.

52. See *Irish Press*, 5 Nov. 1952.

53. The only reference that de Valera made to Northern Ireland was his rejection of a resolution requesting that Fianna Fáil extend the organisation into Northern Ireland. See *The Irish Times*, 15 Oct 1953.

54. See Dáil Éireann debates, Nov. 1951–Feb. 1953.

55. UCDA P104/8639–8655, record of 39th – 43rd meetings of the All-Party Anti-Partition Committee, 28 Sept. 1951–2 Nov. 1955.

56. PRONI D2991/B/60/8, MacBride to Healy, 26 Feb. 1953.

57. See UCDA P176/346, meeting of National Executive, 21 Oct. 1946.

58. NAI DT S 9361A, letter from de Valera's personal secretary Kathleen O'Connell to P.J. A. Scott-Manuel, assistant secretary of the central council of Anti-Partition of Ireland League of Great Britain, London, 29 Jan. 1948. Speaking in May 1947, Michael Sheehan, secretary of the London branch of the League, bemoaned that Fianna Fáil gave 'no help' to the movement. 'We have had visits from brilliant secretaries of the party repeatedly', he lamented, 'yet Fianna Fáil TDs have ignored requests to come to London to speak'. See *Evening Standard*, 8 Aug. 1947.

59. UCDA P150/1998, Alf Havekin to de Valera, May 1951. See also UCDA P104/8610, Alf Havekin to Aiken, 23 July 1952.

60. See UCDA P104/8610, Alf Havekin to Aiken, 23 July 1952.

61. Boland noted that if Feehan did decide to go 'it is doubtful whether any assistance given to the League will be used to any good purpose'. UCDA P104/8612, Boland to Nunan, 26 Aug. 1952.

62. UCDA P104/8600, memorandum entitled 'the general position of the Anti-Partition Movement in Britain' from Boland to Nunan, 12 June 1951.

63. UCDA P104/8600, memorandum entitled 'the general position of the Anti-Partition Movement in Britain' from Boland to Nunan, 12 June 1951.

64. The records state that of the 120,000 pamphlets distributed, *Nothing to Do with Me*, made up 70,000; *Ireland's Right to Unity*, constituted 30,000; *One Vote Equals Two*, constituted, 15,000; and *Discrimination*, the remaining 5,000 pamphlets. UCDA P104/8600, memoranda entitled, 'the general position of the Anti-Partition Movement in Britain', Boland to Nunan, 12 June 1951.

65. NAI DFA 305/14/108/5, Boland to Nunan, 12 Jan. 1952.

66. Privately, Havekin noted that Aiken had personally decided that the Irish government would no longer subsidise the League's activities. See UCDA, P104/8612, Havekin to Feehan, 20 Aug. 1952.

67. UCDA, P104/8612, Havekin to Feehan, 20 Aug. 1952.

68. NAI DFA 305/14/108/5, Boland to Nunan, 12 Jan. 1952.

69. See UCDA P104/4639, report from Little on the 'current position of the Anti-Partition of Ireland League of Great Britain', London, 1950/1951.

70. See Michael Farrell, *Northern Ireland: The Orange State* (London: Pluto Press, 1980), 198.

71. Gerald Boland was the only elected representative in the Republic of Ireland to attend the second annual conference of the Anti-Partition League in Dublin (*Irish Press*, 31 May 1948). Also in Nov. 1948 members of the Irish Anti-Partition League wrote to the Fianna Fáil National Executive requesting a speaker for an all-party meeting in Belfast, 23 Nov. 1948. P.J. Little was appointed to attend. UCDA P176/346, meeting of the National Executive, 15 Nov 1948. Also, Frank Aiken and Little addressed rallies in support of Cahir Healy MP, in the run up to the 1950 Westminster election. *Irish Press*, 14 Feb. 1950.

72. UCDA P104/8608, McNally to Aiken, 17 June 1952.

73. McCall was employed by the All Party Anti-Partition Committee from 1949 to 1951. In July 1951, the All Party Anti-Partition Committee terminated McCall's employment. This was further evidence of the inactivity of the Committee considering that McCall was the only person sending reliable information to the Committee on the activities of the numerous branches of the Anti-Partition League in Northern Ireland.

74. NAI DFA 305/14/65, memorandum from McCall to Frank Gallagher, 22 Sept. 1951.
75. NAI DFA 305/14/65, memorandum from McCall to Frank Gallagher, 22 Sept. 1951.
76. UCDA P104/4662, document entitled 'National Anti-Partition (Mansion House Committee) fund, statement of position of the fund as at 15 March 1951'.
77. UCDA P104/8606/7, speech delivered by Jack Lynch at a reception held at the Grant Hotel, Sheffield, 19 Feb. 1952.
78. NAI DT S 9361C, interview given by de Valera on the day of his seventieth birthday to the German News Agency, 14 Oct. 1952.
79. See UCDA P104/4667, meeting between de Valera and a delegation of the Irish Anti-Partition League (Northern Ireland), 3 Aug. 1951.
80. See UCDA P24/1769, Blythe, *Towards a Six-County Dominion?*, Aug 1949.
81. Alvin Jackson, 'Ireland, the Union and the Empire, 1800–1960', in Kevin Kenny (ed.), *Ireland and the British Empire* (Oxford: Oxford University Press, 2004), 146.
82. Henry Patterson, *The Politics of Illusion, Republicanism and Socialism in Modern Ireland* (London: Radius Books, 1989), 117.
83. Patterson, *The Politics of Illusion*, 117.
84. Patterson, *The Politics of Illusion*, 117.
85. Patterson, *The Politics of Illusion*, 118.
86. UCDA P104/4578, meeting between de Valera and Hanna, 19 Sept. 1951.
87. UCDA P104/4578, meeting between de Valera and Hanna, 19 Sept. 1951.
88. NAI DFA P203, Boland to Seán Nunan, 1 Oct. 1951.
89. NAI DFA P203, Boland to Seán Nunan, 1 Oct. 1951.
90. Speech by de Valera, 19 July 1951. See Moynihan, *Speeches and Statements by Eamon de Valera*, 541–544.
91. Chris Reeves, '"Let us stand by our friends": British policy towards Ireland, 1949–1959', *Irish Studies in International Affairs*, Vol. 2 (2000), 100–101.
92. Barry Flynn, *Soldiers of Folly: the IRA Border Campaign, 1956–1962* (Cork: Collins Press, 2009), 27.
93. See *Irish Press*, 29 Oct. 1954.
94. See *Irish Independent*, 14 Feb. 1955.
95. See comments by MacGiolla. *The Irish Times*, 1 Nov. 1954.
96. See comments by MacGiolla. *The Irish Times*, 1 Nov. 1954.
97. See comments by a Sinn Féin supporter in *Irish Press*, 18 April 1955.
98. UCDA P150/2000, copy of Sinn Féin pamphlet, Nov. 1954.
99. UCDA P150/2000, copy of Sinn Féin pamphlet, Nov. 1954.
100. Educated in England (Methodist College, The Leys School, Cambridge) Booth had served as a Captain in the Irish army during Second World War. At the 1954 Fianna Fáil Ard Fheis Booth was appointed to the party's National Executive committee of fifteen. He was subsequently elected Fianna Fáil TD Dun Laoghaire-Rathdown at the 1957 general election. In 1956, he became managing director of Booth Poole and Company Limited, until he became managing director of Brittain Group from 1970.
101. See David Andrews, *Kingstown Republican* (Dublin: New Island, 2007), 37.
102. See comments by Booth. *The Irish Times*, 13 Oct. 1954.
103. See comments by Booth. *The Irish Times*, 15 Oct. 1954.
104. See comments by Booth. *The Irish Times*, 2 Nov. 1954.
105. This is the opinion of Dr Richard Booth (son of Lionel Booth). Interview with Richard Booth, 8 Dec. 2008.
106. UCDA P26/1366, Booth to Blythe, 16 Oct. 1954.
107. Interview with Richard Booth, 8 Dec. 2008.
108. *Irish Independent*, 14 Feb. 1955.
109. *Irish Independent*, 14 Feb. 1955.
110. UCDA Sighle Humphreys Papers P106/2149, copy of *Clann* Bulletin, Vol.2, No. 12, Nov. 1954.
111. UCDA P106/2149, copy of *Clann* Bulletin, Vol.2 No.12, Nov. 1954.
112. UCDA P106/2149, copy of *Clann* Bulletin, Vol.2 No.12, Nov. 1954.

113. For example, at a meeting of the Howth-Finglas Comhairle Dáilcheantair on 27 Sept. 1954 and at a subsequent meeting at Swords Comhairle Dáilcheantair on 29 Sept. 1954, a debate occurred on partition. At both meetings it was decided that each cumann had 'no policy on partition to offer'. UCDA P176/280, record of various Comhairle Dáilcheantair meetings in the Dublin North-East 1954–1957.

114. UCDA P176/277, Brady to Lemass, 2 Nov. 1954.

115. This was the opinion of M. O'Neil, a grocer from Sandycove. UCDA P176/277, Brady to Lemass, 2 Nov. 1954.

116. Andrews, *Kingstown Republican*, 29.

117. UCDA P176/277, Lemass to Brady, 11 Nov. 1954.

118. The Fianna Fáil constituency files for Dún Laoghaire-Rathdown contain no evidence that Lemass contacted Booth during late 1954 and early 1955. See UCDA P176/277.

119. Additionally, Fianna Fáil headquarters sent a letter to each of the twenty-one cumann in Dún Laoghaire-Rathdown outlining the decisions taken at the conference. UCDA P176/277, record of meeting between de Valera and members of the two Dún Laoghaire-Rathdown Comhairle Dáilcheantair (besides the presence of de Valera and Booth those in attendance at the meeting are unknown), held on 12 April 1955.

120. Interview with Richard Booth, 8 Dec. 2008.

121. This was the opinion of members of the Fianna Fáil Barnstown Thomas Ashe cumann, Colestown, Co. Wexford. UCDA P176/276, Miss Ena Moore, honorary secretary Barnstown Thomas Ashe cumann to Lemass, 25 March 1955.

122. See UCDA P176/293, Seamus Babington to Lemass, 1 March 1955.

123. NAUK War Office (WO) 32/21318, conversation between Boland and Laithwaite, 22 Feb. 1955.

124. NAUK WO 32/21318, record of conversation between Boland and permanent under-secretary of state for Commonwealth Relations, Gilbert Laithwaite, 22 Feb. 1955.

125. NAUK WO 32/21318, record of conversation between Boland and Laithwaite, 22 Feb. 1955.

126. NAUK DO 35/7809, Clutterbuck's observation towards the IRA, 24 Oct. 1955.

127. NAUK DO 35/7809, Clutterbuck's observation towards the IRA, 24 Oct. 1955.

128. UCDA P176/347, record of meetings of the Fianna Fáil National Executive, 1951–1954.

129. *Irish Press*, 13 Oct 1954.

130. Lemass noted to Brennan that the resolution needed to be 'constructive and reasonable'. UCDA P176/308, Lemass to Brennan, 6 Sept. 1954.

131. For a copy of the resolution see *The Irish Times*, 13 Oct. 1954.

132. UCDA P176/347, meeting of National Executive, 8 Nov. 1954.

133. It replaced the party's anti-partition sub-committee, which had been established in 1946, but had effectively ceased to operate since 1949, due to the establishment of the All-Party-Anti-Partition committee in Jan. of the same year.

134. See numerous comments by disgruntled Fianna Fáil members at the 1954 Fianna Fáil Ard Fheis as reported in the *Irish Press*, 12 Oct. 1954.

135. *Irish Press*, 12 Oct. 1954.

136. *Irish Independent*, 13 Oct. 1954.

137. Extract from *Gléas*, Oct. 1954.

138. *The Irish Times*, 13 Oct. 1954.

139. See UCDA P176/446, meeting of Fianna Fáil parliamentary party, 27 Oct. 1954.

140. See UCDA P176/446, record of Fianna Fáil parliamentary meetings, 1951–1955.

141. See UCDA P176/446, meeting of Fianna Fáil parliamentary party, 27 Oct. 1954.

142. Fianna Fáil deputies were first informed of the new committee at a meeting of the parliamentary party on 18 Nov. 1954. At the meeting, at which 46 deputies attended, a 'general discussion on partition occurred'. See UCDA P176/446, meeting of Fianna Fáil parliamentary party, 18 Nov. 1954.

143. Brian Farrell, *Seán Lemass* (Dublin: Gill and Macmillan, 1983), 107.

144. UCDA P176/447, meeting of Fianna Fáil parliamentary party, 22 May 1957.

145. Lemass was given a salary out of party funds of £500.00 per annum and re-appointed as joint honour secretary of the party.

146. John Horgan, *Seán Lemass, The Enigmatic Patriot* (Dublin: Gill and Macmillan, 1999), 160.

147. See comments by Lemass. *The Irish Times*, 13 Oct. 1954.

148. An *Irish Times* profile of Mullins recalled that de Valera had proposed the name of 'Fianna Fáil; Seán Lemass had urged the formation of the organisation; and Mullins actually formed the first cumann of the party, before it had a name, on 12 April 1926. See 'The making of a national party', *The Irish Times*, 16 Feb. 1974.

149. UCDA P104/8654, letters sent by Mullins stating that a joint committee comprising of members of the National Executive and the parliamentary party would draw up policy on Northern Ireland, to be held in Jan. 1955.

150. NAUK Foreign and Commonwealth Office (FCO) 33/1599, confidential profile of Liam Cunningham, British Embassy, Dublin, May 1971.

151. See UCDA P176/46, Liam Cunningham to Fianna Fáil headquarters, 29 Dec. 1954.

152. Michael O'Sullivan, *Seán Lemass* (Dublin: Blackwater Press, 1994), 141.

153. Gerald Boland's unpublished handwritten memoirs, pp. 8–9.

154. See, for example, UCDA P176/270, record of Fianna Fáil Longford constituency files and UCDA P176/274, record of Fianna Fáil Kilkenny constituency files.

155. UCDA P176/280, Haughey to Mullins, 15 Jan. 1955.

156. UCDA P176/46, memorandum from Feehan to Mullins, 20 Jan. 1955 (a copy is also present in the Frank Aiken Papers, P104/8654).

157. UCDA P176/46, Mullins to each member of the standing-committee on partition matters, 25 Jan. 1955.

158. O'Donovan was also chairman of Dublin North-East Comhairle Dáilcheantair. He was brother-in-law to Gerald Boland. In 1939, O'Donovan had written to the party's National Executive expressing his frustration towards the lack of progress on ending partition. See UCDA P176/346, meeting of National Executive, 15 May 1939.

159. Other members of the Tomas Ó Cléirigh cumann were D. Ó Aodh, Eugene Ward, Michael Slatter, Richard Mylan, Danny Lions and Mary Colley (wife to George Colley). Harry Boland interview, 22 Feb. 2008.

160. See *Magill*, July 1989. 'And Now the End is Near', 6. Article by Vincent Browne on the political career of Charles J Haughey.

161. See Martin Mansergh (ed.), *The Spirit of the Nation: Speeches and Statement of Charles J. Haughey (1957–1986)* (Dublin & Cork: Mercier Press, 1986), xxxii.

162. Haughey's breakthrough did not come until the following general election in 1957, when he was elected a Fianna Fáil TD for North-East Dublin; at the expense of Harry Colley.

163. See record of Charles Haughey's last known interview with Frank Kennedy, 22 May 2006. *The Irish Times*, 11 June 2009.

164. Henry Patterson, *Ireland Since 1939, The Persistence of Conflict* (Dublin: Penguin Ireland, 2006), 172–173.

165. UCDA P104/2341, typescript copy of an article by Geraldine Kennedy, 'Frank Aiken: the story that was never told', as related by Francis Aiken (Frank Aiken's son), June 1983.

166. Brown, *'And Now the End is near'*, 6.

167. O'Brien, *The Arms Trial*, 100.

168. Arnold, *Haughey*, 15.

169. Patterson, *Ireland Since 1939, Persistence of Conflict*, 173.

170. Arnold, *Haughey*, 14.

171. The FCA was renamed the Irish Reserve Defence Forces (IRF) in 2005.

172. Walsh, *The Irish Times*, 'Charles Haughey Supplement', 31 Jan. 1992.

173. Raymond Smith, *Haughey and O'Malley, the Quest for Power* (Dublin: Aherlow, 1986), 50.

174. Throughout the memorandum the word 'we' is used when referring to the views of the members of the Ó Cléirigh Cumann.

175. A central duty of an honorary secretary of a Fianna Fáil cumann is to submit letters and memoranda to party headquarters. See 'Duties of cumann honorary secretary', in *Córú agus rialacha, Fianna Fáil, the Republican Party, constitution and revised rules 2006*, 11.
176. For example, in the aftermath of Haughey's election as leader of Fianna Fáil in 1979, a post Colley had been confident of securing, the latter only agreed to serve in the former's government, if he was appointed tánaiste and held a veto over who was appointed to the two key security ministries of the Departments of Justice and Defence. See Arnold, *Haughey*, 158–163.
177. Author's written correspondence with Seán Haughey, Feb. 2009.
178. Author's written correspondence with Seán Haughey, Feb. 2009.
179. Interview with Harry Boland, 22 Feb. 2008.
180. Interview with Mary Colley, 18 May 2009.
181. See comments by de Valera. *Irish Independent*, 13 Oct. 1954.
182. Interview with Harry Boland, 22 Feb. 2008.
183. Correspondence with Harry Boland, 16 June 2009.
184. UCDA P176/347, record of National Executive meeting, 6 Sept. 1954. At this meeting members discussed the request from the Ó Cléirigh cumann that Fianna Fáil take a more 'positive line on partition'.
185. Tomas Ó Cléirigh cumann memorandum, 1.
186. Tomas Ó Cléirigh cumann memorandum, 1.
187. Tomas Ó Cléirigh cumann memorandum, 6.
188. Tomas Ó Cléirigh cumann memorandum, 2–3.
189. Tomas Ó Cléirigh cumann memorandum, 3.
190. Tomas Ó Cléirigh cumann memorandum, 3–4.
191. I am indebted to Harry Boland for this information. Interview with Harry Boland, 22 Feb. 2008.
192. See John A. Murphy, 'The New IRA 1925–62', T. Desmond Williams (ed.), *Secret Societies in Ireland* (Dublin: Gill and Macmillan, 1973), 163.
193. Tomas Ó Cléirigh cumann memorandum, 6.
194. J. Bowyer Bell, *The Secret Army: the IRA* (New Jersey, Transaction Publishers, 1997), 283.
195. Tomas Ó Cléirigh cumann memorandum, 6.
196. Tomas Ó Cléirigh cumann memorandum, 6.
197. On three previous occasions Feehan had unsuccessfully ran as a Fianna Fáil candidate in the 1948, 1951 and 1954 general elections in the Dublin North-West constituency. In the 1954 election, Feehan was narrowly defeated by his Fianna Fáil running mate Richard Gogan. Feehan was held in high regard among the party faithful and at the 1955 Fianna Fáil Ard Fheis was appointed a member of the party's committee of fifteen.
198. UCDA P176/46, Mullins to Feehan, Dec. 1954.
199. In total there were 21 policy points outlined in the memorandum.
200. UCDA P176/46, copy of memorandum from Feehan to Mullins, 20 Jan. 1955 (A copy is also available from P104/8654).
201. Feehan partition memorandum, 1.
202. Feehan partition memorandum, 1–3.
203. Feehan partition memorandum, 'Preparing for Unity, point 'c', 5. See also *The Irish Times*, 11 Oct. 1944 and 16 June 1949.
204. Feehan partition memorandum, 4–5.
205. UCDA P104/8654, record of standing-committee on partition matters meetings, 3 Feb. 1955 and 5 April 1955.
206. UCDA P176/46, memorandum by the chairman of the standing-committee on partition matters, April 1955.
207. An earlier version of the memorandum included a demand that the party appoint a 'Cabinet Minister for National Unity'. Although this was ultimately rejected by the committee, the very fact that it was even considered was evidence that for the first time in the party's existence a concerted effort was being made by senior Fianna Fáil members to construct a coherent

Northern Ireland policy. See UCDA P176/46 and P150/1998, for copies of draft version of memorandum by the chairman standing-committee on partition matters, April 1955.

208. Horgan, *Seán Lemass, The Enigmatic Patriot*, 93–94.

209. Kennedy, *Division and Consensus,* 151.

210. *Irish Press,* 30 Jan. 1953.

211. For example, speaking in Ottawa, Canada, in Sept. 1953, Lemass publicly denounced partition as an 'absurdity'. See NAI DFA 305/14/192A, record of speech by Lemass, Ottawa, Canada, 25 Sept. 1953.

212. Kennedy, *Division and Consensus,* 151.

213. This view of Lemass was offered by the British Embassy, Dublin, 1971. See NAUK FCO 33/1599, confidential profile of Seán Lemass, British Embassy, Dublin, May 1971.

214. NAUK Prime Minister's Office (PREM) 8/824, character profile of Seán Lemass, 1947.

215. *Irish Press,* 19 Oct. 1968.

216. Kennedy, *Division and Consensus,* 132.

217. NAUK FCO 33/1599, confidential profile of Seán Lemass, British Embassy, Dublin, May 1971.

218. See Chapter Five, pp.218-219

219. Although the memorandum did not mention specific constitutional changes it would seem most probable that the document referred to Articles two, three and forty-four of the Irish constitution.

220. See speech by Lemass. *Irish Press,* 8 Feb. 1954.

221. Booth made this observation in a letter to Ernest Blythe. UCDA P24/1389, Booth to Blythe, 9 Feb. 1955.

222. The reference to the 'special position of the Catholic Church' enshrined within the 1937 Irish constitution was removed by referendum in 1973.

223. Diarmaid Ferriter noted that de Valera did make concessions within the 1937 Irish constitution for the possibility of a federal solution. Article 15.2 contained a clause that suggests that the Northern Ireland Parliament could continue, or as the Article stated, 'Provision may be made by law for the creation or recognition of subordinate legislatures'. Ferriter, *Judging dev*, 149.

224. UCDA Seán MacEntee Papers P67/588, copy of speech by Seán MacEntee at UCD Fianna Fáil Kevin Barry meeting, precise date unknown, during his time in opposition, 1951–1954.

225. Record of a debate on partition between Blythe and Northern Nationalist Senator J. Lennon, Armagh, 7 Feb. 1954. *Irish Press,* 8 Feb. 1954.

226. Two months early, in Feb. 1955, de Valera had informed an audience in Manchester that 'Britain must accept her share of the responsibility for the continuation of partition and not wash her hands of it'. *The Irish Times,* 18 Feb. 1955.

227. Chris Reeves, 'Let us stand by our friends', 95–96.

228. See Henry Patterson, 'Seán Lemass and the Ulster question, 1959–65', in *Journal of Contemporary History,* Jan. 1999; 34 (1), 148.

229. NAUK DO 35/7853, record of British Ambassador to Ireland (1955–59), Alexander Clutterbuck's observations of Lemass, 3 July 1959.

230. Patterson, 'Seán Lemass and the Ulster question, 1959–65', 148.

231. Michael Sheehy, *Divided we Stand, a Study of Partition* (London: Faber and Faber, 1955), 94. See also J. L. McCracken, *Representative Government in Ireland, a Study of Dáil Eireann 1919–48* (London: Oxford University Press, 1958), 199–204.

232. Sheehy, *Divided We Stand,* 94.

233. The letter proposed that 'the National Executive should issue a statement on partition on the following lines and incorporate such a statement in any publication dealing with the Fianna Fáil policy and programme'. UCDA P176/46, memorandum by the chairman standing-committee on partition matters, April 1955.

234. UCDA P176/46, de Valera to Lemass, 7 April 1955.

235. See Brian Farrell, 'The unlikely marriage: De Valera, Lemass and the shaping of modern Ireland', *Etudes Irelandaises*; 10, 1985, 217.

236. *Irish Press*, 29 Jan. 1969.

237. *Irish Press*, 4 Feb. 1969.

238. See UCDA P150/1998, Mullins to Máire Ní Cheallaigh, 21 Jan. 1958.

239. Some within the party had commented on supporters of Sinn Féin, who had become 'very sore with Fianna Fáil for coming out against them while the fight was still on'. This was the opinion of Fianna Fáil TD for Cork-South, Seán McCarthy. UCDA P176/286, McCarthy to Lemass, 30 Jan. 1957.

240. See UCDA P24/1769, Blythe, *Towards a Six-County Dominion?*, Aug. 1949.

5

1956–1961

'The man or men that would solve partition would deserve an outstanding place in Irish history'.

[Eamon de Valera, 19 Nov. 1957][1]

'Mr. Lemass is ... the most hard headed and least sentimental of our Statesmen, with an intuitive understanding that the true approach to the North is by ways of deeds, rather than of threats and blandishments ... it is not hard to guess that his approach to the Six-Counties will be along the line of economic co-operation.'

[*The Irish Times*, 30 June 1959][2]

'CONDITIONAL CONSTITUTIONALISTS': FIANNA FÁIL, NORTHERN IRELAND AND THE IRA BORDER-CAMPAIGN, 1956–1959

The unrest witnessed by the Fianna Fáil hierarchy during 1954 and 1955 because of grass-roots' sympathy for the new IRA activity had by early 1956 quietened down. This momentary period of calm was dashed following the recommencement of IRA violence in late 1956. On 12 November 1956, the IRA attacked six customs posts along a seventy-mile section of the Irish border in counties Armagh and Fermanagh. The attacks signalled a new border offensive by the movement, later termed 'Operation Harvest'. The method was to be guerrilla warfare, with an ambitious plan to use flying columns from the Republic of Ireland to attack targets in Northern Ireland.[3]

The following month, in mid-December, the IRA's long-anticipated border-campaign (1956–1962) swung into action. With approximately 150 men, the IRA attacked several of the Northern Ireland security forces' key military positions. On 11–12 December, counties Armagh and Fermanagh were again the targets. Eight miles from the border in the city of Armagh, the IRA raided Gough Barracks; the scene of the successful Gough Barracks arms raid in 1954. On the same night, in Derry city, five members of the local unit of the IRA blew up the British Broadcasting Corporation (BBC) radio transmitter in the Rosemount district and in the County Derry market town of Magherafelt, the movement attacked the town's courthouse. Two days later, on the morning of 14 December, the IRA exploded four bombs outside Lisnaskea RUC police-station in Co. Fermanagh.[4]

It was the military shambles of 1 January 1957, following an IRA ambush of Brookeborough RUC police-station, Co. Fermanagh, which exposed a growing divergence within Fianna Fáil towards the use of violence to end partition. During the ambush two young IRA men, Seán South and Fergal O'Hanlon were killed.[5] The raid became a legend overnight and South and O'Hanlon were martyrs within a week. Their deaths were to cause a 'powerful spasm of public emotion' as the dead 'Volunteers' entered the pantheon of martyrs of both Fianna Fáil and of the extra-constitutional republican movement.[6]

Significantly, their deaths witnessed a split within the Fianna Fáil parliamentary party and were to demonstrate just how strong the mystique of self-styled republicanism in the 1950s was in the Republic of Ireland. As Dermot Keogh noted, both men enjoyed the status of popular martyrs and were viewed by many, including a large number of traditional Fianna Fáil supporters, as being part of the 'purer, unsullied "republican" tradition, which was contrasted with politicians caught up in the materialist world of Yeats' "greasy till"'.[7] Gerald Boland, Fianna Fáil TD for Roscommon, eloquently described this mindset some years later, lamenting that the Irish nationalist community were inspired by a 'philosophy of death rather than life'.[8]

The funerals of South and O'Hanlon were a public relations coup for the IRA. The men's coffins, which were draped with the Tricolour once they crossed the border, were removed from Enniskillen, Co. Fermanagh to St Macartan's Cathedral, Co. Monaghan.[9] Throughout Monaghan town flags flew at half-mast, blinds were closed in houses and businesses closed. A guard of honour made up of thirty youths dressed in black berets marched alongside the coffins of the dead men.[10] At O'Hanlon's funeral emotional speeches were made, which had the wholehearted participation of a number of clergymen, in support of 'Volunteer Fergal O'Hanlon'.[11]

On 5 January, South's funeral in Co. Limerick was a huge affair. Thousands of people lined the streets of Drogheda, Dundalk and Dublin to pay their last respects, as the remains of South made their way to his native county. In Limerick city alone a reported 25,000 people lined the streets as the hearse made its way through Denmark Street to St Michael's Church in the early hours of the morning.[12] The funeral pictures in the *Irish Press* of the dead men spoke for themselves, and reflected a clear ambivalence in Irish society towards the use of violence. Indeed, the Catholic Dean of Limerick, informed an official from the British Embassy in Dublin that the 'whole of the South seemed now to have become infected with the nationalist virus, which was spreading like an epidemic'.[13]

The public reaction to the two young men's deaths forced the taoiseach, John A. Costello to deliver a radio broadcast, in which he spoke of the IRA as an illegal force and categorically ruled out the use of force to secure a united Ireland.[14] In a well-choreographed offensive de Valera offered his full public support to Costello's statement.[15] An editorial in the *Kerryman* encapsulated the mood amongst a section of the population sympathetic to the actions of South and O'Hanlon:

> We do not think the same unity of opinion with regard to the action of the young men will be found amongst the people of the twenty-six counties as there is at Leinster House. The people and their deputies are not in full accord in this matter. Not that the people are prepared to give their active support to armed incursions, or anything of that kind, into the Six-Counties, but they cannot withhold their admiration for young men who risk their all – life and liberty – to achieve the unity of Ireland, even though their methods are considered by most people unwise and foolhardy.[16]

The widespread public outburst of sympathy for the two 'dead volunteers' was visibly apparent at numerous meetings of local county councils throughout the country.[17] Dublin City Corporation and Clare City Council witnessed differences of opinion concerning a passing of a vote of sympathy for the relatives of South and O'Hanlon, respectively; appeals were made by some councillors to adopt an 'unqualified vote of sympathy' for the dead men.[18] In de Valera's constituency of Clare, councillor Vincent McHugh, remarked that it was not a 'regrettable thing to find young men ready to fight the common enemy'.[19] At South Tipperary County Council, Sligo Corporation, Cork Corporation, Wexford Corporation and Kerry Corporation, resolutions were also passed offering sympathy to the families of South and O'Hanlon.[20]

Unrest was stirring at Fianna Fáil grass-roots following the deaths of South and O'Hanlon. A vocal minority of party members expressed their frustration at the lack of progress on partition; one disgruntled supporter from Dublin recorded that if 'something was not done people would forget that there was a border at all'.[21] In January 1957, Lemass received correspondence from the Seán MacDermott cumann, Dublin North-East, informing party headquarters that a resolution was passed by majority vote in 'adoration of the courage and selflessness of Seán South and Fergal O'Hanlon in fighting for Ireland and giving their lives in the cause'.[22] The resolution expressed a desire for 'a leadership that will not hesitate to adopt the most radical measures to secure the reunification of our Country'.[23] In reference to the increased support for the recent IRA activities, the resolution stated that 'it was not surprising that the youth of Ireland, silk of platitudes and hungering for a new more visile [sic] leadership should turn to the IRA'.[24]

For the Fianna Fáil leadership the fact that local representatives agreed that a vote of sympathy should be passed by their respective county councils was a worrying development. In early January 1957 Lionel Booth, in a letter to the *Irish Press*, objected to any vote of sympathy for anyone that did not recognise the authority of the Oireachtas and was a member of an illegal organisation. Booth put it in refreshingly simple terms:

> If these two men had survived, they would, if found by the Gardaí, have now been under arrest on a criminal charge ... anyone, therefore, who attempts to glorify the actions of this illegal organisation is joining in the present defiance of our Constitutional Government.[25]

Booth's comments caused offence among many members of his own constituency of Dún Laoghaire-Rathdown, as two cumainn threatened to resign from the party.[26] The Meaghen Neary cumann and Joseph Hudson cumann, Sallynoggin, wrote to Fianna Fáil headquarters to protest at the actions of Booth as they had 'shown that he is not a loyal member of Fianna Fáil'.[27]

Lemass fully endorsed Booth's remarks. He similarly noted that the passing of a vote of sympathy by public representatives would 'only do more harm'.[28] Writing in response to a letter he received from the honorary secretary of the Meaghen Neary cumann, Seán O'Dalaigh, he was unambiguous: 'Such expressions of sympathy' for the IRA, Lemass said, 'should be voiced as to make clear beyond doubt or ambiguity that Fianna Fáil did not endorse the IRA's actions'.[29] In correspondence with Fianna Fáil TD for Cork-South, Seán MacCarthy, Lemass wrote that the party was at a 'crossroads'. He warned his parliamentary colleague that if party supporters did not 'speak in the same voice' on partition 'they might as well wind up Fianna Fáil'.[30] Frontbench party TD for Cork-North, Seán Moylan followed the Lemass-line. He scornfully protested that there was no future for Fianna Fáil if supporters accepted as official policy 'speeches made at those gravesides'.[31]

The uneasiness among Fianna Fáil members, as noted by John Bowman, exposed that many of those originally recruited to the party could be termed as 'conditional constitutionalists'.[32] While the majority of party members understood the futility of violence, there was evidentially a small number of supporters who still had an 'each way bet' on the use of force.[33] The recent IRA activities highlighted how the difference between policy and ideology was a central Fianna Fáil position on Irish unity. As Matthew Feehan wisely explained, two years earlier, the 'young generation is unable to distinguish between the physical force tradition and the national tradition ... Fianna Fáil as the true "Republican Party" must endeavour to win over the young IRA'.[34]

A selection of Fianna Fáil members saw in their elected representatives only empty rhetoric and unanswered promises. The *Kerryman* articulated Irish republicans' anxieties: 'the people might very well say to their deputies in Leinster House 'You condemn and jail those who are trying their way of ending partition: let us hear how you propose to end it'.[35] The paper concluded:

> Leinster House cannot escape its responsibilities. No solution,
> no leadership in regard to partition has been forthcoming
> from either Fine Gael or Fianna Fáil ... by common consent

they seem to have united in pushing the matter into the background.[36]

In early January 1957, Fianna Fáil Limerick-East TD and future cabinet minister, Donogh O'Malley wrote to de Valera suggesting that considering many party representatives had been 'making goats of themselves' and showing the party in a 'bad light' a meeting should be held so as to make sure that any votes that were passed in local Councils were in accordance with official Fianna Fáil policy.[37] Fianna Fáil TD for Clare, Patrick Hillery, recalled that at this time a lot of party deputies were coming under pressure in their constituencies because of the renewed IRA campaign, including himself.[38] Brian Lenihan, a recently elected Fianna Fáil Senator and future party deputy president, remembered that during the emotive year of 1957 the 'perennial question of Northern Ireland was causing an acute problem'. It was a 'problem', he noted, that was causing many within Fianna Fáil to permit emotions to cloud their judgement.[39]

De Valera recognised that he needed to restate official Fianna Fáil policy towards the IRA and the party's stance on Northern Ireland. Following O'Malley's advice, he scheduled a meeting of the parliamentary party for 15 January 1957. In an unprecedented manner, the parliamentary party convened over an eight-hour period.[40] De Valera chaired proceedings, while over eighty deputies attended, including all senators.[41] On the subject of partition the meeting was the most hostile since the party's foundation. Fianna Fáil TDs openly quarrelled with one another over whether the use of physical force was a legitimate Fianna Fáil policy. Some of those present expressed sympathy for the IRA campaign, one TD even argued that peaceful methods to secure Irish unity had failed. The result of which was that Lemass, 'in a quite untypical display of emotion, erupted'.[42] The problem with peaceful means, he told the meeting, was that it had 'never been given a chance'. Lemass explained that 'every time there was the prospect of some advance in North–South relations, the IRA devastated it by some dastardly act ...'[43]

Hillery recalled some years later that during the course of the meeting, in which tempers were fraught, he was tempted 'twice or more' to stand up and express his opposition to the imprisonment of IRA members. 'I stood up to say so', he wrote, 'but as if he knew my mind, Ted Sullivan TD west Cork grabbed my coat and held me down. After a while, confident of Ted's friendship I got the message and watched as the party found its way to the position it always held'. In a clear indication of Lemass's stature within Fianna Fáil, Hillery noted that 'Lemass's intervention was one of those swift and perhaps unprepared ones which have to be made to bring a meeting to think of relatives'. 'At the time', he remembered,

> I was visited not by the thought of how the Party was [*sic*] swing back on its own rails re IRA but how it was Lemass and *not* Dev who saw the way the meeting might go out of control and swiftly came in to lead. It was during that period '57 to '59 before I was a member of the Govt and while Dev was still Taoiseach.[44]

Privately Lemass believed that Fianna Fáil should not 'pussyfoot about'.[45] As a public representative his job, he noted in private, was to 'lead public opinion and not to follow it slavishly'.[46] He saw the recent IRA border-campaign as merely putting the goal to end partition 'back generations'.[47] Instead, he insisted that resources should be focused on practical ways to end partition.[48] Violence had no place in Lemass's Northern Ireland policy. Fianna Fáil resources, he argued, should be focused towards encouraging cross-border co-operation between Dublin and Belfast. The recent IRA raids and the show of support by Fianna Fáil members towards the IRA left Lemass feeling extremely frustrated. As the voice of pragmatic republicanism he had grown weary of de Valera's inability to forge ahead with a new approach to Northern Ireland.

Lemass's intervention at the parliamentary meeting did not prove altogether successful. The minutes record that the majority of members present contributed on the recent raids carried out in Northern Ireland. After considerable debate, those present decided that 'there could be no armed force here except under the control and direction of the government' and that the 'employment of force at any time in the foreseeable future would be undesirable and likely to be futile'.[49] Paddy Hillery remembered that while it was a 'decision not easily arrived at', party members had 'definitely' agreed that 'whatever happens in the North we're not going in there'.[50] His recollection is, however, at variance with the official minutes of the parliamentary party meeting. The minutes record that 'concerning the feasibility of the use of force by any future government as a means of solving partition ... no definite decision was taken'.[51] It is apparent, therefore, that at the conclusion of the meeting de Valera had failed to secure agreement from those present that the Fianna Fáil Party was against the use of physical force to secure Irish unity, if, in the future, the suitable circumstance arose.

This was significant, not least because the meeting had lasted over eight hours. Such lengthy meetings were a classical example of de Valera's leadership techniques, in which he always wanted to achieve unanimity and he sought this unanimity by the simple process of keeping the debate going, until those who were in the minority, out of sheer exhaustion, conceded the case made by the majority.[52] On this occasion, however, this technique was unworkable, for the fact that too many deputies could not agree that the use of force by a future Fianna Fáil government was not a legitimate policy. Such scenes of antagonism within the party exposed a deep fault-line on the emotive subject of partition. It was not until the turbulent years of 1969 to 1971 that the Fianna Fáil parliamentary party was to again experience bitter scenes between those in the party who supported and those who were against the use of physical force to end partition.[53]

In an attempt to present a united front within the Fianna Fáil parliamentary party, at the close of the meeting, leading members of the Fianna Fáil frontbench reminded both the general public and party supporters that the use of force was not official Fianna Fáil policy. Gerald Boland remarked that 'it was the height of folly to think that we in the Twenty-Six Counties had force enough, if we wished to use it, to compel the Six-Counties to join our State'.[54] Seán Moylan boisterously announced that he could 'see no possible value for the nation in the policy of the use of force in the Six-Counties'.[55] Indeed, de Valera's son, Vivion, stressed that the young men of the IRA needed 'friendly sympathy and advice' to desist from violence.[56]

During the Irish general election campaign in February 1957, on the rare occasions that partition was mentioned, Fianna Fáil deputies propagated the well-trodden claim that only a Fianna Fáil government could eventually secure Irish unity. De Valera reminded the Irish electorate that there had not been a day when he was in office that he 'did not keep the idea of a united Ireland' fully before his mind.[57] The note struck by Fianna Fáil speakers during the campaign was the need to make a division between the will to end partition and the futility of the use of violence: that the IRA's resort to force was understandable but counter-productive. Indeed, the election campaign highlighted the *modus vivendi* that Fianna Fáil and Fine Gael had reached on ending partition, in which both parties were 'resolutely opposed' to the use of force.[58] Fine Gael candidates maintained that 'the people of the North are Irish and that armed attacks against Brother Irishmen' would only result in civil war.[59] A Fianna Fáil government, recorded Seán MacEntee, would have the 'unity, capacity, and the will to curb the IRA'.[60]

Lemass masterminded Fianna Fáil's election campaign with the slogan 'let's get cracking'.[61] The economy not partition dominated his campaign message. He reminded his audiences that there was 'only one issue ... how to get the country back on its feet'.[62] He was determined that Ireland's priority should not be the question of Irish unity, but instead the state of Ireland's economy.[63] He candidly noted that 'nobody would have the neck to urge the Six-Counties to come in until we can show we can lick this economic problem'.[64] The election result heralded a superb victory for Fianna Fáil. The party gained an additional thirteen seats from sixty-five to seventy-eight and its highest ever share of the poll at 53%. It was the party's first overall majority since the wartime victory of 1944.

FIANNA FÁIL AND 'THE OFFENCES AGAINST THE STATE ACT', JULY 1957

Fianna Fáil's entry into government in February 1957 came as a breath of fresh air for de Valera and his newly-appointed cabinet colleagues following three years in opposition. However, the honeymoon period quickly ended as a result of the new government's suppression of the IRA. For a minority of party members the Fianna Fáil hierarchy's determination to crack down on the IRA border-campaign was greeted by a sense of indignation. It had been bad enough that the party had supported the previous Inter-Party government's policy against the IRA, now party members were being asked to endorse a Fianna Fáil government led attack of the IRA: this was a bridge too far for a sizeable minority of Fianna Fáil supporters.

The initial signs of a rift developing between the new Fianna Fáil government and a cohort of disgruntled party supporters surfaced following de Valera's decision to enact 'The Offences Against the State Act' in July 1957. The legislation was in response to IRA border-campaign in Northern Ireland. De Valera's action led to the imprisonment of the Sinn Féin Ard Comhairle, the IRA army council and the IRA general headquarters staff.[65] On the same day that the legislation was enacted, 25 July 1957, de Valera issued a public statement on the recent wave of violence. He maintained that the arrest of Sinn Féin activists was because they were believed to be members of the IRA.[66] He explained that a Fianna Fáil government could not tolerate a secret army which denied the validity of the state and undermined the authority of the cabinet and the Dáil. The government's response was widely praised due to its 'no nonsense' stand against the IRA.[67] The British secretary of state for Commonwealth Relations, Lord Douglas-Home, described de Valera's actions as 'extremely courageous'.[68] In reference to de Valera's crackdown of the IRA, the British Ambassador, Alexander Clutterbuck remarked that 'whatever his defects, he is not lacking in the courage of his conviction'.[69]

The government's suppression of the IRA, however, was greeted with resistance from a vocal section within Fianna Fáil. At a meeting of the Cork Corporation, in late July 1957, Fianna Fáil councillor, TD for Cork-South and former Lord Major of Cork, Seán McCarthy spoke in defence of Sinn Féin councillor, Tomás MacCurtáin. MacCurtáin had been previously arrested as part of the government crackdown on IRA activity.[70] Later that year in December, at a meeting of Dublin Corporation, several unidentified Fianna Fáil councillors publicly recorded their sympathy towards those arrested IRA members. A cohort of Fianna Fáil elected representatives reportedly gave their support to a motion which demanded that all persons imprisoned under the provisions of 'The Offence Against the State Act' should be accorded the status of political prisoners.[71] In the same month, in the border county of Monaghan, at a meeting of Clones Urban Council, councillor S. O'Connor, with the support of a number of unnamed Fianna Fáil councillors, unsuccessfully proposed a resolution calling for the immediate release of IRA internees from the Curragh.[72]

Given such public displays of sympathy for the IRA campaign by elected representatives de Valera realised the recent events could have a destabilising effect on Fianna Fáil – as had been the case in January 1957 following the deaths of the IRA members Seán South and Fergal O'Hanlon. Therefore, in April 1958, de Valera scheduled a meeting of his parliamentary party to reaffirm Fianna Fáil's policy against the IRA and towards partition. In response to deputy McCarthy's actions, at a meeting of the Cork Corporation the previous July 1957, de Valera warned all those present at the parliamentary meeting that any deputy who wished to disagree with government policy 'could resign from Fianna Fáil'.[73] In support of de Valera's comments, Fianna Fáil TD for Cork Borough and minister for education, Jack Lynch, noted that McCarthy's defence of IRA activity was 'unsatisfactory'.[74] De Valera also instructed his parliamentary secretary, Donnchadh Ó Briain, to send a copy of his public statement of 25 July 1957, to all Fianna Fáil TDs, to clarify that the IRA campaign was 'at variance with official government policy'.[75] De Valera concluded the parliamentary party meeting expressing his hope that 'the air had now been cleared'.[76] He was to be disappointed, as much worse was to follow.

During de Valera's remaining years as taoiseach from 1957 to 1959, at meetings of the parliamentary party and National Executive, he routinely spoke of the need for Fianna Fáil elected representatives to condemn IRA violence.[77] Working closely with a collection of cabinet ministers, which included minister for external affairs, Frank Aiken; minister for justice, Oscar Traynor; minister for health, Seán MacEntee; and Jack Lynch, the Fianna Fáil leadership pleaded with party TDs to adhere to government policy against the IRA. Each maintained that to do otherwise would result in the 'loss of everything that has hitherto been gained'.[78] Local party canvas officers also received instructions from party headquarters to notify grass-roots supporters that official Fianna Fáil policy was resolutely against the use of private armies and that if 'the use of force were desirable, only the government would be entitled to employ it'.[79]

Speaking in 1959, on the eve of his retirement from active politics, de Valera again appealed to Fianna Fáil supporters to realise that the alternative to non-violence was 'anarchy and national frustration'.[80] Instead he educated party supporters that it was unrealistic to assume that the ending of partition was a reasonable short-term objective.[81] Publicly, de Valera conceded that there was 'no clear way' to end partition and said that 'the man or men that would solve partition would deserve an outstanding place in Irish history'.[82] Indeed, Aiken and MacEntee each acknowledged it would be naïve to say that partition would be ended in their life time.[83]

Such public declarations by frontbench Fianna Fáil ministers, although a logical assessment of the partition conundrum, were viewed by a minority of party members as an act of treachery. A representative of the Fianna Fáil cumann in Mountmellick, Co. Tipperary, accused de Valera and his cabinet colleagues of 'not giving an answer to the question of partition'.[84] A dejected supporter from Neagh, Co. Laois claimed that 'any ray of hope in the quest to find a solution to the problem had lapsed'.[85] De Valera personally received criticism for his failure to undo partition and his firm stance against the IRA. In early February 1958 an outraged Fianna Fáil member from Co. Tipperary wrote to the *Kerryman* accusing de Valera of helping to 'openly maintain partition'.[86] In July 1958, a Kerry native living in Derbyshire, England, wrote to de Valera to express his 'amazement, regret and disgust at the Fianna Fáil government's shameful treatment of patriotic' IRA men. Comparing the Fianna Fáil government tactics to those of the Gestapo, he warned de Valera that 'back in Kerry' many prominent Fianna Fáil supporters were 'outraged and disgusted at their party's persecution of Republicans'.[87]

Of even greater concern was the worrying development that a consortium of Fianna Fáil elected representatives opposed their government's actions against the IRA; the previous public outbursts by Fianna Fáil elected representatives, notably by Seán McCarthy had been isolated cases, but worse was to follow. At meetings of the Fianna Fáil strong-holds of South Tipperary and Cavan County Councils, respectively, in late 1958 and early 1959, Fianna Fáil councillors voted in favour of resolutions calling for the release of IRA internees.[88] During a meeting of the South Tipperary County Council, in early January 1958, six Fianna Fáil councillors voted in support and four other party councillors abstained, for a motion requesting that de Valera grant a political amnesty for IRA internees.[89] The successful motion was proposed by the prominent Fianna Fáil activist, J. Ahessy and seconded by his party colleague T. Duggan.[90] Abuse was hurled across the council floor against Fianna Fáil councillor and future party member of the Seanad, William Ryan, because he objected to the motion. Ahessy, who had previously spent time in jail and on hunger-strike, branded his fellow Fianna Fáil colleague, Ryan an 'Armchair Republican'.[91]

On hearing of this unrest among Fianna Fáil grass-roots members de Valera again immediately instructed that copies of his Dáil statement, originally issued in July 1957, be sent to every registered Comhairle Ceantair and Comhairle Dáilcheantair throughout the Republic. Attached to the statement was a cover letter that gave details of an amendment that should be used by Fianna Fáil councillors in the event that a resolution in defence of internees was moved at any future local County Council meetings.[92] The situation was perceived to have become so unstable in South Tipperary that in early 1959 de Valera arranged a secret meeting with the three local Fianna Fáil TDs, Daniel Breen, Michael J. Davern and Francis Loughman. At the meeting de Valera reaffirmed to his colleagues the necessity to make sure Fianna Fáil members in South Tipperary adhered to official Fianna Fáil policy against the IRA.[93] Arrangements were also made to send a member of the government to attend a meeting of South Tipperary Comhairle Dáilcheantair so as to 'remind' Fianna Fáil members of official party policy.[94]

On the issue of Northern Ireland, de Valera's final two years as taoiseach were governed by his determination that Fianna Fáil supporters would not switch their allegiance to the IRA. In the immediate term, de Valera managed to keep discontent among party supporters over the IRA campaign to a minimal level. His successful personal intervention in the dispute in South Tipperary revealed his ability to galvanise support for his stance against the IRA. Nevertheless, his actions were only successful in the short-term; a response to isolated events. As usual no long-term strategy to deal with Fianna Fáil members offering support to IRA activities was implemented. Due to his inability to formulate a lucid overall strategy towards Northern Ireland, there remained a tangible gap between the hierarchy and the anti-partitionist-wing of Fianna Fáil towards what constituted official Northern Ireland policy. This divide was never reconciled under de Valera's leadership of the party. When he retired as president of Fianna Fáil in 1959 the party remained divided between those members who acknowledged that only constitutional means could secure an end to partition and those who sympathised, and in some cases supported, the use of physical force to secure Irish unity.

PERCEPTION VS. REALITY: DE VALERA, LEMASS AND NORTHERN IRELAND

In the short term de Valera may have been successful in securing support from Fianna Fáil members up and down the country for this Northern Ireland policy. He did, however find it a more arduous task to maintain harmony on Northern Ireland policy within his own cabinet; Lemass being the main opponent. Fianna Fáil's return to government emphasised the widening gap that had developed between de Valera and Lemass in relation to Fianna Fáil's Northern Ireland strategy. Their main difference lay in how both men *perceived* the role of Ulster Unionists in the equation to secure Irish unity. De Valera had acknowledged that partition could not be ended without the support of the Northern Ireland majority. He had made some attempts to foster North–South co-operation, notably through the Erne Scheme and the Lough Foyle fishery.

However, he was unwilling to view North–South co-operation as independent from ending partition. Lemass, on the other hand, had by the 1950s, accepted they were two separate policies in the short term and only when the first was achieved could attention be turned to the second.

Lemass's growing frustration became evident following a cabinet meeting in April 1957 at which de Valera instructed all government departments to proceed with a study on partition.[95] The study had originally been discussed by the Second Inter-Party government in January 1957,[96] and had called for an examination of 'the practical problems arising on the re-integration of the National Territory'.[97] De Valera's enthusiasm was not shared by his cabinet colleagues many of whom viewed the initiative with disdain.[98] Lemass was the main objector to his leader's proposal. In an astute note to secretary to the Department of the Taoiseach, Maurice Moynihan, Lemass explained that the preparation of such a memorandum could 'not be justifiable'.[99] Instead he remarked that the study should be deferred because of 'the uncertainty as to the future position which has been introduced by the [William B. Stanford] Free Trade area proposals'.[100] Two months previously in January 1957, Belfast-born Protestant, Senator Professor William B. Stanford (Trinity College Dublin) had proposed, in the Seanad, a thirty-two-county free trade area between North and South.[101]

Lemass's desire to defer de Valera's request exposed a central area of contention between both men concerning Fianna Fáil's Northern Ireland policy. Lemass had no time for his chief's proposal. He believed that Irish unity was a long-term objective. Therefore, the compiling of lengthy memoranda, statistics and data on the 'practical problems arising' from Irish reunification was a waste of time. His main concern was for immediate policies that could be implemented by the Fianna Fáil government to lead to the establishment of a thirty-two-county free trade area between Dublin and Belfast; hence his reference to the 'Stanford Free Trade' proposals. Stanford's wish for an all-Ireland free trade area had become an area of conflict between de Valera and Lemass. Since the mid-1950s Lemass had championed an internal crusade within Fianna Fáil designed to foster closer North–South economic co-operation. Specifically, he wished to establish a thirty-two-county free trade area that would see the removal of tariffs between both jurisdictions.[102]

In October 1957 an enthusiastic Lemass requested that a cabinet meeting be held to discuss Stanford's proposals, which were scheduled for debate in the Seanad in January 1958. His eagerness, however, was not shared by his cabinet colleagues and in particular not by de Valera, who ordered that the cabinet would not consider Stanford's proposal.[103] Lemass's willingness to support the proposal at cabinet level was a brave, but unsuccessful tactic, given that de Valera had previously informed Lemass that he did not favour the removal of trade barriers between Dublin and Belfast.[104] Indeed, during the Stanford debate in the Seanad, on 29 January 1958, de Valera objected to the proposal on the premise that it offered 'no real practical value'.[105]

De Valera's reluctance was not altogether surprising considering that it was under his Fianna Fáil administration in the early 1930s that the Irish government originally erected tough tariffs against Northern Ireland goods, which effectively denied Northern Irish manufacturers and distributors access to the Southern market. Unlike his lieutenant, who realised that Ireland's economic protectionism had merely helped to entrench partition, de Valera proved incapable of progressing beyond the outdated Sinn Féin economic mentality.

In a private conversation with the British permanent under secretary for state for Commonwealth Relations, Gilbert Laithwaite, de Valera revealed the differences between himself and Lemass on the issue of tariff barriers between Dublin and Belfast. De Valera noted that excluding the existing areas of co-operation, it would be difficult to find new areas that would benefit both jurisdictions. Specifically, on the issue of the removal of the customs posts between North and South, de Valera recorded that while 'an attractive notion' it was a 'non-starter'.[106] Exposing his inability to grasp the economic realities of the late 1950s de Valera explained that it would 'in effect subject industry in the South to the full force of British competition'.[107]

In the post-war period de Valera acknowledged that partition could not be solved unless he could persuade Ulster Unionists that their future lay within a united Ireland; hence his attempts at North–South economic co-operation.[108] Yet, as taoiseach, he lacked the practical capabilities of fostering such a policy. It was his overall reluctance to maintain a debate on the issue which underlined his lack of vision. He admitted that he saw huge problems in trying to create free trade between North and South and acknowledged that he did not know what steps the government should now take.[109] Indeed, the week before the Stanford motion was scheduled to be debated in the Seanad de Valera had instructed his personal secretary, Maire Ní Cheallaigh, to locate the memorandum on partition issued by the standing-committee on partition matters in April 1955: a document he had previously rejected out of hand.[110]

Conor Cruise O'Brien of the Department of External Affairs summed up the problem for government policy makers arising out of Stanford's motion, in a letter to Irish permanent representative at the United Nations, Freddie Boland. O'Brien explained that linking co-operation with an anti-partitionist agenda had merely negative results in North–South relations. It allowed 'orthodox or right-wing unionists to spotlight moderates as dupes or traitors, who are succumbing to the wills of the enemies of Ulster'. O'Brien envisaged that the government should be seen to develop and encourage economic co-operation in isolation to seeking a solution to partition.[111] O'Brien had unknowingly spotted the differences between de Valera and Lemass in connection with North–South co-operation. For too long de Valera had failed to avoid linking practical proposals with the political objective of Irish unity.

The Stanford debate also exposed the internal division within Fianna Fáil in relation Northern Ireland. Although de Valera was in a position to constrain Lemass within the cabinet, the same could not be said of the former's ability to dictate policy at party level. The initial signs of a desire for change in the face of de Valera's lack of mobility on policy occurred at a meeting of the Fianna Fáil parliamentary party on 5 February 1958. The meeting took place a little under a week after the Stanford debate. Deputy Lionel Booth moved a motion urging that steps be taken to initiate discussions at high level between 'the government and Stormont to promote co-operation and close liaison between the two governments and all their departments' and to lay the 'foundations for maximum joint planning of agriculture and industry'.[112]

The proposals were ruled out by de Valera on the dubious assertion that any action taken would have to be along the 'proper lines'.[113] Booth's proposal should not, however, be viewed merely as an example of a disgruntled party backbencher challenging official policy. On the contrary, the Dún Laoghaire-Rathdown deputy was a respected businessman, representing the industrial wing of the party. He was previously a member of the party's committee of fifteen and included Lemass as one of his closest associates within Fianna Fáil.[114] Since the early 1950s Lemass had nurtured the idea of cross-border co-operation with Belfast on the issues of tourism and transport. He believed that these early exchanges on areas of common interest only marked the beginning of a process that had the ultimate objective of establishing official contact between the Dublin and Stormont governments.

While de Valera remained as leader of Fianna Fáil the liberal economic advances advocated by Lemass, Booth and others within the party remained impeded. De Valera's inability to recognise the advantages of encouraging a free trade area between Dublin and Belfast was yet another example for an increasingly frustrated Lemass of his leader's unwillingness to deal with partition on a rational basis. Lemass, however, remained quiet, biding his time. He realised that de Valera would sooner rather than later step aside and as is discussed below, the moment he did, Lemass pounced. Upon assuming the leadership of Fianna Fáil in 1959 his first major Northern Ireland policy initiative was to offer Belfast a thirty-two-county free trade area for goods of Irish or Northern Ireland origin.[115]

OUT OF TOUCH WITH POLITICAL REALITIES: DE VALERA, A 'BRITISH DECLARATION' AND THE COMMONWEALTH 'DEBATE'

There were two strands of Fianna Fáil's traditional strategy towards partition which further exposed the party's inability, under de Valera's leadership, to make substantial revisions to its Northern Ireland policy. The first was de Valera's continued badgering of the London government to make a declaration in support of Irish unity; the second was the flawed belief that Ireland's possible re-entry to the British Commonwealth could help facilitate an end to partition.

The first point dealt with the arena of Anglo-Irish relations, where during de Valera's final years in government, partition became an almost dirty word for London. British ministers avoided a debate on the issue on every suitable occasion.[116] In his few meetings with British ministers and officials, de Valera was reported to offer only a 'rambling conversation' on partition.[117] British prime minister, Harold Macmillan maintained that he was 'not prepared to enter into a discussion on partition'.[118] While Macmillan privately confessed that he personally 'would like to see a united Ireland', he believed that the Fianna Fáil government had made little, if any, attempts to secure the support of Ulster Unionists.[119] Writing in July 1957, he lamented that the 'right way for the Republic to make for closer understanding with Northern Ireland is to woo Northern Ireland'. 'They have', he said, 'made no effort whatever to do anything of the sort ...'[120]

From a British perspective de Valera's continued presence in power as Fianna Fáil leader had implications for partition. Throughout the

1930s and the war period de Valera was a prominent figure in Anglo-Irish relations. By the end of the 1950s, however, the British concluded that de Valera was out of touch with political realities. Unlike Lemass they viewed him as a leader that was incapable of dealing with partition on a rational basis. The British Embassy in Dublin reported that de Valera looked 'downhearted ... old and tired' and worried not merely about partition, but with Ireland's stagnating economy.[121]

Ironically, Aiken offered de Valera's impending retirement as a reason why the British government should seek to find a solution to partition. On at least two occasions in 1958, while meeting British officials, he explained that de Valera would 'not be around forever and because of his stature in the Country any solution which he might endorse would in all probability be acceptable to the people in Ireland'.[122] Clutterbuck noted that given de Valera's impending retirement it was not altogether 'unreasonable to assume he may make a final effort to crown his career with the ending of partition'.[123] Aiken's comments, nonetheless, were greeted by little more than condescending amusement from London. The British maintained that the ending of partition was unattainable in the immediate-term.[124]

Aiken was undeterred and throughout late 1957 and 1958 routinely requested that the British make 'a conciliatory gesture' towards the undoing of partition.[125] By the conclusion of the 1950s Aiken was viewed by London as encapsulating the inherent anti-partitionists mindset endemic within the Fianna Fáil organisation. Though now 'somewhat mellowed', he was reported to have 'always had a violent anti-British bias',[126] a man, as recorded by the British Embassy in Dublin, who saw partition as the 'supreme issue'. The Embassy warned that Aiken's approach to Anglo-Irish relations would be dictated by a single-minded pursuit to gain Irish unity.[127] Indeed, during a meeting with Aiken in July 1957, Clutterbuck complained that the former gave a 'fresh tirade against partition' and it took him sometime 'to calm down'.[128]

Left frustrated that the British had no intention of taking any new initiatives on partition de Valera focused his attention on a traditional ingredient of his Northern Ireland policy: a declaration from the British in support of Irish unity. Privately, de Valera admitted that this represented his 'last desperate effort' to find a solution to partition.[129] This policy had been routinely evoked by Fianna Fáil administration since the party's coming to power in the 1930s. It had received its most sympathetic hearing from London during the Chamberlain–MacDonald era of Anglo-Irish relations in the late

1930s. Malcolm MacDonald actually pressed for such a declaration from his cabinet colleagues during the 1938 Anglo-Irish negotiations and had sent a draft to de Valera for his consideration. Although it was ultimately dropped by London, due to disputes over North–South trade concessions, it left de Valera with a deep-rooted, but ultimately flawed, conviction that the British could be eventually persuaded to make a declaration in favour of Irish unity.

The political landscape of the 1950s was entirely different to that of the 1930s. The passing of the Ireland Act of 1949 by Westminster had effectively seen the veto on Irish unity being switched from London to Belfast. This, together with Ireland's neutrality during the Second World War and removal from the Commonwealth in 1948, meant that a British declaration was no longer a realistic demand. De Valera, however, ignored this political reality and had throughout the 1950s made a British declaration one of Fianna Fáil's central Northern Ireland policies.[130] During de Valera's last two years in power the Irish government routinely inquired whether the British would consider making a declaration.

Dublin's latest efforts to convince London to make a declaration in support of Irish unity were immediately rejected. On each occasion that the Irish raised the issue the British response was rudimentary: London could see 'no solution to partition in the immediate term and therefore a British declaration would be futile'.[131] Clutterbuck described Dublin's request for a declaration as 'fanciful notions'.[132] He wrote that the dropping of the 'vendetta against the North and its replacement by a new sustained effort at conciliation' was a veiled attempt by the Fianna Fáil government to give the perception that it wished to win the support of Ulster Unionists.[133]

London's reluctance to maintain a debate on partition may help to explain de Valera's willingness to open up a second front of his Northern Ireland strategy; his support of a proposal in favour of Ireland's possible re-entry into the Commonwealth, in return for Irish unity. The proposal was originally suggested by the Roman Catholic Primate, Cardinal John D'Alton, during the Irish general election in March 1957. The proposal was based on a four-stage process that anticipated a federal agreement between the North and South and that a united Ireland, within the Commonwealth, would offer bases to NATO, Britain and America.[134]

Although initially against the proposal on the grounds that it was 'quite impractical',[135] de Valera did – for a brief period at least – give it some consideration. In a secret meeting with Lord Pakenham, who it would seem travelled to London at the behest of Macmillan in September 1957,[136] de Valera informed his British colleague that the Cardinal's offer could be 'regarded as an approach from the Irish'. However, de Valera said that he did not intend to take any initiative, nor did the Irish government have any intention of offering (or seeking) the association of Ireland with the Commonwealth as a step independent of a solution to partition.[137] What de Valera did propose, as revealed from an examination of Pakenham's record of the meeting, was that he 'would personally favour association with the Commonwealth on the Indian model, i.e. membership of the Commonwealth without direct allegiance to the Crown, provided that Ireland could return as a united country'.[138] During a meeting between de Valera, Aiken and Home, in March 1958, de Valera proposed that Northern Ireland should surrender its 'direct allegiance to the Queen in return for a united Republic of Ireland within the Commonwealth recognising the Queen as the Head'.[139]

Nothing came of de Valera's overtures to London. The British privately expressed concern for Dublin's sudden wish to reopen the Commonwealth debate. Macmillan wrote that the Fianna Fáil 'Republican government' was merely using the proposal in an attempt to 'bring off a coup', so to 'compensate them for any ground they may have lost for their ... action in arresting those various IRA people'.[140] Although some attempts were made by British officials to further explore the proposal, Aiken, in particular, had by 1958 become privately sceptical as to whether London was genuinely supportive of the initiative.[141] Given Dublin's reluctance to officially endorse the Cardinal's proposals, by the end of 1958' the British no longer wished to keep the debate alive. Macmillan was reported to not be overly enthusiastic, 'doubting if a united Ireland – with de Valera as a sort of Irish Nehru – would do us much good'.[142] Indeed, he recorded that there was 'no question of its being politically possible for Éire to rejoin the Commonwealth'.[143] Consequently, the proposal disappeared into the political undergrowth not to be reawakened again during de Valera's remaining time in government.

The available evidence would suggest that on balance de Valera did not support the proposal. Nevertheless, that he had at least given the proposal consideration demonstrated the futility of his Northern Ireland policy; for the offer to be effective it required the support of the Northern Ireland government. This was never a realistic objective. Ulster Unionists detested any of de Valera's advances, describing the proposal as 'economic suicide'.[144] On Lemass's election as taoiseach, he recognised this fundamental anomaly. He conceded that the Northern Ireland government were uninterested in the proposal.[145] Ever the political realist, he questioned, 'why would Ireland's re-entry into the Commonwealth help to end partition?' Partition, he said 'had been instituted when Ireland was in the Commonwealth'.[146] During Lemass's leadership the Irish government never gave the proposal serious consideration.[147]

By the time de Valera had completed his final two years as taoiseach he realised that for all his pronouncements and protests the British government cared little of Dublin's demands for an end to partition. It was a depressing period for him. Privately he confessed to the former British representative to Ireland, Lord Rugby that the 'inevitability of gradualness' was all he had left. He explained that 'an intermediate period was first required in which the people of North and South would have to co-exist on good neighbourly terms'.[148] De Valera's confession to Rugby exposed the former's recognition that Irish unity was an unattainable medium-term objective.

Writing to MacDonald, on the eve of his retirement from active politics in 1959, de Valera remembered that only Neville Chamberlain had ever really wished to find a solution to partition. All Chamberlain's successors as British prime minister, he lamented, could 'never envisage the real solution of the Irish-English problem'.[149] His comments to MacDonald encapsulated de Valera's inability to deal with partition in the post-war era. He seemed stuck in political limbo, unable to realise the extent that the political landscape had changed over the preceding decades. Thus, when he retired from active politics in the summer of 1959, he left behind him no coherent or, indeed realistic, Fianna Fáil Northern Ireland policy. Years of neglect had meant that de Valera's only positive legacy towards partition was his habitual pronouncements that physical force was not a legitimate policy to secure Irish unity; a policy he had made central to Fianna Fáil's strategy towards Northern Ireland during the early 1930s.[150]

He had admitted that it was the threat of partition that had first prompted his involvement in politics.[151] But as he faced the end of his career in mainstream politics he had failed to fulfil the number one objective of Fianna Fáil: the party's promise of a thirty-two county Irish Republic. It would be unfair to be overly critical of de Valera for failing to attain that which he never actually claimed to be able to achieve. What he can be criticised for, nevertheless, was his stubbornness and myopic attitude towards partition. He was incapable of disregarding outdated nationalist prejudices. In particular, he would not acknowledge the huge stumbling block that Ulster Unionism represented in the drive to secure Irish unity.

He simply believed that if he could eventually persuade the British government to make a statement in support of ending partition, Ulster Unionists would somehow be impelled to join a united Ireland. Indeed, writing in 1975, Seán MacEntee recalled with frustration that throughout de Valera's political career 'his chief' was 'firm in his conviction that the trouble there [Northern Ireland] was due to British guile and nothing else'. 'The nucleus' of de Valera's political strategy on partition, MacEntee wrote, was focused almost entirely on Britain.[152] While de Valera did make some conciliatory gestures towards Belfast, notably on cross-border co-operation, these were but isolated cases. Indeed, he failed to comprehend the extent that he was personally ridiculed in Unionist circles. He was seen as the 'bogeyman' of Ulster Unionism. For Ulster Unionists he was a political leader who encapsulated the anti-partitionist mindset inherent within mainstream Irish nationalism in the Republic.

In January 1959 de Valera announced his intention to retire as Fianna Fáil president; it was a further six months, June of that year, that he finally stepped aside.[153] Party deputies were 'dumbfounded that he should ever think of retiring', his decision came as a 'bombshell'.[154] The spotlight immediately turned on who would replace de Valera as Fianna Fáil leader and taoiseach. Lemass was undoubtedly popular among party deputies and at 58 years old was viewed as the most realistic and practical man in the government. He had, nevertheless, made critics in a ministerial career spanning more than two decades; some supporters felt that by 1959 Lemass was 'old and tired'.[155] Lemass realised that no one could replace de Valera – to do so would have been futile – he had not Dev's magic appeal, nor did he hold the "chief's" domineering and authoritarian qualities. He was, however, a superbly gifted political tactician who possessed a work horse ethos. He believed he was what Ireland in the twentieth century needed, a hard-headed tycoon rather than a romantic visionary. He was, as noted by Clutterbuck, 'down to earth', a leader that London '... could do quite a lot of business with'.[156]

The result of the succession race was never really in doubt; even if there was a little discontent among a select few of deputies.[157] After the furore of de Valera's election as president of Ireland, the parliamentary party and the National Executive gathered on 22 June 1959 to elect a new leader. MacEntee duly proposed and Aiken seconded Lemass as the second president of Fianna Fáil.[158] Soon after the National Executive met to ratify the decision;[159] the following day he was officially elected taoiseach by the Dáil. Except for Fine Gael leader, Enda Kenny, no national leader, or prime minister, North or South, before or since, spent as long as an elected representative before assuming the highest office. He was now the head of the youngest cabinet in Europe and resembled a relatively old man in a hurry; although it would be wrong to view him as representing the dawning of a new era. Instead he was to be the link between the old and the new generation within Fianna Fáil.

'A NEW LOOK AT THE OLD POLICY OF PARTITION':[160]
SEÁN LEMASS AND NORTHERN IRELAND, 1959–1961

Seán Lemass's appointment as Fianna Fáil leader and taoiseach in June 1959 raised hope to a new generation of Fianna Fáil supporters that he would cast aside the ghosts of the past and deal with Irish unity, not as a theoretical aspiration, but as a long-term reality. Lemass offered Fianna Fáil members a new interpretation of the partition question. Guided by one central motivation – the Irish economy – his entire approach to Northern Ireland was based on securing support from Ulster Unionists for his wish to establish a free trade area between Dublin and Belfast. He wished to portray partition not so much as the artificial division of the country, but a tangible political, social and cultural division – a division that could only be healed through a process of understanding and co-operation between North and South.

Significantly, under Lemass, partition and economic policies became intrinsically linked as he adapted Fianna Fáil's traditional approach towards Northern Ireland to the new economic realities of the 1960s. The Irish government's 1958 programme for economic expansion, inspired and implemented by the secretary of the Department of Finance, T.K. Whitaker, emphasised the importance of an open market free trade area between Ireland and the United Kingdom. Particular emphasis was placed on dismantling the Irish protectionist regime in preparation for European Economic Community (EEC) membership.[161] This new initiative had ramifications for partition. Lemass believed that the first step in securing a free trade area between the Republic and Great Britain was the dismantling of Dublin's protectionist system against Belfast within the island of Ireland.

Like his predecessor, de Valera, Lemass retained sole control and management of Fianna Fáil's Northern Ireland policy. Throughout his period as taoiseach from 1959 to 1966 policy initiatives towards Northern Ireland rarely came from anywhere else within the Fianna Fáil party but from Lemass personally. The Department of the Taoiseach, with Lemass at the helm, dictated what constituted the Fianna Fáil government's Northern Ireland policy. He would consult others from within the civil service and his own party if required, but his decision was always final. Unlike de Valera, Lemass did not give his Fianna Fáil colleagues an opportunity to debate Northern Ireland strategy. On no occasion during his premiership was Northern Ireland policy discussed at a meeting of either the Fianna Fáil parliamentary party or National Executive.[162] This approach was also followed at government level. While he did encourage his ministers to develop their own policies within their particular departments,[163] when it came to Northern Ireland, this was always Lemass's sole responsibility.

Lemass's firm hold over Northern Ireland policy revealed his style of management. As Jack Lynch later recalled, Lemass's style was 'brusque and peremptory'.[164] He was direct and forceful in handling government and party meetings.[165] He believed that a quick decision was always better than the long delayed decision.[166] Lemass was unlike de Valera. The latter would chair a meeting of the cabinet or parliamentary party for hours on end to achieve unanimous agreement on Northern Ireland policy. Lemass simply choose not to place Northern Ireland on the agenda, so as not to allow deputies raise any objections that they may have harboured. Indeed, Seán MacEntee was to recall that more often than not Lemass was inclined to come to a cabinet meeting with his mind already made up.[167]

Lemass's first major policy development towards Northern Ireland was his offer to the Ulster Unionist government of a thirty-two-county free trade area between North and South for goods of Irish or Northern Ireland origin;[168] a move that de Valera would have never contemplated, as he believed that to do so would grant legitimacy to the Northern Ireland state. The offer was rejected by the Northern Ireland prime minister, Lord Brookeborough. He described any attempts at improving North–South relations as a 'dirty word' in the context of renewed IRA activity.[169] Moreover, Brookeborough was resolute that cross-border co-operation between Dublin and Belfast was impossible so long as the Irish government refrained from granting constitutional recognition to Northern Ireland.[170]

Lemass's willingness, nevertheless, to encourage constructive dialogue on economic policy with the Northern Ireland government demonstrated that a metamorphosis was gradually occurring within Fianna Fáil. During the 1938 Anglo-Irish negotiations, Lemass had supported the de Valera line of not agreeing to the granting of free entry for Northern goods to the South. Since the mid-1950s, however, Lemass believed that Dublin should end its protectionist policies towards Belfast and instead establish a free trade area between both jurisdictions.

Despite Lemass's progressive stance on the economic realities of partition it would be incorrect to say that Lemass's Northern Ireland policy was a significant departure from that of his predecessor, de Valera. Under Lemass's leadership no radical policy development regarding partition occurred; as with de Valera, he did not advocate a substantial change of principle or priorities towards Northern Ireland. Lemass freely admitted that his policy for unity was 'not a new policy'. It was 'a reaffirmation of the traditional republican policy', since de Valera.[171] Short-term considerations motivated Lemass's initiatives on Northern Ireland. His early years as taoiseach saw no fundamental changes occur towards Fianna Fáil's approach to partition. His Oxford Union speech in October 1959, shortly after he became taoiseach, best highlights how Lemass's ultimate objectives in relation to Northern Ireland differed little to de Valera. Its significance is apparent given that on the recommendation of Lemass, it was decided that his speech at Oxford would be published as a pamphlet entitled, *One Nation* and distributed among Fianna Fáil members as an official policy document.[172] During Lemass's years as taoiseach the pamphlet was routinely distributed whenever a request was made by members of Fianna Fáil and from the general public, enquiring what constituted the Irish government's Northern Ireland policy.[173]

The Oxford speech represented Lemass's most important pronouncement on partition during his first term as taoiseach from 1959 to 1961. The address contained three policies that were in accordance with Fianna Fáil's traditional Northern Ireland policy: his government maintained that Northern Ireland Protestants could not be coerced into a united Ireland; that a federal solution between Dublin and Belfast constituted a legitimate settlement of partition; and lastly, that the British government was required to make a declaration that Irish unity was in London's interests.[174]

That the Protestant majority in Northern Ireland could not be coerced into a united Ireland by physical force constituted a central tenet of Fianna Fáil's Northern Ireland policy under Lemass.[175] Throughout his seven years as leader he attempted to institute effective dialogue with Ulster Unionists and to increase social and economic co-operation between North and South, in an effort to marginalise the appeal that the IRA had for the younger generation of Ireland.[176] He routinely pronounced that Irish unity could not be achieved until the 'barriers of hostility and distrust', which separated Irish nationalists and unionists, were first removed.[177]

Additionally, Lemass's offer to Ulster Unionists of a federal agreement between Dublin and Belfast, whereby the Northern Ireland government would retain its own parliament in Belfast and the powers currently held by Westminster would be transferred to the Dublin parliament, was a reoccurring feature of Lemass's speeches on Northern Ireland.[178]

Traditionally, a British declaration in support of Irish unity had been a central theme of Fianna Fáil's Northern Ireland policy under de Valera. Under Lemass this policy was demoted to a distinctly secondary role. He believed that the constant harassing of the British government was a scapegoat used by nationalists to relieve themselves of any responsibility for partition. In Lemass's meetings with his British counterparts, during his time as Fianna Fáil taoiseach, he did not raise the issue of a declaration.[179] Instead, on suitable occasions, usually at the Fianna Fáil annual Ard Fheiseanna, Lemass demanded a British declaration to placate the anti-partitionists within the party. His reluctance to 'badger' the British to support an end to partition exposed his wish to channel Fianna Fáil's Northern Ireland policy towards Belfast rather than London. He certainly did not absolve Britain of a responsibility to end partition. Nevertheless, he did believe that Irish unity was primarily about securing reconciliation between North and South.[180]

This approach rejected a traditional Fianna Fáil view of the North, as the 'fourth green field', tragically separated from the rest of the nation by the means of the British. This policy was not confined to Fianna Fáil, but to the wider Irish nationalist community. From the inception of the Northern Ireland state the Irish government had refused to accept its legitimacy as a political unit. For many nationalists, in both parts of Ireland, the right to rule of the Stormont government was illegitimate; republicans repeatedly pronounced that no one in Ireland, including the unionist population, had voted for what they termed the 'Partition Act'.[181] Northern Ireland was viewed as the missing piece in the jigsaw, the stolen, sundered territory, which rightly belonged to the Irish nation. Lemass had become tired of this time-honoured anti-partitionist mentality and realised a change of direction was necessary.

LEMASS AND THE EVOLUTION OF TERMINOLOGY: FROM A 'SIX-COUNTIES' TO A 'NORTHERN IRELAND' POLICY

Although apparent that Lemass was unwilling to make drastic alterations to Fianna Fáil's Northern Ireland policy, he did seek to move away from the anti-partitionist rhetoric that had dominated the party's stance on partition since its foundation. The single greatest change was Lemass's subtle development of political terminology regarding Northern Ireland. Through the imaginative use of language he attempted to create a climate which favoured a softer policy of near-recognition of the Northern Ireland government and of the Northern Ireland state so as to foster closer North–South relations.

Lemass epitomised the 'politics of nuance' in which shades of difference in the articulation of certain ideas had profound implications for political ideology and action.[182] Importantly he introduced a process of reinterpretation – rather than replacing – key principles of Fianna Fáil's attitude to partition. This change, however, was always limited as Lemass was unable to go any faster than his supporters would allow, owing to the constant battle within the party among the traditionalists and modernisers over Northern Ireland policy.

On the day he became taoiseach, Lemass illustrated his wish to end Irish nationalists' constant use of irredentist language. In a break from the past, he said that he preferred to cease to use the negative term 'Anti-Partition' and replace it with the more positive phrase 'restoration of national unity'.[183] Symbolically this was a huge step forward. The phrase had become synonymous with de Valera and Fianna Fáil. One only had to remember the ill-fated All Party Anti-Partition Committee that had so recklessly spearheaded the anti-partition campaign in the South during the early 1950s. Indeed, although the All-Party Anti-Partition Committee continued to meet occasionally during the 1950s and into the late 1960s and early 1970s, under Lemass, the committee never gathered.[184]

Lemass's most important public pronouncement of his desire to leave behind the outdated nationalist rhetoric came at the thirtieth Fianna Fáil Ard Fheis in early November 1959; his first party conference as president.[185] Lemass remained loyal to a central tenet of Fianna Fáil's Northern policy maintaining that it was 'impossible' to recognise the existence of the Northern Ireland state.[186] He was, however, willing to move the goal posts and instead said that he recognised that partition existed.[187] This was unprecedented and was a brave gamble on Lemass's part – it is easy to underestimate the political tremor that was caused by a Fianna Fáil taoiseach's decision to include the two words 'partition' and 'recognise' in the same sentence.[188] Of even greater significance was Lemass's reference, throughout his speech to the party faithful, to the 'parliament and government of Northern Ireland' and 'the Constitution of Northern Ireland'.[189] It was an initiative that de Valera would never have contemplated. Lemass's usage of terminology highlighted a distinctive feature of his Northern Ireland policy and his willingness to progress beyond the traditional Fianna Fáil anti-partitionist mentality.

Since the early years of the Irish Free State the standard practice in political and administrative circles in the South of Ireland was the constant usage of the term 'Six-Counties' to refer to Northern Ireland. This formula was an easy way for Irish nationalists to propagate their non-recognition of the Northern Ireland state and was endorsed by not only de Valera, but also by the leaders of Fine Gael Party and the Labour Party, respectively. Lemass was no longer willing to adhere to such nationalist rhetoric. Although he had no intention of succumbing to Ulster Unionist demands that Northern Ireland should be recognised *de jure* as part of the United Kingdom, Lemass did want to deal with the political realities of North and South relations.[190]

Writing to Vivion de Valera, in May 1960, Lemass explained that 'the use of terms like "Belfast government", "Stormont government", "Belfast authorities" has been the outcome of woolly thinking on the partition issue'.[191] He wrote that if Ulster Unionists were to ever agree to enter a united Ireland under a federal solution, which would grant local autonomy to a subordinate Northern Ireland Parliament with a government in Belfast, it was nonsensical that the Irish government continue to refrain from using the title 'government of Northern Ireland'. He, therefore, argued that it was merely 'commonsense that the current name would be kept'.[192] Lemass also believed that if he was to achieve his policy of establishing effective co-operation in the economic sphere with Ulster Unionists, the Fianna Fáil government, as expressed by Lemass's son-in-law and future taoiseach, Charles J. Haughey, 'needed to take a less rigid line in the matter of nomenclature'.[193]

Both *The Irish Times* and *Irish Independent* drew attention to the new policy, suggesting that the use of a 'changed terminology' had now been informally communicated to the media and was to be a welcome departure from the use of the derogatory term 'Six-Counties'.[194] The Director of the Government Information Bureau, Pádraig Ó hAnnracháin, informed the political correspondent of the *Irish Independent*, P. Quinn, that although 'no government decision' had been communicated to the officials concerned, Lemass had 'officially encouraged' such an approach.[195] The British warmly welcomed Lemass's willingness to abandon the use of the 'Six-Counties'. The British Ambassador to Ireland, Alexander Clutterbuck, reported back to Whitehall that Lemass's references in the Dáil to partition were 'couched in notably moderate terms'.[196]

Support for Lemass's new initiative from within Fianna Fáil was mixed. Although not attacking Lemass personally, the available evidence suggests there was a certain level of discontent among deputies. Certainly, Jack Lynch, Seán MacEntee and Charles J. Haughey welcomed a change in policy.[197] Haughey, for example, privately informed Aiken that the Fianna Fáil government 'should introduce a greater degree of flexibility in our practice by permitting the use, as occasion may require, of the terms "Republic of Ireland" and "Northern Ireland"'.[198]

Aiken, however, was the main opponent to the move; as were others within the party.[199] The unrest originally surfaced following remarks by Fianna Fáil TD for Dún Laoghaire-Rathdown, Lionel Booth during a debate in the Dáil in July 1959. Booth passionately pleaded to all members of Dáil Éireann to ban the word 'partition forever from the language', remarking that it was a 'misleading word' that only increased the 'whole misconception'. In the mould of Lemass, he too explained the futility of the usage of terms such as 'puppet government', 'occupied territory' and 'police State'.[200]

Reaction from Fianna Fáil circles to Booth's comments was alarming. At a meeting of the Fianna Fáil parliamentary party in July 1959, Longford-Westmeath TD, Michael Joseph Kennedy made a *cri de coeur* in opposition to Booth's remarks. Lemass was forced to intervene, explaining that partition was 'a very difficult question' and notified deputies to be 'extremely careful' when it came to making public utterances on partition.[201] At a subsequent meeting of the party's National Executive, a letter was read from Booth's own County Comhairle Dailcheantair, Dún Laoghaire-Rathdown, denouncing his Dáil statement on partition.[202] Again Lemass spoke on Booth's behalf and reassured those present that he would discuss with Booth 'the advisability of his taking an early opportunity of removing any misconceptions created by his remarks'.[203]

This episode exposed a fault-line within Fianna Fáil on the subject of terminology. Lemass's own comments at the Ard Fheis in November 1959 and the subsequent media attention surrounding his usage of the term 'Northern Ireland', caused such controversy among Fianna Fáil supporters that in June 1960 he was forced to speak in the Dáil on the issue. During the course of the speech Lemass was visibly reluctant to officially record that the government had decided to use the term 'Northern Ireland'. Instead he informed deputies that 'no final decision had been taken by the government on the name of Northern Ireland or to give formal or official recognition to the government of Northern Ireland'.[204] Lemass, ever the pragmatist, was forced to deny the reality of what he was doing and instead he left the matter as undecided so as to satisfy both sides within Fianna Fáil.

This approach, however, had its own problems as it merely meant that there developed a wide variation in practice between government departments and various ministers. Lemass could himself be criticised for the ambiguity of Fianna Fáil government policy on the issue. On viewing a record of his speeches to the Dáil during this time as taoiseach, his usage of terminology varied greatly; in February 1961, Lemass used both 'Northern Ireland' and 'Six-Counties' in the same debate in the Dáil.[205] Albeit within the Department of the Taoiseach it did become invariable policy to use the term 'Northern Ireland', Lemass never officially sanctioned that the term 'Northern Ireland' was to replace 'Six-Counties'.

Indeed, the official files of the 1966 Easter Rising Commemoration Committee show the abandonment by Lemass of the description 'Northern Ireland' and a reversion to the 'Six-Counties' formula.[206] Most revealingly, in March 1966, shortly before his retirement as taoiseach, Lemass privately admitted that he had 'no strong views either way'.[207] Throughout his time as taoiseach, whenever the issue of terminology arose, the standard practise within his department was to cite his Dáil speech of 21 June 1960 as official government policy.[208] This was to remain the official government response throughout the remainder of the 1960s, with Lemass's successor as leader of Fianna Fáil, Jack Lynch happy to leave the matter as undecided.[209]

It is difficult, a generation removed, to convey how significant Lemass's decision was to alternate the phrase 'Northern Ireland' with 'the Six-Counties'. This apparently symbolic gesture was in the early 1960s a great leap forward. One must understand how powerful and intoxicating the usage of anti-partitionist rhetoric had over the nationalist psyche. Abandoning such language was a brave departure on Lemass's behalf. His wish to foster a new discourse of this nature was complicated from the start, as it was developed by the Irish state, whose constitution claimed jurisdiction over the 'Six-Counties' of Northern Ireland. Thus, Lemass's usage of terminology was an important departure and signalled his desire to reconstruct one of the most contentious ideological symbols of the traditional Fianna Fáil mentality.

A RELIC OF THE FAILED ANTI-PARTITION CAMPAIGN: FIANNA FÁIL, THE ANTI-PARTITION OF IRELAND LEAGUE OF GREAT BRITAIN AND NORTHERN NATIONALISTS, 1956–1961

Lemass's relationship with the Anti-Partition of Ireland League of Great Britain and Northern Nationalists continued as it had under de Valera, with the new taoiseach unwilling to offer either any direct line of input into Northern Ireland policy-making. One merely had to read the text of Lemass's first public interview on partition of June 1960. He had informed his interviewee of the need to replace the negative term 'Anti-Partition' for the positive phrase 'the restoration of the national unity'.[210]

Following Fianna Fáil's election victory in 1957 de Valera had deliberately remained aloof from the Anti-Partition of Ireland League of Great Britain and Northern Nationalists.[211] Years of neglect by successive Fianna Fáil governments had meant that by the turn of the 1960s both movements were on the brink of collapse. In the summer of 1957 the Irish Ambassador in London, Con Cremin, communicated to Dublin that the Anti-Partition of Ireland League of Great Britain was 'not thriving'. Its decline, Cremin remarked, was due to a lack of enthusiasm, which in some cases was even replaced by one of cynicism.[212] Since the late 1940s, de Valera had been reluctant to financially support the movement. He believed that the organisation was a hangover from his failed anti-partition campaign and its continued existence merely represented a conflict of interests.[213]

Moreover, Fianna Fáil's relationship with Northern Nationalists and the Irish Anti-Partition League in Belfast had eroded during de Valera's last term in government. In a letter from the secretary to the Department of the Taoiseach, Maurice Moynihan, in May 1957, the Fianna Fáil government's apathy for the League's activities were glaringly exposed. Moynihan noted that the anti-Stormont campaign abroad had failed.

He explained that a large current of cynicism and disillusion had developed towards anti-partition activities and that the Irish people had become 'puzzled about the whole question'.[214] Privately, Aiken had repeated such utterances. He believed that the League had produced an ill-disciplined abstentionist opposition to a 'well oiled Unionist machine' and because of its parish-based structure it had been 'given ... a sectarian character'.[215] Officials in the Department of External Affairs maintained that the League served 'no useful purpose'.[216] It was merely an 'allegiance that offered no policy'.[217]

The arrival of Lemass as taoiseach mattered little to the plight of the Anti-Partition of Ireland League of Great Britain or to Northern Nationalists. During his first term as taoiseach Lemass devoted little energy towards either anti-partition body. His relationship with the Anti-Partition of Ireland League of Great Britain was characterised with at best a sense of indifference and at worst hostility. Throughout his time as taoiseach he routinely turned down invitations from the League to attend their annual conference.[218] Under his authority he did not permit the Irish government to offer the movement either practical or financial assistance.[219] He viewed the League as an outdated anti-partitionist talking shop, which offered no actual workable policies to help end partition.

Tadhg Feehan, general secretary of the Anti-Partition of Ireland League of Great Britain, was the first within the movement to acknowledge that a change of direction was necessary. Privately, Feehan noted that he was not altogether happy about the term 'Anti-Partition League' describing it as 'cumbersome'.[220] In October 1960, at the organisation's annual conference he pleaded with delegates to support a resolution calling on the movement to change its name to 'The United Ireland League'. His appeals, however, fell on deaf ears and the resolution was rejected.[221] Over the next couple of years the League continued to disintegrate and by 1962, Feehan acknowledged that the League 'had served its purpose'.[222]

In June 1962 the vice-chairman of the League, Maurice Roche offered a frank evaluation of the movement's future. His observations were not optimistic. He envisaged that the League should be either radically revised or completely wound up. He noted that partition was not a 'live issue in British politics'. What was most revealing about Roche's analysis was his confession that the League had proved 'an embarrassment to the Irish government'. He explained that it was 'representative of a vociferous Irish political organisation actively engaged in removing the border right away'.[223]

Roche's assessment proved to be the shot in the arm that the League needed as in early 1963 the decision was finally made to change the name of the movement to that of the 'United Ireland Association'. Writing to the Irish Embassy in London, in March 1963, Feehan remarked that the decision to change the name 'had benefited greatly' the organisation. Because of the positive title, Feehan said, 'more influential people had become interested in the objectives of the Association'.[224] It is apparent that the movement's change in direction was welcomed by Fianna Fáil. In 1965, under the authority of Frank Aiken, minister for external affairs, the Fianna Fáil government reinstated its financial support to the newly remodelled Association. This was a marked shift in policy. Between 1965 and 1969 the government gave over £3,000 to the movement, with an average of over £600 per annum.[225] Aiken, in his capacity as minister for external affairs, lodged the monies to the credit of the Trustees of the United Ireland Association.[226]

Lemass, likewise, welcomed the change in emphasis that the Association offered; although his approval was always couched with a sense of indifference. He viewed the remodelled movement as moving away from a stale anti-partitionist formula, towards the recognition of the need to encourage a bond of goodwill between Ulster Unionists and Irish nationalists. Throughout the remainder of Lemass's premiership he sent a message to the annual conference of the Association.[227] Although more accommodating towards the Association, Lemass did not offer the movement any direct input towards Fianna Fáil's approach to partition. His unwillingness to accord the Association a voice on Northern Ireland policy was conditioned on his wish to move the emphasis of Fianna Fáil's Northern Ireland policy away from the British government and instead towards Ulster Unionists. After all, de Valera had first formed the anti-partition movement in Great Britain in 1938 as a means of 'educating' the British government and citizens of the injustice of partition. This approach was no longer relevant in the changed political landscape of the 1960s. Lemass, therefore, believed that the movement could offer nothing of benefit to the Fianna Fáil government's approach towards Northern Ireland.

On becoming taoiseach Lemass's relationship with Northern Nationalists was as equally frosty to that of the anti-partition movement in Great Britain. During his first years as taoiseach, he had little time for those he regarded as being as conservative and sectarian as Ulster Unionists.[228] In particular, Lemass disliked Northern Nationalists' unwillingness to participate as the official opposition to Ulster Unionists at Stormont. He maintained that if his federal approach to a united Ireland was to prove successful, Northern Nationalists would be required to play an active role in electoral politics of Northern Ireland.[229] By the early 1960s Lemass had become increasingly exasperated by Northern Nationalists' attempts to influence the Fianna Fáil government's Northern Ireland policy. This was a matter that Lemass believed was for the government alone. Just as de Valera had explained in the 1950s, Northern Nationalists should know their place and would not be permitted to have any direct input into policy-making.

Lemass was to later concede that he had attributed a part of the responsibility for Northern Ireland's problems to the 'narrow attitudes' of the Nationalist Party.[230] His criticisms were justified. Since the mid-1950s the anti-partition campaign in Northern Ireland had been in a state of turmoil.[231] Although the League had a general policy that elected members should attend the Northern Ireland parliament, there were no official policy guidelines. The political reality was indeed worrying; there was no Nationalist Party organisation in the strict sense of the word; no constituency organisations such as the Ulster Unionist Party or the Northern Ireland Labour Party; no party offices, no headquarters, no secretary, no membership cards and no members. Instead there were only individual MPs at the Northern Ireland parliament who came together in a loose form of a parliamentary party organisation.[232]

Nationalist MP for Foyle Derry, Eddie McAteer had frequently called for a reassessment of the tactics used by Anti-Partitionist MPs at Stormont. In early January 1959, at meeting of the Executive of the Anti-Partition League, McAteer expressed his desire that the League be abolished.[233] Although his petition was rejected, McAteer continued to lobby members of the League to abandon their abstentionist policy – thus acknowledging the constitutional position of Northern Ireland – and participate as a functional political machine at Stormont. Yet for many within the League such moves were nothing less than 'treacherous'.[234] As is demonstrated in the following chapter, it would take almost a further five years of political wrangling before the party agreed to assume the position as the official opposition at Stormont.

The establishment of a new organisation 'National Unity' in Northern Ireland, in late 1960, placed mainstream Northern Nationalists on the defensive. The movement was designed as a 'sort of a discussion group to bring together people of widely different opinion' to discuss ways and means towards Irish reunification.[235]

It was the focus of middle-class Catholic discontent with the calibre and electoral effectiveness of the majority of Northern Nationalist MPs.[236] Importantly it sought to promote greater understanding of the nationalist case within the Ulster unionist community and to pursue its aims by seeking support from the existing parties representing the nationalist people with the exception of Sinn Féin.[237] It represented the initial steps towards a revisionist approach to nationalist thinking, which was to fully manifest itself in 1965, with the formation of the politicised National Democratic Party.

Lemass supported the new movement from its inception. He viewed it as a welcome alternative to the sterile anti-partitionist rhetoric offered by the Nationalist Party.[238] Although he turned down an offer to attend a meeting of National Unity in April 1961,[239] he was impressed by the early progress of the movement. Throughout his time as taoiseach he received reports on the movement from his 'eccentric' Protestant cabinet colleague, minister for posts and telegraphs, Erskine Childers.[240] A politician with a 'first class mind ... a glutton for work, enthusiastic, loyal and conscientious',[241] Childers was a valuable source of intelligence for Lemass's insight into Northern Ireland affairs.

As a consequence of a request from Lemass that he be supplied with additional information on the National Unity's objectives,[242] in mid-1961, he received a forward-thinking pamphlet *Unity, New Approaches to Old Problems*. Written by Michael McKeown, a member of National Unity, its preamble was inexplicitly unambiguous. Partition, McKeown wrote, could only be ended with the consent of the majority of the Northern Ireland population, not only that, but the raising of the issue at the United Nations or at Church door collections had proved a failure.[243]

National Unity's willingness to publicly acknowledge that Irish unity could only be achieved with the consent of the majority of Northern Ireland citizens was controversial within nationalist circles. Traditionally, the Dublin government and elected Northern Nationalist representatives had maintained that Ulster Unionists did not have the right to vote themselves out of a united Ireland. Irish nationalists North and South of the border had opposed the 1949 Ireland Act, which had enshrined the principle that partition could not be ended without the 'consent of the majority of Northern Ireland'. Significantly, as is argued in the following chapter, there is evidence available to suggest that Lemass was a supporter of National Unity's readiness to offer concessions on the issue of consent to Ulster

Unionists.[244] For the meantime, however, he kept his views hidden, aware that to speak on the issue could cause a division between the anti-partitionist and liberal-wing of his own party.

Indeed, Lemass's positive view of the new organisation was not shared by officials in the Department of External Affairs. Some warned that Lemass's flirtation with the organisation made him guilty of 'ultimate heresy' in that the aims of the movement 'at achieving a united Ireland by the consent of the people of Northern Ireland' was in effect a recognition of the constitutional position of Northern Ireland.[245] There was a founded apprehension that any new departure envisaged by Lemass towards Northern Nationalists might be viewed as a betrayal and would merely encourage some within the nationalist community to support more extreme measures, thus defeating the object of the exercise.

Lemass was not to be discouraged and he even advised his Fianna Fáil backbench TD for Dublin North-East, George Colley to approach 'a selected private person to raise funds for the movement's magazine, *New Nation*, because a public grant would require a Dáil vote';[246] financial assistance that Lemass was intentionally slow to offer to the Nationalist Party.[247] Lemass's willingness to support the new organisation further underlined his desire to mould a new approach towards Northern Ireland and replace the anti-partition mentality which had held such a firm grip over the psyche of Fianna Fáil. His relationship with Northern Nationalists during his first term as taoiseach exposed his contempt for their outdated and 'negative' involvement with Northern Ireland politics.[248] It would not be until Lemass's last four years as taoiseach that relations improved with the Northern minority.

*   *   *

In conclusion, although all the walls did not come down during Lemass's first period in government, on the issue of partition, some of the stones had been removed. As a file prepared by the British Embassy in Dublin, recorded in July 1959, Lemass's approach to partition was driven by a determination to secure Ireland's economic prosperity. 'Improvements could be got', the memorandum noted, 'brick by brick and it was his [Lemass's] intention to lay a few of these bricks'.[249] He showed a willingness to disregard traditional illusions and prejudices and deal with Northern Ireland how it was and not how he wished it to be. He was openly more accommodating towards Ulster Unionists, helping to foster cross-border relations in the hope that a unity of wills would eventually emerge among all people of Ireland.

As is discussed in the following chapter, Lemass continued this theme during his second term as taoiseach from the winter of 1961 to April 1965. Following Fianna Fáil's election victory in October 1961, he sought to convince Ulster Unionists of the economic and political merits of entering a united Ireland. It was, however, to prove an ominous task; not least because of Northern Ireland prime minister, Lord Brookeborough's sceptical reception of Lemass's Northern Ireland initiatives. In particular, Ulster Unionists resolutely maintained that any practical co-operation between Dublin and Belfast was impossible as long as the Republic continued not to recognise the *de jure* existence of Northern Ireland. Relations were made all the more precarious because of the recommencement of the IRA border-campaign in Northern Ireland in January 1962. Moreover, if Lemass was to find it an arduous task securing support from Ulster Unionists for his approach towards Northern Ireland, he was to find it as equally difficult to convince a small, but vocal, cohort of anti-partitionists within Fianna Fáil to fall behind his Northern Ireland strategy; particularly because of his ruthless suppression of the IRA.

A glimmer of hope, however, surfaced following the arrival of Terence O'Neill as Northern Ireland prime minister in March 1963. Sensing that O'Neill may have been more susceptible to Dublin's overtures on cross-border co-operation than his predecessor, Lemass seized the initiative. In a change in policy, he sought to 'encourage' Northern Nationalists to end their policy of abstentionism and agree to become the official opposition party at Stormont. Significantly, risking a huge backlash from Fianna Fáil rank-and-file, on the delicate constitutional issue of recognition, he offered *de facto* recognition of Northern Ireland. As is analysed Lemass's policies, at least in the short term, proved successful and this was acknowledged by O'Neill's decision to officially meet Lemass at Stormont in January 1965. The Lemass–O'Neill meeting represented a milestone for Lemass, signifying the culmination of ten years of policy development towards Northern Ireland.

NOTES

1. University College Dublin Archives (UCDA) Eamon de Valera Papers P150/2075, copy of de Valera's Presidential speech, 1957 Fianna Fáil Ard Fheis, 19 Nov. 1957.
2. *The Irish Times*, 30 June 1959.

3.   Barry Flynn, *Soldiers of Folly: the IRA Border Campaign, 1956–1962* (Cork: Collins Press, 2009), 48–81. See also John Maguire, *IRA Internments and the Irish Government: Subversives and the State, 1939–1962* (Dublin: Irish Academic Press, 2008).
4.   Flynn, *Soldiers of Folly*, 66–70 & 82–83.
5.   Richard English, *Armed Struggle, A History of the IRA* (London: Pan Macmillan, 2003), 74.
6.   Henry Patterson, *The Politics of Illusion, Republicanism and Socialism in Modern Ireland* (London: Radius Books, 1989), 81.
7.   Dermot Keogh, *Twentieth Century Ireland, Nation and State* (Dublin: Gill and Macmillan, 1994), 229.
8.   *Irish Press*, 19 Oct. 1968.
9.   *Irish Press*, 4 Jan. 1957.
10. Flynn, *Soldiers of Folly*, 120.
11. *Irish Press*, 4 Jan. 1957.
12. Flynn, *Soldiers of Folly*, 124–125.
13. National Archives of the United Kingdom (NAUK) Dominions Office (DO) 35/4987, note of conversation between the Dean of Limerick and P.A. Clutterbuck, 16 Jan. 1957.
14. UCDA John A. Costello Papers P190/683, text copy of Costello's speech, 6 Jan 1957.
15. See *Irish Press*, 7 Jan. 1957.
16. *Kerryman*, 12 Jan. 1957.
17. J. Bowyer Bell, *The Secret Army: the IRA* (Dublin: Poolbeg, 1997), 301.
18. This appeal was made by the Lord Mayor of Dublin, Robert Briscoe; he was also Fianna Fáil TD for Dublin South-West. He said that in passing such a vote the Dublin Corporation did not approve the activities of the IRA. *The Irish Times,* 8 Jan. 1957.
19. *The Irish Times*, 17 Jan. 1957. *Irish Press*, 7 Jan. 1957.
20. Flynn, *Soldiers of Folly*, 128.
21. This was the opinion of J. Brennan, Fianna Fáil Dublin County Comhairle Dáilcheantair. *The Irish Times*, 13 Nov. 1956.
22. UCDA Fianna Fáil Party Papers P176/280, D. Uas. Mac Phroinsias, honorary secretary of Seán MacDermott cumann, Dublin North-East, to Fianna Fáil headquarters, 15 Jan. 1957.
23. UCDA P176/280, Mac Phroinsias to Fianna Fáil headquarters, 15 Jan. 1957.
24. UCDA P176/280, Mac Phroinsias to Fianna Fáil headquarters, 15 Jan. 1957.
25. *Irish Press*, 7 Jan. 1957.
26. UCDA P176/277, E. P. Leonard, honorary secretary Fianna Fáil Joseph Hudson cumann, Sallynoggin, to Fianna Fáil headquarters, 10 Jan. 1957.
27. UCDA P176/277, Leonard to Fianna Fáil headquarters, 10 Jan. 1957. See also UCDA P176/277, Lemass to Seán O'Dalaigh, honorary secretary Fianna Fáil Meaghen Neary cumann, Dún Laoghaire-Rathdown, 15 Jan. 1957.
28. UCDA P176/286, Lemass to MacCarthy, 25 Jan. 1957.
29. UCDA P176/277, Lemass to Seán O'Dalaigh, honorary secretary of Meaghen Neary cumann, Dún Laoghaire-Rathdown , 15 Jan. 1957.
30. UCDA P176/286, Lemass to MacCarthy, 25 Jan. 1957.
31. *Irish Press*, 21 Jan. 1957.
32. See John Bowman, *De Valera and the Ulster Question, 1917–1973* (Oxford, Oxford University Press, 1982), 287. Indeed, Seán MacCarthy pleaded with Lemass to 'listen to the ordinary citizens in the bars and buses' who had become 'increasingly supportive to the IRA activity'. UCDA P176/286, MacCarthy to Lemass, 24 Jan. 1957.
33. Bowman, *De Valera,* 287.
34. UCDA P176/46, memorandum from Feehan to Mullins, 20 Jan. 1955.
35. *Kerryman*, 12 Jan. 1957.
36. *Kerryman*, 12 Jan .1957.
37. O'Malley explained that it would look 'appalling if any members, councillors [*sic*] carried away by popular sentiment agree to a vote which congratulates these youngsters'. UCDA P150/3095, Donogh O'Malley to de Valera, 8 Jan. 1957.
38. UCDA Patrick Hillery Papers P205/101, record of Hillery's recollections of conversation with one of his Co. Clare constituents 'Hurley'. Hillery's handwritten diary entry, 10 Jan. 1978.

39. See Brian Lenihan, *For the Record* (Dublin, 1991), 5.
40. The meeting began at 3.00pm and did not conclude until 11.00pm. UCDA 176/446, meeting of Fianna Fáil parliamentary party, 15 Jan. 1957. This comment was made by Lemass. UCDA P176/286, Lemass to MacCarthy, 25 Jan. 1957.
41. Seán MacEntee, Jack Lynch, Edward Cotter, John Flynn and Thomas Harris were absent with permission, while Dan Breen, Bernard Butler, Thomas McEllistrim and Peadar Maher were absent without permission. See UCDA 176/446, meeting of Fianna Fáil parliamentary party, 15 Jan. 1957.
42. Horgan, *Lemass*, 173.
43. UCDA P205/101, record of Hillery's recollections of Fianna Fáil parliamentary party meeting, 15 Jan. 1957. Hillery's handwritten diary entry, 10 Jan. 1978.
44. UCDA P205/101, record of Hillery's recollections of Fianna Fáil parliamentary party meeting, 15 Jan. 1957. Hillery's handwritten diary entry, 10 Jan. 1978. The use of italics is this author's insertion.
45. UCDA P176/286, Lemass to MacCarthy, 25 Jan. 1957.
46. UCDA P176/286, Lemass to MacCarthy, 25 Jan. 1957.
47. UCDA P176/286, Lemass to MacCarthy, 25 Jan. 1957.
48. This comment was made by Lemass. See UCDA P176/286, Lemass to MacCarthy, 25 Jan. 1957
49. UCDA 176/446, meeting of Fianna Fáil parliamentary party, 15 Jan. 1957.
50. Ronan Fanning, 'Playing it cool: The response of the British and Irish governments to the crisis in Northern Ireland, 1968–9', *Irish Studies in International Affairs*, Vol. 12 (2001), 70.
51. UCDA 176/446, meeting of Fianna Fáil parliamentary party, 15 Jan. 1957.
52. Farrell records an interview he had with Lemass in which the latter noted that de Valera relied upon 'the force of physical exhaustion'. Brian Farrell, *Seán Lemass* (Dublin, Gill and Macmillian, 1983), 107.
53. For example at a meeting of the parliamentary party on 5 Oct. 1969, heated exchanges occurred among deputies concerning the party's Northern Ireland policy. At the meeting, Fianna Fáil leader and taoiseach, Jack Lynch requested that 'deputies not to give the appearance of cashing in on the situation' in Northern Ireland. UCDA P176/448, meeting of Fianna Fáil parliamentary party, 5 Oct. 1969. See also meetings of the Fianna Fáil parliamentary party, 3 June 1970, 27 Oct. 1970 and 28 July 1971. See UCDA P176/448.
54. Boland noted that the recent raids 'will only delay the inevitable reunion of the country'. *Irish Press*, 21 Jan. 1957.
55. *Irish Press*, 21 Jan. 1957.
56. See Bowman, *De Valera*, 290.
57. *The Irish Times*, 4 March 1957.
58. This view was expressed in a pamphlet issued on behalf of Fine Gael in the run-up to the election in Dublin South-west. See UCDA P176/311.
59. UCDA Seán MacEntee Papers P67/391, copy of Fine Gael 1957 general election leaflet issued on behalf of Gerald Sweetman, Kill, Co. Kildare.
60. Bowman, *De Valera*, 290.
61. Farrell, *Lemass*, 95.
62. *Irish Press*, 27 Feb. 1957.
63. Three days after the parliamentary meeting, on 15 Jan., he delivered a 12,500–word address to the party's Consultative Council in Dublin in which he focused his entire speech on a plan for economic recovery for Ireland. *The Irish Times*, 18 Jan. 1957.
64. UCDA P176/286, Lemass to MacCarthy, 25 Jan. 1957.
65. Bell, *The Secret Army*, 306–307.
66. UCDA P150/3117, statement issued on behalf of de Valera, July 1957.
67. *The Irish Times*, 16 Sept. 1957.
68. National Archives of Ireland (NAI) Department of Foreign Affairs (DFA) P203/2, meeting between Cremin and secretary of state for Commonwealth Relations, Home, 27 July 1957.
69. NAUK DO 35/7812, Clutterbuck to Laithwaite, 9 July 1957.

70. See *Cork Examiner* for the month of July 1957.
71. *The Irish Times*, 31 Dec. 1957.
72. *Evening Mail*, 21 Dec. 1957.
73. UCDA P176/447, meeting of the parliamentary party, 16 April 1958.
74. UCDA P176/447, meeting of the parliamentary party, 16 April 1958.
75. UCDA Donnchadh Ó Briain Papers P83/266, de Valera to Ó Briain, 23 Aug. 1957.
76. UCDA P176/447, meeting of the parliamentary party, 16 April 1958.
77. See for example UCDA P176/447, meeting of the parliamentary party, 24 Oct. 1957 and UCDA P176/348, meeting of National Executive, 12 Jan. 1959.
78. See for example UCDA P176/447, record of meetings of the parliamentary party, 24 Oct. 1957, 16 April 1958, and 22 Jan. 1959.
79. See UCDA P176/312, document entitled 'Notes for Canvassers', located within the Fianna Fáil constituency files for Dublin North-Central. Oct. 1957.
80. See *Irish Press*, 15 March 1959, speech by de Valera.
81. See speeches by de Valera, *Irish Press*, 9 March 1957, 19 Oct. 1957 and 19 March 1958.
82. UCDA P150/2075, copy of de Valera's Presidential speech, 1957 Fianna Fáil Ard Fheis, 19 Nov. 1957.
83. See comments by Aiken during a meeting with secretary of state for Commonwealth Relations, Lord Home. NAI DFA P203/2, meeting between Aiken and Home, 4 July 1958. See also speech by MacEntee, *Irish Press*, 18 March 1958.
84. This was the opinion of Mr Culleton representative of the Fianna Fáil Mountmellick cumann, Co. Tipperary. *Irish Press*, 20 Nov. 1957.
85. This was the opinion of Mr M. McGrath representative of the Fianna Fáil Nenagh cumann, Co. Laois. *Irish Press*, 20 Nov. 1957.
86. This was the opinion of Jack Meagher, Annfield House, Cudville, Nenagh. See *Tipperary Star*, 7 Feb. 1959.
87. NAI Department of the Taoiseach (DT) 97/9/1273, 'Government policy: letters of advice and criticism, 1957–1959', Pádraig Ó Bhrosnaeain to de Valera, 29 July 1958.
88. See *Tipperary Star*, 10 Jan. 1959 and *The Irish Times*, for the month of Jan. 1959.
89. *Tipperary Star*, 10 Jan. 1959.
90. Seán Tracey, Labour councillor and future Ceann Comhairle and G. Meskil also supported the motion. See *Tipperary Star*, 10 Jan. 1959.
91. *Tipperary Star*, 10 Jan. 1959.
92. UCDA P176/348, meeting of National Executive, 12 Jan. 1959.
93. UCDA P176/348, meeting of National Executive, 12 Jan. 1959.
94. UCDA P176/348, meeting of National Executive, 12 Jan. 1959.
95. NAI Cabinet minutes (CAB) 2/18, extract from cabinet meeting, 26 April 1957.
96. NAI CAB/2/17, extract from Inter-Party government cabinet meeting, 2 Feb. 1957.
97. NAI DT S 9361G, copy of 'Memorandum for the Government, Partition: study of practical problems arising on re-integration of the National Territory', 16 April 1957.
98. By early Aug. 1957 other departments, namely Justice, Education, Health, Lands and Gaeltacht all reported that there was 'no value in pursuing the study', with Finance commenting that they felt that there was 'no urgency'. No replies were received from Local Government, Social Welfare or Posts and Telegraphs. NAI DT S 16220, Belton to Moynihan, 1 Aug. 1957.
99. NAI DT S 9361G, secretary of the Department of Industry and Commerce to Moynihan, 23 April 1957.
100. NAI DT S 9361G, letter from secretary of the Department of Industry and Commerce to Moynihan, 23 April 1957.
101. NAI DT S 16272, copy of memorandum for the Government: 'Co-operation with the Six-Counties – Seanad motion by Prof. William B. Stanford', 18 Oct. 1957.
102. As chairman of the standing-committee on partition matters, in April 1955, Lemass advocated the establishment of a free trade area between North and South. See Chapter Four, pp.177-184.
103. Michael Kennedy, *Division and Consensus, the Politics of Cross-Border Relations in Ireland, 1925–1969* (Dublin: Institute for Public Administration, 2000), 169.

104. UCDA P176/46, de Valera to Lemass, 7 April 1955.
105. Seanad Éireann debate (SE), 29 Jan. 1958. Vol. 48, cols. col. 413–414.
106. NAUK DO 35/5210, meeting between Gilbert Laithwaite and de Valera, 8 April 1957.
107. NAUK DO 35/5210, meeting between Gilbert Laithwaite and de Valera, 8 April 1957.
108. See de Valera's 'concurrence of wills' speech. Dáil Éireann debate (DE), 24 June 1947. Vol.107, col. 79. See also de Valera's 1957 Ard Fheis speech. *Irish Press*, 20 Nov. 1957.
109. *The Irish Times*, 30 Jan. 1958.
110. UCDA P150/1998, letter from Ní Cheallaigh to de Valera attached to which a copy of the memorandum was issued on behalf of the standing-committee on partition matters, 21 Jan. 1958.
111. NAI DFA 305/14/169/3, O'Brien to Boland, 14 Feb. 1958
112. UCDA P176/447, meeting of parliamentary party, 5 Feb. 1958.
113. UCDA P176/447, meeting of parliamentary party, 5 Feb. 1958.
114. I am indebted to Dr Richard Booth (son of Lionel Booth) for this information. Interview with Richard Booth, 8 Dec. 2008.
115. See Lemass's Oxford Address, 15 Oct. 1959. *The Irish Times*, 16 Oct. 1959.
116. See NAI DFA P203/2, meeting between Aiken and Home, 18 March 1958; and meeting between Aiken and Home, 4 July 1958.
117. See NAUK DO 35/5210, meeting between Laithwaite and de Valera, 8 April 1957. See also NAUK Prime Minister's Office (PREM) 11/2374, meeting between Macmillan and de Valera, 18 March 1958.
118. See NAUK PREM 11/2374, meeting between Macmillan and de Valera, 18 March 1958.
119. NAUK PREM 11/1901, Macmillan's observations re: 'the Fianna Fáil government, partition and the IRA', 17 July 1957.
120. NAUK PREM 11/1901, Macmillan's observations re: 'the Fianna Fáil government, partition and the IRA', 17 July 1957.
121. NAUK DO 35/5210, meeting between Gilbert Laithwaite and de Valera, 8 April 1957.
122. NAI DFA P203/2, meeting between Aiken and Home, 18 March 1958; and meeting between Aiken and Home, 4 July 1958.
123. NAUK PREM 11/2374, Clutterbuck to Prime Minister's Office, March 1958.
124. See, for example, NAI DFA P203/2, meeting between Aiken and Home, 18 March 1958; meeting between Aiken and Home, 4 July 1958.
125. See for example NAUK PREM 11/1901, letter entitled: 'recent suggestions from Irish Republican quarters as to a means of ending partition', April/May 1957. See also NAUK DO 35/7812, record of conversation between Aiken and Laithwaite, mid-July 1957.
126. NAUK PREM 8/824, character profile of Frank Aiken, 1947.
127. See NAUK PREM 11/2374, letter from British Embassy, Dublin to Commonwealth and Relations Office, London, recording Aiken's views on partition, 3 March 1958.
128. NAUK DO 35/7812, meeting between Aiken and Clutterbuck, 8 July 1957.
129. UCDA P150/2940, de Valera to Lord Rugby, 17 April 1957. See also NAUK PREM 11/901 for a copy of the letter.
130. See, for example, P104/8037, meeting between Aiken and Lord Salisbury, leader of the House of Lords, 28 Oct. 1952.
131. This was the opinion of the British permanent under secretary to the Commonwealth Office, Sir Gilbert Laithwaite. NAI DFA P203/2, meeting between Cremin and Laithwaite, 1 May 1957. See also NAI DFA P203/2, meeting between Aiken and Home, 18 March 1958.
132. NAUK PREM 11/2374, Clutterbuck to Laithwaite, 2 Feb. 1958.
133. NAUK PREM 11/2374, Clutterbuck to Laithwaite, 2 Feb. 1958.
134. The Cardinal's proposal was based on a four stage process: (a) the application of the County option system to Northern Ireland, which would allow each of the Six-Counties to decide whether it would remain under the Northern Ireland parliament or come under the jurisdiction of the Dublin parliament; (b) the second stage was to consist of the agreement of the Northern Ireland government to 'unite with the South as a federal unit'; (c) the third would be the association of federal Ireland 'within the Commonwealth as an

independent republic on the same basis as India'; and finally (d) a united Ireland would offer basis to NATO, Britain and America. *The Irish Times*, 4 March 1957.

135. See *Irish Press*, 17 March 1951 and UCDA P150/2940, de Valera to Rugby, 8 June 1957.

136. UCDA P104/8046, memorandum from Cremin to Murphy recording a meeting between Pakenham and Macmillan, 20 Aug. 1957.

137. NAI DFA 203/2, meeting between de Valera and Pakenham, 18 Sept. 1957.

138. See NAUK PREM 11/1901, Pakenham's record of meeting between himself and de Valera, 11 Sept. 1958.

139. NAUK PREM, 11/2374, meeting between de Valera, Aiken and Home, 18 March 1958.

140. NAUK PREM 11/1901, Macmillan's observations re: 'the Fianna Fáil government, partition and the IRA', 17 July 1957.

141. See NAI DFA 203/2, confidential meeting between Aiken and Home, 21 Oct. 1957; meeting between Aiken and Home, 18 March 1958; and meeting between Aiken and Home, 4 July 1958.

142. NAUK PREM 11/1901, Macmillan's views re: 'Ireland and the Commonwealth', 14 Aug. 1957. See also Deirdre McMahon, 'Ireland, the Empire, and the Commonwealth', in Kevin Kenny (ed.) *Ireland and the British Empire* (Oxford: Oxford University Press, 2004), 217.

143. NAUK PREM 11/1901, Macmillan's views re: 'Ireland and the Commonwealth', 14 Aug. 1957.

144. See William A. Carson, *Ulster and the Irish Republic* (Belfast, 1957), viii. See also, *Belfast Telegraph*, 4 March 1957.

145. NAI DT S/9361 K/61, interview between Lemass and Count Jean de Madre, 7 July 1961.

146. NAI DT S/9361 K/61, interview between Lemass and Count Jean de Madre, 7 July 1961.

147. In March 1961, Lemass refuted claims by Lord Pakenham in the latter's article 'Ireland and the New Commonwealth' published in the *Sunday Observer* that Irish unity could be achieved if Ireland re-entered the Commonwealth. See *Irish Independent*, 30 March 1961 for Lemass's comments and the *Sunday Observer*, 8 Jan. 1961 for a copy of Pakenham's proposal.

148. UCDA P150/2940, de Valera to Rugby, 8 June 1957.

149. UCDA P150/2553, de Valera to MacDonald, June 1959.

150. For example, speaking at the 1931 Fianna Fáil Ard Fheis de Valera noted that 'force was out of the question. Were it feasible, it would not be desirable'. UCDA P176/42, 1931 Fianna Fáil Ard Fheis, Oct. 1931.

151. Earl of Longford and Thomas P. O'Neill, *Eamon de Valera* (London: Hutchinson, 1970), 470.

152. See UCDA P67/ 475–478, Seán MacEntee, 'The man I knew', *Iris*, *Fianna Fáil*, winter 1975 (draft copy).

153. UCDA P176/447, meeting of parliamentary meeting, 14 Jan. 1959. On 19 Jan. 1959, at a meeting of the National Executive, Oscar Traynor proposed and it was unanimously agreed, that de Valera be selected as the party's candidate for the Presidency of Ireland. UCDA P176/348, meeting of National Executive, 19 Jan. 1959.

154. Longford and O'Neill, *Eamon de Valera*, 447.

155. This was the opinion of Todd C.S. Andrews. See Tom Garvin, *Preventing the Future, Why was Ireland so Poor for So Long?* (Dublin: Gill and Macmillan, 2004), 213.

156. NAUK DO 35/7853, record of Clutterbuck's observations of Lemass, 3 July 1959.

157. At the parliamentary party meeting, Joseph Kennedy was the most vocal, believing that Lemass would quickly replace the old guard with a younger generation of deputies that could be easily manipulated. See Michael O'Sullivan, *Seán Lemass, a Biography* (Dublin: Blackwater Press, 1994), 146.

158. UCDA P176/348, meeting of National Executive, 22 June 1959.

159. UCDA P176/447, meeting of parliamentary party, 22 June 1959.

160. See speech by Seán Lemass, *The Irish Times*, 23 May 1960.

161. Etain Tannam, *Cross-border co-operation in the Republic of Ireland and Northern Ireland* (New York: St Martin's Press, 1999), 50.

162. See UCDA P176/44718, record of Fianna Fáil parliamentary party meetings, 1959–1965. On the rare occasions that the subject of Northern Ireland was debated at a meeting of

the National Executive these usually concerned local cumann disputes and not official Fianna Fáil policy. See UCDA, P176/347–348, record of Fianna Fáil National Executive meetings, 1959–1965.

163. Farrell, *Seán Lemass*, 105.
164. See 'My life and times' by Jack Lynch, *Magill*, Nov. 1979, 40.
165. See 'My life and times' by Jack Lynch, *Magill*, Nov. 1979, 40.
166. Lemass recalled that once he had a 'clear concept of a problem ... you rarely added to your wisdom by going back and looking at it again and again and again, delaying the decision'. *Irish Press*, 3 Feb. 1969.
167. See Terence de Vere White, *The Irish Times* supplement 'Fifty Years of Fianna Fáil', 19 May 1976.
168. See Lemass's Oxford Address, 15 Oct. 1959. Reprinted, *The Irish Times*, 16 Oct. 1959.
169. *The Irish Times*, 15 Jan. 1960.
170. See speeches by Brookeborough, *Northern Whig*, 5 Feb. 1958; *Irish Press*, 5 July 1958; and *The Irish Times* 23 May 1960 and 29 Aug. 1960.
171. See NAI DT 97/9/1504, copy of speech by Lemass at a Fianna Fáil dinner, Imperial Hotel, Castlebar, 14 Dec. 1959. See also NAI DT 97/9/1550, copy of speech by Lemass at a dinner of the South Louth Fianna Fáil Comhairle Ceantair, White Horse Hotel, Drogheda, 5 Feb. 1961.
172. UCDA P176/348, meeting of National Executive, 12 Oct. 1959.
173. See, for example, NAI DT S 9361 K/63, 'Government policy on partition, Jan. 1963–Dec. 1963'.
174. See Lemass's Oxford Address, 15 Oct. 1959. Reprinted, *The Irish Times*, 16 Oct. 1959.
175. See NAI DT S 9361 K/61, speech by Lemass, 5 Feb. 1961. See also NAI DT 97/9/1504, speech by Lemass, Fianna Fáil dinner, Imperial Hotel, Castlebar, 14 Dec. 1959.
176. See NAI DT S 9361 K/61, copy of speech by Lemass, 5 Feb. 1961.
177. See NAI DT 97/9/1504, copy of speech by Lemass, Fianna Fáil dinner, Imperial Hotel, Castlebar, 14 Dec. 1959.
178. See, for example, Lemass's 'Tralee speech', *Irish Press*, 30 July, 1963.
179. See NAI DFA P203/2, meeting between Macmillan and Lemass, 13 July 1959. See also NAUK PREM 11/5151, meeting between MacMillan and Lemass, 18 March 1964.
180. See, for example, Lemass's 'Tralee speech'. *Irish Press*, 30 July, 1963.
181. See comments by de Valera, *Irish Press*, 26 Oct. 1948.
182. See Kathy Hayward, 'The politics of nuance: Irish official discourse on Northern Ireland', *Irish Political Studies*, 19:1 (2004): 19.
183. *Irish Press*, 30 June 1959.
184. See UCDA P104/8642–8670, record of 43rd – 46th meetings of the Al-Party Anti-Partition Committee, 2 Nov. 1955–26 Oct. 1971.
185. *The Irish Times*, 11 Nov. 1959.
186. See *Irish Press*, 30 June 1959.
187. *Irish Press*, 11 Nov. 1959.
188. See Horgan, *Seán Lemass*, 258 & 260–265.
189. *Irish Press*, 11 Nov. 1959.
190. NAI DT S 16272 D/62, Lemass to Ernest Blythe, 7 Dec. 1962.
191. NAI DT S 16699B, Lemass to Vivion de Valera, 14 May 1960.
192. NAI DT S 16699B, Lemass to Vivion de Valera, 14 May 1960.
193. This was the opinion of Charles J. Haughey, a view Lemass certainly held. UCDA P104/8822, Haughey to Aiken, 14 March 1967.
194. See *The Irish Times* 23 May 1960 and *Irish Independent*, 24 May 1960.
195. NAI DT S 1957/63, record of conversation between Ó hAnnracháin and Quinn, 23 May 1957.
196. NAUK DO 35/5379, Clutterbuck to Home, 1 Sept. 1959.
197. See NAI DT S 96/6/23, Lemass to Jack Lynch, 18 March 1966, and NAI DT 1957/63, record of reply received by the Department of the Taoiseach from MacEntee.
198. UCDA P104/8822, Haughey to Aiken, 14 March 1967.

199. See NAI DT S 10467/ F/64, secretary to the Department of External Affairs, John Molloy to secretary in the Department of Education, 27 Sept. 1963.
200. DE, 7 July 1959. Vol. 176, col. 646.
201. Michael Joseph Kennedy was parliamentary secretary to the minister for social welfare, Seán McEntee. UCDA P176/447, meeting of parliamentary party, 15 July 1959.
202. UCDA P176/348, meeting of National Executive, 27 July 1959.
203. UCDA P176/348, meeting of National Executive, 27 July 1959.
204. DE, 21 June 1960. Vol. 183, cols. 3–4.
205. See DE, 22 Feb. 1961. Vol. 186, col. 677. On a further occasion Lemass only referred to 'Northern Ireland' and made no reference to the 'Six Counties', see DE, 13 Dec. 1962. Vol. 198, col. 1408. Furthermore, on two further occasions he referred to the 'Six Counties', but refrained from using the term 'Northern Ireland', see, DE, 8 Feb. 1961. Vol. 186, col. 10 and DE, 7 March 1963. Vol. 200, col. 892.
206. See Horgan, *Seán Lemass*, 285.
207. NAI DT S 96/6/23, Lemass to Jack Lynch, 18 March 1966.
208. See NAI DT S 1957/63.
209. See speech by Lynch. DE, 11 Nov 1969. Vol. 242, col. 1.
210. *The Irish Times*, 30 June 1960.
211. Following Fianna Fáil's return to government in 1957 de Valera rejected an invitation from the Anti-Partition of Ireland League of Great Britain to send a party representative to the League's annual conference in Bradford in May 1957.
212. NAI DFA P203/1, Cremin to Murphy, 20 May 1957.
213. The government's apathy for the Anti-Partition of Ireland League of Great Britain was exposed during a lunch appointment in Oct. 1958 between Hugh McCann, the new Irish Ambassador in London and Alf Havekin, president of the Manchester branch of the League. The latter protested 'rather bitterly' about the delay's in replies to any correspondence he had with the Department of External Affairs and in some cases to the absence of any reply at all. UCDA P104/8628, McCann to Cremin, 13 Oct. 1958.
214. NAI DT S 9361G, Maurice Moynihan to unknown recipient, 9 May 1957.
215. Enda Staunton, *The Nationalists of Northern Ireland* (Dublin: Columba Press, 2001), 220.
216. This was the opinion of John Belton. NAI DFA 305/14/2/4, Belton to unknown person in the Department of External Affairs. 9 May 1958.
217. This was the opinion of Conor Cruise O'Brien. NAI DFA 305/14/2/4, O'Brien to unknown person in the Department of External Affairs, 1 May 1958.
218. See, for example, NAI DT 97/9/1341, folder 'Taoiseach's messages to Anti-Partition of Ireland League (Britain)'.
219. See NAI DFA 305/14/108A and 305/14/108 b/11.
220. NAI DFA 305/14/108A, Feehan to Cremin, 15 Sept. 1959.
221. NAI DFA 305/14/108 b/11, record of annual report of the Anti-Partition of Ireland League of Great Britain, Oct. 1960.
222. NAI DFA 305/14/108 b/11, Feehan to Keating, 3 May 1962.
223. UCDA P104/8633, M. Roche to T. Feehan, 8 June 1962.
224. NAI DFA 305/14/108A, Feehan to Irish Embassy, London, 14 March 1963.
225. See UCDA P104/8634, record of financial lodgements made to the Trustees of the United Ireland Association on behalf of the Irish government, April 1965–April 1969.
226. See UCDA P104/8634, record of financial lodgements made to the Trustees of the United Ireland Association on behalf of the Irish government, April 1965–April 1969.
227. NAI DFA 305/14/108A, Feehan to Irish Embassy, London, 14 March 1963.
228. Patterson, *Ireland Since 1939*, 157.
229. See NAI DFA 305/14/303, Lemass to Eddie McAteer, 6 Jan. 1964, and Lemass's interview with, *The Guardian*, 28 May 1965.
230. Patterson, *Ireland Since 1939,*157.
231. For a concise analysis of Northern nationalism during the 1950s, see Staunton, *The Nationalists of Northern Ireland*, 181–229.
232. *The Irish Times*, 5 May 1960.

233. NAI DT 305/14/2/4, Eoin MacWhite to O'Brien, 9 Jan. 1959.
234. This was the opinion of Cahir Healy, a prominent member of the Anti-Partition League. See *Irish News*, 18 March 1960.
235. NAI DT S 16272B, Childers to Lemass, 21 Dec. 1960.
236. See *The Irish Times*, 5 May 1964.
237. Michael McKeown, *The Greening of a Nationalist* (Dublin: Murlough Press, 1986), 19.
238. Indeed, National Unity was the first political group that Garret FitzGerald joined. See Garret FitzGerald, *All in a Life, Garret FitzGerald, An Autobiography* (Dublin: Gill and Macmillan, 1991), 64.
239. NAI DT S 16272 C/61, Childers to executive secretary of National Unity, B. McFadden, 18 March 1961.
240. See David Andrews, *Kingstown Republican* (Dublin: New Ireland, 2007), 21.
241. NAUK FCO 33/1599, confidential profile of Erskine Childers, British Embassy, Dublin, May 1971.
242. NAI DT S 16272 C/61, Department of Taoiseach to McFadden, 18 March 1961.
243. A copy of the pamphlet is available from NAI DT S 16272 C/61.
244. See Chapter Six, pp.273-274.
245. Horgan, *Seán Lemass*, 270.
246. Horgan, *Seán Lemass*, 270.
247. In Oct. 1963 Healy appealed to Lemass for financial assistance for the forthcoming election; a request that he 'politely ignored'. Horgan, *Seán Lemass*, 270.
248. See NAI DFA 305/14/303, Lemass to Eddie McAteer, 6 Jan. 1964
249. NAUK DO 35/7853, British Embassy, Dublin, note on Lemass and partition, 3 July 1959.

6

1962–1965

'Irish freedom will not be finally secure[d] until it rests on firm and unshakable economic foundations'.

[Seán Lemass, 29 July 1963][1]

'The [Lemass-O'Neill] meeting is the most important development that has taken place in North–South relations since the actual establishment of the Border'.

[*Anglo-Celt*, 16 Jan. 1965][2]

'A SIN TOO FAR': LEMASS, THE IRA AND NORTHERN IRELAND, 1961–1962

During Lord Brookeborough's last years as prime minister of Northern Ireland relations between Dublin and Belfast remained cold. Ulster Unionists maintained that cross-border co-operation was impossible while the Republic refused to recognise the *de jure* existence of Northern Ireland and because the IRA continued its border-campaign.[3] Indeed, Brookeborough reportedly believed that North–South co-operation had become a 'dirty-word'.[4] Lemass rejected Brookeborough's wish for *de jure* recognition of Northern Ireland. He did, however, pinpoint the crushing of the IRA as a major objective of his second term in government from 1961 to 1965. Lemass was optimistic that if his government defeated the IRA, the contentious constitutional question could be put to one side and attention could instead focus on cross-border co-operation between Dublin and Belfast.

Following Fianna Fáil's return to government in October 1961 Lemass was determined to tackle the IRA head on. Although he commanded only a minority position in the Dáil, he considered Fianna Fáil's position safe enough to wage a campaign against the IRA. Throughout 1961 the IRA carried out a number of horrific murders. On 27 January, of that year, the movement shot dead a young RUC Corporal, Norman Anderson. This was followed by further IRA attacks in 1961. The most brutal of these was carried out in November, when the IRA ambushed an RUC police patrol in Jonesborough, Co. Armagh; during the ambush an RUC policeman, Constable William Hunter was killed.[5] These attacks, which were an increasing source of embarrassment for the Irish government, reinforced the Republic's opposition to physical force republicanism.

In response to the renewed IRA campaign the Irish government, led by Lemass's son-in-law, minister for justice, Charles J. Haughey, reactivated the Special Criminal Courts by filling vacancies caused by retirements or deaths.[6] Working closely with Lemass and Frank Aiken, Haughey orchestrated a publicity campaign portraying the IRA as an illegal organisation that did not 'serve the cause of national unity'.[7] The government's propaganda offensive was a success and by the early months of 1962 public sympathy for the IRA had waned. However, Dublin's crackdown of the movement was not welcomed by a vocal minority of Fianna Fáil grass-roots members. Letters of protest from a small number of dismayed party supporters arrived to the Department of the Taoiseach condemning Lemass's policy towards the IRA.

A Fianna Fáil member, Seán Ó'Fionn, originally from Co. Kerry, but living in London, wrote to Lemass to express his anger at the government's failure to tackle partition. 'Instead of sending soldiers to the Congo', he pronounced, 'couldn't they send them into Northern Ireland?'[8] Those outside Fianna Fáil circles also expressed their anger towards the government-led suppression of the IRA. Rev. P.F. Malone, from Westport Co. Mayo, wrote to Lemass in early February 1962 denouncing the government's decision to imprison 'freedom fighters'. Rev. Malone's letter, in both its tone and content, typified the feelings of some Fianna Fáil grass-roots to the government suppression of the IRA. He asserted that those IRA men arrested had acted on the 'same principles' that many within Fianna Fáil fought against the British during the Irish War of Independence. Rev. Malone expressed his anger that 'even tinkers' had the right to trial by jury, but the opposite was the case for the members of the 'once historic Sinn Féin'.[9]

Rev. Malone's closing comments epitomised the inherent ambiguity that many supporters of Fianna Fáil (and indeed the general public at large) held towards the use of violence to deliver Irish unity:

> I honestly say – that if certain members of the Dáil came to confession to me and admitted that they were lax regarding it [partition] – and that suffering is caused by it, I could not in conscience absolve them ... some make a terrible error. They think there's no practical sin – that anything 'put over' is o.k. They believe that what they don't do is no harm in politics – whereas sins of omission can be and are frequently the greater sins of all.[10]

For a collection of Fianna Fáil members Lemass's willingness to arrest and imprison members of the IRA represented a 'sin' too far. The IRA, as the only movement that openly endorsed the use of violence to achieve Irish unity, appealed to a minority within Fianna Fáil. For the anti-partitionists within Fianna Fáil constitutionalism had merely been a strategy which could legitimately be resorted to, but only for as long as 'it proved promising'.[11] Conor Cruise O'Brien discussed the prevalence of ambivalence towards political violence in the Fianna Fáil tradition. Within Fianna Fáil there was a 'sneaking respect for the IRA, the only category of the population not deemed to be less truly Irish than Fianna Fáil'. O'Brien acidly wrote, 'as true descendents of the Republican side in the Civil War the IRA has to look more plausible, *even to Fianna Fáil*, than Fianna Fáil does'. He concluded, 'the boys' might have to be 'disciplined from time to time, but your heart went out to them all the same'.[12]

Evidently some party supporters had grown increasingly wary of professional politicians' pronouncements in support for an end to partition. Merely on suitable occasions, such as the party's annual Ard Fheiseanna or at a local cumann meeting, Fianna Fáil elected representatives made jaded pronouncements against partition so as to jump on the anti-partition 'bandwagon'.[13] Indeed, even those within Fianna Fáil who supported the government's internment of republicans in the Republic, saw no contradiction in their vocal endorsement of the IRA campaign in Northern Ireland. This contradiction was easily overlooked by some within Fianna Fáil as they regarded the Ulster Unionist controlled Northern Ireland as virtually an enemy state. The renewed IRA campaign permitted some within Fianna Fáil to allow their emotions to distort the reality of the situation, wherein the underlining psychological obsession with the injustice of partition resonated in the collective consciousness of a vocal minority of party followers.

This was Lemass's first occasion, since becoming taoiseach in 1959, to receive criticism from Fianna Fáil supporters for his policy towards the IRA and his stance on Northern Ireland. Like his predecessor, Eamon de Valera, Lemass was determined to retain absolute control of the government's handling of the latest IRA campaign. In a strongly worded letter in reply to Mr. James C. Heaney, an American Attorney at Law from Buffalo, New York, in November 1961, Lemass made clear his policy. He condemned the suggestion from Mr. Heaney that IRA members were 'brave men'. Such description he noted, 'is debasement of the words ... A government which failed to take action to protect their peoples' democratic rights would not be worthy of the name'. Lemass concluded by delivering a hard assessment of the IRA campaign. Their actions, he said, had left Irish citizens 'feeling shame .... and horror'.[14] Speaking in the Dáil the following month, in December, he was even blunter of the IRA's campaign: 'No sane person could think that such murderous activities serve any national purpose'.[15]

Lemass's rejection of IRA violence was a central theme of his speeches in 1961 and 1962. At the thirty-second Fianna Fáil Ard Fheis, in January 1962, he reminded delegates that the use of violence by 'irresponsible elements' was a futile exercise. Speaking during his Presidential address Lemass explained to those in attendance that 'such actions cannot serve the cause of national unity'. What was required, he said, 'was for all Irishmen of all classes and creeds to work together through democratic institutions to achieve re-unification'.[16] Aiken, also speaking at the 1962 Ard Fheis, rejected the proposition that physical force was a legitimate policy of Fianna Fáil. 'Only when all Irishmen of all classes and creeds work together through democratic institutions', he protested, could reunification be achieved.[17] Haughey also followed the Lemass-line, condemning the IRA's resort to violence as 'foolish'.[18]

By February 1962 the government's actions against the IRA proved successful. The IRA leadership realised that its military position was futile and issued orders for the movement to 'dump arms'.[19] The movement acknowledged that the general public's apathy for the IRA border-campaign was the central reason for its decision to cease military operation.[20] As Barry Flynn noted, 'so in February 1962, the curtain fell on a campaign that had failed, and failed utterly to achieve any of its primary objectives'.[21]

An examination of regional newspapers from November 1961 to March 1962 demonstrates that the vast majority of Fianna Fáil members and indeed the general public, offered no objections to the government's actions against the IRA.[22] An editorial in the Cork-based *Southern Star*, following the IRA's cessation of military activities, typified such attitudes. The paper pronounced, 'the IRA at last conceded defeat ... the few hundred die-hards realise the folly of their misguided activities'. The editorial continued, 'do they understand that it costs the Irish people £400,000 a year to keep a check on their misdeeds'.[23] Furthermore, at a Fianna Fáil convention attended by approximately two hundred people in the border county of Cavan, only days after the IRA announcement in early March 1962, no reference was made to the IRA. In attendance at the meeting were two senior Fianna Fáil representatives, minister for lands, Paddy Smith and his parliamentary secretary, Brian Lenihan. Seven resolutions were placed on the agenda for discussion, ranging from secondary school education to the problem of itinerants. There was, however, no resolution relating to the government's handling of the IRA or partition.[24]

The cessation of IRA violence was the catalyst that Lemass now hoped would compel the Northern Ireland government to agree to North–South cross-border co-operation. With the IRA defeated Lemass was anxious that Belfast would not make the recognition of Northern Ireland a prerequisite for the commencement of cross-border co-operation. As is discussed below, he was to be disappointed. Under Brookeborough, Ulster Unionists still demanded that Dublin officially recognise Northern Ireland. Faced with yet another stalemate in North–South relations Lemass decided that the time had arrived to take some bold initiatives on the issue of recognition.

FLYING KITES AND THE *'DE FACTO'* RECOGNITION OF NORTHERN IRELAND: THE SHELBOURNE SYMPOSIUM, APRIL 1963

To understand Lemass's approach to Northern Ireland it is important to lay emphasis on his indirect and private initiatives to bring about a revision of Fianna Fáil's traditional Northern Ireland policy. Central to this approach was Lemass's use of senior Fianna Fáil elected representatives. On two separate occasions during 1962, Lemass sent two of his leading government frontbenchers, minister for commerce and industry, Jack Lynch and minister for justice, Charles J. Haughey, to Northern Ireland on a kite flying exercise. The aim of their respective visits to Belfast was to reopen a debate on the commencement of cross-border trade between North and South, in the light of the end to the IRA border-campaign.

In February, within days of the IRA announcing an end to their campaign, Lynch spoke at a debate on North–South relations at Queen's University Belfast. He expressed the Irish government's desire to establish an all-Ireland free trade area for goods of Irish and Northern Ireland origins.[25] It was a policy publicly advocated by Lemass since becoming leader of Fianna Fáil in 1959.[26] By this time Lynch was a rising figure within Fianna Fáil. According to a file from the British Embassy in Dublin, by the early 1960s, he was 'one of the bright young men' of the party, with a 'relaxed attitude to partition'.[27] He was trusted by Lemass and over the subsequent years made numerous similar visits to Belfast to encourage cross-border co-operation.

Later that year in November, Haughey spoke at a debate organised under the auspices of the New Ireland Society, again at Queen's University Belfast. Proposing the motion that 'minorities have nothing to fear in a united Ireland', Haughey said that Protestants had nothing to fear if Ireland was united as the 'constitution of the Irish Republic guaranteed freedom of religion to every citizen'.[28] Haughey was following Lemass's policy that the religious division between the two communities would need to be tackled in order for Protestants to agree to enter a united Ireland based on a federal model.[29]

Importantly, both speeches failed to mention the delicate issue of the recognition of Northern Ireland. Instead, Lemass fostered the idea that economic co-operation should be independent of recognition. Privately Lemass spoke of his desire to separate the issue of recognition from that of cross-border co-operation. The Fianna Fáil government, he wrote, should urge 'whatever co-operation' which can be beneficial, without seeking to 'impose any pre-condition of acceptance of any historical theory'.[30]

By early 1963 it was apparent that the sending of Fianna Fáil ministers to Northern Ireland had proved ineffective. Lemass realised that Belfast would not agree to cross-border co-operation until Dublin offered concessions on the thorny and sensitive issue of recognition of Northern Ireland. The *Southern Star* noted that the time had arrived for the Republic to take the initiative and to 'accept the North's right as a separate entity'.[31] An editorial in *The*

Irish Times recorded the dilemma that faced the taoiseach: 'Lemass cannot hope to negotiate with a body whose existence he does not recognise'.[32] He now sought to rectify this anomaly. He made up his mind that the Fianna Fáil government should now accord *de facto* recognition to Northern Ireland, in the hope that he could persuade Ulster Unionists to commence cross-border co-operation.

Through a series of 'kite flying' exercises, particularly through his use of backbench Fianna Fáil TDs, Lemass orchestrated a campaign to accord Dublin's *de facto* recognition of Northern Ireland. On the night of 16 April 1963, Fianna Fáil TD for Dublin North-East, George Colley, spoke at a major symposium on North–South co-operation. Subsequently described as representing the 'conscience of Fianna Fáil', a man of honesty and who was 'conscious of the position of the minority in the North', he firmly endorsed Lemass's Northern Ireland policy.[33] The event was held under the auspices of the Fianna Fáil Dublin Comh-Chomhairle [*sic*], at the Shelbourne Hotel, Dublin. Chaired by Dublin North-Central TD Philip Brady, the event was attended by several high-profile Fianna Fáil members. These included Jack Lynch, Oscar Traynor, former minister for justice, James Gallagher, Fianna Fáil TD for Sligo-Leitrim, Aindrias Ó Caoimh, attorney general, Fianna Fáil senators Thomas Mullins and Seán O'Donovan, and Colley's father, retired Fianna Fáil TD, Harry Colley.

Significantly Colley's speech was the first occasion that a Fianna Fáil elected representative officially granted *de facto* recognition to Northern Ireland. Although never publicly acknowledging that he was the instigator of Colley's speech the circumstantial evidence does confirm that Lemass did instruct his backbench colleague to speak on the subject of recognition. In a 2009 interview Mary Colley, wife to George Colley, remembered that it was under Lemass's instructions that her husband delivered the speech. She recalled that during this period a small group within Fianna Fáil, which included her husband, Lemass, Lynch and Fianna Fáil TD for Dún Laoghaire-Rathdown, Lionel Booth, sought to re-examine the party's relationship with Ulster Unionism. She remarked that this modern-wing within the party had commenced a 'gradation of initiatives' in the hope that it would 'open up a new way' towards the party's official stance on Northern Ireland.[34]

In an interview with Michael Mills of the *Irish Press* in 1969, Lemass recalled how he was an adroit exploiter of the press as a means of accelerating executive action 'as part of the art of political leadership'.[35] He was ready to 'plant a good story, fly a kite' in order to test public opinion.[36] By using Colley as a front man Lemass was attempting to manoeuvre his party, Ulster Unionists and indeed the general public, ever closer to his line of thinking.

Speaking to a packed ballroom in the Shelbourne Hotel, Colley dealt with the sensitive question of recognition of the Northern Ireland government. He said it was 'the greatest – perhaps the only barrier to effective co-operation between North and South on economic matters'. His choice of terminology was noteworthy:

> The government of Northern Ireland is in effective control of the territory of Northern Ireland and as such we in the South have always accorded *de facto* recognition to the government. Consequently the demand from the North is not for *de facto* recognition but for *de jure* recognition of the constitutional position of Northern Ireland ... What we have not been prepared to do is grant *de jure* recognition to the claim of the British parliament to legislate for any part of Ireland.[37]

Colley's usage of the terms 'Northern Ireland' and 'recognition' in the same sentence was a deliberate attempt by the Fianna Fáil deputy to place on the record Dublin's official position on the issue of the recognition of Northern Ireland. Four years previously, speaking at the 1959 Fianna Fáil Ard Fheis, Lemass had similarly acknowledged 'that partition existed'.[38] Colley now went further. He recorded that a Fianna Fáil government would never grant *de jure* recognition to Northern Ireland, as this would give legitimacy to the British government's territorial claim on Northern Ireland. He did, nevertheless, publicly concede that Dublin recognised the *de facto* existence of the Northern Ireland state.

Lemass's orchestrated scheme to place on record Dublin's recognition on Northern Ireland was a brave gamble. For the traditionalist-wing within Fianna Fáil any move towards the recognition of Northern Ireland was viewed as an abandonment of a central tenet of the party's traditional Northern Ireland policy – a sell-out of Fianna Fáil's republicanism. From the inception of the Northern Ireland state the Irish government had refused to accept its legitimacy as a political unit. Under de Valera, Fianna Fáil maintained that the state of Northern Ireland did not exist, that the right to rule of the Stormont government was illegitimate.

Since the late-1950s Lemass was at the forefront of an ongoing internal debate within Fianna Fáil on the issue of *de facto* recognition of Northern Ireland. Working closely with a small select group within the party, which included Lionel Booth;[39] National Executive committee member Anthony Hederman;[40] and party Senator Eoin Ryan,[41] Lemass was determined to re-examine the contentious issue of recognition. Privately, he argued that if Irish unity was to be obtained, based on a federal solution, the Belfast government must be granted *de facto* recognition.[42]

During this period respected Irish nationalists outside Fianna Fáil circles also attempted to nurture innovatory thinking on Dublin's relationship with Belfast and particularly the *de facto* recognition of the Northern Ireland government. The catalyst for this was the publication of a pamphlet by a young lawyer, Donal Barrington, entitled, *Uniting Ireland.*[43] Barrington argued that although all Southern parties agreed that 'unity of wills' was the sole prerequisite for the ending of partition, this agreement needed to be translated into practical terms, if it was to ever convince Ulster Unionists to enter a united Ireland. Thus, he argued, recognition of the Northern Ireland government was imperative if the long-term goal of Irish unity was to be achieved.[44]

Veteran Irish nationalists, John J. Horgan,[45] Ernest Blythe,[46] Senator Owen Sheehy-Skeffington,[47] and future Fine Gael leader and taoiseach, Garret FitzGerald, had all argued that *de facto* recognition merely implied that the Irish recognised the existence of the 'Six-Counties' as a provincial administration and not as the government of a sovereign state.[48] There is evidence to suggest that Lemass had become receptive to such innovatory thinking on the issue of recognition. As Liam de Paor claimed, the policy suggested by Barrington 'was, in effect, put into operation by Mr. Lemass's government'.[49] Thus, by orchestrating Colley's Shelbourne speech Lemass was attempting to convert his privately held convictions on the subject of recognition into official Fianna Fáil policy. It would prove a difficult policy to implement.

The timing of the meeting was not coincidental. It had been hurriedly arranged by Fianna Fáil to take place in the weeks after Terence O'Neill succeeded Lord Brookeborough as Northern Ireland prime minister in late March 1963. O'Neill's appointment was warmly welcomed by Dublin. *The Irish Times* reported that O'Neill was a 'dynamic man' who, like Lemass, wished to transform the economic conditions in his jurisdiction.[50] He had no record of drum-beating militancy or fundamentalist Protestantism. Northern Nationalists likewise greeted his appointment, viewing him as a welcome departure from his predecessor.[51] The *Belfast Telegraph* wondered whether O'Neill would permit North–South economic co-operation, even if Dublin had not granted formal recognition to the Belfast government.[52] Lemass held a similar opinion. By instructing Colley to offer *de facto* recognition Lemass believed he could bypass Ulster Unionists' demand for the formal *de jure* recognition. With the recognition debate resolved, Lemass hoped to focus instead on cross-border co-operation.

The attendance at the Shelbourne symposium of three leading members of the young liberal-wing of the Ulster Unionist Party, Robin Baillie, John Hutchinson and R. Cooper, was significant. There as individuals and not necessarily officially representing the Ulster Unionist Party, their presence, nonetheless, showed that within Unionist circles there was a desire to foster a new chapter in cross-border relations.[53] The arrival of O'Neill as Northern Ireland prime minister had permitted a fresh examination of Ulster Unionists' relationship with Dublin.[54] Tellingly the previous month, in March 1963, George Colley accompanied by his wife Mary, had visited Belfast to attend a St Patrick's Day dinner hosted by National Unity.[55] During their stay in Belfast, Mary recalled that she and her husband had met Robin Baillie. She remembered that both men were 'engrossed for hours' in conversation concerning relations between Dublin and Belfast.[56]

Baillie's father, J.O. Baillie, was chairman of the Ulster Unionist Party in Terence O'Neill's own constituency of Bannside, Co. Antrim. O'Neill had told the two young Unionists, Hutchinson and Baillie that provided that they 'did not go overboard', he believed their visit to Dublin would be a welcome improvement in relations.[57] Given Colley's visit to Belfast and the direct input of O'Neill into the actions of the unofficial Young Unionist delegation the available evidence does suggest that both O'Neill and Lemass were attempting to improve North–South relations. The symposium was a huge step forward after decades of mistrust and suspicion between Dublin and Belfast. In the words of Mary Colley 'you couldn't imagine how wonderful it was to have Ulster Unionists down here'.[58]

Speaking at the Shelbourne symposium Baillie argued that full recognition of the Northern Ireland state was paramount for official North–South negotiations to commence. However, he noted that he 'did not believe that it must be a prerequisite to all forms of contact at political level between the Belfast and Dublin governments'.[59] Hutchinson put it clearly: 'unionists were not prepared to compromise their constitutional position or their political sovereignty, but this should not be a barrier to mutually beneficial co-operation'.[60]

The meeting was equally important for internal politics within Fianna Fáil. Lemass also used the event, through a speech delivered by his confidant Anthony Hederman, to secure support for his economic policy. In particular, Lemass wished to reassure Fianna Fáil members that his desire to secure a thirty-two-county free trade area between North and South for goods of Irish or Northern Ireland origin was the correct policy. Hederman's speech was important for the emphasis that he placed on the need for the end of economic trade barriers between Dublin and Belfast. 'There was no reason', he said, 'why a unified trade movement should not work for the betterment of the working men on both sides of the border'.[61]

Lemass's determination for closer economic co-operation with Ulster Unionists and particularly his wish to grant tariff concessions to the Northern Ireland government had previously caused a division within the Fianna Fáil cabinet. Minister for agriculture, Co. Cavan resident, Paddy Smith was the first to break ranks with cabinet policy by openly defying Lemass's proposals; Smith was to eventually resign from the cabinet in October 1962. Smith was not the only minister to disagree with Lemass's policy. Minister for finance, James Ryan, threw his weight behind Smith and opposed the tariff reductions.[62] The available evidence suggests that, at the very least, Lynch, Haughey, Childers and Aiken, fully supported Lemass.[63] Aiken explained that he 'felt that the existing economic situation in the Six-Counties provides a particularly appropriate opportunity for a gesture of this kind'. Any attempt to not encourage North–South relations, he said, would 'be a very retrograde step'.[64]

It is evident that Lemass carefully choreographed the scheduling of the Shelbourne symposium. The use of Colley and Hederman as a means to articulate central tenets of his Northern Ireland policy exposed a shrewd managerial style. He was aware that his willingness to offer *de facto* recognition of Northern Ireland, together with his desire to establish a thirty-two county all-Ireland trade agreement, would meet resistance from Fianna Fáil members. By using Colley and Hederman as front men, Lemass was attempting to test public opinion and win support for his new Northern Ireland initiative.

The Fianna Fáil government did receive some conciliatory replies from several Ulster Unionist MPs following Colley's Shelbourne speech.[65] O'Neill, however, quickly poured cold water on the prospect of North–South co-operations. Speaking at Stormont he categorically ruled out 'general discussions so long as the Dublin government refused to recognise the constitutional position of the Six-Counties'.[66] O'Neill's remarks led to a stalemate. He had failed to understand the importance of Colley's speech, which was the first occasion that a member of Fianna Fáil had recognised the legitimacy of the Northern Ireland government. The simple fact that the speech had been made was significant, as it marked a departure from the traditional Fianna Fáil policy as espoused by de Valera.

O'Neill's rebuttal of Colley's speech was also a reflection of the pressure that he faced from traditionalists within the Ulster Unionist Party. Michael Kennedy has argued that O'Neill was in 'no position to officially open relations with Dublin' given the strength of the hardcore traditionalist-wing within the Ulster Unionist Party.[67] This observation was made clear by Sir Robert Gransden, Northern Ireland secretary to the cabinet from 1939 to 1957 and agent for the Northern Ireland government in London from 1957 to 1962. He informed the Irish Ambassador to London, Hugh McCann that he believed O'Neill's continual demand that the Irish government grant official recognition to the Northern Ireland government was 'unrealistic'. Gransden explained that Dublin must realise that the Northern Ireland government 'cannot get out of step with the thinking of its own supporters'. He added, 'we should recognise that, if the prime minister there attempted to do certain things, he might be "shot out on his ear"'.[68]

'DE FACTO' RECOGNITION OF NORTHERN IRELAND: LEMASS'S TRALEE SPEECH, JULY 1963

Lemass was confronted by yet another rejection from Belfast for cross-border co-operation prior to Dublin granting *de jure* recognition to Northern Ireland. He now decided that the time had arrived for him to personally deliver a public statement on the Irish government's policy towards recognition of Northern Ireland. His decision to speak in Tralee, Co. Kerry, in July 1963, at a dinner given in honour of veteran Fianna Fáil TD, 'the Ballymac man' Tommy McEllistrim, was a courageous undertaking. Traditionally, Kerry was a hotbed of militant republicanism, which had a strong Fianna Fáil grass-roots tradition.

The government information bureau maintained that the speech did not mark 'any change from past policy'.[69] In fact, the reality was that the speech was one of Lemass's most important pronouncements on Northern Ireland policy throughout his time as taoiseach. It presented a calculated policy statement which had been developing for the previous four years. It was aimed directly at Ulster Unionists and significantly it deliberately omitted any mention of the role of the British government in ending partition.

Lemass delivered his speech to a packed room of Fianna Fáil supporters, at the Manhattan Hotel. Those in attendance included party Senator, Patrick O'Reilly and party TD for Limerick-West, James Collins. Using the *de facto/de jure* argument that Colley had given a trial run at the symposium on North–South relations the previous April, Lemass explained that he understood O'Neill's demands for recognition of the Northern Ireland government. He had no problem recognising the Northern Ireland state *de facto*. He explained that if the Northern majority were to agree to a united Ireland based on a federal agreement, Ulster unionists would still require their own government and parliament. His choice of words was significant: 'We recognise that the government and parliament there exist with the support of the majority in the six county area – artificial though that area is'.[70]

While not recognising Northern Ireland as part of the United Kingdom *de jure*, Lemass did accord *de facto* recognition to the state. *The Irish Times* noted that on the issue of recognition 'grudging and half-hearted though this admission, it none the less represents an important step forward'.[71] Significantly, although Lemass had referred to Northern Ireland as 'an artificial area', no Southern political leader since the foundation of the Irish state had ever been so explicit in public on the issue of recognition. Indeed, during the mid-1920s, Desmond FitzGerald, as minister for external affairs under the Cumann na nGaedheal government, had merely inferred rather than stated openly his support for *de facto* recognition.[72]

Nationalist reaction both North and South of the border to Lemass's recognition of *de facto* existence of Northern Ireland was hostile. An editorial in the *Sunday Independent* noted that to give recognition to the Northern Ireland government would 'make a mockery of all that Ireland has fought for over the centuries'.[73] The *Kerryman* reported that the people of Kerry had not expected Lemass to make a pronouncement of such 'national importance' and questioned what he hoped to achieve by making the statement.[74] The *Derry Journal* was likewise dismissive of the recognition debate. The paper quoted Ernest Blythe's repeated calls for the Irish government to grant *de facto* recognition to Northern Ireland. The editorial rhetorically pondered:

> How a particular six county portion of the historic Ireland could suddenly have acquired the quality of a separate and indefeasible entity as if of a God-given right, but which was never heard of as any such entity until Lloyd George came about.[75]

Importantly, in the same manner that Lemass never formally ordered that the term 'Northern Ireland' should be used in place for the term 'Six-Counties', throughout his time as Fianna Fáil president and taoiseach, the Irish government never formally acknowledged the *de facto* position of Northern Ireland.[76] Indeed, under Jack Lynch's leadership from 1966 to 1979, Fianna Fáil routinely implied that *de facto* recognition of Northern Ireland was only envisaged within the context of a federal agreement between Belfast and Dublin.[77] Lemass realised that to overtly accord official recognition of Northern Ireland would have caused a serious and possibly irreconcilable split within Fianna Fáil. Yet, the fact remains that Lemass's Tralee speech did grant *de facto* recognition to Northern Ireland.

That Lemass never officially accorded Northern Ireland *de facto* recognition was to be expected considering that de Valera had been the main opponent of the initiative. He had publicly spoken of a 'concurrence of wills' approach, based on agreement between Dublin, Belfast and London, as a solution to partition. He had, however, always maintained Dublin would not recognise the constitutional position of Northern Ireland.[78] Articles two and three of de Valera's constitution of 1937 had in effect withdrawn the *de facto* recognition of the 1925 boundary commission between Dublin and Belfast, by asserting the thirty-two county national claim over the island of Ireland. Privately senior Fianna Fáil members, notably Kevin Boland[79] and Michael Joseph Kennedy[80] had expressed their objection to *de facto* recognition of Northern Ireland. Theirs were not lonely voices. Lemass, therefore, was forced to deny the reality of what he was doing. Conscious that the issue of recognition could expose an inherent division among the traditionalist and pragmatists within Fianna Fáil, he decided to leave the policy as undecided.[81]

Ulster Unionists gave Lemass's Tralee speech a guarded welcome. Ulster Unionist MP for South Down, Capt. L.P.S. Orr, said that it presented a 'change of spirit' from Dublin. He did, nevertheless, regret that really 'the speech contained nothing new'.[82] This was an opinion shared by Northern Ireland minister for commerce, Brian Faulkner.[83] Privately, O'Neill noted that although the statement 'fell short of the constitutional recognition which Northern Ireland has always sought from the Republic, its general tone was regarded as not unfriendly'.[84] Publicly he waited for some time, almost three months, before he officially replied to Lemass's speech. He seemingly wished to take the temperature of his supporters before making his own position clear. He described Lemass's speech as 'not without courage'. However, he maintained that it was Northern Ireland's 'indisputable right' to remain by its own right within the United Kingdom.[85]

Lemass's response to O'Neill was to try and tempt his political foe to look beyond the recognition debate in the immediate term and instead focus on the 'practical' considerations between North and South. Speaking in September 1963, he noted that the political position should be placed to one side. Lemass could not conceal his hope for unity, neither could he reject O'Neill's determination to remain within the United Kingdom. 'This is why I have spoken of consultations without preconditions', he said, 'I should like to see some system of regular consultation, if this cannot be established at ministerial level, it may be possible at civil service level'.[86]

O'Neill's reply to Lemass's overtures was slow in coming, but when it did Lemass was quick to act. In mid-September 1963 O'Neill said that co-operation would now depend on the ability of the Irish government to control the IRA, together with Dublin acknowledging that the restriction put in place on trade with the United Kingdom by the Irish government were the main obstacles to co-operation.[87] This was Lemass's opportunity to bring forward proposals at cabinet level for discussions at civil service level on cross-border co-operation between Dublin and Belfast. On 16 September 1963, Lemass wrote to all government ministers requesting that their respective departments should draw up a list of areas where cross-border co-operation would be 'beneficial'.[88] The departmental response to Lemass's memorandum was quick. Within two weeks the Department of the Taoiseach had received detailed memoranda from several departments.[89] Although some ministers, notably Kevin Boland, James Ryan and Paddy Smith, did express reservations concerning the merits of the proposal, the general response was encouraging.[90] On receipt of the various departmental submissions on cross-border co-operation, the assistant secretary in the Department of the Taoiseach, Tadhg Ó Cearbhaill, drafted a fifty-six point list of areas which dealt with North–South relations. It proved a valuable undertaking, offering an up-to-date synopsis of cross-border co-operation and providing details of the key individuals involved.[91]

Lemass's decision to personally accord *de facto* recognition of Northern Ireland, based on his federal offer, was a brave gamble: a gamble that in the short-term did pay off. O'Neill, himself wishing to initiate cross-border co-operation, understood that by acknowledging Northern Ireland *de facto* Lemass had gone as far as he could possibly go. O'Neill's pronouncement in September 1963 that he would consider discussions with Dublin on cross-border co-operation certainly gave Lemass a personal sense of gratification. His prolonged efforts since becoming taoiseach to entice Belfast to agree to North–South co-operation was one step closer to becoming a reality. It was, as is discussed below, to be a false dawn. Unfortunately, it was Lemass's own pronouncements on partition, while on a trip to America and subsequently in a speech to rank-and-file supporters, at Arklow, Co. Wicklow, which threatened to destroy the recently acquired cordial relations between Dublin and Belfast.

THE 'PRINCIPLE OF CONSENT' AND LEMASS'S ARKLOW SPEECH, APRIL 1964

In October 1963 Lemass, accompanied by Aiken, travelled to America. The former's time abroad revealed his sometimes muddled approach to his Northern Ireland policy. His speeches in America exposed the discriminatory practices of the Ulster Unionist regime against the Catholic minority within Northern Ireland. Such pronouncements, however, were at variance with his previous conciliatory speeches in Ireland. In his American speeches he challenged the very legitimacy and permanence of the Northern Ireland state. Speaking at the National Press Club, Washington, for example, he was critical of the Northern Ireland electoral system. He lamented that the people of Northern Ireland, irrespective of their religion, required a system 'which would give proper representation to all sections'.[92]

The extent that Lemass's continually accused the Stormont authorities of carrying out a systematic programme of political and social discrimination against Northern Ireland Catholics infuriated O'Neill and destroyed the prospect of improvements in North–South co-operation.[93] O'Neill reacted bitterly to Lemass's American speeches: 'where is the Tralee speech now?' he mockingly enquired of Lemass.[94] Within Dublin circles it was reported to Lemass that his speeches in America had been a source of 'embarrassment' to O'Neill. As a consequence of Lemass's remarks, O'Neill reportedly found himself in a 'very awkward' position with his supporters.[95] Privately, O'Neill informed the British prime minister, Sir Alex Douglas-Home that Lemass's speech came as a 'considerable surprise' to him.[96] Interestingly, O'Neill noted that it was Lemass's decision to raise the issue of partition at the National Press Club which had annoyed him the most. 'Had the issue been raised before a partisan audience of Irish-Americans', O'Neill noted, 'the reference might have been interpreted as nothing more than a bow to "patriotic" sentiment'. 'It's gratuitous introduction at an important forum of opinion such as the National Press Club was, on the other hand', O'Neill bemoaned, 'regarded as a very deliberate démarche'.[97]

When O'Neill eventually decided to publicly reply to Lemass, selecting an Ulster Unionist rally in Co. Antrim, in November 1963, his words were stern. He maintained that Lemass's comments in America 'have wiped out all those remarks which he [Lemass] made in Tralee last July'.[98] In hindsight, Lemass had overplayed his hand in America and his trip abroad merely resulted in a return of megaphone diplomacy between Dublin and Belfast. However, one should not be overly critical of Lemass. After all, this was his first occasion in America as leader of Fianna Fáil and taoiseach. To have not mentioned his desire to see an end to partition would have damaged his political reputation in America and Ireland.

On Lemass's return from America he did attempt to end the deadlock in North–South co-operation caused by his anti-partition speeches during his time in America. In the final months of 1963 he sent two of his closest Fianna Fáil colleagues, both of whom were Protestant, to Northern Ireland. In November, minister for posts and telegraphs, Erskine Childers, spoke at the Historical Society of Queen's University Belfast. Subsequently reported by the British Embassy in Dublin to be 'distrusted by his own party' because of his 'English accent ... Protestant faith and Anglo-Irish background',[99] Lemass respected Childers's insight into Northern Ireland affairs. Speaking at Queen's University, Childers emphasised the need for Dublin and Belfast to agree to closer economic co-operation as this would permit greater economic prosperity on the island of Ireland.[100]

The following month, in early December, backbench Fianna Fáil TD, Lionel Booth, also spoke in Belfast in defence of his party leader's speeches in America. His speech was important for it was the first occasion that a senior Fianna Fáil representative acknowledged that Irish unity could only be secured with the consent of the majority of Northern Ireland. Booth spoke to a packed audience at a Methodist Church on University Road, Belfast. He assured those present, speaking with his authoritative British accent, that there could be 'no change' to the political set-up of Northern Ireland unless by the 'free consent of the people of the North'.[101] His words recognised that partition could not be ended without the 'consent of the majority of Northern Ireland', as enshrined in the Ireland Act, passed by Westminster in 1949.

It was no coincidence that Booth selected a Methodist Church to make his announcement. He was educated in The Leys, a Methodist funded school in Cambridge. Within Fianna Fáil, along with Childers, he represented the 'Protestant voice' of the party. His presence in Belfast allowed Lemass to offer Northern Protestant an 'acceptable face' of Fianna Fáil.[102] For Northern Protestants, Booth represented the antithesis of the traditional interpretations of a Fianna Fáil TD. He was, after all, not a republican die-hard hell bent on securing Irish unity at any cost. This may be an overly simplistic statement. Nevertheless, there is no doubt that the Northern Ireland majority were extremely sceptical of any overtures from a Fianna Fáil-lead Dublin government. Indeed, during his speech in Belfast, Booth admitted that he had more in common and could relate better with Ulster Unionists than he could with all Irish politicians from the Republic.[103]

There is no available evidence to suggest that Lemass ordered his colleague to officially speak on the 'principle of consent' in Belfast. However, the circumstantial evidence does support the theory that Lemass, in fact, endorsed Booth's pronouncements. As confirmed by Booth's son Richard, during the 1960s, his father and Lemass would routinely gather at the Booth family home in Sandycove, Dún Laoghaire-Rathdown, to discuss Northern Ireland policy. Mr Booth recalled that his father admired Lemass greatly and would be very surprised if his father's decision to speak in Belfast was not at the behest of Lemass.[104] Lemass's endorsement of National Unity, which publicly conceded that Irish unity could not be achieved without the consent of the majority of Northern Ireland, also lends weight to this hypothesis.[105]

It is true that officially Lemass never publicly spoke of his support for the 'principle of consent'. Nevertheless his Tralee speech of July 1963 had recognised that Northern Ireland existed with the support of the

majority of its citizens.[106] Within Fianna Fáil there was a determination
to re-examine the 'principle of consent'. As early as 1938, Seán
MacEntee had privately expressed to de Valera that Irish reunification
could not be achieved without the support of the Protestant majority in
Northern Ireland.[107] Indeed, writing in the Irish Jesuit journal *Studies*
in 1934, the widely regarded rabid anti-partitionist, Aodh de Blacam
had likewise acknowledged that the ending of partition could only be
secured 'by a settlement of consent' between Southern Catholics and
Northern Protestants.[108] Most tellingly, in March 1967, shortly after
Lemass's retirement as taoiseach and leader of Fianna Fáil, Charles J.
Haughey wrote to Frank Aiken regarding the 'principle of consent'.
Haughey advised his party colleague that because Northern Ireland
had over time become a 'firmly established political reality', Dublin
must acknowledge that Irish unity could only be secured 'through a
majority decision of the people of the North', to be 'moulded by the
positive publicity of the government in the Republic'.[109]

Lemass, as ever unwilling to create a divide within Fianna Fáil, never
formally adopted the 'principle of consent' as official policy. He was
painfully aware, as had been the case concerning *de facto* recognition,
that to officially concede on the issue would meet with fierce resistance
from the fundamentalists within the party, many of whom would have
viewed such a move as a 'sell out' and the abandonment of Fianna Fáil's
republican ethos. In fact, the 'principle of consent', was not formally
adopted by a political party in the South until September 1969. Fine
Gael then made the policy decision that Irish reunification required the
consent of the majority of the Northern Ireland population.[110] It took
a further two decades, until the late 1980s, before Fianna Fáil official
acknowledged the 'principle of consent'.[111]

Booth's speech in Belfast was not reported widely within the press
on either side of the border. The result was that his reference to
'the free consent of the people of the North' was not accorded the
importance that it deserved.[112] The issue, as a consequence, faded
into the political wilderness, not to be reopened for the remainder
of Lemass's leadership. Instead the emphasis shifted back to the
divisive issue of recognition of Northern Ireland. Not since his Tralee
speech in July 1963 had Lemass spoken of his wish to accord *de
facto* recognition to Northern Ireland. O'Neill's announcement in
September 1963 that he would consider cross-border co-operation
had allowed Lemass to bypass the issue of recognition.

In April 1964, at a Fianna Fáil constituency convention at Arklow,
Co. Wicklow, Lemass spoke on the need to separate the issue of

recognition from that of cross-border co-operations. By selecting Arklow, a 'centre of Republicanism' as later described by an official from the British Embassy in Dublin, Lemass attempted to keep the anti-partitionists within Fianna Fáil firmly behind his Northern Ireland policy.[113] Speaking to over three hundred grass-roots party members he explained that the issue of recognition had merely helped to prevent the 'economic salvation of both North and South'. Instead, he said, 'we should try to persuade Ulster unionists that the dispute over recognition should not inhibit cross-border co-operation'.[114]

Lemass's argument that the subject of recognition should be placed to one side in favour of cross-border co-operation was a legitimate request considering that he had publicly accorded *de facto* status on Northern Ireland. His speech, however, contained one major ill-advised element which proved disastrous in his efforts to secure support from Ulster Unionists. His declaration that the British government had no longer any desire to maintain partition infuriated Ulster Unionists. In a private discussion with the secretary of state for Commonwealth Relations, Duncan Sandys, the previous March, Lemass had pressed London to permit Dublin and Belfast to find a permanent solution to partition without Britain's interference; this request was firmly rejected.[115] His decision, therefore, to publicly speak on the issue at Arklow was intended for home consumption, to keep afresh in Fianna Fáil circles that he was committed to securing Irish unity.

His Arklow speech, as noted by the *Irish Press*, effectively signalled an end to any chance of a resumption of dialogue between Dublin and Belfast over economic co-operation.[116] Given O'Neill's anger and indeed disappointment, over Lemass's speeches in America the previous year, his reference that London no longer wished to maintain a partitioned Ireland was certainly a misguided move. O'Neill was reported to be furious at Lemass's reference to Britain's alleged disinterest in maintaining partition. Speaking at Stormont, O'Neill was unequivocal: 'So long as he continues to adopt this attitude he will get nowhere with me'.[117]

Lemass's American speeches had resulted in a damping down of the prospect of North–South co-operation. His Arklow speech had brought outright suspicion and even hostility from Ulster Unionists. *The Irish Times* reported that 'the "no surrender" echo will be more raucous and even resemble the cries of 40 years ago'.[118] The Belfast *News Letter* was more forthright: 'one cannot take Mr. Lemass seriously at all: this because of the essential hypocrisy of a policy that permits one hand out stretched in friendship while the other conceals a wounding dagger'.[119] The official British response was swift. A spokesman for the Commonwealth Relations Office in London said that the London government must wait for agreement between Northern Ireland and the Republic of Ireland before they could 'engage in discussions'.[120]

Lemass seemed unperturbed by Belfast and London's public condemnation of his Arklow pronouncement. Within days of delivering the speech he oversaw a revision of the September 1963 departmental memorandum on cross-border relations. The memorandum was condensed into a focused list of fourteen areas suitable for cross-border relations. Lemass judged that the points 'could not give rise to political problems' and as a consequence 'would be worth examining on their merits'.[121] As is discussed below, this fourteen-point plan agenda bore the crux of the brief that Lemass brought to Belfast when he met O'Neill in January 1965.

On reflection, the net result of Lemass's speeches in America and at Arklow was that the economic co-operation between Dublin and Belfast reached its lowest ebb since Lemass assumed power in 1959. Thus, by April 1964, his Northern Ireland policy of promoting North–South co-operation was left in tatters. His orchestrated campaign to win support from Ulster Unionists for cross-border co-operation on issues of common concern, had failed. Even his willingness to offer Belfast concessions on recognition of Northern Ireland had proved ineffective. Privately, O'Neill noted that Lemass's overtures on economic co-operation and the 'constitutional issue' were merely a reincarnation of the 'old anti-partition campaign conduced in a new and more sophisticated way'.[122] AQ8

Given O'Neill's anger at Lemass's anti-partitionist speeches it was somewhat ironic that it was the former who eventually commenced a series of secret negotiations in order to arrange a meeting with Lemass. The driving motivation for O'Neill, in his sudden willingness to meet Lemass, was because of pressure that he faced from within his own party; his minister for commerce, Brian Faulkner being the main intimidator.[123] In December 1964, in a preconceived attempt to outmanoeuvre O'Neill, Faulkner expressed his willingness to meet minister for industry and commerce, Jack Lynch to discuss North–South trade.[124] An invitation that Lynch suggested he would be willing to accept in the early months of 1965.[125]

O'Neill read the signals. He feared that Faulkner would steal the political headlines by becoming the first Unionist politician to meet a minister from the Republic for the first time since the mid-1950s.[126]

Consequently in early January 1965, O'Neill instructed his private secretary, Jim Malley, to offer Lemass an invitation to Belfast. On receiving the invitation Lemass did not hesitate and working through secretary of the Department of Finance, T.K. Whitaker, arrangements were made for Lemass to travel to Belfast for mid-January.[127]

THE LEMASS–O'NEILL MEETING: THE CULMINATION FOR LEMASS OF TEN YEARS' OF POLICY DEVELOPMENT TOWARDS NORTHERN IRELAND

On the morning of 14 January 1965, Lemass, in the company of Whitaker, left Dublin en-route to Belfast. At 1.00pm, the Irish party arrived in Belfast and were greeted by O'Neill at his official residence at Stormont. The agenda of the meeting between the two premiers provided a comprehensive list on cross-border issues. Importantly, the agenda avoided discussions on political and constitutional matters, careful to respect the jurisdiction of the Northern Ireland government. Writing in the aftermath of the meeting, the secretary of the Northern Ireland government, Cecil Bateman, informed Whitehall that the discussions were 'conducted in a most amicable atmosphere'. Political and constitutional questions were 'not an issue' and this was 'fully accepted by both sides'.[128]

The historiography of the Lemass–O'Neill meeting has customarily portrayed the event as significant simply for the fact that it took place.[129] These explanations severely underestimate Lemass's revision of Fianna Fáil's strategy towards partition and Northern Ireland since the mid-1950s. In fact, the true importance of the meeting (from Lemass's perspective, at least) was that it signified the culmination of ten years of policy development on Northern Ireland. As chairman of an internal Fianna Fáil National Executive standing-committee on partition matters, in April 1955, Lemass had first advocated the need to develop cross-border relations with Belfast on issues of common concern. His discussions with O'Neill at Stormont, ten years later, on practical cross-border issues were almost identical to proposals first put forward by Lemass in 1955.

Under Lemass's chairmanship, the 1955 standing-committee on partition matters had produced a revolutionary memorandum. Containing several recommendations, the memorandum advised that a Fianna Fáil government should seek to develop cross-border co-operation with Belfast and 'encourage the establishment of joint authorities to manage affairs of common interest, including transport, electricity generation and distribution, sea lights and marks, drainage programme and tourist development'. Central to the memorandum was the request 'to eliminate as far as possible all impediments to the free movement of goods, persons and traffic across the border' and most importantly to dismantle trade barriers and 'alter the Customs Law' between Dublin and Belfast.[130]

The meeting with O'Neill was a personal milestone for Lemass's Northern Ireland policy. Ten years after first compiling a comprehensive list of possible areas of cross-border co-operation between Belfast and Dublin, Lemass now sat face to face discussing those very same items with the prime minister of Northern Ireland. During his one-hour meeting with O'Neill, both men discussed tourism, education, health, industrial promotion, agricultural research, trade, electricity and justice matters.[131] Lemass must have found the entire episode a rewarding experience. After so long in de Valera's long shadow, he was in a position to fully implement his economic-motivated Northern Ireland strategy.

Lemass achieved what de Valera could have never done. Unlike his predecessor, he was a not a prisoner of history. His visit to Belfast, as the *Irish Press* promulgated, had taken 'courage', greatly helping to 'eliminate the atmosphere of mistrust which had prevailed for so long'.[132] He attempted finally to lay to rest Fianna Fáil's anti-partitionist approach to Northern Ireland. In its place he commenced a policy of *realpolitik*, which positioned North–South relations on a functional basis.

There had been occasional agreements between Dublin and Belfast over the preceding decades. In 1933, for example, the Fianna Fáil government sanctioned the possibility that the Electricity Service Board (ESB) might access supplies of electricity from Northern Ireland. During the 1950s this process continued, as Dublin and Belfast negotiated cross-border agreements in relation to the Foyle Fisheries Commission, the Great Northern Railway and the Erne Hydro-Electric scheme. These, however, had been isolated cases.

After decades of suspicion and prejudice the Lemass-O'Neill meeting had brought the two governments together and had asked all Irishmen to live in harmony irrespective of religious and political differences. Lemass was the first taoiseach to treat Northern Ireland not as 'non-entity', but as a neighbouring state requiring the development of friendly relations. A parallel can be made between Lemass's approach to Northern Ireland and that of the West German socialist politician Willy Brandt's policy of *Ostpolitik*. Like Brandt, who during the 1960s and 1970s, overcame divisions and introduced a normalisation policy between communist East and democratic West, Lemass nurtured change through a policy of *rapprochement*.[133]

The encounter was highly symbolic among the few meetings that had taken place between the leaders of Northern Unionism and Southern Nationalism to that date. Not since the James Craig – William T. Cosgrave meeting, forty years previously in 1925, had an official meeting occurred between the prime ministers of the two states in Ireland. Indeed, the sensational reaction to the Lemass–O'Neill meeting was not rivalled until the celebrated handshake between taoiseach, Bertie Ahern and the first minister of Northern Ireland, the Rev. Ian Paisley in 2007.[134]

In fact, Lemass's meeting with O'Neill was unique. Lemass achieved what no leader of Irish nationalism had done before. For the first time the political leaders of Southern nationalism and Northern unionism officially gathered to facilitate discussions on practical matters of mutual concern, which affected every person on the island of Ireland. Indeed, any comparisons to the meetings between Cosgrave and Craig in 1923 and 1925 are ill-founded. The Cosgrave–Craig meetings were concerned about working out the final terms of the conditions laid down in the 1921 Anglo-Irish Treaty. Thus, it was in Craig's interest to meet Cosgrave as, due to the abolishment of the Council of Ireland, the meetings effectively copper fastened partition.

Albeit a success in the immediate term, Lemass's approach towards Northern Ireland was always based on his desire for stronger cross-border co-operation between Dublin and Belfast. A determination to see Ireland's economy grow dictated his views towards partition. How could he help improve the Irish economy and foster better relations with Ulster Unionists? This was the question that he sought to answer. And he did, by sponsoring stronger economic ties with the Stormont government. He encouraged Fianna Fáil to replace its anti-partitionist agenda towards Ulster Unionism with that of cross-border co-operation between Dublin and Belfast. Nevertheless, as it argued in the following chapter, upon Lemass's retirement, he left behind him no coherent Northern Ireland policy for the long-term. No policies that his successor, Jack Lynch, could comfortably declare as preordained official Fianna Fáil strategy on Northern Ireland.

THE REACTION OF FIANNA FÁIL CABINET MINISTERS, BACKBENCH TDS AND GRASS-ROOTS TO THE LEMASS–O'NEILL MEETING

Writing in the *The Irish Times* shortly after Lemass's visit to Belfast, Garret FitzGerald wondered whether the decision of a Fianna Fáil taoiseach to formally meet the prime minister of Northern Ireland would 'flush the hidden partitionists' within Fianna Fáil out of the woodwork?[135] Lemass must have also pondered the same question. He was to be pleasantly surprised. Reaction from the Fianna Fáil organisation from cabinet ministers down to grass-roots towards Lemass's visit to Belfast was overwhelmingly supportive.

Wary of the undue press coverage of the meeting Lemass asked that the announcement of his visit would not be made until the actual day of the planned meeting. He did not even inform his wife, Kathleen, of his impending visit to Belfast.[136] Lemass's decision to keep the entire affair secret was a calculated gamble. He realised that by not informing Fianna Fáil members of his intention to travel to Belfast he could have met criticism from anti-partitionists within the party. Yet, by keeping the meeting secret he also knew he would inhibit extremists from either the republican or unionist camps from organising protests.

Privately, Lemass had informed one source that he feared 'fanatical demonstrations' would sabotage his visit.[137] Indeed, following Lemass's trip, it was widely reported that if his meeting with O'Neill had become public, he would have cancelled his journey to Belfast.[138] O'Neill, writing in his autobiography several years later, recalled that prior publicity of Lemass's visit to Belfast could have 'endangered the life of my distinguished guest'.[139]

The timing of the scheduled meeting for 14 January was no coincidence. Lemass scheduled the visit during the Oireachtas Christmas recess. The majority of TDs were in their constituencies and political correspondents were less active. Lemass, therefore, had a far greater chance of keeping his planned trip secret. One political correspondent admitted that the visit had 'caught most journalists napping'.[140] Fine Gael leader, James Dillon subsequently conceded that, like the vast majority of deputies at Leinster House, he had been unaware of Lemass's impending visit to Belfast.[141]

On originally receiving the invitation from O'Neill, Lemass had telephoned his minister for external affairs, Frank Aiken. Although somewhat surprised, he fully supported Lemass's plan to meet O'Neill.[142] Writing some years later, in 1968, Aiken described his leader's decision to travel to Belfast as 'historic'.[143] There was also some speculation in the press that Lemass consulted de Valera before he made his decision; although there is no evidence to support this.[144] Besides Aiken, Lemass informed two other unknown cabinet ministers of his impending visit to Belfast.[145] Jack Lynch was not one of the unnamed ministers. He later recalled that Lemass had kept the planned trip to Belfast strictly confidential.[146]

Interestingly, in the immediate aftermath of Lemass's visit to Belfast, some within the media speculated that like O'Neill's pre-emptive strike against his minister for commerce, Brian Faulkner, Lemass had similarly wished to outmanoeuvre his minister, Lynch. In the days before the Lemass–O'Neill meeting, Lynch informed his taoiseach that Faulkner had invited the former to Northern Ireland: 'Do nothing about that until you hear from me', was Lemass's cryptic instructions.[147] Lemass was reportedly worried about his political legacy. He was reputedly concerned that his younger minister might steal the headlines by being the first Fianna Fáil minister to officially meet a member of the Northern Ireland government, in this instance, Faulkner. The *Connacht Tribune* recorded that Lemass 'as the supreme political tactician ... skilled in infighting', wanted to be remembered as 'the man who bridged the border'.[148] There is no available evidence to support this observation. Nevertheless, such comments do reveal the heightened sense of paranoia and intrigue that surrounded the meeting.

Unfortunately, given the nature of the Irish cabinet minutes there is no official record of ministers' reaction to Lemass's announcement of his intent to travel to Belfast.[149] Members of Lemass's cabinet differ in their recollection of whether or not he informed the government before he met O'Neill. Minister for agriculture, Charles J. Haughey recalled that Lemass did raise his planned meeting with O'Neill, but he did not permit a debate on the subject.[150] Minister for local government, Neil Blaney subsequently noted that Lemass, in fact, did not raise his scheduled meeting with O'Neill with his cabinet colleagues.[151] Blaney's observations seem inadmissible, considering he did not attend the last cabinet meeting, on 12 January, prior to Lemass's trip to Belfast.[152]

Speaking in 1969, as tension mounted in Northern Ireland between the Catholic and Protestant communities, Lemass recalled that he had faced no criticism from his cabinet colleagues over his planned visit to Belfast. He did, however, remember that he felt O'Neill was in for a 'rough ride'.[153] Asked by Michael Mills of the *Irish Press* if the meeting with O'Neill was objected to by 'old Republicans', Lemass was unapologetic: 'if we are ever to have unity in Ireland, we are going to have to bring all the people of the country into it and to cherish them all equally'.[154] He admitted publicly that there were not many other occasions in his life when he was 'so completely certain that what I did was right'.[155] Such words epitomised Lemass's approach towards Northern Ireland. He believed that if significant progress was to be made Fianna Fáil supporters needed to dispel the traditional anti-partitionist mentality and deal with Northern Ireland on a functional basis.

The circumstantial evidence suggests that the vast majority of his cabinet colleagues welcomed the meeting with O'Neill. As mentioned, on hearing of Lemass's planned visit Aiken had offered his full support. Lynch, Haughey and minister for transport and power, Erskine Childers, had all spoken of the need to improve relations with Ulster Unionism. These three ministers, in the months prior to the meeting, had travelled to Northern Ireland to hold discussions with their Northern Ireland ministerial counterparts. Indeed, Lynch remembered how he had 'enthusiastically supported' Lemass's initiative. He stated that it had 'introduced an element of rationality to what was essentially an absurd situation'.[156]

Ministers Patrick Hillery (minister for education), Seán MacEntee (tánaiste and minister for health), and Brian Lenihan (minister for justice), neither then nor subsequently voiced opposition to the Lemass–O'Neill meeting. Hillery's support of Jack Lynch's Northern Ireland policy during the turbulent years from 1969 to 1971, lends weight to the fact that he supported his leader's initiative. In his official biography Hillery recorded that he had always maintained that only peaceful methods could deliver Irish unity. He spoke of his lifelong wish to see an end of partition. He 'despised' the Ulster Unionist government, but said that use of violence was out of the question.[157] MacEntee, likewise, supported Lemass's visit to Stormont. Born in Belfast, he remained a consistent critic of de Valera's myopic attitude towards Ulster Unionism. The only biography of Lenihan records that he too supported the meeting.[158]

Besides two of the youngest members of Lemass's cabinet, Neil Blaney and Kevin Boland (minister for social welfare) the available evidence suggests that the remainder of the cabinet endorsed Lemass's meeting with O'Neill.[159] The response from Boland and Blaney to their leader's new initiative is not known. Neither man publicly recorded their feelings towards Lemass's decision to travel to Belfast. Nevertheless, both men harboured a visceral anti-partitionist outlook on the division of the border. They represented the rugged face of the traditional Fianna Fáil stance on Northern Ireland. They were hard men, unapologetic of their desire to see Ireland united.

Blaney, the quintessential localist, was a Fianna Fáil TD in the border county of Donegal. He represented the firebrand 'conditioned constitutionalist' within the organisation.[160] Only three years after

Lemass's visit to Belfast, in 1968, he publicly asserted that the use of physical force to end partition was a legitimate policy.[161] Thereafter, under Jack Lynch's leadership, he remained a consistent critic of Fianna Fáil's Northern Ireland policy, until his eventual expulsion from the party in 1972. Boland equally detested the continuance of partition. His bitter opposition in 1967 to the proposed amendment of article three of the Irish constitution by the All-Party Committee on the Constitution (on which Lemass was a member),[162] together with his resignation from Fianna Fáil in 1971, in protest of the party's Northern Ireland policy, offers strong evidence that like Blaney, he too opposed Lemass's visit to Belfast.

The reaction from backbench Fianna Fáil deputies to the Lemass–O'Neill meeting was, in public at least, unanimously supportive. On first meeting O'Neill, Lemass had told him he would receive criticism from Dublin for his decision to travel to Belfast.[163] In fact, on his return from Belfast none of his backbenchers either at a meeting of the parliamentary party or National Executive raised any opposition to the Lemass–O'Neill meeting.[164] This was surprising. On previous occasions during the 1950s backbenchers had not been shy to express opposition to certain aspects of the party's strategy towards Northern Ireland, particularly in relation to the party's firm stance against the IRA.

In the immediate days and weeks following Lemass's return to Dublin several Fianna Fáil backbench TDs recorded support for the meeting. The day after Lemass's visit to Belfast parliamentary secretary for lands, George Colley, wrote to congratulate Lemass on 'the historic breakthrough'.[165] Colley's wife, Mary, recalled that her husband had known of the meeting prior to Lemass's departure. According to Mary, T. K. Whitaker had kept George 'well in on it'.[166] Party TD for Carlow-Kilkenny, Jim Gibbons, speaking at a Fianna Fáil cumann meeting in Kilkenny, offered his overwhelming approval. He described the meeting as 'probably the most significant meeting since partition was established'. Echoing in public what Lemass believed in private, he noted that 'only a sorry and lunatic fringe ... seek to perpetuate the hatred upon which the border defends [sic], let us hope they, too, may soon see the light'.[167] Donnchadh Ó Briain, TD Limerick-West spoke in support of his party leader, arguing that Fianna Fáil had 'a mandate' to make tough decisions.[168] Parliamentary secretary to the minister for finance, Donogh O'Malley, Limerick-East TD, publicly endorsed the meeting. Speaking in early February 1965 he noted that the meeting was 'acclaimed by all reasonable people'.

However, he warned that it should be 'clearly understood that our ultimate aim is the reunification of our country'.[169]

Any apprehensions that Lemass harboured concerning a negative reaction from the general public to his meeting with O'Neill also proved unwarranted. Indeed, on his return to Dublin, Lemass privately confessed to a small circle of journalists that what particularly pleased him about the meeting was 'the sane and sensible reaction to it on the part of the general public'.[170] The *Evening Echo* did publish a letter to the editor protesting to the Lemass–O'Neill meeting from an irate Corkman, Seán Mac Gabhaim. He wrote that Lemass's visit to Belfast 'can be interpreted as a permanent acceptance of an immoral situation'.[171] His, however, was a lonely voice of protest. The files of the Department of the Taoiseach contain no letters objecting to Lemass's visit from party supporters.[172] The few letters that Lemass did receive from the general public were complimentary. An Irishman living in London, G.P. Lawrence, hailed the meeting as a 'great step forward'.[173] Writing to Lemass from Portadown, Co. Armagh, Joseph Gibson noted that the meeting was 'a good and wise' move.[174] Ernest Blythe believed it was a 'definite turning point'.[175]

An examination of the files of the Prime Minister's Office, Northern Ireland, offers further evidence that Irish nationalists from the Republic supported the meeting. Colm Breathnach, Ardara, Co. Donegal wrote personally to O'Neill in the aftermath of Lemass's visit to express 'as an Irishman I wish to congratulate you most sincerely and warmly on your recent meeting with Mr. Lemass'.[176] The honorary secretary of the United Societies of Castleblaney, Co. Monaghan, M. Hanatty, likewise wrote to 'offer his congratulations to O'Neill'.[177] Most revealingly, a representative of the Leinster Association, IRA 1916–1921, wrote to O'Neill to inform him that 'our organisation is very pleased concerning the recent visit of Mr. Lemass to Stormont ... we desire to see our little country united, but we desire more to see our people united in friendship'.[178]

In fact, the general reaction from the public was to greet Lemass's visit to Belfast and O'Neill's subsequent trip to Dublin in February with a sense of indifference. The vast majority of local and regional newspapers, in the immediate days and weeks after the Lemass–O'Neill meeting, gave minimal space to the event.[179] It is a striking feature of the local press that the meeting was not even mentioned by several regional newspapers. In counties Wexford, Galway, Roscommon, Tipperary, Limerick, Cork and the border county of Donegal, the local newspapers did not refer to the Lemass–O'Neill meeting.[180]

Lemass was eager on his return to Dublin to talk down the importance of his meeting with O'Neill. Speaking to waiting reporters at Government Buildings the day after his visit to Belfast, on 15 January, he noted 'its significance should not be exaggerated'.[181] In the Dáil several days later he argued that the meeting should not be given greater importance than was warranted.[182] At the Fianna Fáil Ard Fheis in October, later of that year, he again recorded that he was at 'pains to discourage any exaggeration of the significance' of the meeting.[183]

Lemass's desire to play down the importance of the meeting was based on the belief that despite the widespread public support for his visit to Belfast it was inevitable that a cohort of anti-partitionists would depict the event as a signal that Fianna Fáil had abandoned its republican ethos. The *Kerryman* warned that although Lemass had set out bravely on a new approach to Northern Ireland, it would earn him criticism from 'die-hearts in our midst'. The paper commented that it could even 'harm him politically'.[184] Lemass had taken a calculated gamble in travelling to Belfast. As Tom Garvin observed, Lemass was trying to transcend a considerable amount of remembered history, bitterness and political passion.[185] This would explain Lemass's reluctance, on his return to Dublin, to make any public comment on the issue of recognition of Northern Ireland.[186] He did not want to return to a subject which he realised could have a destabilising effect within Fianna Fáil. The reality was that his visit confirmed *de facto* recognition of Northern Ireland, which Lemass had already conceded in his Tralee speech in July 1963.

Predictably the largest protest against the meeting came from the extremists within the nationalist and unionist communities. President of Sinn Féin, Tomás MacGiolla denounced Lemass's visit to Belfast as 'a shameful betrayal'. He accused Fianna Fáil of abandoning its 'Republican ideal'.[187] The leader of the Free Presbyterian Church of Ulster, Rev. Ian Paisley was equally dismissive of the meeting. He bemoaned 'in a veil of secrecy you succeeded in smuggling this IRA man into Stormont'.[188] Fearing further protests and demonstrations, Lemass cancelled a scheduled address on 9 February 1965 to the Literary and Scientific Society of Queen's University Belfast. His decision not to visit the Northern capital so soon after his successful meeting with O'Neill was understandable. He realised that there was a real danger, in the words of the *Evening Echo*, that 'ultra nationalists and unionists' would carry out demonstrations.[189]

Lemass's decision to speak at a meeting of the Fianna Fáil Joseph Hudson cumann, on 26 January 1965, was an attempt to appease the anti-partitionists within his own party. He was aware that some supporters, although not making their feelings known publicly, may have harboured resentment towards his visit to Belfast. He therefore selected the anti-partitionist hotbed of Sallynoggin, Dún Laoghaire-Rathdown, to declare his ultimate aspiration for Irish unity. This was a classical political manoeuvre by Lemass. By speaking directly to the hardliners, he was reassuring a sceptical audience that Fianna Fáil was committed to the cause for Irish unity. He later described this technique as a 'process of public education'. He explained that 'this was what a successful politician had to do'. Political leaders, he said, 'have to be able to sense the groundswell of public opinion' and keep the development of 'his policy on a line which enables him to build upon the foundation of public support'.[190]

Lemass's speech was important for his announcement that he believed that the British government no longer had 'any desire to maintain partition'. 'That the problem', he said, 'was one to be settled in Ireland by Irishmen'.[191] Lemass was responding to a speech by British foreign secretary, Gordon Walker. During the course of a by-election in his own constituency, Walker had inadvertently stated that he felt that the British government did not wish to maintain partition.[192] His comments were quickly rebuffed by a spokesman for the Commonwealth Relations Office.[193] Lemass, however, seized upon the minister's off-the-cuff remarks, eager to keep afresh in his supporters' minds that, as head of a Fianna Fáil government, he was doing all he possibly could to secure Irish unity. Commenting on Lemass's Sallynoggin speech the *Irish Press* proclaimed the taoiseach was 'a man who would not sacrifice his political principles at the cost of cross-border co-operation'.[194]

Like Lemass's speeches in America in 1963 and in particular his speech at Arklow the following year in April 1964, his Sallynoggin speech frustrated Ulster Unionists. One Unionist source remarked: 'we get the warm handshake, then in the next we get the cold shoulder'.[195] Lemass realised that his Sallynoggin speech would upset Belfast. It was a risk, however, he was willing to take so as to appease the anti-partitionists within Fianna Fáil. Fortunately, O'Neill, not wanting to get into another round of megaphone diplomacy between North and South, did not respond to Lemass's speech. Indeed, O'Neill was to later concede that such speeches were inevitable, as both he and Lemass could never 'surrender our own constitutional principles'.[196]

Over the remainder of January and February 1965 Lemass sought to put his discussions with O'Neill in Belfast on cross-border co-operation into action. On 4 February, Lynch and Childers held separate meetings with Faulkner in Dublin, on issues relating to cross-border trade and tourism.[197] On 9 February, cross-border relations reached a further highpoint when O'Neill travelled to Dublin to meet Lemass for a second summit. This was the first occasion that the prime minister of Northern Ireland visited Dublin in an official capacity since Sir James Craig had met Michael Collins in 1922. O'Neill was warmly received by Dublin. Accompanied by his wife he had lunch with Lemass, Aiken, Lynch and Ryan at Iveagh House. Following lunch, discussions commenced with a general informal conference on cross-border relations. The meeting planned future co-operation at ministerial level and it was hoped that Haughey and Colley would be in a position to meet their Northern Ireland counterparts in the near future.[198] The very fact that Dublin and Belfast had commenced discussions on cross-border issues at ministerial and civil-service level was significant, signifying the commencement of a policy of normalisation in North–South relations which only a few years before seemed unattainable.

ABSTENTIONISM AND DISCRIMINATION: LEMASS AND NORTHERN NATIONALISTS, 1962–1965

With relations between Dublin and Belfast at their most cordial in over a generation, Lemass next turned his attention to a second front of his reformist approach towards Northern Ireland: his wish that Northern Nationalists end their policy of abstentionism and agree to become the official opposition party at Stormont. On becoming taoiseach in 1959, in the mould of his predecessor, Lemass had been unwilling to offer little help or support to the Nationalist Party. He routinely maintained that it was 'undesirable' for the Fianna Fáil government to provide the Nationalist Party advice on policy matters.[199]

By 1964, on the eve of Lemass's visit to Belfast, this traditional attitude towards Northern Nationalists took a marked change. Lemass now attempted to convince Northern Nationalists to end their 'negative' policy of abstentionism and assume the position as official opposition in Northern Ireland politics.[200] Aiken fully supported Lemass's line, arguing that Northern Nationalists must end their policy of abstentionism so as to take 'a firm logical basis for effective political action'.[201] This was a selfish policy, as Lemass, by effectively using Northern Nationalists, manipulated Northern Ireland politics in the pursuit of his own political ambition. He was resolute that the Nationalist Party would not be permitted to contribute to Fianna Fáil's Northern Ireland policy. Northern Nationalists were to be consulted on policy issues if requested by Dublin, but on Lemass's terms. Lemass realised that by granting Northern Nationalists too much influence he would run the risk of offending Ulster Unionists – a risk he could not afford to take, given that he was trying to encourage closer co-operation between Dublin and Belfast.

It is no coincidence that by 1964 Lemass's sudden preoccupation with Northern Nationalists took place; this was a period when he sought to intensify cross-border co-operation with the government of Northern Ireland. This sudden change in policy was motivated by Lemass's long-term strategy of securing support for his federal proposal from Ulster Unionists. For Lemass this was simply a pragmatic consideration. Under a federal agreement, the Northern Ireland parliament would remain at Stormont. Therefore, Northern Nationalists, as the official opposition, would be required to play a full and active role in Northern Ireland politics. Lemass maintained that Nationalists' participation at Stormont could be without prejudice to their position on Irish unity.[202]

As early as January 1964, in correspondence with the leader of the Nationalist Party, Eddie McAteer MP, Lemass inferred that the Nationalist Party must end its abstentionist policy. He remarked that the time had arrived for the party to use its 'patriotic dedication' and 'make a far more effective and positive contribution to the economic and social development of the area'.[203] Personally, McAteer was in favour of Northern Nationalists ending their abstentionist policy. Since the late 1950s he had championed a personal crusade to persuade members of the Executive of the Anti-Partition League to assume the position as the official opposition at Stormont. His efforts, however, were defeated by the 'older generation' within the movement who were 'horrified' by the request.[204]

Eager to gauge the level of support for the ending of abstentionism within the rank-and-file of the Northern Nationalism, in May 1964, Lemass sent Erskine Childers on a fact-finding mission to Northern Ireland. Childers's letters to Lemass were not reassuring. He reported his visit to a meeting of National Unity, a non-political body founded in 1960, which had explicitly pronounced that Irish unity could only be achieved with the consent of the people of Northern Ireland. National Unity, Childers wrote, 'faced an extremely difficult task of uniting nationalist opinion'. On the issue of recognition of Northern

Ireland, Childers remarked that there was 'a bankruptcy of thought and a fractional division of opinion'.[205]

Lemass was not the only person that viewed Northern Nationalists' abstentionist policy with contempt. Within the Catholic community of Northern Ireland there was a sense of frustration at the lack of progress made by Nationalist politicians down through the years. The fact was that the position and attitude of the Northern Nationalists had barely changed in the four decades since partition. On the whole, the Nationalist Party offered only a grudging acceptance of the Belfast parliament and its authority to govern. For many Northern Ireland Catholics this 'bunker mentality', which had shaped political attitudes for a generation, was no longer an appropriate policy.[206] By the mid-1960s, led by social activists, Patricia and Conn McCluskey and their 'Campaign for Social Justice' (CSJ), Northern Ireland Catholics focused their resources on social and economic concerns, rather than political aspiration for a united Ireland.[207] This approach was to signify a radical new departure.

It was the disastrous showing of republican candidates during the British general election of October 1964 that finally forced the bulk of Northern Nationalists to abandon their abstentionist policy. The participation of republican candidates for the first occasion in a British general election had ensured that the election became a contest over Northern Ireland's future as part of the United Kingdom. Large-scale sectarian riots marred the election campaign. O'Neill's declaration that the border issue was the supreme theme of the election was McAteer's moment to finally force through reforms within the Northern Nationalist Party. Arguing that the result showed that Ulster Unionists were in the ascendancy, McAteer led calls for Northern Nationalists to launch a renewed political programme.[208]

McAteer refrained from committing the movement to becoming the official opposition party: he realised that such a step would prove too far for some of the old-guard within the organisation. Nonetheless, in a sign of the changed political atmosphere, in November 1964, for the first time, the movement announced that it would establish formal constituency structure and hold annual conferences. McAteer also issued a thirty-nine points policy statement, which he explained would help give Northern Ireland Catholics equal rights and eventually help to end partition.[209] This was the first policy document issued by Northern Nationalists since partition.[210] The policy statement ranged from voting rights to a better deal for small farmers, the subject of local government, housing, employment, land and fisheries.[211] Thus, for both McAteer and Lemass the seeds of change had been sown. Northern Nationalists' eagerness to form official constituency branches and release a policy document was the beginning of the movement's move away from sterile anti-partitionism, which had dominated its members' mindset for over a generation.

Significantly, it was Lemass's visit to Belfast in January 1965, which finally compelled Northern Nationalists to end their abstentionist policy and agree to assume the role as official opposition party at Stormont. On Lemass's return from his talks with O'Neill, he commenced intense negotiations with McAteer in an attempt to convince the movement to take up the role as official opposition in Stormont.[212] On 21 January 1965, Lemass held talks with McAteer at Government Buildings in Dublin. He again pushed his Northern colleague to make a statement that Northern Nationalists would finally end its policy of abstentionism.[213] Lemass's pressure eventually paid off.[214] Following consultation between McAteer and his party colleagues, who in turn sought out opinion in their own constituencies, on 2 February 1965 the Northern Nationalist Party became the official opposition in Stormont.[215] The party replaced the Northern Ireland Labour Party, which with four MPs, had previously been accorded recognition as the official opposition by the Speaker of the House. McAteer would be the leader of the new official opposition. The movement consisted of nine Nationalist MPs in the House of Commons and Senator James G. Lennon, as leader of the opposition in the Senate.

Effectively, as Michael Farrell has commented, since 1925 the position of the Nationalist Party had 'come full circle'. Then Northern Nationalists had shelved their opposition to partition and entered Stormont to work within it for immediate reforms. The complete lack of response had forced them into a futile policy of abstentionism. Following the conclusion of the Second World War they returned to parliament, where the party placed immediate reforms in second place to a campaign to end partition. During the 1950s they drifted directionless. With their decision to take their seats at Stormont they had now committed themselves to working within the system so as to reform it.[216]

By agreeing to work from within the Northern Ireland political system the entire context of the partition question had changed for Northern Nationalists. They did not demand an immediate end to partition: they realised that this was unattainable. Instead they sought full civil rights within the United Kingdom. As Northern Nationalist MP for Down South, Joe Connellan commented, 'what had to be accepted was that reunification ... cannot be brought about miraculously overnight'. Therefore, 'one of the most immediate and urgent duties is to help in the building of prosperity, tolerance and mutual respect among all our people in the part of the country in which we live'.[217]

This dramatic shift in policy had implications for Fianna Fáil's relationship with Northern Nationalists. By the Nationalist Party agreeing to enter Stormont Lemass's long-term strategy of securing Irish unity based on a federal agreement was one stage closer. The Nationalist Party had served its purpose. In Lemass's eyes the party as the official opposition at Stormont could now pursue its own policies independent of Dublin.[218] Lemass's detached attitude to Northern Nationalists was most apparent given the Fianna Fáil government's unwillingness to publicise the widespread instances of gerrymandering and discrimination of the Catholic minority by the Stormont authorities. At the Fianna Fáil Ard Fheis the previous year, in November 1964, grass-roots demanded that the party intervene in Northern Ireland politics, so as to highlight discrimination against Northern Catholics and remedy the perceived organisational weakness of the Northern Nationalist organisation.[219] Lemass and his fellow ministers, however, blatantly ignored grass-roots appeals for assistance to Northern Nationalists. Outward criticism of the Northern Ireland state served no useful political value at a time when Dublin was intensifying cross-border co-operation with Belfast.

McAteer, in particular, kept his frustration towards the Fianna Fáil government well hidden. Privately, he expressed his resentment towards the Fianna Fáil government's apathy regarding social and political discrimination of Northern Catholics. Recalling a meeting following Lemass's return from Belfast, in January 1965, McAteer remembered that he was 'more worried than ever. I got neither the encouragement nor the understanding of our position'.[220] McAteer noted that Lemass had accused Catholics in Northern Ireland of being 'as intractable' as their Protestants neighbours. He wrote, 'it was hardly the reaction I expected from a Taoiseach with his Republican background to the representative of the oppressed Irish minority in the Six-Counties'. 'I came away with the conviction that as far as Seán Lemass was concerned, the Northern Irish were very much on their own'.[221]

Writing several years later, McAteer explained that whenever he travelled to Dublin for talks with Fianna Fáil ministers he felt that he rarely received 'real support'.[222] He complained that he was a 'little concerned about the growing lack of contact' between Northern Nationalists and the Irish government.[223] 'Dáil deputies', McAteer said, had 'more contact with parliamentarians abroad than with Nationalists in Stormont'.[224] Journalist Fionnuala O'Connor, writing retrospectively in the 1990s about traditional Northern Ireland Catholics' attitude towards the Republic, accurately illustrated McAteer's criticisms. She recalled interviews with many Northern Catholics, many of whom expressed their belief that Southern politicians and the media had less sympathy for Northern Catholics than for their Protestant neighbours.[225] As expressed by an unidentified lady from a strong republican area of South Co. Derry: 'Dublin was our capital ... but Dublin neglected us'.[226] Frank Curran, former editor of the *Derry Journal*, was more forthright in his condemnation of the Irish government: The Dublin 'guarantee' of Northern Ireland Catholics, he wrote, 'was no guarantee at all. It was a myth, pure and simple'.[227]

Since the formal partition of Ireland, successive Irish governments had been reluctant to involve themselves in the day-to-day grievances of the Catholic minority. The Fianna Fáil government was concerned that its involvement would have effectively given acceptance to the legitimacy of Northern Ireland.[228] By Lemass's first period as taoiseach the comprehensive amount of data on discrimination and gerrymandering in Northern Ireland compiled by the All-Party Anti-Partition Committee during the 1950s was by then out-of-date. Additionally, the 'fact finding' trips made by Conor Cruise O'Brien in the early 1950s, to meet Northern Nationalists had been discontinued, as the official anti-partition campaign faded into the political undergrowth.

Indeed, O'Brien later noted that by the 1960s consecutive Fianna Fáil governments were 'not concerned' about the discrimination of Northern Ireland Catholics. He recalled that within Fianna Fáil government circles there was a feeling that Northern Ireland Catholics 'had brought ... most of their trouble on themselves, and it was now up to them to come to terms with reality'.[229] By Lemass's second term as taoiseach, within the Department of External Affairs, there were no facts or figures on the discrimination of Catholic in Northern Ireland. Lemass privately admitted that the Irish government had no up-to-date 'reliable' statistics of discriminations.[230] He even inquired if Northern Ireland Nationalist MP for South Fermanagh, Cahir Healy, could collect all the relevant material available and forward it to the Dublin government.[231]

During Lemass's premiership the only reliable briefings that the Irish government received on conditions of the Catholic community within Northern Ireland came from McAteer directly. In a clear indication of the Fianna Fáil government's lack of resources towards the plight of Northern Ireland Catholics, in late 1964, officials within the Department of External Affairs asked McAteer to send the most recent annual report of the Derry Catholic Registration Association. The report contained the most up-to-date information on discrimination and was requested by the department as it had no available figures.[232] Within the Department of External Affairs there was reluctance by senior civil servants to establish formal communications with Northern Nationalists. For instance, in the summer of 1964, McAteer sent a new pamphlet on discrimination practices against Northern Catholics to officials in the Irish government. His pamphlet, however, was dismissed by the top officials within the department as inappropriate.[233]

The lack of involvement that Aiken allocated towards Northern Ireland was a further reason why Dublin was so out of touch with the plight of Northern Catholics. Throughout the 1950s, Aiken in particular, had kept himself abreast of the political and social problems of the Catholic minority. More than any other Fianna Fáil minister, in his dealings with London, Aiken routinely urged British ministers to help alleviate the widespread political and social discrimination of Northern Ireland Catholics by the Stormont government.[234] Yet, by the 1960s Aiken was noticeably silent on Northern Ireland; it was not until the aftermath of the RUC attacks on a civil rights march in the city of Derry, in early October 1968, that Aiken fully reengaged with the partition question.[235] Prior to this period as minister for external affairs, his central interest lay, not with partition, but in Ireland's involvement at the United Nations. He believed that Northern Ireland policy was a 'constitutional issue' and thus not his concern.[236] According to the British Embassy in Dublin by this time Aiken had 'mellowed considerably' and was no longer viewed as 'bitterly anti-British'; that said, he was still perceived to be a fierce opponent of partition.[237]

Aiken's detached attitude towards Northern Ireland suited Lemass. John Horgan noted that Lemass's relationship with Aiken was 'problematic', characterised by a sense of reserve at best.[238] According to Brian Lenihan, Lemass regarded Aiken 'as a fool' and was delighted to see him disappear over the horizon in the direction of the United Nations for three months every year.[239] Todd Andrews recorded that there was a 'known coolness' between Lemass and Aiken.[240] It was not merely Lemass who was sceptical of Aiken's abilities. Writing in the early 1960s, Aiken's long-serving ministerial colleague, Gerald Boland, recorded that 'a worse minister for external affairs could not be found'.[241]

While there may have been differences between both men, Aiken did adhere, in general, to Lemass's Northern Ireland policy. Like Lemass, Aiken repeatedly denounced the use of physical force to end partition,[242] recognised that the support of Ulster Unionism was necessary to bring an end to partition[243] and did not support the official raising of partition at the UN.[244] Since the late 1950s Aiken acknowledged that Dublin should seek to improve North–South relations and in particular remove trade barriers between both jurisdictions.[245] As mentioned above, he also offered his support for Lemass's visit to O'Neill in 1965 and sought to convince Northern Nationalists to assume the position as the official opposition at Stormont. Although against the use of the term 'federal agreement', he did endorse Lemass's calls for an agreement between Dublin and Belfast, whereupon the powers of Westminster would be transferred to a Dublin parliament, with Ulster Unionists retaining their own 'local' parliament in Belfast.[246]

Where he differed from Lemass on Northern Ireland was that he found it difficult to fully detach himself away from Fianna Fáil's anti-partitionist agenda. He was, as stated by Conor Cruise O'Brien 'consistent' with Lemass on Northern Ireland policy, but Lemass's was 'from a pragmatic point of view, while Aiken's was more idealistic'.[247] Aiken made it known to Lemass that he favoured the traditional usage of the term 'Six-Counties' to that of 'Northern Ireland', while he also refused to grant *de facto* recognition to Northern Ireland. Unlike Lemass, even into the 1960s, he placed primary responsibility on Britain's shoulders for ending partition.[248] He also was less than enthusiastic for Lemass's endorsement of National Unity; although this was to be expected considering that the movement acknowledged that the 'consent' of the majority of Northern Ireland was required to end partition. Whatever differences there were between Aiken and Lemass on Northern Ireland, they remained relatively minor. Aiken was more than content to permit his leader to pursue his Northern Ireland agenda.

For the remainder of his leadership of Fianna Fáil, until his retirement as taoiseach in November 1966, Lemass's main focus was on intensifying cross-border co-operation with Belfast. He was satisfied to leave O'Neill to implement reforms in Northern Ireland. Instead, the Fianna Fáil government decided to step to one side and permit the Nationalist Party to publicise the internal problems facing the Catholic minority of Northern Ireland. During Lemass's final two years as taoiseach, the government's main priority was cross-border co-operation with Belfast. Northern Catholic grievances were to be ignored. Indeed, when one unidentified Fianna Fáil cabinet minister was questioned by a journalist on the plight of Roman Catholics in Northern Ireland in 1966, he exclaimed: 'Ah, we don't worry about them. Sure the English Roman Catholic MPs at Westminster will look after them'.[249] This attitude to Northern Nationalists continued under the authority of Lemass's successor as Fianna Fáil leader, Jack Lynch. It was not until 1968 – impelled by the civil rights campaign and the impending violence on the streets of Northern Ireland – that the Fianna Fáil government was forced to confront the politically sensitive issue of discrimination against Northern Catholics.

In summarising Lemass's relationship with Northern Nationalists one could argue that it had begun with an inbuilt sense of distance and reserve and ended in an atmosphere little short of open hostility.[250] The deterioration of friendly relationship with Northern Nationalists was a price that Lemass was willing to pay so as to secure support from Ulster Unionists. Lemass was unapologetic. His wish to secure cross-border co-operation outweighed any perceived loyalties that Fianna Fáil may have held to expose discrimination against Northern Catholics. In fact, the Fianna Fáil government's policy of encouraging cross-border co-operation with Belfast, at the expense of relations with Northern Nationalists, was to ultimately prove unsuccessful. As is discussed in the following chapter, the failure was not to be directed at the hands of Lemass or his Fianna Fáil government, but to the escalation of religious and political tension in Northern Ireland.

* * *

In conclusion, as Fianna Fáil entered the general election campaign during April 1965, Lemass felt confident that his meeting with O'Neill would be viewed as a positive factor by the Irish electorate. As in previous elections, the economy, not Northern Ireland, dominated the election trail.[251] Lemass admitted publicly that as far as he was concerned there was 'an unspoken' agreement between all Southern political parties to keep the partition question out of the campaign.[252] When pushed by reporters to outline his Northern Ireland policy he was realistic: 'It is going to be a long process'. 'But the recent developments', he noted, 'which have been taken to ensure effective co-operation to our mutual advantage will I hope help to create this new atmosphere'.[253] When the election results were announced, on 13 April, Fianna Fáil won exactly half the seats, seventy-two, a gain of two seats. The result did not give Lemass the overall majority that he desperately wanted. The very closeness of the result, as noted by John Horgan, suggests that without the Northern issue he might have been forced into another minority government.[254]

For the meantime at least, relations between Dublin and Belfast looked as though they were at their most cordial since that of the Cumann na nGaedheal government's dealings with Ulster Unionists during the early 1920s. This was to prove a momentary period of the melting of hostile relations between the governments. Unfortunately, old agendas and prejudices were to soon return. Whitaker, writing in the 1970s of Lemass's visit to meet O'Neill in 1965, recalled with poignant accuracy how quickly the political landscape of the island of Ireland changed within the space of a few years: 'We started back on the road to Dublin with new hope in our hearts. We had no presentiment of the tragic events to 1969 and the years since'.[255]

NOTES

1. *Irish Press*, 30 July 1963.
2. *Anglo-Celt*, 16 Jan. 1965.
3. See, for example, comments by Lord Brookeborough. *The Irish Times*, 16 Jan. 1960.
4. See 'North and South 1: Mr Lemass's Approach', *The Irish Times*, 15 Jan. 1960.
5. Tim Pat Coogan, *The IRA* (London, Pall Mall Press, 1971), 417–418.
6. See 'The Peter Barry papers', *Magill*, June 1980, 48.
7. See University College Dublin Archives (UCDA) Fianna Fáil Party Papers P176/769, record of 32nd Fianna Fáil Ard Fheis, 16–17 Jan. 1962.
8. See National Archives of Ireland (NAI) Department of Foreign Affairs (DFA) 305/14/19 D11, Seán Ó'Fionn to Lemass, 23 June 1962.
9. NAI Department of Taoiseach (DT) S/9361 K/62, Rev. P.F. Malone to Lemass, 8 Feb. 1962.
10. NAI DT S/9361 K/62, Rev. P.F. Malone to Lemass, 8 Feb. 1962.
11. John Bowman, *De Valera and the Ulster Question* (Oxford: Oxford University Press, 1982), 287.

12. Conor Cruise O'Brien, *Herod: Reflections on Political Violence* (London: Hutchinson, 1978), 137.
13. See Kevin Boland's observations on Fianna Fáil grass-roots' ambiguity towards IRA violence, Kevin Boland, *The Rise and Decline of Fianna Fáil* (Dublin: Mercier Press, 1982), 61.
14. UCDA Frank Aiken Papers P104/8812, Lemass to Mr Heaney, 25 Nov. 1961.
15. Dáil Éireann Debate (DE), 6 Dec. 1961. Vol. 192, col. 1213.
16. UCDA P176/769, record of 32nd Fianna Fáil Ard Fheis, copy of Lemass's Presidential address, 16–17 Jan. 1962. This was the first of two Ard Fheiseanna in 1962 due to the previous general election in Oct. 1961. See also UCDA P176/769, record of 33rd Fianna Fáil Ard Fheis, 20–21 Oct. 1962.
17. See NAI DT S/9361 K/62, extract of speech by Aiken, 1962 Fianna Fáil Ard Fheis, 17 Jan. 1962.
18. See Haughey's comments. *Anglo-Celt*, 3 March 1962.
19. 'The Peter Barry papers', *Magill*, June 1980, 48.
20. *Anglo Celt*, 3 March 1962.
21. Barry Flynn, *Soldiers of Folly: the IRA Border Campaign, 1956–1962* (Cork: Collins Press 2009), 203.
22. The *Meath Chronicle, Connacht Tribune, Anglo-Celt* and *Kerryman* made minimal, if any, reference to the IRA border campaign during Nov. 1961–March 1962.
23. The *Southern Star*, 3 March 1962.
24. See *Anglo Celt*, 10 March 1962.
25. *Irish Times*, 20 Feb. 1962.
26. See Lemass's Oxford Address, 15 Oct. 1959. *The Irish Times*, 16 Oct. 1959.
27. National Archives of the United Kingdom (NAUK) Foreign and Commonwealth Office (FCO) 33/1599, confidential profile of Jack Lynch, British Embassy, Dublin, Feb. 1971.
28. See Haughey's comments. *Belfast Telegraph*, 13 Nov. 1962.
29. See Lemass's Oxford Address, 15 Oct. 1959. *The Irish Times*, 16 Oct. 1959.
30. See UCDA Ernest Blythe Papers P24/1421, Lemass to Blythe, 7 Dec. 1962.
31. The *Southern Star*, 3 March 1962.
32. *The Irish Times*, 30 July 1963.
33. See the *The Irish Times*, 19 Sept. 1983.
34. Interview with Mary Colley, 18 May 2009.
35. *Irish Press,* 4 Feb. 1969.
36. See Brian Farrell, *Seán Lemass* (Dublin, Gill and Macmillan, 1983), 106.
37. See speech by Colley. *Irish Press*, 17 April 1963.
38. *Irish Press*, 11 Nov. 1959.
39. Speaking in the Dáil in July 1959, Booth spoke in support of recognising the Northern Ireland government *de facto*. He argued that not to do so was a policy of futility and accused mainstream nationalism as being 'far too greedy'. DE, 7 July 1959. Vol.176, col. 646.
40. A resident of Dartry, Co. Dublin, Hederman was a solicitor and attorney general under the Fianna Fáil government from 1977 to 1981. At a meeting of the Fianna Fáil National Executive, in February 1958, Hederman had 'requested that the Irish government should recognise the government of Northern Ireland *de facto*'. UCDA P176/348, meeting of Fianna Fáil National Executive, 10 Feb. 1958.
41. At the National Executive meeting of 10 Feb. 1958, Ryan had seconded Hederman's motion for the *de facto* recognition of Northern Ireland. UCDA P176/348, meeting of National Executive, 10 Feb. 1958.
42. NAI DT S/16699B, Lemass to Vivion de Valera, 14 May 1960.
43. Barrington was married to, Eileen, daughter of Seán O'Donovan, Fianna Fáil Senator. Barrington was appointed a Fianna Fáil Senator in 1961.
44. Donal Barrington, *Uniting Ireland* (Dublin, 1957). A copy is available from NAI DT S 9361 G.
45. See comments by Horgan, *The Irish Times*, 16 Dec. 1957.

46. See comments by Blythe, *The Irish Times*, 5 Aug. 1957.

47. See Seanad Éireann debate (SE), 29 Jan. 1958. Vol. 48, col. 1404–1408.

48. See Garret FitzGerald's comments, *National Observer*, June 1959.

49. Liam de Paor, *Divided Ulster* (Harmondsworth: Penguin Press, 1970), 137–138.

50. See *The Irish Times*, 26 March 1963.

51. Brendan Lynn, *Holding the Ground: The Nationalist Party in Northern Ireland, 1945–72* (Aldershot: Ashgate, 1997), 161.

52. See *Belfast Telegraph*, 27 March 1963.

53. Five years previously, in 1959, the Young Unionist Council had categorically rejected a proposal from the Central Branch of Fine Gael for a debate between the two movements until the Dublin government recognised the constitutional of Northern Ireland and dealt more firmly with the IRA. *The Irish Times*, 14 Dec. 1959.

54. See Graham Walker, *A History of the Ulster Unionist Party, Protest, Pragmatism and Pessimism* (Manchester,: Manchester University Press, 2004), 154–156.

55. National Unity founded in 1960 was a Nationalist organisation that sought to encourage closer relations with Ulster Unionists. Its major significance was that it recognised that a united Ireland could only be secured with the consent of the majority of Northern Ireland.

56. Interview with Mary Colley, 18 May 2009.

57. Michael Kennedy, *Division and Consensus, The Politics of Cross-Border Relations in Ireland, 1925–1969* (Dublin: Institute for Public Administration, 2000), 196.

58. Interview with Mary Colley, 18 May 2009.

59. *Irish Press*, 17 April 1963.

60. *Irish Press*, 17 April 1963.

61. *Irish Press*, 17 April 1963.

62. Kennedy, *Division and Consensus*, 188.

63. This is apparent given the fact that on separate visits to Belfast, each minister publicly spoke in favour of cross-border co-operation. See speech by Lynch, *The Irish Times*, 20 Feb. 1962. See also speech by Haughey, *Belfast Telegraph*, 13 Nov. 1962. See also Childers's speech, *Irish Press*, 15 Nov. 1963.

64. Kennedy, *Division and Consensus*, 188.

65. See comments by Ulster Unionist Senator, Albert Walmsley, *Irish News*, 8 May 1963. See also remarks by Unionist MPs for North Down and North Antrim, Robert Nixon and Henry Clarke, respectively, Kennedy, *Division and Consensus*, 192.

66. *Irish Press*, 1 May 1963.

67. Kennedy, *Division and Consensus*, 198.

68. NAI DT S/9361K/63, note by McCann, 15 July 1963.

69. *The Irish Times*, 2 Aug. 1963.

70. *Irish Press*, 30 July, 1963.

71. *The Irish Times*, 30 July 1963.

72. Clare O'Halloran, *Partition and the Limits of Irish Nationalism* (New Jersey: Humanities Press International, Inc., 1987), 121.

73. See *Sunday Independent*, 14 July 1963.

74. *Kerryman*, 3 Aug. 1963.

75. *Derry Journal*, 12 July 1963.

76. See Lemass's comments during a debate on recognition of Northern Ireland. DE, 10 Feb. 1965. Vol. 214, col. 3–4.

77. See Lynch's Tralee speech, 20 Sept. 1969. *The Irish Times*, 21 Sept. 1969.

78. DE, 24 June 1947. Vol.107, col. 79.

79. See Boland, *The Rise and Decline of Fianna Fáil*, 145–150.

80. At a meeting of the Fianna Fáil National Executive in July 1959 Kennedy apposed Lionel Booth's previous calls for the Irish government to accord *de facto* recognition to Northern Ireland. See UCDA P176/447, meeting of National Executive, 15 July 1959.

81. In fact the notion of amending the 1937 constitution, so as to remove the Irish government's territorial claim over the Island of Ireland, was again revisited in 1967,

with the establishment of a Committee on the Constitution in which Lemass, although retired as leader of Fianna Fáil, chaired. For a detailed recollection of the workings of this committee, see Boland, *The Rise and Decline of Fianna Fáil*, 145–150. See also, Bowman, *de Valera*, 323–331.

82. *The Irish Times*, 2 Aug. 1963.
83. See O'Neill's comments. *The Irish Times*, 31 July 1963.
84. NAUK Prime Minister's Office (PREM) 11/4874, memorandum by O'Neill entitled: 'Aspects of relations with the Irish Republic', 22 Nov. 1963.
85. *Irish Press*, 12 Sept. 1963.
86. See Kennedy, *Division and Consensus*, 200. See also interview by Lemass, *Sunday Press*, 3 Oct. 1963.
87. Kennedy, *Division and Consensus*, 200.
88. UCDA P104/8814, Lemass to all government ministers, 16 Sept. 1963.
89. See Kennedy, *Division and Consensus*, 202–210.
90. See Kennedy, *Division and Consensus*, 204–206.
91. See Kennedy, *Division and Consensus*, 209–210.
92. See speech by Lemass. *Irish Press*, 16 Oct. 1963.
93. See Lemass's comments. *The Irish Times*, 17 Oct. 1963 and *Irish Press*, 18 Oct 1963.
94. Michael Kennedy 'Northern Ireland and cross-border co-operation', in Brian Girvin and Gary Murphy (eds.), *The Lemass Era-Politics and Society in the Ireland of Seán Lemass* (Dublin: UCD Press, 2005), 114.
95. NAI DT S/9361K/63, Cremin to McCann, 5 Dec. 1963.
96. NAUK PREM 11/4874, memorandum by O'Neill entitled: 'Aspects of relations with the Irish Republic', 22 Nov. 1963.
97. NAUK PREM 11/4874, memorandum by O'Neill entitled: 'Aspects of relations with the Irish Republic', 22 Nov. 1963.
98. *Irish Press*, 8 Nov. 1963.
99. NAUK FCO 33/1599, confidential profile of Erskine Childers, British Embassy, Dublin, May 1971.
100. See Childers's comments. *Irish Press*, 15 Nov. 1963.
101. Booth also remarked that 'his ancestors had come to Ireland with Oliver Cromwell and that his Portadown born wife's ancestors had come over with King William'. *The Irish Times*, 9 Dec. 1963.
102. Interview with Richard Booth, 8 Dec. 2008
103. *The Irish Times*, 9 Dec. 1963.
104. Interview with Richard Booth, 8 Dec. 2008. Mary Colley also remembered that 'off the record meetings' on Northern Ireland occurred at the home of Booth. She and her husband would regularly have dinner at the Booths' family home. Interview with Mary Colley, 18 May 2009.
105. See Chapter Five, p.229.
106. *Irish Press*, 30 July, 1963.
107. In a draft letter to de Valera, MacEntee wrote that 'The partition problem cannot be solved except with the consent of the majority of the Northern non-Catholic population. It certainly cannot be solved by their coercion'. UCDA Seán MacEntee Papers P67/155, (draft) MacEntee to de Valera, 17 Feb. 1938.
108. Aodh de Blacam, 'Some thoughts on partition', *Studies, An Irish Quarterly Review* (Vol. XXIII, 1934), 559–576; 576.
109. UCDA P104/8822, Haughey to Aiken, 14 March 1967.
110. Garreth Ivory, 'Revisions in nationalist discourse among Irish political parties', *Irish Political Studies*, 14:1, (1999), 84–103: 89–90.
111. For further analysis of Fianna Fáil and the 'principle of consent' see Stephen Kelly, 'The politics of terminology: Seán Lemass and Ulster question, 1959–1966', in Caoimhe Nic Dháibhéid and Colin Reid (eds.), *From Parnell to Paisley: Constitutional and Revolutionary Politics in Ireland, 1879 – 2008* (Dublin: Irish Academic Press, 2010), 151–153.
112. See *Belfast Newsletter* and *Irish Press* for Dec. 1963.

113. NAUK FCO 33/1596, David Blatherwick to R. Bone, 21 Dec. 1971.

114. *Wicklow People*, 18 April 1964.

115. NAUK Dominions Office (DO) 182/130, meeting between Lemass and Duncan Sandys, 18 March 1964.

116. *Irish Press*, 13 April 1964.

117. See O'Neill's comments. *The Irish Times*, 14 April 1964.

118. *The Irish Times*, 14 April 1964.

119. *News Letter*, 14 April 1964.

120. *The Irish Times*, 14 April 1964.

121. See Michael Kennedy and Eoin Magennis, 'North–South agenda setting in the 1960s and 1990s: plus ca change?', *Journal of Cross Border Studies in Ireland*, No.2 (spring, 2007), 34–53:37.

122. NAUK PREM 11/4874, memorandum by O'Neill entitled: 'Aspects of relations with the Irish Republic', 22 Nov. 1963.

123. Thomas Hennessey argued that O'Neill's decision to meet Lemass was based on his wish to secure Northern Ireland's constitution against the Republic's 'empty' territorial claim to the region. Such observations underestimate the internal pressure from within the Ulster Unionist Party, which effectively compelled O'Neill to finally agree to meet Lemass. Significantly, faced with the threat posed by Faulkner, politics not pragmatism guided O'Neill's ultimate decision to meet Lemass. See Thomas Hennessey, *A History of Northern Ireland, 1920–1996* (Dublin: Gill and Macmillan, 1997), 125.

124. See Faulkner's comments, *The Irish Times*, 15 Dec. 1964.

125. See Lynch's comments, *The Irish Times*, 1 Jan. 1965.

126. Another reason for O'Neill's willingness to meet Lemass was to show the British prime minister, Harold Wilson, that he was implementing reforms in Northern Ireland. See Kennedy 'Northern Ireland and Cross-Border Co-operation', 115. See also Henry Patterson, *Ireland Since 1939, The Persistence of Conflict* (Dublin: Penguin Ireland, 2006), 190–191.

127. NAI DFA P363, Whitaker to Malley, 5 Jan. 1965.

128. Public Records Office of Northern Ireland (PRONI) Cabinet Files (CAB) 9U/5/1, 'Meeting with the Prime Minister of the Irish Republic' (date unknown).

129. See Michael O'Sullivan, *Seán Lemass, A Biography* (Dublin: Blackwater Press, 1994), 179; Tom Garvin, *Judging Lemass, The Measure of the Man* (Dublin: Royal Irish Academy, 2009), 6–19; and Dermot Keogh, *Twentieth Century Ireland, Nation and State* (Dublin: Gill and Macmillan, 1994), 287.

130. See UCDA P176/46, memorandum by the chairman standing-committee on partition matters, April 1955.The workings of this committee are examined in full in Chapter Four.

131. See UCDA Kenneth Whitaker Papers P175 (1), record of meeting between O'Neill and Lemass, 14 Jan. 1965.

132. *Irish Press*, 9 Nov. 1966.

133. For more on Brandt and his policy of *Ostpolitik*, see Willy Brandt, *A Peace Policy for Europe* (London: Weidenfeld and Nicolson, 1969).

134. *The Irish Times*, 5 April 2007.

135. *The Irish Times*, 27 Jan. 1965.

136. NAI DFA P363, Whitaker to Malley, 5 Jan. 1965.

137. See report from the 'special correspondent', *Anglo-Celt*, 25 Jan. 1965.

138. See *Kerryman*, 16 Jan. 1965 and *Limerick Chronicle*, 16 Jan. 1965.

139. Terence O'Neill, *The Autobiography of Terence O'Neill* (London: Rupert Hart-Davis, 1972), 75.

140. *Wicklow People*, 16 Jan. 1965.

141. *Irish News*, 15 Jan. 1965. According to Whitaker, however, someone within the cabinet in Dublin did leak the planned trip to the *The Irish Times* and the paper had despatched a cameraman to the border to snap the historic occasion. Whitaker's assertion is dubious as no image was published by the paper the following day. See Garvin, *Judging Lemass*, 4.

142. Kennedy, *Division and Consensus*, 232.

143. See UCDA P104/8774, article by Aiken, 'Unity in Diversity', in *United Ireland Association Review*, Spring, 1968, 2.
144. See *Connacht Tribune*, 23 Jan. 1965.
145. Horgan, *Seán Lemass*, 278.
146. Horgan, *Seán Lemass*, 278.
147. Horgan, *Seán Lemass*, 278.
148. *Connacht Tribune*, 23 Jan. 1965.
149. See NAI 96/5/1, Tenth Government Cabinet Minutes, record of cabinet meeting, 12 Jan. 1965. A subsequent cabinet meeting was not held until 19 Jan. 1965. See also NAI DT 96/4/1, Government Minutes, record of meeting of government, 12 Jan. 1965, 11am – 1pm.
150. O'Sullivan, *Seán Lemass*, 179.
151. O'Sullivan, *Seán Lemass*, 179.
152. See NAI 96/5/1, Tenth Government Cabinet Minutes, record of cabinet meeting, 13 Jan. 1965. Blaney was the only minister recorded as absent from the cabinet meeting.
153. *Irish Press*, 28 Jan. 1969.
154. *Irish Press*, 28 Jan. 1969.
155. *Belfast Telegraph*, Jan. 1965.
156. See 'My life and times' by Jack Lynch, *Magill*, Nov. 1979, 44.
157. See John Walsh, *Patrick Hillery: The Official Biography* (Dublin: New Ireland, 2008), 175–176.
158. See James Downey, *Lenihan, His Life his Loyalties* (Dublin: New Ireland, 1998), 72–73.
159. The remainder of Lemass's frontbench, likewise, did not offer any public comments on the Lemass–O'Neill meeting. They were Michael Hilliard (minister for posts and telegraphs), James Ryan (minister for finance), Gerald Bartley (minister for defence), and Michael Moran (minister for lands and minister for the gaeltacht).
160. See 'Neill Blaney: past and future', *Magill*, 2 May 1985.
161. See Blaney's speech to his Donegal constituents, *Irish Press*, 9 Nov. 1968.
162. To Boland's amazement and indeed disgust the Report of the Committee on the Constitution recommended that a new provision, to replace article three, be inserted into the Irish constitution. Boland believed to remove the provision in article three, which referred to the right of the Dáil to legislate for the whole of the island of Ireland, was tantamount to recognising the British claim to Northern Ireland. Boland subsequently wrote that any attempts to amend article three of the constitution would represent a 'sell-out' and an 'abandonment' of Fianna Fáil's republicanism, and he would never tolerate this. See Donnacha Ó Beacháin, *Destiny of the Soldiers: Fianna Fáil, Irish Republicanism and the IRA, 1926–1973* (Dublin: Gill and Macmillan, 2011), 265 and Boland, *The Rise and Decline of Fianna Fáil*, 147.
163. See Joseph J. Lee, *Ireland 1912–1985 Politics and Society* (Cambridge: Cambridge University Press, 1989), 411.
164. From an examination of over twenty local newspapers in the immediate days and weeks after the Lemass–O'Neill meeting this author has found no evidence that backbench Fianna Fáil deputies opposed the meeting. See also UCDA P176/447–448.
165. NAI DT 96/6/23, Colley to Lemass, 15 Jan. 1965.
166. Interview with Mary Colley, 18 May 2009.
167. *Kilkenny Journal*, 23. Jan 1965.
168. *Anglo-Celt*, 30 Jan. 1965.
169. *Limerick Weekly Echo*, 6 Feb. 1965.
170. See *Connacht Tribune*, 23 Jan. 1965.
171. See *Evening Echo*, 21 Jan. 1965.
172. See NAI DT 97/9/1277, Government policy: letters of advice and criticism, 1964–1965. See also UCDA P176/311–348, record of Fianna Fáil constituency files, 1959–1966.
173. NAI DT 97/9/1277, G.P. Lawrence to Lemass, 26 Jan. 1965.
174. NAI DT 97/9/1277, Joseph Gibson to Lemass, 12 May 1965.
175. See UCDA P24/1824, copy of remarks regarding Blythe's views on the Lemass–O'Neill meeting, 1 March 1965.

176. PRONI Prime Minister's Office (PREM) 5/7/6, Colm Breathnach to O'Neill, 4 Feb. 1965.
177. PRONI PREMM 5/7/6, M. Hanatty to O'Neill, 3 March 1965.
178. PRONI PREM 5/7/6, J. Doyle, Woodpark, The Rise, Glasnevin, Dublin to O'Neill, (undated).
179. The *Munster Express, Wicklow People and Northern Standard* gave minimal attention to the Lemass–O'Neill meeting, see each paper during Jan. 1965.
180. The *Eniscorthy Guardian, Galway Observer, Roscommon Champion, Tipperary Star, Limerick Weekly Echo, Cork Evening Echo* and the *Donegal Democrat*, made no reference to the Lemass–O'Neill meeting, see each paper during Jan. 1965.
181. *The Irish Times*, 16 Jan. 1965.
182. See *Belfast Telegraph*, 11 Feb. 1965.
183. UCDA P176/772, record of 1965 Fianna Fáil Ard Fheis, 16–17 Oct. 1965.
184. *Kerryman*, 23 Jan. 1965.
185. Garvin, *Judging Lemass*, 6.
186. See also Lemass's speech in the Dáil, 10 Feb. 1965. Dáil Éireann (DE), 10 Feb. 1965. Vol. 214, col.3. He skilfully dodged explicitly granting recognition to the Northern Ireland state.
187. *Kerryman*, 16 Jan. 1965.
188. *Irish Press*, 16 Jan. 1965.
189. *Evening Echo*, 18 Jan. 1965.
190. *Irish Press*, 4 Feb. 1969
191. See NAI DFA 96/6/250, copy of Lemass's speech at a dinner of the Joseph Hudson cumann of Fianna Fáil, 26 Jan. 1965.
192. *The Irish Times*, 28 Jan. 1965.
193. *The Irish Times*, 28 Jan. 1965.
194. *Irish Press*, 27 Jan. 1965.
195. *The Irish Times*, 28 Jan. 1965.
196. O'Neill made these comments during an interview on RTÉ, 18 Feb. 1965. See *The Irish Times*, 19 Feb. 1965.
197. At civil service level, the Northern Ireland cabinet secretary, Cecil Bateman and Whitaker commenced a series of negotiations designed to formulate an agenda for future North–South meetings. Discussions also occurred between the Department of Justice and the Ministry of Home Affairs and the Gardaí and RUC on co-operation over extradition and the IRA. See Kennedy, *Division and Consensus*, 239–242.
198. See Kennedy, *Division and Consensus*, 245–246.
199. See Enda Staunton, *The Nationalists of Northern Ireland, 1918–1973* (Dublin: Columba Press, 2001), 231.
200. NAI DFA 305/14/303, Lemass to McAteer, 6 Jan. 1964.
201. See NAI DT S/16272G, Aiken to Lemass, 26 Jan. 1965.
202. See NAI DT S/16272G, See NAI DT S/16272G.
203. NAI DFA 305/14/303, Lemass to McAteer, 6 Jan. 1964.
204. See *Belfast Newsletter*, 5 March 1964, which quotes from *Focus* a Dublin-based magazine.
205. NAI DT 172697/95, Childers to Lemass, 11 May 1964.
206. Brendan Lynn, 'Revising Northern nationalism, 1960–1965: the Nationalist Party's response', *New Hibernia Review*, Vol. 4 No. 3 (autumn, 2000), 78–92, 78.
207. In early 1963, Patricia and Conn McCluskey and other local people from Dungannon Co. Tyrone, formed the Homeless Citizens League (HCL), which sought to bring to the attention of a wider audience the chronic housing shortage in the region, particularly against working-class Catholic families. Conn McCluskey wrote to McAteer requesting that the Northern Nationalist Party move away from the 'Border' issue and instead 'concentrate on getting our rights and trying to overcome gerrymandering'. In January 1964, the McCluskeys expanded their protest and helped to launch the Campaign for Social Justice (CSJ). Significantly this movement sought to win for Northern Catholics the same ordinary rights that British citizens held throughout the United Kingdom. See Lynn, 'Revising Northern nationalism, 1960–1965', 80.

208. See Lynn, 'Revising Northern nationalism, 1960–1965', 85–90.
209. *Irish News*, 21 Nov. 1964.
210. *The Irish Times*, 23 Nov. 1964.
211. *The Irish News*, 21 Nov. 1964.
212. See Kennedy, *Division and Consensus*, 236–237.
213. Horgan, *Seán Lemass*, 282.
214. McAteer subsequently acknowledged that the party's decision had been accelerated following 'pressure' from the Irish government. See *The Irish Times*, 3 Feb. 1965.
215. Lynn, 'Revising Northern nationalism, 1960–1965: the Nationalist Party's response', 90.
216. See Michael Farrell, *Northern Ireland: The Orange State* (London: Pluto Press, 1980), 239–240.
217. Brendan Lynn, *Holding the Ground: The Nationalist Party in Northern Ireland, 1945–72* (Aldershot: Ashgate, 1997), 182–183.
218. See Patterson, *Ireland Since 1939*, 159.
219. See UCDA P176/771, record of 1964 Fianna Fáil Ard Fheis, Nov. 1964. Lemass, however, in the mould of de Valera, rejected grass-roots demands for the extension of the organisation into Northern Ireland. Speaking at the 1964 Ard Fheis Lemass was unapologetic: Fianna Fáil would not participate in Northern Ireland politics as it would be conceived by Ulster Unionists 'as a kind of Southern interference in the North's affairs'.
220. Lynn, 'Revising Northern nationalism, 1960–1965: the Nationalist Party's response', 92.
221. Lynn, 'Revising Northern nationalism, 1960–1965: the Nationalist Party's response', 92.
222. Patterson, *Ireland Since 1939*, 157.
223. Kennedy, *Division and Consensus*, 202.
224. Patterson, *Ireland Since 1939*, 157.
225. See Fionnuala O'Connor, *In Search of a State, Catholics in Northern Ireland* (Belfast: Black Staff Press, 1993), 223–271.
226. This was the opinion of Colette (surname omitted). O'Connor, *In Search of a State*, 236.
227. Frank Curran, *Derry: Countdown to Disaster* (Dublin: Gill and Macmillan, 1986), 37.
228. For an excellent analysis of Fianna Fáil's traditional relationship with the Catholic minority of Northern Ireland prior to the 1960s see O'Halloran, *Partition and the Limits of Irish Nationalism*.
229. See Conor Cruise O'Brien, *States of Ireland* (New York: Viking, 1972), 145–148.
230. NAI DT TAOIS S 9361 K/62, Lemass to Healy, 31 March 1962.
231. NAI DT TAOIS S 9361 K/62, Lemass to Healy, 31 March 1962.
232. NAI DFA 305/14/360, official in the Department of External Affairs to McAteer, 24 Nov. 1964.
233. See Patterson, *Seán Lemass and the Ulster Question, 1959–65*, 150.
234. See, for example, UCDA P104/8724, conversation between Aiken and Lord Ismay, 14 Feb. 1952 & NAUK PREM 11/2374, meeting between de Valera, Aiken and Home, 18 March 1958.
235. See, for example, UCDA P104/7006, record of Aiken's interview to assembled members of the press, New York, 23 April 1969.
236. Ronan Fanning, *Dictionary of Irish Biography*, Frank Aiken (Dublin, 2010), 55.
237. NAUK DO 182/131, British Embassy, Dublin, profile of Frank Aiken, 1966.
238. Horgan, *Seán Lemass*, 193.
239. Horgan, *Seán Lemass*, 193.
240. Horgan, *Seán Lemass*, 340.
241. Boland admitted that in 1957/1958 he pleaded with de Valera not to appoint Aiken as minister for external affairs. See Gerald Boland's unpublished handwritten memoirs, 7(x). See also file marked '1957–58' (pp. 3 &4).
242. See, for example, comments by Aiken. *Irish Press*, 6 May 1940.
243. See, for example, UCDA P104/8035, meeting between de Valera, Aiken and Pakenham in Dublin, 2 May 1952.
244. See, for example, record of Aiken's views regarding raising the partition question at the UN during the late 1950s and early 1960s as recorded by Conor Cruise O'Brien, UCDA

P104/6115, O'Brien to Boland and Cremin, 24 Jan. 1958. See also UCDA P104/6117, Boland's memorandum on raising partition at the UN, 17 Feb. 1958 and UCDA P104/6117, Cremin to O'Brien, March 1958. See also Kennedy, *Division and Consensus*, 160.

245. UCDA P104/8035, meeting between de Valera, Aiken and Pakenham in Dublin, 2 May 1952.

246. See NAI DFA 1995 release, Secretary's files, P363, Aiken to Lemass, 26 Jan. 1965.

247. Horgan, *Seán Lemass*, 193.

248. See, for example, UCDA P104/8047, record of meeting between Aiken and Home, 21 Oct. 1957; UCDA P104/8052, record of conversation between Aiken and British Ambassador to Ireland, Clutterbuck, 4 March 1959; and lastly, UCDA P104/7006, record of speech by Aiken, New York, 23 April 1969.

249. Tom Gallagher, 'Fianna Fáil and partition 1926–84', *Éire Ireland*, Vol. 20, No.1 (1985), 51–52.

250. See John Horgan's observations on this point, Horgan, *Seán Lemass*, 288.

251. See *Irish Press* during the first week of April 1965. See also UCDA P176/840, Fianna Fáil 1965 general election leaflet.

252. See NAI DFA 305/16/361, copy of speech by Lemass during a press conference to members of the 'Foreign Press Association', in London, 5 April 1965.

253. See NAI DFA 305/16/361, copy of speech by Lemass during a press conference to members of the 'Foreign Press Association', in London, 5 April 1965.

254. Horgan, *Seán Lemass*, 283.

255. UCDA P175 (8), personal recollection of Whitaker's visit to Belfast with Lemass on 14 Jan. 1965 (early 1970s, precise date unknown).

7

1966–1971

'I have always been interested in the criticism of politicians. Political leaders always have to look over their shoulder as well as forward. Unfortunately sometimes they can get a crick in the neck'.

[Kenneth Bloomfield, 2006][1]

THE 1966 EASTER RISING COMMEMORATIONS AND THE DETERIORATION OF NORTH–SOUTH RELATIONS

The fiftieth anniversary commemorations of the 1916 Easter Rising, held during April 1966, presented Fianna Fáil with a dilemma. Here was an event celebrating Irish nationalists' violent rebellion against Britain to secure an independent thirty-two county Republic. Many Fianna Fáil stalwarts, including Seán Lemass and Eamon de Valera, participated in the 1916 Easter Rising and had openly endorsed the use of physical force. Times, however, had changed. Over the proceeding fifty years an entire generation had grown up, unaffected by the revolutionary events of 1916. Under Lemass's leadership, consecutive Fianna Fáil governments consistently maintained that the use of violence to deliver a united Ireland was illegal. Only the sovereign Irish government, he argued, had the right to take up arms.[2] He now found himself, however, responsible for overseeing the organising of a series of nationwide events to celebrate an illegal rebellion against the might of the British Empire. As noted by Conor Cruise O'Brien, 1966 was 'the year in which the ghosts had to walk and the traditional rhetoric had to be heard again'.[3]

Fearful that republican extremists might hijack the celebrations, Lemass was determined that the 1966 commemorations would remain staunchly pacifist. In his commemoration speeches he offered a new symbol of Irish patriotism. The industrialists, not the militant insurgent, were to represent nationalist Ireland. He spoke of patriotism, not as a symbol of armed revolt, but of economic modernity. In one speech he explained that 'the Technical College, the planning officer, the busy executive of industry ... the builders ... the workers, these people represented the next fifty years of patriotism'.[4] Reverence to the past offered minor importance for Lemass; the future economic prosperity of Ireland, not the events of fifty years ago, was his main concern in 1966.

Traditionally the 1966 Easter Rising commemorations have been interpreted as playing a part in the outbreak of violence in Northern Ireland: that the commemorations encouraged a new generation of Irish nationalists to take up arms in the fight for Irish reunification.[5] Such observations are overly simplistic. Roisín Higgins demonstrated that the Irish government wanted a commemoration that celebrated the idea of 1916, but not the violence.[6] 'The Lemass government', Higgins implored , 'paid lip service to the patriot dead, gestured to the nationalist past but sought to shape the future in the allegedly "normal" modernity of the state'.[7]

In particular, Lemass's preoccupation with Ulster Unionism was a significant factor in his attitude to the 1966 commemorations. Mindful of the eroding effect that the event could have for relations between Dublin and Belfast, he refrained in his commemoration speeches from permitting partition to assume a prominent position. For the first time in the history of the state the Dublin government was working hand in hand with their Belfast counterparts at government and civil service level to encourage cross-border co-operation on matters of common interest. Thus, the last thing Lemass wanted was for the Irish government to encourage an event that could bring relations with Ulster Unionists to a grinding halt. The British government was aware of Lemass's moderate tone and although reportedly 'gloomy' about violence in Northern Ireland over the 1966 commemorations, they noted that 'there is growing evidence of the Republican government's desire to take a firm stand against the IRA lawlessness and to co-operate with the Northern Ireland authorities'.[8]

Fianna Fáil grass-roots adhered to the Lemass line that the celebrations should not be interpreted as an endorsement of physical force to secure Irish unity. The nationwide celebrations commemorated the men of 1916, but did not link a physical force past with the present. The cross-county insight offered by the regional newspapers shows no evidence that the commemorations endorsed violence to secure Irish unity; indeed Fianna Fáil grass-roots, as well as the general public alike, were far more concerned with the plight of emigration and unemployment than ritualistic pledges for Irish unity.[9] Revealingly, a minor incursion of British army troops across the Irish border in early April 1966 resulted in far greater anti-partitionists outcries than that of the fiftieth commemorations of the Rising.[10]

The commemorations, while passing off relatively quietly in the Republic, did expose the simmering sectarian tensions in Northern Ireland. Although the Fianna Fáil government was able to dampen down the debate on Irish unity in the South, this was in stark contrast to events across the border. On Easter Monday 1966, approximately 10,000 Northern nationalists marched in Belfast and numerous other locations throughout Northern Ireland in celebration of the 1916 Rising.[11] In May, Lemass spoke of his hope that the Easter celebrations had not destroyed the prospect for further cross-border trade between Dublin and Belfast.[12] His hopes were to be soon dashed as religious tensions quickly increased in Northern Ireland. Following commemorations of the Battle of the Somme in July of that year, together with the upsurge in sectarian killing by the Ulster Volunteer Force (UVF) later that summer, relations between Dublin and Belfast soon soured.

Thereafter, Lemass's Northern Ireland policy of cross-border co-operation gradually disintegrated. Under pressure from his own supporters, particularly his chief rival within cabinet, minister for commerce, Brian Faulkner, O'Neill returned to the thorny issue of recognition. By October 1966 Belfast demanded that Dublin once again officially recognise Northern Ireland.[13] O'Neill argued that the issue was a 'major irritant' in the development of relations between both jurisdictions.[14] Although North–South co-operation continued at civil service level, ministerial meetings were placed to one side. For the meantime, at least, Lemass's master plan of establishing a long-term working relationship with the Northern Ireland government seemed a distant aspiration, rather than a medium-term policy.

As the events of the Easter commemorations faded, Lemass contemplated his own future. In June 1966 he informed close friends of his intention to resign as taoiseach and Fianna Fáil president.[15] After serving nine years as taoiseach and a further twenty-one years as a Fianna Fáil minister, Lemass, 67 years old, had grown tired of the day-to-day hustle and bustle of political life. On 9 November of that year, he notified a gathering of the Fianna Fáil parliamentary party of his intention to resign. He asked deputies to offer no sympathetic speeches.[16] Lemass's announcement left his cabinet colleagues shocked. Seán MacEntee was outraged by his leader's decision. He could not believe that the taoiseach should 'wash his hands of responsibility for the country's affairs'.[17]

Frank Aiken was likewise upset. He recorded that he had tried his 'upmost to persuade him [Lemass] to carry on at least for another few years'.[18] At the parliamentary party meeting a vote was taken on Lemass's successor so as to avoid 'acrimonious discussions and intemperate statements that could cause unnecessary division in the party'.[19] The contest between Jack Lynch and George Colley was a one-sided affair. When the votes were counted Lynch was declared new Fianna Fáil leader, beating his rival on a margin of fifty-two votes to nineteen.[20] The following day, on the morning of 10 November 1966, Lemass announced to the Dáil chamber his resignation as taoiseach. He offered no fancy pretentious speech, but simply recorded with his customary fondness for brevity: 'I have resigned'.[21]

How does one assess Lemass's attitude to Northern Ireland as leader of Fianna Fáil? His determination to nurture cross-border co-operation with Belfast was a positive legacy of his stance on partition and Northern Ireland. The themes and topics he and O'Neill discussed in the expectant years before 1969 were those that Dublin, Belfast and London would return to again and again and which were finally codified in 1999, with the establishment of the North–South Ministerial Council and the British–Irish Council.[22] Additionally, Lemass's ability to move away from the use of anti-partitionist language, his desire to accord *de facto* recognition to Northern Ireland and his visit to Belfast in January 1965, were all a brave gamble.

However, it was a gamble that Lemass lost. Ever the pragmatist and unwilling to create a split within Fianna Fáil, Lemass was forced to deny the reality of what he was doing. Due to pressure from the traditionalist-wing of Fianna Fáil, Lemass was regularly impeded as he attempted to revise core principles of the party's stance towards Northern Ireland. Therefore, despite his positive legacy on North–South co-operation, upon his retirement Lemass left behind him an incoherent and ultimately unofficial Northern Ireland policy for his successor Jack Lynch and the Fianna Fáil Party. As is discussed below, the lack of long-term planning within Fianna Fáil towards Northern Ireland goes a considerable way in explaining and understanding why the party was so ill-prepared for the outbreak of violence in the summer of 1969.

JACK LYNCH AND NORTHERN IRELAND, 1966–1969

On assuming the role of taoiseach and leader of Fianna Fáil, Lynch declared his ultimate aspiration for a united Ireland, maintaining that the border was 'unnatural'.[23] *The Irish Times* recorded that on the subject of Northern Ireland the new taoiseach 'remained probably even more doctrinaire than Lemass on fundamental attitudes'.[24] The British Ambassador in Dublin, Sir Geofroy Tory, noted that Lynch's Northern Ireland policy would seek to encourage a policy to 'abolish suspicion and distrust', however, Tory predicated that Lynch had 'no intention of abandoning basic principles' of a united Ireland.[25]

Although the new taoiseach's comments were couched in anti-partitionist sentiments, on a practical level, Lynch genuinely sought to follow Lemass's conciliatory approach towards Ulster Unionists and to try and kick-start the stalled cross-border co-operation between Dublin and Belfast. In the mould of his predecessor, Lynch explained that he wished for his Fianna Fáil government to 'promote the reunification of Ireland by fostering a spirit of brotherhood among all sections of the Irish people'.[26] During his first press conference as taoiseach, on 17 November 1966, he expressed his eagerness to meet O'Neill so as to continue cross-border co-operations between Dublin and Belfast. Asked about the anti-Catholic discrimination in Northern Ireland, Lynch noted, while he was aware of the discriminatory practices against the Catholic minority, he was confident that O'Neill was taking adequate steps to resolve the problem.[27] For Lynch, like Lemass before him, cross-border co-operation, not the plight of Northern Ireland Catholics, was Dublin's central preoccupation.

After one year as taoiseach, on 11 December 1967, O'Neill eventually invited Lynch to Belfast for formal cross-border discussions. Over the previous several months, under pressure from members of his own cabinet, O'Neill was forced to tread lightly in his dealings with Dublin.[28] Lynch was accompanied by the secretary of the Department of Finance, T.K. Whitaker and by the secretary of the government, Nicholas Nolan ('Meticulous Nicholas' as he was widely known). Lynch's meeting with O'Neill was not universally welcomed by the Protestant community. As he entered the gates of Stormont and rounded the statue of Edward Carson, Lynch's car was met by a storm of snowballs from Ian Paisley, a prominent member of the Free Presbyterian Church of Ulster and his supporters.[29] Lynch paid little attention to the meagre protest, humorously dismissing it as 'just the sort of thing one might expect from the boys if one drove through a village. It was also very seasonable'.[30] Despite Paisley's frosty protests, O'Neill greeted Lynch with a warm welcome. Lunch was held in the Prime Minister's residence and all the members of the Northern Ireland government and the attorney-general were present. A general discussion at Stormont Castle followed and like Lemass's meeting with O'Neill three years previously, no constitutional or political topics were discussed and instead attention was on issues of common concern, including electricity, tourism and cross-border concessions on furniture and carpets.[31]

The following month, in the early days of the new-year, on 8 January 1968, O'Neill made his expected return visit to Dublin. Again, constitutional and political concerns were not on the agenda and instead both men discussed, among other things, tariffs and the metric system.[32] Unbeknown to either man, this was the last occasion that a bipartite meeting would occur between the prime ministers of both jurisdictions. In the aftermath of the two meetings Lynch emphasised that his discussions with O'Neill, as well as between other ministers and officials on both sides, had 'helped to confirm the desirability and good sense of this policy of contact and co-operation in order to contribute to a better understanding and appreciation of our common interests'.[33]

Again, in a similar tone to the Lemass–O'Neill meetings, reaction from the South was overwhelmingly supportive of the Lynch–O'Neill initiative. However, the agenda had clearly moved on and opposition parties in the Dáil rounded on Lynch, arguing that mere formal contacts with Belfast were no longer sufficient. Irrespective of the benefits of cross-border co-operation, both Fine Gael and Labour pronounced that the issue of anti-Catholic discrimination, so prevalent in Northern Ireland, could no longer be ignored.[34] For the meantime, however, Lynch was content to ignore the plight of Northern Catholics. He seemed so fixated with the idea of cross-border co-operation that he failed to realise that on the streets of Northern Ireland the political temperature was reaching boiling point.

The repressive reaction of the civil authorities and the Royal Ulster Constabulary (RUC) towards the Civil Rights movement in Northern Ireland, particularly the actions of the Northern Ireland Civil Rights Association (NICRA), proved the final nail in the coffin for cross-border co-operation between Dublin and Belfast. The catalyst for this end in functional co-operation was the attack by the RUC on a civil rights march in the centre of Derry on 5 October 1968. Broadcast throughout the world, ugly scenes emerged of the

RUC indiscriminately attacking marchers with batons, including Nationalist MP for Foyle Derry, Eddie McAteer. Nationalist opinion was only galvanised in response to the attacks and soon after McAteer announced that the Nationalist Party would no longer act as the official opposition at Stormont. In response, speaking in the Dáil, Lynch tried to play down the events in the hope to continue his conciliatory relations with Ulster Unionists.[35] The seeds, however, were sown.

In the space of a few months, Lynch's attempt to cultivate a conciliatory relationship with Ulster Unionists was in tatters. The events in Derry acted as a wakeup call for the Dublin government. No longer was it acceptable, in the eyes of Southern nationalists, to ignore the plight of the Catholic minority of Northern Ireland. In the words of the *Kerryman*, 'for better or worse', the riots in Derry, had brought the question of partition 'back in the consciousness of the people'.[36] Lynch, however, seemed unsure as how to act. In a speech delivered in the immediate aftermath of the violence in Derry, on 6 October, he spoke of the need to continue cross-border co-operation with Belfast and at the same time promote civil rights for Northern Ireland Catholics.[37] Yet, two days later, the goal posts had shifted. Speaking in Clonmel, Co. Tipperary, on 8 October, Lynch now declared that the aim of Fianna Fáil's Northern Ireland policy was to get Britain to recognise its responsibility for maintaining the partition of Ireland.[38]

Lynch's visit to London to meet British prime minister, Harold Wilson, on 30 October, also witnessed a sharp rebuttal from Ulster Unionists. Although the meeting secured no guarantees from London on the issue of partition, Lynch's visit and his pronouncements on Northern Ireland, infuriated O'Neill. The Northern Ireland prime minister was left to bemoan that Lynch had returned to the 'war horse of anti-partition activity'.[39] Within Fianna Fáil the signs were ominous. The following month on 8 November, at a meeting of a Fianna Fáil Comhairle Ceantair, in Letterkenny, Co. Donegal, minister for agriculture, Neil Blaney spoke strongly against the maintenance of partition. He described O'Neill as a 'sham' and significantly said that cross-border government discussions had proved 'a futile exercise'.[40] This was a deliberate and calculated attack on his leader's Northern Ireland policy and was to open up a can of worms within Fianna Fáil. It was an attempt by the disgruntled minister to counteract what he believed was an undesirable shift from Fianna Fáil's traditional stance on Northern Ireland. It was also an obvious attack on Lynch's leadership. Blaney had copies of his statement circulated to the press, but not to Lynch, who was traditionally regarded as the sole spokesperson on Northern Ireland.[41]

Lynch was evidentially under pressure from the anti-partitionists within his own party to defend his approach to Northern Ireland. His minister's attack of the maintenance of partition was to be expected, given Blaney's republican pedigree and the respect he held among the rank-and-file of Fianna Fáil. Indeed, Lynch had, likewise, placed heavy emphasis on the illegality of partition over the previous months.[42] The taoiseach, nonetheless, would have certainly disagreed with Blaney's assertion that North–South co-operation had become a 'futile exercise'. His unwillingness to reign in his minister exposed the vulnerability of Lynch's position around the cabinet table; he was viewed as a relatively new and inexperienced leader of Fianna Fáil, with little republican credentials.

As Pádraig Faulkner, a member of Lynch's consecutive Fianna Fáil cabinets from 1969 to 1973, explained: Lynch 'was the first Fianna Fáil leader not to have had any involvement, personal or family, with the struggle for Irish independence or with the Civil War. In the eyes of some party supporters ... the lack of a Republican pedigree was a problem'.[43] This was certainly the case in Blaney's eyes and he always retained a dislike of Lynch. Patrick Hillery, a confidant to Lynch, later recalled that at this time Blaney was using the Northern Ireland issue as a 'useful' instrument in an attempt to try and oust Lynch as leader of Fianna Fáil. Hillery recorded that Blaney was 'riding high' and was a 'rough shod'. Hillery prophetically wrote that by this stage he came to the conclusion that Blaney and his fellow anti-partitionists within Fianna Fáil, chiefly Boland, 'will destroy the country now'.[44] Indeed, one Dubliner was left to ponder 'who is in control of sagging fortunes of Fianna Fáil – sorrowful Jack or arrogant Blaney?'[45]

Privately, three days after Blaney's remarks, on 11 November, T.K. Whitaker, who had accompanied Lynch to Belfast a little under one year previously, spelt out what should constitute the basis of Lynch's Northern Ireland policy. Whitaker was Lynch's key adviser on Northern Ireland from 1966 to 1971. Personally, they had been close ever since Lynch's period as minister for finance. Previously, on intermediate occasions, Whitaker had advised Lemass on Northern Ireland and had been a key player in instigating the Lemass–O'Neill meetings. As taoiseach, Lynch now continued this informal, but important, function. Whitaker's report to Lynch was unambiguous: firstly, Whitaker noted that 'the use of force to overcome Northern

Unionists would accentuate rather than remove basic differences and'; secondly, he said, 'It would be militarily impossible in any event'. Therefore, he explained the Irish government was left with 'only one choice, a policy of seeking unity in Ireland by agreement between Irishmen'.[46] Lynch fully endorsed his civil-servant's rational objection to the use of physical force to end partition. Importantly, Whitaker's comments helped to galvanise Lynch's resolve as he made his way to a meeting of the Fianna Fáil National Executive, held later that evening on 11 November. At the gathering, at which Blaney was absent, Lynch avoided mentioning his minister's statement directly and instead spoke of how partition aroused 'deep feelings and emotions'. Instead, he depicted Blaney's obvious challenge to his Northern Ireland policy as a momentary example of frustration, on his colleague's behalf, because of the lack of progress on partition. Fianna Fáil's main focus Lynch stressed, must be to 'strengthen contacts and promote co-operation' between Dublin and Belfast. 'It is inevitable', he told those in attendance, 'that this disappointment should be strongly voiced by different people, lacking neither in courage nor in sincerity'. But he warned 'that we must not allow this frustration and disappointment to force us to abandon this course, tedious and irksome though it may be'.[47]

It was a classic example of Lynch fudging the issue, in the hope that he could maintain a united front within Fianna Fáil on the emotive subject of partition. In fact, Lynch's intervention had the opposite effect. On the very night that Lynch attempted to win support for his Northern Ireland policy from Fianna Fáil National Executive members, Blaney once again publicly undermined his leader. Speaking at a party function in Listowel, Co. Kerry, on 11 November, he told those in attendance that 'the recovery of the Six-Counties ... by whatever means possible ... is the foremost plank in the platform policy of Fianna Fáil'.[48] *The Irish Times*, in a wonderfully adept critique of Blaney's remarks, wrote that 'the middle aged politician may play with words and lay them aside; it is otherwise with young, impressionable men and boys. Words kill, and it is the young men who die'.[49] *The Irish Times* piece echoed Lynch's own thoughts.

Yet, Lynch seemed unsure as how to respond to Blaney's blatant attack of Fianna Fáil's conciliatory approach to Ulster Unionism and the party's general stance on partition. Lynch's chief rival for control of Fianna Fáil during the 1966 leadership contest, George Colley, reportedly advised Lynch to sack Blaney, but Lynch refused.[50] Maybe

Lynch believed that in the volatile climate of 1969 the sacking of Blaney might divide the party and, possibly even worse, bring down the government. Blaney was a powerful figure within the party, a son of a founding member of the organisation; he had built up a strong power base and had a reputation as a hardline republican. Addressing a meeting of the Fianna Fáil parliamentary party two days later, on 13 November, Lynch confusingly noted that 'everyone agreed with what he [Blaney] had said, but that it was the wrong time to say it'.[51] Such comments were hardly the words of a confident and assertive leader. In public, however, Lynch was more forthright. Speaking in the Dáil, later that same day, he said that Blaney's speech had been made without his approval and that Fianna Fáil sought a peaceful solution to partition.[52]

In the short-term, Lynch's rebuttal seemed effective and Blaney remained quiet on the partition issue. However, it did not take long for the Donegal native to again undermine his leader's stance on Northern Ireland. In early April 1969, speaking at a dinner in Derry in honour of Eddie McAteer, Blaney once again demanded that the British government hand over Northern Ireland to the Republic, describing partition as a 'temporary expedient'. He offered a federal council for all-Ireland as his preferred solution to partition. He passionately declared that it was time that 'a real beginning was made in the task of dismantling partition'. Ulster Unionists, he argued, had no right to retain a veto over unity given that the 'Irish border had no ultimate permanency'.[53] O'Neill described Blaney's remarks as 'wholly unacceptable' and advised Lynch that he keep 'this party hatchet-man' out of the affairs of Northern Ireland.[54] This was to be one of O'Neill's last comments on partition prior to his replacement as Northern Ireland prime minister by James Chichester-Clark on 1 May 1969.

Blaney's speech, rather than rebuffed by Fianna Fáil headquarters, was widely endorsed. On 14 April 1969, at a meeting of the party's National Executive, attended by approximately forty-five senior party members, 'congratulations' were offered to Blaney for his partition speech in Derry.[55] Lynch's silence was noteworthy. The problem that Blaney's periodic attacks created, as noted by Donnacha Ó Beacháin, was not that he was opposing Fianna Fáil policy: 'in fact it was the reverse'. By offering the traditional anti-partitionist approach to Northern Ireland Blaney was impairing Lynch's ability to formulate government strategy on partition, as his actions placed an 'ideological straitjacket on Lynch'.[56]

Blaney's outbursts heralded the outbreak of a partition virus, which by the summer of 1969, infected the Southern body politic. Unbeknown to Lynch the virus was to spread like an epidemic throughout Fianna Fáil, infecting every strand of the organisation from cabinet ministers to grass-roots supporters. Although Lynch tried to introduce quarantine measures, as is discussed below, they proved to be too little and too late. In early August 1969, the recently appointed minister for external affairs, Patrick Hillery predicted that some skirmishes would invariably break out on the streets of Derry following the annual Apprentice Boys' march, scheduled for 12 August.[57] Hillery, however, like the rest of his cabinet colleagues in Dublin, severely underestimated the scale of the crisis that was to unfold. Consequently, the Fianna Fáil government's reaction to the commencement of the Troubles in Northern Ireland was both ineffective and incompetent.

FIANNA FÁIL AND THE BATTLE OF THE BOGSIDE, AUGUST 1969

The Battle of the Bogside of mid-August 1969, which was televised around the world, represented a total breakdown of law and order on the streets of Northern Ireland. The crisis was initiated by the holding of the annual Apprentice Boys' march in the heart of the city of Derry on the afternoon of 12 August. Following skirmishes between young Catholic youths, mostly from the Bogside, and members of the procession, the RUC intervened to end the violence. However, by the evening of 12 August, after enduring an onslaught of missiles and stones, members of the RUC began to retaliate and throw stones at the Bogsiders. In the heat of the moment some Protestant onlookers joined forces with the police and supported the RUC in their quest the gain access to the Bogside area, located in the immediate outskirts of the city centre.

Images were broadcast via the assembled television broadcasters showing the Bogside Catholics desperately trying to halt the RUC and Protestant hooligans from entering the Bogside. The RUC, equipped with armoured cars and water cannons, made the fateful decision to permit the use of CS gas. In retaliation, a large crowd of Catholics built numerous barricades around the entranceways to the Bogside. The Battle of the Bogside, as it subsequently became known, was underway. From this relatively small episode developed a riot, which enveloped the city of Derry for over two days and nights and was not brought under control until the arrival of the British army into Londonderry on the evening of 14 August 1969.[58]

As the battle continued on the streets, the government in Dublin desperately tried to deal with the unfolding political crisis. The drama exposed the fact that Fianna Fáil had no coherent, or indeed realistic, Northern Ireland policy. It brought Fianna Fáil face to face with one of its most blatant contradictions – the gap between its rhetoric and the reality of its attitude to Irish unity. Conor Cruise O'Brien accurately described the dilemma felt by many within Fianna Fáil in August 1969:

> Fianna Fáil was a party which exploited a Republican – revolutionary mystique, while practising very ordinary pragmatic middle-class politics. The effect of Bogside was to bring the mystique exploited into sharp collision with the pragmatism practised ... In the cabinet, in the party and in the country, there were men and women to whose emotional lives, and to whose conception of the meaning of life and its glory, the mystique of 1916 was central. For most of these, the Bogside meant the re-lighting of the fire.[59]

The Fianna Fáil cabinet first met to discuss the unfolding crisis in Northern Ireland on the afternoon of 13 August. At the meeting a consortium of vocal anti-partitionist ministers bitterly argued with Lynch and his supporters over what constituted official Fianna Fáil Northern Ireland policy. Ministers Neil Blaney, Kevin Boland and Charles J. Haughey all demanded that the Irish army be sent into Derry or Newry or both to offer, at the very least, support to the beleaguered Catholic populations.[60] Led by an aggressive Blaney, both Boland and Haughey maintained that physical force had always represented official Fianna Fáil policy and that the outbreak of the violence was an opportunity to undermine partition and force Britain to concede a united Ireland.[61]

Tempers were fraught; even known moderate ministers, such as Brian Lenihan, were 'very excited'.[62] Lynch was under huge pressure as he desperately tried to advocate that only peaceful actions could secure Irish unity. Some in the cabinet looked despairingly at Lynch, believing that he lacked a Republican pedigree. The absence of minister for foreign affairs, Patrick Hillery, a rational and moderate figure within the government and a close ally of the taoiseach, gave more leeway to extremists in the cabinet. After several hours of heated discussions, the anti-partitionists' request to send the Irish army into

Northern Ireland was rejected by the pragmatists within the cabinet. Led by Lynch it was instead decided that later that evening the taoiseach would deliver a statement on national television declaring Ireland's right to reunification and denouncing the actions of the Ulster Unionist government and the RUC.[63]

Lynch's televised address to the Irish nation on the night of 13 August was calculated to offer the illusion that the Fianna Fáil government was doing all it could to defend Northern Ireland Catholics. Lynch did not mix his words. Spurred on with a few glasses of whiskey to calm his nerves, he not only attacked the very legitimacy of the Northern Ireland state, but demanded the 'British government to enter into early negotiations with the Irish government to review the present constitutional position of the Six-Counties of Northern Ireland'. Declaring that the RUC could no longer be 'accepted as an impartial police force', he also rejected the possibility of deploying the British army on the streets of Northern Ireland.[64]

Upon hearing Lynch's address, Northern Ireland prime minster, Chichester-Clark was furious. 'This clumsy and intolerable intrusion into our internal affairs', he exclaimed, 'I must hold Mr Lynch personally responsible for any worsening of feeling his inflammatory and ill-considered remarks may cause'.[65] The British home secretary was, likewise, taken aback by Lynch's strong words. 'When I heard this late at night', James Callaghan was to later write, 'it really seemed to be putting the fat in the fire. We had to consider the possibility that within the next twenty-four hours we might face possible civil war in the North and an invasion from the South. I frankly could not believe the second was possible'.[66]

On the morning of 14 August, the British Ambassador in Dublin, Andrew Gilchrist sent a telegram to the Foreign and Commonwealth Office, explaining Lynch's dilemma. 'Derry', he reported, 'came too soon', for the worried taoiseach. 'There is this to be said for Lynch', Gilchrist said, 'he warned us that when the pressure grew too great he would be compelled to string along with the Nationalist/ Sinn Féin/ IRA line ...'[67] Hinting at the possible outbreak of violence in the South, the ambassador pessimistically noted that 'the Irish are a dangerously emotional people ... if I were a fire insurance company I would not like to have the British Embassy on my books'.[68] Gilchrist's prediction, with regard to the fate of the British Embassy in Dublin, ironically proved correct. The following day, on 15 August, the Embassy building was stoned and the Union Jack flag ripped down from the pole outside the building and torn up by Irish protestors.

At 11.00am, as Gilchrist was offering his observations on that state of Irish politics, the second Irish government meeting in as many days, commenced. To Lynch's relief, Hillery was present having returned from his holidays on Achill Island. On arriving at the cabinet meeting Hillery was aghast to find that some ministers were calling for the Irish army to intervene in Northern Ireland, describing the meeting as 'a ballad singing session'.[69] Hillery subsequently noted that 'Frankly, the army was not equipped or capable of doing what some people would like it to do. It is silly to think that the cartoonist in office saying that the army if fully equipped, would put up a better show than if not equipped at all [sic] ...' He sarcastically noted that the anti-partitionists within the cabinet 'smothered in lashings of creamy patriotic ballad singing type of thing', were all 'talk' and no action. 'It would appear to me', he said, 'that their hearts were not in it. It would appear to me that they want to take the right posture but get no scratches'.[70]

As at the meeting on 13 August, after heated discussions, the majority of ministers firmly opposed military intervention or covert support for political violence in Northern Ireland; they instead sought to place diplomacy at centre stage. In an attempt to placate the anti-partitionists' demands to send the Irish army across the border, the decision was instead made that Hillery, as minister for external affairs, should seek a meeting with the British secretary of state for Foreign and Commonwealth Affairs or the secretary of state for the Home Office, as soon as possible.[71]

By the time the cabinet meeting in Dublin concluded events in Northern Ireland took a drastic change. Following Lynch's televised address the previous night on 13 August, rumours were rife on the streets of Derry that the Irish government was genuinely going to attempt to help the people of the Bogside. However, the nature of that assistance was not clear. The first daily *Barricade Bulletin*, which was circulated among the Catholic population in Derry, during the Battle of the Bogside, reported that following Lynch's televised address the people of Derry were 'Not alone'. 'The Irish taoiseach', the paper reported, 'has made it clear that the Irish government can no longer stand by ... the best help our comrades in the 26 counties can give us is to respond to the appeal of the Citizen's Defence Association for able bodied men to come to Derry'.[72]

In some quarters this call for, 'able bodied men to come to Derry', was interpreted by many Bogsiders that the Irish government intended to send the Irish army into Derry. This view was reinforced by Eamonn McCann, a leading figure on the streets of the Bogside during this period and one of the original founders of the Derry Committee Defence Association (DCDA). McCann, although pointing out that he never actually believed that the Irish army might arrive, did emphasise that a large number of the Bogside population, 'in the chaos of the moment thought the Irish government would send in the Irish army to help resolve the situation'.[73]

The Bogside residents were to be disappointed. Rather than the Irish army entering the streets of Northern Ireland, at 5.00pm on 14 August, a company of the First Battalion of the Prince of Wales Own Regiment arrived in Waterloo Place, in the heart of Londonderry. Under mounting pressure and faced with a depleted RUC force, the Northern Ireland authorities were forced to make the fatal decision to request the assistance of the British army in Northern Ireland.[74] This decision was to have severe long-term implications for the stability of Northern Ireland and in hindsight, was the first nail in the coffin of the Stormont regime. As then deputy cabinet secretary to the Northern Ireland government, Kenneth Bloomfield later stated in a 2006 interview with this author, the rioting in Derry and elsewhere had underlined the extent that the public uprising had tested the credibility of the Northern Ireland government. 'If you cannot preserve order in your own society', he noted, 'within your own means then you're not really a government but more like a county council'.[75]

The arrival of the British army was initially welcomed by the Bogside Catholics. On the morning of 15 August the *The Irish Times* led with the title: 'Troops greeted by Bogside defenders'. It reported that 'the troops had been welcomed by the defenders of the Bogside, who joked with them and at one point gave three cheers for the British'. It continued, 'The British soldiers and the Bogside rebels joked with each other as they moved the barbed wire to let in the brigade'.[76] Eddie McAteer, however, greeted the British army's presence on the streets of his native city with a little more caution. 'As long as the police stay out we have a chance of peace', he explained, 'It's not that we love the British troops more, it is that we hate the RUC'.[77] Eamonn McCann described the initial good relations between the Bogside residents and the British army as a 'honeymoon period'.[78] 'I'm never happy to see British troops on Irish soil', he told assembled reporters, but it was better than 'having the hated police or B-Specials in the Bogside'.[79]

News of the British army's arrival to Northern Ireland caught Lynch by surprise and in the words of Gilchrist left the taoiseach 'shaken'.[80] Although the army's presence had calmed tensions in Derry, by the early hours of 15 August, Lynch received reports of fierce gun battles occurring across Northern Ireland. On the night of 14 August, a total of six people, including a child, were killed in Belfast and Armagh, respectively. Alarmed by the unfolding events, in the early hours of the morning of 15 August, the taoiseach sent a Garda car to the house of T.K. Whitaker, who was renting a holiday home in Carna, Co. Galway.[81] Lynch was under severe pressure and sought the advice of Whitaker on the situation in Northern Ireland. Lynch greatly valued his friend's recommendations, knowing he could talk to him in absolute confidence.

At 10.00am Whitaker travelled to the Garda barracks in Carna where he contacted the taoiseach via telephone.[82] During the conversation Whitaker advised Lynch on a number of key points, and later that day, Whitaker posted a summarised letter of the conversation from Galway city to Dublin. Firstly, Whitaker informed the taoiseach of the importance of trying to 'woo' the Protestant population of Northern Ireland and of the importance of the Irish government's public statements. Whitaker had in mind the controversy which the taoiseach's televised speech had caused on the night of 13 August. He warned that 'there is a terrible temptation to be opportunist – to cash in on political emotionalism – Every effort should be made in any Govt. statement from Dublin to avoid identifying the government solely with the Catholics or Nationalists of Northern Ireland'. It was the responsibility of Irish politicians, he noted, '... to make it clear that the aim of a United Ireland would be a scrupulously fair deal for all ... that the position of Northern Ireland Protestants would be particularly respected'.[83]

Whitaker's words were nothing new; instead they acted as encouragement for the taoiseach. Whitaker's final point was his most significant and sobering. It brought the reality of the current situation straight back to the forefront of the taoiseach's mind. 'But where do we go from here?', Whitaker rhetorically pondered, 'We can't take over Britain's financial contributions, nor do we want the terrifying task of keeping sectarian and anarchical mobs in order. Better confine ourselves to preventing groups from here intervening by strict control of the Border'.[84] Whitaker spelt it out to Lynch in a clear manner. The Irish government could not financially afford to take control of Northern Ireland. Thus, Whitaker emphasised that 'We have to envisage a slow – phased movement towards some form of unification. There should be no rigid clinging to pre-conceived formulae. Even condominium may be a useful transitional concept'.[85]

Following Lynch's council from his colleague, at 11.30am, the Irish cabinet convened. All ministers were present, except for Patrick Hillery who was in London. Ministers discussed the present situation in Northern Ireland and it was decided that Hillery should inform the British government that in 'anticipation of their agreement to the proposal regarding a United-Nations Peace-Keeping Force in the Six-Counties ... the Government have authorised the mobilisation of the First-Line Reserve of the Defence Forces'.[86] Kevin Boland was not satisfied with the government's decision. Instead, he called for Irish soldiers on United Nations peace-keeping duty to be recalled to the country immediately. Boland recollected that:

> I had gone to the Cabinet meeting intending to resign unless the Cabinet was prepared to give a real indication to the United Nations of the seriousness of the position in the country by the recall of our troops from Cyprus and by calling up a second-line reserve.[87]

By this meeting Boland had ruled out the use of the Irish army because it would have undoubtedly invited the massacre of nationalists in Northern Ireland. However, he failed to realise the danger of threatening an invasion by recalling the Irish troops in such a public manner. Pádraig Faulkner, minister for education, later wrote that if the troops were recalled from Cyprus, in his view, 'it would have been interpreted by the Unionists and British government as a sign that we were preparing to use military force'. Although, Boland was on record as being opposed to such action, he did not see the contradiction involved at the time. Faulkner later explained that, 'If we'd agreed to his proposal it would have involved us in a futile and dangerous gesture'.[88] This would have only led to heightening the tensions that had reached almost fever pitch following Lynch's televised speech two days earlier.

Boland was to later confess, 'I looked around the Cabinet and saw a no-good pathetic lot'.[89] He promptly announced his resignation and walked out of the meeting. The Irish president, Eamon de Valera, was asked to try and convince Boland to reconsider his resignation, which he quickly did. In a 2006 interview, Faulkner recalled how he was, 'particularly perturbed as Kevin left the meeting'. At previous meetings, Faulkner explained, Boland had walked out of gatherings because he had not been given enough money for social services and he felt that this was simply another instance of Boland venting his frustration.[90] Such spontaneous decisions by Boland eventually came back to haunt him following his resignation surrounding the fallout from the Arms Crisis and the dismissal of Haughey and Blaney from the cabinet. As is discussed below, Lynch accepted his colleague's resignation.

At 4.00pm, on 15 August, the day's events reached their pivotal climax. In accordance with the Irish government decision of 14 August, Patrick Hillery, with the aid of secretary to the Department of External Affairs, Hugh McCann, met their British counterparts Lord Chalfont, minister of state at the Home Office, Lord Stoneham, and first secretary at the Irish desk in Foreign and Commonwealth Office, Edward Peck. As had become customary over the previous decades, Lord Chalfont asserted that the Irish government could have no input into the affairs of Northern Ireland. Chalfont noted that 'we regard Northern Ireland as an integral part of the United Kingdom ... this is an internal matter to be dealt with by the Home Office'.[91] Chalfont also ruled out the deployment of either a UN or a British-Irish force into Northern Ireland.

Hillery, clearly incensed by the British response, made his first and not his last, patriotic outcry during the meeting: 'Northern Ireland', he declared, 'is part of Ireland. Our people do not accept that it is part of the United Kingdom'. The British troops, he said, 'are a provocation. Our people do not accept them in Northern Ireland.' Hillery stated, 'I was sent here ... Our Government assumed that you must accept a combined force. My next sailing orders may well be to go to the United Nations'.[92] Hillery's demands, however, fell on deaf ears; Lord Chalfont merely viewing Hillery's calls as the typical anti-partitionist rant from an irate Irish minister.

Although Hillery made little progress with his British counterparts, the Irish government were aware of the importance of using the media to publicise their attempts to intervene with regard to the violence in Derry and elsewhere. Upon his arrival at Dublin Airport, Hillery gave a brief press conference to the waiting media. He informed reporters that he had received, 'a courteous brush off' in London and that Lord Chalfont had assured him that the British government felt confident it was in control of the situation. Hillery did not seem so sure, telling journalists that, 'He did not give me the reason why they were confident and I cannot say I am confident'.[93]

Soon after Hillery's interview at Dublin Airport the British army arrived on the streets of Belfast. What had begun as a minor riot in the

Bogside of Derry had now erupted into a full-scale humanitarian and indeed political crisis. The events in Northern Ireland caught Lynch off guard. Prior to August 1969, he had recognised that Derry might erupt. However, recognising a problem and adequately dealing with the realities of a volatile situation was an entirely different matter. In the aftermath of the summer of 1969, confronted by the gap between Fianna Fáil's anti-partitionist rhetoric and the reality that the party had no immediate solution to partition, Lynch desperately attempted to formulate a conciliatory approach towards Ulster Unionism and reaffirm the Fianna Fáil government's commitment to Irish unity by peaceful means. Speaking to a gathering of the Fianna Fáil parliamentary party in early September 1969, he appealed to party deputies to adhere to his Northern Ireland policy and 'not to give the appearance of cashing in on the situation'. Those who wished to speak publicly on Northern Ireland, he informed his party colleagues, must first receive permission from the party chief whip.[94] Clearly, Lynch was laying down the law to his senior colleagues. Time would tell if they would tow the party-line.

'BY PEACEFUL MEANS': LYNCH'S TRALEE SPEECH AND THE MCCANN MEMORANDUM

In the immediate aftermath of the August riots, a revision took place within government circles towards Fianna Fáil's Northern Ireland policy. In late August, tánaiste and minister for health, Erskine Childers produced a lucid and thought-provoking memorandum. In the shadow of Lemass, he wrote that Fianna Fáil must follow a 'gradualist' Northern Ireland policy. The government, he explained, must re-think 'our unity policy'. Dissecting Fianna Fáil's traditional stance on Northern Ireland, he noted that 'in 1932 we compromised our 1916 position as political realists'. He asked, was there not a case for 'taking a leaf out of the 1932 to 1938 record?' In a wonderfully constructed paragraph he challenged his Fianna Fáil cabinet colleagues to reassess their stance on Northern Ireland:

> After forty-eight years of self-government in the twenty-
> six counties would our electors not accept a gradualist
> policy? After six years of Fianna Fáil government under the
> 1922 Constitution (gradually revised); after ten years of
> Commonwealth membership as a Republic, 1938–48; after

five years of extremely benevolent semi-neutrality in a world
war; after 21 years of Republican government in increasingly
close economic cooperation with the U.K. – there is at least
a case for considering a new forum of policy. If we were now
joining the EEC the present official policy would look to some
people extremely rigid.[95]

Childers's adept memorandum concluded by mentioning the
possibility of making constitutional changes in the hope of enticing
Northern Protestants into a united Ireland and rejecting any idea
that physical force and in particular the actions of the IRA, could
secure Irish unity. The following month, taking inspiration from his
tánaiste's comments, Lynch decided that the time had arrived for
him personally to clarify the Fianna Fáil government's stance on
Northern Ireland.

On 20 September 1969, Lynch delivered his 'Tralee speech' to
the party faithful in Tralee, Co. Kerry. Devised by Whitaker, the
speech restated the Fianna Fáil government's commitment 'to seek
reunification of the country by peaceful means'.[96] In fact, the speech
was extremely similar to Lemass's Tralee speech of July 1963. In
both tone and content Lynch echoed the words of Lemass. Lynch
said, 'that we have no intention of using force' and that Irish unity
was a 'long-term' goal.[97] Based on the traditional model of a federal
agreement between Dublin and Belfast, Lynch noted that the Irish
government were willing to consider 'constitutional' changes in order
that the Protestants of Northern Ireland would have 'no fear of any
interference with their religious freedom or civil liberties and rights'.
On the issue of the constitutional recognition of Northern Ireland,
again in the shadow of Lemass, Lynch maintained that Dublin would
only recognise the *de facto* position of Northern Ireland based on
Dublin's federal offer.[98] The significance of the speech, as noted by
Ronan Fanning, was that although it reiterated the Irish government's
right to be consulted by the British, importantly it publicly set out the
principles of moderation and conciliation that became the hallmark
of Lynch's policy on Northern Ireland.[99]

The crisis at cabinet level in August 1969, not only served as
a wakeup call for politicians, but also for the Irish civil service.
In particular, the Department of External Affairs was caught off
guard and was clearly out of touch with events at street level in
Northern Ireland by the late 1960s. It had failed to take account of

the developing civil rights movement since 1968 and had not sent officers across the border on fact-finding missions since the 1950s.[100] Worryingly a trend had developed within the Department of External Affairs whereby its most senior officials had little direct knowledge of Northern Ireland or its population, nationalist or unionist. In Brussels, Ambassador Gerald Woods wrote that 'a vacuum was allowed to develop in our cognisance of the mental outlook and conditions of existence of our people in the North'. Ambassador to Sweden, Timothy J. Horan, admitted that both parts of Ireland simply did not know each other: 'I know no Six-County unionists, and have no direct knowledge of what these people think and how they feel. As far as I can remember I have only on two occasions had contact with Six-County Protestants'.[101]

Patrick Hillery recalled that as minister for external affairs, during the early 1970s, he could get more information from the embassy in Lagos about the civil war between Nigeria and Biafra, than he could in regard to information on Northern Ireland.[102] It is not surprising, therefore, that by September 1969 a process of reflection was underway within Iveagh House, where Eamonn Gallagher had become a key policy adviser on Northern Ireland. Familiar with Northern Ireland on a personal level, he had decided to travel to Belfast on his own initiative on 15 August 1969. Although not present in Northern Ireland in an official capacity, the Department of External Affairs did not object to his presence there. Indeed, secretary in the Department of External Affairs, Hugh McCann had secretly encouraged Gallagher's escapade. Thereafter, Gallagher, who had been under-employed as a first secretary in the Economic Section of the Department of External Affairs, soon filled a vacuum in relation to Northern Ireland policy.[103]

Gallagher's sister Anna, who lived in Letterkenny, paved the way for his introduction to nationalist leaders in Northern Ireland, including Ivan Cooper Independent MP for Mid-Londonderry and most importantly, John Hume Independent Nationalist MP for Foyle. Gallagher's reports on his frequent visits to Northern Ireland were sent directly to the Department of the Taoiseach. By October 1969, Lynch was relying on the Department of External Affairs, or more appropriately Gallagher, for his speeches on Northern Ireland. Significantly, under Gallagher's instructions, he advised Lynch to pin responsibility for the crisis in Northern Ireland on Britain's shoulders and not at the feet of Belfast: this marked a deliberate change in policy from his predecessor in the Department of the Taoiseach, Seán Lemass.[104]

Inspired by Lynch's Tralee speech and Gallagher's arrival, in November 1969, McCann devised a memorandum on Northern Ireland policy for the attention of the Irish government. Its contents were the brainchild of McCann, Irish permanent representative to the UN, Con Cremin and Irish Ambassador to Nigeria, Paul Keatinge. Focused on a long-term programme for an end to partition, the memorandum noted that Irish unification 'should be sought by peaceful means through cooperation, agreement and consent between Irishmen'. The use of force was also dismissed as a foolish policy. Instead it advised that, in the short-term, 'nothing should be done' that might impede the implementation of reforms in Northern Ireland. It also warned against using international forums, such as the UN or Council of Europe, to merely voice Irish grievances against partition.[105]

The focus, instead, the memorandum outlined, should be towards convincing London that Dublin has 'a right to be heard on matters affecting the North and Britain's ultimate responsibility for the situation should be emphasised'. In line with the Lemass approach, the memorandum advised maximising 'cooperation with the North'. Ministerial and official changes should facilitate academic, commercial, cultural, and economic ties between Dublin and Belfast. Interestingly, it also noted that barriers to unity should be removed 'to convince Northern Protestants that they would enjoy full civil rights and equality in a United Ireland'. In words echoing Childers's memorandum of August 1969, on the subjects of birth control and divorce, it advised that special consideration should be given 'to constitutional and statutory difficulties' arising from reform of these two sensitive issues.[106]

The concluding and most significant proposal in the memorandum urged the establishment of a section in the Department of External Affairs to deal specifically with Northern Ireland. It was envisaged that this new section would be responsible for keeping in touch with 'all aspects of Anglo-Irish relations having a bearing on the North'; studying in depth long-term solutions as well as short-term problems; and acting as 'a clearing-house for the activities of other Departments in relation to the North'.[107] Despite some opposition from the Department of the Taoiseach (which wished to control Northern Ireland policy), these policies formed the blueprint of what became the Anglo-Irish division within the Department of External Affairs, which was established in 1970. This was followed, a year later, in 1971, with the creation of the Interdepartmental Committee on Northern Ireland, which brought together influential civil servants from the main departments, namely, the Departments of Taoiseach,

Foreign Affairs, Finance and Justice to develop and co-ordinate the government's approach to Northern Ireland.[108]

For the time being, however, the Dublin government remained unsure about how precisely to advance in its approach to Northern Ireland. Within the Fianna Fáil cabinet differences were still apparent towards what constituted official policy. Blaney, once again, was the leading opponent to Lynch's recent conciliatory approach to Ulster Unionism. Speaking to a gathering of the party faithful in Letterkenny, Co. Donegal, in December 1969, Blaney argued that while peaceful means were the 'ideal way' to end partition, he said that 'no one has the right to assert that force is ruled out'.[109] Ulster Unionist MP, Robin Baillie called Blaney's speech a 'typical Blaney rant'.[110] The British government labelled Blaney's comments as 'rather silly'.[111]

Privately, Lynch would have agreed with such descriptions. In response, the taoiseach issued a statement quoting his Tralee speech and again asserted that the policy of unification could only be secured by peaceful means.[112] Compelled by Lynch's rebuttal of his comments, Blaney issued a statement to clarify his position. 'I did not advocate use of force', he said, there is 'no split in cabinet on Northern policy'.[113] Questioned again on the issue on RTÉ radio, he denied that Lynch had taken him to task over his speech and again said that there was no rift in the cabinet.[114] Speaking at the Fianna Fáil Ard Fheis in January 1970, Lynch was unequivocal: 'the Government are firm in this conviction, that only peaceful means can achieve the abolition of Partition'. Although refraining from mentioning Blaney, directly, it was obvious that Lynch had his cabinet colleague in his sights. The partition of Ireland, Lynch pronounced, 'eats into the Irish consciousness like a cancer'. However, 'Emotionalism', he said, cannot solve partition. 'It is not enough for our hearts to be in the right place – our decisions, too, had to be made in the right way and at the right time'. Lynch argued that Fianna Fáil supporters must 'realise the nature and magnitude' of partition and 'face up to the fact' that there was no 'short-term solutions'. Instead he spoke of the 'long-term' policy of seeking Irish unity by 'only peaceful means'.[115]

For the immediate time it seemed that Lynch's moderation had won out over the extremists within Fianna Fáil. His success, however, was to be short-lived. As the violence increased in Northern Ireland and the death toll mounted, many within Fianna Fáil turned their back on Lynch's conciliatory policy towards partition. Lynch pleaded with supporters to encourage 'tolerance, forbearance – neighbourly love' with Northern Protestants. 'Shooting each other', he exclaimed, would preserve rather than help solve partition.[116] Lynch's pleas were to fall on deaf ears. From the early months of 1970 the division at cabinet level spread like wildfire throughout the Fianna Fáil organisation, from party backbench TDs down to grass-roots supporters. The catalyst for this simmering division between the constitutionalists and militants within Fianna Fáil had its origins in the Arms Crisis.

FIANNA FÁIL AND THE ARMS CRISIS

The infamous story of the Arms Crisis can be traced back to the turbulent events of mid-August 1969. At an Irish cabinet meeting on the afternoon of 16 August, government ministers, collectively, authorised the establishment of a four-man Northern Ireland sub-committee to deal with certain aspects of Northern Ireland affairs. Along with Haughey, three border county TDs, Blaney, Joseph Brennan and Pádraig Faulkner were appointed. In reality the committee was defunct from the start. The only 'committee', as such, comprised Haughey and Blaney. Haughey combined his role on the new sub-committee with control of a special Northern Ireland relief fund of £100,000, voted for by the Dáil, to provide 'aid for the victims of the current unrest in the Six-Counties'.[117] As minister for finance, he held most power and was responsible for ensuring that £100,000 was used for its intended purpose; what actually occurred, however, was that at the very least, approximately £50,000 was used to buy guns.[118]

In the immediate aftermath of the crisis of mid-August 1969, with tensions extremely high, many within Irish government circles argued that if the Irish army was not going to intervene to help the besieged Northern Catholics, at the very least, Northern nationalists should receive guns on purely defensive grounds. On 16 August, three Nationalist MPs, Paddy Devlin, Paddy O'Hanlon and Paddy Kennedy arrived at Dáil Éireann demanding to see the taoiseach. Unable to meet Lynch or Hillery, they stressed to External Affairs officials the plight of Catholics in Derry and Belfast and noted that if 'Irish troops were not sent into the North, they wanted guns';[119] Devlin was reportedly so angry at Lynch's cold-shoulder that the police armed guard protecting the taoiseach's house was increased.[120] Although rebuffed by Lynch, Haughey and Blaney met Devlin and both expressed their determination to obtain guns for Northern nationalists.[121] Indeed, Blaney subsequently claimed that he knew the names of 25 deputies and senators, who in August 1969 had given their own guns for use in Northern Ireland. He said that 'truck loads of surplus small arms were at the time loaded in trucks ready to be moved to the North'.[122]

From the beginning Haughey played a prominent role in what became known as the Arms Crisis; although he always maintained he never had any involvement in the importation of arms. The circumstantial evidence, however, paints a very different picture. In secret, with the support of Blaney and members of the Irish military intelligence, Haughey purportedly used Irish government monies and resources to help arm Northern nationalists with guns and ammunition.[123] Captain James Kelly, an officer of the Irish military intelligence, later testified to the Public Accounts Committee that he had acted with the knowledge and approval of Haughey[124] and that the importation of arms was to be cleared through customs by the Department of Finance.[125]

By August 1969, Haughey was allegedly under surveillance by the Irish special branch because of his secret discussions with leading IRA figures, including the chief of staff of the IRA, Cathal Goulding.[126] Blaney subsequently recalled that on one occasion, following the Ballymurphy explosions in Belfast in April 1970, himself and the Irish minister for defence, Jim Gibbons, with Haughey's knowledge, sent over 500 rifles, 80,000 rounds of ammunition and 3,000 respirators to Dundalk to arm Northern nationalists; the rifles, however, were never actually sent across the border.[127]

Haughey and Blaney were, thus, effectively conducting their own Northern Ireland policy, which was at odds with official government policy. Their fellow cabinet colleague, Hillery later concluded that 'there was a government within a government'.[128] Blaney's involvement with the Arms Crisis was not surprising; like Boland, his visceral anti-partitionism was not in question. However, many then and still today, question Haughey's motivations, seeing his involvement as little more than shrewd political opportunism in a bid to topple and replace Lynch.[129] Prior to the summer of 1969, Haughey is portrayed as caring little about Northern Ireland or indeed Irish unity. Blaney and Boland were reportedly as surprised as the rest of the cabinet when Haughey joined them in the argument for a stronger line on Northern Ireland.[130] Boland subsequently argued that Haughey's active participation in the Northern situation was motivated solely by a desire to enhance his republican credentials within Fianna Fáil.[131]

In particular, writers point to Haughey's period as minister of justice during the early 1960s, when under the Seán Lemass-led government he showed no remorse for his suppression of the IRA border campaign.[132] However, Haughey's clampdown of the IRA and his general endorsement of Lemass's Northern Ireland policy, do not necessarily contradict his perceived alleged 'greening' by 1969/1970. For an ambitious young minister, as he ascended the ranks of the party and government, there was little to be gained in emphasising the gap between rhetoric and reality in relation to Northern Ireland. Better for Haughey to bide his time. As mentioned earlier in this book, since the early 1950s, particularly during his tenure as honorary secretary of the Fianna Fáil Tomas Ó Cléirigh cumann, Dublin North-East, he had demonstrated a strong and virile anti-partitionist mentality.[133] Of course, political ambition was a motivating factor. Nonetheless, the outbreak of violence on the streets of Northern Ireland and the harassment of the Catholic minority by the RUC, struck a chord within Haughey; his passion for Irish unity was revealed and his well hidden anti-partitionist feelings reignited.

Haughey wanted action, not words. Indeed, by the winter of 1969, the British government recognised Haughey's deep-rooted 'passion for unity', as British Ambassador to Ireland, Gilchrist said.[134] In October 1969, during a private meeting between Haughey and Gilchrist, the former noted that 'there was nothing he would not sacrifice', including the position of the Catholic Church and Irish neutrality in order to 'get a united Ireland'. Haughey said if Britain wanted Ireland back in the Commonwealth or requested Irish bases he would 'accept that'.[135] Such strongly worded comments can not merely be written off as political opportunism on Haughey's behalf. Spoken privately, they reveal his genuine republicanism.

Under instructions from Haughey and Blaney, Captain Kelly eventually made arrangements with a German arms dealer, Albert Luykx, to buy 500 pistols and approximately 180,000 rounds of ammunition. The shipment of cargo was to be flown from Vienna to Dublin on 21 April 1970. It was Haughey's failure to arrange clearance for the arms at Dublin Airport that precipitated the Irish state's most serious crisis since its formation.[136] Haughey's former secretary at the Department of Justice, Peter Berry, informed Haughey that the guns would be seized by the Irish special branch if the attempted shipment arrived at Dublin Airport. Although Berry informed Lynch of the plot, the taoiseach accepted the denials from both Blaney and Haughey. Blaney, who had been interviewed in the Taoiseach's office, protested his innocence and refused to resign. Haughey, who was in the Mater Hospital, was visited by the taoiseach; Haughey had purportedly injured himself either falling from his horse or after having been badly beaten with an iron bar during an altercation in a public house on the morning of 22 April.[137] He too protested his innocence. Because of his ill-health, Lynch felt that he could not continue his meeting with his frail minister.[138]

On 1 May 1970, Lynch addressed a meeting of the government. He informed those in attendance that serious allegations of attempts to import arms had been made against both Blaney and Haughey. Both, he said, vehemently denied the allegations. Pádraig Faulkner recalled that he was shocked by the allegations and noted that if they proved to be true the taoiseach would have no choice but to demand the resignation of the two accused.[139] In his memoirs, Faulkner wrote, 'I can still clearly recall Neil Blaney, minister for agriculture, vigorously arguing a point on the subject [of agriculture]. It was as if the Taoiseach had said nothing of any significance'.[140] George Colley was reportedly left dumbfounded, with his mouth wide open, demanding to learn more about the requested resignations.[141] Hillery's recollection of the meeting is most revealing. He recalled that he felt that his 'heart would burst with the excitement' as Lynch 'stood beside me speaking'.[142]

Over the coming days, Lynch weighed up the situation, seeking council from the old guard within Fianna Fáil. He visited Seán Lemass, who informed him: 'you're the Taoiseach: do what you have to do'.[143] Although Lynch was not reported to have spoken to de Valera directly, the Irish president, on meeting Hillery at Áras an Uachtaráin, reportedly 'whispered' that 'we were right and stick it out the people will see we are right'.[144] Frank Aiken, by then a backbencher TD, was more forthright. In a meeting with the taoiseach at government buildings, in which Lynch supplied him with 'files on the two' ministers, Aiken demanded that the whip be withdrawn from Haughey and Blaney. Aiken said that 'you are the leader of the Irish people – not just the Fianna Fáil Party'.[145]

As Lynch considered the fate of his ministers, events outside his control, forced his hand. On 5 May 1970, the leader of Fine Gael, Liam Cosgrave, received a tip-off about the plot to import arms. Later that evening Cosgrave confronted Lynch regarding his news. After some procrastinating Lynch eventually approached Blaney and demanded his resignation. He refused. Lynch then phoned Haughey in hospital. He too refused to resign. Returning home, Lynch consulted a small number of his closest circle of advisers. Soon afterwards, on the morning of 6 May, the Government Information Bureau issued a statement announcing the sacking of Blaney and Haughey for their alleged involvement in an illegal attempt to import arms.[146] In the space of five days the Fianna Fáil government had lost four of its ministers; Lynch having also forced the resignation of his weak minister for justice, Micheál Ó Moráin, the previous day, on 5 May and following Kevin Boland's resignation from the cabinet in protest at the sacking of Blaney and Haughey.[147]

In the immediate aftermath of the ministerial sackings Hillery telephoned Lemass to enquire 'if he wished to speak to me after Haughey and the others had been fired from government'. Lemass did not object to the sacking and cryptically informed Hillery that what Haughey 'must avoid now is doing anything that would make it impossible to recover'.[148] It was the most bizarre series of events since Fianna Fáil first entered the Dáil in 1927 and there was widespread public anxiety, not only about the stability of the government, but whether the institutions of the state could cope with the unfolding events.

Pádraig Faulkner recalled that when the Fianna Fáil cabinet met on the morning of 6 May he looked around the table and saw 'the four vacant chairs, like black holes, in the circle'.[149] At the cabinet meeting Lynch proposed the immediate filling of the vacant ministerial posts. He appointed Desmond O'Malley as the new minister for Justice. George Colley was promoted to minister for finance and Jim Gibbons was appointed minister for agriculture and fisheries. Joseph Brennan was given the Department of Social Welfare. Patrick Lalor took over responsibility for Industry and Commerce, while Jeremiah Cronin was assigned the Department of Defence. Gerald Collins was given the Department of Posts and Telegraphs and Robert Molloy received Local Government. The other ministers retained their posts.[150]

Later that evening, at 6pm, the Fianna Fáil parliamentary party gathered to discuss the fallout from the ministerial sackings. To Lynch's relief, he received 'unanimous' support for his actions; even Kevin Boland spoke in a conciliatory tone. Lynch concluded the meeting noting that he was 'very grateful to the Party for its unanimous decision'. He even 'paid tribute' to the three sacked ministers for the 'outstanding service that they have given'.[151] Despite such pronouncements Lynch was in no mood to compromise. He decided to seize the initiative and firmly clampdown on the last remaining outward critic of his Northern Ireland policy within the cabinet. Later that night, at 10pm, in the aftermath of the parliamentary party meeting, Lynch announced that he had asked the

Irish president to accept the resignation of Kevin Boland. In protest, Paudge Brennan resigned as parliamentary secretary to the minister for Local Government.[152]

Lynch's ability to retain 'unanimous' support from his parliamentary party (in the public dominion at least) was, in the words of *The Irish Times* correspondent Dick Walsh, 'probably the most remarkable example of an Irish party's instinct for self-preservation overcoming its internal divisions, an example of pragmatism without parallel in the history of constitutional nationalism in Ireland'.[153] A plausible explanation for the muted response of Fianna Fáil TDs to Lynch's actions was provided by party deputy for Co. Clare, Sylvester Barrett. Patrick Hillery noted that in the aftermath of the parliamentary party meeting of 6 May he asked Barrett: 'Will we have great trouble with the Party for firing them?'. Barrett replied that 'the more he fired the better', referring to the ever present ambitions for promotion among many members of Fianna Fáil.[154] For Fine Gael the crisis merely reinforced its argument that behind the 'childish impertinence and imposture' Fianna Fáil, in the words of Senator John Kelly, was '*pretending* to be a Republican Party'.[155]

In the aftermath of the affair, Frank Aiken privately criticised Lynch for failing to expel Blaney, Haughey, Boland and Paudge Brennan from the Fianna Fáil Party. In a handwritten letter to Lynch, Aiken wrote that the 'crisis of confidence in Fianna Fáil will not just fade away'. 'Ireland and the Irish people', Aiken lamented, 'must go down in confusion before long', unless immediate action was taken against Blaney and his co-anti-partitionist collaborators. 'I would appeal to you for the sake of the people of the North and for the sake of the Irish people as a whole', he concluded, 'to summon a party meeting and take the action I suggested to you the other night in getting rid of them out of the party'.[156]

Lynch, however, refused to act decisively. A few days after receiving Aiken's letter the Fianna Fáil parliamentary party duly met on 13 May 1970. At the meeting no motion was tabled calling for the removal of the four mentioned Fianna Fáil deputies.[157] Aiken was incensed. Shortly after the conclusion of the meeting he again wrote to Lynch to express his 'grave disappointment that at the party meeting this morning you did not move to withdraw the Whip from the four members, who by their actions and statements have publicly repudiated the policy of non-violence in regard to the Six Counties'.[158]

On 28 May 1970, Haughey and Blaney were arrested and charged with conspiracy to import arms. Reaction to the news from within

Fianna Fáil was extreme. Kevin Boland again led the protests. He accused Lynch of 'felon-setting' and demanded a special meeting of the Fianna Fáil parliamentary party. The party faithful thus met on 3 June. Speaking at the meeting Lynch noted that any attempts to import arms into Northern Ireland would only lead to 'civil war' throughout the island of Ireland. Boland refused to withdraw his 'treachery' allegations against Lynch. The taoiseach described Boland's accusations as 'inadequate and unacceptable'. After three and a half hours of heated exchanges, the meeting was adjourned until the following day.[159] The next day the party convened once more. This time Lynch was in no mood to compromise and following a secret ballot, Boland was expelled from the Fianna Fáil parliamentary party, by sixty votes to eleven.[160]

The dust was allowed to settle for a few days. However, tensions again came to the fore on the evening of 22 June, at a specially arranged meeting of the Fianna Fáil National Executive. At the gathering, which lasted over four hours, Lynch demanded Boland's removal as joint secretary of Fianna Fáil.[161] Seán MacEntee was the taoiseach's principal defender; he seconded a motion calling for Boland's removal as joint secretary and for Dermot Ryan's expulsion from the party's National Executive.[162] 'Jack Lynch,' MacEntee noted, 'whose record and conduct since he came into public life in the dark days of 1948, has entitled him to nothing but respect and esteem'. He accused Boland of intentionally trying to divide Fianna Fáil. 'No state, no party, no organisation', he bemoaned, 'will prosper if it is encumbered with two leaders! Yet dual leadership is in effect what Kevin Boland is asking us to accept'. 'As this government cannot have two leaders', he said, 'neither can it have two policies'. If the National Executive endorsed Boland's policies, he warned, than Fianna Fáil was in danger of imploding. 'It will be the death too of any likely reunification ...'[163]

After much debate Boland and Ryan resigned as members of the National Executive. In protest, Boland's father Gerald Boland resigned as vice-president and trustee of the party, although he retained his Fianna Fáil membership. 'I want no part of a party', Gerry Boland complained, 'where an honourable man like my son appears to be an embarrassment'.[164] There was also speculation that Kevin's brother, Harry Boland would also resign from Fianna Fáil.[165] Hillery subsequently wrote that Kevin Boland's resignation ended the latter's 'spoilt child days' around the cabinet table. Boland, Hillery noted, had 'expected to be coerced to withdraw his resignation. But this time Jack did not coax him'.[166]

The rift between MacEntee and Boland soon became public. Writing in *The Irish Times* on 30 June, MacEntee publicly held Kevin Boland personally responsible 'for the fires and killings which occurred in Belfast over the weekend'. Boland, he said, in advocating that Northern Catholics be supplied with guns for defensive purposes, held a 'moral responsibility' for 'those who used their weapons against five Protestant Irishmen – now dead'.[167] By this time, sectarian conflict in Northern Ireland was widespread. Severe rioting broke out in Derry, while Orange parades down the Crumlin Road ignited conflict on the streets of Belfast. The Provisional IRA had intensified its bombing campaign, while the British army's heavy-handed security operations, only further alienated Northern Catholics. On 27 June alone, a reported ninety-six people were injured in Northern Ireland.[168] In a statement Lynch appealed for calm, but the violence went from bad to worse in the first week of July.[169] The British army began a security crackdown in West Belfast and imposed a curfew lasting thirty-four hours. It was within this sense of despair and confusion that the Fianna Fáil government found itself trying to operate.

On 2 July the charges of the attempted importation of arms were dropped against Blaney. Haughey, however, with his three co-accused, Albert Luykx, James J. Kelly and John Kelly, were returned for trial in the Central Criminal Court. The infamous story of the Arms Trial itself, from the collapse of the first trial to Haughey's eventual acquittal has been told on numerous occasions.[170] Haughey was eventually acquitted in October 1970; the jury possibly finding it difficult to accept that the arms importation did not have at least covert government sanction. Haughey was carried shoulder-high from the court to the cheers of 'We want Charlie' and jeers demanding 'Lynch must go'.[171]

On his acquittal Haughey demanded Lynch's resignation; albeit in an ambiguous fashion.[172] The taoiseach, however, was able to use party members' overwhelming desire to maintain unity and stay in government against the protests of the anti-partitionists within the organisation. An opinion poll carried out after Haughey's dismissal showed that 72% of the electorate supported Lynch's decision and 89% of those who voted for Fianna Fáil in the last election still supported him as their preferred choice as taoiseach.[173] Following Lynch's return from a meeting of the General Assembly of the United Nations, he was met at Dublin Airport by the entire government and some fifty TDs and senators. It was a brilliant public display of support for Lynch and as *The Irish Times* noted 'if anyone, after that display, wishes to say that they are better Republicans than Mr Lynch in Fianna Fáil, then they have a formidable task ... it was the Republic *par excellence*'.[174] In the end, realising that he had little hope of defeating Lynch, Haughey backed down and within days voted confidence in the Dáil for his taoiseach and Jim Gibbons; the very minister whose word could have put him behind bars for twenty years![175]

That said, the sacking of Blaney and Haughey and their subsequent public humiliation, caused uproar among some Fianna Fáil supporters, including party elected representatives. Not for the first time Blaney led the protests. An *Irish Times* editorial quoted him as having stated on British television that had he been taoiseach he would have sent the Irish army into Northern Ireland in August 1969.[176] Within the Fianna Fáil parliamentary party several TDs reportedly supported the two disgraced former ministers. They included Wicklow TD, Paudge Brennan; North-County Dublin TD, Desmond Foley; South-West Cork TD, Flor Crowley; South Tipperary TD, Noel Davern; and South Kerry TD, Timothy O'Connor.[177] Indeed, by the close of 1970, Blaney, Brennan and Foley were either expelled or resigned from the Fianna Fáil parliamentary party.

A consortium of Fianna Fáil grass-roots was equally incensed. The *Evening Herald* quoted Haughey's election agent, Pat O'Connor, who announced that the people of Dublin North-east were in a rebellious mood.[178] Haughey's own Fianna Fáil branch, the Tomas Ó Cléirigh cumann, issued a resolution to party headquarters calling for the reinstatement of Haughey and Blaney in the cabinet and Lynch's resignation.[179] In Donegal, preparations were made to give Blaney a hero's welcome. 'Bonfires blaze for Blaney' was the headline in the *Evening Herald*.[180] Fianna Fáil cumainn from Dublin South and Co. Cork also wrote to party headquarters, demanding the Fianna Fáil leadership take a 'stronger' approach towards Northern Ireland.[181] In April 1970, the honorary secretary of the Fianna Fáil Dún Laoghaire Comhairle Ceantair, Brian Davies, wrote to the party's National Executive demanding that the Irish government immediately 'appoint a committee' to examine Northern Ireland policy.[182] Later that year, in October 1970, honorary secretary of the party's Firhouse cumann, South Co. Dublin, Con Corrigan, wrote to the National Executive requesting the 'restoration of the Whip to Deputy Kevin Boland and a public apology by an Taoiseach to him'.[183]

In June 1970, Patrick Hillery received reports from Jack Daly, a prominent Fianna Fáil activist in Clare, that there were 'a number of "malcontents", who were trying to stir up opposition to the Taoiseach ...'[184] In the same month, irate Fianna Fáil members even issued death threats to Seán MacEntee, who had proposed Kevin Boland's removal from the joint secretaryship of Fianna Fáil; they also threatened to burn MacEntee's house to the ground.[185] There was also a subsequent request from Dublin grass-roots for the recalling of Irish troops from Cyprus to serve along the border counties and that 'Fianna Fáil must activate its original Republican policy for a 32–county Ireland'.[186] Clearly, the pledges of loyalty to the Fianna Fáil leadership were seen by the Blaneyites and Haugheyites as empty formulae, intended to gloss over their differences with Lynch, not to eliminate them.

JACK LYNCH, NORTHERN NATIONALISTS AND THE SDLP, 1966–1971

In early July 1970, the same week that the charges of the attempted importation of arms were dropped against Blaney, Lynch was evidently facing increasing pressure from both his own supporters and the opposition parties for his apparent inability to influence the unfolding crisis in Northern Ireland. Moreover, the sectarian violence across the border appeared to vindicate the militant rhetoric of his opponents within Fianna Fáil. Hillery, therefore, decided to make a bold symbolic show of support for Northern Ireland Catholics. He visited the Falls Road on 6 July, the day after the curfew was lifted.[187] Hillery recalled that his actions were as a direct response to the political pressure on Lynch. Although Lynch did not ask him to do anything specifically, Hillery was well aware of the taoiseach's concerns and took the hint. He later noted that on hearing of his decision to travel to Belfast Lynch said 'you are taking an awful lot on you and I am very grateful to you and I said not to worry'.[188]

Without informing either the Belfast government or British army, in the company of Eamonn Gallagher, Hillery secretly travelled to Belfast. Hillery's decision was one of the most spectacular actions taken by an Irish government minister since Eamon de Valera's visit to the German embassy on 30 April 1945, to pay his condolences on the death of Adolf Hitler.[189] The visit to the Falls Road permitted Hillery to meet several community leaders and representatives of Northern nationalist opinion, including James Doherty of the Nationalist Party. He was brought on a tour of the Falls and was taken aback at the extent of the destruction to property caused by the British army throughout the house searches. The visit, as Hillery later recalled, reinforced his belief that the British government was required to play a key role if the situation in Northern Ireland was to change. 'My own belief', he wrote, 'is that the British need fierce pushing at this time and I am going to give it to them'.[190]

Hillery's decision to visit Belfast in such a remarkable manner highlighted the differences between himself and Lynch in relation to Northern Ireland policy. On the one hand, Lynch's attentions focused on attacking the IRA and maintaining his conciliatory approach to Ulster Unionism. On the other, Hillery channelled his energies directly upon the British government for their continued support for partition. William O'Brien offered the adept observation that if Lynch was 'the dove and the trio of Blaney, Boland and Haughey the hawks, then Hillery was a hybrid of the two'.[191] The irredentist void left following the departure of the ministers in the aftermath of the Arms Crisis, arguably, was filled by Hillery. At this time, it was this hybrid of an overall moderate policy, coupled with the pursuance of it in an aggressive manner, which characterised the Irish government's attitude towards Northern Ireland and comparably Britain. Hillery, along with Gallagher, pursued the aggressive approach, while Lynch was moderation personified. The relationship between Lynch and Hillery was essentially that of good cop, bad cop. As Hillery put it, 'we had a balance without agreeing to do so'.[192]

For politics within Fianna Fáil, the visit gave Lynch some much-needed breathing space, acting as a buffer against accusations within his party that he had abandoned Northern Catholics to British and Ulster Unionist oppression. Passivity would have alienated the Irish government from the Catholics in Northern Ireland and those in the Republic whose views were similar to those of Blaney and Boland. The *Financial Times* observed on 8 July that Hillery's visit to the Falls Road allowed Lynch to 'insist to his own militant back-benchers, and to the opposition parties in the Dáil, that he is not neglecting the welfare "of our people in the North"'.[193] On hearing of Hillery's visit to Belfast, Seán MacEntee emphatically supported the decision. Writing to Hillery he described the 'escapade' as 'like holing with your tee-shot!' (Hillery was an enthusiastic amateur golfer).[194]

In fact, by this period, with the support of the Derry constitutional nationalist, John Hume, Lynch sought to provide Northern Ireland nationalists with a democratic alternative to the emerging Provisional Sinn Féin and IRA. In mid-February 1970, Eamonn Gallagher, upon receiving confidential reports from Hume, informed Lynch that there was a move on foot in Northern Ireland to create a new political party.[195] This new party, which was a hybrid of intellectualism, socialism and moderate nationalism, was eventually launched under the title: the Social Democratic and Labour Party (SDLP), in August 1970.

The Fianna Fáil government's public endorsement of the SDLP marked a significant change of policy. Under Lemass and indeed de Valera, consecutive Fianna Fáil governments had looked disparagingly towards Northern Nationalists; Lemass in particular had always believed that the Northern Nationalist Party was of little value to Dublin and would not permit the movement of any input into Fianna Fáil's Northern Ireland policy. In the aftermath of the Lemass–O'Neill meeting in January 1965 Lemass had successfully convinced the Nationalist Party to assume the role as the official opposition party at Stormont. Thereafter, he distanced Fianna Fáil away from the plight of Northern Ireland Catholics and instead concentrated on nurturing cross-border co-operation with Ulster Unionists.

At Lynch's first press conference as leader, in November 1966, he clearly demonstrated his adherence to the Lemass-line: the strengthening of cross-border co-operation, not the plight of Northern Ireland Catholics, Lynch said, was his central concern.[196] He also distanced himself away from Northern nationalists and their programme for civil rights. The political, economic and social discrimination practices against the Catholic minority of Northern Ireland would have to be quietly put to one side so as not to antagonise Ulster Unionists or threaten a policy of functional co-operation between Dublin and Belfast. Hugh McCann made this policy decision blatantly clear in a confidential letter to all Irish missions aboard. Although the letter was produced in February 1969 its contents reflected the traditional attitude of the Department of External Affairs to the issue of civil rights in Northern Ireland during the 1960s. 'On the question of civil rights and current political developments in the Six Counties', McCann explained, 'it is considered that our policy should continue to be one of constraint, with little active involvement as possible and the less said the better'. 'The reasoning behind this policy', he said, 'is simply that there is nothing at this stage that we could do to improve the situation in the North ...'[197]

Since becoming taoiseach, Lynch selected the Northern Nationalist Party for particular criticism. Speaking in November 1967, in language which echoed Lemass, he spoke of the 'narrow attitudes' of the Nationalist Party and berated the movement for relying on the religious affiliations of constituents rather than on social and economic policies.[198] Indeed, the previous month, in October 1967, the retired taoiseach, Lemass reportedly told an audience at Queen's University Belfast that Northern Ireland politicians and this included Northern Nationalists, were unable to move with the times and look beyond religious labels.[199]

In the aftermath of Lynch's public criticisms Eddie McAteer travelled to Dublin to voice his complaints. Lynch, however, was unavailable to meet McAteer. In his absence, secretary of the Department of Taoiseach, Nicholas Nolan, agreed to meet McAteer. The latter expressed his concern that Lynch's speech reflected government policy and he explained his frustration that Fianna Fáil ministers seemed more interested in meeting Ulster Unionists than Northern Nationalists. He inquired if the taoiseach would consider inviting Northern Nationalists to Dublin, occasionally, and if members of the Irish government would make courtesy visits to Northern Ireland.[200] McAteer's requests, however, came to nothing. When Lynch brought the issue to cabinet in early December 1967 he decided, without encountering any dissent, that if McAteer sought a meeting with the Irish government, the latter should take the initiative. Thereafter, the matter was quietly ignored.[201] McAteer was left to exclaim that 'Nationalists feel that they are now nobody's children'.[202]

By this time the Nationalist Party only existed in a vague parliamentary sense, offering their MPs an umbrella under which they could convey an impression of cohesion. This apparent cohesion was paper-thin, since it was really only a consensus on the constitutional issue that united MPs, that is, opposition to unionism and the attainment of a united Ireland.[203] Although Eddie McAteer (spurred on by pressure from Dublin) and Austin Currie Nationalist Party Stormont MP for East Tyrone had sought to reform the 'movement' in the aftermath of the Lemass–O'Neill meetings, MPs lacked a coherent organisational structure and had only recently begun to convene annual conferences. In reality, the party was worn-out. It had taken its eye off the ball over the preceding years, with its political focus on partition rather than the wider social and economic difficulties facing its constituents throughout Northern Ireland.

Although in November 1969, in the aftermath of Lynch's Tralee speech, Fianna Fáil TD, Ray McSharry, attended the Northern Nationalists' annual convention, the signs were already ominous.[204] Addressing the Dáil, in December 1969, Lynch publicly distanced the Fianna Fáil government from the Nationalist Party. He noted that 'it would be wrong ... and rather divisive to have consultation' only with the Northern Nationalist Party.[205] By February 1970,

Fianna Fáil's reluctance to offer the Nationalist Party involvement in Dublin's Northern Ireland policy was made visibly clear. On 14 February, the executive secretary of the Nationalist Party wrote to Lynch requesting the establishment of a 'combined committee' of its party and the Fianna Fáil government, so as 'to keep the situation in the Six-Counties under review'. Lynch's reply, drafted by officials in the Department of the Taoiseach, was unequivocal.

Firstly, in the traditional Fianna Fáil stance, which echoed both Lemass and de Valera, the letter stated that it was unacceptable for 'reasons of principle' that a 'formal connection' be established between Dublin and the Nationalist Party. Secondly, given the disorganised condition of the Nationalist Party and its possible demise in the 'foreseeable time', the letter argued that it would be pointless to establish a formal connection. In conclusion, the letter described the current policies of the Nationalist Party as outdated and noted that the 'ideas and techniques' of the Civil Rights Movement proved to be 'far more successful in changing the situation in the North'.[206] Indeed, by this period, the Dublin government realised that street protests and demonstrations, organised by civil rights groups such as the Derry Housing Action Group and NICRA, assumed far greater priority among Northern Catholics than Nationalist political parties or their political representatives.

It was within this context that Lynch believed that it was an opportune time to nurture a new alternative to the outdated and sterile Nationalist Party. Within Fianna Fáil others had called for a change in policy. In late August 1969, Childers circulated a memorandum on Northern Ireland to all government ministers. Its contents helped form the basis of Fianna Fáil's approach to Northern Nationalists over the coming years. Referring to the government's joint programme of reviving nationalism in Northern Ireland and securing support from the media, Childers noted that between 1932 and 1947 'the Nationalist parties' polices have been weak, contradictory and unrealistic'. He wrote of the outcome of the Lemass–O'Neill meetings and the positive impact on the growth of ecumenism since the Papacy of Pope John XXIII. Middle-class groups in Northern Ireland, he explained, were meeting socially 'on a basis unheard of ten years ago'. If that policy was to succeed, he suggested the need to have a 'policy for ending partition'.[207]

It was within this revisionist thinking that Fianna Fáil embraced the formation of the SDLP. The new movement constituted a left-of-centre, non-sectarian party. Its founding members consisted of six MPs and one senator. Its appointed leader, Gerry Fitt and his

Belfast colleague, Paddy Devlin, were crucial to the party's origins and survival, given their respective base in the capital city. Both men held powerful personalities and labour socialist views. Since 1966, Fitt was Republican Labour MP for West Belfast, while Devlin represented the Northern Ireland Labour Party for Falls constituency, Belfast. Hume, who took Eddie McAteer's Foyle constituency seat at the 1969 Stormont elections, represented the intellectual non-violent Irish nationalist voice of the party. Of the three other founders, Ivan Cooper was previously a member of the Northern Ireland Labour Party and an active civil rights campaigner; Austin Currie held the constituency of East-Tyrone for the Nationalist Party; and Paddy Wilson – murdered in June 1973 – was a Republican Labour Senator.

The SDLP's nationalism was expressed in a moderate and democratic form: 'To promote co-operation, friendship and understanding between North and South with a view to the eventual reunification of Ireland through the consent of the majority of the people in the North and South'.[208] On the issue of consent, the party formed its roots from the revisionist nationalist thinking associated initially with National Unity in the early 1960s and then with the more politicised challenge to the Nationalist Party that emerged with the formation of the National Democratic Party in 1965. Under the influence of Michael McKeown, the National Democratic Party aimed to 'promote the cause of Irish unity; to promote the economic, social and cultural welfare of the Irish people; to promote the creation of a society in the community in which social justice prevails'.[209] Importantly, the party advocated that Irish unity could only be secured by the consent of the majority of Northern Ireland. This dramatic policy change was central to the SDLP's political makeup.

Electorally, the Nationalist Democratic Party had only limited success; by December 1969 the party had branches in only ten out of forty-eight territorial constituencies and no representation at Stormont.[210] Nonetheless, its high-profile, its socio-economic agenda and its modern outlook inspired the genesis of the SDLP's policies. The National Democratic Party was predictably enthusiastic about the formation of the SDLP and by October 1970 had decided to disband and defect *en masse*. Of the almost 400 people who joined the SDLP, nearly 80% had been National Democratic Party members.[211]

From the outset, the SDLP was anxious to establish good working relations with the Fianna Fáil government; the new party was likewise eager to form good relations with Fine Gael and the Labour Party, respectively. Prior to the party's official launch, Hume had asked Gallagher to convey to the taoiseach that 'notwithstanding the necessary inclusion of the word Labour in the name of the party, there will be no connection between it and the British, Irish and Northern Ireland Labour parties'.[212] There was, however, reluctance within the SDLP towards formalising official links with Fianna Fáil. The scandal over the Arms Crisis made some SDLP supporters sceptical of the Dublin government's commitment to non-violence. Moreover, the SDLP's two Belfast-based MPs, Fitt and Devlin, prided themselves on upholding traditional socialist values. In the past, neither lost the opportunity to attack parties like Fianna Fáil for their alleged right-wing big business makeup. On one occasion, following Lynch's speech at the United Nations, in October 1970, where the taoiseach claimed that the Fianna Fáil government was the Nationalist community's 'second guarantor', Devlin took grave exception to such comments. He claimed that the taoiseach's remarks had no validity and had been made without consultation with the SDLP.[213]

Practical, or more appropriately, financial considerations, also motivated the SDLP's eagerness to forge strong relations with the Fianna Fáil government. Although the party received widespread support in Northern Ireland, those who supported the party, in the words of Austin Currie, 'were not monied people, certainly in the early days'.[214] Thus, the party's attention turned to the South. With the support of Dr John Kelly, a Newry man and lecturer at UCD, a support group was formed. Initially, Fianna Fáil was reluctant to help, however, following a lunch between Kelly, Currie, Jack Lynch and Brian Lenihan, the Irish government decided to come on board.[215] Thereafter, the Dublin group became a major contributor to the SDLP war chest. Paddy Devlin subsequently wrote that in the early days 'we made several lucrative trips to Dublin, where a support group of sympathetic business and professional people ... handed over generous sums of money'.[216] Devlin noted that thereafter the Fianna Fáil government 'were running after us – whatever we wanted we got'.[217]

From Lynch's perspective the establishment of the SDLP perfectly suited his long-term strategy to support the emergence of a constitutionalist nationalist party in Northern Ireland. As ever, there were some within Fianna Fáil that were not so supportive. Neil Blaney's political contacts in Northern Ireland were not primarily with John Hume or Gerry Fitt and he felt uneasy about establishing formal relations with the party.[218] Despite Blaney's apprehensions,

Lynch's new policy towards the politics of Northern nationalism was a welcome departure from Fianna Fáil's previous detached attitude to Northern Catholics. Thereafter, the Fianna Fáil government worked in tandem with the SDLP to formalise its working relationship. Although, minister for finance, George Colley confessed that the Fianna Fáil government might have held some difference of opinion with the SDLP leadership, he acknowledged that they were in total agreement on the 'central major issues'.[219] Thus, in the immediate period, acknowledging the long-term aspirations for Irish unity, both endorsed the principle of a power-sharing administration in Northern Ireland.[220]

In the intermediate period, however, any notions of a power-sharing Executive or the prospect of the British government permitting Dublin an input into the affairs of Northern Ireland seemed a distant fantasy. Although Lynch received some respite as a result of Hillery's visit to the Falls Road, the sharp divisions within Fianna Fáil remained on the emotive subject of partition. By October 1970, Hillery admitted to the British Embassy in Dublin that because of the battle between the constitutionalists and anti-partitionists Fianna Fáil could 'crumble'. He said that he felt like a 'hatchet man' trying to twist the arms of the dissidents, in an effort to rally supporters behind Lynch's Northern Ireland policy.[221] Hillery's words were to prove prophetic. Like Lynch, he realised that the forthcoming Ard Fheis, scheduled for February 1971, would witness the ultimate showdown between the two warring factions within Fianna Fáil.

'YE CAN HAVE BOLAND, BUT YOU CANNOT HAVE FIANNA FÁIL':
THE 1971 FIANNA FÁIL ARD FHEIS

The 1971 Fianna Fáil Ard Fheis represented the highpoint of the division between Fianna Fáil members towards the party's attitude to Northern Ireland. Although since becoming taoiseach Lynch had continually advanced a conciliatory and peaceful approach to Northern Ireland, a sizeable proportion of Fianna Fáil members still advocated that physical force was a legitimate policy. Convened, in late February, at the Royal Dublin Society (RDS) and attended by approximately 5,000 Fianna Fáil supporters, tempers were fraught and a sense of hostility dominated proceedings.[222]

Initially, reports in the media predicted that the Ard Fheis would witness little opposition to Lynch's leadership or indeed his Northern Ireland policy. According to Chris Glennon of the *Irish Independent*,

Lynch's support throughout the cumainn seemed quite strong. Glennon said that Lynch was 'so firmly in control, that any dissident elements will await a better time to launch an assault on his policies or his leadership'.[223] A motion signed by twenty-nine cumainn, constituency councils and district councils, recorded confidence in Lynch and his government and pledged unwavering support in their efforts to end partition by peaceful means.[224] Such optimism, however, was quickly dashed.

Declaring the Ard Fheis open, Lynch initially received a standing ovation from party delegates. However, the atmosphere soon changed when the standing orders proposed by the chairman, Paddy Smith, were challenged. When Maurice Downey attempted to speak, another delegate, Joan Buckley, took to the rostrum to protest against the shortening of the speaking time. Paul Butler, of the Robert Emmet cumann, then attacked the attempts to prosecute the defendants in the Arms Trial and accused prominent members of the party of perjury and cowardice.[225] The result was chaos for several minutes. Amid the confusion Lynch received his second standing ovation of the evening, when a member of the audience shouted: 'We will continue under the leadership of our Taoiseach, Jack Lynch'. When Jim Gibbons, minister for agriculture, rose to speak, he could hardly be heard as a group of delegates shouted 'Judas' and 'traitor'. One group shouted: 'We want Jim', while others chanted 'Out, out, out'.[226]

Patrick Hillery rose to his feet and despite coming under a barrage of verbal and physical intimidation, sought to defend his taoiseach. However, as he made his way to the podium, Kevin Boland appeared on the platform as if to speak. Uproar enveloped throughout the hall for several minutes, amid jeers and shouts of 'Free speech', and 'We want Jack'. Lynch then appealed for calm. He was shouted down by a faction of those present as a 'Hypocrite', branded 'Traitor Jack' and mockingly told to 'join the Free Staters'.[227] Erskine Childers was left dumbfounded, sitting on the platform with his head in his hands in disbelief.[228] Parliamentary secretary to the Taoiseach, David Andrews defended his leader, describing one unidentified Donegal delegate as a 'Blue Shirt'. Some below the podium even kicked and punched one another.[229]

Hillery intervened and declared that 'our policy is Jack Lynch's policy, de Valera's policy, Seán Lemass's policy and we will continue that policy in spite of any bully boys within or without the organisation'. Those that were causing disturbances, he said, would not be allowed to prevent the Ard Fheis from deciding policy.[230] He asked the Ard Fheis to make up its mind. He said that they were dealing with the enemies within the party. Boland, with a curled index finger, reportedly, taunted Hillery, inviting him to 'come on, come on'.[231] The rostrum was then toppled over as Boland was led down to the floor of the hall amid scuffles and exchanges of punches between rival delegates.[232] The *Kerryman* reported that 'it will not be easy to forget the sight of the imperturbable Dr Hillery and the solid Kevin Boland roaring in rage at each other'.[233] What followed next has gone down in Irish folklore. Hillery's iconoclastic phrase immortalised by the assembled journalists and cameras, 'Ye can have [Kevin] Boland but you can't have Fianna Fáil', encapsulated the division within the party over its Northern Ireland policy.[234]

An appeal for calm then came from an unlikely source. Neil Blaney made a conciliatory speech. The damage, however, had already been done. By that point delegates were either for or against Lynch. By the night of 20 February, tensions remained at fever pitch. Just after 8.00pm, Seán MacEntee was invited to speak. He began amid boos and chants of 'Boland, Boland'. When he said that Fianna Fáil had never forsaken its principles he was met with cries of 'Who are you fooling'. It was an 'astonishingly sad moment', *The Irish Times* reported, as MacEntee witnessed 'men half his age' standing shaking their fists at one of the founding fathers of Fianna Fáil.[235] Nóirín Ní Scoláin, a member of the outgoing National Executive and a Boland sympathiser, declared that 'for fifty years we have ignored them [Northern Catholics] and have done nothing. Have we lost our souls?'[236]

Next Lynch moved to the podium, to deliver his much anticipated Presidential address. As Lynch began to speak, Boland was carried shoulder-high in a lap of honour around the hall. Others shouted 'Union Jack', while grass-roots delegates from counties Donegal, Dublin, Laois and Offaly reportedly booed and jeered their party leader.[237] Tim Buckley, a grass-roots supporter from the Tullamore cumann, accused the taoiseach of 'hypocrisy'.[238] Lynch sought to ignore the commotions and focused on delivering his speech. Greeted by a burst of applause, he reaffirmed his commitment and that of his Fianna Fáil government to a peaceful solution to partition. He said it was the job of politicians, both North and South, 'to do all possible to calm the situation' and 'encourage a peaceful and prosperous future'. Those that 'keep alive the physical force tradition', he explained, 'do not represent anything significant in our community'. 'We wish to extend an olive branch to the North and we wish the North to accept it'.[239]

After the speech delegates gave Lynch his third standing ovation of the day, which reportedly lasted between two to three minutes. The Ard Fheis, in the words of an official in the British Embassy, Dublin, represented 'hair raising moments' for Lynch.[240] However, the showdown at the Ard Fheis ended in a decisive victory for the taoiseach and a lasting setback for his opponents. The Fianna Fáil Party machine had destroyed all tangible opposition to Lynch's conciliatory stance on Northern Ireland. By the exercise of his political skills and aided by his loyal supporters, Lynch retained the leadership of Fianna Fáil and the endorsement of his policy of a peaceful approach to Irish unity. Indeed, Lynch had managed to retain party unity and to secure the election of his strongest supporters to important posts within the organisation. In replacement of Boland, Patrick Hillery and Joseph Groome were elected joint honorary secretaries. Moreover, George Colley secured the post of joint treasurer, while after a tight battle Anthony Hederman obtained the other joint treasurer post, following a close battle with Blaney.[241]

Predictably, residual dissent remained within Fianna Fáil towards Lynch's leadership and the government's stance on Northern Ireland. In the aftermath of the Ard Fheis, Hillery exclaimed that the party was on the verge of dividing due to a 'crisis of confidence among Fianna Fáil stalwarts – the active party members and officers in the constituencies'.[242] In a speech in Arklow, a month after the Ard Fheis, in April 1971, Blaney made a blistering attack on the Fianna Fáil leadership, in which he denounced the 'peaceful means hypocrites'.[243] In Cork, on 17 August, eight prominent Fianna Fáil members, including James O'Leary, chairman of Lynch's own local party branch, the Brother Delaney cumann, resigned in protest against the party's Northern Ireland policy. A statement issued on behalf of the former members announced that 'Fianna Fáil had abandoned the last vestige of Republicanism'.[244] The following day, on 18 August, two more Fianna Fáil members resigned, Denis O'Brien, chairman of the Seán T. O'Kelly cumann and Diarmuid Traynor, chairman of the Fianna Fáil youth cumann.[245]

Despite the inevitable opposition from a cohort of 'wild men' within Fianna Fáil, the Ard Fheis successfully alienated the anti-partitionist wing of the party. In the words of the British Ambassador to Ireland, Sir John Peck, despite his public outbursts, Blaney was pleading quietly for 'tolerance', Haughey 'never uttered a word', while Lynch finally cooked 'Mr Boland's goose'. 'Mr Lynch is master', Peck noted, 'the party of Republicanism has formally and overwhelmingly endorsed the policy laid down by Mr Lynch'.[246] In the aftermath of the Ard Fheis, the Fianna Fáil National Executive rallied behind Lynch pledging its '... approval and full support ...' for his 'handling of the position'.[247]

Likewise, the parliamentary party, and this included Haughey, recorded that they 'fully supported' Lynch's Northern Ireland policy.[248] The vast majority of Fianna Fáil grass-roots equally expressed their endorsement of Lynch's stance on Northern Ireland and offered 'full confidence' in his leadership.[249] Henceforth, under Lynch's leadership the means of securing a united Ireland was settled. Fianna Fáil members could no longer be under any illusions. Physical force was unequivocally ruled out and Lynch's conciliatory and peaceful stance formed the basis of Fianna Fáil's Northern Ireland policy for the remainder of his leadership until his resignation in 1979.[250]

* * *

In conclusion, as the turmoil surrounding the 1971 Fianna Fáil Ard Fheis receded into the background, the party's commitment to peaceful policy in the attainment of a united Ireland remained steadfast. Lynch categorically stated that there could be no room for compromise between the position of the Fianna Fáil leadership and the view of the anti-partitionists. Under Lynch's leadership force would never be the answer. Instead, based on the principle that Irish reunification was a long-term goal, the Fianna Fáil government sought a three-flank approach. Firstly, Dublin would maintain pressure on London to ensure that the reforms programme in Northern Ireland was fully implemented. Secondly, the Irish government would seek to woo Ulster Unionists offering co-operation and assistance in economic and development planning and other matters of mutual interest. Lastly, by pursuing the concept of a united Ireland, embracing the two traditions and religions, the Fianna Fáil government would envisage making constitutional and social changes so as to accommodate the fears of Northern Protestants.

Writing subsequently, Kevin Boland pinpointed the 1971 Ard Fheis as representing a turning-point for Fianna Fáil's stance on Northern Ireland. He acidly wrote that on the subject of partition, 'there was no Fianna Fáil policy on that matter any more'. Instead there was the bi-partisan policy of a unified approach. 'It was', he exclaimed, 'the policy of Cumann na nGaedheal, the one-time government "under contract with the enemy to maintain his overlordship"'.[251] Boland argued that the first aim of Fianna Fáil had been replaced 'by the entirely new policy that partition was to be solved only by the effluxion of time and without any help from them'.[252] In Boland's eyes, echoing Peck's comments above, Fianna Fáil was now the 'Party of Pragmatism' rather than the 'Republican Party'.[253] Although Boland's writings must be taken with a pinch of salt given his dislike of the Lynch leadership, his observations did, in fact, hold some credence. Since the late 1920s, under de Valera's guidance, Fianna Fáil had rejected the use of physical force as a 'viable' policy to end partition. Over the following decades, however, and chiefly during the turbulent years from 1969 to early 1971, a widespread misconception enveloped the organisation, seeming to indicate that the use of violence constituted official Fianna Fáil policy.

Lynch's 'victory' at the 1971 Fianna Fáil Ard Fheis, forever dispelled the *suggestion* that physical force was a legitimate policy. Under Lynch's leadership, he successfully stood out against those within Fianna Fáil that advocated physical force nationalism. He mobilised the institutions of the state to fight against the subversion of a reconstituted IRA; a subversion that had run to the heart of his own cabinet. With the support of loyal cabinet colleagues, such as Patrick Hillery, he had managed to repel the challenge from the Blaney–Haughey anti-partitionist wing of Fianna Fáil.

Thereafter, Fianna Fáil, Fine Gael and indeed the Labour Party, shared a bi-partisan non-violent Northern Ireland policy. Of course, there were differences of emphasis among Oireachtas parties in relation to Northern Ireland.[254] However, all mainstream Southern political parties agreed that Irish unity could not be secured in the immediate term. Most significantly, they agreed that only a peaceful – non militant – policy constituted a workable solution to ending partition. As Lynch articulated, in a speech in honour of Frank Aiken in May 1971, 'There is no substitute for a peaceful approach [to partition] and all parties in Dáil Éireann have repeatedly and unambiguously emphasised this'.[255]

Akin to Fianna Fáil, when the violence first broke out in Northern Ireland in 1969, Fine Gael had been caught off guard. By this time, they too had no concrete policy towards Northern Ireland. Garret FitzGerald recalled that when the Bogside erupted in 1969, there was an 'absence of any clear framework of party policy in relation to Northern Ireland'. The result, he said, in a clearly veiled dig at Fianna Fáil, was that it 'left a dangerous vacuum, that atavistic filling of which in conditions of great tension carried evident dangers'.[256] Fitzgerald, thus, took upon himself to draw up Fine Gael's Northern Ireland policy. Partition, he maintained, could never be secured by physical force and that only with the consent of the majority of the population of Northern Ireland could Irish unity be secured.[257] These two policies, thereafter, formed the crux of Fine Gael's official stance on Northern Ireland.[258] While it would take until the mid-1980s before Fianna Fáil officially acknowledged the 'principle of consent', like Fine Gael, by 1971, both parties were in broad agreement on the issue of a peaceful solution to partition.[259]

Equally, by 1971, the Labour Party, under the leadership of Brendan Corish and the party's spokesman on Northern Ireland, Conor Cruise O'Brien, was a firm proponent of finding a peaceful solution to partition. Prior to the outbreak of the Troubles, in a similar vein to Fianna Fáil, Labour, in the words of Niamh Puirséil, had 'not really had a policy on the North. It had supported civil rights and still professed its support for a united Ireland, but beyond these vague goals there was nothing concrete'.[260] Thereafter, O'Brien's conciliatory and non-violent policies on Northern Ireland became those of the party.[261]

Disgusted with Fianna Fáil's alleged *volte face* on Northern Ireland, in May 1971, Kevin Boland resigned from the party. Later that year he established a new political party, Aontacht Éireann. Seán Sherwin TD soon followed, leaving Fianna Fáil and defecting to Boland's new party.[262] Aontacht Éireann failed to make an impact on Irish politics and eventually disbanded in 1976. Boland was left to complain that the people 'didn't want a Republican Party'.[263] The British Embassy in Dublin wrote that Boland's departure from Fianna Fáil, for the immediate period, at least, was the 'last sign of open revolt' against Lynch's leadership and his stance on Northern Ireland.[264]

Boland's exit was soon followed by Blaney's expulsion in 1972. Blaney easily retained his seat in Donegal as an independent Fianna Fáil TD, but remained in the political wilderness thereafter. He never wavered from his absolute belief that the use of physical force had always and still did represent legitimate Fianna Fáil policy, 'that force could not be ruled out if the circumstances in Northern Ireland demanded'.[265] Although Haughey had no intention of joining his former allies in the wilderness, he found himself marginalised within Fianna Fáil. He publicly accepted Lynch's leadership and towed the party-line.

Thus, by the summer of 1971, the Fianna Fáil government had not only survived the most turbulent period in the party's history, but in the process became a much more effective and cohesive unit. The removal of Lynch's leading opponents from the cabinet eliminated the division that had paralysed and distorted the government's stance on partition. Speaking at a gathering of the Fianna Fáil parliamentary party in September 1971, Lynch reminded those in attendance that 'a united Fianna Fáil party was the only possible hope of achieving' a united Ireland.[266] Henceforth, Fianna Fáil's Northern Ireland policy, channelled through Lynch, followed a moderate and conciliatory approach. Ambiguity, sympathy or support for political violence was unequivocally rejected by the Lynch-led Fianna Fáil government.

NOTES

1. Author's interview with Kenneth Bloomfield, 2 June 2006.
2. See, for example, Lemass's Oxford Address, 15 Oct. 1959. Reprinted, *The Irish Times*, 16 Oct. 1959.
3. *The Irish Times*, 27 March 1975.
4. See Lemass's comments, *Kerryman*, 23 April 1966.
5. See Conor Cruise O'Brien, *States of Ireland* (London, Viking, 1972), 143. See also Richard English's comments, *Irish Freedom, the History of Irish Nationalism in Ireland* (London: Pan Macmillan, 2006), 371–372.
6. Roisín Higgins, 'Sites of memory and memorial in 1966', in Mary E. Daly and Margaret O'Callaghan (eds.) *1916 in 1966, Commemorating the Easter Rising* (Dublin: Royal Irish Academy, 2007), 275.
7. Mary E. Daly and Margaret O'Callaghan, 'Introduction – Irish Modernity and "The Patriot Dead" in 1966', in Daly and O'Callaghan (eds.), *1916 in 1966, Commemorating the Easter Rising*, 15.
8. National Archives of the United Kingdom (NAUK) Prime Minister's Office (PREM), 13/980, memorandum addressed to British prime minister, Harold Wilson, 4 April 1966.
9. See the *Anglo-Celt*, *Connacht Tribune*, *Kerryman*, and *Southern Star*, during April 1966.
10. Clones County Council, Co. Monaghan, issued a resolution to the Irish government in protest at the British Army crossing the Irish border at Lackey Bridge on the outskirts of Clones. See *Anglo-Celt*, 11 April 1966.
11. Michael Kennedy, *Division and Consensus, the Politics of Cross-Border Relations in Ireland, 1925–1969* (Dublin: Institute for Public Administration, 2000), 267.
12. *The Irish Times*, 4 May 1966.
13. See *The Irish Times*, 3 Oct. and 20 Oct. 1966.
14. *Irish Press*, 20 Oct. 1966.
15. See Dick Walsh, *Irish Times* supplement, *After Lemass, deluge or desert?*. 19 May 1976.
16. University College Dublin Archives (UCDA) Fianna Fáil Party Papers P176/448, meeting of Fianna Fáil parliamentary party, 9 Nov. 1966.
17. See UCDA Seán MacEntee Papers P67/734, draft letter by MacEntee concerning Lemass's decision to resign as taoiseach and leader of Fianna Fáil, Nov. 1966. (It is unclear if MacEntee actually read this letter at a meeting of the parliamentary party).
18. UCDA Frank Aiken Papers P104/2083 (2), note by Aiken on Lemass's decision to retire, 10 Nov. 1966.
19. UCDA P176/448, meeting of Fianna Fáil parliamentary party, 9 Nov. 1966.
20. UCDA P176/448, meeting of Fianna Fáil parliamentary party, 9 Nov. 1966.
21. See John Horgan, *Seán Lemass, The Enigmatic Patriot* (Dublin: Gill and Macmillan, 1999), 339.
22. These two councils were established under the British–Irish Agreement Act of 1999. See Michael Kennedy 'Northern Ireland and cross-border co-operation', in Brian Girvin and Gary Murphy (eds.), *The Lemass Era-Politics and Society in the Ireland of Seán Lemass*

(Dublin: UCD Press, 2005), 120.

23.   *The Irish Times*, 18 Nov. 1966.

24.   *The Irish Times*, 18 Nov. 1966.

25.   NAUK Dominions Office (DO) 215/20, British Ambassador to Ireland, Sir Geofroy Tory to secretary of state for Commonwealth Relations, Arthur Bottomley, 18 Nov. 1966.

26.   National Archives of Ireland (NAI) Department of Taoiseach (DT) 2000/6/657, address by Lynch to the Anglo-Irish Parliamentary Group, 30 Oct. 1968.

27.   *The Irish Times*, 18 Nov. 1966.

28.   Terence O'Neill, *The Autobiography of Terence O'Neill* (London: Rupert Hart-Davis, 1972), 73–75.

29.   See 'My life and times' by Jack Lynch, *Magill*, Nov. 1979, 44.

30.   Kennedy, *Division and Consensus*, 297.

31.   Dermot Keogh, *Jack Lynch, a Biography* (Dublin: Gill and Macmillan, 2008), 136.

32.   NAI Department of External Affairs (DEA) 98/3/33, record of O'Neill's visit to Dublin, 8 Jan. 1968.

33.   See Lynch's comments. Dáil Éireann Debate (DE), 30 Jan. 1968. Vol. 232, No. 1, col. 8.

34.   See, for example, leader of the Labour Party, Brendan Corish's comments. DE, 30 Jan. 1968. Vol. 232, No. 1, col. 7–8.

35.   See Lynch's comments. DE, 30 Jan. 1968. Vol. 236, No. 7, col. 1088.

36.   *Kerryman*, 19 Oct. 1968.

37.   *Irish Times*, 7 Oct. 1968.

38.   *The Irish Times*, 9 Oct. 1968.

39.   *The Irish Times*, 31 Oct. 1968.

40.   *Irish Press*, 9 Nov. 1968.

41.   See Donnacha Ó Beacháin, *Destiny of the Soldiers: Fianna Fáil, Irish Republicanism and the IRA, 1926–1973* (Dublin: Gill and Macmillan, 2011), 272.

42.   See, for example, NAI DT 2000/6/657, speech by Lynch, Tipperary town, 8 Oct. 1968 and NAI D/T 2000/6/657, press conference by Lynch, Irish Embassy, London, 30 Oct. 1968.

43.   See Pádraig Faulkner's comments in his work, *As I saw It, Reviewing over 30 years of Fianna Fáil and Irish Politics* (Dublin: Wolfhound, 2005), 89.

44.   UCDA Patrick Hillery Papers P205/101, record of Hillery's recollections of internal Fianna Fáil attitude to Lynch and Northern Ireland. Hillery's handwritten diary entry, 13 Jan. 1978.

45.   See comments by Mr B.L. Markey. *The Irish Times*, 12 Nov. 1968.

46.   NAI DT Jack Lynch Papers, 2001/8/1, Whitaker to Lynch, 11 Nov. 1968.

47.   UCDA P176/348, meeting of Fianna Fáil National Executive, 11 Nov. 1968. See also, *The Irish Times*, Nov. 1968.

48.   *The Irish Times*, 12 Nov. 1968.

49.   *The Irish Times*, 12 Nov. 1968.

50.   UCDA P205/101, record of Hillery's recollections of internal Fianna Fáil attitude to Lynch and Northern Ireland. Hillery's handwritten diary entry, 13 Jan. 1978.

51.   UCDA P176/448, meeting of Fianna Fáil parliamentary party, 13 Nov. 1968.

52.   DE, 30 Jan. 1968. Vol. 237, No. 1, cols. 162–163.

53.   *The Irish Times*, 10 April 1969.

54.   *The Irish Times*, 11 April 1969.

55.   Those in attendance included: Seán Lemass, Seán MacEntee, Kevin and Gerald Boland and Eoin Ryan. UCDA P176/350, meeting of Fianna Fáil National Executive, 14 April 1969.

56.   Ó Beacháin, *Destiny of the Soldiers*, 276.

57.   See, for example, NAI DEA 2000/6/658, meeting between Irish minister for external affairs, Patrick Hillery and secretary for state for the Commonwealth Office, Michael Stewart, 1 Aug. 1969.

58.   The above information is taken from my 2006 MA dissertation: *The Battle of the Bogside: A Comparative Analysis of the Irish, British and Northern Ireland Governments' Reaction to the Outbreak of Violence in Derry, 12–15 August 1969.* This work is available from

    UCDA.

59. O'Brien, *States of Ireland*, 196.

60. As Haughey refrained from publicly speaking on this issue and his general involvement in the arms crisis for the remainder of his life, one cannot state with absolute certainty that he advocated sending the Irish army into Northern Ireland. Nonetheless, within the general literature an agreement has emerged supporting the argument that Haughey did demand that the government send the army into Northern Ireland. See Dick Walsh, *The Party, Inside Fianna* Fáil (Dublin: Gill and Macmillan, 1986), 96; Stephen Collins, *The Power Game, Fianna Fáil Since Lemass* (Dublin: O'Brien Press, 2000), 48; and lastly, Keogh, *Jack Lynch*, 169.

61. John Walsh, *Patrick Hillery, The Official Biography* (Dublin: New Ireland, 2008), 174.

62. Ronan Fanning, 'Playing it cool: the response of the British and Irish governments to the crisis in Northern Ireland, 1968–9', *Irish Studies in International Affairs*, Vol. 12 (2001), 57–85; 73–74.

63. NAI 12 Government Cabinet minutes, 2000/9/1, record of Irish government cabinet meeting, 13 Aug. 1969.

64. For a complete version of Lynch's speech, see NAI DT 2000/6/657, 'Statement by the Taoiseach, Mr J. Lynch', 13 Aug. 1969.

65. *The Irish Times*, 14 Aug. 1969.

66. James Callaghan, *A House Divided, the Dilemma of Northern Ireland* (Glasgow, London: Collins, 1973), 40.

67. NAUK Northern Ireland Files (CJ) 3/22, Telegram no. 176, Gilchrist to Foreign and Commonwealth Office, 14 Aug. 1969.

68. NAUK CJ 3/22, Telegram no. 176 sent by Gilchrist to Foreign and Commonwealth Office, 14 Aug. 1969.

69. UCDA P205/35, record of Hillery's recollections of Irish cabinet meetings, mid-Aug. 1969. Hillery's typed notes, marked 'August 1969'.

70. UCDA P205/35, record of Hillery's recollections of Irish cabinet meetings, mid-Aug. 1969. Hillery's typed notes, marked 'August 1969'.

71. NAI 12 Government Cabinet minutes, 2000/9/1, record of Irish government cabinet meetings, 14 Aug. 1969

72. Museum of Free Derry, *Barricade Bulletin*, 14 Aug. 1969.

73. Author's interview with Eamonn McCann, 22 March 2006.

74. See the *Scarman Report, Violence and Civil Disturbances in Northern Ireland 1969–72* (London, 1972), 34.

75. Author's interview with Kenneth Bloomfield, 2 June 2006.

76. *The Irish Times*, 15 Aug. 1969.

77. See *Irish Independent*, 15 Aug. 1969.

78. Author's interview with Eamonn McCann, 22 March 2006.

79. See *Irish Independent*, 15 Aug. 1969.

80. NAUK CJ 3/22, Telegram sent by Gilchrist to Foreign and Commonwealth Office, 15 Aug. 1969.

81. UCDA T.K. Whitaker Papers P107/104, note recalling a request for Whitaker to contact the taoiseach, 15 Aug. 1969.

82. UCDA P107/104, note recalling a request for Whitaker to contact the taoiseach, 15 Aug. 1969.

83. UCDA P107/105, note of conversation between Whitaker and taoiseach with regard to Northern Ireland, 15 Aug. 1969.

84. UCDA P107/105, note of conversation between Whitaker and taoiseach with regard to Northern Ireland, 15 Aug. 1969.

85. UCDA P107/105, note of conversation between Whitaker and taoiseach with regard to Northern Ireland, 15 Aug. 1969.

86. It was also decided to request that the British agree to send a United Nations peace-keeping force into Northern Ireland; and lastly, that Haughey's department should expand the Garda Síochána intelligence service in Northern Ireland. See NAI 12 Government

Cabinet minutes, 2000/9/1, record of Irish government cabinet meetings, 15 Aug. 1969.

87. T. Dwyer, *A Biography of Jack Lynch* (Cork: Mercier Press, 2001), 183.

88. Faulkner, *As I Saw it*, 90–91.

89. Dwyer, *Jack Lynch*, 183.

90. Author's interview with Pádraig Faulkner, 6 June 2006.

91. NAI DEA 2000/5/38, report of discussion at Foreign and Commonwealth Office London concerning Northern Ireland, 15 Aug. 1969.

92. NAI DEA 2000/5/38, report of discussion at Foreign and Commonwealth Office London concerning Northern Ireland, 15 Aug. 1969.

93. *The Irish Times*, 16 Aug. 1969.

94. UCDA P176/448, meeting of Fianna Fáil parliamentary party, 5 Sept. 1969.

95. NAI DT 2000/6/659 9361O, memorandum by Erskine Childers on Northern Ireland, 26 Aug. 1969.

96. *The Irish Times*, 21 Sept. 1969.

97. *The Irish Times*, 21 Sept. 1969. Speaking in Bray, Co. Wicklow, in Nov. 1969, Lynch again stated that 'we have no intention of using our Defence Forces to intervene in the affairs of Northern Ireland'. See Jack Lynch, *Speeches and Statements, Irish Unity Northern Ireland Anglo-Irish Relations, August 1969 – October 1971* (Dublin, Government information bureau, 1972), 13–14.

98. *The Irish Times*, 21 Sept. 1969.

99. Fanning, 'Playing it cool', 79.

100. See Michael Kennedy, '"This tragic and most intractable problem': the reaction of the Department of External Affairs to the outbreak of the Trouble in Northern Ireland", *Irish Studies in International Affairs*, Vol. 12 (2001), 87–95; 87.

101. Kennedy, 'This tragic and most intractable problem', 88.

102. See Walsh, *Patrick Hillery*, 207–08.

103. Fanning, 'Playing it cool', 80.

104. Fanning, 'Playing it cool', 80.

105. UCDA P205/35, memorandum for the information of the government, 'policy in relation to Northern Ireland', 28 Nov. 1969.

106. UCDA P205/35, memorandum for the information of the government, 'policy in relation to Northern Ireland', 28 Nov. 1969.

107. UCDA P205/35, memorandum for the information of the government, 'policy in relation to Northern Ireland', 28 Nov. 1969.

108. Kennedy, 'This tragic and most intractable problem', 95.

109. *Irish Press*, 8 Dec. 1969.

110. *The Irish Times*, 10 Dec. 1969.

111. NAI DT 2000/6/662, S9361R, record of meeting between Patrick Hillery and British secretary of state for foreign affairs, George Thompson, 10 Dec. 1969.

112. NAI DT 2000/6/662, Government Information Bureau release, 9 Dec. 1969.

113. *The Irish Times*, 15 Dec. 1969.

114. *The Irish Times*, 15 Dec. 1969.

115. See Lynch, *Speeches and Statements, Irish Unity Northern Ireland Anglo-Irish Relations*, 15–17.

116. See Lynch's 'address over Radio Telefis Éireann, 11 July 1970'. Lynch, *Speeches and Statements, Irish Unity Northern Ireland Anglo-Irish Relations*, 22–24.

117. NAI DT 2000/6/658, Draft G. C. 13/14, Cabinet Minutes, 16 Aug. 1969.

118. The investigation by the Public Accounts Committee revealed that a substantial percentage of the relief fund for the victims of distress in Northern Ireland was used to buy arms. The evidence given before the committee reported that approximately £29,000, less than a third of the original allocation of relief, was actually spent on its intended purpose. The rest of the money was, in fact, diverted to other purposes, including the allocation of £32,000 to buy arms in West Germany. See Public Accounts Committee, *Interim and Final Reports* (Dublin, 1972), 45–49.

119. NAI DEA 2001/8/3, record of 'sequence of events from 1 August, 1969 to 18 August 1969'.

See also Martin Mansergh, *The Legacy of History* (Cork: Mercier Press, 2003), 398.

120. NAI DT 2000/9/2, secret memorandum by Seán Ronan, 18 Aug. 1969.
121. Henry Patterson, *Ireland Since 1939, Persistence of Conflict* (Dublin: Penguin Ireland, 2006), 174.
122. NAUK Foreign and Commonwealth Office (FCO) 33/1596, British Ambassador to Ireland, Sir John Peck to the FCO, April, 1971. 'Mr Blaney attacks Mr Lynch', record of Blaney's speech at a Fianna Fáil meeting at Arklow, Co. Wicklow (date unknown).
123. For an account of the attempts to import arms into Ireland, first by boat and subsequently by air, see Bruce Arnold, *Haughey, His Life and Unlucky Deeds* (London: Harper Collins, 1993), 88–89.
124. Public Accounts Committee, *Interim and Final Reports* (Dublin, 1972), 45.
125. Justin O'Brien, *The Arms Trial* (Dublin: Gill and Macmillan, 2000), 118.
126. According to the secretary to the Department of Justice, Peter Berry, on 19 Aug. 1969, the Irish Special Branch informed Berry that an undefined Fianna Fáil minister, the previous week, had held a meeting with the Chief of Staff of the IRA, Cathal Goulding, at which 'a deal had been made' that the IRA would have a 'free hand in operating a cross Border campaign in the North', provided it called off its campaign of violence in the South. The identity of the minister was believed to be Blaney, Boland or Haughey; although Berry could not believe that the latter could have any involvement given Haughey's suppression of the IRA border campaign during the early 1960s. See 'The Peter Berry Papers', *Magill* (1980), 51–52.
127. NAUK FCO/33/1596, British Ambassador to Ireland, Sir John Peck to the FCO, April, 1971. 'Mr Blaney attacks Mr Lynch', record of Blaney's speech at a Fianna Fáil meeting at Arklow, Co. Wicklow (date unknown). See also Patterson, *Ireland Since 1939, Persistence of Conflict*, 175.
128. Walsh, *Paddy Hillery*, 214.
129. See for example, Catherine O'Donnell, *Fianna Fáil, Irish Republicanism and the Northern Ireland Troubles, 1968–2005* (Dublin: Irish Academic Press, 2007), 29; Justin O'Brien, *The Modern Prince: Charles J. Haughey and the Quest for Power* (Dublin: Merlin, 2002), 4 & 6; Arnold, *Haughey, His Life and Unlucky Deeds*, 78–79; and Conor Cruise O'Brien, *States of Ireland* (London: Viking, 1972), 188–190. For a detailed overview of the Arms Crisis and Haughey's involvement with the affair see Justin O'Brien, *The Arms Trial*.
130. Dick Walsh, *The Irish Times* supplement, 31 Jan. 1992.
131. Ó Beacháin, *Destiny of the Soldiers*, 294.
132. Arnold, *Haughey*, 78.
133. See Chapter Four, pp.170-176.
134. NAUK CJ 3/100, record of confidential meeting between Gilchrist and Haughey, 4 Oct. 1969.
135. NAUK CJ 3/100, record of confidential meeting between Gilchrist and Haughey, 4 Oct. 1969.
136. Patterson, *Ireland Since 1939*, 174–175.
137. Keogh, *Jack Lynch*, 259.
138. Keogh, *Jack Lynch*, 260–261.
139. Author's interview with Pádraig Faulkner, 6 June 2006. See also Faulkner, *As I Saw It*, 96.
140. Faulkner, *As I Saw It*, 96.
141. See Neil Blaney, 'Neil Blaney: past and the future', *Magill* (2 May, 1985), 19.
142. UCDA P205/99, recollection of Hillery's memories during the emotive month of May 1970. Hillery's handwritten diary entry, July 1977.
143. Horgan, *Seán Lemass*, 344.
144. UCDA P205/98, recollection of conversation between Hillery and de Valera, 1970/1971. Hillery's handwritten diary entry, 19 Jan. 1977.
145. UCDA P104/2341, typescript copy of an article by Geraldine Kennedy, 'Frank Aiken: the story that was never told', as related by Francis Aiken (Frank Aiken's son), June 1983.
146. Keogh, *Jack Lynch*, 262–263.
147. Keogh, *Jack Lynch*, 262.
148. UCDA P205/99, record of telephone conversation between Hillery and Lemass, May

1970. Hillery's handwritten diary entry, July 1977.

149. Faulkner, *As I Saw It*, 99.

150. Keogh, *Jack Lynch*, 263.

151. UCDA P176/448, meeting of Fianna Fáil parliamentary party, 6 May 1970.

152. Keogh, *Jack Lynch*, 263.

153. Collins, *The Power Game*, 79.

154. Walsh, *Patrick Hillery*, 224.

155. *The Irish Times*, 3 June 1970.

156. UCDA P104/8836, handwritten letter from Aiken to Lynch, undated, sometime from 6 to 12 May 1970.

157. UCDA P176/448, meeting of Fianna Fáil parliamentary party, 13 May 1970.

158. UCDA P104/8836, handwritten letter from Aiken to Lynch, 14 May 1970.

159. UCDA P176/448, meeting of Fianna Fáil parliamentary party, 3 June 1970. See also *The Irish Times*, 4 June 1970.

160. UCDA P176/448, meeting of Fianna Fáil parliamentary party, 4 June 1970. See also *The Irish Times*, 5 June 1970.

161. UCDA P176/348, meeting of Fianna Fáil National Executive, 22 June 1970.

162. See UCDA P67/476 (1), record of 'special meeting of Fianna Fáil National Executive, 22 June 1970 (Monday), Leinster House, 7pm'.

163. UCDA P67/475 (8), copy of MacEntee's handwritten notes, 22 June 1970.

164. *The Irish Times*, 24 June 1970.

165. *The Irish Times*, 25 June 1970.

166. UCDA P205/99, Hillery's handwritten diary entry, July 1977.

167. *The Irish Times*, 30 June 1970.

168. Walsh, *Patrick Hillery*, 258.

169. See 'Statement of 28 June, 1970', Lynch, *Speeches and Statements, Irish Unity Northern Ireland Anglo-Irish Relations*, 18–19.

170. See, for example, O'Brien, *The Arms Trial*, 187–213.

171. Keogh, *Jack Lynch*, 268.

172. See Haughey's comments in *The Irish Times*, 24 Oct. 1970.

173. Patterson, *Ireland Since 1939*, 176.

174. Keogh, *Jack Lynch*, 317.

175. Ó Beacháin, *Destiny of the Soldiers*, 306.

176. *The Irish Times*, 26 Oct. 1970.

177. The remaining TDs reported to have supported the anti-partitionist stance on Northern Ireland were: Dublin North-West TD, Richard Gogan; North-East Donegal TD, Liam Cunningham; Dublin South-West TD, Seán Sherwin; and Dublin South-West TD, Joe Dowling. See NAUK FCO 33/1201, letter entitled 'Fianna Fáil' record of article in *Hibernia*, issued by D.E.S. Blatherwick, British Embassy, Dublin, 12 June 1970.

178. Walsh, *The Party, Inside Fianna Fáil*, 119.

179. NAUK FCO 33/1596, letter entitled 'defection in Fianna Fáil', issued by D.E.S. Blatherwick, British Embassy, Dublin, 19 Aug. 1971.

180. Walsh, *The Party, Inside Fianna Fáil*, 119.

181. NAUK FCO 33/1596, letter entitled 'defection in Fianna Fáil', issued by D.E.S. Blatherwick, British Embassy, Dublin, 19 Aug. 1971.

182. UCD P176/350, meeting of Fianna Fáil National Executive, 27 April 1970.

183. UCD P176/350, meeting of Fianna Fáil National Executive, 26 Oct. 1970.

184. Walsh, *Patrick Hillery*, 239.

185. See O'Brien, *States of Ireland*, 222. O'Brien was married to MacEntee's daughter, Maire.

186. NAUK FCO/33/1596, D.E.S. Blatherwick to A.C. Thorpe Esq., Western European Department, FCO, 19 Aug. 1971.

187. For an excellent analysis of Hillery's visit to the Falls Road, see William O'Brien, 'The Political Implications of Patrick Hillery's Visit to the Falls Road on 6 July'. MA thesis (2006), available from UCDA.

188. UCDA P205/37, typed account of Hillery's decision to travel to Belfast, undated.

189. O'Brien, 'The political implications of Patrick Hillery's visit to the Falls Road on 6 July', 4.

190. UCDA P205/37, typed account of Hillery's decision to travel to Belfast, undated.

191. O'Brien, 'The political implications of Patrick Hillery's visit to the Falls Road on 6 July', 14.

192. O'Brien, 'The political implications of Patrick Hillery's visit to the Falls Road on 6 July', 15.

193. NAI DEA 2001/43/1351, *Financial Times* report of Hillery's Belfast visit, 8 July 1970.

194. UCDA P205/37, MacEntee to Hillery, 11 July 1970.

195. See Enda Staunton, *The Nationalists of Northern Ireland, 1918–1973* (Dublin: Columba Press, 2001), 273–274.

196. Lynch also ruled out the proposal of permitting Northern Ireland Nationalist entry to Dáil Éireann. *The Irish Times*, 18 Nov. 1966.

197. UCDA P104/7003, copy of draft confidential letter from McCann to all Irish missions abroad, Feb. 1969.

198. *The Irish Times*, 2 Nov. 1967.

199. Horgan, *Seán Lemass*, 342.

200. NAI DT 99/1/76, memorandum by secretary of the Department of Taoiseach, Nicholas Nolan, 3 Nov. 1967.

201. Ó Beacháin, *Destiny of the Soldiers*, 264.

202. NAI DT 99/1/76, memorandum by secretary of the Department of Taoiseach, Nicholas Nolan, 3 Nov. 1967.

203. Seán Farren, *The SDLP, the Struggle for Agreement in Northern Ireland* (Dublin: Four Courts Press, 2010), 24.

204. Staunton, *The Nationalists of Northern Ireland*, 273–274.

205. Staunton, *The Nationalists of Northern Ireland*, 273–274.

206. Staunton, *The Nationalists of Northern Ireland*, 274.

207. NAI DT 2000/6/659 S 9361O, memorandum by Erskine Childers on Northern Ireland, 26 Aug. 1969.

208. Patterson, *Ireland Since 1939*, 235–236.

209. Farren, *The SDLP, The Struggle for Agreement in Northern Ireland*, 24.

210. See Michael McKeown, *The Greening of a Nationalist* (Dublin: Murlough Press 1986), 80.

211. Patterson, *Ireland Since 1939*, 233.

212. Farren, *The SDLP, The Struggle for Agreement in Northern Ireland*, 28.

213. Farren, *The SDLP, The Struggle for Agreement in Northern Ireland*, 28.

214. Austin Currie, *All Hell Will Break Loose* (Dublin: O'Brien Press, 2004), 156–158.

215. Currie, *All Hell Will Break Loose*, 156–158.

216. Paddy Devlin, *Straight Left, an Autobiography, Paddy Devlin* (Belfast: Blackstaff, 1994), 145.

217. Staunton, *The Nationalists of Northern Ireland*, 276.

218. Keogh, *Jack Lynch*, 233.

219. See NAUK FCO 33/1596, 'Fianna Fáil policy on Northern Ireland question'. D.W.S. Blatherwick, British Embassy in Ireland to Roger B. Bone, Western European Department, Foreign and Commonwealth Office, 22 Nov. 1971.

220. This was ultimately established in late 1973 with the Sunningdale Agreement, which permitted an 'Irish Dimension' in Northern Ireland affairs and created power-sharing Executive, representing eleven members, including Ulster Unionists and the SDLP.

221. NAUK FCO 33/1201, letter entitled 'Government crisis', issued by D.E.S. Blatherwick, British Embassy, Dublin, 31 Oct. 1970.

222. For an account of the events of the 1971 Fianna Fáil Ard Fheis, See *The Irish Times*, 22 Feb. 1971.

223. *Irish Independent*, 21 Feb. 1971.

224. *Irish Independent*, 21 Feb. 1971.

225. *Irish Independent*, 22 Feb. 1971.

226. The above recollection is taken from Keogh, *Jack Lynch*, 280–281.

227. *The Irish Times*, 22 Feb. 1971.

228. *The Irish Times*, 22 Feb. 1971.

229. *The Irish Times*, 22 Feb. 1971.
230. *The Irish Times*, 22 Feb. 1971.
231. *The Irish Times*, 22 Feb. 1971.
232. Keogh, *Jack Lynch*, 281.
233. *Kerryman*, 27 Feb. 1971.
234. *The Irish Times*, 22 Feb. 1971.
235. Keogh, *Jack Lynch*, 282.
236. *The Irish Times*, 22 Feb. 1971.
237. *The Irish Times*, 22 Feb. 1971.
238. *The Irish Times*, 22 Feb. 1971.
239. See Lynch's Presidential address, Fianna Fáil Ard Fheis, 20 Feb. 1971. Lynch, *Speeches and Statements, Irish Unity Northern Ireland Anglo-Irish Relations*, 41–48.
240. NAUK FCO 33/1596, British Ambassador to Ireland, John Peck to Sir Stewart Crawford, Foreign and Commonwealth Office, 1 June 1971.
241. *The Irish Times*, 22 Feb. 1971.
242. NAUK FCO 33/1596, British Ambassador to Ireland, John Peck to Sir Stewart Crawford, Foreign and Commonwealth Office, 1 June 1971.
243. Ó Beacháin, *Destiny of the Soldiers*, 317.
244. Gerald Carroll P.C.; Denis O'Sullivan (vice-chairman Cork North-West constituency); Pat Lane (Comhairle delegate); Seamus O'Donovan (former secretary, O'Neill Crawley cumann); James Christopher Barry (vice-chairman, Gerard Hourigan cumann); and J. J. O'Donovan (chairman P. H. Pearse cumann); all resigned from Fianna Fáil. See NAUK FCO 33/1596, letter entitled 'new Republican Party', issued by D.E.S. Blatherwick, British Embassy, Dublin, 19 Aug. 1971.
245. NAUK FCO 33/1596, letter entitled 'new Republican Party', issued by D.E.S. Blatherwick, British Embassy, Dublin, 19 Aug. 1971.
246. NAUK FCO 33/1596, British Ambassador to Ireland, John Peck to officials in the Foreign and Commonwealth Office, 9 March 1971.
247. See UCDA P176/350, meeting of Fianna Fáil National Executive, 13 Sept. 1971.
248. See UCDA P176/448, meeting of Fianna Fáil parliamentary party, 22 Sept. 1971.
249. This view was expressed by C.A. Leonard Runai Oinigh, honorary secretary of the North Co. Dublin Comhairle Dáilcheantair. UCD P176/350, meeting of Fianna Fáil National Executive, 22 Nov. 1971.
250. A survey by a Dublin magazine, *This Week*, in May 1970 found that only 17% of those asked were in favour of sending the Irish Army into Northern Ireland in the event of a repetition of Aug. 1969. Only 14% favoured the use of force to end partition. In March 1972, a poll by the *Sunday Telegraph* found that 85% of those surveyed were against the current IRA campaign in Northern Ireland. See O'Brien, *States of Ireland*, 197.
251. Kevin Boland, *The Rise and Decline of Fianna Fáil* (Dublin: Mercier Press, 1982), 70–72.
252. Kevin Boland, *Up Dev* (published by the author, 1977), 41.
253. Boland, *The Rise and Decline of Fianna Fáil*, 72.
254. For an overview of Fine Gael's position on Northern Ireland from Aug. 1969 to Feb. 1973, see Garret FitzGerald, *All in a Life, Garret FitzGerald, an Autobiography* (Dublin: Gill and Macmillan, 1991), 88–111. For an overview of the Labour Party's attitude to Northern Ireland from 1969 to 1973, see Niamh Puirséil, *The Irish Labour Party, 1922–73* (Dublin: UCD Press, 2007), 288–299.
255. NAUK FCO 33/1596, copy of speech by Lynch at a dinner of the South Louth Comhairle Ceantair, Fianna Fáil, at Fairways Hotel, Dundalk, 28 May 1971.
256. FitzGerald, *All in a Life*, 88.
257. FitzGerald, *All in a Life*, 88–89.
258. See Garreth Ivory, 'Revisions in nationalist discourse among Irish political parties', *Irish Political Studies*, 14:1, (1999), 84–103: 89–90.
259. For further analysis of Fianna Fáil and the 'principle of consent' see Stephen Kelly, 'The politics of terminology: Seán Lemass and Ulster question, 1959–1966', in Caoimhe Nic Dháibhéid and Colin Reid (eds.), *From Parnell to Paisley: Constitutional and Revolutionary*

Politics in Ireland, 1879 – 2008 (Dublin: Irish Academic Press, 2010), 151–153.

260. Puirséil, *The Irish Labour Party, 1922–73*, 289.

261. That said, within the Labour Party, there were those who sympathised with the physical force policy. Labour TDs, such as David Thornley and Seán Treacy, were the most prominent in their sympathy for political violence. Labour's grass-roots were equally divided and throughout the early 1970s there was a strong support among the Dublin membership for the IRA's stance. Puirséil, *The Irish Labour Party, 1922–73*, 291.

262. O'Donnell, *Fianna Fáil, Irish Republicanism and the Northern Ireland Troubles*, 39.

263. Boland, *Up Dev*, 41.

264. NAUK FCO 33/1596, British Ambassador to Ireland, John Peck to Sir Stewart Crawford, Foreign and Commonwealth Office, 1 June 1971.

265. See Blaney, 'Neil Blaney: past and the future', 18.

266. UCDA P176/448, meeting of Fianna Fáil parliamentary party, 22 Sept. 1971.

Conclusion

'Fianna Fáil ... pay lip service to the reunification ideal ... I don't believe Dublin wants to see an end to partition'.

[Eric D. O'Gowan, Co. Cavan, 22 June 1951][1]

EPILOGUE: FIANNA FÁIL, PARTITION AND NORTHERN IRELAND, 1971 – 1979

Jack Lynch's victory over the anti-partitionists at the Fianna Fáil Ard Fheis in February 1971 finally dispelled the argument, so prevalent within the party, that the use of physical force was a legitimate policy in the attainment of a united Ireland. In the aftermath of the party conference Lynch repeatedly drove this message home. In a statement, issued in late March 1971, he said that his government 'totally repudiate[d] any recourse to violence'. 'We re-affirm', he pronounced, 'our view that nothing is to be gained by it [the use of force] either within the North or in relation to the eventual unification of Ireland'.[2] Speaking in Dundalk in May of that year, he again stipulated that 'There is no substitute for a peaceful approach and all political parties in Dáil Éireann have repeatedly and unambiguously emphasised this'.[3]

Nonetheless, prior to his expulsion from the party in 1972, Neil Blaney continued to attack Lynch's leadership and Fianna Fáil's Northern Ireland policy. Speaking in Arklow in April 1971, Blaney asserted that Northern Catholics were morally entitled to use violence to defend themselves if they came under 'murderous attacks' from the Northern Ireland apparatus.[4] Lynch reacted immediately to Blaney's outburst and in response the Fianna Fáil National Executive informed all party cumainn of the need to retain a conciliatory and pacifist attitude to the attainment of Irish unity.[5]

It was events outside Fianna Fáil's control that again stirred up the ghosts of physical force nationalism. The escalation of the IRA campaign in Northern Ireland accelerated the ultimate collapse of the Northern Ireland state. Although the Conservative government in London, under prime minister, Edward Heath, strongly supported keeping Northern Ireland prime minister, Chichester Clark in office, by March 1971, the latter's position was untenable. London sought to avert the prospect of direct rule, which would be the direct consequence of the collapse of the Stormont government, by propping up the Chichester Clark regime. However, the murder of three British soldiers in Belfast on 10 March 1971 dealt the final blow to the Northern Ireland prime minister's administration. Chichester Clark resigned on 21 March. His replacement as Northern Ireland prime minister, Brian Faulkner, although an extremely capable politician, was deeply mistrusted by Northern nationalists and the Fianna Fáil government in Dublin.

By this point, in the words of Eamonn Gallagher, Northern Ireland was like a 'volcano', ready to erupt at any time.[6] The first eruption occurred in August 1971, when Lynch received a personal message from Heath that the British government, willed on by Faulkner, intended to introduce internment without trial in Northern Ireland. Operation Demetrius began in the early hours of the morning of 9 August; 464 people (mostly Catholics) were arrested in the initial raids, with 342 being detained without trial.[7] The deployment of internment was a grave blunder, which only heightened Catholic alienation from the Northern Ireland state.

On 11 August, Charles J. Haughey, now a backbencher Fianna Fáil TD, issued an emotive public statement deploring the actions of the British government and foreshadowing his thesis that Northern Ireland was a 'failed political entity'. He pronounced that 'Every day it becomes clearer that the cynical experiment of partitioning Ireland has ended in total, tragic failure'. He described the introduction of internment as a 'historically tragic decision', which had 'brought the North beyond the point of no return'. He said that the British army was no longer a peace-keeping force, having lost the confidence of the people.[8]

Haughey's speech did little to calm the situation. Northern Ireland was in the midst of chaos, with reportedly 4,339 people from the North taking refuge in the South. A special train had brought women and children from Belfast to Dublin, while many took refuge in temporary housing supplied by the Irish army.[9] Lynch attempted to clarify his government's position. On 12 August he issued a public statement condemning the actions of the Ulster Unionist government and the British decision to introduce internment. Significantly, his speech explicitly demanded the abolition of the Northern Ireland government. 'The Stormont regime', he said, 'which has consistently repressed the non-Unionist population and bears responsibility for recurring violence in the Northern community, must be brought to an end'. In its place he called for the creation of a power-sharing executive in Northern Ireland between Unionists and non-Unionists.[10]

This was a bold speech. Lynch had shifted government policy from national unity to an agreed power-sharing administration in Northern Ireland. *The Irish Times* reported that Lynch's remarks were significant for his decision, as head of the Irish government, to make a 'full frontal attack on the elective representatives of the Northern State'.[11] In one fell swoop Lynch rejected the aspirations of the Downing Street Declaration of August 1969, in which London and Belfast had committed themselves to the fair and equal treatment for all citizens of Northern Ireland. Simultaneously, his condemnation of the Stormont regime meant that the Fianna Fáil government's long-term policy of cross-border co-operation between North and South was effectively dead.

Lynch also appealed to London to permit Dublin a voice in the affairs of Northern Ireland. In a telegram to Heath on 20 August, Lynch requested a meeting 'of all the interested parties designed to find ways and means of promoting the economic, social and political wellbeing of all the Irish people North and South...'.[12] Initially, Heath firmly rebuffed Lynch's request to permit Dublin's involvement 'in the affairs of the United Kingdom'.[13] Nevertheless, realising the error of internment, in early September 1971, Heath invited Lynch to a two-day summit to discuss Northern Ireland at the official residence of British prime ministers, at Chequers. Given the fiasco of internment, Lynch worried that he might face criticism from the nationalist community North and South of the border if he took up the British prime minister's offer. Nonetheless, Lynch disregarded the possibility of protests, realising that Heath was, in effect, recognising the Irish government's legitimate right to discuss Northern Ireland. Lynch did not need to worry; members of the Fianna Fáil National Executive, for example, offered Lynch their 'full support'.[14]

The Chequers summit marked a milestone in Anglo-Irish relations. Lynch spoke of his commitment, and that of the Irish people, to a peaceful policy to the attainment of a united Ireland. Support for the IRA, he said, could only be diminished if political initiatives were put in place and all internees released.[15] In reality, the summit did not produce any dramatic breakthrough on Northern Ireland. But like Lemass's visit to Belfast to meet Terence O'Neill in

1965, the fact that it happened was significant in itself. The summit was followed shortly afterwards by a tripartite summit, which also included Faulkner, at Chequers on 27 September 1971. This was the first meeting between the heads of government in Dublin, London and Belfast since the boundary agreement negotiations in 1925. Such discussions would have never been possible if not for the grim backdrop of internment, the IRA campaign and the political stalemate at Stormont.[16]

All the good diplomacy undertaken between Dublin and London, during the latter months of 1971, was shattered by the events in Derry on 30 January 1972. Following a civil rights demonstration from Creggan to the Bogside of Derry, soldiers of the British Parachute Regiment killed fourteen unarmed civilians and seriously injured many more; the finding of the Saville Inquiry in 2010 found no evidence that any of those who died during the protests on 'Bloody Sunday', had carried weapons or explosives.[17] The shootings caused widespread outrage and nationalist revulsion throughout Ireland and unleashed a wave of irredentist emotion, not witnessed since the summer of 1969.

With the events of August 1969 afresh in his mind, Lynch appealed for calm. Parliamentary politics, he argued and not paramilitary violence was the only legitimate policy that a Fianna Fáil government would pursue. Lynch immediately denounced the British army as 'unbelievably and savagely inhuman'.[18] An emergency cabinet meeting was held on 31 January. The government demanded the immediate withdrawal of the British army from Derry and other Catholic areas of Northern Ireland, the end of internment and a declaration on intent by the government to 'achieve a final settlement of the Irish question ...'.[19] The Irish Ambassador in London, Dónal O'Sullivan was recalled in protest and a national day of mourning was proclaimed for the victims in Derry.[20]

Lynch also addressed members of Dáil Éireann where he attacked the idea that physical force was a legitimate solution to end partition. Describing the IRA as 'pseudo patriots', he said their actions would only prove futile and were not supported by the vast majority of Irish people. He also appealed for calm and admitted that on the subject of Irish unity and Dublin's relationship with Ulster Unionism his government 'would have to face up to some change from our present stance and policies'.[21] Indeed, there was some speculation that Lynch might appoint a government minister solely responsible for Northern Ireland.[22] The public mood, however, had reached boiling point. On 2 February, following a march through the city of Dublin, an estimated 20,000 people assembled outside the British Embassy in Merrion Square. A large riot broke out and the embassy was attacked and burned out.[23]

Lynch condemned the attack on the British Embassy, claiming that the 'nation gained no credit' from such actions.[24] Blaney, on the other hand, said he 'shed no tears' in the aftermath of the burning of the embassy. Speaking in the Dáil he attacked the maintenance of partition and Britain's continued presence in Northern Ireland. In language that verged on inciting violence, he demanded that the 'House must now lead or be overwhelmed'. 'If they gave the right leadership', he said, 'the Six-Counties were "theirs for the taking"'.[25] Blaney's cryptic threat of civil war was ridiculed by opposition deputies. Labour TD Dr John O'Connell described Blaney as a 'warmonger'.[26] O'Connell's party colleague, Michael O'Leary was equally forthright, exclaiming that Blaney's 'threat' to Northern Unionists would prove 'calamitous'. 'Only a madman', he said, 'would suggest that way would solve the problem'.[27]

The major political consequence of Bloody Sunday was the British government's dramatic change in policy. Direct rule, not the propping up of the Stormont regime, was London's preferred option. Heath intended to take full control over the security and criminal justice in Northern Ireland. Faulkner was dismayed and threatened to resign. Heath was in no mood for compromise and on 30 March 1972 introduced direct rule. William Whitelaw was appointed as secretary of state for Northern Ireland. The suspension of Stormont transformed the political landscape in Northern Ireland.[28] The British outlined a policy of 'reconciliation' with all parties across the political spectrum in Northern Ireland.[29] The British initiative also permitted a thawing of relations between Dublin and London. The Irish Ambassador, O'Sullivan resumed his post in London.

However, not for the first or the last time, the Provisional IRA thwarted political progress. On 21 July 1972, the IRA committed one of the worst atrocities of the Troubles. On 'Bloody Friday' the movement killed eleven people and injured a further 130 in a carefully co-ordinated series of bombs in Belfast.[30] Such atrocities, excluding the increased dialogue between Dublin and London, proved a brutal reminder that the conflict in Northern Ireland had bypassed both governments. The findings of Lord Widgery's investigative enquiry into Bloody Sunday, in April 1972, only compounded hostilities in Northern Ireland and between Dublin, London and Belfast. To the disbelief of many, Widgery's verdict exonerated the British army for their action in Derry. The Widgery Report, which accused several of those shot and killed of carrying firearms or bombs, was a whitewash from start to finish and merely exasperated sectarian tensions in Northern Ireland.[31]

Thereafter, the situation in Northern Ireland settled into a military and political stalemate. The Ulster Volunteer Force (UVF) and Ulster Defence Association (UDA) escalated their respective campaigns of terror, while the IRA failed to force the withdrawal of the British forces from Northern Ireland. In the 1973 Irish general election Fianna Fáil found itself voted out of office for the first time since 1957. Although the party secured more than 22,000 additional votes compared to the 1969 election, it secured six fewer seats; ironically, two of the sacked Fianna Fáil ministers, Blaney and Haughey, headed their polls with 8,368 and 12,901 respectively, although Kevin Boland, standing for Aontacht Éireann, lost his seat.[32] The result brought Fianna Fáil's sixteen years in government to an abrupt end. Fine Gael and the Labour Party, who had been pursuing independent opposition policies since 1957, suddenly agreed on 6 February to an electoral pact and fought the election as an alternative coalition government. This pact proved somewhat appealing to the electorate and in late February a 'National Coalition' under taoiseach, Liam Cosgrave was formed.

The general election once again exposed the divisions within Fianna Fáil. The election was the first since the Arms Crisis and at least one founding member of the party was worried that the 'wrong sort of people were gaining ground'. This was the view of Frank Aiken and the 'wrong sort of people' was aimed directly at Charles J. Haughey. Aiken informed Lynch that if Haughey was ratified as a Fianna Fáil candidate, he would resign from the party. Aiken also protested that he would write a letter to the papers explaining his reasons for resigning. Lynch asked de Valera to intervene on his behalf, which he duly agreed to do. However, Aiken would not budge. On 12 February, Aiken learned that Haughey had been ratified. Aiken immediately withdrew his nomination. After much arm twisting and the intervention of Paddy Smith and his close friend Joe Farrell, Aiken agreed not to publicly accord his reasons for retiring from public life. Thus, on the night of 13 February 1973, Lynch announced that with great regret the former tánaiste and minister for external affairs was retiring from politics on 'doctors' orders'. It was a sad end to a long and distinguished political career. Thereafter, Aiken never attended another Fianna Fáil Ard Fheis nor took part in party affairs.[33]

Under Lynch's leadership Fianna Fáil in opposition maintained its peaceful commitment to Irish unity.[34] The party leadership fully endorsed the Sunningdale communiqué in 1973, which proposed the establishment of the power-sharing executive in Northern Ireland, which was to consist of the Faulknerite Ulster Unionists, the SDLP and the Alliance Party. However, not all within Fianna Fáil supported the agreement; in private Haughey 'strongly' opposed its implementation.[35] Speaking in the Dáil, Lynch welcomed the power-sharing 'partnership', linking it to the Council of Ireland, as first envisaged under the Government of Ireland Act of 1920.[36] Importantly, the ideal of a united Ireland remained to the fore of Fianna Fáil's Northern Ireland policy, but this, Lynch realised, was to take a back seat in the intermediate period. His attentions instead shifted towards London.

In 1975, following the collapse of the Sunningdale Agreement and the short-lived power sharing-executive, sharp differences emerged within Fianna Fáil over Lynch's Northern Ireland policy. In September of that year and without Lynch's consent, Fianna Fáil's spokesman for foreign affairs, Michael O'Kennedy called on London to make a 'commitment to implement an ordered withdrawal from her involvement in the Six-counties of Northern Ireland'. The British government, he said, should 'Encourage the unity of Ireland by agreement in independence and in a harmonious relationship between the two islands'.[37] Lynch was caught off guard. Hitherto, under Lynch's leadership a request for Britain to make a declaration of its intent to withdraw from Northern Ireland had not constituted official Fianna Fáil policy. Lynch reacted immediately and said O'Kennedy's speech represented a 'conflict of expression rather than of policy'.[38]

However, the signs were ominous. O'Kennedy's remarks were a huge embarrassment for Lynch and his spokesman on Northern Ireland, Ruairí Brugha (the son of Cathal Brugha). An editorial in the *The Irish Times*, 'Shattered consensus', asked why O'Kennedy had selected that time to add his voice to those calling for a British declaration of intent to withdraw from Northern Ireland. The obvious explanation, the paper noted, was that 'he had taken the temperature of his party and found that there is a majority in favour of demanding a declaration of intent – and thereby posing a renewed challenge to Mr Lynch's policies and leadership'.[39]

O'Kennedy's policy statement on Northern Ireland was supported by the rejuvenated Charles Haughey. In October 1975, in view of the abject performance of Fianna Fáil and widespread demands from his restoration, Lynch reluctantly reinstated Haughey to the party frontbench. Both George Colley and Seán MacEntee had strongly counselled Lynch against this move, but Lynch gave in under considerable pressure.[40] Haughey did not wait long to publicly express his views on partition. The following month, in mid-November, he recorded that attainment of Irish unity was central to Fianna Fáil's political composition. Describing Fianna Fáil's Northern Ireland policy as a 'positive approach', like O'Kennedy, he too called for a 'British withdrawal' from the North.[41] Confronted by overwhelming support from within the party for the British 'to make a commitment to implement an ordered withdrawal from Northern Ireland', Lynch, albeit reluctantly, was forced to adopt this policy-line throughout Fianna Fáil's remaining period in opposition.

Fianna Fáil won the 1977 Irish general election with an unassailable majority and Lynch became taoiseach once again. Northern Ireland remained high on his agenda. Initially, Lynch's Northern Ireland policy focused on Anglo-Irish relations. However, faced with little headway in negotiations with the Labour government, under prime minister, James Callaghan, in early January 1978, Lynch publicly called for a British declaration of its intention to 'withdraw' from Northern Ireland. London, however, was unimpressed and ignored Lynch's pronouncements.[42] The election of Margaret Thatcher as Conservative prime minister, in April 1979, did little to heal the rift in Anglo-Irish relations. In preliminary negotiations with Thatcher, Lynch attempted to place political, as well as security issues, on the agenda. London, however, seemed uninterested in Lynch's calls. Northern Ireland secretary of state, Humphrey Atkins, repeated the traditional British government line that responsibility for Northern Ireland rested executively with London. 'There is no responsibility elsewhere', he exclaimed, 'in Dublin or anywhere else'.[43] Indeed, in the aftermath of the IRA assassination of Lord Louis Mountbatten, a cousin of the Queen of England, on 27 August 1979, together with the movement's murder of eighteen British soldiers in an explosion on the Newry–Warrenpoint Road, on the same day, Anglo-Irish relations remained at best cordial, at worst cold.[44]

Within Fianna Fáil the old divisions among the party leadership and the anti-partitionists soon re-emerged. In an article in *The Irish Times*, Fianna Fáil Senator, Patrick Cooney, claimed that Lynch's recent policy initiative on Northern Ireland marked a 'significant shift in Fianna Fáil policy'. He pointed to the agreement with London on security related issues as an indication of the party's 'shelving of a demand for a British declaration of intent to withdraw'.[45] The perception that Lynch had backed down from his previous stance on the issue of a British strategic withdrawal from Northern Ireland was the excuse many had been waiting for to take down their leader. Granddaughter of Eamon de Valera, Síle de Valera led the protests. In a speech delivered at the graveside oration at the commemoration of Liam Lynch, in Fermoy, Co. Cork, in September 1979, she challenged Lynch to 'demonstrate his republicanism' and described the 'so-called solutions' of seeking a power-sharing executive in Northern Ireland as 'half-measures'.[46]

De Valera's speech, which was not sanctioned by the party whip, was condemned by Lynch. He informed his unruly backbencher that her speech was 'contrary to Government policy, wrong, unhelpful and untimely'.[47] De Valera blatantly ignored her party leader's protests. Lynch immediately responded and on the same day that de Valera delivered her address, issued a public statement stressing that his government supported the policy of establishing a devolved administration in Northern Ireland, with the ultimate ambition of securing a united Ireland.[48] In the aftermath of the de Valera/Lynch confrontation the taoiseach stipulated that, in the immediate term, the Fianna Fáil government's Northern Ireland policy was focused on the acceptance of an internal settlement in the North, without first seeking a British declaration.[49] Clearly, this was a deliberate attempt to distance the party away from its 1975 proposal for a British 'withdrawal' from Northern Ireland.

Pressure was mounting on Lynch and not merely in relation to his stance on Northern Ireland. The double defeat in by-elections in Co. Cork, in which Fianna Fáil lost the Cork City seat and Cork North-East seat, came as a personal blow to Lynch. On the back of the election setback two figures from Lynch's recent past remerged to challenge his stance on Northern Ireland. First, the recently appointed minister for health and social welfare, Haughey delivered a 'coded attack' on Lynch in November 1979; the former claimed that the idea of partition was 'totally inconceivable' to Pádraig Pearse. He also noted that Pearse regarded Ireland, by its history, as being emotionally, spiritually, intellectually and politically one 'indissoluble nation'.[50] Lynch, although in America, tried to face down Haughey's challenge. In a prepared statement he recorded that '... we are concerned with the moral, cultural and material well-being of the Irish people and that can be advanced not by killing, not by death or hatred or destruction, but by life'. Rejecting the idea of Pearse's 'blood sacrifice', he concluded, 'The paradox of Pearse's message for the Irish nation today is that we must work and live for Ireland, not die, and most certainly not kill for it'.[51]

Neil Blaney, although no longer a member of Fianna Fáil, stepped into the debate. Like Haughey he undermined Lynch's calls for the establishment of a power-sharing administration in Northern Ireland rather than calls for a British withdrawal. '... the dogs on the streets', Blaney protested in Cork in late November, 'know that the British must go. It is the only realistic initiative left to them'.[52] Speaking several days previously he also declared his support for Haughey assuming the leadership of Fianna Fáil.[53] Lynch, reading the signs, resigned as Fianna Fáil leader and taoiseach on 5 December 1979. On resigning he confidently (and naively) believed that George Colley would secure the leadership of Fianna Fáil. Both he and Colley were to be bitterly disappointed. The leadership campaign, which was fought over a forty-eight hour period, pitted the traditionalist Colley against the flamboyant Haughey. When the vote was counted Haughey emerged triumphant, winning the leadership contest by five votes. He became Fianna Fáil leader on 9 December 1979 and taoiseach four days later, on 13 December.

Soon after, Haughey demonstrated a desire to make fundamental changes to Fianna Fáil's Northern Ireland policy, with an aspiration of achieving a united Ireland. As Fianna Fáil leader, until his forced retirement in 1992, he continually maintained that Northern Ireland was a 'failed political entity' and abandoned his predecessor's policy of fostering a power-sharing executive in Northern Ireland.[54] Although there were hints in the early 1980s that Haughey was willing to embrace constitutional change in relation to Northern Ireland, (consider his summit meeting with Thatcher in 1980 and his participation on the New Ireland Forum in 1983), the threat from Sinn Féin meant that under Haughey Fianna Fáil reverted to its republican anti-partitionist roots; a reversal which depicted Haughey in the mould of Eamon de Valera rather than his own self-declared hero, the pragmatic republican, Seán Lemass. This was particularly true of the party's time in opposition. As noted by Haughey's special adviser on Northern Ireland, Martin Mansergh, faced by the rise of Sinn Féin, Fianna Fáil was determined to 'hold the republican ground and not cede it to anyone else'.[55]

In truth, Haughey's stance on Northern Ireland was dictated by whether his party was in or out of government. From 1981 to 1987, confronted by the electoral threat of Sinn Féin, Haughey consistently played the anti-partitionist card. For instance, his opposition to the 1985 Anglo-Irish Agreement, particularly on the issue of consent and its perceived violation of articles two and three of the Irish constitution, showed his ability to alter Fianna Fáil's Northern Ireland policy depending whether in government or opposition. Despite his heckling that he was 'not emotionally sold on the agreement', on returning to government in 1987, he not only accepted the agreement, but also the principle of consent.[56]

From a more positive perspective, Haughey made a significant contribution during the early stages of the Peace Process in his dealings with the IRA. Haughey's decision to facilitate, as far as possible, Sinn Féin's desire to move republicans away from violence and towards constitutional politics formed the basis of a strong pan-nationalist alliance, which his successor as Fianna Fáil leader Albert Reynolds was able to develop further during the Peace Process.[57]

A SUMMARY OF FIANNA FÁIL'S ATTITUDE TO PARTITION AND NORTHERN IRELAND, 1926–1971

Why, by the early 1970s, was Fianna Fáil bitterly divided on the subject of Northern Ireland? For the preceding five decades the party had played a dominant role in Irish society. However, on Fianna Fáil's self-proclaimed 'number one' objective, Irish reunification, the party was incapable of formulating a realistic long-term Northern Ireland policy. As this book illustrates, there is no single explanation as to why Fianna Fáil was unable to institute a long-term, or indeed, realistic Northern Ireland policy by the late 1960s. Rather, there are several reasons, many dating back to Fianna Fáil's foundations in 1926. Significantly the party's approach to Northern Ireland was a mixture of outdated, piecemeal and short-term ad-hoc policies.

Central to de Valera's Northern Ireland policy, a strategy which continued under Lemass and Lynch was: (a) Fianna Fáil's offer of a federal solution to end partition; (b) that the British government had a responsibility to see Ireland reunited; and lastly (c) that Fianna Fáil would not officially recognise the constitutional existence of Northern Ireland. The rigid maintenance of these three policies under consecutive Fianna Fáil leaders provided ample evidence for why Fianna Fáil was unable to make any headway on partition. They exposed the prevalence of a self-delusional naivety endemic within Fianna Fáil. These three policies formed the crux of the party's entire approach to partition for a generation. By the close of the Second

World War they were already outdated. Nevertheless, they remained at the core of Fianna Fáil Northern Ireland strategy into the 1970s.

(a) A federal solution

Since the early 1920s de Valera had offered Ulster Unionists a federal solution to end partition. The proposal rested on the premise that the Northern Ireland government would retain its own parliament in Belfast and that the powers currently held by Westminster would be transferred to the Irish government. Throughout de Valera's presidency of Fianna Fáil, until his retirement from active politics in 1959[58] and subsequently under Lemass's leadership, a federal proposal constituted a core tenet of the party's Northern Ireland policy.[59]

By the late 1960s, over forty years since Fianna Fáil first mooted a federal proposal, Lynch maintained that the policy was central to the party's Northern Ireland strategy.[60] Four decades passed and Ulster Unionists repeatedly rejected a federal offer, yet from 1966, Lynch still felt an obligation to adhere to the traditional Fianna Fáil dictum towards Northern Ireland. There was no attempt within Fianna Fáil to make considerable alterations to the party's Northern Ireland policy. Thus, by maintaining a hold on tradition the party was unable to modernise its Northern Ireland policy.

(b) A British declaration

That the British government should make a declaration in favour of an end to partition represented a further component of Fianna Fáil's traditional Northern Ireland policy. Although in the aftermath of the Government of Ireland Act, de Valera had turned his attention towards Ulster Unionists to find a solution to partition, his fruitless negotiations with James Craig in May 1921, convinced him that London, not Belfast, held the key for the attainment of Irish unity.[61] Throughout the 1930s de Valera continually maintained that London had a moral responsibility to end partition and that a declaration in favour of Irish unity was the first stage in securing a united Ireland. Whilst British prime minister, Neville Chamberlain, considered the proposal in line with his 'appeasement' policy towards the Irish government, in the aftermath of the Second World War, the British rejected the proposal outright.

London maintained that considering Northern Ireland's participation in the war and the strategic importance of the region in the event of a future war, a declaration was impossible.[62]

The passing of the Ireland Act by Westminster in 1949, which acknowledged that partition could not be ended without the consent of the majority of Northern Ireland (i.e. the Protestant majority), further illustrated London's opposition to such a declaration. For the remainder of de Valera's time as Fianna Fáil leader, however, he desperately insisted that a British declaration was the first step towards ending partition.[63]

In the post-war period, there was an ingrained reluctance within Fianna Fáil to acknowledge that London had no desire to offer a declaration in support of Irish unity. De Valera, in particular, was incapable of dealing with the reality that the British had no interest in facilitating an end to partition. While Lemass did place less emphasis on the issue as leader, he too, was never fully able to divorce himself from the traditional nationalist belief that London had a moral obligation to deliver Irish reunification.[64] Under Lynch, Fianna Fáil returned to the de Valera *modus operandi* of publicly asserting that the British were responsible for partition and therefore should express its desire to see it ended.[65]

There was an underlying contradiction between attempting to secure support from Ulster Unionists for a federal solution to partition, while at the same time badgering the British to make a declaration in support of Irish unity: outward harassment of London only added further evidence to Ulster Unionists' convictions that Fianna Fáil's federal offer was a 'veiled' attempt to secure Irish unity and coerce Northern Ireland Protestants into a Gaelicised, Catholic, all-Ireland Republic.

(c) 'The fourth green field': Fianna Fáil's non-recognition of partition and Northern Ireland

Fianna Fáil's inability to formulate and implement a realistic and coherent Northern Ireland policy was further inhibited by the Irish political establishment's non-recognition of the Northern Ireland state and parliament. This policy was not confined to Fianna Fáil, but to the wider Irish nationalist community. From the inception of the Northern Ireland state, consecutive Irish governments refused to accord official recognition to the Stormont regime. Northern Ireland was perceived as the 'fourth green field', the stolen territory, which legitimately belonged to the Irish nation. In spite of the reality that by the mid-1920s Northern Ireland was a functional entity, Irish nationalists saw the whole of Ireland as 'a distinct geographical entity, bounded by the sea and with no internal divisions'.[66]

As the party in government for over twenty-five years from 1932 to 1973 Fianna Fáil's non-recognition of Northern Ireland had long lasting implications for the party's approach to partition. Indeed, the vast majority of Fianna Fáil members never actually used the term 'Northern Ireland policy' as this, they believed, would entail granting recognition to the Northern Ireland state. Instead terms such as 'Six-Counties policy', 'partition policy' and 'Ulster policy' were used to denote Fianna Fáil's Northern Ireland strategy. Writing in 1957, Donal Barrington explained that because of the Irish government's inability to recognise that partition might be permanent, there had never been an effective Northern Ireland policy. Instead he exclaimed there had been 'a rather slip-shod' approach to formulating policy.[67]

Dublin's approach to Northern Ireland was incoherent as there was no forum within which to try to shape policy.[68] For the first fifty years of the Irish state's existence neither the Department of External Affairs nor the Department of Taoiseach allocated sufficient resources or manpower to devise a Northern Ireland policy. As the distinguished Irish civil servant, Noel Dorr explained in a 2006 interview, prior to the early 1970s there was no minister, official or department, at government and civil servant level, exclusively and specifically assigned to Northern Ireland policy.[69] Indeed, writing in the early 1970s, S.G. Ronan of the Department of External Affairs exclaimed that his department was 'saddled with a number of unfit personas mentally and physically'. 'In my opinion', he recorded, 'probably the single most important factor militating against an effective Department is the personnel and performance situation which is feckless and uneven'.[70]

This anomaly was not rectified until the latter part of 1970, when a new dedicated Anglo-Irish section, with responsibility for Northern Ireland policy, was established within the Department of External Affairs. This was followed, a year later, in 1971, with the creation of the Interdepartmental Committee on Northern Ireland. This committee brought together influential civil servants from the main departments, namely, the Departments of Taoiseach, Foreign Affairs, Finance and Justice, to develop a series of studies on Northern Ireland policy and to co-ordinate the government's approach to Northern Ireland.[71]

When the Troubles broke out in the late 1960s, the Stationery Office, which supplied the Irish government departments with paper and other stationary supplies, had more people working in their office, ten in total, than the Department of the Taoiseach had. Within the Department of the Taoiseach there was no assigned civil servant to deal with Northern Ireland policy.[72] Instead, there were a limited number of individual civil servants trying to shape government policy working within no fixed guidelines, such as T.K. Whitaker during the 1960s and Eamonn Gallagher, from the summer of 1969 onwards. In today's world it seems odd that there was no separate department and so little manpower allocated to Northern Ireland affairs between the turbulent years from 1969 to 1971 and indeed beforehand. Yet, this was the sobering reality and goes a long way to explain why the Fianna Fáil government reacted so incoherently to events in Northern Ireland.

Due to the autocratic and executive dominance of Dáil Éireann, it was effectively the taoiseach of the day who retained sole authority over Northern Ireland policy.[73] Therefore, as this book argues, from 1932 to 1959 de Valera acquired personal responsibility for Fianna Fáil's Northern Ireland policy. Under his watchful eye, Fianna Fáil refused to concede recognition to the Northern Ireland state; he consistently maintained that Northern Ireland was artificial. This was not unexpected as de Valera's constitution of 1937, which gave official claim to the Irish government's legal right to the thirty-two counties, had withdrawn *de facto* recognition of the Northern Ireland state granted by the Cumann na nGaedheal government at the conclusion of the boundary commission in 1925.

Lemass's arrival as Fianna Fáil leader heralded a reassessment within the party of Northern Ireland's constitutional position. His Tralee speech of July 1963 and his subsequent visit to Belfast in 1965 to meet the Northern Ireland prime minister, Terence O'Neill accorded *de facto* recognition to Northern Ireland. Nevertheless, although Lemass's nuances on Northern Ireland were new, under his leadership, the Fianna Fáil government never officially acknowledged the *de facto* existence of Northern Ireland.[74] Constrained by a loyalty to Fianna Fáil's orthodox nationalistic attitude to partition, Lemass was unable to make any major or lasting revisions to the party's Northern Ireland policy. Indeed, under Jack Lynch's leadership from 1966 to 1979, Fianna Fáil routinely implied that *de facto* recognition of Northern Ireland was only envisaged within the context of a federal agreement between Belfast and Dublin.[75]

When the violence broke out in Northern Ireland in 1969, these three policies remained as central to Fianna Fáil's Northern Ireland policy as they had first been almost half a century previously. Over the preceding forty years, however, the political landscape had changed drastically. London had decided that the Irish problem was no longer their concern, while with every passing year the Ulster Unionist controlled Northern Ireland gained an increasing sense of legitimacy and permanence. Fianna Fáil's attitude to Northern Ireland, however, remained rooted in the past. The party was incapable of evolving from beyond the outdated conservative shackles of an anti-partitionist ideology.

THE SHORT-TERM FACETS OF FIANNA FÁIL'S
NORTHERN IRELAND POLICY

Fianna Fáil's implementation of Northern Ireland policy based on short-term considerations was also a defining characteristic of the party's approach to partition from 1926 to the early 1970s. Motivated by immediate preoccupations, the Fianna Fáil hierarchy – usually following the commencement of IRA activity in Northern Ireland or to secure closer cross-border co-operation between North and South – implemented new initiatives towards Northern Ireland and Ulster Unionism. This approach to policy development never considered the long-term implications for Fianna Fáil's Northern Ireland strategy. Therefore, there remained a sizeable gap within Fianna Fáil towards what actually denoted the party's official Northern Ireland policy: this gap was never filled.

In particular, Fianna Fáil's changing relationship with the IRA had lasting implications for the party's approach towards Northern Ireland. This book reveals that the re-emergence of IRA activity, particularly during the Second World War and later under the guise of the IRA border-campaign during the 1950s and early 1960s, exposed a deep fault-line among party members towards Northern Ireland policy. The party leadership's willingness to suppress the IRA disgusted many of the rank-and-file Fianna Fáil members. A large proportion of party grass-roots were appalled that as descendants of the physical force tradition the Fianna Fáil hierarchy could restrain a movement that was continuing a policy first advocated by de Valera, Lemass and their fellow 'soldiers of destiny'.

Nevertheless although the Fianna Fáil leadership endorsed political rather than military means to undo partition, this did not mean that all party members disapproved of force. For many within the organisation the use of violence was seen as a legitimate policy. The party leadership, constrained by a loyalty to their 'Republican' philosophy, was never able to completely detach the organisation away from its militant tradition and refocus on Northern Ireland policy. This is a significant statement. Fianna Fáil, after all, sought to represent republicanism in Ireland: an ideologically radical philosophy whose adherents claimed to be the guardians of the restoration of a united Ireland.[76]

As descendants of the anti-treaty wing of Sinn Féin the party portrayed itself unashamedly as Anglophobic. During the early years of Fianna Fáil's existence it was considered neither necessary nor desirable to sever links with the IRA. De Valera was still regarded by many IRA volunteers as the leader of the republican movement. John A. Murphy explained that Fianna Fáil and the IRA had a common socio-political background and ultimately a common objective – Irish unity.[77] In fact, de Valera more than once expressed his sympathy with the IRA,[78] while Seán Lemass asserted that Fianna Fáil, the 'slightly constitutional' party, was republican by parliamentary means.[79]

This book shows that the outbreak of IRA violence in Northern Ireland was almost always the catalyst for Fianna Fáil supporters to attack the party's approach towards Northern Ireland. Whether in government or in opposition, the party leadership's consent to the arrest and imprisonment of IRA members was viewed as an act of treachery by a vocal minority of party TDs, county councillors and grass-roots members. The research uncovered the extent to which party supporters from counties Donegal to Cork issued resolutions, letters and memoranda to Fianna Fáil headquarters in protest at the party's attitude towards the IRA and Northern Ireland. Within Fianna Fáil there was a 'sneaking respect for the IRA, the only category of the population not deemed to be less truly Irish than Fianna Fáil'.[80] This 'sneaking respect' for the IRA guaranteed that beneath the surface there lay a schism between the Fianna Fáil hierarchy and an element of grass-roots in relation to the party's Northern Ireland policy.

Fianna Fáil's relationship with Northern Nationalists further underlined the party's ad-hoc approach to the formation of Northern Ireland policy. Since Fianna Fáil's establishment, Northern Nationalists had looked to the party as their effective saviours; the party that would help bring partition to an end. By the close of the Second World War, Northern Nationalists' attitudes towards Fianna Fáil had changed drastically. De Valera and his Fianna Fáil colleagues were viewed with suspicion. Fianna Fáil's reluctance to permit their Northern comrades an input into Dublin's Northern Ireland policy was privately loathed by Northern Nationalists. Significantly, in the context of Fianna Fáil's sponsored anti-partition campaigns, de Valera effectively used Northern Nationalists, as a means of articulating the 'crime' of a partitioned Ireland. Northern Nationalists would be consulted if needed, but this was always on Fianna Fáil's terms.

Lemass was equally motivated by short-term considerations in his relationship with Northern Nationalism. During his period as taoiseach he followed a selfish policy. His wish for Northern Nationalists to become the official opposition at Stormont was based on short-term motivations. Northern Nationalists were effectively used in Lemass's political gamble of securing support from Ulster Unionists for his offer of a federal agreement in his attainment of a united Ireland. Once Northern Nationalists agreed to end their abstentionist policy and enter Stormont, in 1965, Fianna Fáil ignored the plight of the Catholic minority of Northern Ireland. Lemass realised that by granting Northern Nationalists too much influence he would run the risk of offending Ulster Unionists – a risk he could not afford to take, given that he was trying to encourage closer co-operation between Dublin and Belfast. It was not until the late 1960s, impelled by the outbreak of the civil rights campaign in Northern Ireland, that the Fianna Fáil government were, for the first time, compelled to confront the politically sensitive issue of discrimination levelled at Northern Catholics by the Stormont authorities.

Fianna Fáil's sponsored anti-partition propaganda campaigns from 1938 to 1939 and later from 1948 to 1950 further exposed the party's narrow-minded attitude to partition. Anti-partitionist propaganda was used by Fianna Fáil in the short-term pursuit to retain the mantle as the party best suited to secure Irish unity. De Valera never seemed to consider the long-term implications that these campaigns would have for Fianna Fáil's Northern Ireland strategy. The net result of the party's persistent use of anti-partitionism was that it further alienated Unionist Unionists. Particularly following de Valera's 1948 to 1950 worldwide anti-partition tour, Belfast maintained that Irish unity was impossible. On becoming Fianna Fáil leader Lemass publicly conceded that Fianna Fáil's anti-partition approach towards Northern Ireland was a useless exercise. Instead his attention turned towards the short-term economic rewards of encouraging closer cross-border co-operation between Dublin and Belfast.

More than any other senior Fianna Fáil politician, Lemass viewed partition through the prism of economic considerations. His desire to establish formal relations at government and ministerial level between Dublin and Belfast on issues of cross-border co-operation guided his Northern Ireland policy. His determination to crackdown on IRA activity; his willingness to change Fianna Fáil's nomenclature on Northern Ireland; his unofficial *de facto* recognition of the existence of partition and his meeting with Northern Ireland prime minister, Terence O'Neill in 1965 were each employed in the hope to secure, in the immediate term, greater cross-border co-operation with Ulster Unionists. Looking to the long-term, Lemass did not offer any radical departure to Fianna Fáil's traditional Northern Ireland policy. The emphasis was on the economic facets of partition, but the fundamental objections to partition remained. Thus, when he retired as leader his successor, Jack Lynch, inherited a Northern Ireland policy that had changed little in a generation. Apart from a more subtly nuanced attitude to partition, Lemass remained loyal to the central tenets of Fianna Fáil's stance on Northern Ireland.

To conclude, as has been demonstrated during the course of this book, Fianna Fáil's approach to partition and Northern Ireland from 1926 to 1971 was a mixture of outdated, piecemeal and short-term ad-hoc policies. Under consecutive Fianna Fáil leaders from de Valera, Lemass and Lynch the party portrayed itself as the 'Republican Party', the custodians of the aspiration for a united Ireland. In reality, Fianna Fáil's entire approach to Northern Ireland was based on the optics of illusion. The party gave the *impression* that it was doing everything possible to secure unity, when in fact, the opposite was true. Impeded by a perceived loyalty to the traditional nationalist prejudices and orthodoxies towards partition, a sense of self-delusion was prevalent within Fianna Fáil. The 'soldiers of destiny', in fact, were prisoners of the past. As noted by a Co. Kerry resident in 1965: 'I think myself that Fianna Fáil are both driven forward and held back by their own past ...'.[81]

NOTES

1. Public Records Office of Northern Ireland (PRONI) Cahir Healy Papers D2991/B/53/8, O'Gowan, Bellamont Forest, Cottehill, Co. Cavan, to Nationalist MP for South-Fermanagh, Cahir Healy, 22 June 1951.
2. See Jack Lynch, *Speeches and Statements, Irish Unity Northern Ireland Anglo-Irish Relations, August 1969 – October 1971* (Dublin, Government Information Bureau, 1972), 51. For an overview of Anglo-Irish relations from 1971 to 1973 see Anthony Craig, *Crisis of Confidence: Anglo-Irish Relations in the Early Troubles* (Dublin: Irish Academic Press, 2010), 85-190.
3. Lynch, *Speeches and Statements, Irish Unity Northern Ireland Anglo-Irish Relations*, 55. See also Lynch's comments on this subject to members of Dáil Éireann, 20 Oct. 1971. Lynch, *Speeches and Statements, Irish Unity Northern Ireland Anglo-Irish Relations*, 100.

4. National Archives of the United Kingdom (NAUK) Foreign and Commonwealth Office (FCO) 33/1596, British Ambassador to Ireland, Sir John Peck to the FCO, April, 1971. 'Mr Blaney attacks Mr Lynch', record of Blaney's speech at a Fianna Fáil meeting at Arklow, Co. Wicklow (date unknown).

5. University College Dublin Archives (UCDA) Fianna Fáil Party Papers P176/350, meeting of Fianna Fáil National Executive, 26 April 1971.

6. John Walsh, *Patrick Hillery, the Official Biography* (Dublin: New Ireland, 2008), 268.

7. See Thomas Hennessey, *The Evolution of the Troubles, 1970–1972* (Dublin: Gill and Macmillan, 2007), 192–197.

8. See comments by Haughey. *The Irish Times*, 12 Aug. 1971.

9. Dermot Keogh, *Jack Lynch, A Biography* (Dublin: Gill and Macmillan, 2008), 312.

10. *The Irish Times*, 13 Aug. 1971.

11. *The Irish Times*, 13 Aug. 1971.

12. Telegram for Lynch to Heath, 19/20 Aug. 1971. See Lynch, *Speeches and Statements, Irish Unity Northern Ireland Anglo-Irish Relations*, 77–78.

13. Telegram for Heath to Lynch, 20 Aug. 1971. See Lynch, *Speeches and Statements, Irish Unity Northern Ireland Anglo-Irish Relations*, 78–79.

14. UCDA P176/348, meeting of Fianna Fáil National Executive, 13 Sept. 1971.

15. National Archives of Ireland (NAI) Department of Foreign Affairs (DFA), 2003/13/6, record of discussions between Lynch and Heath, 6 & 7 Sept. 1971.

16. See NAI DFA 2003/13/7, record of meetings between Lynch, Heath and Brian Faulkner, 27 & 28 Sept. 1971.

17. See *The Guardian*, 15 June 2010. For an overview of the Lynch government's Northern Ireland policy during this period, particularly in relation to the IRA, see Henry Patterson, 'The Border Security problem and Anglo-Irish Relations, 1970-1973', *Contemporary British History*, 26:2 (2012), 231-251.

18. NAI D/T 2003/6/461, Statement issued by the Government Information Bureau on behalf of the Taoiseach, 30 Jan. 1972.

19. NAI D/T 2003/6/461, Statement issued by the Government Information Bureau on behalf of the Taoiseach, 31 Jan. 1972.

20. See *Irish Independent*, 4 Feb. 1972.

21. See comments by Lynch. *Irish Independent*, 4 Feb. 1972.

22. See *Irish Press*, 3 Feb. 1972.

23. *The Irish Times*, 3 Feb. 1972.

24. See comments by Lynch. *Irish Independent*, 4 Feb. 1972.

25. See comments by Blaney. *Irish Independent*, 4 Feb. 1972.

26. See comments by O'Connell. *Irish Independent*, 4 Feb. 1972.

27. See comments by O'Leary. *Irish Independent*, 4 Feb. 1972.

28. J. J. Lee, *Ireland 1912–1985, Politics and Society* (Cambridge: Cambridge University Press, 1989), 440–441.

29. See comments by William Whitelaw. *The Irish Times*, 21 July 1972.

30. Lee, *Ireland 1912–1985*, 442.

31. See The Rt. Hon. Lord Widgery, *Report of the Tribunal Appointed to Enquire into the Events on Sunday, 30th January 1972, Which Led to Loss of Life in Connection with the Procession in Londonderry on that Day ...*, 'Were the deceased carrying firearms or bombs?', 26–33.

32. Dermot Keogh, *Twentieth Century Ireland, Nation and State* (Dublin: Gill and Macmillan, 1994), 321.

33. UCDA Frank Aiken Papers P104/2341, typescript copy of an article by Geraldine Kennedy, 'Frank Aiken: the story that was never told', as related by Francis Aiken (Frank Aiken's son), June 1983.

34. For an excellent analysis of Lynch's and indeed Fianna Fáil's attitude to Northern Ireland during the party's years in opposition from 1973 to 1977 see Keogh, *Jack Lynch, A Biography*, 369–408.

35. Author's interview with Martin Mansergh, Dec. 2010.

36. See speech by Lynch. Dáil Éireann Debate (DE), 28 Nov. 1973. Vol. 269, col. 426.

37. See Martin Mansergh (ed.), *The Spirit of the Nation: Speeches and Statements of Charles J. Haughey (1957–1986)* (Dublin & Cork: Mercier Press, 1986), 207–208. See also Jack Lynch, 'My life and times', *Magill*, Nov. 1979, 45.

38. See comments by Lynch. *The Irish Times*, 15 Oct. 1975.

39. *The Irish Times*, 15 Oct. 1975. Quoted in Keogh, *Jack Lynch, A Biography*, 401.

40. Keogh, *Jack Lynch, A Biography*, 396.

41. See speech by Haughey, Dublin Artane Fianna Fáil constituency organisation, Hollybrook Hotel, 19 Nov. 1975. Mansergh (ed.), *The Spirit of the Nation*, 209.

42. Keogh, *Jack Lynch, A Biography*, 414.

43. Catherine O'Donnell, *Fianna Fáil, Irish Republicanism and the Northern Ireland Troubles, 1968–2005* (Dublin: Irish Academic Press, 2007), 44.

44. See *The Irish Times*, 28 Aug. 1979.

45. O'Donnell, *Fianna Fáil*, 44.

46. See comments by Síle de Valera. *The Irish Times*, 10 Sept. 1979.

47. Keogh, *Jack Lynch, A Biography*, 423.

48. See *The Irish Times*, 10 Sept. 1979.

49. See *The Irish Times*, 18 Dec. 1979.

50. See comments by Haughey. *The Irish Times*, 12 Nov. 1979.

51. See comments by Lynch. *The Irish Times*, 12 Nov. 1979.

52. See comments by Blaney, 26 Nov. 1979.

53. See comments by Blaney. *Irish Press*, 21 Nov. 1979.

54. See Haughey's Presidential address, 49th Fianna Fáil Ard Fheis, 16 Feb. 1980; Haughey's comments at a speech delivered in Co. Wexford, 31 May 1981; and lastly, statement issued on behalf of Haughey, 29 July 1982. Mansergh (ed.), *The Spirit of the Nation*, 335, 501 and 663, respectively.

55. O'Donnell, *Fianna Fáil*, 61.

56. O'Donnell, *Fianna Fáil*, 66.

57. Under the direction of Sinn Féin President, Gerry Adams and with the support of Haughey, it was envisaged that this 'pan-nationalist' alliance would consist of Sinn Féin, the SDLP and the Irish government. See O'Donnell, *Fianna Fáil*, 56–57.

58. See Eamon de Valera, *The Alternative to 'The Treaty': Document No. 2* (Dublin, 1923). A copy is available from UCDA P176/944. See also de Valera's comments, *Evening Standard*, 17 Oct. 1938 NAI DFA 203/2, record of conversation between de Valera and Lord Pakenham, 18 Sept. 1957.

59. See Lemass's Oxford Address, 15 Oct. 1959. *The Irish Times*, 16 Oct. 1959.

60. See Jack Lynch's Tralee speech, 20 Sept. 1969, *The Irish Times*, 21 Sept. 1969. See also Lynch's comments in the Dáil. DE, 22 Oct. 1969. Vol. 241, cols. 1407–1408.

61. See John Bowman, *De Valera and the Ulster Question* (Oxford, 1982), 46–48.

62. See NAI DFA P203/2, meeting between Aiken and Home, 22 March 1958; and meeting between Aiken and Home, 4 July 1958.

63. See, for example, speech by de Valera. DE, 24 June 1947. Vol. 107, cols. 78–81. See UCDA P104/8724, conversation between Aiken and Lord Ismay, 14 Feb. 1952. See also NAUK Prime Minister's Office (PREM) 11/2374, meeting between Macmillan and de Valera, 18 March 1958.

64. See UCDA P176/769, Lemass's Presidential speech, 1962 Fianna Fáil Ard Fheis. See also Lemass's Sallynoggin speech, *Irish Press* 27 Jan. 1965.

65. See Lynch's address to the United Nations, 22 Oct. 1970. See *Speeches and Statements by Jack Lynch*, 'Irish unity Northern Ireland Anglo-Irish relations', 34.

66. Clare O'Halloran, *Partition and the Limits of Irish Nationalism* (New Jersey: Humanities Press International, Inc., 1987), 1.

67. See Donal Barrington's seminal work, *Uniting Ireland* (Dublin, 1957). A copy is available from NAI Department of the Taoiseach (DT) S 9361 G.

68. Ronan Fanning, 'Playing it cool: The response of the British and Irish governments to the crisis in Northern Ireland, 1968–9', *Irish Studies in International Affairs*, Vol. 12 (2001), 57–85; 58.

69. UCD, School of History and Archives, Postgraduate Seminar Series: Noel Dorr interview, 11 April 2006.
70. UCDA Patrick Hillery Papers P205/42, copy of confidential memorandum concerning the structure of the Department of External Affairs by S.G. Ronan, Jan. 1971.
71. See Michael Kennedy, '"This tragic and most intractable problem": the reaction of the Department of External Affairs to the outbreak of the Trouble in Northern Ireland', *Irish Studies in International Affairs*, Vol. 12 (2001), 87–95; 95.
72. This information is sourced from my 2006 MA dissertation: *The Battle of the Bogside: A Comparative Analysis of the Irish, British and Northern Ireland Governments' Reaction to the Outbreak of Violence in Derry, 12–15 August 1969*, 32. (This work is available from UCDA).
73. Brian Farrell, *The Foundation of Dáil Eireann, Parliament and National Building* (Dublin: Gill and Macmillan, 1971), 51. See also Basil Chubb, *The Government and Politics of Ireland* (Dublin, Gill and Macmillan, 1992), 151–167.
74. See Lemass's comments during a debate on recognition of Northern Ireland. DE 10 Feb. 1965. Vol. 214, col. 3–4.
75. See Lynch's Tralee speech, 20 Sept. 1969. *The Irish Times*, 21 Sept. 1969.
76. Tom Garvin, 'The destiny of the soldiers: tradition and modernity in the politics of de Valera's Ireland', *Irish Political Studies*, Vol. XXVI, 26 (1978), 328.
77. See John A. Murphy, *The Irish Times* supplement 'Fifty Years of Fianna Fáil', 19 May 1976.
78. For example, in 1947, de Valera admitted that, while misguided, he sympathised with the younger generation of IRA volunteers. Indeed, he confessed to the British that if 'he were a young man' he might possibly 'take up arms' to secure Irish unity. NAUK DO 35/3924, record of meeting between de Valera and secretary of state for Commonwealth Relations, Philip Noel-Baker, 4 Nov. 1947.
79. See comments by Lemass. DE, 21 March 1928. Vol. 22, col. 1615.
80. See Conor Cruise O'Brien, *Herod: Reflections on Political Violence* (London: Hutchinson, 1978), 137.
81. PRONI Prime Minister's Office (PREM) 5/7/6, letter from unidentified (name censored) Fine Gael supporter, Killarney, Co. Kerry to Northern Ireland prime minister, Terence O'Neill, 26 March 1965.

Bibliography

PRIMARY SOURCES

Archival institutions

IRELAND (REPUBLIC)

National Archives of Ireland (NAI)

- Cabinet Minutes
- Department of Foreign Affairs (DFA)
- Department of the Taoiseach (DT)
- Government Cabinet Minutes
- Jack Lynch Papers

National Library of Ireland (NLI)

- Frank Gallagher Papers (MS 18375)
- Seán T. O'Kelly (MS 8469)

University College Dublin Archives (UCDA)

- Frank Aiken Papers (P104)
- Todd Andrew Papers (P91)
- Ernest Blythe Papers (P24)
- John A. Costello Papers (P190)
- Eamon de Valera Papers (P150)
- Fianna Fáil Party Papers (P176)
- Patrick Hillery Papers (P205)
- Sighle Humphreys Papers (P106)
- Seán MacEntee Papers (P67)
- Donnchadh Ó Briain Papers (P83)
- Desmond Ryan Papers (LA10)
- Moss Twomey Papers (P69)
- Kenneth Whitaker Papers (P175)

NORTHERN IRELAND

Public Records Office of Northern Ireland (PRONI)

- Cabinet Papers (Cab)
- Cahir Healy Papers (D2991)
- Prime Minister's Office (PREM)
- Ellison Spence Papers (D2481)

The Archives of the Archdiocese of Armagh (ARCH)

- The Cardinal Joseph MacRory Papers

GREAT BRITAIN

National Archives of the United Kingdom (NAUK)

- Dominion's Office (DO)
- Foreign and Commonwealth Office (FCO)
- Northern Ireland Office (CJ)
- Prime Minister's Office (PREM)
- Security Service Files (KV)
- War Office (WO)

University of Birmingham Special Collections (UBSC)

- Neville Chamberlain Papers (NCP) 18/1

University of Oxford (UO), Bodleian Library (BO)

- Clement Attlee Papers (MS. Dep. 83)

PRIVATE PAPERS

- Gerald Boland unpublished handwritten memoirs, copy in author's possession.

INTERVIEWS AND CORRESPONDENCE

- Dermot Ahern, (phone interview), 17 Sept. 2012

- Niall Blaney (Jnr.), correspondence, Feb. 2008
- Kenneth Bloomfield, interview, 2 June 2006
- Richard Booth, interview, 8 Dec. 2008
- Harry Boland, interview, 22 Feb. 2008
- John Bowman, interview, 17 Feb. 2007
- Mary Colley, interview, 18 May 2009
- Liam Cullen (former head of research, Fianna Fáil), interview, Dec. 2007
- Garret FitzGerald, interview, 19 Jan. 2009
- Pádraig Faulkner, interview, 10 July 2006
- Desmond Hanafin, correspondence, Sept. 2009
- Seán Haughey, correspondence, Feb. 2009
- Ciarán Ó Cuinn (personal adviser to Dermot Ahern), interview, Jan. 2010

PUBLISHED PRIMARY SOURCES

Documents on Irish Foreign Policy (Vol. IV 1937–1939 and Vol. V 1939–1941), Royal Irish Academy (Dublin), (eds.) Catriona Crowe, Ronan Fanning, Michael Kennedy, Dermot Keogh, Eunan O'Halpin.
Moynihan, Maurice, *Speeches and Statements by Eamon De Valera 1917–1973* (Dublin, 1980).
Speeches and Statements by Jack Lynch, 'Irish Unity Northern Ireland Anglo-Irish Relations, August 1969 – October 1972', Government Information Bureau (Dublin, 1972).

PARLIAMENTARY SOURCES

Dáil Éireann debates (DE)
Seanad Éireann debates (SE)

NEWSPAPERS, PERIODICALS, ETC.

Anglo-Celt
Auckland Star
Belfast Newsletter
Belfast Telegraph
Catholic Digest

Kilkenny Journal
Limerick Weekly Echo
Magill
Meath Chronicle
Munster Express

Claire Champion
Clare People
Cork Evening Echo
Cork Examiner
Connacht Tribune
Daily Telegraph
Derry Journal
Donegal Democrat
Eniscorthy Guardian
Evening Echo
Evening Post
Evening Mail
Evening Standard
Galway Observer
Gléas

Nation
Newry Journal
Newry Reporter
Northern Standard
Nusight
Ottawa Journal
Roscommon Champion
Southern Cross
Southern Star
Sunday Independent
Sunday Observer
Sunday Telegraph
Tipperary Star
The Guardian
The Independent
The Irish Times
The Irish Press
The Kerryman
Wicklow People

SECONDARY SOURCES

WORKS OF REFERENCE

Dictionary of Irish Biography (Dublin: Cambridge University Press, 2010).

Córú agus Rialacha, Fianna Fáil The Republican Party, Constitution and Revised Rules 2006 (not for public publication).

WORKS OF HISTORY AND POLITICS (SELECTED)

Allen, Kieran, *Fianna Fáil and Irish Labour, 1926 to the Present* (London: Pluto Press, 1997).

Andrews, C.S., *Man of No Property* (Cork: Mercier Press, 2001).

Andrews, David, *Kingstown Republican* (Dublin: New Ireland, 2007).

Arnold, Bruce, *Haughey, his Life and Unlucky Deeds* (London: HarperCollins, 1993).

Arthur, Paul, 'Anglo-Irish relations and the Northern Ireland problem', *Irish Studies in International Affairs,* Vol. 2 (1985), 37–50.

Barrington, Donal, *Uniting Ireland* (Dublin, 1957).

Bell, Bowyer, John, *The Secret Army: the IRA* (Dublin: Poolbeg, 1997).

Bew, Paul, *The Politics of Enmity, 1789–2006* (Oxford: Oxford University Press, 2007).

– (ed.) *The memoir of David Gray: A Yankee in De Valera's Ireland* (Dublin: Royal Irish Academy, 2012).

– and Patterson, Henry, *Seán Lemass and the Making of Modern Ireland 1945–66* (Dublin: Gill and Macmillan, 1982).

Boland, Kevin, *The Rise and Decline of Fianna Fáil* (Dublin: Mercier Press, 1982).

– *Under Contract with the Enemy* (Dublin: Mercier Press, 1988).

Boyce D. George, *Nationalism in Ireland* (London: Gill and Macmillan, 1991).

Bowman, John, *De Valera and The Ulster Question, 1917–1973* (Oxford: Oxford University Press, 1982).

Brandt, Willy, *A Peace Policy for Europe* (London: Weidenfeld and Nicolson, 1969).

Chubb, Basil, *The Government and Politics of Ireland* (Dublin: Gill and Macmillan, 1992).

Coakley, John (ed.), *Changing Shades of Orange and Green: Redefining the Union and the Nation in Contemporary Ireland, Perspectives in British-Irish Studies* (Dublin: UCD Press, 2002).

– 'The north–south institutions: from blueprint to reality', *Institute for British-Irish Studies*, working paper No.22, 2002, 1–20.

Collins, Stephen, *The Power Game, Fianna Fáil Since Lemass* (Dublin: O'Brien Press, 2000).

Craig, Anthony, *Crisis of Confidence: Anglo-Irish Relations in the Early Troubles* (Dublin: Irish Academic Press, 2010).

Cronin, Seán, *Washington's Irish Policy 1916–1986* (Dublin: Anvil Books, 1987).

Davis, D. Troy, *Dublin's America Policy, Irish – American Diplomatic Relations 1945–1952* (Washington D.C: Catholic University of America Press, 1998).

De Blacam, Aodh, 'Some thoughts on partition', *Studies* Vol. XXIII (1934), 559–576.

De Paor, Liam, *Divided Ulster* (Harmondsworth: Penguin Press, 1970).

De Valera, Terry, *A Memoir, Terry de Valera* (Dublin: Currach Press, 2005).

Downey, James, *Lenihan, His Life his Loyalties* (Dublin: New Island Books, 1998).

– *Irish Times* supplement 'Fifty Years of Fianna Fáil', 19 May 1976.

Dunphy, Richard, *The Making of Fianna Fáil Power in Ireland* (Oxford: Oxford University Press, 1995).

Dwyer, T. Ryle, *De Valera's Finest Hour: In Search of National Independence 1932–1959* (Dublin: Mercier Press, 1982).

– 'Eamon de Valera and the partition question', in *De Valera and His Times*, (eds.) J. P. O'Carroll and John A. Murphy (Cork: Cork University Press, 1986) 74–91.

– *Nice Fellow, Jack Lynch* (Cork: Mercier Press, 2001).

Edwards, Aaron, 'Social democracy and partition: the British Labour Party and Northern Ireland, 1951–64', *Journal of Contemporary History*, Oct. 2007; 42 (4), 595–612.

English, Richard, *Armed Struggle, A History of the IRA* (London: Pan Macmillan, 2003).

– *Irish Freedom, the History of Irish Nationalism* (London: Pan Macmillan, 2006).

Evans, Bryce, *Seán Lemass, Democratic Dictator* (Cork: Collins Press, 2011).

Fanning, Ronan, 'Anglo-Irish relations: partition and the British dimension in historical perspective', *Irish Studies in International Affairs*, Vol. 2 (1985), 1–20.

– *Independent Ireland* (Dublin: Helicon, 1983).

– 'Playing it cool: The response of the British and Irish governments to the crisis in Northern Ireland, 1968–9', *Irish Studies in International Affairs*, Vol. 12 (2001), 58–85.

– 'Small states, large neighbours: Ireland and the United Kingdom', *Irish Studies in International Affairs* Vol. 9 (1998), 21–29.

– '"The rule of order": Eamon de Valera and the IRA, 1923–1940', in *De Valera and His Times*, (eds.) J. P. O'Carroll and John A. Murphy (Cork: Cork University Press, 1986), 160–172.

Farrell, Brian, *Seán Lemass* (Dublin: Gill and Macmillan, 1983).

– *The Foundation of Dáil Eireann, Parliament and National Building* (Dublin: Gill and Macmillan, 1971).

–'The unlikely marriage: De Valera, Lemass and the shaping of modern Ireland', *Etudes Irelandaises*; 10 (1985), 215–222.

Farrell, Michael, *Northern Ireland: The Orange State* (London: Pluto Press, 1980).

Faulkner, Pádraig, *As I saw It, Reviewing over 30 years of Fianna Fáil and Irish Politics* (Dublin: Wolfhound, 2005).

Feeney, Tom, *Seán MacEntee, A Political Life* (Dublin: Irish Academic Press, 2009).

Ferriter, Diarmaid, *Judging Dev* (Dublin: Royal Irish Academy, 2007).

– *The Transformation of Ireland, 1900–2000* (London: Profile Books, 2005).

Fisk, Robert, *In Time of War* (London: Andre Deutsch, 1983).

FitzGerald, Garret, *All in a Life, Garret FitzGerald, An Autobiography* (Dublin: Gill and Macmillan, 1991).

Flynn, Barry, *Soldiers of Folly: The IRA Border Campaign, 1956–1962* (Cork: Collins Press, 2009).

Gallagher, Tom, 'Fianna Fáil and partition 1926–84', *Éire – Ireland*, Vol. 20, No.1 (1985), 28–57.

Garvin, Tom, *Judging Lemass, The Measure of the Man* (Dublin: Royal Irish Academy, 2009).

Gellner, Ernest, *Nations and Nationalism* (London: Verso, 2006).

Girvin, Brian, *The Emergency: Neutral Ireland 1939–45* (London: Macmillan, 2006).

– *Preventing the Future, Why was Ireland so Poor for so Long?* (Dublin: Gill and Macmillan, 2004).

– 'The destiny of the soldiers: tradition and modernity in the politics of de Valera's Ireland', *Irish Political Studies*, Vol. XXVI, 26 (1978), 328–347.

Hanley, Brian, *The IRA, 1926–1936* (Dublin: Four Courts Press, 2002).

Harkness, David, 'The north and de Valera', in *The "De Val-Era" in Ireland, 1916–1975*, (ed.) Sidney Poger (Boston, 1984), 63–86.

Hayward, Kathy, 'The politics of nuance: Irish official discourse on Northern Ireland', *Irish Political Studies*, 19:1, (2004), 18–38.

Hennessey, Thomas, *Northern Ireland, The Origins of the Troubles* (Dublin: Gill and Macmillan, 2005).

Heslinga M.W., *The Irish Border as a Cultural Divide* (Netherlands: Van Gorcum Assen, 1979).

Higgins, Roisín, 'Sites of memory and memorial in 1966', in Mary E. Daly and Margaret O'Callaghan (eds.) *1916 in 1966, Commemorating the Easter Rising* (Dublin: Royal Irish Academy, 2007), 272–302.

Hobsbawm J. Eric, *Nations and Nationalism Since 1780* (London: Cambridge University Press, 1990).

Horgan, John, *Seán Lemass, The Enigmatic Patriot* (Dublin: Gill and Macmillan, 1999).

Ivory, Garreth, 'Revisions in nationalist discourse among Irish political parties', *Irish Political Studies*, 14:1, (1999), 84–103.

Jackson, Alvin, *Home Rule, An Irish History, 1800–2000* (London: Phoenix, 2003).

– 'Ireland, the Union and the Empire, 1800–1960', in Kevin Kenny (ed.) *Ireland and the British Empire* (Oxford: Oxford University Press, 2004), 123–153.

Kedourie, Elie, *Nationalism* (London: Hutchinson, 1993).

Kelly, Stephen, "Conditional constitutionalists", the reaction of Fianna Fáil grass-roots to the IRA Border Campaign, 1956–1962', in *Riotous Assemblies: A history of Riots and Public Disorder in Ireland* (eds.) William Sheehan and Maura Cronin (Cork: Mercier Press, 2011).

– '"Derry came too soon"': The Irish government's reaction to the outbreak of violence in Derry, 12–15 August 1969', *University College Dublin History Review* (Dublin, 2006), 54–76.

– *The Battle of the Bogside: A Comparative Analysis of the Irish, British and Northern Ireland Governments' Reactions to the Outbreak of Violence in Derry, 12–15 August 1969* (unpublished 2006 MA thesis available from the UCDA).

– 'The politics of terminology: Seán Lemass and Ulster question, 1959–1966', in *From Parnell to Paisley:Constitutional and Revolutionary Politics in Ireland, 1879 – 2008*, (eds.) Caoimhe Nic Dháibhéid and Colin Reid (Dublin: Irish Academic Press, 2010), 139–158.

Kennedy, Michael, *Division and Consensus, The Politics of Cross-Border Relations in Ireland, 1925–1969* (Dublin: Institute for Public Administration, 2000).

– 'Northern Ireland and cross-border co-operation', in Brian Girvin and Gary Murphy (eds.) *The Lemass Era-Politics and Society in the Ireland of Seán Lemass* (Dublin: UCD Press, 2005), 99–121.

– Kennedy and Magennis, Eoin. 'North–South agenda setting in the 1960s and 1990s: plus ca change?', *Journal of Cross Border Studies in Ireland,* No.2 (spring, 2007), 34–53.

– '"This tragic and most intractable problem", the reaction of the Department of External Affairs to the outbreak of the Trouble in Northern Ireland', *Irish Studies in International Affairs*, Vol. 12 (2001), 87–95.

Keogh, Dermot, *Jack Lynch, a Biography* (Dublin: Gill and Macmillan, 2008).

– *Twentieth Century Ireland, Nation and State* (Dublin: Gill and Macmillan, 1994).

– and Doherty, Gabriel, (eds.), *De Valera's Ireland* (Cork: Cork University Press, 2003).

Laffan, Michael, *The Partition of Ireland 1911–1925* (Dundalk: Dundalgan Press, 1983).

Lee, J. J., *Ireland 1912–1985, Politics and Society* (Cambridge: Cambridge University Press, 1989).

Longford and O'Neill – The Earl of Longford and Thomas P. O'Neill, *Eamon de Valera* (London: Hutchinson, 1970).

Lynn, Brendan, *Holding the Ground: the Nationalist Party in Northern Ireland, 1945–72* (Aldershot: Ashgate, 1997).

– 'The Irish Anti-Partition League and the political realities of partition', *Irish Historical Studies*, Vol. XXXIV, No. 135 (May 2005), 321–332.

– 'Revising northern nationalism, 1960–1965: the Nationalist Party's response', *New Hibernia Review*, Vol. 4 No. 3 (autumn, 2000), 78–92.

Maguire, John, *IRA Internments and the Irish Government: Subversives and the State, 1939–1962* (Dublin: Irish Academic Press, 2008).

Manning, Maurice, *James Dillon, A Biography* (Dublin, Wolfhound Press, 1999).

Mansergh, Martin (ed.), *The Spirit of the Nation: Speeches and Statements of Charles J. Haughey (1957–1986)* (Dublin & Cork: Mercier Press, 1986).

– *The Legacy of History, For Making Peace in Ireland* (Cork: Mercier Press, 2003).

Mansergh, Nicholas, *The Prelude to Partition: Concepts and Aims in Ireland and India* (Cambridge: Cambridge University Press, 1976).

– 'Eamon de Valera: Life and Irish times', *Studies* (spring, 1971), 13–21.

Maume, Patrick, 'Anti-Machiavel: Three Ulster Nationalists of the Age of De Valera', *Irish Political Studies,* 14 (1999), 43–63.

McCracken, J. L., *Representative Government in Ireland, A Study of Dáil Eireann 1919–48* (London: Oxford University Press, 1958).

McDermott, Eithne, *Clann na Poblachta* (Cork: Cork University Press, 1998).

McGarry, Fearghal, 'Twentieth century Ireland revisited', *Journal of Contemporary History*, Jan. 2007; 42 (1), 137–148.

McKeown, Michael, *The Greening of a Nationalist* (Dublin: Murlough Press, 1986).

McMahon, Deirdre, 'Ireland, the empire, and the commonwealth', in Kevin Kenny (ed.) *Ireland and the British Empire* (Oxford, Oxford University Press, 2004), 182–219.

McNabb, Joe, *'More Rancour than Reason', The Irish Government's Policy on Partition, 1948–51* (unpublished 2000 M.Litt. thesis available from UCDA).

Moynihan, Maurice, *Speeches and Statements by Eamon de Valera* (Dublin: Gill and Macmillan 1980).

Murphy, John A., *Irish Times* supplement 'Fifty Years of Fianna Fáil', 19 May 1976.

– 'The New IRA 1925–62', in *Secret Societies in Ireland*, (ed.) T. Desmond Williams (Dublin: Gill and Macmillan, 1973), 150–164.

Nehru, Jawaharlal, *Glimpses of World History* (India, 1934).

Nic Dháibhéid, Caoimhe, 'Throttling the IRA: Fianna Fáil and the subversive threat, 1939–1945', in *From Parnell to Paisley, Constitutional and Revolutionary Politics in Modern Ireland*, (eds.) Caoimhe Nic Dháibhéid and Colin Reid (Dublin: Irish Academic Press, 2010), 139–158.

Ó Beacháin, Donnacha, *Destiny of the Soldiers: Fianna Fáil, Irish Republicanism and the IRA, 1926–1973* (Dublin: Gill and Macmillan, 2011).

O'Brien, Conor Cruise, *Herod: Reflections on Political Violence* (London: Hutchinson, 1978).

– *Memoir my Life my Times* (Dublin: Poolbeg Press, 1999).

– *States of Ireland* (London: Viking, 1972).

O'Brien, Justin, *The Arms Trial* (Dublin: Gill and Macmillan, 2000).

O'Brien, Máire Cruise, *The Same Age as the State* (Dublin: O'Brien Press, 2003).

O'Carroll, J. P. and Murphy, John A., *De Valera and his Times* (Cork: Cork University Press, 1986).

O'Donnell, Catherine, *Fianna Fáil, Irish Republicanism and the Northern Ireland Troubles, 1968–2005* (Dublin: Irish Academic Press, 2007).

– 'Pan-nationalism: explaining the Irish government's role in the Northern Ireland peace process, 1992–1998', *Contemporary British History*, 21, 2 (June, 2007), 223–245.

O'Halloran, Clare, *Partition and the Limits of Irish Nationalism* (New Jersey: Humanities Press International, Inc., 1987).

O'Halpin, Eunan, 'British intelligence, the Republican movement and the IRA's German links, 1935–45', in *Republicanism in Modern Ireland*, (ed.) Fearghal McGarry (Dublin: UCD Press, 2003), 108–131.

– 'Long fellow, long story: MI5 and de Valera', *Irish Studies in International Affairs* Vol. 14 (2003), 185–203.

–'Parliamentary party discipline and tactics: the Fianna Fáil archives, 1926–32', *Irish Historical Studies*, Vol. XXX (1996–7), 581–590.

O'Malley, Kate, *Ireland, India and Empire, Indo-Irish Radical Connections, 1919–1964* (Manchester: Manchester University Press, 2008).

O'Sullivan, Michael, *Seán Lemass* (Dublin: Blackwater Press, 1994).

Patterson, Henry, *Ireland Since 1939, The Persistence of Conflict* (Dublin: Penguin Ireland, 2006).

– 'Seán Lemass and the Ulster question, 1959–65', *Journal of Contemporary History*, Jan. 1999; 34 (1), 145–159.

'The Border Security problem and Anglo-Irish Relations, 1970-1973', *Contemporary British History*, 26:2 (2012), 231-251.

– *The Politics of Illusion, Republicanism and Socialism in Modern Ireland* (London: Radius Books, 1989).

Phoenix, Eamon, *Northern Nationalism, Nationalists Politics, Partition and the Catholic Minority in NI, 1890–1940* (Ulster Historical Foundation, 1994).

Poger, Sidney (ed.), *The 'De Val-Era' in Ireland, 1916–1975* (Boston: Northeastern University Press, 1984).

Puirséil, Niamh, *The Irish Labour Party, 1922–73* (Dublin: UCD Press, 2007).

Reeves, Chris, '"Let us stand by our friends": British policy towards Ireland, 1949–1959', *Irish Studies in International Affairs*, Vol. 2 (2000), 85–102.

Reynold, Raymond James, 'David Gray, the Aiken mission, and Irish neutrality, 1940–41', *Diplomatic History*, Vol. 9, No. 1 (winter, 1985), 55–71.

Ryan, Desmond, *Unique Dictator, A Study of Eamon de Valera* (Dublin, 1936).

Sheehy, Michael, *Divided we Stand, A Study of Partition* (London: Faber and Faber, 1955).

Smith, Raymond, *Haughey and O'Malley, The Quest for Power* (Dublin: Aherlow, 1986).

Staunton, Enda, *The Nationalists of Northern Ireland, 1918–1973* (Dublin: Columba Press, 2001).

Tannam, Etain, *Cross-Border Co-operation in the Republic of Ireland and Northern Ireland* (New York: St Martin's Press, 1999).

Travers, Pauric, *Eamon de Valera (Life and Times)* (Dundalk: Dundalgan Press, 1994).

Walker, Graham, *A History of the Ulster Unionist Party, Protest, Pragmatism and Pessimism* (Manchester: Manchester University Press, 2004).

Walsh, Dick, *The Party, Inside Fianna Fáil* (Dublin: Gill and Macmillan, 1986).

– *Irish Times* supplement, *After Lemass, Deluge or Desert?*, 19 May 1976.

Walsh, John, *Patrick Hillery, The Official Biography* (Dublin: New Ireland, 2008).

Welch, David, *The Third Reich, Politics and Propaganda* (London: Routledge, 2002).

Whelan, Noel, *Fianna Fáil, A Biography of the Party* (Dublin: Gill and Macmillan, 2011).

Index